FIXED INCOME ANALYTICS

FIXED INCOME ANALYTICS

Kenneth D. Garbade

The MIT Press
Cambridge, Massachusetts
London, England

Third printing, 1999

This book was set in Times Roman by Asco Trade Typesetting Ltd., Hong Kong

Printed and bound in the United States of America.

Library of Congress Cataloging-in-Publication Data

Topics in fixed income analytics / [edited, with some additions, by] Kenneth D. Garbade.
    p.   cm.
    "A collection of articles ... that appeared between 1983 and 1990 in Topics in money and securities markets, a series of occasional papers written by members of the Cross Markets Research group at Bankers Trust Company"—P.   .
    Includes bibliographical references and index.
    ISBN 0-262-07176-2 (hc : alk. paper)
    1. Fixed-income securities. I. Garbade, Kenneth D.
HG4650.T66   1996
332.63′2044—dc20

96-19251
CIP

for Bernice and our joys:
Larissa Louise, Edward Arthur, and Rachel Rose

Contents

Acknowledgments

This book is a collection of articles on fixed income analytics that appeared between 1983 and 1990 in *Topics in Money and Securities Markets*, a series of occasional papers written by members of the Cross Markets Research group at Bankers Trust Company. Kenneth Baron, Steven Dym and Marcia Recktenwald coauthored several of the papers printed below, and Tom Daula made important contributions to one of the papers. The *Topics* series was introduced as, and continues to be, a vehicle for preserving and communicating information about institutional arrangements and analytical methodologies in markets for publicly traded financial instruments. The Cross Markets Research group was supervised by Alan Lerner during the 1980s and early 1990s and more recently by Howard Schneider and P. Daniel Borge, with Walter Callender acting as business manager.

Thomas Urich, a member of the Cross Markets Research group, applied many of the analytical methods described below to non-dollar-denominated sovereign bonds. Only space limitations prevented the inclusion of this important body of related research. Some of his papers have been reprinted in *U.K., German and Japanese Government Bond Markets*, (Monograph Series in Finance and Economics, Monograph 1991-2, New York University Salomon Center, Leonard N. Stern School of Business, New York University, 1991).

The research reported in the papers printed below was materially advanced by conversations with market participants and members of the academic community, including Yakov Amihud, Betsy Battle, Franco Continolo, Ned Elton, Bill Feezer, Stephen Figlewski, Robert Garry, Ron Grobel, Martin Gruber, Mark Hinckley, Kose John, Arlen Klinger, Carolyn Kohn, Paul LeGrand, Clinton Lively, Andrew Lo, William Melton, Belita Ong, Marcia Recktenwald, Alan Rogers, Ehud Ronn, William Silber, Douglas Skolnick, Rita Skolnick, Michael Stock, Marti Subrahmanyam, Timothy Thompson, Garret Thunen, and Barney Tumey.

Many of the topics addressed in this book required substantial computational programming and/or data analysis. These activities were greatly facilitated by the help of Kenneth Abbott, Robert Apsel, Neil Berkowitz, Len Paquette, and Louise Scarpati.

Anyone who has been involved with the mechanics of publishing is familiar with the extraordinary efforts required of those who work on text and artwork. Alice Fortino prepared the original typescripts for the papers, and Bruce Revels prepared the revised typescripts. Frank Ching and the Graphics Department in the Presentation Group at Bankers Trust Company prepared the graphics. We acknowledge the guidance of

Ann Sochi at the MIT Press as we readied the manuscript for publication, the editing by Dana Andrus, and the book design by Sharon Warne.

Finally, this book would not have been written without the encouragement over many years of William Silber and the generous comments of Arthur Warga.

About the Book

This book examines a variety of topics important to participants in the markets for U.S. Treasury bills and bonds and zero coupon securities stripped from Treasury bonds. Broadly stated, it addresses the quantification of risk and return and/or the identification of securities that are relatively cheap or expensive compared to other similar securities.

The chapters focus narrowly on the analysis of securities that promise to pay, and historically have paid without exception, specified amounts of money on specified future dates, that is, "truly" fixed income securities. They do not address matters of credit risk (such as exists for conventional corporate bonds) or equity risk (such as exists for convertible corporate debt) or commodity price risk (such as exists for commodity linked bonds). They also do not address topics commonly associated with mortgage-backed securities (such as prepayment speed models) or derivative instruments.

The book is divided into four parts. Part I presents basic concepts of bond yield and bond duration. Here we show the close relationship between yield (as a measure of average rate of return on capital) and duration (as a measure of the interval of time over which yield has relevance) when the yield curve is flat and can shift up and down but cannot otherwise change shape. This relationship is associated with the concept of immunization, or the elimination of risk by matching the duration of a bond to an investor's investment horizon. We also point out two phenomena that can limit the utility of conventional measures of yield and duration: change in the shape of the yield curve and large, discontinuous yield changes.

Part II examines yield curves and the problem of assessing relative value. In view of the close relationship between yield and duration identified in part I, we suggest that it is reasonable to sort fixed income securities in order of increasing duration and to define a prototypical yield curve as the variation of yield with duration. However, we observe that this basic framework has to be modified to account for nontrivial security characteristics other than duration, such as the superior liquidity of Treasury bills and the relative desirability of high and low coupon bonds. We suggest that the relative value of a Treasury security can be assessed by comparing the yield on the security to yields on comparable securities with similar durations and—in the case of a bond—coupon rates.

Part III addresses topics in fixed income portfolio management associated with change in the shape of the yield curve. The topics include yield curve trades, butterfly trades, and hedging. We also consider the problem of constructing an immunizing bond portfolio when the yield curve can change shape as well as level and/or when an investor has to fund multiple future liabilities and hence does not have a single well-defined investment horizon.

Part IV examines the characteristics and consequences of fluctuations in the shape of the yield curve. We show that, on average, shifts in the curve can be characterized as changes in level, slope, and curvature and that these changes are statistically independent of each other. We further suggest that the shape of the curve may reflect a relationship between (1) the short-run expected rate of return on a bond or bond portfolio and (2) the short-run risks of the bond or bond portfolio that stem from fluctuations in the level and shape of the curve. This relationship leads directly to an algorithm for pricing securities whose future payments (or payoffs) are contingent on the future structure of yields.

This book was written by and for practitioners in the U.S. Treasury securities markets. This has affected its content in two ways. First, some of the chapters pay extremely close attention to institutional practices in the marketplace, including yield conventions, the accrual of interest, and the mechanics of financing long and short positions in securities. (We do not describe in detail the mechanics of financing positions. See Marcia Stigum, *The Repo and Reverse Markets*, Irwin, 1989.) Second, the analytical methodologies do not rely on unobservable variables like expectations of future short-term interest rates. Thus there is little mention of traditional academic theories of the yield curve such as pure expectations or liquidity preference.

The chapters do not have a uniform expository style for two reasons. First, they were written at various dates between 1983 and 1990 and hence reflect natural changes in emphasis associated with the accumulation of knowledge and the development of new ideas. Second, different chapters were prepared originally for different purposes. Some are no more than simple expositions of existing information. (This is especially true of the early chapters.) Other chapters, such as chapters 13 and 14, seek to clarify a possibly misunderstood topic or to report new research results, such as chapters 18, 19, and 20. Several chapters have a Subsequent Remarks section added to clarify or expand on a matter addressed in the chapter or to relate it to subsequent work.

I YIELD AND DURATION

Yield and duration are the two most important and best known characteristics of a bond. The chapters included in this part define the two characteristics and examine their properties.

Chapter 1 begins by specifying the principal and interest payments on a Treasury bond and showing how the Street and the Treasury conventionally compute a bond's yield. Chapter 2 describes how zero coupon securities are stripped from a bond and states the relationship between the price of a zero and its yield.

Chapter 3 introduces the concept of duration and shows how duration can be used to assess the sensitivity of the price of a bond to yield changes. It also describes the process of immunization, or matching the duration of an investment to an investor's investment horizon in order to eliminate the risk of gains or losses attributable to subsequent changes in interest rates. Chapter 4 examines in more detail the behavior of duration through time and shows that duration jumps sharply when a bond pays a coupon but otherwise declines on a day-for-day basis with the passage of time. The chapter points out the implications of this behavior for managing an immunized portfolio and for yield curve analysis.

Chapters 5 and 6 offer critical appraisals of yield and duration. Chapter 5 proposes a measure of the "true" yield on a bond or zero coupon security which, we suggest, is more useful in analytical applications than the conventional yields described in the first two chapters. Chapter 5 also questions the utility of matching the duration of a bond to an investor's horizon when the shape as well as the level of the yield curve can change. Chapter 6 reconsiders bond immunization when interest rates change substantially, either in a single large jump or in a sequence of small jumps.

1 Invoice Prices, Cash Flows, and Yields on Treasury Bonds

This chapter describes the computation of invoice prices, future cash flows, and yields on noncallable Treasury bonds for a given valuation date (usually the settlement date of a trade or proposed trade). The first section focuses on a "regular" bond which pays one-half of its annual coupon every six months to maturity. The second section examines the special case of an "odd first coupon" bond. This is a bond for which there is more (or less) than six months from the date of issue to the date of payment of the first coupon. In this case the first interest payment will be more (or less) than subsequent payments.

Even though there are only about a dozen odd first coupon bonds in the market at any point in time they are important because they appear regularly in the 5-year, 7-year, and 20-year auctions. An odd first coupon can also appear on other bonds if the usual issue date of a bond (the last day of the month for 2-year and 4-year bonds and the 15th of the month for 3-year, 10-year, and 30-year bonds) is a weekend or holiday, and the bond is therefore issued on the next business day.

This chapter also points out the difference between Street practices in yield calculations and how the Treasury calculates yield. The difference is important because auctions are bid on a yield basis rather than by price. Since the Treasury uses a different method to calculate bond prices from bond yields, market participants should be aware that their auction bid yields, and yields in pre-auction when issued trading, are not directly comparable to conventionally computed yields on outstanding bonds.

1.1 Bonds without Odd First Coupons

Analyzing the yield on a bond proceeds along the following lines: First, we specify the future cash flow from the bond—how much we get and when we get it—including periodic coupon payments and the return of principal. Next we calculate the price we pay for the bond (the "invoice price"), including both the quoted price and any accrued interest. Finally, we derive the yield on the bond by computing the discount rate which makes the present value of its future cash flow equal to its invoice price.

This section examines cash flows, invoice prices, and yields on regular bonds which will pay one-half of their annual coupon every six months to maturity. The following section examines bonds with odd first coupons.

Cash Flows

Two parameters are needed to describe fully the cash flow on a regular Treasury bond. The first is the *maturity date* of the bond, at which time the

Written December 1983.

principal, or face amount, of the bond is paid and the bond retired. At the present time Treasury bonds mature either on the 15th of the month (3-year, 5-year, 7-year, 10-year, 20-year, and 30-year issues) or on the last day of the month (2-year and 4-year issues). If a stated maturity date is a weekend or holiday, the principal is paid on the next business day.

The second parameter needed to describe a Treasury bond is the *coupon rate*. A regular bond pays one-half of its coupon rate times its principal value every six months up to and including the maturity date. Thus a bond with a 10% coupon maturing on August 15, 1984, valued on October 25, 1983, will make future coupon payments of 5% of principal value on February 15, 1984, and August 15, 1984. A 9% bond valued on the same date and maturing on September 30, 1984, will pay a 4.5% coupon on March 31, 1984 and September 30, 1984. (This follows the convention of paying interest at the end of a month on bonds that mature at the end of a month rather than on a particular date such as the 30th). If a scheduled payment date is a weekend or holiday the coupon is paid on the next business day.

The "semi-annual anniversary dates" of a bond are its maturity date and the sequence of dates preceding maturity which are spaced an even six months apart. For example, a bond maturing on August 15, 1984 has the following semi-annual anniversary dates:

August 15, 1984 (maturity and last coupon),

February 15, 1984 (second to last coupon),

August 15, 1983 (third to last coupon),

and so on.

Note that these dates are all on the 15th of a month because the bond matures on the 15th of a month. A bond maturing on June 30, 1984, has the following semi-annual anniversary dates:

June 30, 1984 (maturity and last coupon),

December 31, 1983 (second to last coupon),

June 30, 1983 (third to last coupon),

and so on.

These are end-of-month dates because the bond matures at the end of a month.

The scheduled coupon payment dates of a regular bond correspond to the future semi-annual anniversary dates of that bond. As we will see later, however, some odd first coupon bonds to not pay interest on their first semi-annual anniversary date.

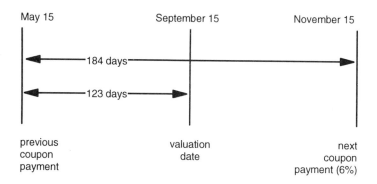

Accrued interest to September 15:
    A = (123/184) · 6%
        = 4.0109% of face amount

Figure 1.1
Calculating accrued interest on a 12% bond paying coupons on May 15 and November 15

Prices

The quoted price of a Treasury bond is expressed as a percent of principal value with fractions of a percent expressed in 32nds, 64ths, or 128ths. The *invoice price* of a Treasury bond is its quoted price plus accrued interest on the next coupon, where the interest is accrued to the valuation date.

Accrued Interest

Accrued interest on a Treasury bond is computed using an actual-over-actual day count method. Consider, for example, a 12% bond paying a 6% coupon on May 15 and November 15 each year. Suppose that this bond is bought for settlement on September 15. As shown in figure 1.1 there are 123 days between the previous coupon payment (May 15) and the settlement date (September 15), and there are 184 days between the previous coupon payment and the next coupon payment (November 15). Thus the accrued interest to September 15 is 123/184ths of the November 15 coupon, or 4.0109%: $4.0109\% = (123/184) \cdot 6\%$.

Yields

We now know to describe fully the future cash flow on a regular Treasury bond, and we know how to compute the invoice price of the bond. In principle, this is all we need to know: the amounts and dates of the cash payment for, and cash receipts on, the bond. However, market participants frequently want to compare different bonds to assess whether one is cheap or expensive compared to another. Schedules of cash flows are not directly comparable in any simple way. Thus market participants want, and need, to reduce those schedules to a few simple summary numbers suitable for making comparisons. Yield to maturity is one useful summary number. (Duration is another.)

The yield to maturity on a bond is the discount rate which makes the present value of the bond's future cash flow equal to its invoice price (not to its quoted price). We will examine the computation of bond yields for three progressively more complex cases:

1. The yield on one of a bond's coupon payment dates (when there is no accrued interest on the bond).

2. The yield on a bond with only one coupon remaining to be paid (when there is accrued interest on the bond).

3. The yield on a bond with multiple coupons remaining to be paid (when there is accrued interest on the bond).

The first case illustrates the basic principle of semi-annual compounding. The second and third cases illustrate how cash flows can be discounted over a fractional part of a 6-month interval.

Yield on a Coupon Payment Date

The simplest place to begin in defining bond yields is a bond that pays a coupon on the valuation date. In this case there is no accrued interest, and the remaining coupon payments are regularly spaced every six months to maturity.

Suppose that a bond has just paid a coupon, has n coupons remaining to be paid, has an annual coupon rate of Rcp, and has a quoted price P in the market. The yield to maturity, compounded semiannually, on this bond is the value of Rm which satisfies the equation:

$$P = \frac{\frac{1}{2}Rcp}{(1 + \frac{1}{2}Rm)} + \frac{\frac{1}{2}Rcp}{(1 + \frac{1}{2}Rm)^2} + \frac{\frac{1}{2}Rcp}{(1 + \frac{1}{2}Rm)^3} + \cdots$$

$$+ \frac{\frac{1}{2}Rcp}{(1 + \frac{1}{2}Rm)^n} + \frac{100}{(1 + \frac{1}{2}Rm)^n} \tag{1.1}$$

The term $1 + \frac{1}{2}Rm$ is the discount factor for a full 6-month interval, that is, one plus one-half of the annualized yield. The present value of the first coupon, payable in 6 months, is the amount of that coupon, $\frac{1}{2}Rcp$, divided by $1 + \frac{1}{2}Rm$ to discount it back to the valuation date. The present value of the second coupon, payable in 12 months, is the amount of that coupon divided by $(1 + \frac{1}{2}Rm)^2$. That is, $\frac{1}{2}Rcp$ is the value of the payment in 12 months, $\frac{1}{2}Rcp/(1 + \frac{1}{2}Rm)$ is the value of that payment discounted back to 6 months in the future, and $\frac{1}{2}Rcp/(1 + \frac{1}{2}Rm)^2$ is the value of the payment discounted back to the valuation date. The equation shows, quite literally, that the price of the bond is equal to the discounted present value of (1) the n coupons remaining to be paid and (2) the payment of principal at maturity.

It should be noted that equation (1.1) does not take account of the actual number of days in any 6-month interval. Depending on the semi-annual anniversary dates of a bond, its 6-month intervals can be 181 and 184 days or 182 and 183 days. The convention of the market is to ignore these variations in the length of a 6-month interval when computing bond yields.

It should also be noted that equation (1.1) does not take account of any delay in payment of principal or interest which will occur if a scheduled payment date falls on a weekend or holiday. This is again a convention of the market. However, in this case a bond will usually look "cheap" compared to bonds that make their payments on the scheduled dates; that is, it will appear to have an unusually high yield.

Yield on a Bond with One Coupon Remaining

Let us consider next a bond that is both simpler and more complex than the bond described above: a bond with only its final payment of interest and principal remaining to be paid but on which there is accrued interest.

The computation of accrued interest is illustrated in figure 1.2. There are x days between the semi-annual anniversary date preceding valuation and the valuation date and y days between the semi-annual anniversary date preceding valuation and the next (and last) semi-annual anniversary date. This means we are a fraction x/y through the current 6-month period, so the accrued interest on the bond is $A = (x/y) \cdot \frac{1}{2}Rcp$.

To compute the yield to maturity on this bond, we need a discount factor that makes the present value of the future payment $\frac{1}{2}Rcp + 100$ equal to the invoice price $P + A$. The question is, How do we discount over the fraction of the 6-month period left on the life of the bond, given that a full period is discounted by the factor $1 + \frac{1}{2}Rm$?

There are two answers to this question. First, we can compound over the fractional period and write:

$$P + A = \frac{\frac{1}{2}Rcp + 100}{(1 + \frac{1}{2}Rm)^w} \tag{1.2}$$

where w is the fraction of the six-month period left on the life of the bond (see figure 1.2). Second, we can multiply the semi-annual yield $\frac{1}{2}Rm$ by the

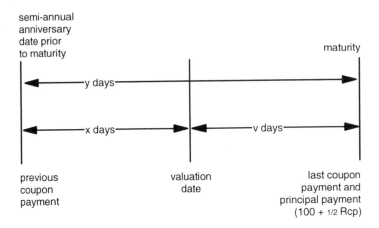

Accrued interest to valuation date:
    A = (x/y) · 1/2Rcp

Fraction of a 6-month period remaining on the life of the bond:
    w = v/y

Figure 1.2
Calculating accrued interest and the fraction of a 6-month period remaining to maturity on a bond with one coupon remaining

fraction w remaining in the six-month period and write:

$$P + A = \frac{\frac{1}{2}Rcp + 100}{(1 + w \cdot \frac{1}{2}Rm)} \tag{1.3}$$

Equation (1.3) says that interest over a fractional period is computed as simple interest.

As might be expected, equations (1.2) and (1.3) lead to different values for the yield on a bond. As shown in figure 1.3, the yield on a bond can be 9.08% per annum if equation (1.2) is used and 8.90% if equation (1.3) is used. This is a general result. Given the invoice price and cash flow of a bond, the assumption of compounding over a fractional period will give a greater yield than the assumption of simple interest over the same fractional period. It should be noted that neither of these yields is "the" correct yield. A yield is just a summary measure of the cash flow on a bond, and we can choose how we want to measure that cash flow. What matters is that we consistently use the same measure so that we can make reasonable comparisons between bonds.

Figure 1.3 also shows that if we calculate the price of a bond from a given yield, we will get a higher price provided that we use compound

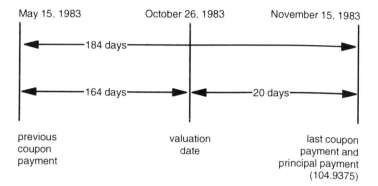

Maturity payment:
$$100 + 1/2Rcp = 100 + 1/2(9.875)$$
$$= 104.9375$$

Accrued interest to valuation date:
$$A = (164/184)\cdot 1/2(9.875)$$
$$= 4.4008$$

Fraction of a 6-month period remaining on the life of the bond:
$$w = 20/184$$
$$= .1087$$

Suppose the quoted price is 100 1/32, or 100.0313, so the invoice price is 104.4321 (104.4321 = 100.0313 + 4.4008). If the yield is calculated with compound interest over the fractional period remaining between October 26, 1983 and November 15, 1983 we have:

$$104.4321 = \frac{104.9375}{(1 + 1/2Rm)^{.1087}}$$

or:

$$Rm = 9.08\% \text{ per annum}$$

If the yield is calculated with simple interest we have:

$$104.4321 = \frac{104.9375}{(1 + .1087\cdot 1/2Rm)}$$

or:

$$Rm = 8.90\% \text{ per annum}$$

Now suppose the quoted yield is 10% per annum. If the invoice price is calculated with compound interest we have:

$$P + A = \frac{104.9375}{(1 + 1/2(.10))^{.1087}}$$

or:

$$P + A = 104.3824$$

If the invoice price is calculated with simple interest we have:

$$P + A = \frac{104.9375}{(1 + .1087\cdot 1/2(.10))}$$

or:

$$P + A = 104.3702$$

Figure 1.3
Calculating yields and prices on October 26, 1983, for a 9.875% bond maturing November 15, 1983, using compound interest and simple interest over the fractional period

interest over a fractional period instead of using simple interest. This is also a general result. When we specify the yield and the future cash flow on a bond, we will compute a larger invoice price if we use compound interest over a fractional period rather than if we use simple interest.

It might seem surprising that compounding interest over a fractional period leads to both a higher yield (for a given price) *and* a higher price (for a given yield). The appendix examines this peculiarity of bond yield in more detail.

For the case of bonds with one coupon remaining, equation (1.3) is used by everybody. As we will see next, however, the problem of discounting over fractional 6-month intervals also arises with bonds with more than one coupon remaining, and in that case the Street uses one convention and the Treasury uses a different convention.

Yield on a Bond with More Than One Coupon Remaining

The third case of defining the yield on a regular Treasury bond is a bond with coupon rate Rcp, quoted price P, n coupons remaining to be paid, and for which accrued interest must be added to the quoted price to calculate the invoice price. This is illustrated in figure 1.4. As shown in that figure, the bond is a fraction x/y through the current six-month period, so the accrued interest on the bond is $A = (x/y) \cdot \frac{1}{2} Rcp$.

To compute the yield on the bond, we have to discount the future coupon and principal payments so their present values sum to the invoice price of the bond. As shown in figure 1.4, the first coupon has to be discounted for the fraction w of a six-month period remaining to its date of payment, the second coupon has to be discounted for $1 + w$ 6-month periods, and so on.

As in the preceding case, there are two ways to discount over the fractional period. First, we can compound the factor $1 + \frac{1}{2} Rm$ over the fractional period and write:

$$P + A = \frac{\frac{1}{2} Rcp}{(1 + \frac{1}{2} Rm)^w} + \frac{\frac{1}{2} Rcp}{(1 + \frac{1}{2} Rm)^{1+w}} + \frac{\frac{1}{2} Rcp}{(1 + \frac{1}{2} Rm)^{2+w}} + \cdots$$

$$+ \frac{\frac{1}{2} Rcp}{(1 + \frac{1}{2} Rm)^{n-1+w}} + \frac{100}{(1 + \frac{1}{2} Rm)^{n-1+w}} \tag{1.4}$$

This equation is directly analogous to equation (1.2). Second, we can discount over the fractional period with simple interest using the factor $1 + w \cdot \frac{1}{2} Rm$ and write:

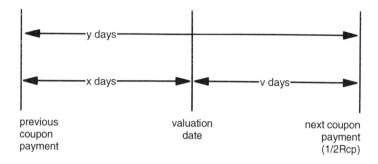

Accrued interest to valuation date:
   $A = (x/y) \cdot 1/2 Rcp$

Fraction of a 6-month period remaining to the next coupon payment:
   $w = v/y$

Discounting of future cash flows (showing the number of 6-month periods between valuation and the future cash flows):

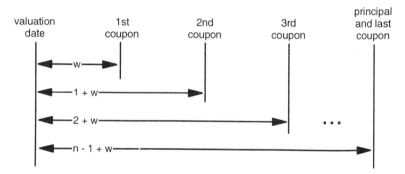

Figure 1.4
Calculating accrued interest and the fraction of a 6-month period remaining to the next coupon payment on a bond with n coupons remaining

$$P + A = \frac{\frac{1}{2}Rcp}{(1 + w \cdot \frac{1}{2}Rm)} + \frac{\frac{1}{2}Rcp}{(1 + w \cdot \frac{1}{2}Rm)(1 + \frac{1}{2}Rm)}$$

$$+ \frac{\frac{1}{2}Rcp}{(1 + w \cdot \frac{1}{2}Rm)(1 + \frac{1}{2}Rm)^2} + \cdots$$

$$+ \frac{\frac{1}{2}Rcp}{(1 + w \cdot \frac{1}{2}Rm)(1 + \frac{1}{2}Rm)^{n-1}} + \frac{100}{(1 + w \cdot \frac{1}{2}Rm)(1 + \frac{1}{2}Rm)^{n-1}}$$

$$(1.5)$$

As was the case for bonds with one coupon remaining, for a given invoice price the use of fractional compounding (equation 1.4) leads to a bond yield greater than that computed with simple interest (equation 1.5). Similarly, for a given yield, we will compute a higher price if we compound interest over the fractional period instead of using simple interest over that period.

Market participants other than the Treasury conventionally compound yields over a fractional period; they use equation (1.4) while the Treasury uses simple interest over a fractional period. To appreciate the significance of this difference in the context of bidding in Treasury auctions, consider the auction of 30-year bonds in the February 1983 refunding. The Treasury announced that instead of selling a new bond, it was reopening the $10\frac{3}{8}\%$ bond maturing November 15, 2012, which had been issued on November 15, 1982. Since the next coupon on that bond was scheduled to be paid on May 15, 1983, the bonds bought in the auction for settlement on February 15, 1983, had 92 days of accrued interest and 89 days remaining before their next coupon payment. The average bid yield in the auction was 11.01%. Using equation (1.5) with $w = .4917$ ($.4917 = 89/181$), the Treasury computed an invoice price of 97.038 for that average yield. At this invoice price the Street, using equation (1.4), calculated an 11.014% yield on the bond. Thus, for the same dollar price, the Treasury and the Street showed a difference in yield of .4 basis points.

It should be noted that the only time the difference between Treasury and Street calculations for a *regular* bond is important is in an auction for a reopening of an old issue for settlement between coupon payments, such as the February 1983 auction described above. If a regular bond is auctioned as a new issue rather than as a reopening, or as a reopening for settlement on a coupon payment date, it will necessarily be issued on a semi-annual anniversary date. In either case there is no fractional period, and equation (1.1) would be used by everybody. If a new bond is not issued on a semi-annual anniversary date, it must have an odd first coupon and thus cannot be a regular bond. Auction prices would then be computed from yields by one of the methods described in section 1.2 below.

1.2 Bonds with Odd First Coupons

If a Treasury bond is issued on one of its semi-annual anniversary dates, it pays a full coupon (equal to one-half of its annual coupon) every six months to maturity. If a bond is not issued on a semi-annual anniversary date, its first coupon pays more or less than its subsequent full coupons. Such a bond is said to have an "odd first coupon."

To appreciate the significance of odd first coupons, consider two examples:

1. 9.5% 2-year note of April 30, 1985, issued May 2, 1983 (because April 30, 1983 was a Saturday)

First coupon: 4.69837% on October 31, 1983.

Subsequent coupons: 4.75%.

2. 11.875% 20-year bond of November 15, 2003, issued October 4, 1983

First coupon: 7.26053% on May 15, 1983.

Subsequent coupons: 5.9375%.

The first example shows a *short* first coupon, so called because the bond pays its first coupon less than six full months after its issue date. The amount of the coupon is consequently less than a full coupon. Short first coupons typically occur when the usual issue date of what would otherwise be a regular bond falls on a weekend or holiday and the bond is issued the following business day.

The 20-year bond shown above is a *long* first coupon bond, so called because the bond pays its first coupon more than six months after its issue date. The amount of that coupon is therefore more than a full coupon. New issues of 5-year, 7-year, and 20-year bonds typically have long first coupons.

An odd first coupon bond poses unique problems in calculating accrued interest, determining cash flow, and computing yield to maturity. However, these problems vanish after the first coupon has been paid because all of the remaining coupons are full coupons payable on the bond's semi-annual anniversary dates. Thus we need only examine the pricing of odd first coupon bonds at valuation dates between issue and payment of the first coupon. We will begin by considering short first coupon bonds and then turn to the more complicated case of long first coupon bonds.

Bonds with Short First Coupons

There are three separate problems encountered with a short first coupon bond: specifying the size of the first coupon, computing accrued interest, and calculating the yield to maturity. We will consider each in turn.

Size of the First Coupon

As with regular bonds, specifying the cash flow on a short first coupon bond requires the maturity date of the bond and the coupon rate. In addition the *issue date* and the *first coupon payment date* are needed to compute the size of the first coupon.

Figure 1.5 illustrates how the size of a short first coupon is computed with an actual-over-actual day count. As shown in the figure, there are 184

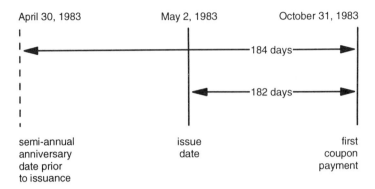

Size of first coupon:
    Q = (182/184) · 1/2 · (9.50%)
      = 4.6984%

Figure 1.5
Calculating the size of the short first coupon on the 9.50% 2-year note issued May 2, 1983, and maturing April 30, 1985

days between the semi-annual anniversary date of the bond preceding its first coupon payment (April 30, 1983) and the date of that payment (October 31, 1983). There are 182 days between the date of issue (May 2, 1983) and the date of the first coupon payment. Thus the Treasury will pay only 182/184ths of a full coupon on the first coupon payment date, or 4.6984% of the face value of the bond: $4.6984\% = (182/184) \cdot \frac{1}{2} \cdot 9.50\%$. It will pay a full 4.75% coupon on subsequent coupon payment dates.

Accrued Interest

Computing accrued interest during a short first coupon period is analogous to computing accrued interest on regular bonds. The differences are attributable to (1) a less-than-full coupon payment and (2) a maximum accrual period shorter than six months.

Figure 1.6 illustrates the computation of accrued interest on a short first coupon bond. As shown, the computation is based on the actual number of days between issue and the valuation date (177—this is the accrual period) and the actual number of days between issue and the date of the first coupon payment (182—this is the number of days for which the first coupon is paid). The valuation date is therefore 177/182nds of the way through the coupon period, so the accrued interest is 177/182nds of the first coupon, or 4.5693% of the face amount of the bond: $4.5693\% = (177/182) \cdot 4.6984\%$.

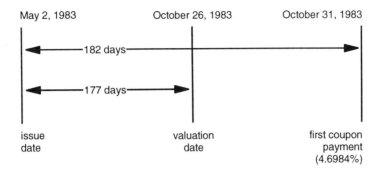

Accrued interest to October 26, 1983:
      A = (177/182) · 4.6984%
        = 4.5693%

Figure 1.6
Calculating accrued interest to October 26, 1983, on the 9.50% 2-year note issued May 2, 1983, and maturing April 30, 1985

Yields

As with regular bonds there are two conventions for computing the yield on a short first coupon bond. Suppose that there is a fraction w of a 6-month interval remaining before payment of the first coupon, where w is computed as the number of days between the valuation date and the date of payment of the first coupon divided by the number of days between the semi-annual anniversary date preceding the first coupon and the date of payment of that coupon. Let Rcp be the annual coupon rate, and let Q be the size of the first coupon payment (expressed as a percent of face amount).

If we assume the yield is compounded over a fractional period the price/yield equation is

$$P + A = \frac{Q}{(1 + \frac{1}{2}Rm)^{w}} + \frac{\frac{1}{2}Rcp}{(1 + \frac{1}{2}Rm)^{1+w}} + \frac{\frac{1}{2}Rcp}{(1 + \frac{1}{2}Rm)^{2+w}} + \cdots$$

$$+ \frac{\frac{1}{2}Rcp}{(1 + \frac{1}{2}Rm)^{n-1+w}} + \frac{100}{(1 + \frac{1}{2}Rm)^{n-1+w}} \qquad (1.6)$$

where P is the quoted price and A is the accrued interest, computed as described above. Comparing this equation to equation (1.4) for the yield on a regular bond shows the two equations look the same except for the first coupon, which is Q above and $\frac{1}{2}Rcp$ in equation (1.4). In particular, the fraction w is the same in both cases: How much is left in the 6-month interval ending on the date of payment of the first coupon and beginning at the semi-annual anniversary date prior to that payment. For the short first coupon bond, the beginning of this interval predates the issuance of the bond. For the regular bond, the beginning of the interval is the date of issuance.

If we assume that payments over a fractional period are discounted with simple interest the price/yield equation for a short first coupon bond is

$$P + A = \frac{Q}{(1 + w \cdot \frac{1}{2}Rm)} + \frac{\frac{1}{2}Rcp}{(1 + w \cdot \frac{1}{2}Rm)(1 + \frac{1}{2}Rm)}$$

$$+ \frac{\frac{1}{2}Rcp}{(1 + w \cdot \frac{1}{2}Rm)(1 + \frac{1}{2}Rm)^2} + \cdots$$

$$+ \frac{\frac{1}{2}Rcp}{(1 + w \cdot \frac{1}{2}Rm)(1 + \frac{1}{2}Rm)^{n-1}} + \frac{100}{(1 + w \cdot \frac{1}{2}Rm)(1 + \frac{1}{2}Rm)^{n-1}}$$

$$(1.7)$$

Comparing this equation to equation (1.5) for the yield on a regular bond using simple interest over a fractional period shows the two equations look the same except for the size of the first coupon payment.

For short first coupon bonds the Treasury uses equation (1.7) to go from yield to price and price to yield, while the Street uses equation (1.6). Given the price of a bond, this means the Treasury will show a lower yield than the Street. Conversely, for any given yield, the Treasury will price a bond more cheaply than the Street. For example, the average bid yield in the April 1983 auction of the 2-year bonds mentioned above was 9.61%. After putting a 9.5% coupon on the bonds, the Treasury calculated an issue price of 99.805 at the average yield. However, at that price the Street saw the yield as 9.611%, or .1 basis points higher than the Treasury.

Bonds with Long First Coupons

As with short first coupons there are three separate problems encountered with a long first coupon bond: specifying the size of the first coupon, computing accrued interest for a valuation date prior to the first coupon payment, and calculating the yield for such a valuation date.

Size of the First Coupon

Figure 1.7 uses the 11.875% bonds issued on October 5, 1983, and maturing November 15, 2003, to illustrate how the size of the first coupon on a long first coupon bond is computed. The first semi-annual anniversary date of that bond is November 15, 1983. However, no interest is paid on that date. Instead, the first coupon is paid on the next semi-annual anniversary date: May 15, 1984. The size of the May 15, 1984, coupon is

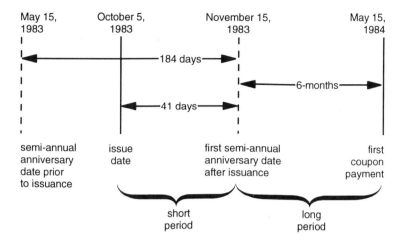

Size of first coupon:
    Q = 5.9375% + (41/184) · 5.9375%
      = 5.9375% + 1.3230%
      = 7.2605%

Figure 1.7
Calculating the size of the long first coupon on the 11.875% 20-year bond issued October 5, 1983, and maturing November 15, 2003

computed as follows. First, a full 5.9375% payment is made for the 6-month interval from November 15, 1983, to May 15, 1984 (5.9375% = one-half of the 11.875% annual coupon rate). The Treasury then adds a payment for the interval from the October 5, 1983, issue date to November 15, 1983. The size of this added payment is figured as the fraction of the 184 day May 15, 1983–November 15, 1983, 6-month period included in the 41-day October 5, 1983–November 15, 1983, interval, times a full semi-annual coupon. As shown in the figure, the total size of the first coupon is 7.2605% of face value: 7.2605% = 5.9375% full coupon plus (41/184) · 5.9375% partial coupon.

Accrued Interest

The discussion above showed that there are two separate parts to the time between issue and first coupon payment on a long first coupon bond: a "short period" running from the issue date to the first semi-annual anniversary date of the bond and a "long period" running from the first semi-annual anniversary date to the second semi-annual anniversary date when the first coupon is paid. Distinguishing between these two periods is important in computing accrued interest to a given valuation date.

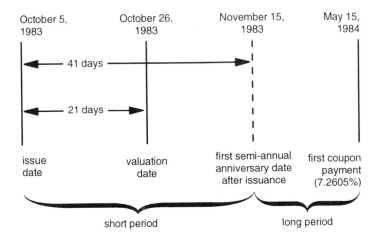

Accrued interest to October 26, 1983:
    A = (21/41) · (1.3230%)
      = .6776%

Note that 1.3230% is the portion of the first coupon payment attributable to the short period.

Figure 1.8
Calculating accrued interest to October 26, 1983, on the 11.875% 20-year bond issued October 5, 1983, and maturing November 15, 2003

Valuation in the Short Period   If a valuation date is in the short period, accrued interest is figured on the partial coupon part of the first coupon using an actual-over-actual day count for computing the fraction of the short period. This is illustrated in figure 1.8.

Valuation in the Long Period   If the valuation date is in the long period, accrued interest is figured as the partial coupon part of the first coupon *plus* a fraction of the full coupon part of the first coupon, where the fraction is computed using an actual-over-actual day count within the long period. This is illustrated in figure 1.9.

In summary, interest on a long first coupon bond accrues separately over the short period and the long period making up the time between issuance and the first coupon payment.

Yields

As with regular bonds and short first coupon bonds, there are two conventions for computing the yield on a long first coupon bond, depending on whether interest over a fractional part of a 6-month interval is compounded or figured as simple interest. In addition we need to be careful

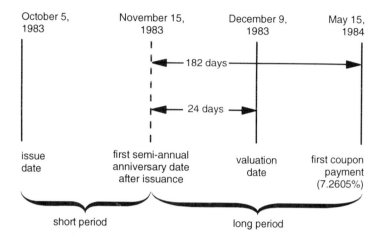

Accrued interest to December 9, 1983:
$$A = 1.3230\% + (24/182) \cdot 5.9375\%$$
$$= 2.1060\%$$

Note that 1.3230% is the portion of the first coupon payment attributable to the short period.

Figure 1.9
Calculating accrued interest to December 9, 1983, on the 11.875% 20-year bond issued October 5, 1983, and maturing November 15, 2003

about whether the valuation date is in the short period preceding payment of the first coupon, in which case that coupon payment is more than 6 months in the future, or in the long period, in which case the first coupon payment is less than 6 months in the future. We will examine both possibilities.

Valuation in the Short Period   Suppose that the valuation date falls between the date of issuance and the first semi-annual anniversary date of the bond. Let w be the number of days between the valuation date and the semi-annual anniversary date following issuance (November 15, 1983, for the 11.875% bonds of 2003), divided by the number of days between the semi-annual anniversary date preceding issuance (May 15, 1983 for the 11.875% bonds of 2003) and the semi-annual anniversary date following issuance. Let n be the number of coupons to be paid, Rcp the annual coupon rate, and Q the size of the first coupon payment, expressed as a percent of face amount.

The first coupon payment will be received in $1 + w$ semi-annual periods. That is, we have a fraction w remaining in the current (May 15, 1983–November 15, 1983) 6-month period plus another full 6-month period (November 15, 1983–May 15, 1984) before the first coupon is paid. Similarly the second coupon will be received in $2 + w$ semi-annual periods, and so on.

If we assume the yield to maturity is compounded over a fractional period the price/yield equation is

$$P + A = \frac{Q}{(1 + \frac{1}{2}Rm)^{1+w}} + \frac{\frac{1}{2}Rcp}{(1 + \frac{1}{2}Rm)^{2+w}} + \frac{\frac{1}{2}Rcp}{(1 + \frac{1}{2}Rm)^{3+w}} + \cdots$$

$$+ \frac{\frac{1}{2}Rcp}{(1 + \frac{1}{2}Rm)^{n+w}} + \frac{100}{(1 + \frac{1}{2}Rm)^{n+w}} \tag{1.8}$$

where P is the quoted price and A is the accrued interest computed over that portion of the short period elapsed between issuance and the valuation date.

If we assume that yield is computed as simple interest over a fractional period the price/yield equation is

$$P + A = \frac{Q}{(1 + \frac{1}{2}Rm)(1 + w \cdot \frac{1}{2}Rm)} + \frac{\frac{1}{2}Rcp}{(1 + \frac{1}{2}Rm)^2(1 + w \cdot \frac{1}{2}Rm)}$$

$$+ \frac{\frac{1}{2}Rcp}{(1 + \frac{1}{2}Rm)^3(1 + w \cdot \frac{1}{2}Rm)} + \cdots$$

$$+ \frac{\frac{1}{2}Rcp}{(1 + \frac{1}{2}Rm)^n(1 + w \cdot \frac{1}{2}Rm)} + \frac{100}{(1 + \frac{1}{2}Rm)^n(1 + w \cdot \frac{1}{2}Rm)} \tag{1.9}$$

As in the case of short first coupon bonds, the Treasury uses simple interest (equation 1.9) while the Street uses compound interest (equation 1.8). For a given yield the Treasury will therefore compute a lower price than the Street on a long first coupon bond. Similarly, for a given price, the Treasury will compute a lower yield than the Street.

Valuation in the Long Period   Suppose next that the valuation date falls between the first semi-annual anniversary date of the bond following issuance and the date of payment of the first coupon. Let w denote the fraction of the 6-month period remaining before payment of the first coupon, computed as the number of days between the valuation date and the bond's first coupon payment date divided by the number of days between the bond's first semi-annual anniversary date and first coupon payment date. The first coupon will then be received in w semi-annual periods. The second coupon will be received in $1 + w$ semi-annual periods, and so on.

If we assume that the yield on the bond is compounded over a fractional period the price/yield equation is

$$P + A = \frac{Q}{(1 + \frac{1}{2}Rm)^w} + \frac{\frac{1}{2}Rcp}{(1 + \frac{1}{2}Rm)^{1+w}} + \frac{\frac{1}{2}Rcp}{(1 + \frac{1}{2}Rm)^{2+w}} + \cdots$$

$$+ \frac{\frac{1}{2}Rcp}{(1 + \frac{1}{2}Rm)^{n-1+w}} + \frac{100}{(1 + \frac{1}{2}Rm)^{n-1+w}} \tag{1.10}$$

Comparing this equation to equation (1.6) for short first coupon bonds shows the two are quite similar in form. More particularly, in both cases the first coupon will be paid in w 6-month periods, the second coupon in $1 + w$ periods, and so on. Moreover the fraction w is calculated the same way in both cases: based on the first coupon payment date and the preceding semi-annual anniversary date. The difference between the two equations lies in the size of the first coupon ($Q > \frac{1}{2}Rcp$ for the long first coupon bond and $Q < \frac{1}{2}Rcp$ for the short first coupon bond) and in the computation of accrued interest.

If we assume that the yield on the bond is computed using simple interest over a fractional period, the price/yield equation is

$$P + A = \frac{Q}{(1 + w \cdot \frac{1}{2}Rm)} + \frac{\frac{1}{2}Rcp}{(1 + w \cdot \frac{1}{2}Rm)(1 + \frac{1}{2}Rm)}$$

$$+ \frac{\frac{1}{2}Rcp}{(1 + w \cdot \frac{1}{2}Rm)(1 + \frac{1}{2}Rm)^2} + \cdots$$

$$+ \frac{\frac{1}{2}Rcp}{(1 + w \cdot \frac{1}{2}Rm)(1 + \frac{1}{2}Rm)^{n-1}} + \frac{100}{(1 + w \cdot \frac{1}{2}Rm)(1 + \frac{1}{2}Rm)^{n-1}}$$

$$\tag{1.11}$$

As in the previous cases of odd first coupon bonds, the Treasury uses the simple interest convention over the fractional period, while the Street uses the compounding convention.

1.3   Appendix: The Effect of the Interest Convention for a Fractional 6-Month Period on Bond Prices and Bond Yields

This appendix examines how the interest convention for a fractional 6-month period affects bond prices and bond yields.

The discount factor for a full 6-month period is $1 + \frac{1}{2}Rm$, where Rm is the yield. For a fractional part of a 6-month period, we can define two alternative discount factors:

Using compound interest, $d_c(Rm) = (1 + \frac{1}{2}Rm)^w$. $\tag{A1.1}$

Using simple interest, $d_s(Rm) = 1 + w \cdot \frac{1}{2}Rm$. $\tag{A1.2}$

Here w is the length of the period, expressed as a fraction of a 6-month period. Note that $0 < w < 1$.

The key fact needed to understand the effect of different interest conventions is the inequality:

$$(1 + \tfrac{1}{2}Rm)^w < 1 + w \cdot \tfrac{1}{2}Rm \tag{A1.3}$$

for all yields Rm and for all values of the fraction w. This means that, given yield, the discount factor is smaller if we use compound interest instead of simple interest:

$$d_c(Rm) < d_s(Rm) \tag{A1.4}$$

Equation (A1.4) has direct implications for the computation of bond prices and bond yields.

Consider first computing the present value of a future payment FV where the payment will be made in a fraction w of a 6-month period in the future and where we are to discount the payment at yield Rm. If we use compound interest the present value is

$$PV^c = \frac{FV}{d_c(Rm)} \tag{A1.5}$$

If we use simple interest the present value is

$$PV^s = \frac{FV}{d_s(Rm)} \tag{A1.6}$$

Since $d_c(Rm) < d_s(Rm)$ by equation (A1.4), we have $PV^c > PV^s$. More particularly, we can compute a higher present value if we use compound interest instead of simple interest.

Consider next the problem of computing the yield on a security priced at P that will pay FV at maturity in a fraction w of a 6-month period in the future. If we compute the yield using simple interest we have to solve the following equation for Rm:

$$P = \frac{FV}{d_s(Rm)} \tag{A1.7}$$

Let Rm^s be the solution so that

$$P = \frac{FV}{d_s(Rm^s)} \tag{A1.8}$$

We can compute the yield using compound interest by solving the equation

$$P = \frac{FV}{d_c(Rm)} \qquad\qquad\qquad (A1.9)$$

Let Rm^c be the solution so that

$$P = \frac{FV}{d_c(Rm^c)} \qquad\qquad\qquad (A1.10)$$

Comparing equations (A1.8) and (A1.9) shows that

$$d_c(Rm^c) = d_s(Rm^s) \qquad\qquad\qquad (A1.11)$$

It is clear that Rm^c cannot equal Rm^s because equation (A1.4) would then imply that $d_c(Rm^c) < d_s(Rm^s)$, and this would violate equation (A1.11). To force the equality of equation (A1.11), we have to push up Rm^c so that

$$Rm^c > Rm^s \qquad\qquad\qquad (A1.12)$$

Thus, for a given price and a given future payment, we will compute a higher yield if we use compound interest instead of simple interest.

1.4   Subsequent Remarks

Several things have changed since this chapter was written in late 1983. First, the Treasury has stopped issuing 4-year, 7-year, and 20-year bonds. The last 20-year bond was issued on January 15, 1986 (the 9.375% bond of February 15, 2006), the last 4-year bond was issued on December 31, 1990 (the 7.625% bond of December 31, 1994), and the last 7-year bond was issued on April 15, 1993 (the 5.5% bond of April 15, 2000).

Second, at the end of 1990 the Treasury changed the issuance schedule for 5-year bonds from quarterly to monthly. Prior to that time 5-year bonds were usually auctioned in late February for issuance in early March, in late May for issuance in early June, and so on. The bonds matured about 5 years and $2\frac{1}{2}$ months after issuance (on the 15th of the second month of a quarter) and had long first coupons. Since January 1991 the Treasury has issued, at the end of every month, 5-year bonds that usually mature in exactly 5 years, that is, that have regular first coupons.

Third, the Treasury now issues 10-year and 30-year bonds as regular bonds even if the issue date is delayed after the 15th of a month. It does this by selling the bonds with accrued interest computed from (1) the semi-annual anniversary date preceding the first coupon payment date to (2) the date of issue. For example, the 9.875% 30-year bond maturing November 15, 2015, was auctioned on November 22, 1985, and issued on November 29, 1985, with a full first coupon due on May 15, 1986, and with accrued interest computed from November 15, 1985, that is, with 14 days of accrued interest.

These changes mean that the Treasury no longer issues any bond with a long first coupon and that only 2-year, 3-year, and 5-year bonds can come with a short first coupon.

Yields on Treasury Bills

It may be helpful to state here the market conventions for quoting bids and offers on Treasury bills and for computing yields on bills.

Treasury bills are quoted in terms of a "discount rate" rather than a price. Consider a bill quoted at discount rate D which matures n days after the valuation date. The invoice price of the bill, expressed as a percent of face amount, is

$$P = 100 - \frac{n}{360} \cdot D \qquad \text{(S1.1)}$$

For example, if $n = 171$ and $D = 7.23\%$, then $P = 96.5658\%$ of face amount: $96.5658 = 100 - (171/360) \cdot 7.23$.

The so-called bond-equivalent yield on a bill is most commonly computed as the value of Rm that satisfies the equation

$$P = \frac{100}{1 + \dfrac{n}{365} Rm} \qquad \text{if } n < 183 \qquad \text{(S1.2)}$$

or the equation

$$P = \frac{100}{(1 + \frac{1}{2}Rm) \cdot \left(1 + \dfrac{n - 182.5}{365} Rm\right)} \qquad \text{if } n > 182 \qquad \text{(S1.3)}$$

Thus $Rm = .07591$, or 7.591% per annum, for a 171-day bill quoted at a discount rate of 7.23%, since $100/(1 + (171/365) \cdot .07591) = 96.5658$. Observe that the bond-equivalent yield on a bill with less than 183 days remaining to maturity is computed with simple interest (see equation S1.2) and that the yield on a bill with more than 182 days remaining to maturity is computed with compound interest over one-half year (182.5 days) and simple interest over the remaining term of the bill (see equation S1.3).

2 Zero Coupon Strips and Custodial Receipts

Zero coupon securities ("zeros") created from ordinary Treasury bonds are among the most innovative instruments to appear in the credit markets in recent years. Simply stated, zeros divide the interest and principal obligations of a whole bond into individual, separated claims. Investors can then acquire the claims best suited to their needs. An investor with a cash requirement in the near future can purchase an early interest claim from a longer maturity bond while an investor with a longer horizon can purchase a later interest claim or a principal claim from the same bond.

Short maturity zeros compete directly with Treasury bills and short-term Treasury notes and do not expand significantly the opportunities available to an investor with a short investment horizon. On the other hand, longer maturity zeros provide important new opportunities for an investor with a long horizon. In particular, they eliminate the risk inherent in reinvesting interest payments from a whole bond at uncertain future yields.

This chapter describes the characteristics of two classes of zero coupon securities: physical strips created from a bearer Treasury bond ("strips"), and custodial receipts created from any bond ("receipts"). The first section describes how strips and receipts are created from noncallable Treasury debt. The second section examines yields and prices on zeros.

2.1 Strips and Receipts from Noncallable Bonds

Consider a noncallable Treasury bond bearing a 10% coupon that matures in two years and pays $1,000 at maturity. The bond is a bundle of five separate obligations:

1. Pay $50 interest in 6 months.
2. Pay $50 interest in 12 months.
3. Pay $50 interest in 18 months.
4. Pay $50 interest in 24 months.
5. Pay $1,000 principal in 24 months.

This section examines how zeros can be created from the bond.

Strips

Figure 2.1 shows the two-year bond described above as it would appear in bearer form. A large engraving sets forth the Treasury's promise to pay the

Written May 1984.

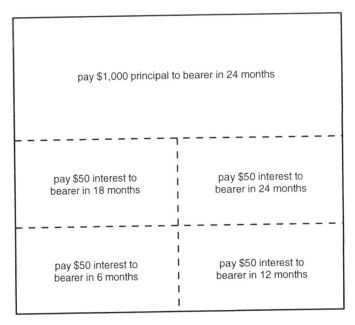

Figure 2.1
Representation of a 2-year bearer treasury bond with a 10% coupon

principal. Smaller engravings, called *coupons*, set forth the promises to make each of the four interest payments. When an interest payment comes due the holder of the bond clips off the appropriate coupon and presents it for payment. When the principal and last interest payment come due the holder presents the bond itself for payment—which by then consists of only the corpus, or principal, and the last coupon.

Creating zeros by stripping the bearer bond in figure 2.1 is simplicity itself: The holder takes scissors and separates each of the coupons from the corpus. As shown in figure 2.2, this leaves him with five separate pieces of paper consisting of the four coupons and the corpus. Each piece of paper is a promise of the Treasury to pay to the bearer a specified amount of dollars on a specified future date; in other words, each piece of paper is a zero coupon security.

Receipts

If all Treasury bonds were available in bearer form, there would be no compelling reason to create zeros other than by stripping. However, since July 1983 Federal tax law has effectively prohibited the issuance of bearer securities with more than one year to maturity, and the Treasury now issues bonds in registered form only. Interest and principal payments on

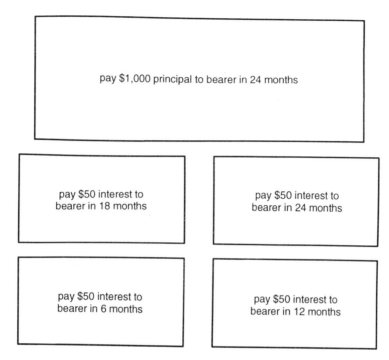

Figure 2.2
Representation of a stripped 2-year bearer treasury bond with a 10% coupon

a registered bond are made to the owner recorded on the books of the Treasury and are not made in response to presentation of an engraved coupon or corpus. The engraved piece of paper typically associated with a registered bond is really not much more than a memorandum which can be filled out with instructions for re-registration in the event of a change in ownership. (Even this piece of paper is absent when title is established by book entry at a Federal Reserve bank.) Thus, stripping cannot be extended to Treasury bonds issued after July 1983 and available only in registered form.

Zeros are created from registered Treasury bonds through custodial receipt programs. The basic elements of such a program are illustrated in figure 2.3. As shown, a bank becomes the owner of record of a Treasury bond (either by book entry with a Federal Reserve bank or directly on the books of the Treasury) and issues separate and individual receipts for each of the bond's interest payments and for the principal payment. When the Treasury makes an interest or principal payment to the bank, the bank passes the payment along to holders of receipts for that payment. Each receipt is itself a zero coupon security.

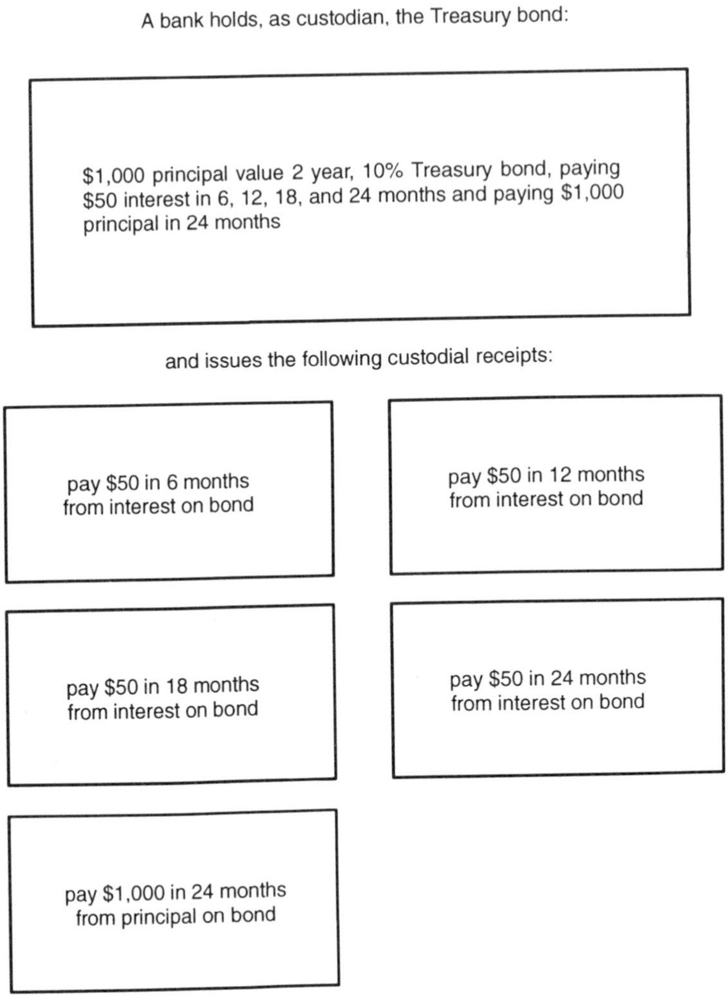

A bank holds, as custodian, the Treasury bond:

$1,000 principal value 2 year, 10% Treasury bond, paying $50 interest in 6, 12, 18, and 24 months and paying $1,000 principal in 24 months

and issues the following custodial receipts:

pay $50 in 6 months
from interest on bond

pay $50 in 12 months
from interest on bond

pay $50 in 18 months
from interest on bond

pay $50 in 24 months
from interest on bond

pay $1,000 in 24 months
from principal on bond

Figure 2.3
Representation of custodial receipts on a 2-year treasury bond with a 10% coupon

It is important to note that the bank neither owns the Treasury bond for its own account nor issues the receipts as its own liabilities. Instead, the bank acts as a custodian, holding the bond for the benefit of the owners of the receipts and passing through the payments made by the Treasury. This custodial function is not different from the bank holding a whole bond on behalf on an investor and issuing a receipt for the bond as a record of its agency function, except that in the present case it issues separate receipts for each of the bond's payments instead of one receipt for all of the payments.

2.2 Denominations, Prices, and Yields

Zeros, including both strips and receipts, are denominated in terms of face amount. For example, an offering of $10 million of a May 15, 1992, maturity means a zero paying $10 million on the stated date and making no other payment. It *does not* mean a zero with a present market value of $10 million.

Zeros are quoted and traded on a yield basis rather than on a price basis. The price of a zero can be computed only if we know how price and yield are related.

Price/yield calculations for zeros follow the conventions of the Treasury bond market. Interest is compounded semi-annually and compounded over the fractional part of a semi-annual period instead of being computed as simple interest. (There is one exception to this convention that is noted below.) In addition the length of the fractional part of a semi-annual period is computed using an actual-over-actual day count method.

The price calculation for a zero is most easily described with a concrete example. Suppose that a May 15, 1992, zero is offered at a yield of 12.75% for settlement on May 1, 1984. There are a bit more than 8 years between settlement and payment, so there are 16 full semi-annual periods between the two dates. To calculate the length of the additional fractional period, we note that there are 14 days remaining between settlement (May 1, 1984) and the beginning of the first full semi-annual period following settlement (May 15, 1984) and that there are 182 days in the current period (November 15, 1983, to May 15, 1984). This means there is only the fraction .07692 of a semi-annual period left in the current period (.07692 = 14/182).

The price of the zero as a percent of face amount is computed by discounting the face amount over 16.07692 semi-annual periods at the 12.75% offering yield with semi-annual compounding

$$P = \frac{100}{(1 + \frac{1}{2}(.1275))^{16.07692}}$$

$$= 37.026$$

Thus we would pay $3,702,600 for $10 million of May 15, 1992, zeros offered at a 12.75% yield for settlement on May 1, 1984 ($3,702,600 = 37.026% of $10 million face amount).

An Exception

There is one exception to the above method for computing prices on zeros. When a zero has less than one full semi-annual period remaining before its payment, interest over the remaining fractional part of a period is computed as simple rather than compound interest. This follows an identical convention for Treasury bonds with only a single coupon remaining to be paid.

To illustrate the pricing of a short maturity zero, suppose that an August 15, 1984, zero is offered at a yield of 10.50% for settlement on May 1, 1984. There are 106 days between settlement and payment, and there are 182 days in the current semi-annual period (February 15, 1984, to August 15, 1984). This means there is a fraction .582418 of a semi-annual period left on the zero (.582418 = 106/182). The price of the zero as a percent of face amount is

$$P = \frac{100}{(1 + \frac{1}{2}(.582418)(.1050))}$$

$$= 97.033$$

If we had compounded the yield over the remaining part of a period (instead of using a simple interest convention), we would have computed the higher price of

$$P = \frac{100}{(1 + \frac{1}{2}(.1050))^{.582418}}$$

$$= 97.064$$

2.3 Subsequent Remarks

As indicated in this chapter, the first zero coupon securities created from ordinary Treasury bonds were obtained by physically separating a bearer bond into its several interest claims and its principal claim. The first custodial receipts, called TIGRs or Treasury Investment Growth Receipts, were innovated by Merrill Lynch in August 1982. This was followed within a matter of days by the CATS, or Certificates of Accrual on Treasury Securities, program of Salomon Brothers and subsequently by a variety of similar programs from other investment and commercial banks.

In January 1985 the Treasury announced that it would itself sponsor a custodial receipt program, called STRIPS (Separate Trading of Registered Interest and Principal of Securities), using the 12 district Federal Reserve banks as custodian and providing the receipts in book-entry form. The STRIPS program subsequently displaced the private sector programs.

Duration: An Introduction to the Concept and Its Uses

Consider three statements:

1. The prices of bonds with equal maturities are equally sensitive to changes in interest rates.

2. The sensitivity of the price of a bond to changes in interest rates increases with the maturity of the bond.

3. If an investor buys a bond whose maturity matches the date on which he requires funds, subsequent interest rate movements have no effect on his total return over the investment interval.

These statements, although popularly believed, are not true. They are more nearly true, however, if "maturity" is replaced with "duration."

The purpose of this chapter is to introduce the concept of duration as a measure of the "futurity" of a bond's payment stream, show how duration is a measure of a bond's interest rate sensitivity, and demonstrate how, given an investment horizon, proper choice of duration can "immunize" the exposure of a portfolio to the risk of interest rate fluctuations over the horizon. For expositional simplicity we will assume that all bonds pay coupons annually. The analysis can be extended readily to semiannual payments.

3.1 Concepts of Futurity

A bond's stream of payments, or cash flow, consists of (1) coupon payments during the life of the bond and (2) repayment of principal at maturity. For some purposes it is useful to have a measure of the futurity of a bond's cash flow. We will examine three possible measures: maturity, dollar-weighted mean waiting time, and duration.

Maturity

Although frequently used, term to maturity is not a useful measure of the futurity of a bond's cash flow because it refers only to the time remaining to the repayment of principal and disregards earlier coupon payments. To see why maturity is not what is desired, consider three bonds with the same maturity but different patterns of cash flow:

Payments from bond

Bond	Year 1	Year 2	Year 3	Year 4	Year 5
A	5	5	5	5	105
B	20	20	20	20	120
C	0	0	0	0	100

Written January 1984 with Steven Dym.

Bond *A* looks pretty ordinary, with most of its payments coming at maturity (year 5). An approximation of a 5 year wait for *A*'s cash flow would seem reasonably accurate. However, bond *C*, which is a "zero coupon" bond, has a cash flow with a futurity that is *exactly* equal to its 5 year maturity. Reasoning from this benchmark, it is clear that the futurity of bond *A*'s cash flow must be less than five years. This follows because only the principal and final coupon payment on bond *A* have a futurity of five years. The earlier coupons all have futurities of less than five years, so the overall futurity of the bond must also be less than five years. Similar reasoning shows that the futurity of bond B's cash flow must be even smaller than that of bond *A* because it makes larger coupon payments prior to maturity.

Dollar-Weighted Mean Waiting Time

Another way of measuring the futurity of a bond's cash flow is to compute a simple average time to payment where each payment interval is weighted by the number of dollars the bond pays at the end of that interval. For example, a number close to 5 would be expected for the average waiting time for bond *A*, since its coupons are small relative to its principal—in fact its mean waiting time is 4.6 years. For bond *B* the mean is less than 4.6 years (it is 4.0 years) because its coupons are larger relative to its principal. Finally, *C*'s mean waiting time is exactly 5 years because it make no payments prior to maturity.

The average waiting time described above weights each year by the amount of dollars paid that year. Note, however, that it assigns equal weight to each dollar, regardless of when a dollar is paid. Since the present value of a dollar decreases with the amount of time that must pass before it is paid, a better method might be to weight each year by the *present value* of the dollars paid that year. This would put the weights on a comparable basis. In addition it leads to a definition of futurity that is exactly equal to duration.

Duration

To begin, assume that the yield per annum is the same for all bonds and equal to *R*, that is, that the yield curve is flat. The present value of *X* dollars payable in *n* years is then $X/(1 + R)^n$. (To avoid cumbersome notation, we assume annual compounding as well as annual interest payments.) The present value of a bond paying a coupon of *C* dollars per year for *n* years and repaying principal at maturity is the sum of the present values of its cash payments:

$$P = \frac{C}{(1 + R)} + \frac{C}{(1 + R)^2} + \cdots + \frac{C}{(1 + R)^{n-1}} + \frac{C + 100}{(1 + R)^n} \qquad (3.1)$$

P is of course equal to the market price of the bond.

To define the duration of the bond, we need to weight the time to each payment by the present value of the payment and then divide the result by the sum of the weights. This gives a measure of waiting time corrected for present value discounting. Thus duration is defined as

$$D = \frac{\dfrac{1 \cdot C}{(1+R)} + \dfrac{2 \cdot C}{(1+R)^2} + \cdots + \dfrac{(n-1) \cdot C}{(1+R)^{n-1}} + \dfrac{n \cdot (C+100)}{(1+R)^n}}{\dfrac{C}{(1+R)} + \dfrac{C}{(1+R)^2} + \cdots + \dfrac{C}{(1+R)^{n-1}} + \dfrac{C+100}{(1+R)^n}} \qquad (3.2)$$

Noting from equation (3.1) that the denominator of equation (3.2) is just the price of the bond, we have that

$$D = \frac{\dfrac{1 \cdot C}{(1+R)} + \dfrac{2 \cdot C}{(1+R)^2} + \cdots + \dfrac{(n-1) \cdot C}{(1+R)^{n-1}} + \dfrac{n \cdot (C+100)}{(1+R)^n}}{P} \qquad (3.3)$$

If we assume a yield of 10% per annum, the duration of bond A (paying a 5% coupon) is 4.5 years, the duration of bond B (paying a 20% coupon) is 3.8 years, and the duration of the zero coupon bond C remains at 5 years. As suggested by the table below, the duration of a bond is never greater than its maturity and it is never greater than its dollar-weighted mean waiting time. It will be less than both if the bond pays any coupon at all.

	Term to maturity	Dollar-weighted mean waiting time	Duration
Bond A	5 yr	4.6 yr	4.5 yr
Bond B	5	4.0	3.8
Bond C	5	5.0	5.0

Duration of a Zero Coupon Bond

There is one special case of duration worth noting. Suppose that a bond pays no coupons. Since $C = 0$, the definition of duration in equation (3.2) becomes

$$D = n \qquad (3.4)$$

In this case the duration of the bond is always and identically equal to its term to maturity. This special case has important implications noted below.

Some Examples

To get some sense of typical duration numbers for real bonds the table below shows the duration (in years) of the actively traded Treasury bonds outstanding at the end of December 1983.

Coupon rate	Maturity date	Term to maturity	Duration
10.875%	12/31/1985	2.0 yr	1.8 yr
11.0	11/15/1986	2.9	2.5
11.25	12/31/1987	4.0	3.3
11.375	2/15/1989	5.2	4.0
11.75	1/15/1991	7.0	5.0
11.75	11/15/1993	9.9	6.0
11.875	11/15/2003	19.9	7.8
12.0	8/15/2013	29.6	8.1

Note that duration *does not* increase on a year-for-year basis with maturity and that the duration of the 12% bond maturing in 2013 is only 8.1 years, even though it has a maturity of almost 30 years.

3.2   Properties of Duration

From the definition of duration in equation (3.2), it is clear that a bond's duration depends on three variables:

1. The maturity of the bond.
2. The coupon on the bond.
3. The bond's yield to maturity.

Increasing the coupon on a bond—leaving the maturity and yield unchanged—will reduce the duration of the bond. This follows because bonds with higher coupons pay relatively more of their cash flows sooner and hence have shorter durations.

Increasing the yield on a bond—leaving the maturity and coupon unchanged—will also reduce the duration of the bond. This follows because a higher yield leads to lower present values for more distant payments relative to the earlier payments and hence relatively lower weights attached to the years remaining to those payments. This reduces the duration of the bond.

At first glance it would seem that increasing the maturity of a bond should also increase the duration of that bond. However, this is strictly true only for bonds trading at a premium to principal value. If a bond is trading at a discount increasing maturity will initially increase—but can later decrease—the bond's duration.

The only exception to the foregoing comments is the case of a zero coupon bond. Since the duration of such a bond is identically equal to its maturity, it does not change with interest rates.

3.3   Using Duration to Measure Interest Rate Sensitivity

It is often useful to know the effect of changing interest rates on the prices of different bonds. There is no general relationship between bond maturity and interest rate sensitivity. However, it is easy to prove a simple and direct relationship between interest rate sensitivity and duration (as is shown in appendix A). Algebraically the result is

$$\frac{\Delta P}{P} = \frac{-D}{(1 + R)} \cdot \Delta R \tag{3.5}$$

where

P = price of the bond,

R = yield on the bond,

D = duration of the bond.

Here ΔP is the change in price associated with a change in yield of ΔR. This equation says that the *relative* change in the price of the bond (which is $\Delta P/P$) is proportional to the *absolute* change in yield (ΔR) where the factor of proportionality, $-D/(1 + R)$, is a function of the bond's duration.

Equation (3.5) implies that for a given change in yield, longer duration bonds have greater relative price volatility. The intuition for this result is clear. The longer a bond's duration, the greater will be the average time that must elapse to receive a dollar of its cash flow. Since the present value of a dollar is more sensitive to interest rate movements the further in the future the dollar is to be paid, longer duration bonds have a greater price sensitivity than shorter duration bonds.

Any scenario described in the previous section that causes an increase in a bond's duration serves to raise its interest rate sensitivity, and vice-versa. Therefore, if rates are expected to fall, bonds with lower coupons can be expected to appreciate faster than higher coupon bonds of the same maturity. In the extreme, zero coupon issues should afford the greatest capital appreciation in a rising market. Conversely, zero coupon and low coupon bonds may be relatively less desirable if the market is expected to decline.

3.4   Duration and Immunization

Another important use of duration is in evaluating the risk exposure of a bond. Consider an investor who contemplates buying bonds and who needs his money back in exactly h years, no earlier and no later. His *investment horizon* is then said to be *h* years. By assumption, any coupons received before year *h* will be reinvested and any bond that matures after year *h* will be sold at the end of year *h*.

Reinvestment Risk and Market Risk

The hypothetical investor described above can buy any of a wide variety of bonds. Let us examine the consequences of two possible choices.

Suppose that the investor has a 2-year investment horizon and purchases a 2-year bond with a 9% coupon yielding 10% to maturity. The price of the bond is

$$P = \frac{9}{(1 + .10)} + \frac{9 + 100}{(1 + .10)^2} = 98.26 \tag{3.6}$$

Since the investor wants his funds at the end of two years and not any earlier, he is only interested in the total cash return from his investment on that date. If the first $9 coupon can be reinvested at 10%, the cash flow at the end of his horizon will be $109 + (9) \cdot (1 + .10)$. The yield per annum on his investment will be the value of Q such that

$$\text{Purchase price} = \frac{\text{Cash return}}{(1 + Q)^2}$$

or

$$98.26 = \frac{109 + (9) \cdot (1 + .10)}{(1 + Q)^2} \tag{3.7}$$

Comparing equation (3.7) with equation (3.6) shows that Q is equal to .1, or the 10% yield prevailing at purchase. More specifically, the investor earns (over his 2-year investment horizon) a return equal to the original yield on the bond if he can reinvest all coupon payments at that yield. However, if the reinvestment rate is lower than the bond's yield at the time of purchase, then the investor's yield over his horizon will also be lower than the bond's original yield, and conversely.

The foregoing argument demonstrates that an investor who buys a bond with a maturity matched to (or less than) his investment horizon is exposed to *reinvestment* risk—if rates go up, the investor is better off, and if rates go down, the investor is worse off.

There is a reciprocal kind of risk that appears when an investor buys a bond that has too long a maturity relative to his investment horizon. This risk is called *market* risk.

To understand the nature of market risk, suppose that the investor has a 1-year horizon and buys a 2-year 9% coupon bond yielding 10% per annum. As in the example above, the purchase price of the bond is

$$P = \frac{9}{(1 + .10)} + \frac{9 + 100}{(1 + .10)^2} = 98.26 \tag{3.8}$$

Since the investor wants his funds at the end of one year and not any later, he is interested in the market value of his bond only at that time. If the bond can be sold at a 10% yield after one year, the cash return on his investment will be $9 + 109/(1 + .10)$, that is, the initial $9 coupon plus the maturity value of the bond discounted at a yield of 10%. The yield on his investment will be the value of Q such that

$$\text{Purchase price} = \frac{\text{Coupon} + \text{Sale proceeds}}{(1 + Q)}$$

or

$$98.26 = \frac{9 + 109/(1 + .10)}{(1 + Q)} \tag{3.9}$$

Comparing equation (3.9) with equation (3.8) shows that Q is equal to .1, or 10% per annum. More specifically, the investor earns (over his investment horizon) a return equal to the original yield on the bond if he can liquidate the bond at that yield. If the yield when he sells is lower than the original yield, his earnings will be greater than that yield, and conversely. Stated another way, if rates go up, the investor is worse off, and if rates go down, the investor is better off. This phenomenon is called *market risk.*

Balancing Reinvestment Risk and Market Risk

We have thus far shown that an investor who buys bonds with a maturity shorter than or equal to his investment horizon is exposed to reinvestment risk, that is, he is worse off if interest rates go down. On the other hand, if he buys bonds with too long a maturity, he is exposed to market risk, that is, he is worse off if interest rates go up. It is therefore natural to ask whether there is any bond that leaves the investor's position unchanged regardless of whether interest rates go up or down. The answer is, *a bond that has a duration equal to the investor's horizon.* As shown in appendix B, in this case the reinvestment risk just offsets the market risk, and the investor earns the bond's original yield over his horizon no matter what happens to interest rates after the purchase date.

A bond is said to *immunize* an investor against interest rate fluctuations if its duration equals the investor's investment horizon. That is, the yield over the specified horizon is free from risk due to interest rate changes. If the duration is less than the horizon, the bond bears reinvestment risk.

Conversely, if the duration exceeds the horizon, the bond bears market risk.

It is important to note that whether a bond immunizes against risk or bears either reinvestment risk or market risk depends on a comparison of (1) the bond's duration with (2) the investor's horizon. It is not possible to assess the riskiness of a bond in terms of its duration alone. Thus longer duration bonds can be less risky than shorter duration bonds for investors —like pension funds with distant horizons.

Some Caveats

Although immunizing bonds are free of both reinvestment and market risk, it is not true that they can be forgotten once they are purchased. In particular, they have to be adjusted in response to changes in interest rates in order to maintain a match between duration and investment horizon as time passes.

As noted above, duration depends on yield, so immunizing bond portfolios have to be "rebalanced" from time to time if interest rates change significantly. Since duration falls (rises) when interest rates go up (down), an immunizing bond portfolio will come to bear reinvestment risk if yields rise and will come to bear market risk if yields fall. This means an investment manager seeking to maintain an immunizing portfolio should switch into shorter duration bonds following a fall in yields and into longer duration bonds following a rise in yields.

It was also noted above that duration does not contract on a year-for-year basis as a bond approaches maturity. To appreciate this effect, consider a 20-year bond with a coupon of 11.875% priced at par. This bond initially has a duration of 8.03 years. After 5 years, however, the duration of the bond falls only .69 years to 7.34 years. After another 5 years, when the bond has 10 years remaining to maturity, its duration will be 6.41 years. Thus the bond ages (in a financial sense) more slowly than time passes. Table 3.1 shows the relation between maturity and duration for this bond in more detail.

Now suppose that the 11.875%, 20-year bond is purchased against a cash requirement 8 years in the future. Since the bond's initial duration of 8.03 years matches the investor's 8-year horizon the investment provides immunization against changes in interest rates. However, after 5 years the cash requirement is only 3 years in the future, while the bond's duration is 7.34 years. Thus the bond is no longer an immunizing investment and has begun to impose market risk on the investor. To maintain an immunized position, the investor should sell the bond and invest the proceeds in a new bond with a shorter, 3-year, duration. This will keep the duration of his investment matched to his now shorter horizon.

Table 3.1
Maturity and duration for a bond with a coupon of 11.875% priced at par

Term to maturity	Duration
20 yr	8.03 yr
19	7.92
18	7.80
17	7.67
16	7.51
15	7.34
14	7.15
13	6.93
12	6.69
11	6.41
10	6.11
9	5.76
8	5.38
7	4.94
6	4.46
5	3.91
4	3.30
3	2.61
2	1.84
1	.97

The only exception to the above comments on the need for rebalancing is the case of zero coupon bonds. Such bonds always have a duration equal to their remaining maturity. Thus the duration of a zero declines on a year-for-year basis as it approaches maturity. In addition the duration of a zero does not depend on the level of interest rates.

3.5 Appendix A: Duration as a Measure of the Interest Rate Sensitivity of a Bond's Price

Consider a bond which has n annual coupons remaining to be paid where each coupon is for $\$C$ per $\$100$ principal amount.

If the bond has a yield of R the price of the bond is

$$P = \frac{C}{(1 + R)} + \frac{C}{(1 + R)^2} + \cdots + \frac{C}{(1 + R)^{n-1}} + \frac{C + 100}{(1 + R)^n} \tag{A3.1}$$

We show in this appendix how duration is related to changes in the price and yield of this bond.

To begin, consider the derivative of the price of the bond with respect to its yield:

$$\frac{dP}{dR} = -\frac{C}{(1+R)^2} - \frac{2 \cdot C}{(1+R)^3} - \cdots - \frac{(n-1) \cdot C}{(1+R)^n} - \frac{n \cdot (C+100)}{(1+R)^{n+1}} \qquad \text{(A3.2)}$$

After multiplying both sides by $1 + R$, this becomes

$$(1+R) \cdot \frac{dP}{dR} = -\left[\frac{C}{(1+R)} + \frac{2 \cdot C}{(1+R)^2} + \cdots + \frac{(n-1) \cdot C}{(1+R)^{n-1}} + \frac{n \cdot (C+100)}{(1+R)^n} \right]$$

$$\text{(A3.3)}$$

Examining the term in brackets on the right-hand side of equation (A3.3) shows that it is $D \cdot P$, or the product of duration and price (see equation 3.3). Thus we can write

$$(1+R) \cdot \frac{dP}{dR} = -D \cdot P \qquad \text{(A3.4)}$$

Using finite changes in yield and price, we have

$$\frac{\Delta P}{\Delta R} = \frac{-D \cdot P}{(1+R)} \qquad \text{(A3.5)}$$

This is the same as equation (3.5).

3.6   Appendix B: Duration as the Balance Point between Reinvestment Risk and Market Risk

Consider an investor with an investment horizon of h years and a bond that has n annual coupons remaining to be paid, where each coupon is for $\$C$ per $\$100$ principal amount. This appendix shows that the bond is riskless for the investor if its duration is just equal to the investor's horizon, that is, that reinvestment risk balances market risk when duration equals investment horizon.

To begin, let us examine the position of the investor at the end of his h-year investment horizon. Assume that m coupons are received before the horizon date and that $n - m$ coupons remain to be paid as of the horizon date. The investor's final wealth can be divided into two components:

1. The proceeds of the m coupons received before the horizon date and reinvested to that date.

2. The liquidation value of the unmatured bond on the horizon date.

Both of these components depend on the level of interest rates following purchase of the bond. If, for example, rates rise, then the first component will be larger, and the second component will be smaller. The bond as a whole is an immunizing or riskless investment if any decrease in one component is exactly offset by an increase in the other component. For simplicity we assume that market yields can change only once, immediately after purchase of the bond.

Let us now derive analytically the two components of the investor's final wealth. Suppose that all the coupons received before the horizon date can be reinvested at interest rate R. (This follows from the assumption in the text of a flat yield curve.) The coupon received at the end of year 1 will be worth $C \cdot (1 + R)^{h-1}$ at the horizon date. Similarly the coupon received at the end of year 2 will be worth $C \cdot (1 + R)^{h-2}$ at the horizon date. It follows that the sum of the values on the horizon date of the reinvested coupons is

$$I = C \cdot (1 + R)^{h-1} + C \cdot (1 + R)^{h-2} + \cdots + C \cdot (1 + R)^{h-m} \qquad \text{(A3.6)}$$

This component of the investor's final wealth is a direct function of R:

$$\frac{\Delta I}{\Delta R} > 0 \qquad \text{(A3.7)}$$

That is, as noted above, higher values of R will lead to larger values of I.

The liquidation value of the bond on the horizon date can be derived by discounting the remaining cash flows on the bond back to that date. Since m coupons have already been received, there are $n - m$ coupons remaining. The liquidation value of the bond computed at a yield of R is

$$L = \frac{C}{(1 + R)^{m+1-h}} + \frac{C}{(1 + R)^{m+2-h}} + \cdots + \frac{C}{(1 + R)^{n-1-h}} + \frac{C + 100}{(1 + R)^{n-h}} \qquad \text{(A3.8)}$$

This component of the investor's final wealth is an inverse function of R:

$$\frac{\Delta L}{\Delta R} < 0 \qquad \text{(A3.9)}$$

That is, higher values of R will lead to lower values of L.

The investor's final wealth is the sum of the two components identified above:

$$W = I + L \qquad \text{(A3.10)}$$

We want to find out if it is possible to have a bond such that $\Delta W / \Delta R = 0$, that is, such that final wealth is invariant with respect to changes in interest rates.

From the expressions for I and L we have

$$W = C \cdot (1 + R)^{h-1} + C \cdot (1 + R)^{h-2} + \cdots + C \cdot (1 + R)^{h-m}$$

$$+ \frac{C}{(1 + R)^{m+1-h}} + \frac{C}{(1 + R)^{m+2-h}} + \cdots + \frac{C}{(1 + R)^{n-1-h}} + \frac{C + 100}{(1 + R)^{n-h}}$$

(A3.11)

Dividing both sides by $(1 + R)^h$ gives

$$\frac{W}{(1 + R)^h} = \frac{C}{(1 + R)} + \frac{C}{(1 + R)^2} + \cdots + \frac{C}{(1 + R)^m} + \frac{C}{(1 + R)^{m+1}}$$

$$+ \frac{C}{(1 + R)^{m+2}} + \cdots + \frac{C}{(1 + R)^{n-1}} + \frac{C + 100}{(1 + R)^n}$$

(A3.12)

The term on the right-hand side of equation (A3.12) is just the price of the bond at the beginning of the investment period when the yield on the bond is R. Denoting this price as P, we have

$$W = (1 + R)^h \cdot P.$$

(A3.13)

The change in W for a given change in R is

$$\frac{dW}{dR} = h(1 + R)^{h-1} \cdot P + (1 + R)^h \cdot \frac{dP}{dR}$$

$$= (1 + R)^h \left[\frac{dP}{dR} + \frac{h \cdot P}{(1 + R)} \right]$$

(A3.14)

From appendix A we have $dP/dR = -D \cdot P/(1 + R)$ so that

$$\frac{dW}{dR} = (1 + R)^h \left[\frac{-D \cdot P}{(1 + R)} + \frac{h \cdot P}{(1 + R)} \right]$$

or

$$\frac{dW}{dR} = P \cdot (1 + R)^{h-1} \cdot (h - D)$$

(A3.15)

It follows directly that the investor's final wealth does not depend on R if the duration of the bond matches the investor's horizon, that is, $dW/dR = 0$ if $D = h$.

It also follows that the bond exposes the investor to market risk if the duration of the bond exceeds his investment horizon, that is, $dW/dR < 0$ if $D > h$. Finally, the bond exposes the investor to reinvestment risk if the duration of the bond is shorter than his investment horizon, that is, $dW/dR > 0$ if $D < h$.

3.7 Subsequent Remarks

For expositional simplicity we assumed in this chapter that bonds make annual coupon payments and that yields are computed with annual compounding. Chapter 4 restores the use (based on Treasury market conventions) of semi-annual coupon payments and yields computed with semi-annual compounding. The next chapter also considers the problem of defining the duration of a bond at a date other than a coupon payment date. (Compare the definition of duration in equations 3.3 and 4.2.)

4 The Effect of Interest Payments on the Duration of a Bond: Implications for Portfolio Management and Yield Curve Analysis

Participants in the fixed income markets frequently use duration to measure the futurity of a stream of cash flows. For example, we characterize one bond as "longer" than a second bond if the duration of its interest and principal payments exceeds the duration of the payments from the second bond. In more analytical applications duration is used to quantify the volatility of the market value of a bond and to identify whether an investment bears market risk, reinvestment risk, or no risk relative to a specified investment horizon.

In view of the significance and widespread used of bond duration, it is important to be aware of peculiarities in its behavior. This chapter discusses one such peculiarity: the increase in the duration of a bond when it pays a coupon. Although this phenomenon is easily (and often) overlooked it is not quantitatively insignificant. We will see that the duration of a new 20-year bond with a 12% coupon trading at a 12% yield starts out at 7.98 years, falls gradually to 7.48 years immediately before its first coupon payment, and then jumps back up to 7.92 years after the payment is made. Thus there is a decline in duration of .50 years over the course of six months but only .06 years of that decline persists beyond the payment of the first coupon.

There are two reasons for seeking to understanding this type of sharp, periodic shift in duration. First, understanding the shift provides some novel insights into duration-based portfolio management, including how interest income is reinvested and when a portfolio must be reallocated to maintain a match between its duration and a given horizon date. Second, some problems in yield curve analysis can be avoided if periodic shifts in duration are recognized.

The chapter is organized as follows: Section 4.1 reviews the definition of bond duration. Section 4.2 describes the behavior of duration through time, including both the general decline in duration as a bond approaches maturity and the increase in duration after a bond pays a coupon. Section 4.3 points out the implications of the latter phenomenon for volatility analysis, portfolio management, and yield curve analysis. Finally, section 4.4 presents an alternative definition of duration that may be more appropriate for yield curve analysis.

4.1 The Conventional Definition of Duration

The duration of a bond is the average time remaining to its future interest and principal payments where the time to a particular payment is

Written July 1984.

weighted by the *present value* of that payment. To calculate duration, we have to describe the size and timing of the bond's future payments, and we have to specify how the present value of a future payment is computed.

Future Payments and Market Value

Consider a Treasury bond with an annual coupon rate of Rcp on which there are n semi-annual coupons remaining to be paid. Suppose that there is a fraction w of a semi-annual period remaining before payment of the next coupon. (w is computed using an actual-over-actual day count method as described in chapter 1.) The first coupon will be paid in the fraction w of a six-month period, the second coupon in $1 + w$ periods, and so on, to the payment of the last coupon and the return of principal in $n - 1 + w$ periods.

The market value of the bond is its quoted price plus accrued interest from the beginning of the current coupon period. Since there is a fraction w of a period left before payment of the next coupon the accrued interest is $(1 - w) \cdot \frac{1}{2} Rcp$. (This is calculated as the size of the next coupon, $\frac{1}{2} Rcp$, times the fraction, $1 - w$, of the current period that has already elapsed.) Denoting the quoted price of the bond as P the total market value is $P + (1 - w) \cdot \frac{1}{2} Rcp$.

We have now described the market value of the bond and the future payments from the bond:

Present market value

$P + (1 - w) \cdot \frac{1}{2} Rcp$

Future payments

in w periods:	$\frac{1}{2} Rcp$
in $1 + w$ periods:	$\frac{1}{2} Rcp$
in $2 + w$ periods:	$\frac{1}{2} Rcp$

.

.

.

in $n - 2 + w$ periods:	$\frac{1}{2} Rcp$
in $n - 1 + w$ periods:	$\frac{1}{2} Rcp + 100$

The yield and duration of the bond are derived from these data.

Yield

The yield on the bond is the discount rate that makes the present value of the future payments equal to the market value. In other words, it is the value of Rm that satisfies the equation

$$P + (1 - w) \cdot \tfrac{1}{2} Rcp = \frac{\tfrac{1}{2} Rcp}{(1 + \tfrac{1}{2} Rm)^w} + \frac{\tfrac{1}{2} Rcp}{(1 + \tfrac{1}{2} Rm)^{1+w}} + \cdots$$

$$+ \frac{\tfrac{1}{2} Rcp}{(1 + \tfrac{1}{2} Rm)^{n-2+w}} + \frac{\tfrac{1}{2} Rcp + 100}{(1 + \tfrac{1}{2} Rm)^{n-1+w}} \tag{4.1}$$

This definition of yield follows the conventions of the Treasury bond market: semi-annual compounding and compounding over the fractional part of a semi-annual period.

Duration

The duration of the bond is the weighted average time remaining to the future payments. Denoting duration as D, we define it as

$$D = \frac{\begin{aligned}&\frac{\tfrac{1}{2} w \cdot \tfrac{1}{2} Rcp}{(1 + \tfrac{1}{2} Rm)^w} + \frac{\tfrac{1}{2}(1 + w) \cdot \tfrac{1}{2} Rcp}{(1 + \tfrac{1}{2} Rm)^{1+w}} + \cdots \\ &+ \frac{\tfrac{1}{2}(n - 2 + w) \cdot \tfrac{1}{2} Rcp}{(1 + \tfrac{1}{2} Rm)^{n-2+w}} + \frac{\tfrac{1}{2}(n - 1 + w) \cdot (\tfrac{1}{2} Rcp + 100)}{(1 + \tfrac{1}{2} Rm)^{n-1+w}}\end{aligned}}{P + (1 - w) \cdot \tfrac{1}{2} Rcp} \tag{4.2}$$

To appreciate this definition, consider the construction of the second term in the numerator. There are $1 + w$ semi-annual periods or $\tfrac{1}{2}(1 + w)$ years remaining to the second coupon payment. The size of that payment is $\tfrac{1}{2} Rcp$, and its present value is $\tfrac{1}{2} Rcp/(1 + \tfrac{1}{2} Rm)^{1+w}$. The product of these two terms, $\tfrac{1}{2}(1 + w) \cdot \tfrac{1}{2} Rcp/(1 + \tfrac{1}{2} Rm)^{1+w}$, is the remaining time to the payment weighted by the present value of the payment. Construction of the other terms in the numerator follows analogously. The denominator of equation (4.2) is the sum of the present values of the future payments which, from equation (4.1), is equal to the market value of the bond.

Duration in the Standard Case

Equation (4.2) defines the duration of a bond in the general case where the bond is between coupon payments and carries accrued interest. The usual textbook definition of duration implicitly assumes that a coupon has just been paid and that there is no accrued interest on the bond. In this case the duration of a bond with n coupons remaining to be paid is

$$D = \frac{\frac{\tfrac{1}{2} \cdot \tfrac{1}{2} Rcp}{(1 + \tfrac{1}{2} Rm)} + \frac{1 \cdot \tfrac{1}{2} Rcp}{(1 + \tfrac{1}{2} Rm)^2} + \cdots + \frac{\tfrac{1}{2}(n - 1) \cdot Rcp}{(1 + \tfrac{1}{2} Rm)^{n-1}} + \frac{\tfrac{1}{2}(n) \cdot \tfrac{1}{2} Rcp}{(1 + \tfrac{1}{2} Rm)^n}}{P} \tag{4.3}$$

Comparing equations (4.2) and (4.3) shows that equation (4.3) is a special case of equation (4.2) where $w = 1$, that is, where there are six full months remaining to the next coupon.

Here we are concerned with the behavior of the duration of a bond through time, abstracting from changes in bond yields. This behavior can be thought of as follows: When a bond is issued, the first coupon will not be paid for six full months, so equation (4.3) applies. As time passes, the first coupon payment date gets closer, so equation (4.2)—with values of w less than unity—applies. Assuming that the yield on the bond is unchanged, the market value of the bond increases over this interval because of the accumulation of accrued interest. The increases the denominator of equation (4.2) and reduces the bond's duration. Then, upon payment of the first coupon, the accrued interest disappears, and we go back to equation (4.3) but with $n - 1$ coupons instead of n coupons.

We show in the next section that this last event implies an increase in the duration of the bond and that the increase can be large enough to offset much of the decrease experienced over the preceding six months.

4.2   The Duration of a Bond through Time

Examining a concrete example is the fastest way to appreciate the point of this chapter. Figure 4.1 exhibits the duration of a 20-year, 12% bond from

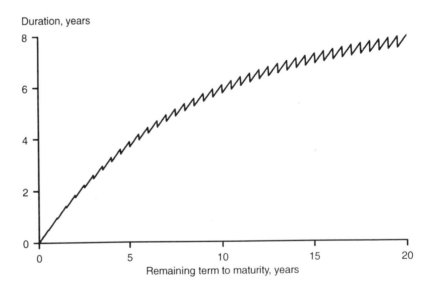

Figure 4.1
Duration of a bond with a 12% coupon priced at a 12% yield from original issue as a 20-year bond to final maturity

its date of issue to its maturity, assuming that the yield on the bond remains constant at 12%. Table 4.1 shows some representative numbers used in plotting the figure.

Two aspects of bond duration are evident in figure 4.1. As a broad proposition the duration of the bond declines as the bond approaches maturity. The decline is slow at first, with duration falling by only a fraction of a year for each contraction of a year in remaining term to maturity. Duration begins to fall more quickly as the bond comes within about five years of its maturity date and ultimately declines on a one-for-one basis with remaining term to maturity.

Figure 4.1 also shows a series of peculiar sawtooth fluctuations in duration superimposed on the general decline. It is evident from table 4.1 that the fluctuations are associated with coupon payments. In particular, the duration of the bond rises whenever the bond pays a coupon. The increase is quite significant when the bond has more than ten years remaining to maturity and becomes smaller as the bond approaches maturity.

Why Does Duration Jump Periodically?

The sawtooth fluctuations in the duration of a bond are a consequence of the market convention for paying interest periodically rather than continuously.

Table 4.1
Duration of a bond with a 12% coupon priced at a 12% yield immediately before and after selected coupon payment dates

| Coupon | Remaining term to maturity | Duration | | Change in duration |
		Immediately before payment	Immediately after payment	
1	$19\frac{1}{2}$ yr	7.48 yr	7.92 yr	.44 yr
2	19	7.43	7.87	.44
3	$18\frac{1}{2}$	7.37	7.81	.44
4	18	7.31	7.75	.43
5	$17\frac{1}{2}$	7.25	7.68	.43
10	15	6.89	7.30	.41
15	$12\frac{1}{2}$	6.39	6.78	.38
20	10	5.74	6.08	.34
25	$7\frac{1}{2}$	4.86	5.15	.29
30	5	3.68	3.90	.22
35	$2\frac{1}{2}$	2.11	2.23	.13
36	2	1.74	1.84	.10
37	$1\frac{1}{2}$	1.34	1.42	.08
38	1	.92	.97	.06
39	$\frac{1}{2}$	.47	.50	.03

Note: Term to maturity at issue = 20 years. Duration at issue = 7.98 years.

The issuer of a bond pays interest semi-annually and makes the entire amount of a payment to whoever holds the bond on the payment date, even if the bond was purchased as recently as the preceding day. (An investor who buys a bond between interest payments compensates the seller for this "inequity" by paying accrued interest in addition to the quoted price. The accrued interest represents an interest return to the seller for holding the bond over the interval since the last payment by the issuer.)

The convention on payment of interest in semiannual "lumps" means that the characteristics of a bond can change sharply when it pays interest. Consider, for example, the 12%, 20-year bond when it has a bit more than $19\frac{1}{2}$ years remaining to maturity and when there are still the original 40 coupons remaining to be paid. Immediately before the first coupon payment date, the bond promises a payment of 6% of principal in just a few days and a series of 39 later payments. Immediately after the payment date, the bond promises only the 39 later payments, the first coupon having been paid. More particularly, the bond's future payments are not the same on the two dates. The bond includes a very short-term future payment on the first date that is absent on the second date.

Since the duration of the bond is the average time to whatever payments are promised by the bond, it is not unreasonable that duration increases when the very near-term payment disappears from the future payment stream. The 39 payments that remain after the first coupon is paid have a longer average time to payment than those same payments *plus* one very near-term payment.

Why Does Duration Jump More on a Longer Maturity Bond?

Having established why the duration of a bond increases when it pays a coupon, we might pose the further question of why the increase is larger on a longer maturity bond. For example, as shown in table 4.1, following a coupon payment the duration of a bond with 19 years remaining to maturity increases by .44 years, but the duration of a bond with 2 years remaining to maturity increases by only .10 years.

The simplest way to think about the size of the jump in duration is to keep in mind the definition of duration as an average time to payment. Many of the payments on a 19-year bond occur far in the future. Dropping a very near-term payment leads to a large increase in the average time to the remaining payments. On the other hand, all of the payments on a 2-year bond are much closer at hand. Dropping a very near-term payment does not lead to much of an increase in the average of the times to the remaining payments.

A more graphic illustration of this argument might be helpful. Example 1 shows the individual and average heights of the players and coach of two

Example 1
Computing the average height of a basketball team

Consider the heights of the players on two basketball teams:

	High school team	Professional team
Center	6′2″	7′1″
Forward	5′10″	6′11″
Forward	6′	6′6″
Guard	6′	6′8″
Guard	6′2″	6′10″

Suppose that each team has a coach who is 5′10″ tall. A little effort with a desk calculator shows the average heights of the teams, including and excluding the coaches:

	High school team	Professional team
Average with coach	5′11$\frac{3}{4}$″	6′7$\frac{1}{4}$″
Average without coach	6′$\frac{1}{2}$″	6′9$\frac{1}{2}$″
Change in average height	$\frac{3}{4}$″	2$\frac{1}{4}$″

basketball teams. The players on the high school team are not very tall. Excluding the coach in computing the average height produces an increase of only $\frac{3}{4}$ inch in that average. Excluding the coach in computing the average height of the professional team makes a difference of $2\frac{1}{4}$ inches.

The Behavior of Duration Between Interest Payments

Close examination of table 4.1 reveals a third important characteristic of the behavior of bond duration. *Between* coupon payments the duration of a bond always declines on a one-for-one basis with the passage of time. For example, the duration of the 20-year bond at original issue is 7.98 years and the duration six months later is 7.48 years, for a decline of .50 years. Following payment of the first coupon the duration is 7.92 years, and it is 7.43 years six months later, for a decline of .49 years. This pattern of declines in duration of .5 years *between* consecutive coupon payments continues throughout the life of the bond.

The present section began with a broad characterization of figure 4.1 to the effect that the duration of a bond declines over time—slowly at first and then at an accelerating rate as the bond approaches maturity. We now see that this general behavior is the result of two very different phenomena. First, *between* interest payments the duration of a bond declines by one day every day; that is, it declines on a one-for-one basis with the passage of time. Second, *across* interest payment dates the duration of a bond increases sharply. If the bond has a long remaining maturity, the increase following an interest payment is nearly as large as the preceding decline, so the net decline is small. This is why the duration of a long maturity bond tends to decline slowly.

The increase in duration associated with payment of a coupon is much smaller when a bond has only a few years remaining to maturity, so the net decline over several coupon periods is larger. This is why the duration of a short maturity bond declines almost as rapidly as the bond's remaining term to maturity.

4.3 Consequences of Periodic Jumps in Duration

Having established that the duration of a bond increases following payment of a coupon, we might wonder whether the phenomenon matters in any practical sense. In fact the "fine structure" of secular changes in bond duration is more than a matter of academic interest. We will see in this section that it has important implications for the use of duration as a measure of the volatility of bond values and in defining the shape of the yield curve. We will also see that it has especially important implications for a duration-managed portfolio, including how interest payments are reinvested and how and when the portfolio as a whole must be reallocated to maintain a match between its duration and the time remaining to a given horizon date.

Duration as a Measure of Volatility

One use of duration is as an index of the volatility of bond values. The longer the duration of a bond, the more sensitive is its value to a given change in interest rates.

The discussion in section 4.2 suggests that a bond is more volatile immediately after a coupon payment (after its duration has jumped) than before that payment. This may seem a little unusual because we do not usually think of a bond becoming more volatile merely because it has paid a coupon. However, greater volatility follows almost trivially from the way volatility is measured.

The general relationship between duration and bond volatility is as follows: Let V be the market value of a bond, that is, the quoted price plus accrued interest, and let D be the bond's duration. If the yield on the bond changes by an amount ΔR, from R to $R + \Delta R$, the market value of the bond changes by an amount ΔV, where

$$\Delta V = V \cdot \left(\frac{-D}{1 + \frac{1}{2}R} \right) \cdot \Delta R \qquad (4.4)$$

Table 4.2
Change in market value of a $19\frac{1}{2}$ year 12% bond for a 10 basis point change in yield

	Day before coupon payment	Day of coupon payment
Value at 12% yield	105.97[a]	100.00[c]
Value at 12.10% yield	105.22[b]	99.25[c]
Change in value	−.75	−.75
Percent change in value	−.71%	−.75%

a. 105.97 equals quoted price of 100.00 plus accrued interest of 5.97.
b. 105.22 equals quoted price of 99.25 plus accrued interest of 5.97.
c. No accrued interest.

For example, the value of a new 20-year bond with a 12% coupon declines from 100.00 to 99.25 ($\Delta V = -.75$) when the yield on the bond increases from 12% ($R = .12$) to 12.10% ($\Delta R = +.001$). This change in value can be predicted with equation (4.4) from the 7.98-year duration of the bond:

$$\Delta V = V \cdot \left(\frac{-D}{1 + \frac{1}{2}R} \right) \cdot \Delta R$$

$$= 100 \cdot \left(\frac{-7.98}{1 + \frac{1}{2} \cdot 12} \right) \cdot (.001)$$

$$= -.75$$

Now consider the volatility of the market value of the same bond immediately before and immediately after its first coupon payment. As shown in table 4.2, an increase in yield of 10 basis points leads to a price decline of .75 points in both cases. However, this price decline represents .71% of the value of the bond immediately before the coupon payment (when the bond carries almost six points of accrued interest) and .75% of the value of the bond after the coupon payment (when the bond carries no accrued interest).

The sense in which a bond becomes more volatile after a coupon payment should now be clear. Volatility is measured as the relative change in the value of the bond for a given change in yield rather than as the absolute change in value. The value of a bond falls when the bond pays a coupon, even if its yield and quoted price are unchanged, because accrued interest is paid off. Thus, a given change in value is *relatively* more significant after a coupon payment.

Duration as a Measure of Risk

In general, the riskiness of a bond cannot be judged independently of the requirements of a buyer. A corporate cash manager needing funds in three months would accept a 3-month Treasury bill as riskless, but he might be unwilling to bear the market risk of buying a 2-year note. Conversely, a pension fund manager might view a 20-year bond as riskless whereas a 2-year Treasury note would expose him to reinvestment risk. The difference in the perception of risk by these two investors is a function of the different cash payments they are funding. The corporate cash manager needs his money back in the near future and hence has a short investment horizon. The pension manager has to fund long-term benefit payments and has a long horizon.

Duration can be used to assess the risk of a particular bond for a particular buyer. If the bond's duration exceeds the buyer's investment horizon, the bond will add market risk or reduce reinvestment risk. If the duration of the bond is shorter than the buyer's horizon the bond will add reinvestment risk or reduce market risk.

The discussion in section 4.2 might seem to suggest that a bond can become "inappropriate" for a particular investor as a result of a coupon payment. For example, suppose that an investor with an 8-year horizon buys the 20-year 12% bond described in table 4.1 at a 12% yield on its issue date. Since the bond has a duration of 7.98 years at the time of purchase, the bond is a nearly riskless investment.

Over the course of the following six months the duration of the bond falls to 7.48 years, and the investor's horizon contracts to $7\frac{1}{2}$ years, so the bond remains a nearly riskless investment. Then, on the first coupon payment date, the duration of the bond jumps to 7.92 years. Does this mean that the bond suddenly begins to impose market risk on the investor, since its duration now exceeds the investor's remaining horizon?

The answer is no. The duration of the bond surely does increase as a result of the coupon payment. However, the duration of the investor's *portfolio* does not change because his portfolio now includes cash (with a zero-year duration) as well as the bond. It is the duration of this total portfolio that matters, not the duration of an individual item in the portfolio. Thus mere payment of the coupon is not sufficient reason for the investor to sell the bond on the premise that it has become "risky" compared to his horizon.

The foregoing argument not withstanding, payment of interest on a bond does require that a portfolio manager make some risk management decisions. Specifically he has to decide (1) how to reinvest the new cash and (2) how much of his original bond position he should continue to hold in light of his reinvestment decision. These decisions have to be made jointly.

Using duration analysis, payment of interest can be seen to have two direct implications for a portfolio manager investing to a fixed horizon date. First, he should not invest the new cash in more of the same bond because that would leave him with a portfolio whose duration exceeds his horizon. This is a direct result of the jump in the bond's duration following the coupon payment.

Second, if the investor invests the cash in a security with any significant duration, such as one-year Treasury bills, he will have to sell off some of this original bond position and invest the proceeds in shorter duration debt to keep the average duration of his portfolio unchanged. This is a simple consequence of the fact that investment of cash is an extension trade so the duration of his other assets must be shortened if he is to keep his average duration unchanged.

When a Portfolio Must Be Reallocated to Maintain a Match between Its Duration and a Given Horizon Date

The last observation has an important implication for duration-managed portfolios. It is widely recognized that since the duration of a bond does not decline on a year-for-year basis with the passage of time, a bond portfolio invested to a fixed horizon date has to be rebalanced from time to time. For example, if an investor initially buys a 20-year bond to fund a cash requirement in eight years, it is clear he cannot remain invested only in that bond for the entire 8-year interval. After, say, 4 years he will have only a 4-year horizon, but the bond will have 16 years remaining to maturity and a duration of 7.5 years (assuming a 12% coupon and a 12% yield). Thus he will be selling some of his bond position and buying shorter duration securities as time goes by.

Our analysis of the effect of interest payments on duration suggests that this "rebalancing" should occur on or around coupon payment dates. It is on those dates that the investor has to make an extension trade, that is, reinvest his interest income, and hence must shorten the duration of his other assets to keep the average duration of his portfolio matched to the time remaining to his ultimate horizon.

We have also established that a duration-managed portfolio *does not* have to be rebalanced between interest payments. As noted in section 4.2, the duration of a bond declines on a one-for-one basis with the passage of time between its coupon payments. Similarly the duration of a portfolio of bonds will decline on a one-for-one basis with the passage of time as long as none of the bonds in the portfolio make a payment. This means that if the duration of a portfolio matches a particular horizon date at some point in time, it will continue to match that date for as long as no payments are received.

The preceding paragraphs can be summarized by observing that in the absence of interest payments, a duration-managed portfolio does not have to be rebalanced to maintain the match to its horizon date and that it must be rebalanced when interest is received. It is therefore not surprising that many Treasury bond portfolio managers trade actively around the February 15, May 15, August 15, and November 15 dates when many Treasury bonds pay interest and that they trade less actively at other times.

Duration and the Yield Curve

The concept of a yield curve, or the structure of yields on bonds with different maturities, is well-known to market participants. Rather than think about yield and maturity, however, many investors prefer to analyze yield and duration. The latter is a more natural approach if one starts with the premise that bonds whose durations match a specified investment horizon are immunizing investments. A yield-duration curve shows directly the consequences for yield of moving into securities that carry reinvestment risk (have a duration shorter than the horizon) or market risk (have a duration longer than the horizon).

The jump in the duration of a bond following a coupon payment creates problems for any simple comparison of yield and duration. For example, suppose that at some point in time the yields on bonds of different durations fall nicely along a curve, as shown by the solid line in figure 4.2. (They never do of course because of differences in the tax treatment of premium and discount bonds and because of technical conditions of supply and demand in different issues, but it makes sense to start out by thinking about the simplest case.) Now suppose that all the bonds pay a coupon and that their durations increase. Assuming market prices do not change, the yield-duration curve shifts to the right, as shown in figure 4.2 by the movement to the dashed line. In addition the yield curve appears to flatten, since the duration of a longer bond increases more than the duration of a shorter bond.

The problem with the evident flattening of the yield curve is that it is a transient phenomenon. As time goes on, the duration of each bond declines, and the curve will shift to the left and re-steepen (again assuming prices are unchanged). This in-and-out movement occurs around some "average" yield curve and is not usually of interest compared to analysis of the shape of the "average" curve itself.

There is another implication of jumps in duration for yield curve analysis. Not all bonds pay interest on the same semi-annual cycle. For

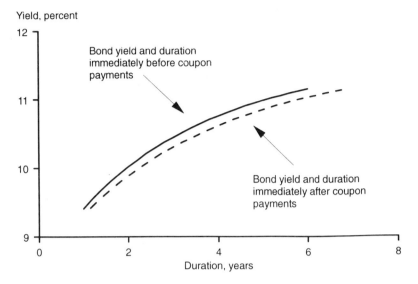

Figure 4.2
Change in the level and slope of the yield curve when bonds pay interest

example, some Treasury bonds pay interest on May 15 and November 15 while others pay interest on February 15 and August 15. If the yield curve has a positive slope and if we compare different bonds in terms of their yields and conventional durations, a bond that has just paid a coupon will look expensive compared to other bonds. That is, it will have a yield that is low in light of its currently longer duration. This relationship will reverse when the other bonds pay their coupons and show a suddenly greater duration.

The upper panel of table 4.3 illustrates this phenomenon. Between February 10, 1984, and February 14, 1984, the yield on the $10\frac{3}{4}\%$ bond of May 15, 2003, rose 4 basis points and its duration declined by .02 years. Between the same two days the yield on the $10\frac{3}{4}\%$ bond of February 15, 2003, rose a virtually identical 5 basis points, but its duration increased by .43 years. This sharp increase in duration resulted from the latter bond paying its February 15 coupon. Since the yield curve had a slight negative slope in the 20-year sector in February 1984, the February 2003 bond went from being a bit expensive to a bit cheap (compared to the May 2003 bond) when it paid its coupon. The lower panel of table 4.3 shows that exactly the reverse phenomenon occurred in May 1984 when the May 2003 bond paid a coupon. These reversals of the yield and duration relationship suggest that simple comparisons of yield and duration may sometimes be misleading. In particular, we should not try to analyze bond yields as a stable function of conventionally defined bond durations.

Table 4.3
Comparison of yield and duration for the $10\frac{3}{4}\%$ bond of February 15, 2003, and the $10\frac{3}{4}\%$ bond of May 15, 2003, around coupon payment dates

Bond maturity	Change in yield	Change in duration
Change in yield and duration from 2/10/84 (2/14/84 settlement) to 2/14/84 (2/15/84 settlement)		
2/15/2003	11.96 → 12.01%	7.59 → 8.02 yr
5/15/2003	11.96 → 12.00	7.83 → 7.81
Change in yield and duration from 5/11/84 (5/14/84 settlement) to 5/14/84 (5/15/84 settlement)		
2/15/2003	13.77 → 13.71%	7.16 → 7.18 yr
5/15/2003	13.77 → 13.70	6.94 → 7.42

For yield curve analysis it may be preferable to measure the duration of a bond in a way that captures the general level of duration without also reflecting the decline in duration associated with the accrual of interest and the jump in duration associated with an interest payment. We consider this issue in the next section.

4.4   An Alternative Definition of Duration

In section 4.2 we observed that the duration of a bond jumps when the bond pays a coupon. In section 4.3 we explored the implications of the jump and concluded that it does not create any analytical inconsistencies for either volatility analysis or portfolio immunization but that it can create a misleading impression in yield curve analysis. For the latter application it may be desirable to use a measure of the futurity of the cash flow on a bond which changes smoothly over time.

Figure 4.3 shows an example of such a smooth measure. The thin line in that figure is the same as the line in figure 4.1: the conventional duration of a 12% bond at a 12% yield from its issue date to its maturity 20 years later. The heavier line in figure 4.3 is a smooth approximation of the thin line. It shows the tendency of the bond's duration to decline as the bond approaches maturity, but it does not exhibit the sawtooth fluctuations in duration associated with semi-annual interest payments.

The smoothed duration of a bond, denoted D_s, can be computed as

$$D_s = \frac{\dfrac{\frac{1}{2}w \cdot \frac{1}{2}Rcp}{(1 + \frac{1}{2}Rm)^w} + \dfrac{\frac{1}{2}(1 + w) \cdot \frac{1}{2}Rcp}{(1 + \frac{1}{2}Rm)^{1+w}} + \cdots + \dfrac{\frac{1}{2}(n - 2 + w) \cdot \frac{1}{2}Rcp}{(1 + \frac{1}{2}Rm)^{n-2+w}} + \dfrac{\frac{1}{2}(n - 1 + w) \cdot (\frac{1}{2}Rcp + 100)}{(1 + \frac{1}{2}Rm)^{n-1+w}}}{P + \frac{1}{2} \cdot \frac{1}{2}Rcp} \qquad (4.5)$$

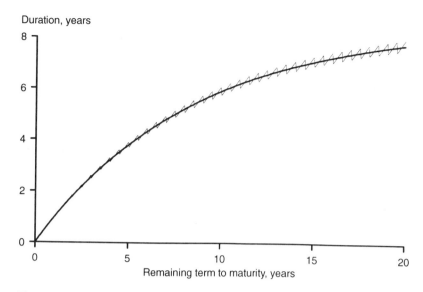

Figure 4.3
Duration (thin line) and smoothed duration (heavier line) of a bond with a 12% coupon priced at a 12% yield from original issue as a 20-year bond to final maturity

A comparison of this equation to the conventional duration defined in equation (4.2) shows that the only difference is the denominator. The denominator of equation (4.2) is the quoted price of the bond plus the accrued interest to the date of valuation. The denominator of equation (4.5) is the quoted price plus the *average* amount of accrued interest midway between two interest payments.

There is no analytical justification for the duration defined by equation (4.5). The justification is pragmatic: obtaining a measure of the futurity of a bond's payments that captures the secular trend of the bond's true duration but that does not exhibit the fine structure of the latter measure.

4.5   Subsequent Remarks

The concept of duration expressed in equation (4.2) is commonly known as *Macaulay* duration, so named for the innovator Frederick R. Macaulay. *Modified* duration is a related concept sometimes used on the Street.

The modified duration of a bond paying interest semi-annually can be computed from the bond's Macaulay duration as

$$D_{\text{mod}} = D \cdot (1 + \tfrac{1}{2}R)^{-1} \tag{S4.1}$$

where D is Macaulay duration, D_{mod} is modified duration, and R is the semi-annually compounded yield on the bond. From equation (4.4) we have

$$D = -\frac{\Delta V}{\Delta R} \cdot \frac{(1 + \frac{1}{2}R)}{V} \tag{S4.2}$$

where ΔV is the change in the value of a bond with a yield of R and a Macaulay duration of D associated with a change in yield of ΔR. Substituting this expression for D into the right-hand side of equation (S4.1) gives

$$D_{\text{mod}} = -\frac{\Delta V}{\Delta R} \cdot \frac{1}{V} \tag{S4.3}$$

This shows that modified duration is a measure of the sensitivity of the price of a bond to a change in its yield relative to the level of the bond's price. Unlike Macaulay duration this measure is not affected directly by the level of the bond's yield—compare equations (S4.2) and (S4.3).

5 Rate of Return and Futurity of Cash Flow from a Bond: Are Yield and Duration Good Measures?

Investors buy and sell bonds for many reasons, sometimes premised on a "feel" for the market and other times stemming from more quantitative analysis. On the analytical side, two security characteristics—yield and duration—play an especially prominent role in appraising fixed income securities. Yield gives some indication of the average rate of return on invested capital. Duration indicates the time span over which that rate of return has relevance; that is, it reflects the "futurity" of a bond's cash flow.

Unfortunately, there are almost as many ways to compute a yield as there are securities in the market. While none of the methods for calculating yield are wrong, it seems clear that they cannot all be equally right. Similar comments apply to duration.

The multiplicity of yield conventions sometimes creates problems for market participants. At the most basic level it confounds attempts to compare securities solely on the basis of their yields. For example, we describe below a Treasury bill and a zero coupon security that have the same dollar price and the same maturity but have yields of 10.82% and 10.91%, respectively. The nine basis points difference in yield has nothing to do with cash flows. It stems from differences in the conventions used to compute yield.

The variety of duration calculations would also seem to hinder the comparison of different securities. Duration is a powerful device for examining whether, for instance, a high coupon bond is "equivalent" in a risk sense to a low coupon or zero coupon bond of shorter maturity. However, bonds that look the same with respect to one definition of duration may appear different if another definition is used.

In sum, while good analysis and good decision making is difficult without good measurement, it appears that present measures of the two most basic characteristics of a bond leave something to be desired.

This chapter examines, almost from first principles, the problem of measuring the rate of return on a bond and the futurity of its cash flow. Section 5.1 begins by exploring simple single-payment securities like Treasury bills and zero-coupon securities. We note some properties that yield "should" have and ask whether conventional definitions of yield have those properties. For example, the yield on a single-payment security should depend on the purchase price, the amount of money received at maturity, and the number of days between purchase and maturity, but it should not also depend on extraneous security characteristics such as the specific calendar date of maturity. Treasury bill yields have this property,

Written December 1984.

but yields on zeros do not. Because conventional definitions of yield do not have "nice" properties, we offer an alternative definition that does have desirable characteristics

Section 5.2 extends the new definition of yield to bonds that make multiple payments. Section 5.3 questions the relevance of yield calculations for bonds. It notes that we really want to measure the average rate of return on the capital invested in a bond and the span of time over which that rate of return is relevant. Given some special assumptions on the behavior of interest rates, section 5.3 demonstrates that the new definition of yield is in fact the single appropriate measure of return and that Macaulay duration is the single appropriate measure of bond futurity. This is important because it means that (given the special assumptions) market participants really are measuring what they think they are measuring.

Unfortunately, these results fall apart when we examine, in section 5.4, bond return and bond futurity in the context of less restrictive assumptions about the behavior of interest rates. In particular, the results do not hold if the yield curve is not always flat. Moreover, if the curve can change shape in any of several ways, there may be no objective measure of either the rate of return on a bond or the futurity of a bond's cash flow.

The conclusions of section 5.4 are discouraging. They imply that we cannot measure objectively two of the most crucial characteristics of a bond. Section 5.5 examines the quantitative significance of the problem. We conclude that yield is an adequate, if somewhat imperfect, measure of the rate of return on a bond. Moreover Macaulay duration is an acceptable measure of futurity as long as the yield curve does not change shape. However, it may not be an acceptable measure if there is substantial uncertainty about the future shape of the curve.

5.1 Money-in/Money-out Yields

The best place to begin examining a complex problem is with the simplest case. In the present context this means a security that makes only a single future payment, such as a Treasury bill or a zero-coupon security. Such a security is sometimes called a *money-in/money-out* (MIMO) instrument because an investor pays for the security on one date (puts money in) and is paid back a specified amount on a specified later date (gets money out).

This section first describes several properties of the conventionally defined yield on a Treasury bill and on a zero. Peculiarities in the behavior of these yields lead us to offer a new definition of the yield on a MIMO instrument.

Some Peculiarities of Conventional Yields

Suppose that an investor is offered a Treasury bill maturing on November 15, 1984, at a 10.41% discount rate for settlement on August 23, 1984. To calculate the yield on the bill, the investor must first compute its price. There are 84 days between settlement and maturity, so the bill has a price of 97.571% of face amount: $97.571 = 100 - (84/360) \cdot 10.41\%$.

The yield on a Treasury bill priced at P with less than 183 days remaining to maturity is the value of Rm that satisfies the equation

$$P = \frac{100}{(1 + v \cdot \frac{1}{2}Rm)} \tag{5.1}$$

where v is the fraction of a semi-annual period remaining in the life of the bill. v is calculated as the number of days from settlement to maturity, divided by 182.5. (Bill yield calculations assume there are 182.5 days in a semi-annual period.) The November 15, 1984, bill at a price of 97.571 on August 23, 1984, has a yield of 10.817% per annum,

$$97.571 = \frac{100}{1 + (84/182.5) \cdot \frac{1}{2}(.10817)}$$

Note that the fraction v is 84/182.5 or .46027 semi-annual periods.

Now suppose that the investor is offered a zero-coupon security maturing November 15, 1984 at a price of 97.571 percent of face amount for settlement on August 23, 1984. If he fails to notice that this zero is identical in terms of cash flow to the previously described bill (pay 97.571 on August 23, 1984, receive 100.0 on November 15, 1984), he might compute its yield to compare to the yield on the bill.

The yield on the zero is the value of Rm that satisfies the equation

$$P = \frac{100}{(1 + w \cdot \frac{1}{2}Rm)} . \tag{5.2}$$

where w is the fraction of a semi-annual period remaining to the maturity of the zero. The fraction w is figured as the number of days from settlement to maturity divided by the number of days in the six calendar months preceding maturity. There are 184 days between May 15, 1984, and the November 15, 1984, maturity date of the zero, so $w = 84/184 = .45652$. The yield on the zero is 10.906% per annum because

$$97.571 = \frac{100}{1 + (84/184) \cdot \frac{1}{2}(.10906)}$$

This would suggest that the zero is a better buy than the Treasury bill because it has a yield of 10.906%, while the yield on the bill is only 10.817%.

What is peculiar about these two yields is that the cash flows on the underlying instruments are identical: Pay 97.571 and receive 100.0 in 84 days. The reason for the difference in yields is the assumed number of days in a full semi-annual period. The bill calculation uses 182.5 days, and hence the bill appears to have .46027 semi-annual periods remaining to maturity. The zero calculation uses 184 days, so the zero appears to have .45652 periods remaining. The yield on the zero appears to be greater because the zero has a shorter time remaining to maturity when "time" is measured in semi-annual periods.

This result is of course nonsense. Any reasonably defined yield should be the same for both the bill and the zero because the money in (97.571), the money out (100.00), and the investment interval (84 days) are the same for both securities.

The nature of this peculiarity can be illuminated further with a third example. Suppose that an investor is offered a zero maturing August 15, 1985, at a price 97.571 for settlement on May 23, 1985. The settlement date is again 84 days before maturity, so this third case is identical to the two preceding examples in a cash flow sense. The yield on the zero, however, would be calculated as 10.728% per annum. This follows because there are 84 days to maturity and 181 days in the six calendar months preceding maturity (February 15, 1985, to August 15, 1985), so $w = 84/181 = .46409$ in equation (5.2).

We have now described three securities with identical cash flows but with yields of 10.728% (the August 15, 1985, zero), 10.817% (the November 15, 1984, bill), and 10.906% (the November 15, 1984, zero). The reason for the yield differences is the assumed length of a semi-annual period: 181 days for the August 15, 1985, zero, 182.5 days for the bill, and 184 days for the November 15, 1984, zero. Note that bills *always* assume 182.5 days in a semi-annual period, while short-maturity zeros use the day count in the six calendar months preceding maturity. Thus the yield on a zero depends on its calendar maturity date as well as on its price and the number of days from purchase to maturity. The yield on a bill depends only on its price and the number of days from purchase to maturity.

With these comparisons in mind we can state the first property that yield should have:

Property 1   The yield on a MIMO security should depend on the amount of money committed, the amount of money received at maturity, and the number of days in the investment interval.

Example 1

Comparing the yield on two sequential 6-month Treasury bills to the yield on a 1-year Treasury bill

---

1. Invest \$100 in a 182-day Treasury bill at a 10.68% yield:

$$\text{Maturity value} = \$100 \cdot \left(1 + \frac{182}{182.5} \cdot \frac{1}{2} \cdot .1068\right)$$

$$= \$105.325$$

2. Invest \$105.325 in a 182-day Treasury bill at a 10.68% yield:

$$\text{Maturity value} = \$105.325 \cdot \left(1 + \frac{182}{182.5} \cdot \frac{1}{2} \cdot .1068\right)$$

$$= \$110.934$$

3. Invest \$100 in a 364-day Treasury bill at a 10.68% yield:

$$\text{Maturity value} = \$100 \cdot \left(1 + \frac{1}{2} \cdot .1068\right) \cdot \left(1 + \frac{364 - 182.5}{182.5} \cdot \frac{1}{2} \cdot .1068\right)$$

$$= \$110.934$$

Note that investment 3 is equivalent to the combination of investments 1 and 2 on a money-in/money-out basis over the 364-day investment interval.

This property is satisfied by the conventional yield on a Treasury bill but not by the yield on a zero.

We turn now to a second peculiarity of MIMO yields. Suppose that an investor buys a 6-month Treasury bill at a 10.68% yield and at maturity invests the proceeds in another 6-month bill at the same yield. As shown in example 1, he would have been in essentially the same position if he bought a 1-year bill at a 10.68% yield in the first place. Thus the yield on a 6-month bill exhibits "stability under reinvestment." Two sequential investments at the same yield are economically equivalent to a single combined investment at that yield.

As shown in example 2, the yield on a 3-month bill is not stable under reinvestment. Two successive 3-month bills at a yield of 10.40% are equivalent, on a money-in/money-out basis, to a 6-month bill at a 10.53% yield. The reason is that the bill yields are computed with simple interest over the fractional part of a semi-annual period (see equation 5.1) and hence do not reflect the compounding implicit in reinvestment. Bills with a 6-month maturity are a special case because their term to maturity is almost a full semi-annual period, so the use of simple interest does not matter much.

The yields on some MIMO securities, such as zeros with more than six months to maturity, are computed with compound interest over both full

Example 2
Comparing the yield on two sequential 3-month Treasury bills to the yield on a 6-month Treasury bill

---

1. Invest \$100 in a 91-day Treasury bill at a 10.40% yield:

$$\text{Maturity value} = \$100 \cdot \left(1 + \frac{91}{182.5} \cdot \frac{1}{2} \cdot .1040\right)$$

$$= \$102.593$$

2. Invest \$102.593 in a 91-day Treasury bill at a 10.40% yield:

$$\text{Maturity value} = \$102.593 \cdot \left(1 + \frac{91}{182.5} \cdot \frac{1}{2} \cdot .1040\right)$$

$$= \$105.253$$

3. Invest \$100 in a 182-day Treasury bill at a 10.534% yield:

$$\text{Maturity value} = \$100 \cdot \left(1 + \frac{182}{182.5} \cdot \frac{1}{2} \cdot .10534\right)$$

$$= \$105.253$$

Note that investment 3 is equivalent to the combination of investments 1 and 2 on a money-in/money-out basis over the 182-day investment interval.

and fractional semi-annual periods (see chapter 2). Their yields are stable under reinvestment. This is illustrated in example 3 with a 9-month zero.

Defining a yield on a MIMO security that is stable under reinvestment is desirable because it facilitates comparison of yields on securities of different maturities. It is convenient to be able to say that two successive investments in a 6-month bill at 11% yields the same as a 1-year bill at 11%. Conversely, it is inconvenient to remember that two sequential 3-month bills at 10.40% are equivalent to a 6-month bill at 10.54%. This leads to the second property which yield should have:

Property 2   The yield on a MIMO security should exhibit stability under reinvestment and hence should be computed with compound rather than simple interest over the fractional part of a semi-annual period.

This property is satisfied by the conventionally defined yield on a zero with more than six months remaining to maturity, but it is not satisfied by yields on shorter maturity zeros or by yields on Treasury bills.

A "True" Yield

We are now ready to define a yield on a MIMO security that has both of the properties described above.

Example 3
Comparing the yield on two sequential 9-month zeros to the yield on an 18-month zero

1. Invest \$100 in a 9-month zero at a 10.75% yield:

$$\text{Maturity value} = \$100 \cdot \left(1 + \frac{1}{2} \cdot .1075\right)^{9/6}$$

$$= \$108.170$$

2. Invest \$108.170 in a 9-month zero at a 10.75% yield:

$$\text{Maturity value} = \$108.170 \cdot \left(1 + \frac{1}{2} \cdot .1075\right)^{9/6}$$

$$= \$117.007$$

3. Invest \$100 in an 18-month zero at a 10.75% yield:

$$\text{Maturity value} = \$100 \cdot \left(1 + \frac{1}{2} \cdot .1075\right)^{18/6}$$

$$= \$117.007$$

Note that investment 3 is equivalent to the combination of investments 1 and 2 on a money-in/money-out basis over the 18-month investment interval.

Consider a MIMO security priced at P that pays 100 in n days. We define the "true" yield on the security as the value of Rm that satisfies the equation

$$P = \frac{100}{(1 + \frac{1}{2}Rm)^x} \tag{5.3}$$

The exponent x is the number of semi-annual periods between settlement and maturity, where a full semi-annual period is assumed to have 182.625 days. (This derives from the length of a year: 365 days except for a 366-day year every four years, so the average year is 365.25 days and the average semi-annual period is 182.625 days.) Note that the definition retains the assumption of semi-annual compounding but assumes that interest is compounded over both fractional and full semi-annual periods.

To illustrate equation (5.3), consider a MIMO security priced at $P = 97.571$ that matures in 84 days. The "true" yield on the security is the value of Rm that satisfies the equation

$$97.571 = \frac{100}{(1 + \frac{1}{2}Rm)^{84/182.625}}$$

or $Rm = .10983$, or 10.983% per annum. This yield differs from the conventional yield of 10.817% on an 84-day bill priced at 97.571 because the latter yield assumes simple interest over the investment interval whereas

Table 5.1
Treasury bill yields on September 19, 1984, for settlement September 20, 1984

Maturity	Days to maturity	Conventional yield	True yield	Difference
Nov. 1, 1984	42	10.425%	10.643%	.219%
Nov. 29, 1984	70	10.646	10.829	.183
Dec. 27, 1984	98	10.658	10.797	.139
Jan. 24, 1985	126	10.834	10.932	.098
Feb. 21, 1985	154	10.947	11.001	.054
Mar. 21, 1985	182	11.017	11.025	.009
Apr. 18, 1985	210	11.031	11.073	.042
May 16, 1985	238	11.063	11.121	.058
Jun. 13, 1985	266	11.144	11.205	.061
Jul. 11, 1985	294	11.247	11.301	.054
Aug. 8, 1985	322	11.312	11.352	.040
Sep. 5, 1985	350	11.323	11.344	.020

the true yield assumes compound interest. The true yield of 10.983% can also differ from the conventional yield on an 84-day zero priced at 97.571 because of the interest convention and also because of the day count convention used with zeros.

Table 5.1 shows conventional yields and true yields on a variety of Treasury bills on September 19, 1984. The difference between the two yields is largest for short maturity bills and for bills with about nine months to maturity. This is a result of using simple interest over the fractional part of a semi-annual period in computing the conventional yield on a bill and compound interest in computing the true yield. For bills with about 6 months to maturity (the March 21, 1985, bill) and 12 months to maturity (the September 5, 1985, bill) the two yields are nearly the same because those bills have nearly an integer number of semi-annual periods remaining before maturity. The assumption on how to discount over a fractional period is largely irrelevant for such bills.

Table 5.2 shows conventional yields and true yields for a variety of zeros on July 24, 1984. The largest difference is 35 basis points on the August 15, 1984, zero. This difference is attributable to the assumption (in conventional yield) of simple interest for a zero with less than six calendar months remaining to maturity versus the assumption of compound interest in true yield. Beginning with the February 15, 1985, zero both the conventional yield and the true yield use compound interest over both full and fractional periods. The differences in the yields on such longer zeros result from the way a fractional semi-annual period is measured: actual-over-actual day counts for the conventional yield and actual over 182.625 for the true yield. As can be seen in table 5.2, this difference becomes irrelevant in computing the yield on a zero with more than about four years remaining to maturity.

Table 5.2
Zero coupon yields on July 24, 1984 for settlement on July 31, 1984

Maturity	Days to maturity	Conventional yield	True yield	Difference
Aug. 15, 1984	15	11.17%	11.52%	.35
Nov. 15, 1984	107	11.50	11.55	.05
Feb. 15, 1985	199	11.90	11.82	−.08
May 15, 1985	288	12.23	12.27	.04
Aug. 15, 1985	380	12.55	12.56	.01
Nov. 15, 1985	472	12.78	12.76	−.02
Aug. 15, 1986	745	13.13	13.14	.01
Aug. 15, 1987	1110	13.32	13.31	−.01
Aug. 15, 1988	1476	13.42	13.42	0
Aug. 15, 1989	1841	13.51	13.51	0
Aug. 15, 1990	2206	13.56	13.56	0
Aug. 15, 1995	4032	13.45	13.45	0
Aug. 15, 2000	5859	13.25	13.25	0
Aug. 15, 2005	7685	12.92	12.92	0

Example 4 shows that the true yield on a MIMO security is stable under reinvestment. That is, earning 11.25% for two successive intervals is equivalent to earning 11.25% over the combined interval. This follows because "true" yield does not assume simple interest over the fractional part of a semi-annual period.

A Comment

At this early stage in the analysis, there is a temptation to ask whether we really need yet another definition of yield? There are two reasons for giving an affirmative answer.

We discussed in this section three securities with identical cash flows (pay 97.571, receive 100.0 in 84 days) but with conventional yields ranging from 10.728% to 10.906% depending on the details of the securities. This state of affairs obviously does not facilitate comparison of the securities. The proposed true yield is a convenient way to assess return on capital that is not influenced by irrelevant security characteristics.

The second reason for the new definition is that it provides a better foundation for examining the return on securities that make multiple payments. This will become clear in the following sections.

5.2 Bond Yields

Having established how we want to compute the yield on a MIMO security, we are ready to consider the more complex case of yields on bonds.

Example 4
Comparing the true yield on two sequential 250-day MIMO securities to the true yield on a 500-day MIMO security

---

1. Invest \$100 in a 250-day MIMO security at an 11.25% true yield:

$$\text{Maturity value} = \$100 \cdot \left(1 + \frac{1}{2} \cdot .1125\right)^{250/182.625}$$

$$= \$107.779$$

2. Invest \$107.779 in a 250-day MIMO security at an 11.25% true yield:

$$\text{Maturity value} = \$107.779 \cdot \left(1 + \frac{1}{2} \cdot .1125\right)^{250/182.625}$$

$$= \$116.164$$

3. Invest \$100 in a 500-day MIMO security at an 11.25% true yield:

$$\text{Maturity value} = \$100 \cdot \left(1 + \frac{1}{2} \cdot .1125\right)^{500/182.625}$$

$$= \$116.164$$

Note that investment 3 is equivalent to the combination of investments 1 and 2 on a money-in/money-out basis over the 500-day investment interval.

The most widely understood way to compute the yield on a bond is to discount each of the bond's future payments at the same interest rate and to define the yield as the interest rate that makes the sum of the discounted values of the individual payments equal to the price of the bond. The present section examines how we can combine this approach with our MIMO yield convention on discounting single payments to define the "true" yield on a bond. The following sections address whether this yield actually measures the rate of growth of capital invested in a bond.

A "True" Bond Yield

Consider a bond that will make a total of n future payments. In the most common case the payments prior to the last payment will be interest equal to one-half of the annual coupon rate, and the last payment will be interest plus return of principal. (However, the first payment may be different from subsequent interest payments if the bond has an odd first coupon.)

Let F_i denote the amount of the ith payment, and let n_i denote the number of days between purchase and the ith payment. In keeping with the true yield convention on the length of a semi-annual period, we will say the ith payment occurs in $x_i = n_i/182.625$ semi-annual periods following settlement. For example, a payment made 2,415 days after settlement occurs 13.224 semi-annual periods after that settlement (13.224 = 2,415/182.625).

At interest rate R the sum of the total discounted value of the bond's future payments is

$$\frac{F_1}{(1 + \frac{1}{2}R)^{x_1}} + \frac{F_2}{(1 + \frac{1}{2}R)^{x_2}} + \cdots + \frac{F_n}{(1 + \frac{1}{2}R)^{x_n}} \tag{5.4}$$

This equation discounts each future payment back to the settlement date using the MIMO convention of equation (5.3).

We define the true yield on the bond as the interest rate that leads to a total discounted value equal to the quoted price of the bond plus the accrued interest on the bond. Letting P denote the quoted price and A the accrued interest, the true yield is the value of Rm that satisfies the equation

$$P + A = \frac{F_1}{(1 + \frac{1}{2}Rm)^{x_1}} + \frac{F_2}{(1 + \frac{1}{2}Rm)^{x_2}} + \cdots + \frac{F_n}{(1 + \frac{1}{2}Rm)^{x_n}} \tag{5.5}$$

To understand how this true yield differs from the conventional yield on a security, it may be helpful to examine some examples.

Comparison of True Yield and Conventional Yield on Treasury Bonds

Consider the 13.375% Treasury bond of March 31, 1985. This bond was quoted at a price of $101\frac{2}{32}$ on September 24, 1984, for settlement on September 25. To calculate either the true yield or the conventional yield, we must first derive (1) the invoice price of the bond and (2) the amounts and dates of the bond's future payments.

The invoice price of the bond is the quoted price plus accrued interest since the last coupon payment. The September 25, 1984, settlement date is 178 days after the preceding (March 31, 1984) coupon, and there are 183 days between that last payment and the next (September 30, 1984) coupon payment. Thus the accrued interest on the bond is $(178/183) \cdot \frac{1}{2} \cdot 13.375$, or 6.505. The invoice price of the bond is therefore 107.567 ($107.567 = 101\frac{2}{32}$ plus 6.505).

The scheduled future payments on the bond are

September 30, 1984   6.6875 (interest)

March 31, 1985   106.6875 (interest plus principal)

However, both of these dates are Sundays, and the payments will not be made until the following Mondays. The *actual* number of days from settlement to payment are

October 1, 1984   6.6875   6 days

April 1, 1985   106.6875   188 days

These payments are, respectively, .03285 (6/182.625) and 1.02943 (188/182.625) semi-annual periods from the settlement date.

Having defined the bond's price and cash flows, we can compute its true yield from equation (5.5). The yield is the value of Rm that satisfies the equation:

$$107.567 = \frac{6.6875}{(1 + \frac{1}{2}Rm)^{.03285}} + \frac{106.6875}{(1 + \frac{1}{2}Rm)^{1.02943}} \tag{5.6a}$$

This implies that $Rm = .11152$, or 11.152% per annum.

The definition of the conventional yield on a Treasury bond differs from the definition of the true yield in three respects. First, delays in payments due to weekends and holidays are ignored. Second, the time between settlement and the first payment is computed using an actual-over-actual day count instead of an actual-over-182.625 day count. Finally, successive payments are presumed to be spaced exactly one semi-annual period apart regardless of the actual day counts between the payments.

Following these conventions, we compute the first payment on the 13.375% bond of March 31, 1985, as .02732 periods following settlement (.02732 = 5/183, where there are 5 days between 9/25/1984 and 9/30/1984 and 183 days between 3/31/1984 and 9/30/1984) and the second payment as 1.02732 periods following settlement (1.02732 = .02732 periods to the first payment plus 1.0 additional periods to the second payment). The conventional yield on the bond is the value of Rm that satisfies the equation

$$107.567 = \frac{6.6875}{(1 + \frac{1}{2}Rm)^{.02732}} + \frac{106.6875}{(1 + \frac{1}{2}Rm)^{1.02732}} \tag{5.6b}$$

This implies that $Rm = .11179$, or 11.179% per annum.

Comparing equations (5.6a) and (5.6b) shows why the true yield is less than the conventional yield by almost three basis points: the payments in equation (5.6b) appear to come sooner after settlement than the payments in equation (5.6a). For example, the first payment is .02732 periods following settlement in equation (5.6b) and .03285 periods in equation (5.6a). This is a result of ignoring the delays in the payments when computing the conventional yield.

True Yield and Conventional Yield on Short-Term Treasury Bonds

Table 5.3 shows the true yield and the conventional yield on a variety of short term Treasury bonds on September 24, 1984. Several comments will help in understanding the differences in the two measures. First, the conventional yield on a Treasury bond with less than six months remaining to maturity uses simple interest rather than the compound interest used in

Table 5.3
Short maturity Treasury bond yields on September 24, 1984, for settlement September 25, 1984

Coupon	Maturity	Conventional yield	True yield	Difference
9.875%	Nov. 30, 1984	10.77%	10.93%	.16[a]
9.625	Feb. 28, 1985	11.15	11.30	.15[a]
9.875	May 31, 1985	11.39	11.42	.03
10.625	Aug. 31, 1985	11.59	11.52	−.07[b]
10.500	Nov. 30, 1985	11.69	11.64	−.05[b]
10.875	Feb. 28, 1986	11.81	11.85	.04
12.625	May 31, 1986	12.13	12.11	−.02[b]
12.375	Aug. 31, 1986	12.14	12.13	−.01[c]

a. Conventional yield assumes simple interest.
b. Saturday maturity.
c. Sunday maturity.

Table 5.4
Intermediate and long maturity Treasury bond yields on September 24, 1984, for settlement September 25, 1984

Coupon	Maturity	Conventional yield	True yield	Difference
12.500%	May 15, 1987	12.26%	12.28%	.02%
12.375	Aug. 15, 1987	12.27	12.26	−.01
12.000	Mar. 31, 1988	12.31	12.32	.01
13.625	Jun. 30, 1988	12.43	12.43	0
13.875	Aug. 15, 1989	12.52	12.52	0
12.750	Nov. 15, 1989	12.48	12.48	0
12.375	Apr. 15, 1991	12.50	12.50	0
13.750	Jul. 15, 1991	12.54	12.54	0
13.125	May 15, 1994	12.53	12.53	0
12.625	Aug. 15, 1994	12.49	12.48	−.01
12.375	May 15, 2004	12.40	12.40	0
13.750	Aug. 15, 2004	12.37	12.36	−.01

the true yield. As we observed in section 5.1, this reduces the conventional yield below the true yield. Second, conventional yield overstates true yield when a bond matures on a weekend. Finally, the two yields can differ because they figure the number of semi-annual periods from settlement to payment differently.

True Yield and Conventional Yield on Intermediate and Long-Term Treasury Bonds

We noted in section 5.1 that true yield and conventional yield are virtually the same for long zeros. As shown in table 5.4, this is also the case for longer maturity bonds. Simply put, when a bond makes payments far in the future, delays in some of those payments of a day or two and fine points of day counts don't matter much for yield.

5.3 Does the Yield on a Bond Measure Return on Capital?

Equation (5.5) defines the yield on a bond by analogy to the definition of the yield on a MIMO security (see equation 5.3). However, similarity of definition does not necessarily mean that the yield on a bond measures return on capital in the same way the yield on a MIMO instrument measures return. A yield of 11% on a 73-day Treasury bill means that capital committed to buy the bill will grow at an average rate of 11% per annum, compounded semi-annually, over the 73 days remaining in the life of the bill. It is not obvious that capital committed to purchase a 10-year bond at a yield of 12% will grow at an average rate of 12% per annum over the following 10 years or over any other interval of time. More generally, we have yet to establish what, exactly, the yield on a bond measures.

Thinking about Rate of Return on a Bond

In examining the meaning of the yield on a bond, we begin with the simplest case. Consider again the MIMO security described in section 5.1: Pay 97.571 and receive 100.0 in 84 days. The meaning of the true yield of 10.983% per annum on this security is unambiguous: it is the average rate of return on capital from purchase to maturity. Note, in particular, the very specific time span (84 days) associated with the yield. The 10.983% yield does not reflect what the unmatured security might be worth 30 days after purchase, nor does it reflect what the reinvested maturity payment might grow to on a date 270 days after purchase. Rather, the yield measures the rate of growth of capital to *the single future date on which the value of the security is known with certainty.*

We want to think about the return on a bond in a similar fashion. Specifically we will say that the return on a bond is the average rate of growth of capital from purchase to some later date, where that later date is defined as a date on which the value of the bond (including the value of any reinvested coupon payments) is known with certainty. We define the futurity of the bond as the time interval from purchase to the date on which the bond has a known value.

This definition of return seeks to recast a bond into a form identical to that of a MIMO security. We put money into the bond at purchase, and we compute how much we will get out, with certainty, at a specified later date. Return measures the average rate of capital appreciation between purchase and that later date, just as the yield on a MIMO instrument measures an average rate of growth of capital. Futurity measures the interval of time over which the rate of return is relevant and corresponds to the term to maturity of a MIMO security.

There is a good practical reason for analyzing a bond as if it were a MIMO instrument. Many investors purchase bonds to fund cash requirements on specified future dates. One way to fund such a requirement is to purchase a MIMO security maturing on the specified date. If bonds can be analyzed like MIMO securities, an investor can purchase a bond with a futurity equal to the time remaining to the cash requirement. This strategy would also give him a fixed amount of cash on the specified date. Bond portfolios constructed to achieve this objective are known generally as immunizing portfolios. Thus we are essentially analyzing the utility of bonds for immunizing future cash requirements.

The conceptual definition of bond return and bond futurity raises two questions. First, is there any future date on which the value of a bond is known with certainty? For a MIMO security the answer is clearly yes—the maturity date. The future value of a bond, on the other hand, depends on what can be earned from reinvestment of interest payments and on the market value of any part of the bond sold before maturity. Both components are quite unpredictable.

Second, assuming that we can establish a value for a bond on some future date, is the average rate of return on capital from purchase to that date numerically identical to the yield defined in equation (5.5)? That is, does yield measure rate of return in an analytically meaningful way?

The remainder of this section addresses these two questions in the context of an extremely restrictive model of the behavior of interest rates. We will show that given the model, the yield on a bond *is* the average rate of growth of capital over an interval of time equal to the Macaulay duration of the bond. The next section reexamines yield and duration in the context of less restrictive assumptions about the behavior of interest rates.

Measuring Return and Futurity When the Yield Curve Is Flat

We assume the following statement characterizes the behavior of yields on MIMO securities: The yield curve is flat and remains flat, so that all MIMO yields change in parallel (i.e., by the same amount) whenever any yield changes. We also assume that all uncertainty in future interest rates stems from the possibility of a one-time shift in the MIMO yield curve, up or down, immediately following purchase of a security. After that shift the curve remains stationary. Finally, we assume that a bond making multiple payments is valued as if it were a "bundle" of MIMO securities. This means that the price of a bond is the sum of the discounted values of its future payments where each payment is discounted as if it were the payment on a MIMO instrument.

Given this admittedly restrictive model of interest rate behavior and bond pricing, we examine whether we can compute the return on a bond in the sense expressed in the beginning of this section: as the average rate of capital appreciation from purchase to a future date on which the value of the bond is known with certainty.

As in section 5.2 we consider a bond that will make n payments following purchase. Let F_i denote the amount of the ith payment, and let x_i denote the number of semi-annual periods between settlement and the ith payment.

The first step in the analysis is to compute the purchase price of the bond. At the time of purchase yields on all MIMO securities are at some interest rate, which we denote R. Since the bond is valued as a bundle of MIMO instruments, its purchase price, denoted $P + A$, can be computed as

$$P + A = \frac{F_1}{(1 + \frac{1}{2}R)^{x_1}} + \frac{F_2}{(1 + \frac{1}{2}R)^{x_2}} + \cdots + \frac{F_n}{(1 + \frac{1}{2}R)^{x_n}} \tag{5.7}$$

Equation (5.7) is a repeated application of equation (5.3). The first payment on the bond is for an amount F_1 after an interval of x_1 semi-annual periods. At the initial MIMO yield R the discounted value of the payment is $F_1/(1 + \frac{1}{2}R)^{x_1}$. The successive terms in the equation follow a similar form. Example 5 illustrates the use of equation (5.7) as a model of bond pricing.

The second step in the analysis is to examine the value of the bond, including the value of any reinvested interest payments, at an arbitrary date following purchase. Suppose that immediately after purchase the (flat) MIMO yield curve shifts to some interest rate R' and thereafter remains stationary at that level. The value of the bond on a horizon date h semi-annual periods following purchase can be computed from the equation

$$FV(R', h) = \frac{F_1}{(1 + \frac{1}{2}R')^{x_1 - h}} + \frac{F_2}{(1 + \frac{1}{2}R')^{x_2 - h}} + \cdots + \frac{F_n}{(1 + \frac{1}{2}R')^{x_n - h}} \tag{5.8}$$

Equation (5.8) says that the contribution of the ith payment to the future value of the bond is $F_i/(1 + \frac{1}{2}R')^{x_i - h}$. If the ith payment precedes the horizon date, $x_i - h$ will be negative. The payment F_i will then be compounded forward to the horizon date at rate R'. If the ith payment follows the horizon date, $x_i - h$ will be positive, and the payment F_i will be discounted back to that date at rate R'. Thus equation (5.8) implies that

Example 5
Pricing a bond from money-in/money-out yields

Consider a 2-year bond with a 10% coupon that pays interest semi-annually and returns principal at maturity. For simplicity, assume that each payment is an integer number of semi-annual periods from the date of purchase so the amounts of and intervals to the cash flows on the bond are

$F_1 = 5.0 \qquad x_1 = 1.0$

$F_2 = 5.0 \qquad x_2 = 2.0$

$F_3 = 5.0 \qquad x_3 = 3.0$

$F_4 = 105.0 \quad x_4 = 4.0$

Suppose that the MIMO yield curve is flat at a yield of 10% per annum compounded semi-annually. The price of the bond can be computed from equation (5.7) as

$$P + A = \frac{F_1}{(1 + \frac{1}{2}R)^{x_1}} + \frac{F_2}{(1 + \frac{1}{2}R)^{x_2}} + \frac{F_3}{(1 + \frac{1}{2}R)^{x_3}} + \frac{F_4}{(1 + \frac{1}{2}R)^{x_4}}$$

$$= \frac{5}{(1 + .05)^1} + \frac{5}{(1 + .05)^2} + \frac{5}{(1 + .05)^3} + \frac{105}{(1 + .05)^4}$$

$$= 4.762 + 4.535 + 4.319 + 86.384$$

$$= 100.00$$

This result views the bond as a bundle of four MIMO instruments. The first pays 5.0 in 1.0 periods and has a price of 4.762. The second pays 5.0 in 2.0 periods and has a price of 4.535. The third pays 5.0 in 3.0 periods and has a price of 4.319. The last instrument pays 105.0 in 4.0 periods and has a price of 86.384. Thus the bundle of four MIMO securities has an aggregate value of 100.00

---

payments received before time h are reinvested at rate R' and that payments due to be received after time h are discounted at rate R'.

Now consider how the future value of the bond varies with the interest rate R'. If the horizon is short and h small, most of the bond's payments occur after the horizon date. A higher R' will lead to a lower future value FV. Heuristically, if we are valuing the bond at a date close to the date of purchase, most of the future value comes from the proceeds of a sale of the bond. Higher rates will produce a lower sale price and a lower FV. Conversely, lower interest rates will lead to a higher future value. This behavior is characterized by saying that the bond bears "market risk" to the nearby horizon date. Example 6 shows a bond that bears market risk.

If h is large, most of the bond's payments occur before the horizon date. A higher R' enhances the proceeds derived from reinvestment of those earlier payments. If h is large enough, the benefits from reinvesting at a higher rate will more than offset any losses realized from sale of the bond's remaining payments, so higher interest rates will produce a higher FV.

Example 6
Valuing a bond at a short future date

Suppose that we want to value the bond described in example 5 at a date 1.0 semi-annual periods after purchase, assuming that MIMO yields go to 11% immediately after purchase. Using equation (5.8) with $h = 1.0$ and $R' = .11$ gives

$$FV(R',h) = \frac{F_1}{(1 + \frac{1}{2}R')^{x_1-h}} + \frac{F_2}{(1 + \frac{1}{2}R')^{x_2-h}} + \frac{F_3}{(1 + \frac{1}{2}R')^{x_3-h}} + \frac{F_4}{(1 + \frac{1}{2}R')^{x_4-h}}$$

$$FV(.11,1.0) = \frac{5.}{(1. + .055)^{1-1}} + \frac{5.}{(1. + .055)^{2-1}} + \frac{5.}{(1. + .055)^{3-1}} + \frac{105.}{(1. + .055)^{4-1}}$$

$$= 5.0 + 4.739 + 4.492 + 89.419$$

$$= 103.651$$

To see the effect of different interest rates on this future value, we can go through a series of similar calculations for a range of values of R':

R'	$FV(R',1.0)$
11.00%	103.651
10.75	103.986
10.50	104.322
10.25	104.660
10.00	105.0
9.75	105.341
9.50	105.684
9.25	106.028
9.00	106.374

As noted in the text, higher interest rates lead to a lower value of the bond 1.0 periods after purchase. This implies the bond bears market risk to that horizon date.

Conversely, lower interest rates will lead to a lower future value. In this case the bond is said to bear "reinvestment risk" to the horizon date. Example 7 shows a bond that bears reinvestment risk to a distant horizon date.

It should be clear that for some intermediate horizon the future value of the bond will not be affected appreciably by either higher or lower interest rates. Denote this horizon as h^0. At the investment horizon h^0 the bond "looks" like a MIMO security with a term to maturity of h^0 semi-annual periods. Example 8 illustrates this invariance of future value with respect to shifts in the MIMO yield curve.

We can now define an appropriate measure of the rate of return on capital invested in the bond. Let FV^0 be the value of the bond on the date h^0 semi-annual periods following purchase. The rate of return on the bond is the value of Rm^0 that satisfies the equation

Example 7
Valuing a bond at a long future date

Suppose that we want to value the bond described in example 5 at a date 4.0 semi-annual periods after purchase, assuming MIMO yields go to 11% immediately after purchase. Using equation (5.8) with $h = 4.0$ and $R' = .11$ gives

$$FV(R',h) = \frac{F_1}{(1 + \frac{1}{2}R')^{x_1-h}} + \frac{F_2}{(1 + \frac{1}{2}R')^{x_2-h}} + \frac{F_3}{(1 + \frac{1}{2}R')^{x_3-h}} + \frac{F_4}{(1 + \frac{1}{2}R')^{x_4-h}}$$

$$FV(.11,4.0) = \frac{5.}{(1. + .055)^{1-4}} + \frac{5.}{(1. + .055)^{2-4}} + \frac{5.}{(1. + .055)^{3-4}} + \frac{105.}{(1. + .055)^{4-4}}$$

$$= 5.871 + 5.565 + 5.275 + 105.0$$

$$= 121.711$$

To see the effect of different interest rates on this future value, we can go through a series of similar calculations for a range of values of R':

R'	$FV(R',4.0)$
11.00%	121.711
10.75	121.671
10.50	121.631
10.25	121.591
10.00	121.551
9.75	121.511
9.50	121.471
9.25	121.431
9.00	121.391

As noted in the text, higher interest rates lead to a greater value of the bond 4.0 periods after purchase. This implies the bond bears reinvestment risk to that horizon date. (Compare this result to the very different result described in example 6.)

$$P + A = \frac{FV^0}{(1 + \frac{1}{2}Rm^0)^{h^0}} \tag{5.9}$$

where $P + A$ is the quoted price of the bond plus accrued interest. $P + A$ is computed from equation (5.7). The time span h^0 measures the interval over which the average rate of return Rm^0 has relevance. That is, it measures the futurity of the bond's cash flow in a way that is conceptually analogous to the term to maturity of a MIMO security.

It is easy to show that the rate of return Rm^0 defined in equation (5.9) is exactly equal to the initial level of MIMO yields. Recall that FV^0 is the value of the bond h^0 periods after purchase and hence can be computed from equation (5.8), since $FV^0 = FV(R',h^0)$. By definition of the horizon h^0, we know that $FV(R',h^0)$ does not depend on R'. Thus we can set R' to the initial level R of MIMO yields, and compute FV^0 as $FV^0 = FV(R,h^0)$.

Example 8

Valuing a bond at a future date on which value is stable with respect to the level of MIMO yields

Example 6 showed that the value of the bond described in example 5 was an inverse function of interest rates for a horizon date 1.0 semi-annual periods after purchase. Example 7 showed that the value of the same bond was positively related to the level of interest rates on a horizon date 4.0 periods after purchase. These results suggest that at some intermediate date the value of the bond should be invariant with respect the level of interest rates.

Suppose that we want to value the bond described in example 5 at a date 3.723 semi-annual periods after purchase, assuming MIMO yields go to 11% immediately after purchase. Using equation (5.8) with $h = 3.723$ and $R = .11$ gives

$$FV(R', h) = \frac{F_1}{(1 + \frac{1}{2}R')^{x_1-h}} + \frac{F_2}{(1 + \frac{1}{2}R')^{x_2-h}} + \frac{F_3}{(1 + \frac{1}{2}R')^{x_3-h}} + \frac{F_4}{(1 + \frac{1}{2}R')^{x_4-h}}$$

$$FV(.11, 3.723) = \frac{5.}{(1. + .055)^{1-3.723}} + \frac{5.}{(1. + .055)^{2-3.723}} + \frac{5.}{(1. + .055)^{3-3.723}}$$

$$+ \frac{105.}{(1. + .055)^{4-3.723}}$$

$$= 5.785 + 5.483 + 5.197 + 103.454$$

$$= 119.920$$

To see the effect of different interest rates on this future value, we can go through a series of similar calculations for a range of values of R':

R'	$FV(R', 3.723)$
11.00%	119.920
10.75	119.919
10.50	119.919
10.25	119.919
10.00	119.919
9.75	119.919
9.50	119.919
9.25	119.919
9.00	119.920

This table shows that to a very close approximation, the value of the bond 3.723 semi-annual periods after purchase is independent of the value of R'.

This gives

$$FV^0 = FV(R, h^0)$$

$$= \frac{F_1}{(1 + \frac{1}{2}R)^{x_1 - h^0}} + \cdots + \frac{F_n}{(1 + \frac{1}{2}R)^{x_n - h^0}}$$

$$= (1 + \tfrac{1}{2}R)^{h^0} \cdot \left[\frac{F_1}{(1 + \frac{1}{2}R)^{x_1}} + \cdots + \frac{F_n}{(1 + \frac{1}{2}R)^{x_n}} \right]$$

From the definition of $P + A$ in equation (5.7), this becomes

$$FV^0 = (1 + \tfrac{1}{2}R)^{h^0} \cdot [P + A]. \tag{5.10}$$

Comparing equations (5.9) and (5.10) shows that $Rm^0 = R$. This demonstrates that both the bond and a MIMO security with a term to maturity of h^0 periods provide a "locked-in" rate of return of R over an interval of h^0 periods, regardless of whether yields rise or fall following purchase.

This process of defining the rate of return and the futurity of a bond can be illustrated with the data presented in examples 5 and 8. Example 5 describes a 2-year bond with a price of 100.00 when the MIMO yield curve is initially flat at 10%. Example 8 shows that the value of the bond, including reinvested interest payments, is 119.919 on a date 3.723 semi-annual periods following purchase, regardless of whether the MIMO yield curve shifts up or down or remains unchanged. Thus the return on the bond over the interval of 3.723 periods is the value of Rm^0 that solves the equation

$$100 = \frac{119.919}{(1 + \frac{1}{2}Rm^0)^{3.723}}$$

or $Rm^0 = .10$, or 10% per annum.

Relation of Bond Return and Bond Futurity to Yield and Macaulay Duration

We have now derived an unambiguous measure of the rate of appreciation of capital committed to purchase a bond, and we have derived the time span over which that rate of appreciation is relevant. Although neither measure looks familiar, it turns out that they are identical to bond yield and Macaulay duration, respectively.

Consider again the bond that we have been examining. The bond has a price $P + A$ and will make n future payments, where the ith payment is for an amount F_i and will occur x_i semi-annual periods after purchase. The yield on the bond, as defined in equation (5.5), is the value of Rm that satisfies the equation

$$P + A = \frac{F_1}{(1 + \frac{1}{2}Rm)^{x_1}} + \frac{F_2}{(1 + \frac{1}{2}Rm)^{x_2}} + \cdots + \frac{F_n}{(1 + \frac{1}{2}Rm)^{x_n}} \tag{5.11}$$

The Macaulay duration of the bond, measured in semi-annual periods, is

$$
h_M = \frac{\dfrac{x_1 \cdot F_1}{(1 + \frac{1}{2}Rm)^{x_1}} + \dfrac{x_2 \cdot F_2}{(1 + \frac{1}{2}Rm)^{x_2}} + \cdots + \dfrac{x_n \cdot F_n}{(1 + \frac{1}{2}Rm)^{x_n}}}{\dfrac{F_1}{(1 + \frac{1}{2}Rm)^{x_1}} + \dfrac{F_2}{(1 + \frac{1}{2}Rm)^{x_2}} + \cdots + \dfrac{F_n}{(1 + \frac{1}{2}Rm)^{x_n}}}
\tag{5.12}
$$

(The Macaulay duration in years is one-half of h_M.)

Comparing equations (5.7) and (5.11) shows that under the assumptions of the present analysis, the yield Rm on the bond is identical to the initial yield R on MIMO securities. Thus the yield on the bond is also identical to the rate of return on capital invested in the bond. Appendix A shows that the Macaulay duration h_M is exactly the futurity of the bond's cash flows, defined as h^0 above.

These results establish the link between yield and Macaulay duration for fixed income securities. To summarize, a bond with yield Rm (defined by equation 5.11) and Macaulay duration h_M (defined by equation 5.12) "looks" like a MIMO instrument with yield Rm that matures in h_M semi-annual periods. The bond yield Rm measures the average rate of return on capital over the interval of h_M periods in exactly the same way the yield on the MIMO security measures the average rate of return on capital to that security's maturity date. Thus either the bond or the MIMO security can be used to immunize a cash requirement h_M periods in the future.

Some Caveats and Comments

These results on bond yield and bond duration are subject to several caveats. They have been established on the premise that the MIMO yield curve shifts only once, immediately following purchase of the bond, and that it is flat both before and after the shift. However, market participants know that interest rates are always changing, that yield curves are typically not flat, and that they change shape from time to time. Thus we have *not* established any general correspondence between bond yield and the rate of return on a bond or between Macaulay duration and the futurity of a bond.

The restrictive assumptions of the present section can be separated into two categories:

1. The assumption that the yield curve shifts only once, immediately following purchase of a bond.

2. The assumption that the yield curve is flat both before and after the shift.

Let us for the moment maintain assumption 2 and examine the consequences of relaxing the assumption of only a single shift in the curve.

Consider an investor who wants to fund a cash requirement coming due on February 15, 1991. If he buys a MIMO security with a February 15, 1991, maturity date, he will be fully immunized against all possible changes in yields. In the alternative, he may buy a bond on February 15, 1985, with a maturity of 12 years and a Macaulay duration of 6 years. The analysis of this section implies that he will be fully immunized against a one-time shift of the (flat) yield curve immediately after purchase. He will not, however, be immunized against subsequent shifts in the (flat) yield curve. For example, if yields rise on February 10, 1991, he will suffer a loss on the sale of what will then be a 6-year bond. Since all the coupons on the bond were received and reinvested at earlier dates, he will have no reinvestment gains to offset this market loss.

The answer to the problem is that the investor has to *maintain continually* a match between the Macaulay duration of his assets and the time remaining to his horizon date. If there is always a match, the investor will always be immunized against the "next" change in yields. This is known as *rebalancing* an immunized portfolio.

In general, bond portfolios have to be rebalanced on coupon payment dates and when yields change significantly. The former topic is described in chapter 4.

The effect of yield changes on bond duration can be appreciated by looking at the definition of Macaulay duration, h_M, in equation (5.12). For a given set of cash flows, the value of h_M falls as the yield Rm rises. Thus, as yields rise, an investor will generally have to extend into longer maturity bonds, and he will have to act conversely as yields fall. As long as rates do not "jump" sharply, he will have an opportunity to rebalance his portfolio continually and hence to maintain the match between its duration and the time remaining to his cash requirement date.

In summary, relaxing the assumption of a one-time shift in yields does not vitiate the conclusion that a bond with a Macaulay duration of h^0 periods "looks" like a MIMO instrument with a maturity of h^0 periods. The next section reconsiders bond return and bond futurity when the yield curve is not always flat.

5.4   Measuring Bond Return and Bond Futurity without Assuming That the Yield Curve Is Flat

In this section we assess the rate of return on a bond and the futurity of a bond's cash flows without making the extreme assumption that the MIMO yield curve is always flat. We continue to define the futurity of the bond as the interval from purchase to a later date on which the value of the bond is known, and we continue to define rate of return as the average rate of capital appreciation between purchase and that later date.

We show below that in the absence of the flat yield curve assumption of the last section, Macaulay duration is an imperfect measure of futurity and that yield is an imperfect measure of rate of return. In fact we show that there is *no* objective measure of either bond return or futurity. Section 5.5 addresses the implications of these somewhat surprising results for portfolio management.

Assumptions on the MIMO Yield Curve

The analysis in section 5.3 assumed that the MIMO yield curve was initially flat at an interest rate R and moved, up or down, to an interest rate R' immediately following purchase of a bond. In this section we want to think about an initial MIMO yield curve that is not necessarily flat. We also want to think about nonparallel shifts, such as a curve that becomes steeper or flatter. This richer framework means that we can no longer represent the initial curve with a single yield R, nor can we represent the subsequent curve with a single yield R'. Instead, we have to recognize explicitly the relation between yield and term to payment.

Let $R[x]$ denote the initial yield on a MIMO instrument with a term to maturity of x semi-annual periods. If the yield curve is rising the value of $R[x]$ will increase as x increases. If the yield curve is inverted, the value of $R[x]$ will fall as x increases. If the yield curve is humped, $R[x]$ will first rise and then fall as x increases.

As in the last section, we assume that the only uncertainty in the MIMO yield curve stems from a single shift immediately following purchase of a bond. Let $R'[x]$ denote the yield after the shift on a MIMO security with a term to maturity of x periods. We write the function $R'[x]$ as $R'[x] = R[x] + t \cdot S[x]$. The variable t is a scalar, and $S[x]$ is a function whose value varies with maturity.

The function $S[x]$ represents the *type* of yield curve shift being studied and the scalar t reflects the *magnitude* of the shift. If t is zero, then $R'[x] = R[x]$ for all x; that is, the curve did not shift. Larger values of t (positive or negative) indicate greater changes in the curve. The "direction" of the change is expressed through the form of $S[x]$.

It may be helpful to examine some examples of curve shifts. A parallel movement of the initial yield curve is represented by $S[x] = 1.0$ for all x. The curve after the shift will then be $R'[x] = R[x] + t$. If t is positive all interest rates moved up by the same amount. If t is negative the whole curve shifted down.

A rotation of the yield curve with the shortest maturity rate remaining unchanged is represented by $S[x] = x$. In this case the shift is proportional to term to maturity. The curve after the shift is $R'[x] = R[x] + t \cdot x$. A positive value of t would imply a relative steepening of the curve, and a negative value of t denotes a relative flattening (or inversion) of the curve.

Example 9 shows a positively sloped initial yield curve and illustrates two types of change in that curve. Scenario A contemplates a parallel shift, and scenario B contemplates a rotation as described in the paragraph above. Note how the individual members of a whole family of final yield curves are indexed by the scalar t in each of the scenarios.

It might appear that this characterization of the yield curve and the change in the curve is unnecessarily cumbersome. This is not the case. The characterization is a powerful way to specify an *arbitrary* initial structure of interest rates (by the form of the $R[x]$ function) and an *arbitrary* change in rates (by the form of the $S[x]$ function). Thus the characterization is far more flexible than assuming, at the outset, a particular type of shift, as is common an many studies of bond duration.

Measuring Bond Futurity and Bond Return

Measuring bond return and bond futurity when the yield curve can change shape is not conceptually different from the methodology of the last section. We only have to be careful to account correctly for the implications of the change in the shape of the curve for the future value of a bond.

The first step in the analysis is to compute the purchase price of the bond from the initial MIMO yield curve and the specification of the bond's payments. We continue to assume the bond will make n payments with the ith payment for an amount F_i in x_i semi-annual periods following purchase. The price of the bond, denoted $P + A$, can be computed as

$$P + A = \frac{F_1}{(1 + \frac{1}{2}R[x_1])^{x_1}} + \frac{F_2}{(1 + \frac{1}{2}R[x_2])^{x_2}} + \cdots + \frac{F_n}{(1 + \frac{1}{2}R[x_n])^{x_n}}$$

(5.13)

This equation figures the price as the sum of the prices of the MIMO instruments implicitly bundled together in the bond. The first payment, for amount F_1, is discounted over x_1 periods at the yield $R[x_1]$ on a MIMO security with a term to maturity of x_1 periods. The second payment of F_2 is discounted over x_2 periods at the yield $R[x_2]$ on a MIMO instrument with x_2 periods to maturity. Note that each bond payment is discounted at its "own" MIMO yield. Through this process the purchase price of the bond reflects the level and shape of the initial yield curve. Example 10 illustrates the use of equation (5.13) for pricing a bond.

The second step is examining the value of the bond on an arbitrary date after purchase. Suppose that immediately following purchase the MIMO

Example 9
An initial yield curve and two scenarios for shifts in the curve

Consider a MIMO yield curve with an overnight yield of 10% per annum (denoted $R[0] = 10.00\%$) and with the following yields on instruments with maturities of 1, 2, 3, and 4 semi-annual periods:

$R[1] = 10.75\%$

$R[2] = 11.25$

$R[3] = 11.50$

$R[4] = 11.60$

Yields on instruments with intermediate maturities follow from linear interpolation. For example, 2.6 periods is 60% of the way from 2.0 to 3.0, so $R[2.6]$ is 60% of the way from 11.25% to 11.50%, or 11.40%. Roughly speaking, the curve is positively sloped but rises at a decreasing rate.

Now consider two scenarios for a shift in the curve. In scenario A the shift is parallel, so all yields change by the same amount. We can write the final curve as $R'[x] = R[x] + t$. For various values of t we can compute the following final curves:

	$R'[0]$	$R'[1]$	$R'[2]$	$R'[3]$	$R'[4]$
A1 ($t = -1.0$)	9.00%	9.75%	10.25%	10.50%	10.60%
A2 ($t = -.5$)	9.50	10.25	10.75	11.00	11.10
A3 ($t = 0$)	10.00	10.75	11.25	11.50	11.60
A4 ($t = +.5$)	10.50	11.25	11.75	12.00	12.10
A5 ($t = +1.0$)	11.00	11.75	12.25	12.50	12.60

Note that a negative value of t reflects a downward shift of all yields and that a positive value of t reflects an upward shift.

In scenario B the shift in yields is due to a "rotation" of the curve with the overnight rate remaining unchanged. We can then write the final curve as $R'[x] = R[x] + t \cdot x$. For various values of t we can compute the following final curves:

	$R'[0]$	$R'[1]$	$R'[2]$	$R'[3]$	$R'[4]$
B1 ($t = -.25$)	10.00%	10.500%	10.75%	10.750%	10.60%
B2 ($t = -.125$)	10.00	10.625	11.00	11.125	11.10
B3 ($t = 0$)	10.00	10.750	11.25	11.500	11.60
B4 ($t = .125$)	10.00	10.875	11.50	11.875	12.10
B5 ($t = .25$)	10.00	11.000	11.75	12.250	12.60

Note that the yield curve becomes flatter the more negative the value of t and becomes steeper the more positive the value of t. Note also that longer maturity yields are relatively more volatile than shorter maturity yields in this scenario.

Example 10
Pricing a bond from money-in/money-out yields

Consider a 2-year bond with a 10% coupon that pays interest semi-annually and returns principal at maturity. For simplicity assume that each payment is an integer number of semi-annual periods from the date of purchase, so the amounts of and intervals to the cash flows on the bond are

$F_1 = 5.0 \qquad x_1 = 1.0$

$F_2 = 5.0 \qquad x_2 = 2.0$

$F_3 = 5.0 \qquad x_3 = 3.0$

$F_4 = 105.0 \quad x_4 = 4.0$

Suppose that the MIMO yield curve is as described in the beginning of example 9. The price of the bond can be computed from equation (5.13) as

$$P + A = \frac{F_1}{(1 + \frac{1}{2}R[1])^1} + \frac{F_2}{(1 + \frac{1}{2}R[2])^2} + \frac{F_3}{(1 + \frac{1}{2}R[3])^3} + \frac{F_4}{(1 + \frac{1}{2}R[4])^4}$$

$$= \frac{5.}{(1.05375)^1} + \frac{5.}{(1.05625)^2} + \frac{5.}{(1.05750)^3} + \frac{105.}{(1.05800)^4}$$

$$= 4.745 + 4.482 + 4.228 + 83.801$$

$$= 97.255$$

This calculation views the bond as a bundle of four MIMO instruments. The first instrument pays 5.0 in 1.0 periods and has a price of 4.745. The second instrument pays 5.0 in 2.0 periods and has a price of 4.482, and so forth.

Given the price of 97.255 on the bond, we can define its yield as the value of Rm that satisfies the equation:

$$P + A = \frac{F_1}{(1 + \frac{1}{2}Rm)^1} + \frac{F_2}{(1 + \frac{1}{2}Rm)^2} + \frac{F_3}{(1 + \frac{1}{2}Rm)^3} + \frac{F_4}{(1 + \frac{1}{2}Rm)^4}$$

$$97.255 = \frac{5.}{(1 + \frac{1}{2}Rm)^1} + \frac{5.}{(1 + \frac{1}{2}Rm)^2} + \frac{5.}{(1 + \frac{1}{2}Rm)^3} + \frac{105.}{(1 + \frac{1}{2}Rm)^4}$$

This implies that $Rm = .11577$, or 11.577% per annum. It should be noted that this yield is not equal to any of the individual MIMO yields used to price the bond. Instead, it is a complex average of those yields.

yield curve shifts to a new curve represented by the function $R'[x]$. Appendix B shows that the value of the bond on a horizon date h semi-annual periods after purchase can be computed from the equation:

$$FV(R'[\cdot], h) = (1 + \tfrac{1}{2} R'[h])^h$$

$$\cdot \left[\frac{F_1}{(1 + \tfrac{1}{2} R'[x_1])^{x_1}} + \frac{F_2}{(1 + \tfrac{1}{2} R'[x_2])^{x_2}} + \cdots \right.$$

$$\left. + \frac{F_n}{(1 + \tfrac{1}{2} R'[x_n])^{x_n}} \right] \qquad (5.14)$$

This future value includes proceeds derived from reinvestment of coupon payments received before the horizon date as well as proceeds derived from sale of the remaining payments on the horizon date. Example 11 illustrates how equation (5.14) is used to value a bond for two members of the yield curve scenarios constructed in example 9.

The third step in the analysis is assessing how the future value of the bond at a given horizon date varies as a function of the yield curve $R'[\cdot]$. Table 5.5 shows the variation of the 2-year bond described in Example 10 at three alternative horizon dates for the parallel shifts (scenario A) described in example 9. Note that larger values of the scalar t in scenario A correspond to greater upward shifts of the curve.

Looking at the first column of table 5.5, we observe that for a horizon of $h = 1$ semi-annual periods, greater values of t result in a lower bond value. This is a manifestation of market risk, or the adverse effect of higher interest rates on the value of a bond liquidated shortly after purchase.

On the other hand, the last column of table 5.5 shows that greater values of t produce higher bond values at a horizon of $h = 4$ semi-annual periods. This reflects reinvestment risk, or the favorable effect of higher interest rates on the reinvestment of coupon payments from a bond held to maturity.

Taken together, the results suggest that for some horizon between 1 and 4 periods the future value of the bond is independent of the value of t; in other words, the value of the bond is not affected by a parallel shift in the yield curve. The middle column of table 5.5 shows this is the case at a horizon of 3.718 semi-annual periods. This horizon, denoted h^0, is the futurity of the cash flows from the 2-year bond for the case of a parallel shift in the initial yield curve.

We can now define the rate of return on the bond. Let FV^0 denote the value of the bond on the horizon date h^0 periods following purchase. The rate of return is the value of Rm^0 that satisfies the equation

Example 11
Valuing a bond on a future horizon date from money-in/money-out yields

Example 9 constructed a variety of MIMO yield curves from an initial yield curve and a shift of a specified type (parallel or pivot around the front end) and magnitude. We consider the following two curves in this example:

	$R'[1]$	$R'[2]$	$R'[3]$	$R'[4]$
A5	11.75%	12.25%	12.50%	12.60%
B1	10.50	10.75	10.75	10.60

Suppose that we want to value the 2-year bond described in example 10 at a date $h = 2$ semi-annual periods following purchase when the MIMO yield curve changed either to curve A5 or to curve B1 immediately after purchase. The general valuation equation is given by equation (5.14) in the text. For $h = 2$ periods and $n = 4$ the equation becomes

$$FV = (1 + \tfrac{1}{2}R'[2])^2 \cdot \left[\frac{F_1}{(1 + \tfrac{1}{2}R'[1])^1} + \frac{F_2}{(1 + \tfrac{1}{2}R'[2])^2} + \frac{F_3}{(1 + \tfrac{1}{2}R'[3])^3} \right.$$

$$\left. + \frac{F_4}{(1 + \tfrac{1}{2}R'[4])^4} \right]$$

If we use the yields specified in curve A5, the future value is computed as

$$FV = (1. + .06125)^2 \cdot \left[\frac{5.}{(1. + .05875)^1} + \frac{5.}{(1. + .06125)^2} + \frac{5.}{(1. + .0625)^3} \right.$$

$$\left. + \frac{105.}{(1. + .0630)^4} \right]$$

$$= 1.12625 \cdot [4.72255 + 4.43951 + 4.16853 + 82.23492]$$

$$= 107.631$$

If we use the yields specified in curve B1, the future value is computed as

$$FV = (1. + .05375)^2 \cdot \left[\frac{5.}{(1. + .0525)^1} + \frac{5.}{(1. + .05375)^2} + \frac{5.}{(1. + .05375)^3} \right.$$

$$\left. + \frac{105.}{(1. + .0530)^4} \right]$$

$$= 1.11039 \cdot [4.75059 + 4.50293 + 4.27324 + 85.40353]$$

$$= 109.851$$

Table 5.5
Valuing a bond for a parallel shift in the MIMO yield curve

	Horizon (semi-annual periods)		
MIMO yield curve[a]	$h = 1.0$	$h = 3.718$	$h = 4.0$
A1 ($t = -1.0$)	103.809	119.878	121.697
A2 ($t = -.5$)	103.143	119.877	121.777
A3[b] ($t = 0$)	102.483	119.877	121.858
A4 ($t = .5$)	101.828	119.877	121.939
A5 ($t = 1.0$)	101.180	119.877	122.021

a. Details on each yield curve are shown in example 9.
b. Represents no shift from the initial yield curve in example 9.

$$P + A = \frac{FV^0}{1 + \frac{1}{2}Rm^0)^{h^0}} \tag{5.15}$$

where $P + A$ is the price of the bond computed from the initial MIMO yield curve as defined in equation (5.13).

This method of defining return can be illustrated numerically with the data in table 5.5. From that table we identify $h^0 = 3.718$ periods and $FV^0 = 119.877$. The purchase price of the bond is 97.255 (see example 10). It follows from equation (5.15) that the rate of return on the bond is the value of Rm^0 that satisfies the equation

$$97.255 = \frac{119.877}{(1 + \frac{1}{2}Rm^0)^{3.718}}. \tag{5.16}$$

This implies $Rm^0 = .11572$, or 11.572%. Thus capital invested in the 2-year bond will, with certainty, grow at a rate of 11.572% per annum over the course of 3.718 semi-annual periods regardless of whether the parallel shift of the initial yield curve is up or down.

These values for the bond's rate of return and futurity *do not* apply if the yield curve does not shift in a parallel fashion. To verify this claim, consider the rotation shift described in scenario B of example 9. Going back to that example we note that larger positive values of the scalar t correspond to a steepening yield curve with longer maturity rates moving up more than shorter maturity rates. Conversely, negative values of the scalar t correspond to a flattening curve with longer maturity rates falling further than shorter maturity rates.

Table 5.6 shows the variation of the future value of the bond on three different horizon dates for the rotation shift of scenario B. Looking at the first column of table 5.6, we observe that for a horizon of $h = 1$ periods greater values of t, or steepening curves, result in lower future values for the bond. The third column shows that for a horizon of $h = 4$ periods steeping curves produce greater future bond values.

Table 5.6
Valuing a bond for a rotation of the MIMO yield curve around the overnight rate

MIMO yield curve[a]	Horizon (semi-annual periods)		
	$h = 1.0$	$h = 3.796$	$h = 4.0$
B1 $(t = -.25)$	104.124	120.422	121.631
B2 $(t = -.125)$	103.299	120.421	121.744
B3[b] $(t = 0)$	102.483	120.421	121.858
B4 $(t = .125)$	101.675	120.421	121.973
B5 $(t = .25)$	100.877	120.422	122.088

a. Details on each yield curve are shown in example 9.
b. Represents no shift from the initial curve in example 9.

These results suggest that for some horizon between 1 and 4 periods the value of the bond should not be affected by the curve steepening or flattening. As shown in the second column of table 5.6, this is the case at a horizon of 3.796 periods. This horizon, denoted h^0, is the futurity of the cash flows from the 2-year bond for the case of a steepening or flattening of the initial MIMO yield curve.

The return over this horizon can be computed from equation (5.15) with $h^0 = 3.796$ periods, $FV^0 = 120.421$ (the value for FV^0 comes from the middle column of table 5.6), and $P + A = 97.255$ (see example 10):

$$97.255 = \frac{120.421}{(1 + \frac{1}{2}Rm^0)^{3.796}}$$

This implies that $Rm^0 = .11580$, or 11.580% per annum.

Comparing these results to those obtained for scenario A shows the following:

1. If the initial yield curve can only shift up or down in a parallel fashion, the 2-year bond will return, with certainty, 11.572% over an interval of 3.718 periods.

2. If the initial yield curve can only steepen or flatten with short-term rates remaining unchanged, the 2-year bond will return 11.580% over an interval of 3.796 periods.

Unless an investor knows the yield curve is going to undergo either (1) a parallel shift up or down, or (2) a steepening or flattening, he cannot know whether the 2-year bond will, "look" like a 3.718-period MIMO instrument yielding 11.572% or like a 3.796-period MIMO security yielding 11.580%.

There are two important implications of the observation that bond return and bond futurity depend on the prospective behavior of the shape of the yield curve. It is clearly possible to specify a large number of scenarios of possible change in the yield curve. (This is simply a matter of constructing a series of different $S[x]$ functions.) For *each* scenario we can identify the horizon date on which the value of a bond does not depend on either the magnitude or direction of change in the curve, and we can compute a rate of growth of capital to that horizon date. Clearly, therefore, we cannot identify a single objective measure of the futurity of the bond's cash flows nor can we identify a single objective measure of the rate of return on the bond. (The next section assesses the implications of this rather strong conclusion for fixed income portfolio management.)

The second implication relates to the special role of zeros in immunized portfolios. Single-payment securities like zeros are fundamentally different from bonds. A known cash requirement on a specific future date can be funded (or immunized) precisely with zeros that mature on that date. Bonds, on the other hand, cannot be used to accomplish such precise immunization. Since the futurity of a bond's cash flow is not well-defined, an investor cannot be sure whether a particular bond imposes market risk, reinvestment risk, or no risk over a horizon terminating on the given future date. Moreover, since the rate of return on a bond is not well-defined, an investor cannot be sure how much of a particular bond is needed to fund the given cash requirement. There is, consequently, a special niche in fixed income portfolios for zeros that provide precise immunization.

Relation of Bond Return and Bond Futurity to Yield and Macaulay Duration

Relaxing the assumption that the MIMO yield curve is always flat means we can no longer identify the yield on a bond as the bond's rate of return, nor can we identify the Macaulay duration of the bond as the bond's futurity.

For example, the 2-year bond described in example 10 has a yield of 11.577% and a Macaulay duration of 3.718 semi-annual periods. As we have shown, the bond's return and futurity depend on how interest rates might change:

	Scenario A	Scenario B
Rate of return	11.572%	11.580%
Futurity	3.718 periods	3.796 periods

It is particularly interesting to note that yield is not equal to return even when we maintain the assumption of a parallel shift in the yield curve (scenario A). A non-flat initial yield curve is sufficient to create a difference between yield and rate of return.

It can of course be argued that the quantitative differences between yield and return, and between duration and futurity are too small to be of practical interest. This may be true, but the claim requires examination of data on actual bonds and actual yield curves. We undertake that examination in the next section.

5.5   Implications for Portfolio Management

The previous section concluded that there is no analytical way to recast a bond so that it looks exactly like a MIMO instrument. The fact remains, however, that market participants frequently need to analyze bonds with simple measures of return and futurity.

One option is to ignore the implications of section 5.4 and to use yield and Macaulay duration as *the* measures of rate of return and futurity. Unfortunately, a steeply sloped initial yield curve or a flattening or steepening of the curve could leave an investor with a cash balance on his horizon date very different from what he thought he would have.

A better alternative is to use yield and Macaulay duration, but to assess the reliability of those measures in the context of alternative assumptions about the behavior of interest rates. At the very least, an investor would then be prepared to react to unanticipated market developments.

This section examines the sensitivity of bond return and bond futurity to alternative scenarios for the behavior of interest rates. In addition it compares the return and futurity derived from each scenario to ordinary bond yield and Macaulay duration. The major results are:

1. Yield is an acceptable, albeit imperfect, measure of the rate of return on a bond with less than about 10 years remaining to maturity.

2. Yields on bonds over 10 years to maturity understate return when the yield curve is positively sloped.

3. Yields on bonds over 10 years to maturity overstate return when the yield curve is negatively sloped.

4. Macaulay duration is nearly equal to the futurity of a bond if the yield curve undergoes a parallel shift, regardless of the initial shape of the curve.

5. If the initial yield curve flattens or steepens as a result of changing long-term interest rates and unchanged short rates, the futurity of a bond will be greater than its value for the case of a parallel shift. As a result Macaulay duration will generally understate futurity.

6. If the yield curve flattens or steepens as a result of changing short-term rates while long rates remain unchanged, the futurity of a bond will be less than its value for the case of a parallel shift. Macaulay duration will then overstate futurity.

Comments 1 and 4 are clearly comforting to those who use yield and Macaulay duration to quantify return and futurity. However, comments 2 and 3 suggest that yield can not be used to compare the attractiveness of investments in long term bonds when the yield curve has either a positive or negative slope. Comments 5 and 6 suggest that the outcome of an immunization program will be affected by changes in the shape of the yield curve. A portfolio structured with Macaulay duration to immunize a cash requirement seven years in the future may turn out to be "too short" or "too long" if the curve changes shape. Moreover the consequence of a flattening (steepening) curve depends on whether the flattening (steepening) occurs because of a decline (rise) in long-term yields or because of a rise (decline) in short-term yields. Thus managing a fixed income portfolio to maintain a match to a particular horizon date is more than an exercise in number crunching. A portfolio manager must have a view on how the shape of the yield curve might change in the future (in order to assess the futurities of different bonds), even if he does not try to forecast the direction of future changes in the level of interest rates.

The Initial Yield Curve

To carry out the analysis, a sequence of yields on single payment, or MIMO, securities of different maturities is needed. We use the spot yield curve implied by the structure of yields on Treasury bonds. Deriving spot yields from bond yields is described in chapter 10.

We use data from the Treasury market on May 30, 1984, to illustrate the analysis. Figure 5.1 shows, with a solid line, the Treasury bond yield curve on that day and, with a dashed line, the spot yield curve. Note that the bond yield curve was strongly positively sloped out to about a seven-year maturity and declined slightly for maturities beyond ten years. The spot curve reflects this humped behavior of bond yields.

Scenarios for Change in the Spot Curve

The next step is to specify how the spot yield curve might change. We examine three scenarios:

Scenario A: Parallel shift. In this case every spot yield changes by the same amount. The top panel of figure 5.2 illustrates several possible changes (up or down) in the spot curve and the top panel of figure 5.3

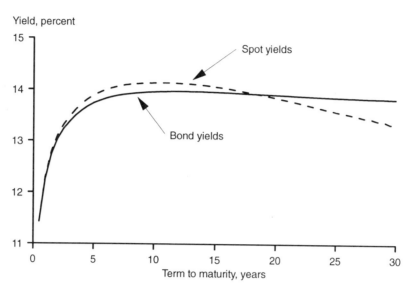

Figure 5.1
Treasury bond yields and spot yields on May 30, 1984

shows the implications for bond yields. Note that the bond yield curve also exhibits a parallel shift.

Scenario B: Rotation around the short end. In this case the spot yield curve pivots or rotates around the short end, as shown in the middle panel of figure 5.2. The bond yield curve also rotates around the short end, but long-term bond yields do not change as much as long-term spot yields. This is because the yield on a bond is an average of its spot yields and because shorter spot yields move less than longer spot yields in this scenario.

Scenario C: Rotation around the long end. In this case the spot yield curve rotates around the 30-year spot yield, as shown in the lower panel of figure 5.2. The bond yield curve also rotates (see the lower panel of figure 5.3), but long-term bond yields do not remain unchanged. This is because, for instance, the yield on a 30-year bond is an average of spot yields from zero to 30 years. Shorter spot yields are not constant in this scenario, so long bond yields cannot remain constant.

These scenarios were chosen as broadly representative of likely and important types of yield curve changes. The parallel shift of scenario A allows us to assess the effect on return and futurity of an initial yield curve that is not flat. It relaxes one assumption from section 5.3 (a flat initial curve) while maintaining the other assumption (a parallel shift of the curve). Scenarios B and C allow us to examine the effect of change in the

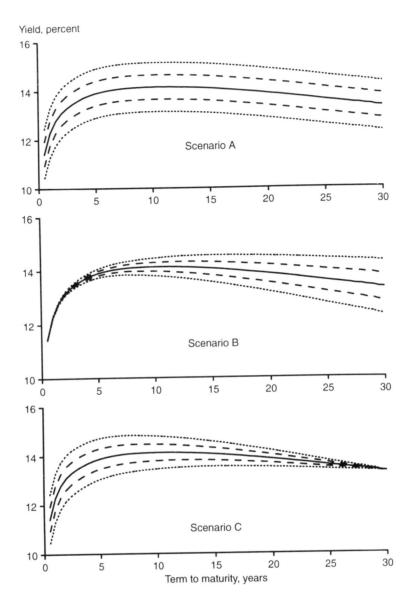

Figure 5.2
Scenarios for shifts in the spot yield curve

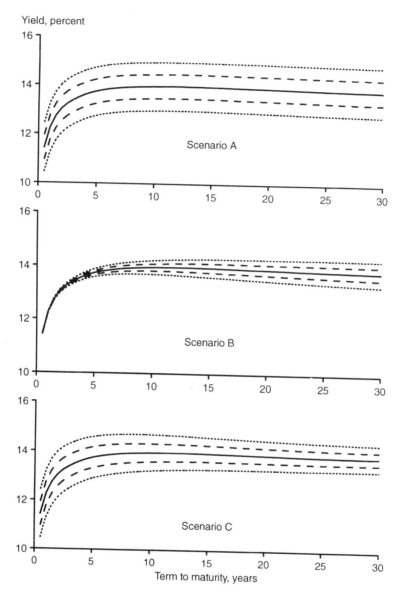

Figure 5.3
Shifts in the bond yield curve implied by shifts in the spot yield curve

Table 5.7
Yields and returns on Treasury bonds priced at par on May 30, 1984

Years to maturity	True bond yield	Bond return, by scenario		
		A	B	C
1	12.35%	12.34%	12.34%	12.34%
2	12.99	12.95	12.97	12.94
3	13.34	13.28	13.32	13.27
4	13.58	13.50	13.56	13.48
5	13.76	13.65	13.73	13.62
6	13.86	13.77	13.87	13.72
7	13.92	13.86	13.96	13.80
8	13.96	13.92	14.01	13.86
9	13.98	13.97	14.05	13.89
10	13.99	14.00	14.08	13.92
11	13.99	14.02	14.11	13.94
12	13.98	14.04	14.13	13.95
13	13.96	14.06	14.14	13.96
14	13.95	14.07	14.15	13.96
15	13.93	14.08	14.16	13.96
16	13.91	14.09	14.17	13.96
17	13.90	14.10	14.17	13.96
18	13.89	14.11	14.18	13.96
19	13.88	14.11	14.18	13.95
20	13.88	14.12	14.18	13.95
21	13.88	14.12	14.17	13.94
22	13.87	14.12	14.17	13.94
23	13.87	14.13	14.17	13.93
24	13.87	14.13	14.17	13.92
25	13.87	14.13	14.17	13.92
26	13.86	14.13	14.17	13.91
27	13.86	14.13	14.16	13.91
28	13.86	14.14	14.16	13.90
29	13.86	14.14	14.16	13.90
30	13.86	14.14	14.16	13.89

slope of the yield curve. In scenario B any change in slope is due to greater relative movement in long-term yields, and in scenario C any change is due to greater relative movement in short-term yields.

Principle Results

Table 5.7 compares the ordinary true yields on a sequence of Treasury bonds priced at par on May 30, 1984, with the rates of return on those bonds to their respective futurities, computed conditional on each of the three scenarios of yield changes. The differences between yield and rate of return are not too significant for bonds with less than 10 years remaining to maturity.

Yield appears to understate significantly the returns on bonds with maturities of 20 years and more. This is a result of the strong positive slope

Table 5.8
Macaulay durations and futurities of treasury bonds priced at par on May 30, 1984

Years to maturity	Macaulay duration	Bond futurity, by scenario		
		A	B	C
1	.93 yr	.93 yr	.93 yr	.93 yr
2	1.78	1.78	1.82	1.77
3	2.53	2.52	2.64	2.50
4	3.17	3.16	3.38	3.10
5	3.73	3.72	4.05	3.60
6	4.22	4.20	4.66	4.01
7	4.64	4.62	5.21	4.34
8	5.01	4.98	5.71	4.60
9	5.34	5.30	6.16	4.80
10	5.62	5.58	6.58	4.96
11	5.88	5.83	6.96	5.07
12	6.10	6.05	7.31	5.15
13	6.29	6.25	7.63	5.21
14	6.47	6.42	7.93	5.24
15	6.62	6.58	8.20	5.25
16	6.76	6.72	8.46	5.25
17	6.86	6.84	8.69	5.24
18	6.97	6.95	8.89	5.22
19	7.05	7.04	9.08	5.19
20	7.14	7.12	9.25	5.16
21	7.22	7.19	9.40	5.12
22	7.26	7.26	9.54	5.08
23	7.31	7.31	9.66	5.04
24	7.37	7.36	9.78	5.00
25	7.39	7.40	9.88	4.97
26	7.43	7.44	9.98	4.93
27	7.47	7.47	10.06	4.89
28	7.49	7.50	10.14	4.86
29	7.53	7.53	10.21	4.83
30	7.55	7.55	10.27	4.80

in the front end of the yield curve on May 30, 1984. Conventional bond yields appear to miss the opportunities available from reinvestment of coupons which will not be paid until several years after purchase. The opposite result, that yield overstates return, will hold if the yield curve is inverted and has a negative slope.

Table 5.8 compares the Macaulay durations of a sequence of par Treasury bonds on May 30, 1984, with the futurities of those bonds. It is evident that Macaulay duration is a good measure of futurity for the case of a parallel shift in the spot yield curve, that is, for scenario A. This implies that the assumption of a flat initial curve is not crucial to the acceptability of Macaulay duration as long as the shift is parallel.

Comparing Macaulay duration to bond futurity for scenarios B and C shows very different results. If long-term yields are assumed to fluctuate more widely than short-term yields (scenario B), Macaulay duration understates the futurity of long bonds. The understatement is not small, exceeding 2 years on a 20-year bond and $2\frac{3}{4}$ years on a 30-year bond.

The reason for the understatement is not hard to guess. Macaulay duration is the horizon at which the market risk on a bond's remaining payments is equal and opposite to the reinvestment risk on its earlier payments, assuming all interest rates move up or down together following purchase. Observe that the Macaulay duration of a 30-year par bond was about $7\frac{1}{2}$ years on May 30, 1984. Now suppose that we change the assumption of rate behavior to that of scenario B, where long-term rates are relatively more volatile than short-term rates. Since a 30-year bond has many long dated payments remaining after it has aged $7\frac{1}{2}$ years, the change in assumption creates a relative increase in the market risk of the bond at a $7\frac{1}{2}$-year horizon date. To restore the balance between reinvestment risk and market risk, we have to increase the horizon date beyond $7\frac{1}{2}$ years. This increases the number of interest payments made before the horizon date and increases the lengths of the reinvestment intervals, thereby increasing reinvestment risk. It also reduces the number of interest payments made after the horizon date and reduces the times remaining to those payments and hence reduces market risk. Table 5.8 shows that a balance between reinvestment risk and market risk is restored at a horizon date about $10\frac{1}{4}$ years after purchase.

If short-term yields fluctuate more widely than long-term yields (scenario C), Macaulay duration overstates the futurity of long bonds. The reason for the overstatement is the reverse of the basis for the understatement in scenario B. Consider again a 30-year bond for which reinvestment risk and market risk balance at a $7\frac{1}{2}$-year horizon if all interest rates move together. Now suppose that we change the assumption of rate behavior to that of scenario C, where short-term rates are relatively more volatile than long-term rates. Since a 30-year bond has many payments remaining to be paid after $7\frac{1}{2}$ years, the change in assumption creates a relative reduction in the market risk on the bond at a $7\frac{1}{2}$ horizon date. The horizon date must contract below $7\frac{1}{2}$ years to restore the balance between reinvestment risk and market risk.

Additional Results

Figure 5.4 plots the bond futurities tabulated in table 5.8 as a function of bond maturity. The general shape of the three curves is well-known: Bond futurity increases with maturity but at a decreasing rate. There is, however, another important implication which can be drawn from figure 5.4.

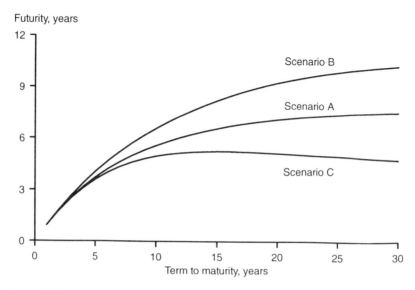

Figure 5.4
Bond futurity as a function of bond maturity on May 30, 1984, for three interest rate scenarios

If interest rates are expected to change as a result of relatively more volatile long-term yields (scenario B) an investor seeking to immunize a given future cash requirement should hold bonds with a maturity shorter than what would be appropriate if all rates were expected to move together. This is a direct result of the expansion of bond futurity due to the change in assumed rate behavior. Conversely, if short-term yields are expected to exhibit greater volatility than longer yields (scenario C), an investor should extend the maturity of his portfolio to maintain an immunized position.

These observations suggest that investors moving from longer maturity bonds into shorter bonds may not always be motivated by expectations of higher interest rates and that investors who extend maturity may not always be responding to expectations of lower rates. They may be seeking to maintain an immunized portfolio position in the face of revised perceptions of how the yield curve might change shape.

Table 5.8 and figure 5.4 also imply that under some interest rate scenarios, an investor may be unable to maintain an immunized position with conventional bonds. For example, an investor can use 30-year bonds to immunize a cash requirement $7\frac{1}{2}$ years in the future if interest rates are expected to shift in parallel. However, if short-term yields are expected to be more volatile than longer rates (scenario C), a 30-year bond will immunize over only a $4\frac{3}{4}$-year horizon. Thus the investor may have to move out of conventional bonds and into $7\frac{1}{2}$-year zeros to maintain an immunized position. Conversely, an investor immunizing over a 9-year horizon can switch out of zeros and into conventional bonds if long-term interest rates are expected to have greater volatility relative to short-term yields.

5.6   Summary

This chapter has reexamined the measurement of rate of return and futurity for fixed-income securities. It began with the simple case of single-payment securities like Treasury bills and zero coupon securities where futurity is identical to maturity. Our concern was deriving a "clean" measure of rate of return, which we called true yield.

Bonds making multiple payments present a more complicated analytical problem. If we assume the yield curve is always flat, a natural extension of true yield, presented in section 5.2, is the right measure of the rate of return on a bond and Macaulay duration is the right measure of a bond's futurity. These results were demonstrated in section 5.3.

If the yield curve is not flat or if it can change shape, yield is an imperfect measure of return, and Macaulay duration is an imperfect measure of futurity. The most significant problem with using yield as a measure of return occurs for bonds with maturities beyond about ten years when the initial yield curve has a sharp slope, either positive or negative. On the other hand, the biggest problem with assessing the futurity of a bond appears when we allow for significant *change* in the shape of the yield curve. Depending on how the curve can change shape, Macaulay duration may either understate or overstate the effective futurity of a bond.

5.7   Appendix A: Analytical Properties of Bond Yield and Macaulay Duration

This appendix shows that under the assumptions of section 5.3 the yield on a bond measures its rate of capital appreciation over an interval of time equal to its Macaulay duration.

Assume the following:

1. The MIMO yield curve is initially flat at yield R.

2. The MIMO yield curve can only shift once, immediately after purchase of the bond, to a yield R'.

3. The bond will make n future payments, where the ith payment is for an amount F_i and will occur x_i semi-annual periods after purchase.

4. The bond is valued as a "bundle" of MIMO securities.

From assumptions 1, 3, and 4 the purchase price of the bond is

$$P + A = \frac{F_1}{(1 + \frac{1}{2}R)^{x_1}} + \frac{F_2}{(1 + \frac{1}{2}R)^{x_2}} + \cdots + \frac{F_n}{(1 + \frac{1}{2}R)^{x_n}} \tag{A5.1}$$

R is also the yield to maturity, as defined in equation (5.5) of the text.

From assumptions 2, 3, and 4 the value of the bond, including reinvested interest payments, after an interval of h semi-annual periods, is

$$FV(R', h) = \frac{F_1}{(1 + \frac{1}{2}R')^{x_1 - h}} + \frac{F_2}{(1 + \frac{1}{2}R')^{x_2 - h}} + \cdots + \frac{F_n}{(1 + \frac{1}{2}R')^{x_n - h}} \tag{A5.2}$$

This future value will be invariant (to a first-order approximation) with respect to R' if the derivative dFV/dR' is zero. The derivative is calculated as

$$\begin{aligned}
\frac{dFV}{dR'} &= \frac{d}{dR'}[F_1(1 + \tfrac{1}{2}R')^{h - x_1} + F_2(1 + \tfrac{1}{2}R')^{h - x_2} + \cdots + F_n(1 + \tfrac{1}{2}R')^{h - x_n}] \\
&= (h - x_1)\tfrac{1}{2}F_1(1 + \tfrac{1}{2}R')^{h - x_1 - 1} + (h - x_2)\tfrac{1}{2}F_2(1 + \tfrac{1}{2}R')^{h - x_2 - 1} + \cdots \\
&\quad + (h - x_n)\tfrac{1}{2}F_n(1 + \tfrac{1}{2}R')^{h - x_n - 1} \\
&= \tfrac{1}{2}(1 + \tfrac{1}{2}R')^{h-1}\left[\frac{h \cdot F_1}{(1 + \frac{1}{2}R')^{x_1}} + \frac{h \cdot F_2}{(1 + \frac{1}{2}R')^{x_2}} + \cdots + \frac{h \cdot F_n}{(1 + \frac{1}{2}R')^{x_n}}\right] \\
&\quad - \tfrac{1}{2}(1 + \tfrac{1}{2}R')^{h-1}\left[\frac{x_1 \cdot F_1}{(1 + \frac{1}{2}R')^{x_1}} + \frac{x_2 \cdot F_2}{(1 + \frac{1}{2}R')^{x_2}} + \cdots + \frac{x_n \cdot F_n}{(1 + \frac{1}{2}R')^{x_n}}\right]
\end{aligned} \tag{A5.3}$$

Setting the derivative to zero at $R' = R$ and letting h^0 denote the solution value of h gives

$$h^0 = \frac{\dfrac{x_1 \cdot F_1}{(1 + \frac{1}{2}R)^{x_1}} + \dfrac{x_2 \cdot F_2}{(1 + \frac{1}{2}R)^{x_2}} + \cdots + \dfrac{x_n \cdot F_n}{(1 + \frac{1}{2}R)^{x_n}}}{\dfrac{F_1}{(1 + \frac{1}{2}R)^{x_1}} + \dfrac{F_2}{(1 + \frac{1}{2}R)^{x_2}} + \cdots + \dfrac{F_n}{(1 + \frac{1}{2}R)^{x_n}}} \tag{A5.4}$$

This is the Macaulay duration of the bond.

Using equation (A5.2) to compute the future value of the bond h^0 periods in the future gives

$$FV(R', h^0) = (1 + \tfrac{1}{2}R')^{h^0}\left[\frac{F_1}{(1 + \frac{1}{2}R')^{x_1}} + \cdots + \frac{F_2}{(1 + \frac{1}{2}R')^{x_n}}\right] \tag{A5.5}$$

Since this value is invariant with respect to R', we can evaluate it at $R' = R$. Noting the definition of $P + A$ in equation (A5.1) then gives

$$FV(R, h^0) = (1 + \tfrac{1}{2}R)^{h^0}[P + A]$$

or

$$P + A = \frac{FV(R, h^0)}{(1 + \tfrac{1}{2}R)^{h^0}} \tag{A5.6}$$

Thus the yield R is the rate of return on the bond over the interval of h^0 semi-annual periods.

5.8   Appendix B: Computing the Future Value of a Bond When the Yield Curve Is Not Flat

This appendix derives the value of a bond on a specified future horizon date, as shown in equation (5.14).

Assume the following:

1. Following purchase of the bond the MIMO yield curve shifts to the function $R'[x]$.

2. The bond will make n future payments, where the ith payment is for an amount F_i and will occur x_i semi-annual periods after purchase.

3. The bond is valued on a date h semi-annual periods after purchase.

The first step in the analysis is to clarify which bond payments have to be reinvested and which payments are to be sold before they are paid. Assume that payments 1 through m are received before the horizon date and that payments $m + 1$ through n are to be received after the horizon date.

Since payments 1 through m are received before the horizon date, they have to be reinvested to that date at contemporaneously prevailing market yields. In particular, the first payment of F_1, to be received x_1 periods after the purchase of the bond, has to be reinvested for $h - x_1$ periods at the yield on a MIMO security with a maturity of $h - x_1$ periods. Similarly the second payment of F_2 has to be reinvested for $h - x_2$ periods at the yield on a MIMO security with a maturity of $h - x_2$ periods.

Let $R'[z, t]$ be the yield prevailing t periods following purchase of the bond on a MIMO security with a remaining maturity of z periods. The total proceeds on the horizon date from reinvestment of earlier payments can be written

$$I = F_1 \cdot (1 + \tfrac{1}{2}R'[h - x_1, x_1])^{h-x_1} + F_2 \cdot (1 + \tfrac{1}{2}R'[h - x_2, x_2])^{h-x_2} + \cdots$$

$$+ F_m \cdot (1 + \tfrac{1}{2}R'[h - x_m, x_m])^{h-x_m} \tag{A5.7}$$

Note that this value depends on yields on MIMO securities of different maturities prevailing on different dates between purchase of the bond and the horizon date.

Since payments $m + 1$ through n will not be received until after the horizon date, they must be sold on that date. The liquidation value of the bond on the horizon date is

$$L = \frac{F_{m+1}}{(1 + \frac{1}{2}R'[x_{m+1} - h, h])^{x_{m+1}-h}} + \frac{F_{m+2}}{(1 + \frac{1}{2}R'[x_{m+2} - h, h])^{x_{m+2}-h}} + \cdots$$

$$+ \frac{F_n}{(1 + \frac{1}{2}R'[x_n - h, h])^{x_n-h}} \tag{A5.8}$$

Note that this value depends on MIMO yields prevailing h periods after the original purchase of the bond.

The value of the bond on the horizon date is the sum $I + L$ where I and L are defined by equations (A5.7) and (A5.8), respectively. We next need to reduce the MIMO yields in those two equations to a familiar form.

Forward Yields

Consider the following problem: At time 0 (the date of purchase of the bond) the yield on a MIMO security with a maturity of x periods is $R'[x, 0]$. If there are no subsequent changes in interest rates, what will a MIMO security with a remaining maturity of $x - t$ periods yield after t periods have elapsed?

The problem can be answered as follows: One dollar invested in an x period MIMO security at time 0 will grow to $(1 + \frac{1}{2}R'[x, 0])^x$ at maturity. On the other hand, an investor can invest one dollar in a t period MIMO security and then at time t reinvest the proceeds in an $x - t$ period MIMO security. The total payment on this second strategy is

$$(1 + \tfrac{1}{2}R'[t, 0])^t \cdot (1 + \tfrac{1}{2}R'[x - t, t])^{x-t}$$

In equilibrium the two strategies should make the same payment after x periods so that

$$(1 + \tfrac{1}{2}R'[x, 0])^x = (1 + \tfrac{1}{2}R'[t, 0])^t(1 + \tfrac{1}{2}R'[x - t, t])^{x-t} \tag{A5.9}$$

This equation can be solved to show how the yield on $x - t$ period debt at time t is related to the yields on x period and t period debt at time 0:

$$(1 + \tfrac{1}{2}R'[x - t, t])^{x-t} = \frac{(1 + \frac{1}{2}R'[x, 0])^x}{(1 + \frac{1}{2}R'[t, 0])^t} \tag{A5.10}$$

The yield $R[x - t, t]$ is called a "forward" yield. It is the yield on an $x - t$ period MIMO security at time t in the future that is consistent with the structure of MIMO yields at time 0.

Valuing the Bond on the Horizon Date

We now want to use equation (A5.8) to simplify expressions (A5.7) and (A5.8).

First, let $x = h$ and $t = x_i$ in equation (A5.10). That equation becomes

$$(1 + \tfrac{1}{2}R'[h - x_i, x_i])^{h - x_i} = \frac{(1 + \tfrac{1}{2}R'[h, 0])^h}{(1 + \tfrac{1}{2}R'[x_i, 0])^{x_i}} \tag{A5.11}$$

Substituting this into equation (A5.7) gives

$$I = (1 + \tfrac{1}{2}R'[h, 0])^h \left[\frac{F_1}{(1 + \tfrac{1}{2}R'[x_1, 0])^{x_1}} + \frac{F_2}{(1 + \tfrac{1}{2}R'[x_2, 0])^{x_2}} + \cdots \right.$$

$$\left. + \frac{F_m}{(1 + \tfrac{1}{2}R'[x_m, 0])^{x_m}} \right] \tag{A5.12}$$

Next, let $x = x_i$ and $t = h$ in equation (A5.10). We then have

$$(1 + \tfrac{1}{2}R'[x_i - h, h])^{x_i - h} = \frac{(1 + \tfrac{1}{2}R'[x_i, 0])^{x_i}}{(1 + \tfrac{1}{2}R'[h, 0])^h} \tag{A5.13}$$

Substituting this into equation (A5.8) gives

$$L = (1 + \tfrac{1}{2}R'[h, 0])^h \left[\frac{F_{m+1}}{(1 + \tfrac{1}{2}R'[x_{m+1}, 0])^{x_{m+1}}} \right.$$

$$\left. + \frac{F_{m+2}}{(1 + \tfrac{1}{2}R'[x_{m+2}, 0])^{x_{m+2}}} + \cdots + \frac{F_n}{(1 + \tfrac{1}{2}R'[x_n, 0])^{x_n}} \right] \tag{A5.14}$$

Adding the expressions for I and L together gives the future value of the bond on a date h periods after purchase:

$$I + L = (1 + \tfrac{1}{2}R'[h, 0])^h \left[\frac{F_1}{(1 + \tfrac{1}{2}R'[x_1, 0])^{x_1}} + \frac{F_2}{(1 + \tfrac{1}{2}R'[x_2, 0])^{x_2}} + \cdots \right.$$

$$\left. + \frac{F_n}{(1 + \tfrac{1}{2}R'[x_n, 0])^{x_n}} \right] \tag{A5.15}$$

This is identical to equation (5.14) in the text.

5.9 Subsequent Remarks

The topics selected for discussion in this chapter reflect a curiosity with exactly what is quantified by the two well-known measures of bond yield and bond duration. More precisely, the topics reflect a curiosity with whether those measures quantify in a reasonable fashion what we think of when we speak of (1) average rate of return on invested capital and (2) the futurity of a bond's cash flows.

The analytics presented here depart from Street conventions in two ways. First, the chapter introduces the concept of "true" yield in order to clear away some of the institutional detail associated with computing yields on Treasury securities (while preserving the central convention of semi-annual compounding). Many of the chapters that follow will continue the use of true yield.

Second, the chapter introduces the possibility of change in the shape of the yield curve in the context of assessing the futurity of a bond's cash flows. It shows that relaxing the assumption of a parallel shift in the curve has serious consequences for the utility of Macaulay duration as a measure of futurity.

Although not known at the time of the writing, subsequent research has established that on average a substantial fraction of the total volatility of Treasury yields stems from essentially parallel shifts of the yield curve (see chapter 16). Thus Macaulay duration survives as an approximate, but clearly imperfect, measure of the futurity of a bond's cash flows.

6 Bond Convexity and Its Implications for Immunization

The most important lesson of recent research in fixed income portfolio management is that an investor who holds bonds with a duration matched to his investment horizon is neither substantially advantaged nor substantially disadvantaged when interest rates change. If rates rise, greater earnings on reinvested coupon payments offset capital losses on the bonds. Conversely, if rates fall higher prices on bonds liquidated before maturity offset the decline in reinvestment income. Some people express this result by saying that immunization makes a bond portfolio "look like" a zero coupon security that matures at the end of an interval of time equal to the portfolio's duration. However, closer analysis reveals that this statement may not be correct.

Consider an investor with a horizon of 8 years choosing between (1) an 8-year zero at a 12% yield and (2) a 20-year bond with a 12% coupon at a 12% yield. A little number crunching shows the bond has a duration of 8 years. It would appear that the investor should be indifferent between the two securities because they have the same yield and a common duration that matches his horizon. Nonetheless, it turns out that the bond may actually be preferable to the zero.

If the investor buys the zero to fund the liability due in 8 years, he will have immunized that liability at a 12% rate of return regardless of how interest rates change. However, if he buys the bond and if interest rates subsequently fall to 8%, he will actually earn 12.40% over his 8-year horizon. (This assumes reinvestment of all coupon payments at 8% and sale of the residual bond payments on the horizon date at an 8% yield.) If interest rates rise to 16%, he will actually earn 12.34% over his horizon. (This assumes coupon reinvestment at 16% and sale of the bond at a 16% yield.) Only if interest rates remain near 12% will the investor earn the original 12% yield over his horizon. Thus the bond is no worse, and sometimes better, than the zero.

The observation that a bond can outperform a matched duration/ matched yield zero is a manifestation of *convexity*. Figure 6.1 illustrates the basic idea for the example described above. The horizontal axis is the assumed yield at which coupons are reinvested and at which the bond is sold on the horizon date. The vertical axis is the average rate of return on capital over the 8-year interval. Observe that the rate of return is a convex function of the reinvestment/liquidation rate. As noted above, an investor's capital will appreciate over the investment interval at an average rate of 12.40% per annum if he can reinvest coupons and sell his bond at an 8% yield (see point *A* in the figure), and it will appreciate at an average rate

Written March 1985.

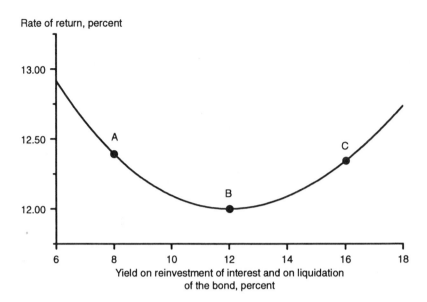

Rate of return, percent

Figure 6.1
Rate of return over an 8-year horizon on a 20-year bond with a 12% coupon purchased at a 12% yield as a function of the reinvestment/liquidation rate

of 12.34% if he can reinvest coupons and sell his bond at a 16% yield (see point *C* in the figure).

If we drew figure 6.1 for an 8-year zero purchased at a 12% yield, we would have a flat line at a rate of return equal to 12%. This is because there is no interest to reinvest and no security to be sold before maturity.

Understanding bond convexity is important for two reasons. First, it negates the proposition that immunization analytically recasts a bond so that it looks like a zero. (The return curve in figure 6.1 certainly does not look like the flat return curve that characterizes a zero of equivalent duration.) Second, the existence of convexity throws the basic tenets of immunization and horizon matching into question.

This chapter analyzes the origins of convexity and discusses its implications for fixed income portfolio management. Section 6.1 examines the mathematics behind figure 6.1. Section 6.2 describes how convexity can be assessed quantitatively and discusses the relation between convexity and bond characteristics such as coupon maturity and yield.

Section 6.3 analyzes the implications of convexity for portfolio management. It concludes that convexity is a mixed blessing. The claim that a bond will outperform a zero of comparable duration is valid only if there are large, sudden shifts in interest rates. If rates change more continuously, convexity does not confer any special advantage on a bond. Moreover convexity can create uncertainty over the actual rate of return that will be earned on a bond if there is uncertainty about future changes in the shape of the yield curve.

6.1   Mathematics of Convexity

This section examines the nature of convexity. We begin by developing an equation for the rate of return on a bond over a specified horizon given an assumed reinvestment/liquidation yield. Basic duration analysis suggests that this rate of return should equal the yield at which the bond was originally purchased, irrespective of the value of the reinvestment/liquidation yield, *if* the bond's duration matches the specified horizon. However, the equation shows that this is not necessarily the case and that the rate of return on the bond is actually a convex function of the reinvestment/liquidation yield.

We turn next to a more qualitative appraisal of the factors that create this convexity. Convexity is attributable to shifts in the duration of a bond that occur when yields change and can be traced ultimately to the presence of multiple payments, that is, coupons paid before maturity. This provides the foundation for measuring convexity, a topic addressed more fully in section 6.2.

Rate of Return on a Bond

Consider an investor contemplating purchase of a bond that will make n payments in the future, where the ith payment is for an amount F_i and will occur x_i semi-annual periods following the settlement date. In most cases the intermediate payments $F_1, F_2, \ldots, F_{n-1}$ will be semi-annual coupon payments and the last payment F_n will be a terminal coupon payment plus return of principal. (The first coupon may be larger or smaller than subsequent coupons if the bond has an odd first coupon.)

If the bond has a quoted price of P and accrued interest of A, the yield on the bond is defined as the value of Rm that satisfies the equation

$$P + A = \frac{F_1}{(1 + \frac{1}{2}Rm)^{x_1}} + \frac{F_2}{(1 + \frac{1}{2}Rm)^{x_2}} + \cdots + \frac{F_n}{(1 + \frac{1}{2}Rm)^{x_n}} \tag{6.1}$$

The duration of the bond, measured in years, is

$$D = \frac{\dfrac{\frac{1}{2}x_1 F_1}{(1 + \frac{1}{2}Rm)^{x_1}} + \dfrac{\frac{1}{2}x_2 F_2}{(1 + \frac{1}{2}Rm)^{x_2}} + \cdots + \dfrac{\frac{1}{2}x_n F_n}{(1 + \frac{1}{2}Rm)^{x_n}}}{\dfrac{F_1}{(1 + \frac{1}{2}Rm)^{x_1}} + \dfrac{F_2}{(1 + \frac{1}{2}Rm)^{x_2}} + \cdots + \dfrac{F_n}{(1 + \frac{1}{2}Rm)^{x_n}}} \tag{6.2}$$

Using equation (6.2) to calculate the duration of a 20-year bond with a 12% coupon at a 12% yield gives a value of 7.97 years. Duration analysis suggests that an investor will earn the 12% yield on this bond over an interval of 8 years regardless of whether interest rates go up or down. To verify or refute this claim, we have to analyze carefully what an investor earns on a bond over a given horizon.

Consider what an investor earns over an interval of h semi-annual periods, or $\frac{1}{2}h$ years, from a bond that makes n payments following purchase, where the ith payment is made in x_i periods and is for an amount F_i. Assume that the first m payments are received before the horizon date and reinvested at yield R to that date, and assume that the residual of the bond, consisting of the last $n - m$ payments, is sold on the horizon date at the same yield.

The value of the reinvested coupons and the liquidated bond on the horizon date, denoted FV, is computed as

$$FV = F_1 \cdot (1 + \tfrac{1}{2}R)^{h-x_1} + F_2 \cdot (1 + \tfrac{1}{2}R)^{h-x_2} + \cdots + F_m \cdot (1 + \tfrac{1}{2}R)^{h-x_m}$$

$$+ \frac{F_{m+1}}{(1 + \tfrac{1}{2}R)^{x_{m+1}-h}} + \frac{F_{m+2}}{(1 + \tfrac{1}{2}R)^{x_{m+2}-h}} + \cdots + \frac{F_n}{(1 + \tfrac{1}{2}R)^{x_n-h}} \qquad (6.3)$$

This expression can be understood as follows: The first payment of F_1 is received after x_1 periods and hence is reinvested over an interval of $h - x_1$ periods at yield R. The second payment of F_2 is reinvested over an interval of $h - x_2$ periods at the same yield. This continues similarly through the first m payments. Payments $m + 1$ to n are sold before they come due. Their values on the horizon date are computed by discounting the payments back to the horizon date at yield R. The $m + 1$st payment is discounted over an interval of $x_{m+1} - h$ periods, the $m + 2$nd payment is discounted over an interval of $x_{m+2} - h$ periods, and so on.

An average rate of return on capital over the investment interval can now be computed. We know what the bond costs $(P + A)$, how much we will get (FV), and the length of time between payment and final liquidation (h semi-annual periods). The average rate of return is the value of Ra that satisfies the equation

$$P + A = \frac{FV}{(1 + \tfrac{1}{2}Ra)^h} \qquad (6.4)$$

Since the future value FV depends on the reinvestment/liquidation yield R (see equation 6.3), the rate of return Ra defined in equation (6.4) will, in general, also depend on the reinvestment/liquidation yield.

Basic duration analysis suggests that, in the special case where the investment horizon equals the bond's duration (as defined in equation 6.2), the rate of return Ra will equal the bond's original yield Rm (as defined in equation 6.1) regardless of the reinvestment/liquidation yield. To verify numerically whether this is true, consider the case of a 12%, 20-year bond purchased at par with a 12% yield and a duration of 7.97 years, or 15.94 semi-annual periods. Using equation (6.3) with a reinvestment/liquidation yield of $R = .10$, or 10% per annum, and a horizon of $h = 15.94$ periods, we have $FV = 254.982$. From equation (6.4) this gives an average rate of return of 12.096% per annum over the investment interval because

$$100. = \frac{254.982}{(1 + \frac{1}{2}(.12096))^{15.94}}$$

This return is close to the original 12% yield on the bond, even if it isn't exactly equal. However, if we reduce the reinvestment/liquidation rate from 10% to 8%, we get a new future value of $FV = 260.773$ and a new average rate of return of $Ra = 12.395\%$ per annum. This rate is significantly different from 12%. The large difference suggests that we look more closely at the relation between the reinvestment/liquidation yield and the rate of return on the bond.

Table 6.1 shows in detail how the rate of return on the 12%, 20-year bond varies as a function of the assumed reinvestment/liquidation rate. Two aspects of the data are worth noting. First, if the reinvestment/liquidation rate is not too far from 12% the average rate of return on capital is very near the 12% yield at which the bond was purchased. Ra varies between 12% and 12.023% for values of R between 11% and 13%. Thus capital invested in the bond does increase at an average rate equal to the original yield on the bond regardless of fluctuations in the reinvestment/liquidation yield as *long as those fluctuations are modest*.

Table 6.1 also shows that Ra will be well above 12% per annum if the reinvestment/liquidation rate is *signficantly* different from 12%. In particular, the rate of return is seen to be a convex function of the reinvestment/liquidation yield. (The data in table 6.1 are the basis for figure 6.1, where the convexity of the relationship is quite evident.) This contradicts the proposition that matching duration and horizon necessarily locks in the yield at which a bond is purchased. The proposition is true as long as interest rate changes following purchase are modest but appears to break down if rates change significantly.

Origins of Convexity

Coping with the effects of convexity requires an understanding of how it arises. A good place to start is by examining how the duration of a bond varies with its yield.

Table 6.1
Rate of return on a 20-year bond with a 12% coupon purchased at a 12% yield over an
interval of 7.97 years as a function of the reinvestment/liquidation rate

Reinvestment/ liquidation rate	Rate of return
6.0%	12.917%
6.5	12.765
7.0	12.628
7.5	12.504
8.0	12.395
8.5	12.300
9.0	12.219
9.5	12.151
10.0	12.095
10.5	12.053
11.0	12.023
11.5	12.006
12.0	12.000
12.5	12.006
13.0	12.023
13.5	12.050
14.0	12.089
14.5	12.137
15.0	12.196
15.5	12.264
16.0	12.341
16.5	12.428
17.0	12.523
17.5	12.627
18.0	12.738

Table 6.2 shows the duration of a 20-year, 12% bond for bond yields
ranging between 6% and 18% per annum. Note that duration is greatest at
low yields and falls as yields rise. This behavior is inherent in the definition
of duration. Recall that duration is a weighted average of the time intervals remaining to a bond's future payments. Higher yields lead to shorter
durations because the times to more distant payments receive relatively
less weight at higher yields.

Now consider the position of an investor with an 8-year horizon who
buys a 20-year 12% bond at a 12% yield. Since the duration of the bond
matches his horizon, his average rate of return is immunized against
modest changes in interest rates. (This is confirmed in table 6.1.) Suppose,
however, that interest rates begin to fall shortly after purchase. Falling
rates lead to an increase in duration beyond the investor's 8-year horizon
(see table 6.2) and thus impose market risk on the investor's net worth.
(Market risk is a situation where lower rates are beneficial and higher

Table 6.2
Duration of a 20-year bond with a 12% coupon as a function of the bond's yield

Yield	Duration
6.0%	10.438 yr
7.0	9.998
8.0	9.567
9.0	9.147
10.0	8.741
11.0	8.349
12.0	7.974
13.0	7.615
14.0	7.273
15.0	6.949
16.0	6.643
17.0	6.355
18.0	6.083

rates are harmful. It exists when the duration of an investor's assets exceeds his horizon.) If interest rates continue to fall, this market risk proves beneficial and leads to an increase in the average rate of return on capital over the 8-year investment interval.

This argument shows that the convexity in figure 6.1 associated with interest rates falling below 12% is a result of a steadily widening gap between the lengthening duration of the bond and the (constant) 8-year investment horizon. Initially the gap is zero or negligible, and changes in the reinvestment/liquidation rate do not affect significantly the rate of return. However, the gap widens as yields decline, and the reinvestment/liquidation rate begins to have an appreciable effect on the rate of return. The lower rates go, the wider the gap and the greater the effect of further rate changes on the return on the bond.

A converse argument applies to the case where interest rates go up following purchase of the bond. As rates rise, the duration of the bond contracts to something shorter than the investor's 8-year horizon. This begins to impose reinvestment risk on the investor's net worth. (Reinvestment risk is a situation where higher rates are beneficial and lower rates are harmful. It exists when the duration of an investor's assets is less than his investment horizon.) If rates continue to rise, the reinvestment risk leads to an increase in the average rate of return. This explains the convexity in figure 6.1 associated with yields rising above 12%.

In summary, the convexity of the rate of return on a seemingly immunized bond investment results from changes in the duration of the bond associated with changes in yield. When yield fluctuations are small, such as between 11% and 13%, duration doesn't change much from its original value (see table 6.2), and convexity is not too important. When, however, yields shift by several percentage points duration may change significantly, and convexity can become quite important.

Why Zeros Have No Convexity

This argument explains why the rate of return on a zero does not exhibit any convexity. The duration of a zero is always exactly equal to its remaining term to maturity, regardless of the level of interest rates. Since duration does not depend on yield, a zero has no convexity.

Convexity of High Coupon Bonds

The argument also suggests that bonds with durations more sensitive to changes in interest rates will exhibit greater convexity. High coupon bonds are a natural place to look for this behavior because they look so different from a single payment zero. Figure 6.2 shows that this is indeed the case. The figure shows the rate of return on three bonds: an 8% bond with 16.3 years remaining to maturity, a 12%, 20-year bond, and a 16%, 26.7-year bond. At a 12% yield all three bonds have a duration of 7.97 years. However, changes in yield have a stronger influence on the durations of the higher coupon bonds (see table 6.3). This stronger influence becomes manifest as greater convexity of return.

Table 6.3
Duration of three bonds as a function of yield

Yield	Durations		
	Bond A^a	Bond B^b	Bond C^c
6.0%	9.91 yr	10.44 yr	11.48 yr
7.0	9.59	10.00	10.80
8.0	9.26	9.57	10.16
9.0	8.93	9.15	9.56
10.0	8.61	8.74	8.99
11.0	8.29	8.35	8.46
12.0	7.97	7.97	7.97
13.0	7.67	7.62	7.52
14.0	7.37	7.27	7.10
15.0	7.07	6.95	6.72
16.0	6.79	6.64	6.37
17.0	6.52	6.36	6.04
18.0	6.26	6.08	5.75

a. Bond A has an 8% coupon and 16.3 years remaining to maturity.
b. Bond B has a 12% coupon and 20.0 years remaining to maturity.
c. Bond C has a 16% coupon and 26.7 years remaining to maturity.

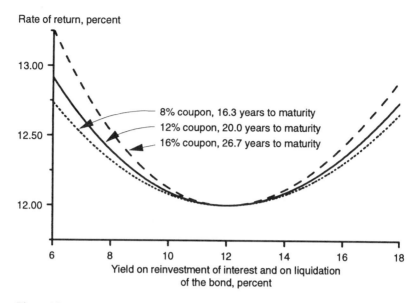

Figure 6.2
Rate of return over an 8-year horizon on three bonds purchased at a 12% yield as a function of the reinvestment/liquidation rate

6.2   Measuring Convexity

The previous section explored in some detail the nature of bond convexity and described how it arises from changes in duration induced by changes in interest rates. In this section we examine how convexity can be measured. This is important for distinguishing between bonds with more and less convexity and for assessing differences in convexity quantitatively.

Any measure of convexity must reflect three stylized facts:

1. All single-payment securities have zero convexity.

2. All multiple-payment bonds have positive convexity.

3. The duration of a bond will be more sensitive to changes in yield the greater its convexity.

We will first propose a measure of convexity and then show that the measure reflects these stylized facts. The last part of the section describes how the measure varies with the characteristics of a bond, that is, maturity, coupon rate, and yield.

Quantifying Convexity

Consider a bond with quoted price P and accrued interest A that will make n payments in the future, where the ith payment is for an amount F_i and will occur x_i semi-annual periods after settlement. The yield Rm on the bond has been defined in equation (6.1) and the bond's duration D has been defined in equation (6.2).

As a measure of the convexity of the bond we propose the expression

$$C = \frac{\dfrac{(\frac{1}{2}x_1 - D)^2 F_1}{(1 + \frac{1}{2}Rm)^{x_1}} + \dfrac{(\frac{1}{2}x_2 - D)^2 F_2}{(1 + \frac{1}{2}Rm)^{x_2}} + \cdots + \dfrac{(\frac{1}{2}x_n - D)^2 F_n}{(1 + \frac{1}{2}Rm)^{x_n}}}{\dfrac{F_1}{(1 + \frac{1}{2}Rm)^{x_1}} + \dfrac{F_2}{(1 + \frac{1}{2}Rm)^{x_2}} + \cdots + \dfrac{F_n}{(1 + \frac{1}{2}Rm)^{x_n}}} \tag{6.5}$$

The parameter C is expressed in units of squared years.

Equation (6.5) says that convexity is a weighted average of the *squared difference* between (1) the time remaining to a future payment and (2) the duration of the bond, where the weight is the present value of the future payment. For example, the second payment is for an amount F_2 and will be made after x_2 semi-annual periods, or after $\frac{1}{2}x_2$ years. The contribution of this payment to the bond's convexity is the squared difference between $\frac{1}{2}x_2$ and the bond's duration, or $(\frac{1}{2}x_2 - D)^2$, weighted by the present value of the payment, or by $F_2/(1 + \frac{1}{2}Rm)^{x_2}$. Example 1 illustrates the calculation of convexity.

Example 1
Computing convexity

As an illustration of calculating convexity, consider a $1\frac{1}{2}$ year note with a 10% coupon priced at par. There are three future cash flows from the note:

$F_1 = 5.$ $x_1 = 1.$ semi-annual periods

$F_2 = 5.$ $x_2 = 2.$

$F_3 = 105.$ $x_3 = 3.$

Since the note is priced at par its yield is $Rm = 10\%$ per annum.
The duration of the note is computed from equation (6.2):

$$D = \frac{\frac{1}{2}x_1 F_1 (1 + \frac{1}{2}Rm)^{-1} + \frac{1}{2}x_2 F_2 (1 + \frac{1}{2}Rm)^{-2} + \frac{1}{2}x_3 F_3 (1 + \frac{1}{2}Rm)^{-3}}{F_1 (1 + \frac{1}{2}Rm)^{-1} + F_2 (1 + \frac{1}{2}Rm)^{-2} + F_3 (1 + \frac{1}{2}Rm)^{-3}}$$

$$= \frac{.5(5.)(1.05)^{-1} + 1.(5.)(1.05)^{-2} + 1.5(105.)(1.05)^{-3}}{(5.)(1.05)^{-1} + (5.)(1.05)^{-2} + (105.)(1.05)^{-3}}$$

$$= 1.43 \text{ yr}$$

The convexity of the note is computed from equation (6.5):

$$C = \frac{(\frac{1}{2}x_1 - D)^2 F_1 (1 + \frac{1}{2}Rm)^{-1} + (\frac{1}{2}x_2 - D)^2 F_2 (1 + \frac{1}{2}Rm)^{-2} + (\frac{1}{2}x_3 - D)^2 F_3 (1 + \frac{1}{2}Rm)^{-3}}{F_1 (1 + \frac{1}{2}Rm)^{-1} + F_2 (1 + \frac{1}{2}Rm)^{-2} + F_3 (1 + \frac{1}{2}Rm)^{-3}}$$

$$= \frac{(-.930)^2 (5.)(1.05)^{-1} + (-.430)^2 (5.)(1.05)^{-3} + (.07)^2 (105.)(1.05)^{-3}}{(5.)(1.05)^{-1} + (5.)(1.05)^{-2} + (105.)(1.05)^{-3}}$$

$$= .0544 \text{ yr}^2$$

Although the definition in equation (6.5) may seem intimidating, it actually has a close and simple relation to duration. Duration is the average time to a bond's future payments. Convexity is the *dispersion*, or spread, of the times to those payments around the average time. Duration and convexity are analogous to the concepts of mean and variance in statistics.

Does the Measure Agree with the Stylized Facts?

Before examining the behavior of our measure of convexity, we want to verify that it agrees with the stylized facts noted in the introduction to this section.

Convexity of a Single-Payment Security

A single-payment security makes only one payment so that n, the number of future payments, is unity.

The definition of duration in equation (6.2) shows that $D = \frac{1}{2}x_1$ when $n = 1$, that is, the duration of a single-payment security is identically equal to the time remaining to its future payment. For the special case where $n = 1$ and $D = \frac{1}{2}x_1$, equation (6.5) becomes

$$C = \frac{\dfrac{(\frac{1}{2}x_1 - \frac{1}{2}x_1)^2 F_1}{(1 + \frac{1}{2}Rm)^{x_1}}}{\dfrac{F_1}{(1 + \frac{1}{2}Rm)^{x_1}}}$$

or

$$C = 0$$

This demonstrates that the convexity of any single payment security is identically equal to zero.

Convexity of a Multiple-Payment Security

A multiple payment security is characterized by a value of n greater than unity. We want to show that convexity is positive if n is two or more.

Looking at equation (6.5), we can see that C will equal zero only when all the squared differences are zero. If even one squared difference is positive, the parameter C will also be positive. Thus a necessary condition for $C = 0$ is $\frac{1}{2}x_1 = D$, $\frac{1}{2}x_2 = D$, ..., $\frac{1}{2}x_n = D$, or that $x_1 = x_2 = \cdots = x_n$.

However, if a bond makes payments at different times, that is, if it makes multiple payments, these equalities cannot all be satisfied simultaneously. This leads to the conclusion that C is positive if n exceeds unity.

Sensitivity of the Duration of a Bond

The third stylized fact asserts that the duration of a bond with more convexity will be more sensitive to a change in yield. Proving that the definition of convexity in equation (6.5) satisfies this assertion is technical and is outlined in appendix A. The results of that appendix can, however, be summarized fairly easily.

Suppose the yield on a bond changes from Rm to $Rm + \Delta Rm$, where ΔRm denotes the amount of change. This change in yield will produce a shift in the duration of the bond denoted by ΔD. The appendix shows that to a first-order approximation,

$$\Delta D = \frac{-C}{(1 + \frac{1}{2}Rm)} \cdot \Delta Rm \tag{6.6}$$

This shows clearly that the duration of a bond will be more sensitive to a change in yield the greater the value of its convexity parameter.

A Note on Convexity and Bond Performance

We can draw an important conclusion from this last stylized fact: The rate of return on a bond (measured over an interval equal to its original duration) will be more sensitive to variations in the reinvestment/liquidation yield the greater its measured convexity. This follows from the convexity of rate of return as a result of changing duration (see the second half of section 6.1) and the greater change in the duration of a more convex bond when yields vary.

The conclusion implies that *among bonds of equal duration* more convex bonds will outperform less convex bonds when interest rates change significantly. This claim is demonstrated in appendix B and illustrated in figure 6.2. The figure shows the rates of return on three bonds with the same duration but with different convexities:

Coupon	Term to maturity	Duration	Convexity
8%	16.3 yr	7.97 yr	33.03 yr^2
12%	20.0	7.97	38.95
16%	26.7	7.97	49.94

If interest rates vary significantly from 12%, either up or down, the more convex bond is seen to outperform the less convex bonds. The observation in the introduction to this chapter that a bond (with positive convexity) will outperform a matched duration single payment security (with zero convexity) if interest rates change significantly—is just a special case of this general characteristic.

Behavior of Convexity

With a few exceptions created by odd first coupons, a bond can be described completely by its maturity, coupon rate, and yield. From the maturity and coupon rate we can specify fully the future cash flows from the bond. We can calculate the current price of the bond from the cash flows and the bond's yield. It is therefore reasonable to ask how bond convexity varies with maturity, coupon, and yield.

We show below that convexity decreases as a bond approaches maturity. We also show that convexity is not monotonically related to either the coupon rate on a bond or to the bond's yield. Over a reasonable range of coupons and yields, convexity increases with both coupon rate and yield for bonds with not more than 7 years to maturity. It decreases with both coupon rate and yield for bonds with 20 to 30 years to maturity.

Effect of Changing Maturity on Convexity

The best place to begin analyzing the relation between maturity and convexity is with an actual example. Figure 6.3 shows the convexity of a

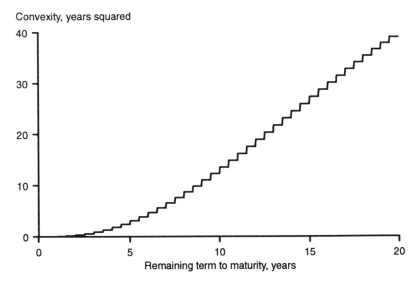

Figure 6.3
Convexity of a bond with a 12% coupon priced at a 12% yield from original issue as a 20-year bond to final maturity

20-year bond with a 12% coupon from issue to maturity, assuming the yield on the bond remains fixed at 12% per annum.

The most striking characteristic of the figure is the way convexity changes as the maturity of the bond declines. Instead of varying smoothly and continuously, it stays constant for a while, then drops to a new lower lever where it remains until the next drop. The data underlying figure 6.3 confirm that convexity is constant *between* coupon payments and falls only when the bond pays a coupon.

Such odd behavior becomes understandable when we recall a related characteristic of duration. Between coupon payments the duration of a bond declines by one day every day, that is, it declines on a one-for-one basis with the passage of time. (This behavior is described in chapter 4.) As long as a bond is between coupon payments the time remaining to each of its future payments also declines on a one-for-one basis with the passage of time. These observations imply that the *difference* between a bond's duration and the time remaining to a given payment is constant between coupon payments. Thus all the squared difference terms in equation (6.5) are constant between coupon payments. Although the present value weights in that equation increase as time passes, they all increase at the same rate, so the *relative* weights on the squared difference terms are also constant. In consequence the weighted average of the squared differences, or the bond's convexity, is constant between coupon payments.

The decline in the convexity of a bond at the time of a coupon payment results from the fact that when a coupon is paid, there are fewer coupons remaining. Thus the dispersion of the times to those remaining payments around the mean time, or duration, must decline. This is similar to removing the shortest person from a group of people and then observing that the heights of the remaining people are less dispersed around the (new) average height.

In summary, the convexity of a bond falls as the bond approaches maturity, but it falls in a series of discrete steps on coupon payment dates rather than smoothly and continuously. Between coupon payments the convexity of a bond is constant (assuming the yield on the bond is unchanged).

A Note on Portfolio Rebalancing

We can now make an interesting observation about an important aspect of managing a fixed income portfolio. Suppose that an investor allocates capital among one or more bonds to achieve a desired mismatch between the duration of his portfolio and his investment horizon (the mismatch can be positive, negative, or zero depending on the investor's appraisal of the market) and to achieve a desired convexity. As long as yields remain unchanged and none of the bonds in the portfolio make a coupon payment, both the mismatch and the convexity will remain unchanged. The duration of the portfolio will decline on a one-for-one basis with the passage of time, as will the time remaining to the investor's horizon date, so the difference (i.e., the mismatch) will remain constant. At the same time convexity will stay constant for the reasons noted above. Thus the portfolio does not have to be adjusted between coupon payments.

On the other hand, portfolio rebalancing is necessary when a bond pays a coupon. At that time the mismatch and the convexity of the portfolio will both change, and, of course the investor will have cash to reinvest.

This may explain why there is so much trading of Treasury bonds around the quarterly dates (February 15, May 15, August 15, and November 15) when longer bonds pay interest. Trading at these times is necessary even to *maintain* a desired convexity and a desired mismatch between duration and horizon.

Effect of Coupon on Convexity

The second bond characteristic we want to analyze is the effect of coupon on convexity. Table 6.4 shows the convexity of bonds of different maturities and coupons at three different yields. Holding yield and maturity fixed, we see that bond convexity increases with coupon rate for bonds

Table 6.4
Bond convexity as a function of yield, coupon, and maturity

Coupon rate	Bond maturity, years							
	2	3	4	5	7	10	20	30
A. Valued at a 14% yield								
14%	.19 yr^2	.65	1.44	2.59	5.79	12.18	34.17	46.73
13	.18	.62	1.41	2.55	5.78	12.30	34.84	47.33
12	.17	.60	1.37	2.50	5.75	12.42	35.60	48.04
11	.16	.57	1.32	2.44	5.70	12.53	36.47	48.87
10	.15	.54	1.27	2.37	5.64	12.63	37.48	49.85
B. Valued at a 12% yield								
14%	.18	.63	1.41	2.52	5.67	12.14	37.43	55.85
13	.18	.61	1.37	2.48	5.64	12.23	38.15	56.66
12	.17	.58	1.33	2.42	5.60	12.32	38.95	57.61
11	.16	.56	1.28	2.36	5.55	12.39	39.87	58.71
10	.15	.53	1.23	2.29	5.47	12.44	40.91	60.01
C. Valued at a 10% yield								
14%	.18	.62	1.37	2.45	5.53	12.02	40.39	66.00
13	.17	.59	1.33	2.40	5.49	12.08	41.12	67.03
12	.16	.57	1.29	2.35	5.44	12.13	41.93	68.22
11	.15	.54	1.25	2.29	5.37	12.16	42.84	69.61
10	.14	.52	1.19	2.21	5.28	12.17	43.86	71.24

with not more than 7 years to maturity and decreases with coupon rate for bonds with 10 years or more remaining to maturity.

The different relationship between convexity and coupon for long bonds versus shorter maturity bonds is attributable to the fact that a higher coupon enhances the importance of payments made prior to maturity relative to the principal payment at maturity. If the bond's mean time to payment, or duration, is comparable to the bond's term to maturity, as is the case for short and intermediate maturity debt, a higher coupon has the effect of increasing the dispersion of the times to payment around that mean; that is, it increases convexity. However, if the mean time is far less than the term to maturity, as with long bonds, increasing the importance of intermediate payments relative to the maturity payment can reduce dispersion.

Effect of Yield on Convexity

Table 6.4 also shows that increasing the yield of a bond, holding coupon and maturity constant, has a different effect on the convexity of long bonds compared to shorter bonds. Higher yield leads to less convexity in long bonds and more convexity in shorter bonds.

The reason for this difference is similar to the reason for the difference in the effect of coupon on convexity. Recall that convexity is computed as a weighted average where the weights are the present values of the future payments. Higher yield has a relatively greater depressing effect on the present value of long dated payments. In crude terms, higher yield enhances the relative importance of early payments and reduces the importance of later payments. Thus higher yield has an effect on convexity similar to higher coupon: It lowers the convexity of long bonds and raises the convexity of shorter bonds.

6.3   Implications of Convexity for Immunization

Duration is an attractive analytical concept because of the simplicity of its implications. It is quite convenient to say that a bond with a duration of 8 years immunizes a liability due in 8 years in essentially the same way that an 8-year zero would immunize that liability. However, we have now seen that bonds and zeros are not similar, even when compared on a matched duration basis, because of their different convexities.

The difference between bonds and zeros that results from convexity raises two questions. First, can we continue to think about immunization with bonds the same way that we think about immunization with zeros— as a simple problem of matching duration to investment horizon? Second, is convexity a favorable or unfavorable characteristic? That is, should an investor be willing to sacrifice yield in order to acquire convexity, or should he demand a yield pickup when swapping into more convex securities?

This section addresses these questions in a slightly indirect fashion. We first examine three situations where convexity is beneficial, irrelevant, and harmful, respectively. This allows us to identify when convexity should matter to a portfolio manager. We then use these results for addressing the questions of ultimate interest.

When Greater Convexity Is Beneficial

Convexity is beneficial for an investor who buys a bond with a duration matched to his horizon if, immediately after purchase, the yield curve becomes flat and shifts to some arbitrary level at which it remains.

This scenario has already been analyzed in section 6.1. To say, as in that section, that all coupons from a bond can be reinvested at a common yield (regardless of when they are paid and regardless of the length of time over which they are reinvested) and to say that the remaining payments on the bond can be sold at that same yield is equivalent to saying that the yield curve becomes flat and stationary following purchase of the bond. However, since the analysis in section 6.1 did not require that the reinvestment/liquidation yield equal the yield at which the bond was purchased that analysis explicitly allowed for a one-time change in yield immediately following purchase. Figure 6.2 shows that the average rate of return on the bond will be greater, the greater the convexity of the bond and the greater the change in yield following purchase. Thus, in this case, more convexity is better.

Assuming that the yield curve becomes flat and remains stationary following purchase of a bond is obviously quite stringent. Market participants know that yields change continuously through time, that the yield curve is usually not flat, and that it can change shape. These elements of added realism have an important influence on the desirability of convexity.

When Convexity Is Irrelevant

Convexity is a nearly irrelevant characteristic of a bond for a portfolio manager seeking to maintain an immunized position if yields change smoothly and continuously rather than in large, sudden jumps.

To appreciate the merits of this claim, we have to recall the origins of convexity discussed in section 6.1. Convexity is attributable to the lengthening of a bond's duration when yields fall and to the shortening of duration when yields rise. If yields change only once, immediately following purchase of a bond, the change in duration occurs contemporaneously with the change in yield. An investor has, by definition, no opportunity to adjust the duration of his portfolio at yields between the initial purchase yield and the subsequent, final yield.

Suppose, however, that interest rates change in small increments and that investors can buy and sell bonds after each incremental change. (This is not to say that yields cannot change by a large amount but that any large change must be the cumulative result of a series of small shifts.) In this scenario an investor seeking to immunize a future liability will observe the duration of his portfolio gradually drifting away from the time remaining to his horizon date as yields change. If yields are falling, he will observe the duration of his portfolio lengthening. If yields are rising, he will observe the duration shortening. In either case he has an opportunity to rebalance his portfolio and to restore the match between its duration and his horizon before the mismatch becomes appreciable.

In an environment of continuously but smoothly changing yields, where an investor maintains continuously the correspondence between portfolio duration and horizon, the gains from convexity are small. In simple terms the gap between duration and horizon, which is the *sine qua non* of convexity, never appears.

It may be argued that this scenario of continual rebalancing is unrealistic. If interest rates are going up (and duration contracting), why should an investor extend duration (to restore the match between duration and his horizon)? Conversely, if interest rates are going down, why should an investor shorten duration? The answer is that failure to rebalance the portfolio when rebalancing is possible is equivalent to accepting risk—market risk if duration has lengthened beyond the horizon and reinvestment risk if duration is too short. Such acceptance of risk conflicts with the initial premise that the investor is seeking to eliminate risk through duration management.

It is important to appreciate the distinction between a single large change in interest rates and a large change that is the cumulative result of a series of incremental changes. In the first case an investor has no opportunity to adjust his portfolio while rates are changing. In the second case the investor has an opportunity to adjust his portfolio after each small shift in yields. He also has an incentive to adjust if he does not know whether yields will continue to move in the same direction or whether they will reverse.

When Greater Convexity Is Harmful

Convexity is an undesirable characteristic if there is significant uncertainty about whether and how the yield curve will change shape in the future.

The problem of analyzing a bond in the context of a yield curve with changing shape was addressed in chapter 5. There we saw that the conventional duration of a bond is not a good measure of the average time to the bond's future payments if the yield curve can steepen or flatten. A bond with a conventional duration of 8 years may behave as if it had a 6-year duration if short-term rates are more volatile than long-term rates, and it may behave as if it had a 10-year duration if the reverse is true.

In general, the effect of changes in the shape of the yield curve on the duration of a bond will be greater, the greater the convexity of the bond. This is because greater convexity implies greater dispersion of cash flow and hence more sensitivity of duration to changes in relative yields across the curve. This is illustrated, in reverse, by zeros, which have no convexity and whose duration is not influenced by how the curve may change shape.

Managing a bond portfolio by matching duration to horizon is obviously more complex if the effective duration of the portfolio depends on how the curve might change shape in the future. Convexity is harmful when there is uncertainty about change in the shape of the curve because it creates uncertainty over whether the portfolio is truly immunized.

Some Conclusions

The three scenarios that we have examined are simplified representations of a complex marketplace, but they suggest when and why convexity is desirable, undesirable, or irrelevant to a portfolio manager.

If interest rates change in modest increments, for instance, on the order of 5 to 10 basis points a day, convexity is, at best, an irrelevant characteristic of a bond. Such small changes give a portfolio manager ample opportunity to maintain a match between the duration of his portfolio and his investment horizon even over the course of cumulatively large shifts in interest rates. If we add an assumption that the yield curve can change shape, convexity becomes undesirable as a result of uncertainty about the effective duration of the portfolio.

Gradually changing yields and yield curves of changing shape appear to be an appropriate characterization of the credit markets. Thus it would appear that investors should generally prefer to limit the convexity of their portfolios and that they should demand a yield pickup before swapping into bonds of great convexity.

More important, convexity by itself does not require any change in the implications of basic duration analysis. We only need to add the caveats that (1) duration changes as interest rates change, so immunization must be an ongoing process of portfolio appraisal and adjustment, and (2) the possibility of change in the shape of the curve can jeopardize any simple balancing of conventional duration and horizon.

Adding only one other assumption on the behavior of interest rates can mitigate, and possibly reverse, the tentative conclusion that convexity is undesirable. If interest rates occasionally shift sharply, by 25 or 50 basis points, convexity may carry significant benefits. In this case an investor can maintain an immunized position while yields change gradually, get the benefits of convexity that arise from an occasional sharp shift in yields, and then reestablish promptly a new immunized position after any such shift. It is not necessary that interest rates only change in large jumps in order to benefit from convexity. A few large shifts from time to time may suffice to make convexity desirable on balance.

The problem, for a portfolio manager, is assessing whether there are likely to be enough, and large enough, sharp changes in interest rates to make the benefits of convexity outweigh the disadvantages associated with the duration uncertainty of more convex bonds. If sharp market moves seem likely, convexity may be very desirable. Conversely, if interest rates are most likely to change smoothly, convexity may be undesirable on balance.

Does the Market Value Convexity?

The desirability of convexity can be addressed from a different perspective by asking whether the structure of Treasury bond prices is such that investors are paid, in higher yield, to accept greater convexity or whether they have to give up yield as the price of adding convexity. There is empirical support both for and against the proposition that the market as a whole places a positive value on convexity.

Section 6.2 pointed out that high coupon intermediate maturity bonds have more convexity than otherwise comparable current coupon bonds. Such bonds are also known to trade at relatively depressed prices; that is, they trade "cheap" to the current coupon Treasury yield curve. Thus the bond market offers a yield pickup to those willing to accept greater convexity, implying that convexity is generally not a desirable characteristic.

At the same time, however, zero coupon securities (which have no convexity) also trade cheap to the current coupon yield curve. This phenomenon may be more closely related to the relative liquidity of zeros versus whole Treasury bonds than to demand for convexity, but it does raise a caution flag over any hasty pronouncements on the value of convexity.

6.4   Summary

In a simple sense this chapter has expanded the vocabulary of bond analytics to include convexity along with the better-known characteristics of yield and duration. Section 6.1 examined the origins of convexity and its effect on the return on capital invested in bonds. Section 6.2 proposed a measure of convexity and described how the measure varies as a function of different bond characteristics.

The preliminary description of convexity suggested that more convex bonds ought to be more valuable than less convex bonds of the same duration and certainly more valuable than zero coupon securities. However, section 6.3 demonstrated that this result depends on how interest rates change over time. If they change smoothly and continuously, convexity may be a largely irrelevant bond characteristic for an investor seeking to maintain an immunized portfolio allocation. Moreover, if the shape of the yield curve can change unpredictably, the very properties that lead to convexity (i.e., multiple payments) also create uncertainty over the effective duration of a bond. Thus the value of convexity depends on an investor's appraisal of the future behavior of interest rates, both with respect to the likelihood of sharp changes and with respect to his confidence in forecasting the relative volatility of short-term and long-term yields.

6.5   Appendix A: Convexity as a Measure of the Sensitivity of the Duration of a Bond to Changes in Yield

This appendix demonstrates that the convexity of a bond, as defined in equation (6.5) in the text, is a measure of the sensitivity of the bond's duration to changes in yield.

To begin, recall the definition of duration in equation (6.2) in the text:

$$D = \frac{\sum_{i=1}^{n} \frac{1}{2} x_i \cdot F_i \cdot (1 + \frac{1}{2} Rm)^{-x_i}}{\sum_{i=1}^{n} F_i \cdot (1 + \frac{1}{2} Rm)^{-x_i}} \tag{A6.1}$$

We want to compute the derivative of duration with respect to yield, or dD/dRm. After some manipulation of equation (A6.1), we get

$$\frac{dD}{dRm} = \frac{-C}{(1 + \frac{1}{2} Rm)} \tag{A6.2}$$

where C is the convexity measure defined in equation (6.5). This is identical to equation (6.6) in the text.

6.6   Appendix B: A Second-Order Approximation to the Rate Return on a Bond as a Function of the Reinvestment/Liquidation Yield

This appendix develops a second-order approximation to the rate of return on a bond over a specified horizon.

To begin, recall how the future value of a bond on a date h semi-annual periods in the future was defined in equation (6.3) of the text:

$$FV = F_1 \cdot (1 + \tfrac{1}{2}R)^{h-x_1} + \cdots + F_n \cdot (1 + \tfrac{1}{2}R)^{h-x_n} \qquad (A6.3)$$

where FV is the future value and R is the assumed reinvestment/liquidation yield.

If the bond is purchased at a price of $P + A$, the average rate of return on the bond over the interval h is the value of Ra that satisfies the equation:

$$P + A = \frac{FV}{(1 + \tfrac{1}{2}Ra)^h} \qquad (A6.4)$$

Since FV depends on R, the value of Ra defined implicitly in equation (A6.4) will also depend on R.

Let $Ra = f(R)$ denote the functional relation between R and Ra. The function f can be expanded in a power series around the yield Rm at which the bond was purchased:

$$Ra = f(Rm) + f'(Rm) \cdot (R - Rm) + \tfrac{1}{2}f''(Rm) \cdot (R - Rm)^2 + \cdots \qquad (A6.5)$$

where $f'(Rm)$ is the first derivative of f evaluated at Rm and $f''(Rm)$ is the second derivative of f evaluated at Rm.

After some manipulation it can be shown that:

$$f(Rm) = Rm \qquad (A6.6a)$$

$$f'(Rm) = 1 - \frac{2D}{h} \qquad (A6.6b)$$

$$f''(Rm) = 2 \left[\frac{C - (\tfrac{1}{2}h - D)D/h}{h(1 + \tfrac{1}{2}Rm)} \right] \qquad (A6.6c)$$

where D is the bond's duration at yield Rm (see equation 6.2) and where C is the bond's convexity at yield Rm (see equation 6.5).

Now suppose that the bond is such that its duration D equals the horizon $\tfrac{1}{2}h$ (where $\tfrac{1}{2}h$ is the horizon in years). Using the terms in (A6.6) for the special case of $D = \tfrac{1}{2}h$ in equation (A6.5) gives

$$Ra = Rm + \frac{C}{2D \cdot (1 + \tfrac{1}{2}Rm)} \cdot (R - Rm)^2 \qquad (A6.7)$$

Equation (A6.7) has three important implications. First, *to a first-order or linear approximation*, the rate of return on the bond is independent of the reinvestment/liquidation yield R. That is, the term involving $R - Rm$ in equation (A6.5) drops out of the expression for Ra when $D = \tfrac{1}{2}h$ because

$f'(Rm) = 0$ in that case (see equation A6.6b). This is the standard result of basic duration analysis. Second, the rate of return is *not* independent of R when we recognize second-order effects. However, the difference between the reinvestment/liquidation yield and the original purchase yield must be fairly large for these second-order effects to be important. Third, the rate of return will be more sensitive to the reinvestment/liquidation yield the greater the value of the convexity parameter C. This demonstrates that a more convex bond will outperform a less convex bond if both bonds have a common duration matched to an investor's horizon.

6.7   Subsequent Remarks

The basic analysis of duration and immunization suggests that a bond with a yield of Rm and a duration of D years is functionally equivalent to a zero coupon security with a yield of Rm and a remaining term to maturity of D years. More concisely, it suggests that a bond can be recast as a zero.

This chapter and the preceding chapter offered critical assessments of the basic analysis. They showed that the returns on a bond and a zero with a common yield and duration will not be the same (over an investment horizon equal to the common duration) if (1) the shape of the yield curve changes or if (2) yields change suddenly by a large amount.

These caveats to basic duration analysis are not trivial, but they also do not negate entirely the utility of categorizing bonds in terms of duration and assessing the relative values of bonds with a common duration in terms of yield. Large, discontinuous yield changes are not common occurrences, and on average, a substantial fraction of the total volatility of Treasury yields stems from essentially parallel shifts of the yield curve. Thus it makes sense, at least as a first approximation, to assess the relative value of fixed income securities using yield and duration. This topic is pursued in part II.

II   YIELD CURVES AND RELATIVE VALUE

It seems reasonable to construct a yield curve for zero coupon securities by graphing yields on different zeros as a function of their term to maturity. Basic duration analysis suggests that a bond can be analyzed "as if" it were a zero with (1) a yield equal to the yield on the bond and with (2) a term to maturity equal to the duration of the bond. By analogy, it therefore seems reasonable to consider constructing a bond yield curve by graphing yields on different bonds against their respective durations. One bond may then be characterized as cheap or expensive compared to another bond of approximately the same duration if it has a materially higher or lower yield than the second bond. However, as suggested in chapters 5 and 6 of part I, basic duration analysis does not account for the consequences of changes in the shape of the yield curve or large, discontinuous changes in yields. This implies that bond yields may vary systematically with security characteristics other than duration and that one bond may not necessarily be cheap compared to another bond of a similar duration merely because it has a higher yield. The premium yield may be justified by differences in bond characteristics other than duration.

Chapters 7 through 10 examine the related problems of (1) depicting bond yield as a function of bond duration and other bond characteristics and (2) assessing the relative values of different Treasury securities, including bonds, bills, and zeros. These chapters show that yield varies with duration and that it also varies with the coupon rate on a bond, with whether a security is a bond, a bill, or a zero, and with the specific maturity date of a bill.

Chapter 7 introduces the variation of yield with duration and other security characteristics and the problem of assessing relative value. A key feature of the chapter is the proposed technique for estimating a Treasury bill yield curve and a par bond yield curve from data on actual Treasury bills and bonds. Bill yield curves and par bond yield curves are crucial analytical constructions which appear frequently in later chapters.

Chapter 8 extends the assessment of relative value to trading in bonds before their issue date and to specialized transactions known as "coupon rolls." Chapter 9 examines whether some bills have special value because they mature, for example, just before the end of a calendar quarter or just before a tax payment date. Finally, chapter 10 considers the problem of assessing the relative value of a zero coupon security that has a term to maturity longer than the duration of every outstanding bond.

7 The Structure of Treasury Yields: Duration, Coupon, and Liquidity Effects

Every business day, participants in the Treasury securities market have to decide what, if anything, should be bought or sold. Broadly speaking, the decision can be factored into three parts:

- Appraising the future direction of the market *as a whole*.
- Examining the best sector to buy or sell within the general market.
- Identifying the best *issue* to buy or sell within a given sector.

Although these topics are not unrelated, each requires some unique analysis. Market timing depends on the prospects for aggregate economic activity, Federal Reserve policy, and Federal tax and expenditure programs. Sector and issue identification, on the other hand, depend on progressively more refined analyses of the structure of yields on Treasury securities.

Almost every appraisal of the structure of Treasury yields begins with some notion of a yield curve. In its simplest form the curve can be represented by a graph of yields and durations of outstanding securities, as shown in figure 7.1. Even without distinguishing further the characteristics of different issues, such a graph is an important analytical device. It captures the intuitive notion that Treasury securities cannot be compared on the basis of their yields alone. At the very least some measure of the futurity of their cash flows is also needed.

Graphs like figure 7.1 are the foundation of traditional yield curve analysis. That analysis is a global analysis directed towards choosing the most appropriate sector to buy or sell. The choice depends on three factors. First, what is the investor's horizon? Second, what is the market outlook? Third, what yields are available in different sectors of the market (i.e., what is the level and shape of the curve)?

An investor who is unsure of the direction of future changes in interest rates might adopt a neutral posture and hold securities with a duration matched to his investment horizon. If he believes interest rates will remain unchanged for the foreseeable future and if the yield curve is positively sloped, he might hold securities with a somewhat longer duration, and thereby bear market risk, in order to pick up additional yield. Finally, he might extend his duration significantly if he has a strongly held expectation that interest rates will fall in the near future.

Despite its obvious significance, global yield curve analysis is not the only type of curve analysis. For example, even if an investor has decided to extend the duration of his portfolio from one year to three years, he still

Written November 1984.

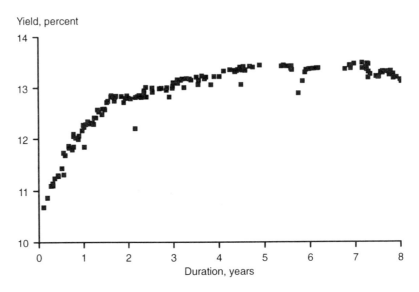

Figure 7.1
Yields and durations of Treasury securities on July 20, 1984

has to decide whether to sell bills or short term bonds and whether to buy low coupon, current coupon, or high coupon intermediate maturity bonds. In addition he has to identify the specific securities to be sold and the specific securities to be purchased. Making these decisions requires an appraisal of relative value more extensive than simply examining the broad market outlook and the general shape of the curve.

This chapter addresses primarily the intensive analysis of small sections of the Treasury yield curve rather than the curve as a whole. We will call this the analysis of the "local" structure of Treasury yields to distinguish it from the more traditional global yield curve analysis described above. To rephrase an old saw, it is a matter of examining the trees, and in some cases the leaves, once the forest has been located.

Section 7.1 describes the topics involved with analyzing the local structure of Treasury yields, including the value of the liquidity of Treasury bills and the comparative desirability of high coupon premium bonds versus low coupon discount bonds. Section 7.2 outlines a framework for representing these factors quantitatively. Section 7.3 shows how a novel representation of the whole Treasury yield curve can be constructed by piecing together the local descriptions provided by the proposed analysis. Finally, section 7.4 presents some applications of the analysis, including especially the evaluation of swap opportunities.

Example 1
Duration and yield comparisons for high and low coupon bonds on December 30, 1983

Case	Bond	Duration[a]	Yield[b]
(1) $14\frac{7}{8}\%$	6/30/1986	2.11 yr	11.02%
$9\frac{3}{8}\%$	5/15/1986	2.12	10.97
(2) $14\frac{1}{2}\%$	5/15/1991	4.77	11.85
$11\frac{1}{2}\%$	10/15/1990	4.75	11.73
(3) $14\frac{5}{8}\%$	2/15/1992	5.05	11.92
$7\frac{1}{4}\%$	8/15/1992	6.08	11.55

a. Duration adjusted for periodic coupon payments as described in chapter 4.
b. "True" yield as defined in chapter 5.

7.1 Factors Affecting the Local Structure of Treasury Yields

Assessing the local structure of Treasury yields begins by expanding the description of a security to include characteristics in addition to duration. This is an important step because it removes the conceptual straitjacket of assuming implicitly that yield depends only on duration and that two securities with the same duration "ought" to have the same yield. Whatever the attractiveness of such an assumption, figure 7.1 shows it is unjustified and that yield is not linked smoothly to duration.

The present section identifies two characteristics in addition to duration which can influence yield: the liquidity of Treasury bills and the coupon on a bond. The next section describes how these characteristics can be incorporated into a quantitative representation of the structure of yields in a particular sector of the Treasury market.

Coupon Rate

Holding duration constant, the coupon on a bond can have a perceptible effect on the bond's yield. Example 1 provides several illustrations of this statement with market data from December 30, 1983. Cases 1 and 2 show pairs of bonds with virtually the same duration but with quite different coupon rates and yields. Case 3 shows a situation where an investor could have sold a low coupon 10-year issue, bought a high coupon issue of comparable maturity, and both shortened his duration and picked up yield. What is remarkable about this example is that the yield curve was generally flat in the 10-year maturity sector (or 6-year duration sector) of the Treasury market at the end of December 1983, so one would not have associated shorter duration with higher yield.

The observation that yields on bonds of the same duration can differ because the bonds have different coupon rates is of interest because yield may then be related systematically to coupon rate. As suggested by example 1, bonds with low coupons commonly have lower yields than current coupon bonds, while high coupon bonds often have higher yields. These "coupon effects" are the result of several supply and demand factors.

Demand Side Influences

Tax considerations were and to some extent remain important for understanding why low coupon bonds usually have low yields. Prior to passage of the Tax Reform Act of 1984, federal tax law treated capital gains more favorably than ordinary income. This created an incentive for investors who were not tax exempt to favor capital gains over interest income—everything else, such as duration, being the same—and strengthened the demand for bonds priced below their principal value. Low coupon bonds consequently traded at low pre-tax yields relative to otherwise comparable current coupon bonds.

The Tax Reform Act of 1984 eliminated entirely the tax-based attractiveness of discount bonds issued after passage of the Act because it defined market discount on such bonds as interest income that must be accrued and recognized periodically. This placed market discount on an even footing with market premium, which was previously treated as an interest expense which could be amortized and recognized periodically. (The Act also defined market discount on a bond issued prior to passage of the Act as interest income, although the cumulative accrued amount of that income does not have to be recognized until the bond matures or is sold. Thus there are still some tax advantages to buying "old" discount bonds.)

There are reasons other than tax treatment to favor either high coupon or low coupon bonds of the same duration. A pension fund (which pays no federal taxes) that has a long dated liability structure due to the presence of many young and middle age beneficiaries may prefer low coupon bonds as a way to minimize the risks inherent in reinvesting coupon income. (These risks are not entirely eliminated by immunization because of the assumption in basic duration analysis that the yield curve is always flat.) In an extreme case such a pension fund may prefer long maturity zero coupon instruments with no reinvestment risk. On the other hand, an investor with a more uniform distribution of future cash requirements may prefer high coupon bonds which generate greater near-term cash flows.

In general, although duration is an important concept for portfolio management, it does not provide a complete measure of the appropriateness of a bond. Depending on the precise size and timing of his future cash needs, an investor may prefer a shorter maturity low coupon bond to a longer maturity high coupon bond of the same duration. In the aggregate such preferences can lead to different market yields on bonds of the same duration.

Supply Side Influences

The direction and magnitude of the coupon effect on bond yields also depends on the relative quantities of high and low coupon bonds available in the market.

For example, as interest rates fall following a contraction in aggregate economic activity the stock of high coupon bonds necessarily increases and the stock of low coupon bonds contracts. (When rates decline a current coupon becomes a high coupon and a low coupon moves toward a current coupon.) The increased stock of high coupon bonds can lead to an expansion of the spreads between their yields and yields on current coupon bonds; that is, it can lead to a relative cheapening of the now more plentiful high coupon bonds. Similarly the contraction in the stock of low coupon bonds can lead to relatively greater advances in their prices and to a similar expansion of the spreads between their yields and yields on current coupon bonds. Conversely, during periods of rising interest rates spreads can narrow as the stock of high coupon bonds falls and the stock of low coupon bonds rises.

There are also important forces that can reduce the stock of particular bonds regardless of the direction of change in the general level of interest rates. During 1983, for example, stripping and zero coupon custodial receipt programs accounted for a significant reduction in the stock of high coupon bonds maturing between 2001 and 2013. Similarly foreign central bank and Federal Reserve purchases during 1983 reduced the floating supply of high coupon bonds maturing between 1988 and 1992. Both factors contributed to a compression of spreads between high coupon bonds and current coupon bonds.

Liquidity

The value of a Treasury security stems from its promise to make interest and principal payments in the future. However, despite promises to make substantially identical payments on substantially identical dates, the prices (and yields) of two securities can differ if one security trades more actively than the other. The reason is that liquidity, or the ability to purchase or sell large amounts of a security without affecting its price, is a valuable characteristic.

Example 2 illustrates this phenomenon. As shown, the same payments had a higher value when packaged as Treasury bills rather than as a short

Example 2
Valuing the cash flows on a Treasury bond with Treasury bill prices

On Monday, June 4, 1984, the following prices for June 5 settlement prevailed in the Treasury market:

Bill maturing 11/15/84:   10.30% discount rate

Bill maturing 5/16/85:   10.75% discount rate

$14\frac{1}{8}$% bound maturing 5/15/85: $101\frac{25}{32}$

The invoice price on the bond was 102.58730 ($102.58730 = 101\frac{25}{32}$ plus .80605 accrued interest since 5/15/1984).

The future cash flows on the bond were

11/15/1984:	7.06250	Coupon payment
5/15/1985:	7.06250	Coupon payment
	100.0	Principal payment
	107.06250	Total payment on 5/15/1985

We want to know how these cash flows were valued in the Treasury bill market.

Consider first a Treasury bill paying 7.0625 on November 15, 1984. This bill was quoted at a 10.30% discount rate, or at an invoice price of 6.73313, for settlement on June 5, 1984. ($6.73313 = 95.33639\%$ of 7.0625, where a 10.30% discount rate on a 163 day bill corresponds to an invoice price of 95.33639% of face value.) Consider next a Treasury bill paying107.0625 on May 15, 1985. Although no such bill actually existed, we could guess that it would have been quoted at about a 10.75% discount rate if it did exist because that was the quote on a May 16, 1985 bill. This corresponds to an invoice price of 96.06480 for settlement on June 5, 1984. ($96.06480 = 89.72778\%$ of 107.0625, where a 10.75% discount rate on a 344 day bill corresponds to an invoice price of 89.72778% of face value.) Thus, the value of the cash flows on the bond computed with Treasury bill prices was 102.79793 ($102.79793 = 6.73313 + 96.06480$.)

The difference between the market price of the bond and the value of the same cash flows computed at Treasury bill prices is .21063 ($.21063 = 102.79793 - 102.58730$.) This corresponds to a yield difference of about 24 basis points on the bond.

maturity Treasury bond. The price difference was equivalent to a yield difference of about 24 basis points on the bond. A holder of the bills could have earned this incremental yield by selling his bills and buying the bond and he would not have altered the timing of his future cash flows by more than one day in the process.

The reason for such a significant difference in the market price of virtually the same cash flows is that Treasury bills trade in a far more liquid market than short maturity Treasury bonds. An investor who faces a substantial likelihood of needing cash before his investment matures will prefer bills and will be willing to pay a higher price for those bills than for bonds. This implies that the yield on a short duration Treasury security is related systematically to whether the security is a bill or a bond.

7.2 Characterizing the Local Structure of Treasury Yields

The preceding section identified two factors in addition to duration that influence yields on Treasury securities:

1. A bond's coupon.
2. The distinction between a bill and a bond.

This section describes how the factors can be incorporated into a quantitative description of yields in a particular sector of the Treasury market. The next section extends the analysis by showing how a series of local descriptions can be pieced together to form a representation of yields in the whole market.

The Par Bond Yield Curve

We begin by defining *the* yield curve. This is important because we are going to analyze coupon and liquidity effects as refinements on a basic duration structure of Treasury yields. An appropriate starting point will facilitate the analysis.

The most common definition of the Treasury yield curve and the definition used in global yield curve analysis is the sequence of yields on active (or recently auctioned) bills and bonds. This turns out to be an inappropriate choice for local analysis for three reasons. First, it ignores any effect of coupon rate on bond yields because it does not distinguish between issues trading at a premium and issues trading at a discount. Second, it obscures the liquidity value of bills because it treats bills and bonds as parts of a single yield curve. Third, it is not a definition of a curve at all but a specification of a sequence of discrete points on a yield-duration graph. It leaves unresolved the problem of connecting the points to form a continuous curve.

None of these objections are important in the context of global analysis where the analyst seeks to identify appropriate sectors to buy or sell. In that case examining yields on active issues alone is economical (in terms of analytical effort and data requirements) and sufficiently complete. The objections are important, however, for an analysis aimed at choosing among securities within a given sector, where differences in, for example, coupon rate can have a larger effect on yield than differences in duration.

For present purposes we define the yield curve as the sequence of yields on par bonds of every maturity. (Although a par bond may not exist for a given maturity we can at least think about what the par yield would be and, as described in the appendix, develop techniques to estimate that

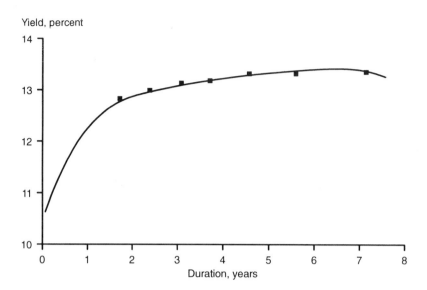

Figure 7.2
Par Treasury bond yield curve and yields and durations of active, or on-the-run, issues on
July 20, 1984

yield.) Using *bonds* priced at *par* establishes a curve that is not confounded
with coupon or Treasury bill liquidity effects.

Figure 7.2 shows (as a solid line) yields on par bonds on July 20, 1984,
and also shows (as solid boxes) yields on active coupon issues on the same
date. It is clear that the general shape of the curve could have been
estimated within close limits simply by knowing the yields on the active
issues. Nonetheless, as indicated in table 7.1, differences of from −6 to +6
basis points did exist between yields on active bonds and yields on par
bonds of comparable duration.

The Local Structure of Treasury Yields

Having defined the basic yield curve, we now narrow our focus to a single
point on the curve and simultaneously expand the breadth of the analysis
to include securities other than par bonds. This leads to examining the
relationship among yield, coupon rate, and the bills or bonds distinction
in a specific sector of the Treasury market.

To appreciate the direction of the analysis consider the following
problems. On July 20, 1984, a par bond with a term to maturity of three
years had a yield of 13.00% and a duration of 2.50 years. Using this as a
starting point, what can we say about yields on bonds with the same
duration but with coupon rates greater or less than 13.00%? Also on July
20, 1984, a par bond with a duration of .95 years had a yield of 12.19%.

Table 7.1
Yields on active issues and on par bonds of comparable duration on July 20, 1984

Sector	Coupon	Maturity	Duration[a]	Yield[b]	Yield[b] on comparable duration[a] par bond	Yield difference
2 yr	13%	6/30/1986	1.72 yr	12.83%	12.77%	6 bp
3	$12\frac{1}{2}$	5/15/1987	2.38	13.00	12.96	4
4	$13\frac{5}{8}$	6/30/1988	3.08	13.14	13.10	4
5	$13\frac{7}{8}$	8/15/1989	3.71	13.19	13.19	0
7	$13\frac{3}{4}$	7/15/1991	4.57	13.32	13.30	2
10	$13\frac{1}{8}$	5/15/1994	5.59	13.32	13.38	−6
20	$13\frac{3}{4}$	8/15/2004	7.14	13.35	13.37	−2

a. Duration adjusted for periodic coupon payments.
b. "True" yield.

What can we say about the yield on a Treasury bill with the same duration?

Non-Par Bonds

Suppose that we pick a particular duration and denote the yield on a par bond of that duration as Rm^p. Let Rcp denote the coupon on an arbitrary bond of the same duration. If Rcp exceeds Rm^p the bond has a high coupon. If Rcp is less than Rm^p the bond has a low coupon.

The relationship between yield and coupon can be represented with the following equation:

$$Rm = Rm^p + c \cdot \max[Rcp - Rm^p, 0] + d \cdot \min[Rcp - Rm^p, 0] \qquad (7.1)$$

where Rm is the yield on the arbitrary bond and c and d are coefficients. (The function $\max[a, b]$ has the value a if a is greater than b and the value b if b is greater than a. The function $\min[a, b]$ has the value a if a is less than b and the value b if b is less than a.)

To understand equation (7.1), consider first the case where the coupon rate exceeds the yield on the comparable duration par bond ($Rcp > Rm^p$) The last term in equation (7.1) then drops out and the equation becomes:

$$Rm = Rm^p + c \cdot (Rcp - Rm^p) \qquad (7.1')$$

The coefficient c reflects the effect of the high coupon on the yield of the bond. For example, c had the value .022 on July 20, 1984, for bonds with a 2.50-year duration. Since Rm^p was 13.00% at a duration of 2.50 years, a bond with the same duration and a coupon of 14.50% would have had a yield of about 13.03% ($13.03 = 13.00 + .022 \cdot (14.50 - 13.00)$). A bond with the same duration and an even higher coupon of 16.00% would have had a yield of about 13.07% ($13.07 = 13.00 + .022 \cdot (16.00 - 13.00)$).

Equation (7.1′) specifies the spread between the yield on a high coupon bond and the yield on a par bond, $Rm - Rm^p$, as a *linear* function of the spread between the former bond's coupon and the yield (and coupon) on the par bond, $Rcp - Rm^p$. The actual relationship may be more complex than a simple linear function. For example, the yield spread may widen at a decreasing rate for larger coupon differences. Equation (7.1′) should be viewed as an approximation to the effect of a high coupon on yield where the approximation is more appropriate for bonds trading closer to par.

Consider next the case where the coupon rate is less than the yield on the comparable duration par bond ($Rcp < Rm^p$). The middle term in equation (7.1) drops out and the equation simplifies to

$$Rm = Rm^p + d \cdot (Rcp - Rm^p) \tag{7.1″}$$

The coefficient d is seen to reflect the effect of the low coupon on the bond's yield. For example, d had a value of .0195 at a duration of 2.50 years on July 20, 1984. Since the yield on a par bond of that duration was 13.00%, a bond with an 8% coupon and the same duration would have had a yield of about 12.90% ($12.90 = 13.00 + .0195 \cdot (8.00 - 13.00)$). The lower yield reflects stronger demand for discount bonds. As with the case for high coupon bonds, equation (7.1″) should be viewed as an approximation to the effect of a low coupon on yield.

It is important to observe that the values of the c and d coefficients in equation (7.1) need not be the same. We have noted that on July 20, 1984, $c = .022$ and $d = 0.195$ at a duration of 2.50 years. This indicates that the weaker demand for high coupon bonds had a marginally larger effect on yield than the stronger demand for low coupon bonds.

It is also important to note that the values of the c coefficients and the values of the d coefficients need not be the same in every sector of the Treasury market. Table 7.2 shows values of c and d at several representative maturities and durations on July 20, 1984. The coefficient c was largest in the 2-year to 4-year duration region, indicating that demand for high coupon bonds was weakest in that range. Note also that c was negative for bonds with a duration less than 1 year and greater than $5\frac{1}{2}$ years. The former characteristic reflects a strong demand by short- and intermediate-term fixed-income mutual funds for bonds with large interest payments that could be passed through to shareholders. The latter characteristic reflects the scarcity of high coupon long maturity bonds created by the stripping and zero coupon custodial receipt programs initiated during 1983. Note finally that d was also negative at durations greater than $6\frac{1}{2}$ years. This reflects the increased stock of low coupon debt created by the rise in interest rates during the first half of 1984.

Table 7.2
Values of c and d coefficients on July 20, 1984

Par bond maturity	Par bond yield[a]	Par bond duration[b]	c	d
1.0 yr	12.19%	.95 yr	−.0025	.0483
2.0	12.79	1.77	.0112	.0293
3.0	13.00	2.50	.0223	.0195
4.0	13.11	3.13	.0205	.0190
5.0	13.19	3.69	.0155	.0194
7.0	13.30	4.61	.0100	.0171
10.0	13.38	5.60	−.0003	.0094
15.0	13.42	6.60	−.0106	−.0010
20.0	13.37	7.14	−.0144	−.0073
25.0	13.29	7.45	−.0152	−.0112

a. "True" yield.
b. Duration adjusted for periodic coupon payments.

Treasury Bills

The next step is to characterize the distinction between a Treasury bill and a bond. Let T_b be a variable describing a security which has a value of zero if the security is a bond and a value of unity if the security is a bill. T_b is a security characteristic just like coupon rate except that it is limited to only two possible values (zero and unity).

The yield Rm on a bill *or* par bond of a given duration might be expressed as

$$Rm = Rm^p + e \cdot T_b \tag{7.2}$$

where Rm^p is, as before, the yield on a par bond with the specified duration. The coefficient e measures the effect on yield of packaging future payments in a Treasury bill instead of a par bond. If the security is a bond so that $T_b = 0$, equation (7.2) becomes $Rm = Rm^p$. If the security is a bill, then $T_b = 1$ and the equation becomes $Rm = Rm^p + e$.

Since Treasury bills are generally more expensive than comparable bonds, we expect the coefficient e to have a negative value. That is, we expect a bill to yield less than a par bond of the same duration. On July 20, 1984, for example, e had a value of −.21% for securities with a duration of .95 years. Thus, an investor gave up approximately 21 basis points of yield by going from one-year par bonds to one-year bills on that date.

In general, the value of the liquidity of Treasury bills will vary across bills of different maturities. The liquidity of a one-year bill compared to a one-year bond was worth 21 basis points on July 20, 1984, but the liquidity of a six-month bill was worth 33 basis points and the liquidity of a three-month bill was worth 37 basis points.

Summary

It may be helpful to review briefly the analysis proposed in this section. To begin, we defined *the* yield curve as the sequence of yields on par bonds of every duration. We then focused on a single point on that curve by isolating a particular sector of the Treasury market, and we asked how we could characterize the yield on a bill of the specified duration and the yields on bonds with different coupons but also of the specified duration.

For bills we introduce a yield spread coefficient to represent the liquidity value of bills in the specified sector. For non-par bonds we introduced two yield spread coefficients representing the differential pricing of high coupon and low coupon bonds, respectively. All three coefficients can vary across sectors of the Treasury market, reflecting variations in the strengths of the underlying market forces.

Obviously an important question is where the par bond yield curve and the values for the yield spread coefficients come from. The answer is set forth in the appendix.

7.3 Characterizing the Global Structure of Treasury Yields

The primary function of any analytical technique is extracting useful information from a mass of data and representing that information clearly and succinctly. Plotting yield against duration for many individual Treasury securities, as in figure 7.1, is a poor technique because it fails to isolate any essential characteristic of the yield curve other than its general shape. In displaying so much undifferentiated data, it conveys little information.

This section describes a technique for representing the Treasury yield curve which presents less data but more information than a diagram like figure 7.1. The proposed technique is a natural extension of the way many participants already think about the Treasury market. In particular, it separates bills from bonds and it separates bonds into low coupon, current coupon and high coupon categories. Thus the technique deals with four homogeneous categories instead of a mass of undifferentiated securities.

The technique is displayed in figure 7.3. As shown, it consists of two yield curves (upper panel)—one for bills and one for par bonds—and two yield spread curves (lower panel). One spread curve shows the difference between the yield on a bond with a coupon 100 basis points below the par yield and the yield on a par bond. (This is the "low coupon" yield spread curve.) The other curve shows the difference between the yield on a bond with a coupon 100 basis points above the par yield and the yield on a par bond. (This is the "high coupon" yield spread curve.) By limiting the data to four categories of securities, the figure shows (more clearly than figure

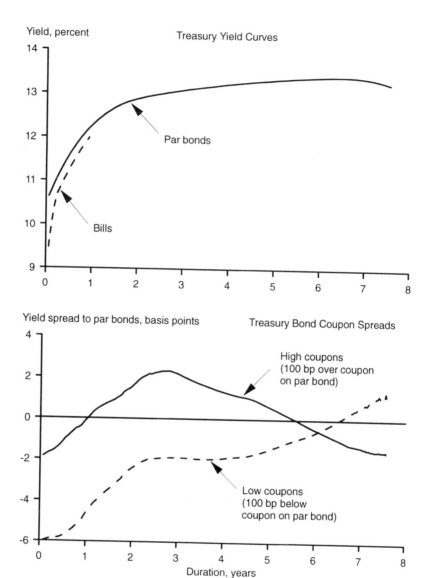

Figure 7.3
The structure of Treasury yields on July 20, 1984

7.1) the shape of the bond yield curve, the effect on yield of different coupon rates in different sectors of the market, and yield spreads between bills and short maturity bonds.

The objective of the curves in figure 7.3 is not to describe yields on individual issues but to represent succinctly the structure of yields in different sectors of the Treasury market. The next section addresses the problem of analyzing yields on individual securities.

Constructing the Curves

The curves in figure 7.3 are constructed by piecing together a series of local descriptions of the Treasury market. Each local description is produced from the analysis described in section 7.2.

We have already examined one part of figure 7.3: the sequence of yields on Treasury bonds trading at par. As before, let Rm^p denote the yield on a par bond of a given duration. From section 7.2 we have the following relationships:

$Rm^p + e$ = yield on a Treasury bill with the same duration.

c = spread between (1) the yield on a bond with the same duration and a coupon 100 basis points above Rm^p and (2) Rm^p.

$-d$ = spread between (1) the yield on a bond with the same duration and a coupon 100 basis points below Rm^p and (2) Rm^p.

The par bond yield Rm^p and the yield spread coefficients c, d, and e vary with duration. The appendix describes a technique for estimating the values of Rm^p, c, d, and e for a given duration. As we let the specified duration vary over all the durations on outstanding Treasury bonds, we can estimate the corresponding values of Rm^p, c, d, and e and hence plot successive points along the yield curves and yield spread curves in figure 7.3.

7.4   Identifying Overpriced and Underpriced Securities

The preceeding sections set forth a method for characterizing the general structure of yields in the Treasury market. This section describes how that characterization can be used as a benchmark against which individual securities can be appraised to assess whether they are cheap or expensive. To place the proposed analysis in a familiar context, let us begin with a discussion of the problem of identifying value.

Identifying Value

The objective of almost any analysis of the Treasury market is identifying value—or identifying whether, and which, securities should be bought or sold. At its broadest this identification is a matter of market timing: deciding that interest rates are likely to go higher and securities should be sold, or conversely. More narrowly the identification is a matter of global yield curve analysis, such as deciding whether the yield curve will flatten and whether some short and intermediate maturity debt should be sold and a weighted amount of longer bonds purchased. At an even finer level the identification comes from local analysis: evaluating opportunities to swap specific securities of nearly equal duration.

These three modes of analysis differ in two significant respects: the extent to which an analysis is one of absolute value versus relative value and the extent to which purchases and sales alter the risk exposure of a particular investor.

Market timing depends most heavily on assessing absolute value—whether interest rates are generally too low and likely to rise or conversely. This requires an appraisal of factors such as aggregate economic activity, Federal Reserve policy, and Treasury financing requirements whose relation to securities prices is rarely clear and quantifiable.

Purchases and sales of securities predicated on market timing often have major risk implications. For example, a pension fund manager who sells 30-year bonds and buys 3-month bills in anticipation of higher interest rates exposes the fund to reinvestment risk. Conversely, a cash manager who sells bills and buys intermediate maturity notes in anticipation of lower rates exposes his portfolio to market risk. These trades will look attractive if the motivating anticipations prove correct but can be disasterous otherwise.

Global yield curve analysis is more a matter of assessing relative value. In some cases the process is straightforward. Thus 3-year notes are probably too expensive if they yield 13.00% when 2-year and 4-year notes are yielding 12.90% and 13.40%, respectively. In other cases the assessment is more qualitative, such as deciding whether 3-year notes at 13.00% are expensive to 6-month bills at 11.80% and 30-year bonds at 14.00%.

It is instructive to consider more fully why the comparison of 3-year notes to 2-year and 4-year notes differs from the comparison to 6-month bills and 30-year bonds. The former comparison relies on the premise that the Treasury yield curve should vary smoothly across continguous sectors. In particular, the curve should not offer an opportunity to increase yield significantly by swapping out of 3-year notes into a portfolio (of weighted amounts of 2-year and 4-year notes) which has virtually the same risk characteristics as the 3-year notes. On the other hand, swapping out of 3-year notes into weighted amounts of 6-month bills and 30-year bonds reduces exposure in the intermediate sector of the market while adding exposure at the very short and very long ends of the market. Thus it alters substantially the exposure of a portfolio to the risk of change in the slope and curvature of the yield curve. The second comparison thus involves some of the qualitative factors that enter into an absolute value analysis.

This section extends the quantitative appraisal of relative value. The analysis does not address whether the yield on a security is too high or too low in absolute terms, nor does it address whether, for example, 3-year notes are cheap or expensive compared to 6-month bills and 30-year bonds. Instead, it seeks to identify whether a particular 3-year note is cheap or expensive compared to other securities with a 3-year maturity and with a comparable coupon. The analysis is oriented toward identifying relative value in small neighborhoods of the Treasury market.

Using the Local Structure of Treasury Yields to Value a Security

To begin the analysis, assume that we have already identified the local structure of Treasury yields as described in section 7.2. In particular, for any duration assume that we know the yield on a par bond and the yield spread coefficients c, d, and e quantifying the effect of high coupons, low coupons, and the liquidity of Treasury bills at that duration. With this data we propose to assess whether a specific security is relatively cheap or expensive.

Consider an example. On June 27, 1984, the active 7-year note (the $12\frac{3}{8}$s of April 15, 1991) had a price of $94\frac{6}{32}$, a yield of 13.705%, and a duration of 4.58 years. On the same date the yield on a par bond with a duration of 4.58 years was 13.756%, and the values of the c and d coefficients for a duration of 4.58 years were $-.0063$ and $.0090$, respectively.

Using equation (7.1), we can calculate the yield we would have expected on a bond with a 4.58-year duration and a $12\frac{3}{8}$% coupon:

$$Rm = Rm^p + c \cdot \max[Rcp - Rm^p, 0] + d \cdot \min[Rcp - Rm^p, 0]$$

$$= 13.756 - .0063 \cdot \max[12.375 - 13.756, 0.]$$

$$\quad + .0090 \cdot \min[12.375 - 13.756, 0.]$$

$$= 13.756 + .0090 \cdot (-1.381)$$

$$= 13.744\%$$

Compared to this benchmark value the active 7-year note at a yield of 13.705% was overvalued by 3.9 basis points.

There is other evidence to support the view that the active 7-year note was an expensive piece of paper on June 27, 1984. On that day Treasury securities were generally financed on repurchase agreements at a rate of $9\frac{7}{8}$%. However, a market participant could have financed the 7-year note at the lower rate of 6%. Several dealers who were short the note needed it to make deliveries and were willing to accept a comparatively low return on their money if they could obtain the note on a reverse repurchase agreement. It is generally true that securities in demand as collateral on RPs are also relatively expensive in the market for outright purchases and sales.

Cheap or Expensive to What?

One aspect of the above analysis requires further elaboration. We identified two yields from the local structure of Treasury yields:

13.756%, the yield on a par bond with a duration of 4.58 years.

13.744%, the yield on a bond with a $12\frac{3}{8}\%$ coupon and a duration of 4.58 years.

At a yield of 13.705% the active 7-year note was 5.1 basis points expensive to the par bond yield curve and 3.9 basis points expensive to the yield on a bond with a $12\frac{3}{8}\%$ coupon and a 4.58-year duration. Although trivial in the example the difference serves to illustrate an important point.

The value of a security can be measured against comparable securities or against the par bond yield curve. The former measure is more appropriate because, for example, even if a low coupon bond is expensive compared to par bonds, it may be fairly priced compared to other low coupon bonds. The expensiveness to par bonds may not represent unusual value but rather a valuation phenomenon shared by all low coupon bonds.

In the specific case of the active 7-year note described above the note was 5.1 basis points expensive to the par bond yield curve. However, 1.2 basis points of the difference in yields was attributable to a characteristic of the note (its low coupon). The note was expensive to *comparable* notes by a net amount of only 3.9 basis points.

Evaluating Swap Opportunities within a Sector of the Treasury Market

Having examined how the local structure of Treasury yields can be used to assess whether a particular security is cheap or expensive, we now want to extend the analysis to the comparative valuation of a group of similar bonds. The extension is important because it is not terribly helpful to assess a single security as either cheap or expensive against an abstract standard. The real objective is identifying a pair of securities, one expensive and one cheap, that provides an opportunity for an attractive swap.

Table 7.3 shows yields and "excess yield" spreads for active and seasoned 2-year, 7-year, and 10-year notes on June 27, 1984. The excess yield spread is a measure of whether an issue is cheap (positive spread) or

Table 7.3
Yields and excess yields on June 27, 1984

Coupon	Maturity	Duration[a]	Yield[b]	Excess yield spread
2-year notes				
$10\frac{5}{8}\%$	1/31/86	1.47 yr	12.728%	2.2 bp
$10\frac{7}{8}$	2/28/86	1.53	12.838	6.5
$11\frac{1}{2}$	3/31/86	1.59	12.997	14.3
$11\frac{3}{4}$	4/30/86	1.66	13.078	16.2
$12\frac{5}{8}$	5/31/86	1.72	13.092	9.3
13^c	6/30/86	1.76	13.134	9.1
7-year notes				
$10\frac{1}{2}$	1/15/90	4.13	13.714	2.5
$10\frac{1}{2}$	4/15/90	4.26	13.714	.9
$10\frac{3}{4}$	7/15/90	4.36	13.760	4.1
$11\frac{1}{2}$	10/15/90	4.42	13.715	−1.4
$11\frac{3}{4}$	1/15/91	4.51	13.735	−.1
$12\frac{3}{8}^c$	4/15/91	4.58	13.705	−3.9
10-year notes				
$10\frac{7}{8}$	2/15/93	5.40	13.758	−.2
$10\frac{1}{8}$	5/15/93	5.57	13.747	−.8
$11\frac{7}{8}$	8/15/93	5.46	13.758	−.4
$11\frac{3}{4}$	11/15/93	5.54	13.767	.7
$13\frac{1}{8}^c$	5/15/94	5.56	13.702	−6.2

a. Duration adjusted for periodic coupon payments.
b. "True" yield.
c. Active issue. Securities not similarly marked are seasoned issues of the same auction sequence.

expensive (negative spread) compared to the local structure of Treasury yields.

7-Year Notes

The middle panel of table 7.3 shows yields and excess yields on 7-year notes. We have already seen that the active 7-year note (the $12\frac{3}{8}$s of April 1991) was expensive compared to the local structure of Treasury yields. The premium for that security did not, however, extend back into seasoned notes of the same series. In fact the $10\frac{3}{4}\%$ note of July 1990 was about 4 basis points cheap to the local structure of Treasury yields.

The relative cheapness of the July 1990 note and the expensiveness of the April 1991 note meant that an investor could have swapped out of the active note into the old note and picked up about 5.5 basis points of yield (from 13.705% to 13.760%) while shortening his duration by .22 years. In view of the different durations and coupons on the two issues, the structure of yields in the 7-year sector called for a yield give-up on the swap of about 2.5 basis points.

10-Year Notes

The bottom panel of table 7.3 shows yields and excess yields on 10-year notes. As with the 7-year sector, the active 10-year note was expensive (by about 6 basis points) compared to the local structure of Treasury yields. However, seasoned 10-year notes were neither cheap nor expensive by more than a basis point.

In terms of swaps the 10-year sector gave a holder of the active 10-year note an opportunity to sell a relatively expensive security and buy any of several fairly priced securities of comparable risk. However, it did not offer any opportunities to swap into a relatively cheap security.

2-Year Notes

The upper panel of table 7.3 shows yields and excess yields on 2-year notes. Observe that those notes were *all* cheap relative to the local structure of Treasury yields, and that the March and April 1986 maturities were especially cheap.

The first observation is characteristic of 2-year notes because the Treasury sells about $8 billion of the notes every month. On a risk-adjusted basis the 2-year sector is the most "overissued" segment of the yield curve. (Year bills also come monthly and in a similar size, but they have only half the volatility of a 2-year note. Longer bonds are only sold quarterly.) In view of this heavy issuance, it is difficult to find investors with a "natural" need for all or most of the securities. The balance of an issue tends to go to investors with shorter horizons who are willing to extend the duration of their portfolios to pick up yield or to investors with longer horizons who are willing to contract duration if they do not have to give up much yield. In either case the 2-year notes must be priced cheap enough to induce investors to hold them even though they do not fit their natural needs.

The March and April 1986 maturities are a more unusual case. Large blocks of those securities were originally purchased in the spring of 1984 by several market participants and then liquidated in secondary sales to dealers. At the end of June 1984 the blocks were still being traded within the dealer community and had not yet been placed with final investors. Observe that an investor could have swapped out of the May 1986 note into the April 1986 note and given up only 1.4 basis points. In a sector of the market where the yield curve was rising, this "local" flatness strongly suggests incomplete distribution of the April note.

As a general proposition the 2-year sector did not offer any opportunities to swap out of a relatively expensive security into a relatively cheap security. At best an investor might have sold a moderately cheap issue like the $10\frac{5}{8}\%$ note of January 1986 at a 12.728% yield and bought a very cheap issue like the $11\frac{3}{4}\%$ note of April 1986 at a 13.078% yield. The 35.0 basis point yield pickup compared favorably to the net pickup of 21.0 basis points that could have been expected from the increase in coupon and duration.

7.5   Summary

In summary, the basic objective was to extend the analysis of the Treasury securities market beyond a simple yield-duration framework and to recognize explicitly that the yield on a security can depend on whether it is a bill or a bond and that the yield on a bond can depend on its coupon.

We modeled these effects in terms of duration-dependent yield spreads. Thus a Treasury bill usually yields less than a par bond of the same duration. A high coupon bond usually (but not always) yields more than a par bond of the same duration and a low coupon bond usually yields less than a comparable par bond. These yield spreads depend on how different the coupon is from a par coupon.

The resulting characterization of the structure of yields on Treasury securities of different duration led to two major results. First, we were able to represent succintly yields in the Treasury market with four curves—a bill yield curve, a par bond yield curve, and high and low coupon yield spread curves. These curves provide an efficient way to represent the different forces operating in different parts of the market, such as unusual demands for bills or high coupon bonds. Second, we asked whether an individual security was cheap or expensive compared to what could be expected given its characteristics. This provided a foundation for evaluating intrasector swap opportunities.

7.6   Appendix: Estimating the Local Structure of Treasury Yields

The structure of yields in a particular sector of the Treasury market can be estimated from yields on actual bills and bonds. Suppose that we are interested in securities with d days remaining to maturity or in securities with a term to maturity of $z = d/182.625$ semi-annual periods. (This parallels the assumption made in computing true yield that there are 182.625 days in a single semi-annual period.) A bond with this maturity will have $n = \text{Int}[z] + 1$ coupons remaining to be paid where $\text{Int}[z]$ is the largest integer not greater than z. For example, if $d = 2,500$ days then $z = 13.6893$ semi-annual periods ($13.6893 = 2,500/182.625$) and $n = 14$ coupons ($14 = \text{Int}[13.6893] + 1$).

Assigning a Tentative Yield, Coupon, and Duration on a Par Bond with the Specified Maturity

The procedure begins by picking a tentative yield for a par bond with the specified maturity. (This initial yield is arbitrary and is refined to a more accurate number as described below.) Denote the tentative yield as Rm^0.

Since the bond is trading at par by hypothesis, we know its coupon equals its yield. Thus the choice of Rm^0 implies a tentative choice Rcp^0 for the coupon such that $Rcp^0 = Rm^0$. Given the tentative yield Rm^0 and the corresponding coupon Rcp^0, we can compute the tentative duration of the par bond:

$$D^0 = \frac{\dfrac{\frac{1}{2}w \cdot \frac{1}{2}Rcp^0}{(1 + \frac{1}{2}Rm^0)^w} + \dfrac{\frac{1}{2}(1 + w) \cdot \frac{1}{2}Rcp^0}{(1 + \frac{1}{2}Rm^0)^{1+w}} + \cdots}{100 + \frac{1}{2} \cdot \frac{1}{2}Rcp^0}$$

$$+ \frac{\dfrac{\frac{1}{2}(n - 2 + w) \cdot \frac{1}{2}Rcp^0}{(1 + \frac{1}{2}Rm^0)^{n-2+w}} + \dfrac{\frac{1}{2}(n - 1 + w) \cdot (\frac{1}{2}Rcp^0 + 100)}{(1 + \frac{1}{2}Rm^0)^{n-1+w}}}{100 + \frac{1}{2} \cdot \frac{1}{2}Rcp^0} \tag{A7.1}$$

w is the fractional part of a semi-annual period remaining to the first coupon payment following settlement and is computed as $w = z - (n - 1)$. (If $z = 13.6893$ so that $n = 14$, then $w = .6893$.) The definition of duration in equation (A7.1) follows the form suggested in equation (4.5).

Equation (A7.1) shows that any choice of a tentative yield on the par bond implies a tentative duration as well as a tentative coupon. As we refine the tentative yield to a more accurate number, we will also be refining the tentative coupon and tentative duration.

Specifying the Structure of Yields on Securities "Close" to the Par Bond

The next step in the analysis is to specify a model of yields on Treasury securities that have durations close to D^0. We assume that the yield on an actual security depends on the following characteristics:

• The security's duration.

• Whether the security is a bill or a bond.

• If the security is a bond, the difference between its coupon and the coupon on a par bond of the same duration.

Section 7.1 outlined the reasons for these assumptions.

Modeling the structure of yields on the basis of these characteristics is a two-step process. The first step is representing the par bond yield curve for durations near D^0. The second step is representing the effect on yield of distinguishing between bills and bonds and the effect of coupon rate on bond yield.

We model the relation between duration and yields on par bonds as

$$Rm^p(D) = b + b' \cdot (D - D^0) + b'' \cdot (D - D^0)^2 \qquad (A7.2)$$

where D is duration and $Rm^p(D)$ is the yield on a par bond of duration D.

Equation (A7.2) specifies that the yield on a par bond is a quadratic function of duration, measured in terms of deviation from the tentative duration D^0. The coefficient b is the yield at the tentative duration, that is, $Rm^p(D) = b$ when $D = D^0$. The coefficient b' measures the slope of the par bond yield curve. If the curve is rising in the neighborhood of D^0, the coefficient b' will be positive. If the yield curve is declining, b' will be negative. The term involving the coefficient b'' allows for curvature of the yield curve in the neighborhood of D^0. If the curve is rising at a decreasing rate, b'' will be negative.

We model the effect on yield of a bond's coupon and whether a security is a bill or a bond as

$$Rm = Rm^p(D) + (c + c' \cdot (D - D^0) \cdot \max[Rcp - Rm^p(D), 0]$$

$$+ (d + d' \cdot (D - D^0)) \cdot \min[Rcp - Rm^p(D), 0]$$

$$+ (e + e' \cdot (D - D^0) + e'' \cdot (D - D^0)^2) \cdot T_b + u \qquad (A7.3)$$

$Rm^p(D)$ is, as defined in equation (A7.2), the yield on a par bond with duration D, Rcp is the coupon on the bond, and T_b is a variable with value zero if the security is a bond and a value of unity if the security is a bill.

The term involving c and c' captures the effect of a high coupon on yield, and the term involving d and d' captures the effect of a low coupon. The magnitudes of these effects vary as linear functions of duration around the tentative duration D^0. The term involving e, e', and e'' reflects the yield spread attributable to packaging future payments as Treasury bills rather than as par bonds. The spread varies as a quadratic function of duration around the tentative duration D^0. The term u reflects other influences, such as a specific issue being unusually cheap or expensive.

Estimating the Structure of Yields on Securities "Close" to the Par Bond

We now have to pull equations (A7.2) and (A7.3) together into a form suitable for estimating the coefficients with actual data. Suppose that we replace the *first* appearance of the variable $Rm^p(D)$ in equation (A7.3) with the expression on the right hand side of equation (A7.2) and rewrite the result slightly:

$$Rm = b + b' \cdot (D - D^0) + b'' \cdot (D - D^0)^2$$

$$+ c \cdot \max[Rcp - Rm^p(D), 0]$$

$$+ c' \cdot (D - D^0) \cdot \max[Rcp - Rm^p(D), 0]$$

$$+ d \cdot \min[Rcp - Rm^p(D), 0]$$

$$+ d' \cdot (D - D^0) \cdot \min[Rcp - Rm^p(D), 0]$$

$$+ e \cdot T_b$$

$$+ e' \cdot (D - D^0) \cdot T_b$$

$$+ e'' \cdot (D - D^0)^2 \cdot T_b$$

$$+ u \tag{A7.4}$$

With one exception equation (A7.4) is a linear equation with fully specified values for the right-hand side variables. We can use multivariate statistics to estimate the values of the coefficients b, b', b'', c, c', d, d', e, e', and e'' from data on yields, durations, and coupons on actual bonds and bills.

The exception is that we do not yet know the relation between duration and yield for par bonds, and hence cannot specify the value of $Rm^p(D)$ for an arbitrary value of D in equation (A7.4). (Note that if we replace the references to $Rm^p(D)$ in equation A7.4 with the right-hand side of equation A7.2, the resulting equation would be highly nonlinear in the unknown coefficients and difficult to estimate.) We finesse the problem initially by assuming a flat yield curve at the tentative yield Rm^0 so that $Rm^p(D) = Rm^0$ for all durations. This assumption will be refined subsequently.

Up to this point we have developed a model of yields on Treasury securities that reflects duration, coupon, and bill liquidity effects and whose coefficients can be estimated. However, attention has yet not focused explicitly on any particular sector of the yield curve beyond writing duration in terms of deviation from the tentative duration D^0. We are now ready to take a step that changes a model of the whole yield curve into a model of the local structure of yields.

We assume the term u in equation (A7.4) is a random variable with a mean value of zero and a variance equal to $\sigma^2 \cdot \exp[g \cdot |D - D^0|] \cdot \exp[h \cdot |Rcp - Rm^p(D)|]$ where g and h are positive real numbers. This specification makes the assumed variance of the random term larger, the greater the difference between the duration of a security and the tentative duration D^0 and the greater the difference between the coupon on a bond and the yield on a par bond of the same duration. The specification has the effect of giving less weight in the estimation procedure to a security with a duration very different from D^0 or to a bond with a coupon very different from $Rm^p(D)$. For this reason we are now estimating the structure of yields on securities which have durations "close" to D^0 and which are either bills or bonds trading "near" par.

Revising the Tentatively Assigned Values

Assume we have obtained estimates of the coefficients in equation (A7.4) predicated on (1) the tentative yield Rm^0 on a par bond maturing in z semi-annual periods and (2) the tentative par bond yield curve $Rm^p(D) = Rm^0$ for all values of D. We now want to revise both of these tentative assignments.

The estimated coefficients allows us to infer the yield on a par bond with a duration of D^0 years and a coupon of Rcp^0. Using equation (A7.4), that yield is just the estimated value of the coefficient b, since all the other terms drop out when $D = D^0$, $Rcp = Rcp^0 = Rm^0$, and $T_b = 0$. This becomes our new tentative yield on a par bond with a remaining term to maturity of z semi-annual periods. From this new yield we can define a new tentative coupon and (using equation A7.1) a new tentative duration.

With the estimated coefficients we can also use equation (A7.4) to define a new tentative par bond yield curve as $Rm^p(D) = b + b' \cdot (D - D^0) + b'' \cdot (D - D^0)^2$. This replaces the old curve of $Rm^p(D) = Rm^0$.

With the new tentative assignments we can recompute the right-hand side variables of equation (A7.4) and reestimate the coefficients of that equation. The iterative process of revision and estimation continues until the estimated coefficients converge to stationary values. We then have our final estimate of the structure of Treasury yields in the neighborhood of a par bond with z semi-annual periods remaining to maturity.

More specifically, we have estimated a set of parameters (D^0, Rm^0, c, d, and e) such that (1) the yield on a par bond of duration D^0 is Rm^0, (2) the yield on a bond with coupon Rcp and the same duration is

$$Rm^0 + c \cdot \max[Rcp - Rm^0, 0] + d \cdot \min[Rcp - Rm^0, 0]$$

and (3) the yield on a Treasury bill with the same duration is $Rm^0 + e$. Thus, this set of parameters characterizes the local structure of Treasury yields at the duration D^0 in the sense set forth in section 7.2 the text.

Going back over the procedures of this section reveals that the analysis began by selecting a maturity z. As z varies from near zero to 30 years or more we can trace out the changing values of the parameters D^0, Rm^0, c, d, and e and hence characterize the structure of Treasury yields along the entire yield curve. This continuous characterization of the curve was described in section 7.3 of the text.

Coupon Rolls

It's 4 PM, Tuesday, March 20, 1984, in the trading room at Bankers Trust. The Dow Jones News Service has just flashed the Treasury's announcement that it will auction 4-year and 7-year notes and 20-year bonds the following week. Rita Skolnick, a saleswoman, calls out, "Arlen, how do you do the 4-year roll?" Arlen Klinger, the intermediate note trader, replies, "I give 8 basis points."

What's going on here?

What's going on is a proposal for a trade in a specialized market known as "the roll." Mr. Klinger is proposing to buy from a customer the most recently issued (outstanding) 4-year Treasury note and simultaneously sell to the same customer an equal principal amount of the just announced (new) 4-year note at a yield 8 basis points higher. For example, he would buy the outstanding note at an 11.93% yield against selling the new note at 12.01%. The customer would be "rolling" his investment from the outstanding note to the new note—which is where the name of the transaction comes from.

Rolls are an integral part of the process of distributing new Treasury securities. They are also among the most complex and least understood transactions in the Treasury market. Deciding whether a roll makes sense at a given yield spread requires an appraisal of maturity and coupon differences and an appreciation for short-term financing and borrowings of bonds.

This chapter describes and analyzes Treasury note and bond rolls. Section 8.1 describes how rolls are quoted. Section 8.2 examines the economic significance of the roll, including its value to dealers and investors and its contribution to the distribution of Treasury securities. Section 8.3 identifies the factors that influence the price of a roll, including maturity, coupon, and financing considerations. Sections 8.4 and 8.5 analyze quantitatively the price of a roll.

8.1 Mechanics

Quotation and settlement conventions for a roll are most readily understood from a concrete example. Consider the 4-year roll noted above. Two securities were involved in that roll, the outstanding 4-year note (the $11\frac{1}{4}\%$ notes of December 31, 1987) and the new 4-year note which would mature March 31, 1988 but which did not yet have a definite coupon rate when its forthcoming sale was announced.

Written June 1984.

Immediately after the auction announcement on March 20, the outstanding 4-year note was quoted at a bid price of $97\frac{30}{32}$, or a yield of 11.93%. In doing the roll at 8 basis points Mr. Klinger was buying the outstanding note at $97\frac{30}{32}$ against selling the new issue at a 12.01% yield. If the outstanding note had strengthened to a bid price of $98\frac{1}{32}$ (or a yield of 11.90%), he would have bought at that price and sold the new issue at an 11.98% yield. In either case the yield spread would be 8 basis points.

The purchase side of the roll, involving the outstanding note, was a conventional transaction. The note was purchased for regular settlement on March 21, the business day following the March 20 trade day, at the quoted price (97 and $\frac{30}{32}$ percent of principal value) plus accrued interest to the settlement date.

The sale side of the roll, involving the new note, was a forward transaction for delivery and payment on April 2, 1984, or 13 days after the March 20, 1984, trade date. Delayed settlement was necessary because the new note would not be issued until April 2. The 4-year trader could negotiate a sale of the new note on March 20, but he could not deliver it until it has been issued. This type of sale is known as a "when issued" (or WI) sale.

There are two quotation conventions for WI trades in notes and bonds. The day after an auction, when the coupon on a new issue is established, the issue trades on a price basis just like an outstanding security (albeit with a forward settlement date). On and before the day of its auction a new issue trades on a yield basis with the ultimate price determined after the coupon is established. An investor buying new 4-year notes before their auction in March 1984 at a 12.01% yield knows they will earn him that yield, but he cannot identify his dollar cost. If the notes carry a 12% coupon he will pay 99.969% of their principal value. If the notes carry an $11\frac{7}{8}$% coupon, he will pay a lower price (99.581), and if the notes carry a higher coupon of $12\frac{1}{8}$%, he will pay a higher price (100.357). Each price results in a 12.01% yield at the corresponding coupon. Since in this chapter we will be concerned with pre-auction rolls, we will focus on yield quotations in WI trading.

At this point it may be useful to summarize the salient aspects of a coupon roll:

• The outstanding security is bid on a price basis for regular settlement on the next business day.

• The new security is offered on a yield basis for forward settlement on its issue date.

• The spread between the dealer's offering yield on the new security and the yield on the outstanding security (computed using the dealer's purchase price and the regular settlement date) is what the dealer "gives" to do the roll.

In some cases there will be a negative spread between the sale yield and the purchase yield on a roll. The dealer is then said to "take" the spread on the roll. For example, a dealer takes 5 basis points if he buys the outstanding issue at a 12.15% yield against selling the new issue at a 12.10% yield.

Reverse Rolls

A dealer does a roll when he buys an outstanding security and sells a new issue. A dealer can also go in the opposite direction, selling an outstanding security and buying a new issue. This is called a "reverse roll." For example, the 4-year trader might propose to take 10 basis points to do the reverse roll in 4-year notes in March 1984. Against a sale price of $97\frac{30}{32}$ (or a yield of 11.93%) on the $11\frac{1}{4}\%$ notes of December 31, 1987 he would buy the new issue at a 12.03% yield.

8.2   Economic Significance of the Roll

Rolls are important for two reasons. First, they are used by dealers to accommodate customers and to position themselves for bidding in Treasury auctions. Second, they are a significant part of the process of distributing new issues of Treasury securities. The two functions are closely related.

As a practical matter a dealer will not aggressively seek to execute a roll unless he is already short the outstanding issue. This short will usually have been established *before* the announcement of the new issue in anticipation of a decline in the market. (Such a pre-announcement short can not be established in the new issue itself because Treasury securities do not trade before their auction announcement.) The short in the outstanding issue may also arise after the announcement of the new issue from sales to customers who want to invest cash immediately rather than wait until the new security is issued.

When a dealer executes a roll, he acquires the outstanding security against selling the new issue short. This has three consequences. First, the dealer closes out his short position in the outstanding security. He no longer has to borrow bonds from day to day to cover that short, and he therefore reduces his operating expenses.

Second, the customer acquiring the new security fixes his purchase yield. Moreover, he fixes the *quantity* of the new issue purchased at the given yield, and he does not have to run the risk of being shut out of the auction and paying more for his new bonds later.

Third, the short in the new issue gives the dealer an incentive to bid actively in its auction and positions him as a key participant in the auction process.

Dealer rolls also provide important benefits to the Treasury. First, if dealers sell a significant part of a new issue against buying outstanding securities to cover earlier shorts much of that new issue will, for all practical purposes, be distributed even before if is auctioned. This reduces the threat of a large part of the issue going onto dealer shelves (where it may have to be marked down in order to be sold) and increases the willingness of all investors to bid for the issue.

Second, rolls create a natural need for dealers to bid aggressively to buy a new issue (to cover their shorts). Such dealer participation in an auction reduces the Treasury's need to rely on bids by the broader investment community to buy the issue.

While rolls confer advantages on dealers, investors, and the Treasury, they do not happen automatically or inexorably, regardless of price. The roll is a trade, and any trade can make sense at one price but appear ridiculous at another price. The 4-year trader was willing to give 8 basis points to do the roll in March 1984, but at a spread of 10 basis points he might have done the reverse roll. Thus the crucial question in quoting or acting on a market for the roll is whether a given yield spread makes sense. The remainder of this chapter addresses that question.

8.3   Factors Influencing the Price of the Roll

Four factors influence the price of a roll: the difference in maturity between the issue bought and the issue sold, the difference in coupon, the return on an investment starting on the regular settlement date applicable to transactions in the outstanding issue and maturing on the forward settlement date for transactions in the new issue, and the scarcity of the outstanding issue. We will use the March 1984, 4-year note roll to illustrate each factor.

Maturity

In mid-March 1984 the outstanding 4-year note had a December 31, 1987, maturity date. The new 4-year note had a March 31, 1988, maturity date. An investor rolling his position from the outstanding note to the new note would therefore extend the maturity of his investment by three months. Since the yield curve was rising in the intermediate sector of the coupon market, this maturity extension should have provided some pickup in yield.

Coupon Rates

In mid-March 1984 the new 4-year note traded at a yield of about 12% in the when-issued market. Barring a dramatic rally or collapse in bond prices this suggested that the issue would carry a 12% coupon (or maybe an $11\frac{7}{8}$% or $12\frac{1}{8}$% coupon). An investor rolling 4-year notes would, therefore, be selling a note with an $11\frac{1}{4}$% coupon and buying a note with, in all likelihood, a 12% coupon. More particularly, he would be selling a low coupon note and buying a current coupon note.

Notes and bonds with low coupons typically have lower yields than otherwise comparable issues with current coupons. Thus an investor rolling 4-year notes in mid-March could expect to pick up some yield simply from swapping out of a low coupon note.

The Return on Funds Invested between Settlement Dates

An investor who rolled a position in 4-year notes on March 20, 1984, sold outstanding notes for settlement March 21 and bought new notes for settlement April 2. The difference in settlement dates left him with cash to invest for 12 days (March 21 to April 2). The return on an investment over this interval was a third factor influencing the yield spread at which he did the roll.

To appreciate the effect of short-term interest rates on the price of a roll consider the 8 basis point roll in 4-year notes, where the dealer would buy the outstanding issue at an 11.93% yield and sell the new issue at a 12.01% yield. Suppose that the rate on a short-term repurchase agreement (RP) was 10%. Investors had to decide whether 8 basis points was enough of a yield pickup to compensate for (1) the maturity extension, (2) the swap out of a low coupon, and (3) earning only 10% for 12 days on the proceeds from the sale of the outstanding note.

It should be clear that the 8 basis point roll was more attractive to investors the higher the RP rate and conversely. Assuming 6 basis points was enough of a yield pickup to compensate for the maturity extension and coupon change, an investor would likely jump at an opportunity to pick up 8 basis points if the RP rate was the same as the 12% yield on 4-year notes, but he may have wanted more than an 8 basis point pickup if the RP rate was only 6%. This argument leads to the conclusion that the yield pickup on a roll will be greater the larger the difference between the yield on the securities involved in the roll and short-term RP rates.

The same argument also suggests that the yield pickup on a roll will get smaller as the issue date of the new security gets closer. A roll in the 4-year note executed on March 20 produced investable funds for 12 days, but a roll executed on March 26 produced investable funds for only 6 days. The impact on the roll of a 10% RP rate versus a 12% 4-year note yield is greater in the first case than in the second.

Scarcity of the Outstanding Issue

The last and most intangible factor influencing the price of a roll is the scarcity of the outstanding issue. If dealers are short that issue and if it is difficult to purchase in the cash market and borrow in the collateral market, they may give more to do the roll than would be indicated by the maturity, coupon, and financing factors already described.

For example, the March 1984, 4-year note roll may have been worth 8 basis points on the basis of maturity, coupon, and financing, but dealers might nonetheless have given 9 or 10 basis points to do that roll if they were having a difficult time covering shorts in the outstanding issue with outright purchases or with bonds borrowed on reverse repurchase agreements. The extra 1 or 2 basis points would be offered to induce more investors into doing the roll and selling the outstanding 4-year note. This would allow dealers to move their shorts from the scarce outstanding issue into the new issue. They could expect to have ample opportunity to cover their shorts in the latter issue in the auction.

8.4 Reopenings—The Case of Financing Rolls

We now want to analyze quantitatively the influence of the factors identified in the preceding section. We begin with the simplest case—when the Treasury raises money in an auction by reopening an outstanding issue instead of offering an entirely new security. In this case the coupon and maturity of the outstanding issue and the forthcoming issue are identical and the price of the roll depends only on financing considerations.

An Example of a Reopening

On February 1, 1984, the Treasury announced a February 8 auction of 10-year notes for delivery and payment on February 15. Rather than offer an entirely new note it stated that it would sell an additional $5.25 billion of the $11\frac{3}{4}\%$ note of November 15, 1993, first issued in November 1983. Thus, following the announcement, the note traded for both regular settlement (as an outstanding issue) and forward settlement (as a new issue).

We are interested in calculating the yield spread a dealer would have given in order to do the 10-year note roll, that is, to buy the outstanding note for regular settlement and to sell the new note for forward settlement.

This is a peculiar roll because the same note is involved on both sides, but analyzing its price will help in understanding more conventional rolls.

Pricing the Roll

Pricing the February 1984, 10-year note roll is mostly a matter of paying attention to details. Against buying the note for regular settlement at a given price, we have to calculate where a dealer could sell the same note for forward settlement and still break even, given the cost of financing between the settlement dates. The analysis is shown in example 1.

As shown in that example, on February 2, the 10-year note was bid at $100\frac{27}{32}$ or 100.84375 for regular settlement. The invoice price for the February 3 regular settlement date was the quoted price plus accrued interest of

Example 1
Pricing the 10-year roll on February 2, 1984, against a 9% RP rate

The outstanding issue and the new issue are the $11\frac{3}{4}\%$ notes of 11/15/1993.

Outstanding 10-year for regular settlement

Quoted price = $100\frac{27}{32}$	100.84375
Accrued interest to 2/3[a]	2.58242
Value for 2/3 settlement	103.42167

Financing from 2/3 to 2/15 at 9%

Funds borrowed on 2/3	103.42167
Funds owed on 2/15	$103.42167 \cdot (1 + .09\frac{12}{360}) = 103.73194$

New 10-year for forward settlement

Value for 2/15 settlement	103.73194
Accrued interest to 2/15[b]	2.96978
Derived price quote	100.76216

Break-even roll

Yield on new issue quoted at 100.76216 for 2/15 settlement (using Treasury yield definition)	11.603%
Yield on outstanding issue quoted at $100\frac{27}{32}$ for 2/3 settlement (using Street yield definition)	11.596%
Break-even roll	.007%, or .7 bp

a. Next coupon pays 5.875; coupon period is 182 days (11/15/83 to 5/15/84), interest accrued over 80 days (11/15/83 to 2/3/84). Therefore accrued interest is $5.875 \cdot (80/182) = 2.58242$.
b. Next coupon pays 5.875; coupon period is 182 days (11/15/83 to 5/15/84), interest accrued over 92 days (11/15/83 to 2/15/84). Therefore accrued interest is $5.875 \cdot (92/182) = 2.96978$.

2.58242 from the issue date of the note. The total invoice price was therefore 103.42617.

The RP rate on February 2 was about 9%. If a dealer financed his purchase of the 10-year note from February 3 to February 15 at 9%, he would owe a total of 103.73194 on February 15 (see example 1). The dealer would break even if he could sell the note at that price on February 2 for forward settlement on February 15.

A February 15 settlement of a sale of the 10-year note would include 2.96978 points of accrued interest (see example 1). Subtracting this accrued interest from a break-even invoice price of 103.73194 gives a break-even quoted price of 100.76216.

The foregoing analysis shows that a dealer would break even if on February 2 he agreed to buy the 10-year note for regular settlement at $100\frac{27}{32}$ and to sell it for forward settlement at 100.76216 and if he financed the security at a 9% RP rate between the settlement dates. The last step in pricing the roll is reducing the purchase and sale prices to yields and computing the spread.

Using the conventional or Street definition of yield a price of $100\frac{27}{32}$ on the 10-year note for settlement February 3 gives a yield of 11.596%. A price of 100.76216 on the same note for settlement February 15 gives an 11.61% yield. The difference in yields indicates a break-even spread on the roll of 1.4 basis points.

However, the offering yield on the new note is *not* expressed using the Street definition of yield but with the definition of yield used by the Treasury in evaluating auction bids. (The difference between Street yield and Treasury yield is described in chapter 1.) Using the latter definition, a price of 100.76216 for February 15 settlement gives an 11.603% yield. Thus dealer willing to do the roll as a break-even proposition would quote it by saying he gives .7 basis points or by bidding the 10-year note at $100\frac{27}{32}$ for regular settlement and offering it at 12.603% (Treasury yield) for forward settlement.

Why Two Different Yields Are Used to Quote the Roll

It might seem odd that the price of a roll is expressed as the difference between yields computed with different definitions, and one might well wonder if this doesn't create a problem of comparing apples to oranges. There are two justifications for the convention.

First, the expression of the price of a roll is a quotation convention adopted for the sake of consistency. Quotes for pre-auction WI trading in notes and bonds are expressed as Treasury yields to make them comparable to yields on auction bids. It would be cumbersome to use a different yield convention merely because a WI trade is part of a roll. On the other hand, market participants use the Street definition of yield in all trading except pre-auction WI purchases and sales, so Street yields are used to price the regular settlement side of a roll.

The second justification for the yield convention on a roll is that it has no "real" consequence. At a quoted price of 100.76216, the Street yield on the new 10-year note is 11.61%, and the Treasury yield is 11.603% for a difference of .7 basis points. It turns out that the yield difference remains .7 basis points over a wide range of prices. Thus an investor can compute his pickup using Street yields for both the sale side and purchase side simply by adding .7 basis points to the quoted spread. If the 10-year roll is quoted at 1.0 basis point, the yield pickup figured with Street yields for both purchase and sale would be 1.7 basis points.

The Roll from an Investor's Perspective

We have argued that a dealer could have executed the 10-year roll as a break-even proposition on February 2, 1984, by buying the outstanding note at $100\frac{27}{32}$, selling the new note at an 11.603% Treasury yield, and financing his position at a 9% RP rate between the settlement dates. An investor would also view the two sides of this roll as equivalent.

Except for the operational costs of settling transactions, it doesn't matter whether an investor (1) bought the 10-year note for $100\frac{27}{32}$ on February 2 for regular settlement or (2) bought the same note on February 2 at an 11.603% Treasury yield for settlement on February 15 and funded his purchase with a 12-day RP beginning February 3. In the first case he pays the quoted price (100.84375) plus accrued interest (2.58242) on the February 3 settlement date or a total of 103.42617. In the second case he needs 103.73194 on February 15 to pay for his forward purchase (an 11.603% Treasury yield implies a quoted price of 100.76216 plus accrued interest of 2.96978) and hence would have to commit 103.42617 to the RP on February 3 ($103.42617 = 103.73194/(1. + (.09) \cdot (12/360))$). In either case he pays out 103.42617 on February 3 and nothing thereafter to obtain the future interest and principal payments on the 10-year note.

Pricing the Roll at a Lower RP Rate

Rolls involving a reopening of an outstanding security provide a simple framework for examining the impact of a change in the RP rate on the price of a roll.

Example 2 shows the same analysis as example 1 but for an 8% RP rate instead of a 9% rate. As observed in section 8.3, a lower financing rate relative to the yield on the securities involved in the roll leads to a greater spread on the roll. A dealer could give .7 basis points to do the roll at a 9%

Example 2
Pricing the 10-year roll on February 2, 1984, against an 8% RP rate

---

The outstanding issue and the new issue are the $11\frac{3}{4}$% notes of 11/15/1993.

Outstanding 10-year for regular settlement

Quoted price $= 100\frac{27}{32}$	100.84375
Accrued interest to 2/3[a]	2.58242
Value for 2/3 settlement	103.42167

Financing from 2/3 to 2/15 at 8%

Funds borrowed on 2/3	103.42167
Funds owed on 2/15	$103.42167 \cdot (1 + .08\frac{12}{360}) = 103.69746$

New 10-year for forward settlement

Value for 2/15 settlement	103.69746
Accrued interest to 2/15[b]	2.96978
Derived price quote	100.72768

Break-even roll

Yield on new issue quoted at 100.72768 for 2/15 settlement (using Treasury yield definition)	11.609%
Yield on outstanding issue quoted at $100\frac{27}{32}$ for 2/3 settlement (using Street yield definition)	11.596%
Break-even roll	.013%, or 1.3 bp

---

a. Next coupon pays 5.875; coupon period is 182 days (11/15/83 to 5/15/84), interest accrued over 80 days (11/15/83 to 2/3/84). Therefore accrued interest is $5.875 \cdot (80/182) = 2.58242$.
b. Next coupon pays 5.875; coupon period is 182 days (11/15/83 to 5/15/84), interest accrued over 92 days (11/15/83 to 2/15/84). Therefore accrued interest is $5.875 \cdot (92/182) = 2.96978$.

RP rate and 1.3 basis points if he can finance his purchase for 12 days at an 8% RP rate.

Pricing the Roll Closer to the Issue Date of the New Securities

Rolls involving a reopening of an outstanding security also provide an opportunity to examine the impact of doing the roll closer to the date of issue of the new securities.

Example 3 shows the same analysis as example 1 but for a regular settlement date of February 9 instead of February 3. As observed in section 8.3, a shorter interval between the regular and forward settlement dates leads to a narrower roll, everything else remaining the same. A dealer could give .7 basis points on February 2 to do the roll for February 3 and February 15 settlements but could do the same roll at

Example 3
Pricing the 10-year roll on February 8, 1984, against a 9% RP rate

---

The outstanding issue and the new issue are the $11\frac{3}{4}\%$ notes of 11/15/1993.

Outstanding 10-year for regular settlement

Price quote = $100\frac{27}{32}$	100.84375
Accrued interest to 2/9[a]	2.77610
Value for 2/9 settlement	103.61985

Financing from 2/9 to 2/15 at 9%

Funds borrowed on 2/9	103.61985
Funds owed on 2/15	$103.61985 \cdot (1 + .09\frac{6}{360}) = 103.77528$

New 10-year for forward settlement

Value for 2/15 settlement	103.77528
Accrued interest to 2/15[b]	2.96978
Derived price quote	100.80550

Break-even roll

Yield on new issue quoted at 100.80550 for 2/15 settlement (using Treasury yield definition)	11.596%
Yield on outstanding issue quoted at $100\frac{27}{32}$ for 2/9 settlement (using Street yield definition)	11.596%
Break-even roll	.0%

---

a. Next coupon pays 5.875; coupon period is 182 days (11/15/83 to 5/15/84), interest accrued over 86 days (11/15/83 to 2/9/84). Therefore accrued interest is $5.875 \cdot (86/182) = 2.77610$.
b. Next coupon pays 5.875; coupon period is 182 days (11/15/83 to 5/15/84), interest accrued over 92 days (11/15/83 to 2/15/84). Therefore accrued interest is $5.875 \cdot (92/182) = 2.96978$.

a zero quoted spread on February 8 for February 9 and February 15 settlements.

8.5 Pricing a Roll in the General Case

Pricing a roll when the new issue is not identical to the outstanding issue requires an appraisal of the value of changes in maturity and coupon as well as an analysis of financing costs. This section describes how a roll can be priced in the more general case under the assumption that the securities involved in the roll trade at yields systematically related to yields on other Treasury issues. More particularly, we assume there is no unusual scarcity of the outstanding issue. The effect of such scarcity on the price of a roll is considered in the following section.

Box 1
A model of yields on bonds in the 4-year sector on March 20, 1984

Using the methodology described in chapter 7, the structure of bond yields on March 20, 1984, indicated that a bond with exactly 8 semi-annual coupons remaining to be paid would trade at its principal value if it had an 11.976% coupon. The duration of such a bond is 3.29 years.

The structure of bond yields also indicated that the yield Rm on an arbitrary bond in the 4-year sector with a duration of D years and a coupon of Rcp would be the value of the following equation:

$$Rm = 11.976 + .320 \cdot (D - 3.29) - .0510 \cdot (D - 3.29)^2$$

$$+ .0437 \cdot \max[Rcp - 11.976, 0]$$

$$+ .0370 \cdot \min[Rcp - 11.976, 0]$$

The first three terms in the equation reflect the level, slope, and curvature of the yield curve, respectively, in the 4-year sector. The second to last term reflects the yield adjustment for a high coupon bond. It is positive if the coupon on the arbitrary bond exceeds 11.976% and zero otherwise. The last term reflects the yield adjustment for a low coupon bond. It is negative if the coupon on the arbitrary bond is less than 11.976% and zero otherwise.

The analysis begins by recalling from chapter 7 the model of bond yields that describes quantitatively the relation between a bond's maturity and coupon and its yield. We then use that model to infer yields for the outstanding issue and the new issue. The spread between the two yields, adjusted for settlement differences and quotation conventions, is the price of the roll. The analysis is illustrated with the March 1984, 4-year note roll.

A Model of Bond Yields

To model the structure of bond yields assume, as in chapter 7, that the yield on a bond trading for regular settlement depends on two characteristics:

1. The bond's duration.

2. The difference between the coupon on the bond and the coupon on a par bond of comparable duration.

Box 1 shows the model for bonds in the 4-year sector trading on March 20, 1984 for regular settlement. As shown, a current coupon 4-year note was estimated to have an 11.976% yield (and coupon rate) and a duration of 3.29 years.

The calculations in example 4 show how the model can be used to infer yields on bonds with durations close to 3.29 years and coupons close to 11.976%. Calculation 1 shows that a note with a 3.5-year duration would

Example 4
Calculating bond yields from the model in box 1

This example shows how the model in box 1 can be used to infer the yield on three bonds with the following characteristics:

	Assumed duration	Assumed coupon
Bond *a*	3.5 years	11.976%
Bond *b*	3.29	13
Bond *c*	3.29	11

The first bond has a coupon identical to the coupon on a 4-year par bond but has a longer duration. The second and third bonds have durations identical to the duration of a 4-year par bond but have different coupons.

1. Putting the values $D = 3.5$ and $Rcp = 11.976$ into the model gives

$$Rm = 11.976 + .320 \cdot (3.5 - 3.29) - .0510 \cdot (3.5 - 3.29)^2$$

$$= 12.041\%$$

This yield is about 7 basis points greater than the 11.976% yield on a 4-year par bond.

2. Putting the values $D = 3.29$ and $Rcp = 13.0$ into the model gives

$$Rm = 11.976 + .0437 \cdot \max[13. - 11.976, 0.] + .0370 \cdot \min[13. - 11.976, 0.]$$

$$= 11.976 + .0437 \cdot (1.024) + .0370 \cdot (0.)$$

$$= 12.021\%$$

This yield is about 5 basis points greater than the 11.976% yield on a 4-year par bond.

3. Putting the values $D = 3.29$ and $Rcp = 11.0$ into the model gives

$$Rm = 11.976 + .0437 \cdot \max[11. - 11.976, 0.] + .0370 \cdot \min[11. - 11.976, 0.]$$

$$= 11.976 + .0437 \cdot (0.) + .0370 \cdot (-.976)$$

$$= 11.940\%$$

This yield is about 4 basis points less than the 11.976% yield on a 4-year par bond.

---

have had a yield about 7 basis points higher than the yield on a current coupon 4-year note. The greater yield associated with the longer duration reflects the positive slope of the yield curve in the 4-year sector on March 20. Calculation 2 shows that a note with a 13% coupon would have had a yield about 5 basis points higher than the yield on a current coupon 4-year note. This reflects a weaker demand for high coupon notes compared to current coupon notes in the 4-year sector. Finally, calculation 3 shows that a note with an 11% coupon would have had a yield about 4 basis points lower than the yield on a current coupon 4-year note. This reflects a stronger demand for low coupon notes.

Pricing the Roll

To price the 4-year note roll on March 20, 1984, we use the model in box 1 to infer yields on the outstanding 4-year note and the new 4-year note. These inferred yields are estimates of where the two notes would trade in the absence of any issue-specific supply or demand pressures; that is, they are consistent with the structure of yields on comparable issues. The difference between the two yields is the inferred price of the 4-year roll.

A Consistent Yield on the Outstanding 4-Year Note

The outstanding 4-year note had an $11\frac{1}{4}\%$ coupon and a December 31, 1987, maturity date. For any given price we can compute the yield and hence the duration of the note. From the $11\frac{1}{4}\%$ coupon and the computed duration we can use the model in box 1 to calculate an inferred yield. The note is priced consistently with the model if that inferred yield equals the yield computed directly from the given price.

After some trial and error it turns out that a yield of 11.908% on the outstanding 4-year note is consistent with the March 20 structure of bond yields in the 4-year sector. A yield higher than 11.908% would shorten the bond's duration and result in an inferred yield from the model less than 11.908%. Similarly a lower yield would lengthen the duration and result in a higher yield calculation from the model.

A Consistent Yield on the New 4-Year Note

We next want to use the model in box 1 to infer a consistent Treasury yield on the new 4-year note for forward settlement on April 2. This is complicated for several reasons.

On March 20 market participants knew the new 4-year note would mature on March 31, 1988, but did not yet know what coupon it would carry. Moreover the model in box 1 is appropriate for valuing securities trading for regular settlement but not for forward settlement. In addition it uses the Street definition of yield rather than the Treasury definition.

The problem of an unknown coupon can be resolved easily: all computations are made for a variety of coupons. We then choose the most appropriate coupon in the last step. The following discussion assumes a 12% coupon but similar calculations were done for other coupon rates.

For any assumed coupon, deriving a consistent Treasury yield for forward settlement is identical to deriving a consistent price for forward settlement. If we find such a price, we can compute easily the equivalent Treasury yield. Thus we have reduced our problem to one of inferring a consistent price for the new 4-year note (assuming a 12% coupon) for forward settlement on April 2.

Table 8.1
Cash flows from the new 4-year note trading in mid-March 1984 assuming a 12% coupon

Payment date	Amount[a]
September 30, 1984	5.93443[b]
March 31, 1985	6.0
September 30, 1985	6.0
March 31, 1986	6.0
September 30, 1986	6.0
March 31, 1987	6.0
September 30, 1987	6.0
March 31, 1988	106.0

a. As a percent of face amount.
b. The 4-year note was issued April 2, 1984, and hence had a short first coupon. A full first coupon period would have been 183 days (March 31, 1984, to September 30, 1984). The actual first coupon period was 181 days (April 2, 1984, to September 30, 1984). The size of the first coupon therefore is 98.907% of a full coupon (181 = 98.907% of 183).

We finesse the problem of forward settlement by analyzing a *combined* position in a 12-day RP (from March 21 to April 2) and a forward purchase of the new note as a purchase of the cash flows from the note for regular settlement. Table 8.1 shows the cash flows from the new 4-year note at the assumed 12% coupon. Suppose that an investor purchases the note on March 20 at a price of 99.845 for settlement on April 2. At the 9.875% RP rate prevailing on March 20, this purchase price is equivalent to paying out 99.517 on March 21. (An investment of 99.517 in a 12-day RP at 9.875% will return 99.845 when the RP matures because 99.845 = $99.517 \cdot (1. + (.09875) \cdot (12/360))$.) That is, an investor (1) lending 99.517, on a 12-day RP beginning March 21 and (2) contracting to buy the new note at a forward settlement price of 99.845 would be in the position of (3) buying the cash flows shown in table 8.1 at a price of 99.517 for settlement on March 21.

This argument shows that we can analyze an RP investment and a forward purchase contract as if it were a purchase for regular settlement. The same idea was used in section 8.4 to derive prices for a 10-year note for two different settlement dates which are equivalent at a given RP rate.

At a March 21 price of 99.517, the cash flows shown in table 8.1 have a yield of 12.033% and a duration of 3.312 years. However, the yield on a security with a 12% coupon and 3.312 year duration inferred from the model in box 1 is 11.982% rather than 12.033%. Thus the price of 99.517 is inconsistent with the structure of yields on bonds trading for regular settlement on March 20.

If we raise the March 21 price of the cash flows in table 8.1 to 99.666, those flows will have an 11.985% yield and a 3.320 year duration. At this longer duration the inferred yield from the model in table 8.1 is also

Table 8.2
Prices and yields on the new 4-year note consistent with the model in box 1 for different assumed coupon rates

Assumed coupon	Price for March 21 settlement	Price for April 2 settlement[a]	Treasury yield for April 2 settlement
$11\frac{3}{4}\%$	98.913	99.239	11.995%
$11\frac{7}{8}$	99.289	99.616	11.999
12	99.666	99.994	12.002
$12\frac{1}{8}$	100.040	100.369	12.006

a. Equal to the price for March 21 settlement plus interest on that price for 12 days at a 9.875% RP rate.

11.985%. Thus a March 21 settlement price of 99.666 for the cash flows in table 8.1 is consistent with the March 20 structure of bond yields. This price corresponds to a price of 99.994 for April 2 settlement (99.994 = 99.666 · (1. + (.09875) · (12/360))).

We have now derived a consistent price for the new note for April 2 settlement assuming a 12% coupon. The same procedure can be used to derive consistent prices at other coupon rates. Table 8.2 shows the resulting prices. The highest April 2 price less than 100.0 occurs when the coupon is 12%. Thus a 12% coupon is the single best guess on March 20 of the coupon on the new note and 99.994 is the single best inference of the price of the note for April 2 settlement.

A price of 99.994 and a coupon of 12% on the new note imply a WI Treasury yield of 12.002%. This is the WI yield on the note that is consistent with the model.

The Price of the 4-year Note Roll

So far we have determined that the structure of bond yields in the 4-year sector of the Treasury market on March 20 implied the following:

1. A yield of 11.908% on the outstanding 4-year note for regular settlement on March 21 (using the Street definition of yield).

2. A yield of 12.002% on the new 4-year note for forward settlement on April 2 (using the Treasury definition of yield).

These yields imply a price for the roll of 9.4 basis points (.094% = 12.002% − 11.908%). This price is tolerably close to the 8 basis point spread at which the 4-year roll was actually executed on March 20.

Table 8.3 shows daily predictions of the price of the 4-year note roll over the interval from the March 20 announcement date of the new issue to the March 27 auction date. The table also shows where the roll actually

Table 8.3
Predicted and actual prices on the 4-year note roll in March 1984

Date	Predicted pickup	Actual pickup	Error
March 20	9.4 bp	8.0 bp	+1.4 bp
March 21	8.7	8.6	+0.1
March 22	7.8	9.3	−1.5
March 23	8.3	8.0	+0.3
March 26	8.2	8.2	0.0
March 27	8.9	8.2	+0.7

traded and the resulting prediction error. The prediction errors are surprisingly small, suggesting that the proposed method of analysis is not without value as a tool for pricing rolls.

8.6   Pricing a Roll When the Outstanding Issue Is Scarce

Thus far we have analyzed two types of rolls. First, when the Treasury reopens an outstanding security, the price of the roll is a matter only of short-term financing rates. Second, when the Treasury offers a new issue, the price of the roll depends on maturity and coupon considerations as well as short-term financing.

The analysis of the second case assumed the new issue and the outstanding security are priced consistently with yields on other Treasury securities. This is a crucial simplifying assumption but one that is not always justified. In reality, different Treasury bonds have some life of their own and their prices cannot be determined from comparative analysis alone.

Market participants know that the yield on a particular bond can diverge sharply from yields on comparable bonds if dealers get short in the issue and find it difficult to buy back. The $15\frac{3}{4}\%$ bond of November 15, 2001, provides an example of this behavior. On September 1, 1983, that bond traded at a yield of 12.15%, while the $14\frac{1}{4}\%$ bond of February 15, 2002—a comparable high coupon bond of a nearly identical maturity—had a yield of 12.17%. By April 2, 1984, the former bond had a yield of 12.16% (hardly any change), while the latter bond had a yield of 12.47% (a 30 basis point increase). The resulting change in relative yields cannot be explained by any comparative analysis of bond yields in general. In simple fact, the $15\frac{3}{4}\%$ bond could not be purchased easily. Scarcity kept its price up even while prices on other bonds were falling.

Issue scarcity can affect the price of a roll. This might seem surprising at first impression. After all, the roll is a trade involving a new security and the most recent issue of the same maturity and neither would usually be

Table 8.4
Predicted and actual prices on the 20-year bond roll in March 1984

Date	Predicted pickup	Actual pickup	Error
March 20	3.1 bp	1.3 bp	+1.8 bp
March 21	2.7	2.3	+0.4
March 22	2.7	2.5	+0.2
March 23	2.0	2.3	−0.3
March 26	1.9	3.8	−1.9
March 27	1.9	4.7	−2.8
March 28	2.1	1.2	+1.9
March 29	1.2	−3.3	+4.5

described as "seasoned" or "put away." Nonetheless, issue scarcity can be important and can vitiate an analysis like that of section 8.5.

Table 8.4 shows an example of the influence of issue scarcity on the price of a roll. The table shows the roll in 20-year bonds in March, 1984. On the March 20 announcement date of the new issue the roll was quoted at 1.3 basis points, a bit tighter than the 3.1 basis point spread inferred from yields on comparable bonds. Between March 21 and March 23 the roll was quoted at virtually the same level as the inferred price. On March 26 the quoted price of the roll widened out to 3.8 basis points, and on March 27 the price widened further to 4.7 basis points. This widening of the roll reflected a growing recognition that the outstanding 20-year bond was difficult to purchase. Dealers began to quote a larger pickup to do the roll and thereby cover their shorts in the outstanding issue, anticipating that they could cover the resulting shorts in the new 20-year in the auction on March 29.

The "specials" market for specific collateral obtained under reverse repurchase agreements provided a parallel indication of the scarcity of the outstanding 20-year bond. General Treasury collateral was financed at a $9\frac{1}{2}\%$ RP rate on March 27, but the outstanding 20-year could be financed at 7%. Market participants who were short the outstanding 20-year were willing to give up 250 basis points of interest income to obtain that bond.

The really interesting aspect of the 20-year roll is what happened on March 28 and 29. As shown in table 8.4, the price of the roll fell to 1.2 basis points on March 28 and to −3.3 basis points on the March 29 auction day. By the latter date the 20-year roll could only be executed by *giving up* yield, even though an investor doing the roll had to extend maturity, swap out of a low coupon bond, and accept a return on investable funds of about $9\frac{1}{2}\%$ from March 30 to the April 5 issue date of the new bond. Moreover this peculiar situation occurred even though the outstanding 20-year bond remained scarce in the collateral market.

What happened is that the *new* 20-year bond got even scarcer than the already scarce outstanding bond. On March 28 a single dealer was rumored to have purchased more than $1 billion of the new bonds from other dealers in when-issued trading. This acquisition was a large portion of the Treasury's $3.75 billion total offering. Dealers who had shorted the new issue became anxious that they would be unable to cover fully their shorts in the auction. To try to cover their shorts before the auction they began to quote a better market for the reverse roll. By March 29 they were offering customers a yield pickup on the reverse roll.

The gyrations of the price of the 20-year bond roll in March, 1984 serve to illustrate the effect of issue scarcity on the price of a roll. More particularly, they demonstrate that anxiety can render moot even a careful analysis of relative value.

9 Treasury Bills with Special Value

One morning in early June 1984, the short maturity Treasury bill trader at Bankers Trust announced to the sales force that he wanted to buy bills maturing on June 28, 1984, at a 7.75% discount rate. Simultaneously he offered to sell June 21 bills at a 10% discount rate and/or July 5 bills at a 9.25% discount rate.

On first impression the bill trader's bids and offers seem irrational. They imply the Treasury bill yield curve had a steep negative slope from June 21 to June 28 and a steep positive slope from June 28 to July 5. Neither of these slopes was consistent with the contemporaneous shape of the short maturity bill curve, which showed a gradual increase in yield of about 10 basis points for each additional week of maturity. The trader's swap proposals also imply that an investor could have increased the yield on part of his bill portfolio by almost 200 basis points (without changing his risk exposure) by selling, say, $10 million of the June 28 bill and buying $5 million each of the June 21 and July 5 bills.

Most market participants would characterize an opportunity to increase yield dramatically without changing risk as a giveaway. On the quite reasonable assumption that traders are not in the business of giving anything away, the proposals of the bill trader demand an explanation. In particular, how can a Treasury bill come to be so evidently "mispriced" compared to other bills that appear to be close substitutes?

The answer lies in the observation that the Treasury bill maturing on June 28 was a "quarter-end" bill, or the last bill maturing before the end of the second quarter in 1984. These bills are particularly attractive to corporate treasurers who like to invest in assets whose maturity payments can be used to liquidate accounts payable and other liabilities before they report their quarterly balance sheets. Such quarter-end "window dressing" allows them to report a less leveraged and presumably less risky enterprise.

A corporate treasurer managing short-term assets in May and June 1984 to minimize the size of his June 30 balance sheet, as well as to maximize profits in general, would not necessarily view the June 21 and July 5 Treasury bills as close substitutes for the June 28 bill. Buying the longer bill would force him to go to the trouble of selling before its maturity date, while buying the shorter bill would force him to reinvest its maturity payment for an additional week. The June 28 bill, on the other hand, matures just when he needs cash and hence has a special "convenience" value. The bill may not have been mispriced in relation to the June 21 and July 5 bills when this convenience value is recognized.

Written December 1985.

This chapter addresses the pricing of Treasury bills with special value attributable to maturities that immediately precede dates when many corporate treasurers need cash to make payments. In addition to quarter-end bills, these include "month-end" bills maturing at the end of a calendar month which is not the third month of a quarter and "tax" bills maturing immediately before the important Federal corporate income tax dates (March 15, April 15, June 15, September 15, and December 15). The chapter also examines the pricing of Treasury bills deliverable against a Treasury bill futures contract on the Chicago Mercantile Exchange. The latter bills do not have special payment dates, but they are widely believed to have special value as a result of their deliverability.

The chapter analyzes two aspects of the pricing of special Treasury bills. First, is a special bill typically expensive compared to other bills—or is it expensive on only a sporadic basis which is negligible on average? Second, if special bills do exhibit consistently high prices and low yields, does any of the premium value spill over to nearby bills, making those bills expensive as well?

Before we can measure and analyze the special value of a Treasury bill, we have to define what we mean by its "normal" value. That is, we have to establish a benchmark against which special value can be assessed. This topic is pursued in section 9.1. We then turn to the analysis of special value.

9.1   The Treasury Bill Yield Curve and Excess Yield

Figure 9.1 and table 9.1 show the structure of yields on Treasury bills on September 9, 1985. Two characteristics are evident. First, yields on longer maturity bills generally exceeded yields on shorter maturity bills. Thus the bill yield curve had a positive slope. Second, a small set of bills appear to have had abnormally low yields (or high prices) because their location in the figure breaks the trend of higher bill yields associated with longer maturities. These bills are identified as the bill maturing on December 26, 1985 (another quarter-end bill), and the next shorter and two longer bills.

We would like to represent in a quantitative fashion the idea of a positively sloped bill yield curve on September 9, 1985, and the idea that the December 26 bill was expensive relative to that curve. More generally, we would like to define a curve reflecting the general structure of bill yields on a given date and then assess whether a particular bill had a yield that falls above or below that curve. The difference—between (1) the actual yield on a bill and (2) the yield that the bill would have had if it were located on the bill curve—is a measure of the bill's abnormal or special value.

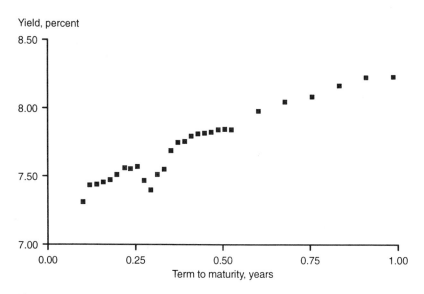

Figure 9.1
Treasury bill yields on September 9, 1985

The Bill Curve

Intuitively, a Treasury bill yield curve should be a smooth (but not necessarily straight) line that reflects the general dependence of bill yields on bill maturities, but it need not follow every bump and wiggle in bill yields. Chapter 7 describes a methodology for constructing such a curve from a set of contemporaneous bill yields. The details of the technique are not as important as the proposition that the resulting curve reasonably reflects the general structure of bill yields.

The graphs in figure 9.2 show, for several dates in the recent past, bill yields and the resulting bill yield curves constructed with the method described in chapter 7. As a broad proposition the curves seem to capture the general behavior of bill yields on each of the respective dates.

Excess Yield as a Measure of Special Value

Having defined the Treasury bill yield curve, we are now ready to focus on the yield on a specific bill.

Figure 9.3 shows bill yields and the bill yield curve for September 9, 1985. Suppose that we want to measure the difference between (1) the actual yield of 7.39% on the December 26, 1985 bill and (2) the yield that the bill would have had if it were located exactly on the curve. Figure 9.3

Table 9.1
Treasury bill yields on September 9, 1985, for settlement on September 10, 1985

Maturity	Term to maturity	Quoted discount rate	True yield[a]
10/3/85	.06 yr	6.95%	7.20%
10/10	.08	6.95	7.20
10/17	.10	7.05	7.31
10/24	.12	7.16	7.43
10/31	.14	7.16	7.44
11/7	.16	7.17	7.45
11/14	.18	7.18	7.47
11/21	.20	7.21	7.51
11/29	.22	7.25	7.56
12/5	.24	7.24	7.55
12/12	.25	7.25	7.57
12/19	.27	7.15	7.46
12/26	.29	7.08	7.39
1/2/86	.31	7.18	7.51
1/9	.33	7.21	7.54
1/16	.35	7.33	7.68
1/23	.37	7.38	7.74
1/30	.39	7.38	7.75
2/6	.41	7.41	7.78
2/13	.43	7.42	7.80
2/20	.45	7.42	7.81
2/27	.47	7.42	7.81
3/6	.48	7.43	7.83
3/13	.50	7.43	7.83
3/20	.52	7.42	7.83
4/17	.60	7.52	7.96
5/15	.68	7.56	8.03
6/12	.75	7.57	8.07
7/10	.83	7.62	8.15
8/7	.91	7.65	8.21
9/4	.98	7.63	8.22

a. As defined in chapter 5.

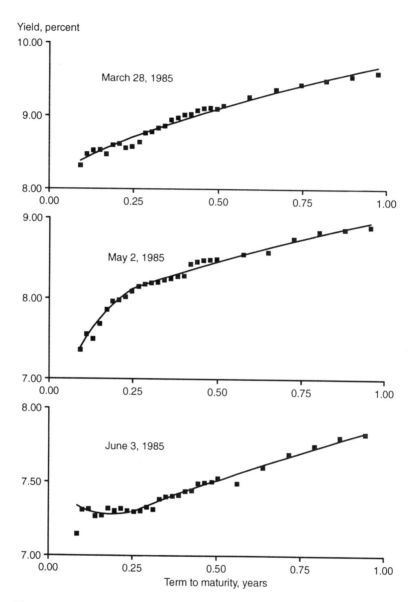

Figure 9.2
Treasury bill yields and yield curves

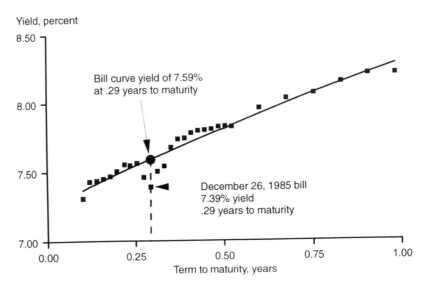

Figure 9.3
Treasury bill yields and the Treasury bill yield curve on September 9, 1985

shows the December 26 bill had .29 years remaining to maturity and that the bill curve had a value of 7.59% at a maturity of .29 years. Thus the yield on the December 26 bill was 20 basis points below the Treasury bill yield curve (20 basis points = .20% = 7.59% − 7.39%).

We will use the difference between the actual yield on a bill and the yield that the bill would have had if it were located on the bill yield curve as a measure of the special value of the bill. Broadly stated, this difference reflects the portion of the bill's yield which cannot be attributed to the contemporaneous structure of bill yields (where the latter is as reflected in the bill curve). The difference is exactly the notion of "excess yield" developed in chapter 7.

Table 9.2 shows excess yields on different Treasury bills on September 9, 1985. A positive excess yield means the yield on the bill is above the bill yield curve and implies that the bill traded "cheap" to the curve. This is illustrated by the bill maturing on January 23, 1986. A negative excess yield means the yield on the bill is below the bill curve and that the bill traded "expensive" to the curve. The quarter-end December 26 bill was 20 basis points expensive, and the nearby bills maturing on December 19, January 2, and January 9 were 10 basis points expensive. This quantifies the observation noted in the beginning of this section that those four bills had some "special" value.

Table 9.2
Treasury bill yields and yield components on September 9, 1985

Maturity	True yield[a]	Components of true yield	
		Curve	Excess
10/3/85	7.20%	7.23%	−0.03%
10/10	7.20	7.27	−0.07
10/17	7.31	7.31	0.0
10/24	7.43	7.35	0.08
10/31	7.44	7.38	0.06
11/7	7.45	7.41	0.04
11/14	7.47	7.44	0.03
11/21	7.51	7.47	0.04
11/29	7.56	7.50	0.06
12/5	7.55	7.52	0.03
12/12	7.57	7.54	0.03
12/19	7.46	7.56	−0.10
12/26	7.39	7.59	−0.20
1/2/86	7.51	7.61	−0.10
1/9	7.54	7.64	−0.10
1/16	7.68	7.66	0.02
1/23	7.74	7.69	0.05
1/30	7.75	7.71	0.04
2/6	7.78	7.73	0.05
2/13	7.80	7.76	0.04
2/20	7.81	7.78	0.03
2/27	7.81	7.80	0.01
3/6	7.83	7.82	0.01
3/13	7.83	7.84	−0.01
3/20	7.83	7.86	−0.03
4/17	7.96	7.94	0.02
5/15	8.03	8.02	0.01
6/12	8.07	8.08	−0.01
7/10	8.15	8.14	0.01
8/7	8.21	8.19	0.02
9/4	8.22	8.24	−0.02

a. As defined in chapter 5.

9.2   Average Excess Yields

Having identified excess yield as a measure of the unusual value of a Treasury bill, we can proceed with an examination of excess yields on special bills. We first describe the data and then review some summary statistics on excess yield.

The Data

The data run from June 1, 1983, to September 30, 1985, and include the quoted discount rate, yield, and excess yield on every outstanding Treasury bill each business day. It should be noted that yield is not the conventional "bond-equivalent" yield used by most market participants but rather the "true" yield introduced in chapter 5.

Table 9.3 identifies all of the special bills in the data set. Any bill which is not a special bill is identified as an "ordinary" bill. Thus the set of all bills is divided into two classes; ordinary bills and special bills, and the latter class is divided further into the four subclasses in table 9.3.

Average Excess Yield

Table 9.4 reports summary statistical measures of excess yield on all bills, special bills, and ordinary bills.

Note first that the average excess yield on *all* bills was essentially zero. This is certainly a reasonable result and in fact is virtually a tautology. An average excess yield computed across all bills which is substantially different from zero would raise serious doubts about the appropriateness of excess yield as a measure of atypical value.

Table 9.4 shows that quarter-end bills are, on average, expensive to the bill curve by about $6\frac{1}{2}$ basis points. The average tax bill is expensive by about $1\frac{1}{2}$ basis points. These results suggest that there is usually strong demand for bills that facilitate window dressing of quarterly balance sheets and at least some unusual demand for bills that facilitate the funding of federal corporate income tax liabilities. On the other hand, there does not seem to be more than a *de minimis* demand, on average, for a bill that matures at the end of a month that is not also the end of a quarter. This suggests that firms may not be as concerned with the precise timing of intraquarterly disbursements and the funding of those disbursements as they are with the timing and funding of federal tax payments and end of quarter payments.

Table 9.4 also shows that deliverable bills trade at premium prices before their delivery dates. The premium is equivalent to a reduction in yield of about 2 basis points. However, following settlement of a Treasury

Table 9.3
Special bills outstanding between June 1, 1983, and September 30, 1985

End-of-quarter bills	Tax bills	End-of-month bills
6/30/1983	6/ 9/1983	7/28/1983
9/29/1983	9/15/1983	8/25/1983
12/29/1983	12/15/1983	10/27/1983
3/29/1984	3/15/1984	11/25/1983
6/28/1984	4/12/1984	1/26/1984
9/27/1984	6/14/1984	2/23/1984
12/27/1984	9/13/1984	4/26/1984
3/28/1985	12/13/1984	5/31/1984
6/27/1985	3/14/1985	7/26/1984
9/26/1985	4/11/1985	8/30/1984
12/26/1985	6/13/1985	10/25/1984
3/27/1986	9/12/1985	11/29/1984
	12/12/1985	1/31/1985
	3/13/1986	2/28/1985
	6/12/1986	4/25/1985
		5/30/1985
		7/25/1985
		8/29/1985
		10/31/1985
		11/29/1985
		1/30/1986
		2/27/1986

Deliverable bills

9/ 8/1983	(deliverable 6/ 9/1983)
12/ 1/1983	(deliverable 9/ 1/1983)
3/22/1984	(deliverable 12/22/1983)
6/14/1984	(deliverable 3/15/1984)
9/ 6/1984	(deliverable 6/ 7/1984)
12/27/1984	(deliverable 9/27/1984)
3/21/1985	(deliverable 12/20/1984)
6/13/1985	(deliverable 3/14/1985)
9/ 5/1985	(deliverable 6/ 6/1985)
12/26/1985	(deliverable 9/26/1985)
3/20/1986	(deliverable 12/19/1985)
6/12/1986	(deliverable 3/13/1986)
9/ 4/1986	(deliverable 6/ 5/1986)

Table 9.4
Statistics on excess yield

	Average	Standard deviation	Number of cases
All bills	0.2 bp	6.5 bp	16,433
Quarter-end bills	−6.5	8.3	1,230
Month-end bills	−0.3	5.7	2,405
Tax bills	−1.6	4.7	1,508
Deliverable bills (before delivery)	−2.0	4.5	1,739
Deliverable bills (after delivery)	2.2	5.9	343
Ordinary bills	1.1	6.3	10,120

bill futures contract, the typical deliverable bill traded about 2 basis points cheap to the bill curve. This suggests, quite reasonably, that deliverable bills have special value as long as they remain deliverable against a futures contract but that their special value evaporates following settlement of the contract.

Finally, table 9.4 shows that ordinary Treasury bills trade cheap to the bill yield curve. This is a direct result of the observation that (1) the average bill trades on the curve and that (2) special bills trade expensive to the curve. It follows that bills other than special bills (i.e., ordinary bills) must trade cheap to the bill curve.

Average Excess Yield as a Function of Bill Maturity

Table 9.4 gives a reasonable general impression of the premium values which attach to special Treasury bills, but it is hardly a complete analysis. It does not, for example, disclose whether a quarter-end bill trades $6\frac{1}{2}$ basis points expensive to the bill curve throughout its life or whether the $-6\frac{1}{2}$ basis points of average excess yield arises because it trades on the curve when it is first issued and then trades very expensive to the curve as it approaches maturity.

The chronological structure of the average excess yield on a special bill is important for deciding the optimal time to purchase such a bill. If the premium value usually appears only as the bill comes within two months of maturity, then it would make sense for an investor to buy the bill before that time. On the other hand, the time of purchase of a special bill is less crucial if the bill typically trades at a constant premium throughout its life.

To assess the chronological structure of the valuation of special bills, we computed average excess yields on bills stratified by their remaining time to maturity. The results are shown in table 9.5.

Table 9.5
Average excess yield, by term to maturity

Weeks to maturity	All bills	Quarter-end bills	Month-end bills	Tax bills	Deliverable bills
5	−5.2 bp	−15.2 bp	−10.5 bp	−8.0 bp	3.6 bp
6	0.8	−10.1	−3.2	−2.9	4.8
7	1.1	−10.4	−2.9	−2.3	1.6
8	−0.1	−11.7	−3.2	−4.9	−0.3
9	0.8	−8.5	−2.3	−2.0	1.0
10	2.4	−5.3	−0.2	0.9	3.7
11	2.6	−5.9	0.6	1.8	4.0
12	1.9	−3.4	2.2	−0.6	−1.1
13	1.2	−3.7	2.5	−2.5	−4.4
14	−0.4	−6.5	0.6	−2.0	−5.0
15	−2.3	−13.9	−1.6	−5.2	−5.7
16	−2.5	−13.4	−0.8	−4.5	−4.4
17	−2.1	−14.6	−0.7	−3.7	−4.2
18	−1.0	−9.5	−0.2	−2.0	−3.9
19	−0.2	−6.1	1.2	−2.0	−3.6
20	0.4	−5.4	1.3	−2.4	−2.6
21	1.1	−3.8	1.2	−0.3	−1.8
22	1.8	−3.8	1.5	0.7	−2.1
23	2.0	−3.5	2.8	0.8	−2.1
24	1.8	−2.4	2.3	1.6	−1.1
25	1.0	−2.8	1.1	0.7	−1.8
26	0.2	−3.4	1.3	−0.2	−2.1
27	0.3	−1.5	2.7	−2.3	−1.2
28	−1.2	−3.5	0.7	−4.4	−3.9
29	−1.8	−4.0	−1.1	−2.3	−3.1
30	−2.5	−7.4	−3.1	−6.0	−4.4
31	−2.8	−6.9	−1.9	−5.4	−3.6
32	−3.0	−4.4	−2.2	−4.0	−2.8
33	−2.8	−8.5	−2.3	−2.8	−3.5
34	−2.7	−7.3	−3.0	−2.6	−3.2
35	−2.1	−2.4	−0.3	−3.4	−2.5
36	−1.6	−3.4	−0.4	−2.5	−2.3
37	−0.9	−4.2	−0.5	−1.7	−2.1
38	−0.8	−2.2	0.0	−1.2	−1.6
39	−0.9	−0.5	0.2	−0.6	−2.0
40	−0.4	−0.9	1.2	−2.5	−2.2
41	0.0	−1.8	2.3	−1.8	−1.0
42	−0.2	−1.3	2.9	−1.0	−0.8
43	−0.4	−1.6	2.8	−0.8	−0.4
44	−0.2	−1.9	2.5	0.0	0.2
45	0.5	−1.3	2.5	0.1	0.2
46	0.5	−0.3	1.4	−0.4	0.2
47	0.5	0.0	0.9	−0.1	0.3
48	0.0	−0.1	0.9	−0.6	−0.3
49	0.4	−1.3	−1.7	−0.8	0.4
50	0.6	−2.2	−2.0	−0.8	0.4
51	0.7	−1.2	1.7	1.2	0.4
52	0.9	−1.8	0.9	1.9	1.7

All Bills

Although the average excess yield on all bills of all maturities is zero (see the first line in table 9.4), the time series average excess yield on bills of a *particular* maturity is not necessarily zero. This is demonstrated by the data in the first column of table 9.5.

The data show that a year bill typically trades quite close to the bill curve from the time it is auctioned as a 52-week bill until it comes to within about 40 weeks of maturity. It then becomes progressively more expensive to the curve until shortly before its reopening as a 6-month bill, at which time it returns to the curve. Following its auction as a 6-month bill, a bill typically trades cheap to the bill curve for about 6 weeks, then becomes expensive until shortly before its reopening as a 3-month bill. Following the 3-month auction a typical bill again trades cheap to the curve for about 4 weeks.

This pattern in the chronology of the average excess yield on an arbitrary bill reflects a "distribution" phenomenon. Prior to its 3-month and (in the case of old year bills) 6-month reopenings, a bill usually trades expensive. Following a reopening (at which time new supplies of the bill are issued) the bill trades cheap to the bill curve. This cheapness persists until the new supply is absorbed—a process that evidently takes about 4 to 6 weeks.

Quarter-End Bills

We now want to begin to assess the chronological structure of average excess yields on special bills in light of what we have established for all bills. The second column in table 9.5 shows the chronology of average excess yields on quarter-end bills. The structure differs from the data for all bills in two respects. First, end-of-quarter bills are almost always expensive to the Treasury bill yield curve. Second, they become extremely expensive when they have about 17 weeks remaining to maturity (average excess yield of $-14\frac{1}{2}$ basis points) and become almost as expensive when they have less than 10 weeks remaining to maturity (average excess yields of -8 to -15 basis points). The data suggest that it is best to plan to purchase quarter-end bills at or shortly after their 6-month auction or 3-month auction and that it is very desirable to avoid purchasing the bills shortly before their 3-month auction. (Note the erosion of negative excess yield from week 17 to weeks 12 and 13.)

Tax Bills

Column 4 of table 9.5 shows that excess yields on tax bills follow a pattern similar to end-of-quarter bills, albeit in an attenuated form.

Month-End Bills

We saw in table 9.4 that the average excess yield on month-end bills of all maturities was only about $-\frac{1}{2}$ basis point. Column 3 of table 9.5 shows that this *de minimis* value does not reflect the typical behavior of month-end bills when they get within about 10 weeks of maturity. In fact, month-end bills usually become more expensive to the bill curve than tax bills as they approach maturity, even though they trade cheaper when they have more than 10 weeks remaining to maturity. This suggests that corporate treasurers have more difficulty making early projections of their need to fund month-end payments compared to tax payments. On the other hand, their month-end funding requirements, once crystalized, appear to have as strong an impact on bill prices as their tax funding requirements.

Deliverable Bills

We have already noted that a deliverable bill usually trades expensive to the bill curve prior to settlement of the futures contract against which it is deliverable and that the reverse holds true following settlement. The last column of table 9.5 adds a little detail to this picture. Deliverable bills begin to exhibit unusual value about 20 weeks before settlement (33 weeks before maturity) and are typically most expensive to the bill curve immediately before settlement (14 to 17 weeks before maturity). They stay expensive to the curve during a settlement week but then cheapen dramatically in the 2 or 3 weeks following settlement.

9.3   Special Bills and Nearby Bills

The preceding section presented evidence that Treasury bills with special maturity dates typically have high prices—or low yields. The special maturity dates include those immediately preceding the end of a calendar quarter, a federal corporate income tax payment, and the end of the first or second calendar month in a quarter. A bill with such a maturity date has value to a corporate treasurer who needs to fund a tax liability or accounts payable at the end of a reporting period. It has a premium price in the market because there are many corporations with the same funding requirements. Similar comments apply to a deliverable Treasury bill, although in this case the premium price stems from a potential need for the bill to liquidate a Treasury bill futures contract rather than to fund a future payment.

A closely related topic is the impact of the premium pricing of special bills on the demand for (and pricing of) nearby bills. We can imagine two possibilities. First, suppose that there are many investors who have a strong preference for holding a 10 week bill to fund a future payment (e.g., a tax liability) but that there are also many investors who do not have the same funding requirement and who are as willing to hold 9-week or 11-week bills as 10-week bills. The strong demand for 10-week bills by the former investors and the resultant low yield on those bills may push the latter investors into 9-week and 11-week bills, leading to higher prices and lower yields on those bills. In this case the special demand for the 10-week bills can be said to "spill over" into stronger demand for nearby bills as well.

A second possibility is that the *bulk* of investors need to fund payments in 10 weeks and that there are relatively fewer investors who view the 9-week and 11-week bills as close substitutes for the 10-week bill. Any spillover of the special demand for the 10-week bill into the 9-week and 11-week bills would then result from investors with a preference for the 10-week bill shortening up on the bill curve, or extending on the bill curve because of the low yield on that bill. In this case the spillover demand may not be as strong as in the previous case, and it may not have the same effect on the two nearby bills. If, for example, investors are more willing to shorten up than to extend, spillover demand will affect the price of the 9-week bill more than it will affect the price of the 11-week bill.

These scenarios for how unusual demand for a special bill can affect yields on nearby bills may seem somewhat hypothetical. However, we will show in this section that they are supported by an analysis of excess bill yields.

All Bills

We examine first the relation between excess yields on bills of consecutive maturities without singling out any special bills. This provides a benchmark against which special bills can be compared.

Consider a set of excess yields on three arbitrary bills with consecutive weekly maturities. We want to compute the average excess yields on the three bills, and we particularly want to compute the correlations of the excess yield on the middle bill with the excess yields on the shorter and longer bills, respectively. These correlations will show whether the excess yields on the bills tend to move up and down together or whether the excess yield on a given bill is unrelated to the excess yields on nearby bills.

The desired statistics are shown in the first line of table 9.6. As in table 9.4 the average excess yield on an arbitrary bill is virtually zero, and the average excess yields on the next shorter bill and the next longer bill are also small.

The correlations of excess yields are more interesting statistics. Table 9.6 shows that excess yields on consecutive bills have coefficients of corre-

Table 9.6
Statistics on excess yields on bills with consecutive weekly maturities

Class of middle bill	Average excess yields			Correlation of excess yield on middle bill with excess yield on:	
	Next shorter bill	Middle bill	Next longer bill	Next shorter bill	Next longer bill
All bills	−0.2 bp	0.3 bp	0.5 bp	0.32	0.37
Tax bills	−0.5	−1.8	−1.2	0.47	0.37
Deliverable bills (before delivery)	−1.2	−3.2	−3.1	0.78	0.55
Quarter-end bills	−2.8	−7.6	0.0	0.30	0.00
Month-end bills	2.3	−0.4	2.3	0.44	0.13

Note: Data includes only those bills for which there existed a bill with a maturity one week shorter and a bill with a maturity one week longer.

lation of about .3. This implies that a 10 basis point rise or decline in the excess yield on an arbitrary bill will usually be accompanied by a 3 basis point rise or decline in the excess yields on nearby bills. More important, it implies that there is some coupling, albeit incomplete, in the pricing of bills with consecutive maturities.

Special Bills

We now want to examine the relationship between the excess yield on a special bill and the excess yield on bills near that bill.

Tax Bills

The second line of table 9.6 shows the average excess yield on the tax bills in our data (−1.8 basis points) and the average excess yields on the next shorter bills (−.5 basis points) and the next longer bills (−1.2 basis points). The data show that bills nearby to tax bills, as well as tax bills themselves, are typically expensive to the Treasury bill curve and imply that the special demand for tax bills spills over to both of the nearby bills. This view is supported by the correlation of the excess yield on a tax bill with the excess yield on a nearby bill. Both correlations are positive and of a nonnegligible magnitude.

Deliverable Bills

The third line of table 9.6 shows similar data and similar results for deliverable bills prior to delivery. It appears that the special demand for a deliverable bill leads some investors to substitute into shorter and longer bills. This substitution in turn produces premium prices on those non-deliverable bills.

Quarter-End Bills

The fourth line of table 9.6 shows quite different results for bills maturing at the end of a calendar quarter. The average excess yields suggest that special demand for a quarter-end bill is associated with premium prices on the next shorter bill as well as on the quarter-end bill itself but that it does not lead to premium prices on the next longer bill. In addition the correlations show that excess yields on quarter-end bills and the next shorter bills tend to move together but that excess yields on quarter-end bills are largely unrelated to excess yields on the next longer bills.

These results support the proposition that there are relatively few investors who view quarter-end bills and the next longer bills as close substitutes and imply that quarter-end funding is a widespread phenomenon. They also suggest that investors concerned with funding end-of-quarter disbursements are reluctant to hold bills maturing after the disbursement date but are willing to substitute into shorter bills. That is, they appear more concerned with the market risks and transaction costs of holding bills that are "too long" for their requirements (and that must be sold before maturity) than with the reinvestment risks and costs of holding bills that are "too short"

Month-End Bills

The fifth line of table 9.6 shows the behavior of excess yield on month-end bills and on the bills nearby to month-end bills. The results, with one exception, follow the same characteristics as quarter-end bills. The exception is the average excess yield on bills maturing one week prior to or after the maturity of month-end bills. These bills appear to trade cheap to the bill curve, implying that special demand for month-end bills does not spill over into either shorter or longer bills. Contradicting this, however, is the observation that excess yields on month-end bills and shorter bills are positively correlated, implying that investors generally view the bills as substitutes.

9.4   Conclusions

This chapter has developed some novel insights into the pricing of Treasury bills. A preliminary analysis of the Treasury bill market separated the yield on a bill into two parts: a component that reflects the bill's location along a smooth yield curve and a component that represents unusual value relative to that curve (either positive or negative). If we stopped here, we might conjecture that any bill trading at a negative excess yield is expensive and should be sold because the premium price of the bill will erode as the bill returns to the curve. Similarly a bill with a positive excess yield might well be purchased because it has a better chance of appreciating as it returns to the curve.

This chapter extended the preliminary analysis by showing that a bill may not be overpriced and in danger of depreciating in value merely because it trades below the bill yield curve. Some bills trade at premium prices because they mature at times when corporate treasurers need to make disbursements and hence are convenient instruments for funding those payments. There is no reason to expect this component of a bill's price to erode as time passes.

More generally, the analysis suggests that the yield on a bill depends not only on the time remaining to the bill's maturity, that is, on the level and shape of the bill yield curve, but also on the bill's specific maturity date. Bills with nearly the same term to maturity may trade at rather different yields if one matures shortly before an important corporate disbursement date. Thus whether a bill is "cheap" or "expensive" depends not only on the relation of the yield on the bill to the bill curve but also on whether the bill matures at a special time.

10 Comparing Yields on Zeros to Yields on Treasury Bonds

Over the last decade duration analysis has become increasingly important for managing fixed income investments. However, the most common fixed income securities—coupon-bearing bonds—have two characteristics which reduce their utility in duration-managed portfolios. First, most bonds currently have durations of less than ten years. This makes it impossible to construct a portfolio matched to any longer investment horizon. Second, a bond portfolio has to be rebalanced from time to time to maintain the match between its duration and a given horizon.

Neither of these limitations exist with zero-coupon securities. For this reason zeros have become a significant part of many institutional portfolios.

This chapter describes some basic elements of the relationship between yields on zeros and yields on bonds. The primary goal is to show how the bond yield curve can be manipulated to obtain a yield curve for hypothetical "spot" obligations which, like zeros, pay no interest before maturity. This spot yield curve provides a benchmark for assessing whether zeros are cheap or expensive to bonds. Put another way, spot obligations provide an analytical bridge between bonds (from which they are derived) and zeros (which they resemble).

10.1 Introduction

A Treasury bond is a complex security to analyze because it makes interest payments to prior to maturity. The most familiar consequence of the payments is that an investor who has cash to invest for, say, five years and contemplates purchasing a five-year bond has to be concerned with the yields at which he will be able to reinvest his early coupons.

Duration is an important device for assessing the suitability of alternative coupon-bearing bonds. If the duration of a bond matches an investor's horizon, then that bond is very nearly riskless, regardless of whether interest rates move up or down following purchase. More specifically, an investor very nearly locks in a fixed yield over his horizon when he buys a bond with a duration equal to that horizon.

Although duration is a powerful tool for evaluating the risks of alternative bond investments, it has some practical drawbacks. One drawback is the absence (at this time) of a Treasury bond with a duration of more than ten years. This means that an investor with a horizon of more than ten years must bear reinvestment risk if he restricts his portfolio to ordinary bonds, regardless of how that portfolio is structured.

Written March 1984.

A second drawback stems from the need to offset changes in bond duration. In particular, duration varies with the level of interest rates, and it does not decline on a year-for-year basis with the passage of time. (For example, if a bond has a three-year duration when purchased, it will have more than a two-year duration one year later.) This means that a portfolio managed to match a particular horizon date has to be rebalanced from time to time to maintain the correspondence between its duration and that date. The investor must of course pay the transactions costs of such rebalancing.

The absence of long-duration bonds and the costs of portfolio rebalancing has created interest in a new class of intermediate- and long-term instruments: zero-coupon securities stripped from ordinary Treasury bonds (see chapter 2). Zeros are important because they overcome both of the practical drawbacks associated with bonds. First, the duration of a zero is *always* identically equal to its *remaining* term to maturity. If a zero had a three-year duration when purchased, it will have a two-year duration after one year has elapsed, regardless of any change in interest rates in the interim. This means that an investment in a zero never has to be rebalanced as a result of changes in yields or the passage of time. Second, zeros are available with maturities (and durations) well beyond the turn of the century, so they can be matched against even very distant horizon dates.

Since zeros are relatively new, there is some uncertainty as to how their yields should be compared to yields on coupon-bearing bonds. It is possible to compare yields on zeros to yields on bonds on a matched duration basis, but this technique is obviously impractical for zeros with maturities (and durations) that exceed the duration of the longest-duration Treasury.

An alternative, and better, device is suggested by the very practice of stripping. As shown in figure 10.1, the payments from a bond can be viewed as a bundle of single-payment "spot" obligations consisting of each of the coupons and the final repayment of principal. If we can derive the present values of each of these individual obligations and compute their respective yields to payment, we would have a natural benchmark for assessing yields on actual zeros. The next section examines a procedure for this computation.

10.2   The Relationship between Bond Prices and Spot Yields

Spot obligations are the building blocks of the cash flow on a coupon-bearing bond. Each obligation, taken by itself, is a promise to pay a specified amount on a single stated date. The present value of a spot

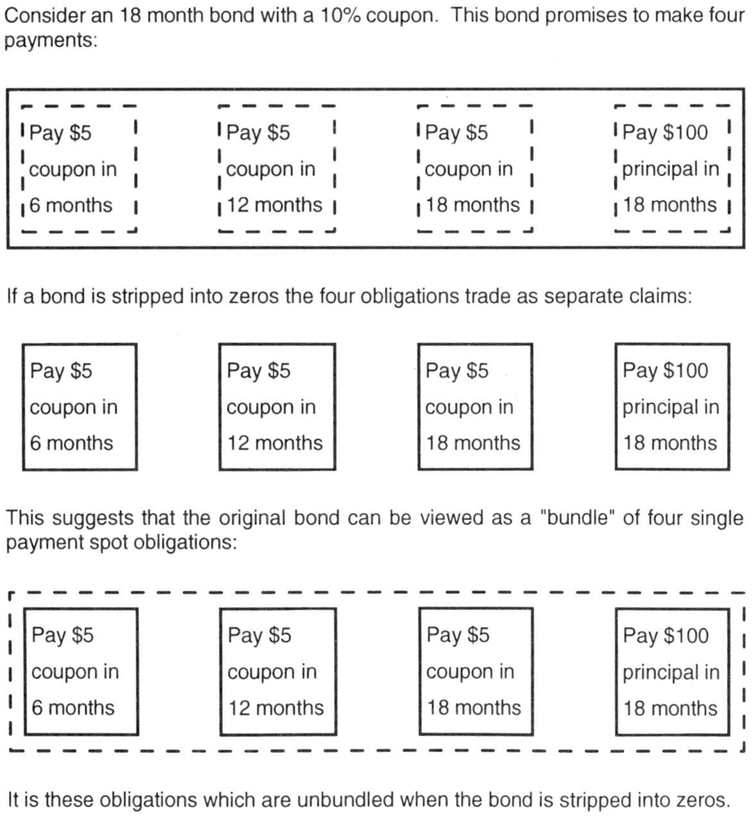

Consider an 18 month bond with a 10% coupon. This bond promises to make four payments:

| Pay $5 coupon in 6 months | Pay $5 coupon in 12 months | Pay $5 coupon in 18 months | Pay $100 principal in 18 months |

If a bond is stripped into zeros the four obligations trade as separate claims:

| Pay $5 coupon in 6 months | Pay $5 coupon in 12 months | Pay $5 coupon in 18 months | Pay $100 principal in 18 months |

This suggests that the original bond can be viewed as a "bundle" of four single payment spot obligations:

| Pay $5 coupon in 6 months | Pay $5 coupon in 12 months | Pay $5 coupon in 18 months | Pay $100 principal in 18 months |

It is these obligations which are unbundled when the bond is stripped into zeros.

Figure 10.1
A Treasury bond as a bundle of spot obligations

obligation is the dollar amount of its promised payment discounted over the time remaining to the payment date. The "cash flow value" of a bond is the sum of the present values of its component spot obligations.

This section first describes how to value the cash flow on a bond from a sequence of spot yields. We then argue that, in some cases, the price of a bond will equal its cash flow value. Finally, we turn the valuation relationship inside out and show how spot yields can be derived from bond prices.

Valuing the Payments from a Bond with Spot Yields

To begin the analysis, denote the yield on a spot obligation payable in k years as r_k, and assume that we know the sequence $r_1, r_2, \ldots,$ of current spot yields. Consider a bond that pays an annual coupon of C. (We assume that bonds pay interest annually for expositional convenience. The

Example 1
Computing the cash flow value of a bond with spot yields

Suppose that we have a 3-year bond paying an annual coupon of $C = 11\%$, and suppose also that the 1-year, 2-year, and 3-year spot yields are as follows:

$r_1 = 9.5\%$

$r_2 = 10.0\%$

$r_3 = 10.5\%$

The cash flow value of the bond can be calculated using equation (10.1) in the text:

$$V = \frac{C}{1 + r_1} + \frac{C}{(1 + r_2)^2} + \frac{C + 100}{(1 + r_3)^3}$$

$$= \frac{11.}{(1 + .095)} + \frac{11.}{(1 + .10)^2} + \frac{11. + 100}{(1 + .105)^3}$$

$$= 101.406$$

Note that (1) the first coupon is discounted for one year at the 1-year spot yield, (2) the second coupon is discounted for two years at the 2-year spot yield, and (3) the final coupon and principal payment are discounted for three years at the 3-year spot yield.

analysis can be extended readily to semi-annual coupons.) We want to compute the present value of the bond's future payments where each payment is discounted back to the present at its *respective* spot yield.

The first coupon is payable in one year and has a present value of $C/(1 + r_1)$. This is the amount C of the future payment discounted for one year at the 1-year spot yield. Similarly the coupon payable in two years has a present value of $C/(1 + r_2)^2$. This is the amount of the second coupon discounted for two years at the 2-year spot yield.

If the bond has a total of n coupons remaining the present value of its cash flow stream, or the sum of the present values of its spot payments, is

$$V = \frac{C}{1 + r_1} + \frac{C}{(1 + r_2)^2} + \cdots + \frac{C}{(1 + r_{n-1})^{n-1}} + \frac{C + 100}{(1 + r_n)^n} \qquad (10.1)$$

Example 1 illustrates the use of equation (10.1) with a numerical example.

If a bond is valued in the marketplace as a function of its cash flows alone, the value of V in equation (10.1) will be identical to the market price of the bond. In practice, however, a bond may have additional value because it is trading below par or it may have lesser value because it is trading at a premium (due to tax laws and accounting conventions for reporting gains and losses on bonds purchased at discounts and premiums). In these cases the market price of a bond can differ from the present value of its future cash flows.

Relation to Yield to Maturity

It should be noted that the form of equation (10.1) is different in an important respect from a somewhat similar equation defining a bond's yield to maturity. If a bond has a price P and n annual coupons remaining to be paid each in the amount C, its yield to maturity is the value of R that satisfies the equation

$$P = \frac{C}{1 + R} + \frac{C}{(1 + R)^2} + \cdots + \frac{C}{(1 + R)^{n-1}} + \frac{C + 100}{(1 + R)^n} \tag{10.2}$$

R is the *single* rate of interest that makes the present value of the future payments on the bond equal to the price of the bond. This single rate is used to discount *all* cash flows, regardless of when they occur. Spot yields as used in equation (10.1) are rates of interest for payments at *specific* future dates. If two payments occur at different dates, they will usually be discounted at different spot yields. The cash flow value of a bond paying funds at n different dates can be computed only when the relevant set of n spot yields are known.

Deriving Spot Yields from Bond Prices

The discussion above showed how the cash flow value of a bond can be derived from spot yields and argued that this value will be comparable to the market price of the bond if the bond is trading near par. This is not very useful because we can observe directly the market price of a bond. Spot yields, however, are not observable, and the real problem is to derive spot yields from bond prices.

To derive spot yields, we begin by supposing we have a sequence of bonds trading at or near par with maturities of one year, two years, etc. Let C_k be the annual coupon payable on a bond maturing in k years, and let P_k be the price of that bond. (Chapter 7 describes how yields (and hence coupon rates) on par bonds can be derived from actual bond prices. The prices of the par bonds are 100% of principal by definition.)

To be consistent with the spot yield curve, a bond maturing in one year must be priced according to the equation

$$P_1 = \frac{C_1 + 100}{1 + r_1} \tag{10.3}$$

That is, the price P_1 of the bond must equal the present value of its interest and principal payments. Since those payments occur in one year, they are discounted at the 1-year spot yield r_1. This equation can be solved readily for r_1.

The price of a 2-year bond must also equal the present value of its interest and principal payments, so

$$P_2 = \frac{C_2}{1 + r_1} + \frac{C_2 + 100}{(1 + r_2)^2} \tag{10.4}$$

Note that the first coupon is discounted at the 1-year spot rate and the second coupon and principal are discounted at the 2-year spot rate. Rearranging equation (10.4) gives:

$$P_2 - \frac{C_2}{1 + r_1} = \frac{C_2 + 100}{(1 + r_2)^2} \tag{10.5}$$

Since we know already r_1, the left-hand side of equation (10.5) can be computed. It follows that the equation can be solved for r_2.

Similarly the price of a 3-year bond must satisfy the equation:

$$P_3 = \frac{C_3}{1 + r_1} + \frac{C_3}{(1 + r_2)^2} + \frac{C_3 + 100}{(1 + r_3)^3} \tag{10.6}$$

or

$$P_3 - \frac{C_3}{1 + r_1} - \frac{C_3}{(1 + r_2)^2} = \frac{C_3 + 100}{(1 + r_3)^3} \tag{10.7}$$

Since we know r_1 and r_2, the left-hand side of equation (10.7) can be computed, and hence the equation can be solved for r_3.

This process can be extended indefinitely, and we can thus compute a sequence of spot yields consistent with the prices and coupons on the specified bonds. Example 2 gives a numerical example showing how spot yields are computed from bond prices.

Two Illustrations

Having described how spot yields can be derived from bond prices, we would now like to illustrate the relationship between spot yields and conventional bond yields.

Table 10.1 and figure 10.2 show yields in the Treasury market on May 17, 1983. The solid line in the figure shows yields on bonds trading at par. Note that this yield curve rises sharply out to about 7 years, then begins to level off (reaching a maximum of 10.70% in the 16- to 21-year area) and finally declines slowly to a yield of 10.52% on 30-year bonds.

The dashed line in the figure shows yields on spot obligations derived from the par bond yield curve. The spot curve rises more sharply than the bond curve and reaches a maximum of 11.09% in the 18-year area. The

Example 2
Computing spot yields from bond prices

Consider the following prices and coupons on a 1-year bond, a 2-year bond, and a 3-year bond, each of which pays an annual coupon:

$P_1 = 101.$ $C_1 = 10\%$

$P_2 = 98.$ $C_2 = 10.25\%$

$P_3 = 97.$ $C_3 = 10.75\%$

From these prices we want to compute the implied 1-year, 2-year, and 3-year spot yields.

The 1-year spot yield can be computed from equation (10.3) in the text:

$$P_1 = \frac{C_1 + 100}{1 + r_1}$$

$$101. = \frac{10 + 100}{1 + r_1}$$

$r_1 = .0891$, or 8.91%

The 2-year spot yield can be computed from equation (10.4) in the text:

$$P_2 = \frac{C_2}{1 + r_1} + \frac{C_2 + 100}{(1 + r_2)^2}$$

Using the specified values of P_2 and C_2 and the computed value of $r_1 = 8.91\%$ gives

$$98. = \frac{10.25}{(1 + .0891)} + \frac{10.25 + 100.}{(1 + r_2)^2}$$

$$88.589 = \frac{110.25}{(1 + r_2)^2}$$

$r_2 = .1156$, or 11.56%

The 3-year spot yield can be computed from equation (10.6) in the text:

$$P_3 = \frac{C_3}{1 + r_1} + \frac{C_3}{(1 + r_2)^2} + \frac{C_3 + 100}{(1 + r_3)^3}$$

Using the specified values of P_3 and C_3 and the computed values of $r_1 = 8.91\%$ and $r_2 = 11.56\%$ gives

$$97. = \frac{10.75}{1 + .0891} + \frac{10.75}{(1 + .1156)^2} + \frac{10.75 + 100.}{(1 + r_3)^3}$$

$$78.492 = \frac{110.75}{(1 + r_3)^3}$$

$r_3 = .1216$, or 12.16%

Table 10.1
Yields on par bonds and spot obligations on May 17, 1983

Years to maturity	Par bond yield	Spot yield	Spread
1	8.98%	8.99%	.01%
2	9.47	9.50	.03
3	9.75	9.80	.05
4	9.92	9.99	.07
5	10.07	10.16	.09
6	10.23	10.36	.13
7	10.32	10.46	.14
8	10.35	10.50	.15
9	10.40	10.55	.15
10	10.43	10.58	.15
11	10.45	10.62	.17
12	10.50	10.69	.19
13	10.55	10.78	.23
14	10.60	10.89	.29
15	10.66	10.99	.33
16	10.69	11.06	.37
17	10.71	11.09	.38
18	10.72	11.09	.37
19	10.71	11.05	.34
20	10.70	10.98	.28
21	10.68	10.90	.22
22	10.66	10.81	.15
23	10.63	10.72	.09
24	10.61	10.62	.01
25	10.59	10.52	−.07
26	10.58	10.46	−.12
27	10.56	10.38	−.18
28	10.55	10.31	−.24
29	10.53	10.25	−.28
30	10.52	10.18	−.34

spot curve then declines, going through the bond curve in the 24-year area and falling to a yield of 10.18% in the 30-year sector.

Why the Par Bond Yield Curve and the Spot Yield Curve Are Different

In thinking about the two yield curves in figure 10.2, it is important to keep in mind the differences in what they measure. The spot curve measures the cost of credit when there is only a single payment on some future date. The bond curve, on the other hand, measures the cost of credit when interest is paid periodically prior to the return of principal. The differences in the timing of the cash flows is the reason why the curves look different. This can be illustrated by comparing spot yields and bond yields in the 1- to 15-year sector and in the 20- to 30-year sector.

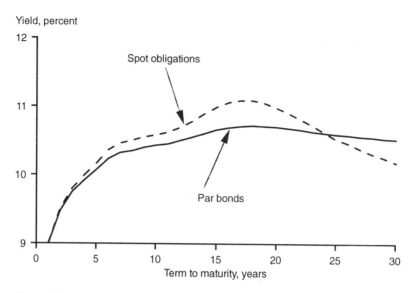

Figure 10.2
Yields on par bonds and spot obligations on May 17, 1983

The shape of the spot yield curve in figure 10.2 implies that longer-dated spot obligations were cheaper (on a relative yield basis) than shorter-dated spot obligations out to 15 years. The positive slope of the spot curve has immediate implications for the relationship between spot yields and bond yields in that sector.

A 5-year spot obligation makes only one payment—at the end of 5 years. Table 10.1 shows the single payment was valued at a yield of 10.16% on May 17. A 5-year bond pays principal and a final coupon at maturity, but it also makes coupon payments at earlier dates. The principal and last coupon payments were valued at a yield of 10.16% on May 17 (since they were spot obligations payable in 5 years), but the earlier coupons were valued at lower spot yields. Since the conventional yield on a bond is a (complex) average of the spot yields on its individual payments, the yield on the 5-year bond must have been less than 10.16% on May 17. (Table 10.1 shows that it was 10.07%.) This illustrates why spot yields exceeded comparable maturity bond yields in the 1- to 15-year sector in figure 10.2. More generally, if the front end of the bond yield curve is rising the spot yield curve will rise more rapidly and lie above the bond curve, and conversely.

The shape of the bond yield curve in figure 10.2 also implies that on a yield basis there was progressively stronger demand for bonds maturing beyond 18 years. Since bonds maturing in, say, 25 years make coupon

payments, throughout their life, and particularly in the less desirable 15-
to 20-year area, this means the market must have been placing progressively higher values (or lower yields) on payments made beyond 20 years.
The spot curve shows that this was in fact the case. A 30-year spot obligation was valued at a 10.18% yield, while a 30-year bond (which makes
payments in the 15- to 20-year area as well as later dates) was valued at a
10.52% yield.

A Second Illustration

The next section compares yields on zeros to spot yields. Some crucial
aspects of that comparison will be facilitated if we note briefly a second
illustration of the relation between spot yields and bond yields.

Table 10.2 and figure 10.3 show yields in the Treasury market on January 24, 1984. Comparing figures 10.2 and 10.3, we see that in both cases
the bond curve was rising out through 15 years and that in both cases the
spot curve was above the bond curve in that sector. The difference in the
two figures is the behavior of yields on bonds with maturities of 15 to 30
years. On May 17, 1983, 15-year par bonds had a 10.66% yield and
30-year par bonds had a 10.52% yield, for a difference of −14 basis points
(see table 10.1). On January 24, 1984, the difference in yields had narrowed
to −3 basis points (see table 10.2), showing that the long end of the bond
curve was much less negatively sloped at the later date. As a result the long
end of the spot yield curve was also less negatively sloped on the later date.
This means that on January 24, 1984, the market was not placing as high
a premium on payments made beyond 20 years, compared to those made
in 15 to 20 years, as it had been on May 17, 1983. We will soon see a similar
change in the comparative structure of spot yields and yields on zeros.

10.3   The Relation between Spot Yields and Yields on Zeros

The previous section described how we can take yields on seasoned par
bonds and convert them into yields on single-payment spot obligations.
We now want to compare the resulting spot yields to yields on zero-
coupon securities. Before we begin, however, it is useful to clarify some
differences between zeros and spot obligations.

The Difference between Zeros and Spot Obligations

Spot obligations have been defined as the hypothetical single payment
claims bundled together in a bond trading at par. Zeros, on the other
hand, are the actual securities that result when the coupon and principal
obligations of a bond are separated and sold individually.

Table 10.2
Yields on par bonds and spot obligations on January 24, 1984

Years to maturity	Par bond yield	Spot yield	Spread
1	10.06%	10.07%	.01%
2	10.62	10.65	.03
3	10.95	11.01	.06
4	11.19	11.29	.10
5	11.37	11.49	.12
6	11.48	11.63	.15
7	11.56	11.72	.16
8	11.60	11.76	.16
9	11.62	11.79	.17
10	11.63	11.77	.14
11	11.63	11.76	.13
12	11.64	11.79	.15
13	11.66	11.82	.16
14	11.68	11.84	.16
15	11.69	11.86	.17
16	11.70	11.87	.17
17	11.70	11.88	.18
18	11.70	11.87	.17
19	11.69	11.83	.14
20	11.69	11.80	.11
21	11.69	11.78	.09
22	11.68	11.76	.08
23	11.68	11.75	.07
24	11.68	11.73	.05
25	11.67	11.71	.04
26	11.67	11.69	.02
27	11.67	11.66	−.01
28	11.66	11.64	−.02
29	11.66	11.62	−.04
30	11.66	11.60	−.06

Because zeros are real securities, their prices and yields are subject to forces of supply and demand on an issue-by-issue basis. A zero will cheapen if investors and/or dealers are selling it. It will richen if investors and/or dealers are buying it. In contrast, spot obligations do not really exist. Their prices and yields are not determined directly in a marketplace but derivatively through the price structure of coupon bearing bonds.

As we will see, the yield on a particular zero can be less than the yield on a spot obligation of the same maturity. This occurs when investors value a single-payment claim of that maturity more highly when it is separated from other claims (when it is a zero) than when it is bundled together with claims of other maturities (when it is a spot obligation wrapped up in a bond).

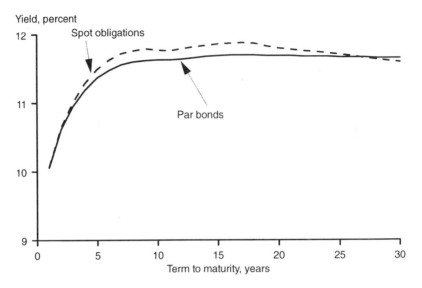

Figure 10.3
Yields on par bonds and spot obligations on January 24, 1984

The yield on a zero can also exceed the yield on a spot obligation of the same maturity. This occurs when investors prefer to hold liquid, readily tradable assets (such as Treasury bonds) and are willing to hold less liquid securities (such as zeros) only at premium yields. If dealers were unwilling to sell zeros at yields greater than spot rates in the face of investor demand for such liquidity, investors would buy more liquid whole bonds (i.e., bundles of spot obligations) with durations matched to their horizons and leave the dealers holding large inventories of zeros. The ability to substitute whole bonds for zeros on a matched duration basis exists in the short and intermediate sectors of the zeros market but it does not exist in the longer end of the zeros market.

Another difference between spot obligations and zeros is that yields on the former are derived from yields on par bonds, while zeros can be created from any bond. There have been instances where high coupon bonds trading "cheap to the (par bond yield) curve" were turned into zeros profitably even though every one of the resulting zeros had to be sold at a yield greater than the yield on a spot obligation of the same maturity.

Having said all this, however, it still makes sense to express the cheapness or dearness of zeros compared to bonds as a function of their spreads to spot yields because the latter best reflect the value placed on single payment Treasury obligations in the coupon market. That is, it is useful to use spot yields as an analytical bridge between zeros and bonds.

Table 10.3
Yields on spot obligations and zeros on May 17, 1983

Years to maturity	Spot yield	Zero yield	Spread
1	8.99%	9.52%	.53%
2	9.50	9.90	.40
3	9.80	10.20	.40
4	9.99	10.39	.40
5	10.16	10.56	.40
6	10.36	10.76	.40
7	10.46	10.81	.35
8	10.56	10.91	.35
9	10.55	10.90	.35
10	10.58	10.88	.30
11	10.62	10.87	.25
12	10.69	10.79	.10
13	10.78	10.78	.0
14	10.89	10.69	−.20
15	10.99	10.59	−.40
16	11.06	10.56	−.50
17	11.09	10.49	−.60
18	11.09	10.49	−.60
19	11.05	10.45	−.60
20	10.98	10.38	−.60
21	10.90	10.40	−.50
22	10.81	10.41	−.40

Two Illustrations

Table 10.3 and figure 10.4 show yields on a selected group of zeros on May 17, 1983, and also show yields on comparable maturity spot obligations on the same day. Two facts are readily apparent.

First, zeros traded cheap to the spot curve for maturities out to 12 years. Investors appeared unwilling to hold less liquid zeros except at yield premiums to Treasuries. In the absence of a sufficient premium, they would have preferred to hold whole bonds of a comparable duration. To get some idea of the size of the yield premiums, table 10.4 shows yields on May 17, 1983, on recently issued Treasury bonds and also shows zero yields on a matched duration basis. Note that the yield premiums on the zeros are somewhat smaller for the longer maturities, where the rebalancing costs of maintaining a match between duration and investment horizon are more significant. Note also that investors with horizons beyond 10 years could not substitute matched duration Treasuries for zeros because there were no Treasuries with such long durations.

The second interesting aspect of figure 10.4 is that zeros traded *expensive* to the spot curve for maturities beyond 13 years. The negative spread

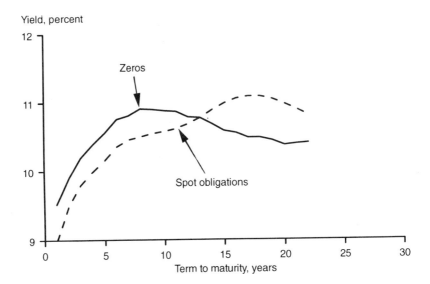

Figure 10.4
Yields on spot obligations and zeros on May 17, 1983

Table 10.4
Yields on active treasury issues and matched duration zeros on May 17, 1983

Active treasury issues			Matched duration zero yield	Spread
Maturity	Duration	Yield		
2 yr	1.8 yr	9.48%	9.89%	.41%
3	2.7	9.64	10.12	.48
4	3.3	9.88	10.29	.41
5	4.0	9.99	10.38	.39
7	5.0	10.33	10.61	.28
10	6.5	10.40	10.83	.43
20	8.5	10.73	10.88	.15
30	9.5	10.56	10.87	.31

indicates that investors were willing to hold long-term single-payment securities at yields lower than the yields placed on long-term spot obligations bundled up in a bond together with short and intermediate-term spot obligations. More generally, investors were willing to "pay up" to have the long-term cash flows on a bond explicitly unbundled from the bond's shorter dated cash flows. This corresponds to the observation derived from figure 10.2 that investors valued very long-term cash flows more highly than intermediate term cash flows on May 17, 1983.

Table 10.5 and figure 10.5 show yields on zeros and spot obligations on January 24, 1984. As was the case in May 1983, shorter zeros traded at a

Table 10.5
Yields on spot obligations and zeros on January 24, 1984

Years to maturity	Spot yield	Zero yield	Spread
1	10.07%	10.37%	.30%
2	10.65	10.92	.27
3	11.01	11.26	.25
4	11.29	11.49	.20
5	11.49	11.66	.17
6	11.63	11.78	.15
7	11.72	11.86	.14
8	11.76	11.88	.12
9	11.79	11.88	.09
10	11.77	11.82	.05
11	11.76	11.76	.0
12	11.79	11.74	−.05
13	11.82	11.72	−.10
14	11.84	11.71	−.13
15	11.86	11.69	−.17
16	11.87	11.67	−.20
17	11.88	11.68	−.20
18	11.87	11.65	−.22
19	11.83	11.61	−.22
20	11.80	11.55	−.25
21	11.78	11.50	−.28
22	11.76	11.48	−.28

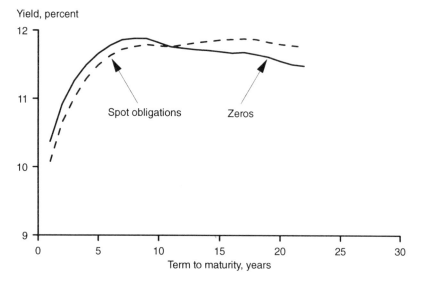

Figure 10.5
Yields on spot obligations and zeros on January 24, 1984

positive spread over spot yields and longer zeros traded at a negative spread. Moreover the spot curve and the zero curve intersect at about the same maturity (around 12 years) in both cases.

The striking difference between the structure of yield spreads on the two dates is the narrowing of zero yields over spot yields in the shorter maturities and the closing of zero yields to spot yields in the longer maturities. More particularly, the two yield curves converged between May 1983 and January 1984 in both their short and long ends.

There are two related reasons for the increase in long-term zero yields relative to long-term spot yields. First, a large quantity of long-term bonds were converted into zeros during the fall and early winter of 1983. The resulting supply of long-dated zeros (from the principal obligations of the stripped bonds) led to a cheapening of those zeros relative to spot yields. Second, as noted above, by January 1984 the long end of the spot curve had flattened from the negative slope prevailing in May 1983, indicating that investors placed a lower relative value on very long-term single-payment obligations. They were also less willing to pay up to have such obligations separated from shorter dated obligations. Thus, for both supply and demand reasons, it is understandable why zeros cheapened relative to spot claims in the long end of the yield curve in the second half of 1983.

The reason for the reduction in short-term zero yields compared to spot yields between May 1983 and January, 1984 is also grounded in changes in both supply and demand. On the supply side, high coupon bonds maturing in 1988 through 1992 that had previously traded cheap to the current coupon yield curve became less cheap and became uneconomical to strip. This shut off the supply of zeros created from the principal obligations of those bonds. The only zeros with maturities shorter than the year 2000 produced in the fall of 1983 were from the coupon obligations of 20- and 30-year bonds. On the demand side, investors became increasingly willing to hold shorter maturity zeros (as the total outstanding stock increased and market liquidity improved) and hence demanded smaller yield premiums.

III BOND PORTFOLIO MANAGEMENT WHEN THE SHAPE OF THE YIELD CURVE CHANGES

If only the level and not the shape of the yield curve could change, bond portfolio management would be largely a matter of choosing the duration of a portfolio in light of the existing level and shape of the curve, an investor's expectations of prospective shifts in the level of the curve, and his or her investment horizon. For example, an investor might choose a duration in excess of her horizon (and thus choose to bear market risk) if she expected interest rates to fall or if she expected rates to remain unchanged and the curve had a positive slope. Characteristics of a portfolio other than its duration would be largely irrelevant, although an investor might be expected to favor relatively cheap bonds and to avoid relatively expensive securities.

In fact, however, the yield curve does change shape, sometimes quite dramatically. This gives rise to investment opportunities beyond simply mismatching the duration of a portfolio relative to an investor's horizon. It also creates difficulties in identifying immunizing bond portfolios.

Chapters 11 through 15 address topics in fixed income investing associated with change in the shape of the yield curve. Chapter 11 examines the construction of bond positions where an investor seeks to profit from a prospective change in the *difference* between the yields on two bonds rather than from a change in the levels of the bond yields. Chapter 12 examines the related matter of cross-hedging bonds of different maturities. It distinguishes between hedge positions constructed to minimize risk and spread positions constructed to assume a particular type of risk, such as the risk of change in the slope or curvature of the yield curve.

Chapter 13 offers a technical appraisal of the problem of computing the yield on a portfolio of bonds from the yields on the bonds in the portfolio. The results of that analysis are used in the two following chapters.

Chapter 14 explores the construction of bond positions where an investor replaces one bond with a balanced position in a shorter maturity bond and a longer maturity bond. Although it is not uncommon to hear the claim that such a butterfly trade leaves risk unchanged (e.g., because it leaves duration unchanged), we show that in fact it increases the risk of loss due to a steepening of the yield curve.

Last, chapter 15 considers the problem of generalizing the concepts of duration and immunization to account for change in the shape as well as the level of the yield curve and to account for a requirement to fund *multiple* future disbursements (where an investor does not have a well-defined investment horizon).

Yield Spread Trades: Weighting, Financing, and Applications

Investors in the government bond market commonly know what position to take if they expect interest rates to fall: They should own bonds with longer (rather than shorter) maturities and with lower (rather than higher) coupons. Conversely, if they expect rates to rise, they should own shorter maturity and higher coupon bonds.

There are, however, expectations of the prospective behavior of interest rates other than the simple view that rates will either rise or fall. An analyst may, for example, believe that a positively sloped yield curve will flatten and that the spread between yields on 2-year notes and 30-year bonds will narrow. Alternatively, he or she might believe that high coupon bonds will outperform low coupon bonds of a comparable maturity, possibly because of a change in tax laws or due to some market innovation such as bond stripping. These appraisals differ from the question of whether interest rates are likely to rise or fall because they involve changes in yield *spreads* rather than yield level.

In general, there is no analytical link between change in a particular yield spread and change in the general level of interest rates. The yield curve can flatten when rates are falling as well as rising (see chapter 16). In consequence it is not generally possible to act on a view of the prospective behavior of a yield spread by purchasing or selling a single security.

An investor with a view on the change in some yield spread will generally want to be both a buyer *and* a seller, buying the security that he believes will appreciate more (or depreciate less) and selling the security that he believes will appreciate less (or depreciate more). More particularly, he will want to construct his position so that he gains or loses *only* as a result of change in the specified spread and so that he has *no* risk exposure with respect to changes in the general level of interest rates. Such a position is commonly termed a "bond spread" because the investor has both a long position and a short position.

This chapter describes two aspects of bonds spreads. Section 11.1 shows how to construct a bond position to eliminate risk with respect to change in the level of interest rates while retaining risk with respect to change in the difference between two yields. Section 11.2 discusses the importance of financing costs.

Section 11.3 shifts focus from the technical aspects of bond spreads to their practical application. We first review some common types of spreads, such as yield curve trades and coupon spreads. We then comment on the applicability of spread trades for investors who cannot sell securities short and who cannot finance bond purchases with borrowed money. These

Written in June 1986 with Marcia Recktenwald.

restrictions have the effect of prohibiting a bond spread unless it can be executed as a swap, as a replacement of one bond by another bond.

11.1 Weighting a Bond Spread

Weighting a spread trade is a matter of deciding the quantity of bonds to be purchased relative to the quantity of bonds sold. The net value of the resulting position should not vary with change in the level of interest rates, but it does of course vary with change in the difference between the yields on the bonds bought and sold. This section describes how to weight a bond spread using the dollar value of a change in yield of one basis point. The appendix describes the more complicated, but no more accurate, weighting of a spread trade using duration.

Weighting with the Value of a Basis Point

Table 11.1 shows price and yield data for a variety of recently issued Treasury bonds on October 8, 1985. It also shows how the value of $1 million principal amount of each bond varied with a change of one basis point in the bond's yield.

Suppose that an investor believed the yield curve was going to flatten but that he had no strong feeling about whether this flattening would occur in an environment of rising or falling interest rates. Suppose further that he believed the flattening would lead to a decline in the 168 basis point yield spread between 2-year notes and 30-year bonds (168 basis points = 10.62% 30-year yield less 8.94% 2-year yield in table 11.1).

Based on his beliefs, the investor wants to buy 30-year bonds and sell 2-year notes, and he wants to execute the trades in quantities that leave

Table 11.1
Bond prices and yields on October 8, 1985, for settlement on October 9, 1985

Sector	Coupon	Maturity	Quoted price	Yield	Dollar value of one basis point[a]
2 yr	9%	9/30/1987	$100\frac{3}{32}$	8.94%	$177.54
3	$9\frac{1}{2}$	8/15/1988	$100\frac{16}{32}$	9.29	246.51
4	$9\frac{5}{8}$	6/30/1989	$99\frac{31}{32}$	9.63	307.04
5	$9\frac{5}{8}$	11/15/1990	$99\frac{5}{32}$	9.82	392.53
7	$10\frac{3}{8}$	7/15/1992	$100\frac{22}{32}$	10.22	481.88
10	$10\frac{1}{2}$	8/15/1995	$100\frac{28}{32}$	10.35	612.49
20	$10\frac{3}{4}$	8/15/2005	$99\frac{16}{32}$	10.80	809.09
30	$10\frac{5}{8}$	8/15/2015	100	10.62	897.97

a. Per $1 million principal amount.

him with no risk exposure with respect to change in the level of interest rates. Assume that he buys $1 million principal amount of the $10\frac{5}{8}\%$ bond of 8/15/2015. As shown in table 11.1, an increase (decrease) in yield of one basis point will decrease (increase) the value of that bond by $897.97 Assuming that he sells the 9% note of 9/30/1987 against his bond purchase, he needs to sell enough of the note so that an increase (decrease) in *its* yield of one basis point will increase (decrease) the value of his (short) 2-year position by exactly $897.97. Gains or losses on the 30-year bond will then be matched by losses or gains on the 2-year note whenever yields on the two securities change by the same amount, that is, whenever yields change without altering the 2-year/30-year yield spread.

Since the value of $1 million of the 2-year note changes by $177.54 for each basis point change in yield (see table 11.1), the investor needs to sell $5.06 million principal amount of the note against his bond purchase (5.06 = 897.97/177.54). He must sell more 2-year notes than the amount of 30-year bonds purchased because the value of a $1 million 2-year note is less sensitive to changes in interest rates than the value of a $1 million 30-year bond.

Table 11.2 shows the initial net value of the investor's note and bond position and the net value of the position for several possible ways in which interest rates can change. The net values are all negative because the value of the investor's short 2-year notes exceeds the value of his long 30-year bonds. Thus, establishing the spread position generates cash rather than uses cash. Conversely, liquidating the position uses cash because the funds needed to buy back the 2-year notes exceeds the amount of cash produced from sale of the 30-year bonds. Ignoring financing considerations, the spread position makes money if the net amount of cash needed to liquidate the position is less than the net amount of cash generated when the position was established.

Observe first in table 11.2 that the investor breaks even if yields on the two securities rise (case I) or fall (case II) by the same amount. The investor earns about $9 thousand if the yield curve flattens by 10 basis points, either because the bond yield falls (case III) or because the note yield rises (case IV). Conversely, the investor loses about $9 thousand if the yield curve steepens by 10 basis points, either because the bond yield rises (case V) or because the note yield falls (case VI).

These results, and similar computations for other possible changes in interest rates, show that being short $5.06 million 2-year notes against $1 million of 30-year bonds held long is the desired spread position for an anticipated flattening of the yield curve. In particular, the value of the position is approximately unchanged for equal changes in interest rates,

Table 11.2
Possible outcomes for a 2-year/30-year bond spread put on and taken off on October 8, 1985

Initial value		
Short	$5.06 million 9% of 9/30/1987, quoted at $100\frac{3}{32}$, to yield 8.945%	−5,064,744
Long	$1.00 million $10\frac{5}{8}$% of 8/15/2015, quoted at 100, to yield 10.622%	1,000,000
	Net value	−4,064,744
I. Value if both yields rise 10 basis points		
Short	$5.06 million 9% of 9/30/1987 9.045% yield, quoted at 99.9156	−5,055,729
Long	$1.00 million $10\frac{5}{8}$% of 8/15/2015 10.722% yield, quoted at 99.1064	991,064
	Net value	−4,064,665
	Change	+79
II. Value if both yields fall 10 basis points		
Short	$5.06 million 9% of 9/30/1987 8.845% yield, quoted at 100.2708	−5,073,704
Long	$1.00 million $10\frac{5}{8}$% of 8/15/2015 10.522% yield, quoted at 100.9046	1,009,046
	Net value	−4,064,658
	Change	+86
III. Value if bond yield falls 10 basis points		
Short	$5.06 million 9% of 9/30/1987 8.945% yield, quoted at 100.0938	−5,064,744
Long	$1.00 million $10\frac{5}{8}$% of 8/15/2015 10.522% yield, quoted at 100.9046	1,009,046
	Net value	−4,055,698
	Change	+9,046
IV. Value if note yield rises 10 basis points		
Short	$5.06 million 9% of 9/30/1987 9.045% yield, quoted at 99.9156	−5,055,729
Long	$1.00 million $10\frac{5}{8}$% of 8/15/2015 10.622% yield, quoted at 100	1,000,000
	Net value	−4,055,729
	Change	+9,015
V. Value if bond yield rises 10 basis points		
Short	$5.06 million 9% of 9/30/1987 8.945% yield, quoted at 100.0938	−5,064,744
Long	$1.00 million $10\frac{5}{8}$% of 8/15/2015 10.722% yield, quoted at 99.1064	991,064
	Net value	−4,073,680
	Change	−8,936
VI. Value if note yield falls 10 basis points		
Short	$5.06 million 9% of 9/30/1987 8.845% yield, quoted at 100.2708	−5,073,704
Long	$1.00 million $10\frac{5}{8}$% of 8/15/2015 10.622% yield, quoted at 100	1,000,000
	Net value	−4,073,704
	Change	−8,960

Note: Values exclude accrued interest.

the value of the position increases if the yield curve flattens as anticipated and the value falls if the curve steepens.

Scaling

It should be clear that what matters for weighting a bond spread is the relative rather than the absolute amounts of the bonds bought and sold. In the example above the investor would have sold $50.6 million of the 9% note of 1987 against buying $10 million 30-year bonds. Similarly he would have sold $101.2 million 2-year notes against buying $20 million 30-year bonds.

Although absolute amounts do not matter for weighting a spread position, they do matter for managing risk. An investor who is short $50.6 million 2-year notes against being long $10 million 30-year bonds has ten times as much risk exposure with respect to the 2-year/30-year yield spread as an investor who is short $5.06 million 2-year notes against being long $1 million 30-year bonds.

Summary

Using the value of a basis point to weight a bond spread leads to a simple rule: The ratio of the principal amounts of the bonds must equal the reciprocal of the ratio of the bonds' values of a basis point. For example, the ratio of the values of a basis point for a 2-year/30-year bond spread is, from table 11.1:

$$\frac{177.54}{897.97} = .1977$$

The reciprocal of this ratio is 5.06. The principal amounts of the 2-year note and 30-year bond must therefore be in the ratio of 5.06 to 1.

It should be noted that a weighting ratio is not necessarily fixed for the life of any two bonds. Table 11.3 shows data similar to table 11.1 for December 26, 1985, when almost three months had passed and yields had declined more than 100 basis points. The ratio of the values of a basis point for the 9% note of 1987 and the $10\frac{5}{8}$% bond of 2015 is $162.51/1092.53 = .1487$, so the relative weighting of a spread position in those securities was 6.73 to 1 on December 26 $(6.73 = 1./.1487)$. Thus, between early October and late December 1985, the weighting ratio rose from 5.06 to 6.73. This demonstrates that the weighting of a spread position has to be adjusted from time to time to maintain the invariance of the value of the position with respect to change in the level of interest rates.

Table 11.3
Bond prices and yields on December 26, 1985, for settlement on December 27, 1985

Coupon	Maturity	Quoted price	Yield	Dollar value of one basis point[a]
9%	9/30/1987	$101\frac{21}{32}$	7.95%	$ 162.51
$9\frac{1}{2}$	8/15/1988	103	8.20	236.65
$9\frac{5}{8}$	6/30/1989	$103\frac{16}{32}$	8.45	304.11
$9\frac{5}{8}$	11/15/1990	$103\frac{29}{32}$	8.61	402.16
$10\frac{3}{8}$	7/15/1992	$107\frac{6}{32}$	8.90	510.13
$10\frac{1}{2}$	8/15/1995	$108\frac{31}{32}$	9.08	672.33
$10\frac{3}{4}$	8/15/2005	$110\frac{30}{32}$	9.51	956.96
$10\frac{5}{8}$	8/15/2015	$112\frac{2}{32}$	9.41	1092.53

a. Per $1 million principal amount.

11.2 Financing Bond Spreads

At this point it might appear that an investor who has properly weighted a spread position has only to wait until the yield spread moves in the desired direction to unwind the trade and take his profits—or to wait until it moves in the opposite direction and take his losses. However, this is true only if the spread changes quickly and the position is liquidated promptly. In cases where a position is held for days and weeks, financing income and expenses can add to or detract from the profitability of the position.

This section describes the importance of financing for bond spreads. We present first a simple analysis that is appropriate if the bonds involved in a spread position are trading close to par and if the bonds held long and short can be financed on comparable terms. The second half of the section provides a more complete analysis for premium and discount bonds and for bonds financed on different terms.

A Simple Analysis

Consider again the 2-year/30-year bond spread described in section 11.1. That position consists of

• $1 million principal amount of the $10\frac{5}{8}\%$ bond of 8/15/2015 held long at a quoted price of 100.

• $5.06 million principal amount of the 9% note of 9/30/1987 held short at a quoted price of $100\frac{3}{32}$.

Assume the 30-year bond can be financed in the market for repurchase agreements (the RP market) at $7\frac{1}{2}\%$ and that the 2-year note can be borrowed in the market for reverse repurchase agreements on special collateral (the specials market) by accepting a rate of $7\frac{1}{2}\%$ on funds lent against the notes borrowed. (This is equivalent to assuming the long and short positions can both be financed at $7\frac{1}{2}\%$.)

We want to calculate how the value of the spread position changes over an interval of one day, net of financing income and costs, assuming that *bond yields* do not change. Since both securities are priced close to their principal value, this is equivalent to assuming that quoted *bond prices* do not change.

There are four components to the financing calculation:

1. The increase in the value of the bonds held long due to accretion of accrued interest.

2. The decrease in the value of the notes held short due to accretion of accrued interest.

3. The cost of financing the bonds held long in the RP market.

4. The income from financing the notes held short in the specials market.

To a good approximation the accrued interest on a note or bond changes by 1/365 times its coupon rate each day. (For a more careful treatment of accrued interest, see chapter 1.) Thus the daily accretion of accrued interest on the 2-year note and 30-year bond are

2-year note:

$$\frac{1}{365} \cdot 9\% \cdot \$5.06 \text{ million} = \$1,247.67 \text{ per day}$$

30-year bond:

$$\frac{1}{365} \cdot 10.625\% \cdot \$1 \text{ million} = \$291.10 \text{ per day}$$

The cost of financing the bond position at an RP rate of $7\frac{1}{2}\%$ is

$$\frac{1}{360} \cdot 7.5\% \cdot \$1 \text{ million} = \$208.33 \text{ per day}$$

The income from financing the note position at a specials rate of $7\frac{1}{2}\%$ is

$$\frac{1}{360} \cdot 7.5\% \cdot \$5.06 \text{ million} = \$1,054.17 \text{ per day}$$

Note that the RP rate and the specials rate both assume a 360-day year, as is the convention in the money markets.

Adding together the effects of accretion of accrued interest and the costs and income of financing gives a net financing cost of $110.73 per day on the spread position:

$-\$1,247.67$	accretion of accrued interest on the short 2-year notes
291.10	accretion of accrued interest on the long 30-year bond
-208.33	cost of financing the 30-year bond
$\underline{1,054.17}$	income from financing the 2-year notes
$-\$110.73$	net financing cost

Holding the position for one week produces a financing loss of $775.11 ($775.11 = 7 days times $110.73 per day).

Table 11.2 demonstrated that a 10 basis point change in the 2-year/30-year yield spread was worth about $9,000, so a 1 basis point change is worth about $900.00 This implies that the spread position will show a net loss unless the 2-year/30-year yield spread narrows by at least one basis point per week.

What "Causes" the Financing Loss?

The financing loss on the 2-year/30-year bond spread arises from the relative costs of carry on the securities held long and short. To a rough approximation, the carry on the 30-year bond is the difference between the bond's coupon ($10\frac{5}{8}\%$) and the RP rate ($7\frac{1}{2}\%$), or 312 basis points. (This is an overstatement of carry because the coupon rate is based on a 365-day year while the RP rate is based on a 360-day year.) Similarly the carry on the 2-year note is 150 basis points (150 basis points = 9% coupon less $7\frac{1}{2}\%$ specials rate). Since the spread position consists of $1 million of the 30-year bond held long and $5.06 million of the 2-year note held short, the net carry is about -447 basis points per $1 million of the 30-year bond ($-447 = \$1$ million 30-year bond times 312 basis points less $5.06 million 2-year note times 150 basis points). More particularly, the spread loses more from the negative carry on the $5.06 million 2-year notes held short than it earns from the positive carry on the $1 million 30-year bonds held long.

This result on the relative costs of carry is a general characteristic of a curve flattening spread trade (where more shorter maturity bonds must be held short than the quantity of longer maturity bonds held long) when the yield curve is positively sloped and financing rates are lower than bond yields. Conversely, carry usually makes a positive contribution to a curve *steepening* bond spread (where shorter maturity bonds are held long against a short position in longer bonds) when financing rates are lower than bond yields.

A More Careful Analysis

There are three problems with the simple analysis of financing presented above. First, the rate on money lent in the specials market is often lower than the cost of financing a long position in the RP market. This reduces the income received from financing the short side of a bond spread and increases net financing costs. Second, if a bond is priced at a substantial premium or discount the assumption of an unchanged yield is *not* equivalent to the assumption of an unchanged price. The quoted price of a discount bond will appreciate over time if the bond's yield remains unchanged and the quoted price of a premium bond will depreciate if its yield remains unchanged. This so-called "pull to par" should be included in the calculation of net financing costs. Finally, the simple analysis assumed that only the principal amount of the bonds had to be financed. It ignored some of the cost of financing a premium bond in the RP market, and it ignored financing of accrued interest.

To appreciate the significance of these finer points of financing, consider a spread position where an investor buys the $12\frac{5}{8}\%$ note of 11/15/1987 against selling a weighted amount of the $7\frac{5}{8}\%$ note of 11/15/1987 on October 8, 1985, for settlement on October 9. The prices, yields, values of a basis point, and financing rates for these bonds are shown in the first four lines of table 11.4. Note that the financing rate for the $12\frac{5}{8}\%$ note held long is the RP rate, while the financing rate for the $7\frac{5}{8}\%$ note held short is a lower specials rate.

From the data in line 3 of table 11.4, the relative weighting on the spread trade is 1.052 to 1. That is, assuming that the investor buys \$10 million principal amount of the $12\frac{5}{8}\%$ note, he will sell \$10.52 million

Table 11.4
Bond prices and yields on October 8, 1985

	$7\frac{5}{8}\%$ note of 11/15/1987	$12\frac{5}{8}\%$ note of 11/15/1987
1. Quoted price (Oct. 9 settlement)	$98\frac{1}{32}$	$106\frac{23}{32}$
2. Yield (Oct. 9 settlement)	8.663%	9.030%
3. Value of one basis point	\$184.84	\$194.47
4. Financing rate	7% (specials)	$7\frac{1}{2}\%$ (RP)
5. Implied quoted price (Oct. 10 settlement)	98.0344 (at 8.663% yield)	106.7113 (at 9.030% yield)
6. Accrued interest (Oct. 9 settlement)	3.0458	5.0431
7. Accrued interest (Oct. 10 settlement)	3.0660	5.0775

principal amount of the $7\frac{5}{8}\%$ note. He has to sell a bit more of the lower coupon note because the dollar value of one basis point is lower for that note.

To compute the daily net financing cost on the spread position, we have to compute the change in the values of the bonds at unchanged yields over a one day interval, and we have to compute the expense and income of financing for one day the long and short bond positions in the RP and specials markets, respectively.

Change in Value at an Unchanged Yield

The change in the value of a bond from one day to the next at an unchanged yield is the sum of (1) the accretion in accrued interest on the bond and (2) the bond's pull to par.

Comparing lines 6 and 7 in table 11.4 shows that the accretions in accrued interest from October 9 settlement to October 10 settlement are

$7\frac{5}{8}\%$ note: .0202% of principal amount
   .0202 = 3.0660 (10/10 settlement) − 3.0458
      (10/9 settlement)

$12\frac{5}{8}\%$ note: .0344% of principal amount
   .0344 = 5.0775 (10/10 settlement) − 5.0431
      (10/9 settlement)

These accretions are essentially identical to what would be calculated from the simple analysis whereby the annual coupon on the bond is divided by 365.

Comparing lines 1 and 5 in table 11.4, we see that the changes in quoted price assuming an unchanged yield from October 9 settlement to October 10 settlement are

$7\frac{5}{8}\%$ note: +.0032% of principal amount
   .0032 = 98.0344 (10/10 settlement) − $98\frac{1}{32}$
      (10/9 settlement)

$12\frac{5}{8}\%$ note: −.0075% of principal amount
   −.0075 = 106.7113 (10/10 settlement) − $106\frac{23}{32}$
      (10/9 settlement)

Note that the low coupon discount bond shows a positive pull to par, while the high coupon premium bond shows a negative pull to par. Both of these changes in quoted price were ignored in the simple analysis.

The daily net changes in value for the two bond positions at unchanged yields are

$7\frac{5}{8}\%$ note: $-\$2,462$

$\qquad -\$2,462 = -\$10.52 \text{ million} \cdot (.0202 + .0032)\%$

$12\frac{5}{8}\%$ note: $\$2,690$

$\qquad \$2,690 = \$10 \text{ million} \cdot (.0344 - .0075)\%$

These changes in value include accretion of accrued interest and pull to par.

Financing Longs and Shorts

The cost of financing $\$10$ million principal amount of the $12\frac{5}{8}\%$ note at a $7\frac{1}{2}\%$ RP rate for one day is

$$\frac{1}{360} \cdot 7\frac{1}{2}\% \cdot \$10 \text{ million} \cdot (106\frac{23}{32} + 5.0431) = \$2,328$$

This calculation assumes the full market value of the note, including the quoted premium and accrued interest, must be financed instead of just the $\$10$ million principal amount of the note as in the simple analysis.

The income from financing a short position in $\$10.52$ million of the $7\frac{5}{8}\%$ note at a specials rate of 7% for one day is

$$\frac{1}{360} \cdot 7\% \cdot \$10.52 \text{ million} \cdot (98\frac{1}{32} + 3.0458) = \$2,067$$

This income is also based on the market value of the note, including accrued interest, rather than on the principal amount of the note.

Net Financing Cost

The net financing cost for the bond spread is a loss of $\$33$ per day:

$-\$2,462$ accretion of accrued interest and pull to par on $7\frac{5}{8}\%$ note held short,

$2,690$ accretion of accrued interest and pull to par on $12\frac{5}{8}\%$ note held long

$-2,328$ financing expense on $12\frac{5}{8}\%$ note

$\underline{2,067}$ financing income on $7\frac{5}{8}\%$ note

$\$-33$ net financing cost

The simple analysis would imply a net financing income of $\$1,224$ per day. This gross overstatement results from ignoring losses due to pull to par on the two notes and the greater cost of financing the premium note.

11.3 Applications

Having analyzed the economics of weighting and financing a bond spread, we are now ready to examine some applications of spread trading. We first describe several common spreads and then look at the applicability of spreading for investors who can neither sell bonds short nor finance bonds held long.

Categories of Bond Spreads

A bond spread has two main characteristics: (1) its value *should not* vary with change in the general level of interest rates and (2) its value *should* vary with change in a specified yield spread. Many types of bond positions have these characteristics.

Yield Curve Trades

Perhaps the most common bond spread is a yield curve trade where an investor anticipates a flattening or steepening of the curve. If he anticipates a flattening, he will buy longer maturity bonds against selling a weighted amount of shorter maturity issues. Conversely, if he anticipates a steepening of the curve, he will buy shorter bonds against selling a weighted amount of longer-term debt.

One of the most important aspects of a yield curve trade is identifying the sectors of the curve to buy and sell. An investor may, for example, deal in 7-year notes and 30-year bonds and thereby span the maturities held by pension funds and other similar investors. Alternatively, he may deal in 2-year notes and 5-year notes (spanning the maturities commonly held by corporations for investment purposes) or he may deal in 3-month Treasury bills and 1-year bills (thereby spanning the money market curve). At the extreme he can span the entire yield curve by dealing in 3-month Treasury bills and 30-year bonds.

Yield spreads within various segments of the yield curve need not move in parallel. This fact is illustrated by the data in table 11.5, showing yields and yield spreads on March 18, July 5, and December 17, 1985. The first date reflects the lows of the Treasury market in 1985, the middle date reflects the highs of the bill market for the year, and the last date reflects the highs for the year in longer maturity notes and bonds.

As shown in the upper panel of table 11.5, yields generally declined from March 18 to July 5. The decline was greatest for shorter maturity bonds, leading to a steepening of the bond yield curve. However, the largest steepening was not in the front end of the curve but in the long end, where the 7-year/30-year yield spread widened from $-.01\%$ to $.48\%$. Perversely,

Table 11.5
Yield levels and yield spreads on three dates in 1985

	A. Yield levels and changes in yield levels						
	3-mn bill	1-year bill	2-year note	5-year note	7-year note	10-year note	30-year bond
1. 3/18/1985	8.95%	10.06%	10.87%	11.72%	11.97%	12.00%	11.96%
2. 7/ 5/1985[a]	6.98 (−1.97)	7.37 (−2.69)	8.36 (−2.51)	9.31 (−2.41)	9.77 (−2.20)	9.94 (−2.06)	10.25 (−1.71)
3. 12/17/1985[a]	7.24 (+0.26)	7.49 (+0.12)	7.94 (−0.42)	8.50 (−0.81)	8.86 (−0.91)	9.02 (−0.92)	9.35 (−0.90)
4. Change, 3/18–12/17	−1.71	−2.57	−2.93	−3.22	−3.11	−2.98	−2.61

	B. Yield spreads and changes in yield spreads				
	3 mn/1 yr	1 yr/2 yr	2 yr/5 yr	5 yr/7 yr	7 yr/30 yr
5. 3/18/1985	1.11%	+0.81%	+0.85%	+0.25%	−0.01%
6. 7/ 5/1985[a]	0.39 (−0.72)	0.99 (+0.18)	0.95 (+0.10)	0.46 (+0.21)	0.48 (+0.49)
7. 12/17/1985[a]	0.25 (−0.14)	0.45 (−0.54)	0.56 (−.39)	0.36 (−.10)	0.49 (+0.01)
8. Change, 3/18–12/17	−0.86	−0.36	−0.29	+0.11	+0.50

a. Change from preceding date in parentheses.

while the bond curve was getting steeper, the bill curve actually flattened (the first columns of lines 5 and 6 show the 3-month/1-year yield spread falling from 1.11% to .39%.

From July 5 to December 17 the yield curve flattened as bond yields (but not bill yields) continued to fall. However, this flattening occurred primarily in the 1-year to 5-year segment of the curve. The 1-year/5-year yield spread fell from 1.94% to 1.01% but the 7-year/30-year yield spread was virtually unchanged over the interval.

This brief historical review suggests that an investor must identify with some care the part of the curve within which he or she expects to see a flattening or steepening. It is entirely possible that one segment of the curve will flatten while another segment is unchanged or even steepening.

Curvature Trades

Having suggested that yield spreads within different segments of the yield curve can behave differently, we can now describe a more exotic category of yield curve trade. Consider an investor who believes that 4-year notes will outperform, on a relative basis, both 3-year notes and 5-year notes. That is, he believes the 3-year/4-year yield spread will narrow *relative* to the 4-year/5-year spread, or that the *curvature* of the yield curve in the 4-year sector will decrease.

In this case the investor will want to buy 4-year notes against selling equal weighted amounts of 3-year and 5-year notes. Suppose, for example, that he buys $10 million principal amount of 4-year notes. Conceptually, he will allocate $5 million principal amount of the notes against a sale of a weighted amount of 3-year notes, and he will allocate the other $5 million principal amount against the sale of a weighted amount of 5-year notes.

The data in table 11.5 provide a nice example of a successful curvature trade. Over the course of the three dates shown in the table, the 2-year/5-year spread and the 5-year/10-year spread behaved as follows:

	2 year/5 year	5 year/10 year	Difference
3/18/1985	85 bp	28 bp	57 bp
7/ 5/1985	95	63	32
12/17/1985	56	52	4

Over both the March 18 to July 5 interval and the July 5 to December 17 interval, an investor would have made money, before financing costs, if he bought 5-year notes against selling equal weighted amounts of 2-year notes and 10-year notes. What is perhaps surprising is that this "curvature decreasing" trade worked while the yield curve was steepening in both the 2-year/5-year sector and the 5-year/10-year sector from March 18 to July 5, *and* while the yield curve was flattening in both sectors from July 5 to December 17. This happened because 5-year notes dramatically outperformed 10-year notes during the first interval (even though they slightly underperformed 2-year notes) and because they dramatically outperformed 2-year notes during the second interval (even though they slightly underperformed 10-year notes during that interval.).

Coupon Spreads

Although less common than yield curve spreads, coupon spreads are a legitimate category of spread trading. They generally involve bonds of comparable maturity (or duration), but with very different coupon rates.

Table 11.6 illustrates the behavior of several coupon spreads over the interval from March 18, 1985, to December 17, 1985, when yields fell by 250 to 300 basis points. Note that in every case but one, the low coupon bond outperformed the higher coupon bond during the rally. This can be explained by observing that more bonds become high coupon bonds when the bond market rallies. The increased supply tends to cheapen those bonds relative to bonds with more current coupons (see chapter 7).

Table 11.6
Changes in yields on high and low coupon Treasury bonds between March 18 and December 17, 1985

Coupon	Maturity	Yield on 3/18/85	Yield on 12/17/85	Change
1. 14%	5/15/1987	11.01%	7.83%	−3.18%
10	2/28/1987	10.89	7.81	−3.08
2. 14⅜	4/15/1989	11.72	8.50	−3.22
11¼	5/15/1989	11.68	8.41	−3.27
3. 12⅝	8/15/1994	12.15	9.15	−3.00
8¾	8/15/1994	12.00	8.80	−3.20
4. 13¾	8/15/2004	12.13	9.63	−2.50
11⅝	11/15/2004	12.19	9.53	−2.66

The exception to the above observation is the first example in table 11.6, where a high coupon short maturity bond outperformed a lower coupon bond. This exception occurred as a result of strong demand for high coupon bonds by short and intermediate maturity fixed income mutual funds who were willing to incur capital losses on premium bonds in order to book the high interest income from those bonds.

Bond Spreading for Investors Who Have Restrictions on Their Activities

We have assumed, up to this point, the absence of any restrictions on bond spreading. In particular, we have assumed an investor can sell bonds short, and we have assumed he can finance bond purchases in the RP market. However, many institutional investors can neither sell bonds short nor finance bonds with borrowed money. These restrictions limit, but do not eliminate, the applicability of bond spreading.

The effect of a restriction on short sales is easy to appreciate. An investor can only sell what he already owns if he cannot sell short. Thus, if he owns only 2-year notes, he will be unable to take advantage of an anticipated widening of the 2-year/5-year yield spread (which would require him to sell 5-year notes and buy 2-year notes). He can, however, take advantage of an anticipated narrowing of the same spread (which would require him to sell his 2-year notes and replace them with a weighted amount of 5-year notes).

For an investor who cannot sell short, bond spreading is tantamount to bond *swapping*. Instead of selling a bond short against the purchase of a weighted amount of some other bond, he will sell a bond that he already owns and replace it with a weighted amount of the second bond. The resulting swap can be analyzed with the same methodology as a conventional bond spread.

The consequences of a restriction on financing is only a bit more difficult to appreciate. As described in section 11.1, every spread trade involves a sale and a purchase. If the cash received from the sale exceeds the cash needed for the purchase, the spread position as a whole generates cash. If the cash needed for the purchase exceeds the cash received from the sale, the spread uses cash.

If an investor cannot finance bonds in the RP market, he will be unable to execute a bond spread, or bond swap, that uses cash (unless of course he has cash available from some other source). Suppose, for example, that an investor owns $20 million market value 30-year bonds and believes the yield curve will steepen but doesn't have any feeling about whether interest rates are going up or down. He would like to sell his bonds and swap into a weighted amount of, say 7-year notes. Unless he can borrow cash, however, he will be unable to switch into those notes on a weighted basis because he would have to invest more than $20 million in the notes. This suggests that institutional investors will generally be blocked from shortening up on the yield curve *on a weighted basis* (in anticipation of the curve steepening) but that they can extend on the curve on a weighted basis (in anticipation of the curve flattening).

11.4   Conclusions

This chapter has described some technical aspects and practical applications of bond spreads. A spread position can be summarized by two characteristics: the net value of the position should not vary with change in the level of interest rates, and it should vary with change in a specified yield spread. These characteristics are obtained by proper weighting, as discussed in section 11.1.

Section 11.2 examined the financing of a spread position. If a position is held for only a short time, financing usually has an insignificant effect on the profit or loss from the position. Financing can, however, become important if a spread position is held for several weeks while an investor waits for an anticipated change in the yield curve. Depending on the specific spread, financing can be either helpful or harmful to the investor's interests.

The last section of the chapter briefly described some common categories of bond spreads and showed how bond spreading can be applied, albeit in a limited fashion, by investors who cannot sell short and who cannot finance bond purchases with borrowed money.

11.5   Appendix: Using Duration to Weight a Bond Spread

Section 1 of this paper showed how to weight a bond spread using the dollar value of a basis point. This appendix examines a second technique for weighting a spread position; with duration. We first describe duration weighting and then relate it to weighting with the dollar value of a basis point.

Weighting with Duration

There is a simple rule for weighting a spread using duration: the product of bond duration and bond value should be the same for both sides of the spread position.

This rule can be illustrated with the 2-year/30-year bond spread described in section 11.1. Table 11.7 shows data on bond prices and yields from October 8, 1985. It also shows for each bond the dollar value of a basis point and the duration of the bond. We will use the duration data in the table to calculate the quantity of the 9% notes of 9/30/1987 which should be sold against a long position in $1 million principal amount of the $10\frac{5}{8}\%$ bonds of 8/15/2015.

The market value of $1 million of the 30 year bond is, from table 11.7,

$$\$1 \text{ million} \cdot (100 + 1.6168) = \$1.016168 \text{ million}$$

Observe that this value includes accrued interest on the bond as well as the quoted price of the bond. Multiplying this value by the bond's duration of 9.321 years gives a product of 9.471702. We must therefore sell enough 2-year notes so that the product of the market value of the notes sold and the duration of the 2-year note is 9.471702.

Table 11.7
Bond prices and yields on October 8, 1985, for settlement on October 9, 1985

Coupon	Maturity	Quoted price	Yield	Dollar value of one basis point	Accrued interest	Duration
9%	9/30/1987	$100\frac{3}{32}$	8.94%	$177.54	.2473	1.846 yrs
$9\frac{1}{2}$	8/15/1988	$100\frac{16}{32}$	9.29	246.51	1.4457	2.529
$9\frac{5}{8}$	6/30/1989	$99\frac{31}{32}$	9.63	307.04	2.6416	3.135
$9\frac{5}{8}$	11/15/1990	$99\frac{5}{32}$	9.82	392.53	.9677	4.113
$10\frac{3}{8}$	7/15/1992	$100\frac{22}{32}$	10.22	481.88	2.8254	4.899
$10\frac{1}{2}$	8/15/1995	$100\frac{28}{32}$	10.35	612.49	1.5978	6.288
$10\frac{3}{4}$	8/15/2005	$99\frac{16}{32}$	10.80	809.09	2.9425	8.326
$10\frac{5}{8}$	8/15/2015	100	10.62	897.97	1.6168	9.321

From table 11.7 the duration of the 2-year note is 1.846 years. It follows that the market value of an appropriately weighted amount of the notes is \$5.130933 million (\$5.130933 = 9.471702/1.846). The principal amount of notes with this value is \$5.11 million (\$5.11 = \$5.130933 million market value divided by a total price of 100.3411, where $100.3411 = 100\frac{3}{32}$ quoted price plus .2473 accrued interest). Observe that this is very nearly the same as the \$5.06 million principal amount of 2-year notes that we calculated in section 11.1 using the dollar value of a basis point.

The Difference between Weighting with Duration and Weighting with the Value of a Basis Point

There are two differences between weighting a bond spread with duration versus the value of a basis point. First, using the value of a basis point gives a weighting ratio directly in terms of principal amounts. Duration weighting, on the other hand, gives a weighting ratio in terms of market values.

The second difference between the two methods is analytical and can be appreciated by examining the definition of duration. The duration D of a bond is related to the value of a basis point F on the same bond by the equation:

$$D = \frac{F \cdot (1 + \frac{1}{2}R)}{P + A} \tag{A11.1}$$

where P is the price of the bond, A is the accrued interest, and R is the yield on the bond, compounded semi-annually. Thus, the duration of the 2-year note in table 11.7 is

$$D = \frac{177.54 \cdot (1 + \frac{1}{2}(.0894))}{100\frac{3}{32} + .2473}$$

$$= 1.84 \text{ yr.}$$

Section 11.1 demonstrated that using the value of a basis point to weight a bond spread leads to the rule that the ratio of the principal amounts of the bonds should equal the reciprocal of the values of a basis point. Algebraically this is equivalent to

$$\frac{Q_1}{Q_2} = \frac{F_2}{F_1} \tag{A11.2}$$

where Q_i is the principal amount of bond i and F_i is the value of a basis point for bond i.

From equation (A11.1) we have

$$F_i = \frac{D_i \cdot (P_i + A_i)}{1 + \frac{1}{2}R_i} \tag{A11.3}$$

where D_i is the duration of bond i, P_i is the quoted price, A_i the accrued interest, and R_i the yield. Substituting this expression for each of the F's in equation (A11.2) gives

$$\frac{Q_1}{Q_2} = \frac{D_2 \cdot (P_2 + A_2)(1 + \frac{1}{2}R_1)}{D_1 \cdot (P_1 + A_1)(1 + \frac{1}{2}R_2)} \tag{A11.4}$$

Equation (A11.4) is quite similar to the rule for duration weighting of a spread trade:

$$Q_1 \cdot (P_1 + A_1) \cdot D_1 = Q_2 \cdot (P_2 + A_2) \cdot D_2 \tag{A11.5}$$

or

$$\frac{Q_1}{Q_2} = \frac{D_2 \cdot (P_2 + A_2)}{D_1 \cdot (P_1 + A_1)} \tag{A11.6}$$

The only difference is due to the ratio of the discount factors in equation (A11.4). This implies that the two weighting techniques will give identical results if the yields on the two bonds are the same and will give quite similar results if the yields are not too dissimilar.

12 Hedging in the Treasury Bond Market: Implications of Imperfect Correlation and Nonuniform Volatility of Yield Changes for the Size of an Optimal Hedge

"Hedging" is a term commonly used in the Treasury bond market. Broadly stated, a hedge is a securities position that reduces uncertainty about prospective net worth. An investor might, for example, hedge a long position in 20-year bonds by selling 30-year bonds short. Losses (due to rising interest rates) on the 20-year bonds would then be offset by gains on the short position, and vice versa, so the investor's future net worth would be relatively more predictable.

Although this description of hedging sounds reasonable it is too vague to be useful. In particular, it fails to specify how the size of a hedge is determined. At one extreme, a short position in $1 million of 30-year bonds is inadequate to hedge $50 million of 20-year bonds. On the other hand, $250 million of 30-year bonds is "too much" of a hedge. While it is reasonable to believe that the correct hedge lies between these extremes, establishing its precise size requires some analysis.

This chapter describes the quantitative aspects of hedging in the Treasury bond market. Section 12.1 reviews a conventional approach to hedging based on matching the changes in value of long and short bond positions associated with equal yield changes. We suggest that this technique is flawed because it fails to recognize that the yield curve does not always move in parallel, or that (1) yields on different securities vary somewhat independently of each other—or lack perfect correlation—and (2) yields on different securities vary over different ranges—or exhibit different volatilities.

Section 12.2 undertakes a more fundamental analysis of hedging in the simple case where one bond is used to hedge another bond. It is shown that the size of an optimal hedge will vary with the relative yield volatilities of the two bonds and with the correlation of changes in the bonds' yields. It is also shown that hedges are not symmetric (if position A is a good hedge for position B, position B will not be a good hedge for position A) and are not necessarily transitive (if position A hedges position B and if B hedges position C, then A will probably not be a good hedge for C). These surprising results are intimately connected with the imperfect correlation of yield changes in different sectors of the Treasury bond market.

Section 12.3 extends the analysis of hedging to the more complicated case where two different bonds are used to hedge a third bond. We show that, in general, it is preferable to have positions in both hedge bonds but that the positions can have opposite signs. For example, a long position in 30-year bonds might best be hedged with a short position in 5-year notes and a *long* position in 2-year notes. This peculiar hedge can be understood

Written in April 1986.

by breaking it into two components. Most of the short 5-year notes are a hedge against the 30 year bonds. However, such a short 5-year/long 30-year position exposes the investor to the risk of loss from a steepening of the yield curve. This curve risk is in turn offset by the long position in 2-year notes and the balance of the short 5-year notes.

Together the analyses in sections 12.2 and 12.3 suggest that as we add more bonds to a hedge position, we are able to reduce more types of risk associated with changes in interest rates; such as changes in the level, slope, and curvature of the yield curve. This proposition is considered briefly in section 4 when we examine hedging in the general case.

12.1   A Conventional Approach to Hedging

Conventional bond hedging is most easily explained with a concrete example. Suppose that an investor has a long position in $100 million principal amount of 2-year notes and wants to hedge against higher interest rates by selling 5-year notes short. If he calculates the hedge with the conventional technique, he will sell enough 5-year notes so that a change in yield of one basis point on both notes changes the value of his long and short positions by equal, but offsetting, amounts. He will then be hedged against gains or losses resulting from equal changes in yield on the two notes.

The first and fourth lines of table 12.1 show characteristics of the actively traded 2-year and 5-year notes relevant for a conventional hedge calculation at the beginning of 1986. The data indicate that a change in yield of one basis point will change the value of $1 million of 2-year notes by $179.84, and will change the value of $1 million of 5-year notes by

Table 12.1
On-the-run Treasury bonds on January 2, 1986

Sector	Coupon	Maturity	Quote	Yield	Value of one basis point[a]
2 yr	$7\frac{7}{8}\%$	12/31/1987	$99\frac{25}{32}$	7.995%	$ 179.84
3	$8\frac{5}{8}$	11/15/1988	101	8.221	251.64
4	$8\frac{3}{8}$	12/31/1989	100	8.374	332.75
5	$9\frac{1}{8}$	2/15/1991	$102\frac{14}{32}$	8.511	413.58
7	$9\frac{3}{4}$	10/15/1992	$104\frac{10}{32}$	8.886	514.13
10	$9\frac{1}{2}$	11/15/1995	$103\frac{4}{32}$	9.012	658.81
20	$10\frac{3}{4}$	8/15/2005	111	9.499	956.96
30	$9\frac{7}{8}$	11/15/2015	$106\frac{4}{32}$	9.265	1057.29

a. Per $1 million principal amount.

$413.58. For example, if the yield on the 2-year note rises from 7.995% to 8.005%, the market value of $1 million of the note will fall by $179.84.

It follows that a one basis point change in yield will change the value of $100 million principal amount of 2-year notes by $17,984. A comparable variation in value would obtain from $43.48 million principal amount of 5-year notes ($17,984 = $43.48 million principal amount times $413.58 value of a basis point per $1 million principal amount of 5-year notes). Thus the conventional approach to hedging indicates a short sale of $43.48 million 5-year notes against a $100 million long position in 2-year notes.

Flaws in the Conventional Approach

There are two flaws to the foregoing approach to bond hedging. First, the approach implicitly assumes comparable volatility of yields on the two notes. Second, it implicitly assumes that yield changes on the two notes are perfectly correlated. To appreciate the significance of these flaws, we will examine the consequences of extreme departures from the assumptions.

Assumption of Comparable Volatility

Suppose first that yield changes on the 2-year and 5-year notes are perfectly correlated but that the yield on the 5-year note changes only half as much as any concurrent change in yield on the 2-year note. If, for example, the yield on the 2-year note rises (falls) by 10 basis points, then the yield on the 5-year note rises (falls) by 5 basis points. We might then say that the yield volatility of the 2-year note is twice the yield volatility of the 5-year note.

In this case it would clearly be incorrect to premise a hedge on matching the dollar values of *equal* changes in yield on the two notes, as we did when we calculated a short hedge of $43.48 million 5-year notes against a $100 million long position in 2-year notes. A 1 basis point yield change on the 2-year note will, as computed above, produce a change in value of $17,984 on $100 million of those notes. However, such a yield change will, by hypothesis, be accompanied by only a $\frac{1}{2}$ basis point change in the yield on the 5-year note and hence by only an $8,991 change in the value of $43.48 million of those notes ($8,991 = $\frac{1}{2}$ basis point change in yield, times $413.58 value of a basis point per $1 million of 5-year notes, times $43.48 million 5-year notes). Thus the short position in 5-year notes effectively hedges only half of the risk of the long position in 2-year notes.

Assumption of Perfect Correlation of Yield Change

The implicit assumption of perfectly correlated yield changes is the second flaw in conventional bond hedging. To appreciate the nature of this flaw, suppose that the 2-year note and the 5-year note have equal yield volatilities but that changes in their yields are uncorrelated. This means that knowing that the yield on the 2-year note went up or down by 1 basis point tells us *nothing* about the contemporaneous change in yield on the 5-year note.

If yield changes on the 2-year and 5-year notes are uncorrelated, it is clear that the latter notes cannot be used to hedge the former securities. By hypothesis, gains and losses on the 2-year notes will be unrelated to losses or gains on the 5-year position.

A Conventional Hedge as a Bond Spread

Although we have suggested two reasons why conventional hedging is flawed, we do not mean to imply that matching dollar values resulting from an equal change in yield on two bonds is a practice without merit. In fact it is the analytical foundation of bond spreading (see chapter 11).

Bond spreading is a trading technique that seeks to take advantage of anticipated change in the difference between the yields on two bonds. If the yield difference changes, a correctly weighted spread position will make (or lose) money. Its value will remain constant if the yield difference remains constant.

Hedging, on the other hand, is a matter of *minimizing* value fluctuations rather than a device for making value a function of some yield spread. As we will see in the next section, hedging and spreading are the same only when yield changes on two bonds are perfectly correlated and of comparable volatility.

12.2   An Analysis of Simple Hedging

The discussion in the preceding section suggests three factors that might affect the size of a bond hedge:

1. The dollar value of a one basis point change in yield for each bond involved in the hedge.

2. The volatility of the yield on each bond.

3. The correlation between changes in yields on pairs of bonds.

This section examines the influence of these factors in the context of a simple hedge where a single bond is used to hedge the risk on a second bond. The two following sections examine more complex hedges.

Table 12.2
Standard deviations and correlations of weekly yield changes for on-the-run Treasury bonds from June 1983 to December 1985

	Sector							
	2-year	3-year	4-year	5-year	7-year	10-year	20-year	30-year
Standard deviation	20.3 bp	20.5	21.2	21.0	20.8	20.3	19.2	18.3
Correlation with								
2 yr	1.000	.984	.973	.956	.927	.921	.891	.886
3	.984	1.000	.983	.970	.945	.939	.909	.904
4	.973	.983	1.000	.988	.972	.965	.940	.933
5	.956	.970	.988	1.000	.985	.978	.953	.949
7	.927	.945	.972	.985	1.000	.993	.973	.969
10	.921	.939	.965	.978	.993	1.000	.982	.982
20	.891	.909	.940	.953	.973	.982	1.000	.988
30	.886	.904	.933	.949	.969	.982	.988	1.000

Yield Volatilities and Correlations

Before beginning the formal analysis of hedging, it may be helpful to look briefly at the empirical structure of yield volatilities and correlations of yield changes on Treasury securities. Table 12.2 shows the standard deviations and correlations of weekly yield changes for actively traded, on the run, Treasury issues from June 1983 to December 1985. Two aspects of the data are worth noting.

First, yield volatility varied significantly across different sectors of the Treasury market. The standard deviation of weekly yield change was 20.3 basis points for 2-year notes; it increased to a high of 21.2 basis points for 4-year notes and then declined to a low of 18.3 basis points for 30-year bonds.

Second, changes in yield were imperfectly correlated. The correlations are highest for "near-by" issues such as the 7-year note and the 10-year note (.993) and lowest for the most "distant" pairings, such as the 2-year note and the 30-year bond (.886). The correlations generally decline the greater the difference in maturity (or duration) between two securities. This is quite reasonable. We expect a 2-year note to behave nearly the same as a 3-year note but less like a 7-year note, and even less like a 30-year bond.

The data in table 12.2 show that the objections raised in section 12.1 to the conventional approach to hedging (the assumptions of uniform yield volatility and perfect correlation) are qualitatively well founded. We now begin to address the objections analytically and assess their quantitative significance.

Risk Minimization

The formal analysis of hedging begins with the premise that we want to minimize the risk of a securities position in the sense of minimizing the variance (or standard deviation) of the value of the position.

Suppose that we have positions in two securities where Q_1 is the principal amount of security 1 and Q_2 is the principal amount of security 2. Let V_1 and V_2 be the dollar values of a basis point for the respective bonds. If the yields on the two issues change by ΔR_1 and ΔR_2, the net value of the position changes by

$$\Delta W = Q_1 \cdot V_1 \cdot \Delta R_1 + Q_2 \cdot V_2 \cdot \Delta R_2 \tag{12.1}$$

The structure of this equation follows from the discussion in section 12.1. For example, the change in value of security 1 is calculated as the quantity of that security (Q_1, denominated in millions of dollars of principal amount), times the dollar value of a basis point per \$1 million principal amount of the security, times the change in the yield on the security.

The variance, or uncertainty, of the change in net value depends on the known quantities $Q_1, Q_2, V_1,$ and V_2 and on the variances and correlation of ΔR_1 and ΔR_2. Let σ_1^2 be the variance of ΔR_1, σ_2^2 the variance of ΔR_2, and ρ the correlation of the changes in yield. The variance of ΔW, denoted σ^2, is

$$\sigma^2 = Q_1^2 \cdot V_1^2 \cdot \sigma_1^2 + Q_2^2 \cdot V_2^2 \cdot \sigma_2^2 + 2 \cdot Q_1 \cdot Q_2 \cdot V_1 \cdot V_2 \cdot \rho \cdot \sigma_1 \cdot \sigma_2 \tag{12.2}$$

In the typical situation we will have a given value for Q_1 (e.g., \$100 million of 2-year notes), and we will want to find the value of Q_2 that minimizes σ^2. It is shown in appendix A that the optimal, variance-minimizing, value of Q_2 is

$$Q_2 = -\frac{\rho \cdot V_1 \cdot \sigma_1}{V_2 \cdot \sigma_2} \cdot Q_1 \tag{12.3}$$

We first illustrate the use of equation (12.3) and then discuss some of its implications.

An Example

As in section 12.1 we want to hedge a long position in \$100 million of 2-year notes by selling 5-year notes short. Identifying the 2-year notes as security 1 (with $Q_1 = 100.$) and the 5-year notes as security 2, we have, from table 12.1,

$V_1 = \$179.84$ per \$1 million principal amount

$V_2 = \$413.58$

From table 12.2 we have

$\sigma_1 = 20.3$ bp

$\sigma_2 = 21.0$

$\rho = .956$

Using these values in equation (12.3) gives the optimal amount of 5-year notes to be sold short:

$$Q_2 = \frac{-(.956) \cdot (179.84) \cdot (20.3)}{(413.58) \cdot (21.0)} \cdot (100.)$$

$$= -\$40.18 \text{ million principal amount} \tag{12.4}$$

Observe that this optimal hedge is $3 million smaller than the conventional hedge of $43.48 million 5-year notes calculated in section 12.1.

Discussion

There are several notable features of equation (12.3). First, the optimal quantity of hedge bonds depends on the yield volatilities of the two securities as well as on the dollar values of a basis point change in yield. In the example, fewer than the conventionally computed quantity of 5-year notes are needed for an optimal hedge, partly because the yield on 5-year notes is more volatile than the yield on 2-year notes.

Second, the size of the optimal hedge depends on the correlation of yield changes, so a lower correlation leads to a smaller hedge position. This result can be appreciated by realizing that a lower correlation implies greater independence in the yield changes on the two bonds. Greater independence means that a greater portion of a given change in yield on security 1 will *not* be accompanied by a concomitant change in yield on security 2 and hence that a larger part of the risk on security 1 will be "unhedgable" with security 2. It is therefore reasonable that an optimal hedge should entail a smaller quantity of the hedge security the lower its correlation with the hedged security.

Third, the conventional approach to bond hedging—using only the values of a basis point—is seen to be a special case of equation (12.3). This case arises when the securities have equal yield volatilities ($\sigma_1 = \sigma_2$) and perfect correlation ($\rho = 1$). We then have the conventional hedge: $Q_2 = (V_1/V_2) \cdot Q_1$.

Two Peculiarities of Optimal Hedges

The analytical implications of optimal hedging may not be generally familiar to market participants, but they are not unreasonable. Many investors recognize that the conventional approach to hedging must be modified when securities have very different yield volatilities and when their yield changes are imperfectly correlated. We have merely specified the quantitative nature of the modification. There are, however, two additional implications of the analysis which are quite striking and counterintuitive.

Optimal Hedges Are Not Symmetric

We showed in the example above that the optimal hedge for $100 million of 2-year notes was a short position in $40.18 million 5-year notes in the beginning of January, 1986. Let us now reverse this problem and consider the optimal 2-year hedge for a short position in $40.18 million of 5-year notes.

This "mirror image" hedging problem can be solved using equation (12.3) by identifying security 1 as the 5-year note (with $Q_1 = -40.18$) and security 2 as the 2-year note. From tables 12.1 and 12.2 we have

$V_1 = \$413.58 \quad \sigma_1 = 21.0 \text{ bp}$

$V_2 = \$179.84 \quad \sigma_2 = 20.3 \text{ bp}$

$$\rho = .956$$

Equation (12.3) then provides

$$Q_2 = \frac{-(.956)\cdot(413.58)\cdot(21.0)}{(179.84)\cdot(20.3)}\cdot(-40.18)$$

$$= \$91.38 \text{ million 2-year notes.} \tag{12.5}$$

Thus the optimal hedge of a short position in $40.18 million 5-year notes is a long position in $91.38 million 2-year notes.

This is a surprising result. Intuitively, if $40.18 million 5-year notes is an optimal hedge for $100 million 2-year notes, then we would expect the symmetric result that $100 million 2-year notes is an optimal hedge for $40.18 million 5-year notes. More generally, intuition suggests that the composition of a hedged position should not depend on the mere labels of the hedge and hedged bonds.

The analysis, however, leads to a contrary conclusion: optimal hedges are not symmetric. This peculiar result can be understood by noting an important difference between the two hedging problems. In the first problem we asked for the quantity of 5-year notes that minimizes risk given that we already own $100 million of 2-year notes. In the second problem we asked for the risk-minimizing quantity of 2-year notes given that we were already short $40.18 million 5-year notes. These are *not* the same problems (in the first we can only buy or sell 5-year notes in constructing the hedge, while in the second we can only buy or sell 2-year notes), so there is no compelling reason why they should lead to the same securities positions.

Optimal Hedges May Not Be Transitive

We saw above that the optimal 5-year hedge for $100 million 2-year notes is a short position in $40.18 million 5-year notes. The upper panel of example 1 shows that the optimal 30-year bond hedge for a long position in $40.18 million 5-year notes is a short position in $17.12 million 30-year bonds. Intuition would suggest therefore that the optimal 30-year hedge for $100 million 2-year notes is a short position in $17.12 million 30-year bonds. However, the lower panel of example 1 shows that the optimal hedge is actually a short position in $16.72 million 30-year bonds.

This is, again, a nonintuitive result. It says that bond position C may not be an optimal hedge of position A even though it is an optimal hedge of position B and B is an optimal hedge of position A. More generally, it demonstrates that optimal hedges are not transitive.

Nontransitivity of optimal hedges can be explained in terms of imperfect correlations. A correlation of less than unity means there is some independence in the changes in yields on two bonds. However, there is no requirement that the degree of independence between securities A and C is determined by the independence between securities A and B and between B and C. Each pairing must be examined directly.

12.3   An Analysis of More Complex Hedging

The preceding section showed how to calculate an optimal, risk-minimizing, hedge in the simple case where a bond is hedged with a single other bond. However, nothing in the analysis suggested that a single bond hedge is superior to hedging with two, three, or more bonds. More specifically, the analysis derived the optimal *size* of a single bond hedge, but it did not address the optimal *number* of hedge bonds.

This section extends the analysis of hedging to the case of two bond hedges as preparation for posing the broader question of the optimal number of hedge bonds. (The latter issue is addressed in the next section.) We will first derive the size of an optimal two bond hedge and then illustrate some aspects of two bond hedges with numerical examples.

Risk Minimization with Two Hedge Bonds

As in single bond hedges the analysis of hedging with two bonds starts from the premise that we want to minimize the risk of a given securities

Example 1
Two hedge calculations

Hedging $40.18 million 5-year notes with 30-year bonds

Identify the 5-year notes as security 1 ($Q_1 = 40.18$) and the 30-year bonds as security 2.

From table 12.1 we have

$V_1 = \$413.58$ per $1 million principal amount

$V_2 = \$1,057.29$

From table 12.2 we have

$\sigma_1 = 21.0$ bp

$\sigma_2 = 18.3$

$\rho = .949$

From equation (12.3) we have

$$Q_2 = \frac{-(.949) \cdot (413.58) \cdot (21.0)}{(1057.29) \cdot (18.3)} \cdot (40.18)$$

$\quad = -\$17.12$ million 30-year bonds

Hedging $100 million 2-year notes with 30-year bonds

Identify the 2-year notes as security 1 ($Q_1 = 100.00$) and the 30-year bonds as security 2.

From table 12.1 we have

$V_1 = \$179.84$ per $1 million principal amount

$V_2 = \$1,057.29$

From table 12.2 we have

$\sigma_1 = 20.3$ bp

$\sigma_2 = 18.3$

$\rho = .886$

From equation (12.3) we have

$$Q_2 = \frac{-(.886) \cdot (179.84) \cdot (20.3)}{(1057.29) \cdot (18.3)} \cdot (100.00)$$

$\quad = -\$16.72$ million 30-year bonds

position in the sense of minimizing the variance (or standard deviation) of the value of the position.

Suppose that we have positions in three securities, where Q_1 is the principal amount of security 1, Q_2 the principal amount of security 2, and Q_3 the principal amount of security 3. Let V_i be the dollar value of a basis point for security i, where $i = 1, 2,$ and 3. If the yields on the three issues change by ΔR_1, ΔR_2, and ΔR_3, respectively, the net value of the position changes by

$$\Delta W = Q_1 \cdot V_1 \cdot \Delta R_1 + Q_2 \cdot V_2 \cdot \Delta R_2 + Q_3 \cdot V_3 \cdot \Delta R_3 \tag{12.6}$$

This is a simple extension of the expression for the change in the value of a portfolio of two bonds shown in equation (12.1).

The variance of the change in net value depends on the known quantities Q_1, Q_2, Q_3, and $V_1, V_2,$ and V_3, and also on the statistical structure of the change in yields on the three securities. Let σ_i^2 be the variance of the change in yield ΔR_i for $i = 1, 2,$ and 3, and let ρ_{ij} be the correlation of ΔR_i and ΔR_j for $i = 1, 2,$ and 3 and $j = 1, 2,$ and 3. The variance of ΔW, denoted σ^2, is

$$\sigma^2 = Q_1^2 \cdot V_1^2 \cdot \sigma_1^2 + Q_2^2 \cdot V_2^2 \cdot \sigma_2^2 + Q_3^2 \cdot V_3^2 \cdot \sigma_3^2$$
$$+ 2 \cdot Q_1 \cdot Q_2 \cdot V_1 \cdot V_2 \cdot \rho_{12} \cdot \sigma_1 \cdot \sigma_2$$
$$+ 2 \cdot Q_1 \cdot Q_3 \cdot V_1 \cdot V_3 \cdot \rho_{13} \cdot \sigma_1 \cdot \sigma_3$$
$$+ 2 \cdot Q_2 \cdot Q_3 \cdot V_2 \cdot V_3 \cdot \rho_{23} \cdot \sigma_2 \cdot \sigma_3 \tag{12.7}$$

This expression involves the variance of the change in yield on each bond and the correlation of the changes in yields on each pair of bonds.

In the typical situation we will have a given value for Q_1 and we will want to find the values of Q_2 and Q_3 which *jointly* minimize σ^2. It is shown in appendix B that the optimal, variance-minimizing, values are

$$Q_2 = \frac{-(\rho_{12} - \rho_{13} \cdot \rho_{23}) \cdot V_1 \cdot \sigma_1}{(1 - \rho_{23}^2) \cdot V_2 \cdot \sigma_2} \cdot Q_1 \tag{12.8a}$$

$$Q_3 = \frac{-(\rho_{13} - \rho_{12} \cdot \rho_{23}) \cdot V_1 \cdot \sigma_1}{(1 - \rho_{23}^2) \cdot V_3 \cdot \sigma_3} \cdot Q_1 \tag{12.8b}$$

We will illustrate the use of equation (12.8a,b) with some numerical examples.

Hedging with Shorter and Longer Bonds

For the first example, suppose that we want to hedge a position in $100 million of 5-year notes ($Q_1 = 100$.) with 2-year notes (identified as security

2) and 30-year bonds (identified as security 3). From table 12.1 we have

$V_1 = \$413.58$ per \$1 million principal amount

$V_2 = \$179.84$

$V_3 = \$1,05729$

From table 12.2 we have

$\sigma_1 = 21.0$ basis points $\sigma_{12} = .956$

$\sigma_2 = 20.3$ $\sigma_{13} = .949$

$\sigma_3 = 18.3$ $\sigma_{23} = .886$

Using the appropriate figures in equation (12.8a) gives the optimal amount of 2-year notes to be sold short:

$$Q_2 = \frac{-(.956 - .949 \cdot .886) \cdot (413.58) \cdot (21.0)}{(1. - (.886)^2) \cdot (179.84) \cdot (20.3)} \cdot (100.)$$

$= -\$127.45$ million principal amount

and the optimal amount of 30 year bonds to be sold short:

$$Q_3 = \frac{-(.949 - .956 \cdot .886) \cdot (413.58) \cdot (21.0)}{(1. - (.886)^2) \cdot (1057.29) \cdot (18.3)} \cdot (100.)$$

$= -\$21.29$ million principal amount

These calculations show that the optimal 2-year note and 30-year bond hedge against \$100 million of 5-year notes is a short position in \$127.45 million 2-year notes and \$21.29 million 30-year bonds. This illustrates the general proposition that it is better to have a position in two hedge bonds than to restrict a hedge to a single bond. In rough terms, some (but not all) of the variation in the 5-year yield is hedgeable by the variation in the 2-year yield, and some (but not all) by the variation in the 30 year yield. Clearly it is preferable to use both the shorter and longer maturity securities in the hedge.

Hedging with Two Shorter Bonds

Suppose that we now change the hedging problem slightly and examine how to hedge a position in \$20 million of 30-year bonds with 2-year notes and 5-year notes.

Example 2 shows the optimal hedge is a short position in \$52.80 million principal amount of 5-year notes and a long position in \$26.16 million 2-year notes. Surprisingly we do not hold a short position in both notes.

Example 2
Hedging $20 million principal amount of 30-year bonds with 2-year notes and 5-year notes

---

Identify the 30-year bond as security 1 ($Q_1 = 20.00$), the 2-year note as security 2, and the 5-year note as security 3.

From table 12.1 we have

$V_1 = \$1,057.29$ per $1 million principal amount

$V_2 = \$179.84$

$V_3 = \$413.58$

From table 12.2 we have

$\sigma_1 = 18.3$ bp $\rho_{12} = .886$

$\sigma_2 = 20.3$ $\rho_{13} = .949$

$\sigma_3 = 21.0$ $\rho_{23} = .956$

From equation (12.8a) we have

$$Q_2 = \frac{-(.886 - .949 \cdot .956) \cdot (1057.29) \cdot (18.3)}{(1 - (.956)^2) \cdot (179.84) \cdot (20.3)} \cdot (20.00)$$

$\quad = +\$26.16$ million 2-year notes

From equation (12.8b) we have

$$Q_3 = \frac{-(.949 - .886 \cdot .956) \cdot (1057.29) \cdot (18.3)}{(1 - (.956)^2) \cdot (413.58) \cdot (21.0)} \cdot (20.00)$$

$\quad = -\$52.80$ million 5-year notes

This anomaly can be explained by observing the consequences of hedging a long position in $20 million 30-year bonds with only 5-year notes. The optimal 5-year note hedge can be shown to be a short position in $42.28 million 5-year notes. While this is an optimal single bond hedge, in the sense of minimizing the variance of the change in net worth of the hedged position, it leads to some significant yield curve risk. In particular, a short 5-year/long 30-year bond position will lose value if the yield curve steepens. This curve risk is reduced in the two bond hedge by "over-hedging" the 30-year bonds with 5-year notes and by taking an additional long position in 2-year notes. If the curve steepens there will be a gain on the long 2-year/short 5-year portion of the composite hedge to offset the loss on the short 5-year/long 30-year portion of the hedge.

A Reinterpretation of Hedging with Shorter and Longer Bonds

The interpretation of the 2-year and 5-year hedge of a 30-year bond position in terms of yield curve risk reduction suggests a reinterpretation of our results on the 2-year and 30-year hedge of a 5-year note position.

We showed above that the optimal hedge of $100 million of 5-year notes was a short position in $127.45 million 2-year notes and $21.29 million 30-year bonds. This "divided" hedge can be viewed as a device to limit yield curve risk. If the hedge consisted of only 2-year notes held short, the position would lose value if the curve steepened. If the hedge consisted of only 30-year bonds held short, the position would lose value if the curve flattened. By dividing the hedge between both 2-year notes and 30-year bonds, the hedge position is less sensitive to changes in the slope of the yield curve.

12.4   Some Comments on Hedging in the General Case

The preceding sections examined two cases of optimal hedging: hedging with a single bond and hedging with two bonds. These cases are obviously only the beginning of a logical sequence that extends to the general case of hedging with an arbitrary number of bonds.

The analysis of hedging in the general case is analytically tractable but does not lead to any qualitatively interesting results. In fact the most interesting aspect of multiple-bond hedging is not the analytics but rather the question of how many different hedge bonds are "enough?" If we can hedge with one or two or three or more bonds, where do we stop?

Some insight into this problem can be gained by comparing our analyses of single-bond and two-bond hedges. Roughly speaking, a one-bond hedge can insulate an existing position against changes in the general level of interest rates but may itself expose a market participant to losses due to changes in the slope of the yield curve. A two-bond hedge, on the other hand, permits hedging the risk of changes in the slope of the curve as well as changes in the level of the curve. This suggests that as we expand the number of bonds in a hedge, we will be able to hedge against more different kinds of changes in interest rates. For example, a three-bond hedge might hedge changes in the level, slope, and *curvature* of the yield curve.

Viewed from this perspective, the issue of the number of bonds sufficient for a good hedge is seen to be a matter of the number of different ways the yield curve can fluctuate. It turns out that this question is closely related to the problem in immunization analysis of how many different kinds of shifts in the yield curve should be immunized. The question will be examined in chapters 15 and 16.

12.5   Conclusion

This chapter has re-examined, from first principles, the problem of hedging a bond position. We showed in section 12.1 that the conventional approach to hedging is flawed because it assumes (incorrectly) that yield changes on different securities are perfectly correlated and of comparable volatility.

Section 12.2 derived the size of an optimal one-bond hedge. The result, equation 12.3, shows explicitly how a hedge should be adjusted for imperfect yield correlation and different yield volatilities. We pointed out that optimal hedges, unlike conventional hedges, are neither symmetric nor necessarily transitive. This means that hedges must be calculated on a case-by-case basis and that there are no simple rules for inferring the optimal size of a particular hedge.

Section 12.3 extended the analysis to two-bond hedges. Some simple examples suggest that a two-bond hedge is better than a one-bond hedge because it reduces the yield curve risk which is generally introduced into one-bond hedges. By analogy, three-bond hedges will reduce the risk associated with changes in the curvature of the yield curve which is introduced into two-bond hedges.

12.6   Appendix A: Minimizing the Variance of the Change in Net Worth for a One-Bond Hedge

Equation (12.2) in the text specifies the variance of the change in net worth for a portfolio of two bonds:

$$\sigma^2 = Q_1^2 \cdot V_1^2 \cdot \sigma_1^2 + Q_2^2 \cdot V_2^2 \cdot \sigma_2^2 + 2 \cdot Q_1 \cdot Q_2 \cdot V_1 \cdot V_2 \cdot \rho \cdot \sigma_1 \cdot \sigma_2 \qquad \text{(A12.1)}$$

We want to minimize σ^2 with respect to Q_2 for a given value of Q_1. This requires that we compute the partial derivative $\partial \sigma^2 / \partial Q_2$, set it equal to zero, and solve for Q_2.

From equation (A12.1) we have

$$\frac{\partial \sigma^2}{\partial Q_2} = 2 \cdot Q_2 \cdot V_2^2 \cdot \sigma_2^2 + 2 \cdot Q_1 \cdot V_1 \cdot V_2 \cdot \rho \cdot \sigma_1 \cdot \sigma_2 \qquad \text{(A12.2)}$$

Setting this equal to zero and solving for Q_2 gives

$$Q_2 = \frac{-\rho \cdot V_1 \cdot \sigma_1}{V_2 \cdot \sigma_2} \cdot Q_1 \qquad \text{(A12.3)}$$

This is exactly equation (12.3) in the text.

12.7   Appendix B: Minimizing the Variance of the Change in Net Worth for a Two Bond Hedge

Equation (12.7) in the text specifies the variance of the change in net worth for a portfolio of three bonds:

$$\sigma^2 = Q_1^2 \cdot V_1^2 \cdot \sigma_1^2 + Q_2^2 \cdot V_2^2 \cdot \sigma_2^2 + Q_3^2 \cdot V_3^2 \cdot \sigma_3^2$$
$$+ 2 \cdot Q_1 \cdot Q_2 \cdot V_1 \cdot V_2 \cdot \rho_{12} \cdot \sigma_1 \cdot \sigma_2$$
$$+ 2 \cdot Q_1 \cdot Q_3 \cdot V_1 \cdot V_3 \cdot \rho_{13} \cdot \sigma_1 \cdot \sigma_3$$
$$+ 2 \cdot Q_2 \cdot Q_3 \cdot V_2 \cdot V_3 \cdot \rho_{23} \cdot \sigma_2 \cdot \sigma_3 \tag{A12.4}$$

We want to minimize σ^2 with respect to Q_2 and Q_3 for a given value of Q_1. This requires that we compute the partial derivatives, $\partial\sigma^2/\partial Q_2$ and $\partial\sigma^2/\partial Q_3$, set them equal to zero, and solve for Q_2 and Q_3.

From equation (A12.4) we have

$$\frac{\partial\sigma^2}{\partial Q_2} = 2 \cdot Q_2 \cdot V_2^2 \cdot \sigma_2^2$$
$$+ 2 \cdot Q_1 \cdot V_1 \cdot V_2 \cdot \rho_{12} \cdot \sigma_1 \cdot \sigma_2$$
$$+ 2 \cdot Q_3 \cdot V_2 \cdot V_3 \cdot \rho_{23} \cdot \sigma_2 \cdot \sigma_3 \tag{A12.5}$$

and

$$\frac{\partial\sigma^2}{\partial Q_3} = 2 \cdot Q_3 \cdot V_3^2 \cdot \sigma_3^2$$
$$+ 2 \cdot Q_1 \cdot V_1 \cdot V_3 \cdot \rho_{13} \cdot \sigma_1 \cdot \sigma_2$$
$$+ 2 \cdot Q_2 \cdot V_2 \cdot V_3 \cdot \rho_{23} \cdot \sigma_2 \cdot \sigma_3 \tag{A12.6}$$

Setting both of these expressions to zero gives two equations in two unknowns (Q_2 and Q_3). Solving for the unknowns gives

$$Q_2 = \frac{-(\rho_{12} - \rho_{13} \cdot \rho_{23}) \cdot V_1 \cdot \sigma_1}{(1 - \rho_{23}^2) \cdot V_2 \cdot \sigma_2} \cdot Q_1 \tag{A12.7}$$

$$Q_3 = \frac{-(\rho_{13} - \rho_{12} \cdot \rho_{23}) \cdot V_1 \cdot \sigma_1}{(1 - \rho_{23}^2) \cdot V_3 \cdot \sigma_3} \cdot Q_1 \tag{A12.8}$$

This is exactly equations (12.8a) and (12.8b) in the text.

13 Approximating the Yield on a Portfolio of Bonds: Value-Weighted Averages versus Value of a Basis Point-Weighted Averages

This chapter addresses a seemingly simple topic: approximating the yield on a portfolio of several different bonds from the yields on the bonds in the portfolio.

Although the topic may sound simple—perhaps even trivial—it is actually quite complicated and has been the occasion of numerous analytical errors, including errors in analyzing dumbbell positions, butterfly trades, and the value of convexity and errors in constructing optimal portfolios and yields on indexed portfolios.

Section 13.1 provides a definition of the exact yield on a portfolio of bonds. The definition does not lead to an algorithm for computing portfolio yield in a practical context, but it does provide a starting point for deriving more useful approximations.

Section 13.2 briefly notes the conventional approximation to portfolio yield as a weighted average of the yields on the bonds in the portfolio in which each bond yield is weighted by the market value of the bond.

Section 13.3 derives a closer approximation of portfolio yield from the exact definition in section 13.1. This approximation is also a weighted average of the yields on the bonds in the portfolio but each yield is now weighted by the bond's *aggregate value of a basis point* rather than its market value.

Finally, section 13.4 illustrates the use of the new approximation in evaluating the yield on a dumbbell position and the yield pick-up on a butterfly trade. We suggest that conventional analyses have systematically misrepresented the yields on dumbbell positions and the yield pick-ups on butterfly trades.

13.1 An Exact Definition of Portfolio Yield

The yield on a bond is typically defined as the discount rate that makes the present value of the bond's future cash flows equal to the invoice price of the bond, or equal to the sum of (1) the bond's quoted market price and (2) the bond's accrued interest. By extension, the yield on a *portfolio* of bonds is the discount rate that makes the present value of the *portfolio's* future cash flows equal to the total market value of the *portfolio*. This section briefly reviews the analytic expressions of these parallel concepts of yield.

The Yield on a Bond

Consider a true fixed income security, that is, a bond with no put or call options and without a market-option sinking fund. Assume the bond will

Written in September 1988.

make a total of K payments in the future, where the kth payment is for the amount C_k and will occur in x_k semi-annual periods. Let P denote the quoted market price of the bond and A the accrued interest on the bond.

The semi-annually compounded yield on the bond is the value of R that satisfies the equation

$$P + A = \sum_{k=1}^{K} C_k \cdot (1 + \tfrac{1}{2}R)^{-x_k} \tag{13.1}$$

The right-hand side of equation (13.1) is the present value of the bond's future payments discounted at the interest rate R. Thus, as noted in the introduction to this section, the yield R is the discount rate that makes the present value of the bond's future cash flows equal to the invoice price of the bond.

The Yield on a Portfolio of Bonds

Now suppose that we have a portfolio of N different bonds. Let P_i and A_i denote the quoted market price and accrued interest per hundred dollars of principal value, respectively, of the ith bond, and let Q_i denote the quantify of the ith bond denominated in hundreds of dollars of principal value. Finally, let $f_i(\cdot)$ denote the present value function for \$100 principal value of the ith bond so that $f_i(R)$ is the present value of the bond's future payments discounted at the interest rate R.

From the discussion above at equation (13.1) the yield on bond i is defined as the value of R_i that satisfies the equation

$$P_i + A_i = f_i(R_i), \qquad i = 1, 2, \dots, N \tag{13.2}$$

By extension, the yield on the *portfolio* of bonds is the value of R that satisfies the equation

$$\sum_{i=1}^{N} Q_i \cdot (P_i + A_i) = \sum_{i=1}^{N} Q_i \cdot f_i(R) \tag{13.3}$$

The left-hand side of equation (13.3) is the total market value of the portfolio, including accrued interest. The right-hand side of the equation is the total present value of the portfolio's future payments, where *every* payment is discounted at the *common* interest rate R. Thus the yield on the portfolio is the discount rate which makes the present value of the portfolio's future cash flows equal to the total market value of the portfolio.

We view equation (13.3) as the exact definition of the yield on a portfolio of many different bonds. Unfortunately, equation (13.3) is not very useful in most practical situations because it requires all of the individual yield-dependent valuation functions $f_1(\cdot), f_2(\cdot), \dots, f_N(\cdot)$. What we need is some way to "average" the yields on the individual bonds $R_1, R_2, \dots, R_N$, as defined by equation (13.2), to approximate the portfolio yield. The next two sections describe two averaging techniques.

13.2   A Value-Weighted Approximation of Portfolio Yield

Suppose, as above, that we have a portfolio of N different bonds. Let R_i continue to denote the yield on the ith bond.

One very simple way to approximate the yield on the portfolio is to add up the individual bond yields and divide by the number of different bonds:

$$R_a = \frac{\sum_{i=1}^{N} R_i}{N} \tag{13.4}$$

where R_a is the approximate yield.

It is widely known that equation (13.4) provides a poor approximation to the yield on the portfolio because it gives equal weight to each different bond regardless of the composition of the portfolio. Analysts generally recognize that the yield on a bond with a disproportionate representation in the portfolio should be given a correspondingly disproportionate weight in approximating the portfolio yield.

The most common way to approximate the yield on the portfolio is to weight the yield on a bond by the total market value of that bond:

$$R_a = \frac{\sum_{i=1}^{N} Q_i \cdot (P_i + A_i) \cdot R_i}{\sum_{i=1}^{N} Q_i \cdot (P_i + A_i)} \tag{13.5}$$

where P_i and A_i denote the quoted market price and accrued interest per hundred dollars of principal value, respectively, of the ith bond and where Q_i is the quantity of the ith bond denominated in hundreds of dollars of principal value.

The approximation of portfolio yield as a value-weighted average has the intuitively appealing attribute that the larger the position in a bond the more the yield on that bond "counts." Indeed this attribute is often taken as so obviously necessary that equation (13.5) has become the conventional definition of portfolio yield. Many analysts have lost sight of the fact that equation (13.5) is really only an approximation to the true definition in equation (13.3).

13.3   A Closer Approximation of Portfolio Yield

We do not dispute the argument that individual bond yields should not be weighted equally when approximating the yield on a portfolio. However, we suggest that the appropriate weight for a bond is its *aggregate value of a basis point* rather than its aggregate market value. This section demonstrates that our alternative approximation follows naturally from the definition of portfolio yield given in equation (13.3).

An Analytic Approximation of Portfolio Yield

Equation (13.3) is the implicit definition of the yield R on a portfolio of bonds:

$$\sum_{i=1}^{N} Q_i \cdot (P_i + A_i) = \sum_{i=1}^{N} Q_i \cdot f_i(R) \tag{13.6}$$

The problem is to approximate R from the yields $R_1, R_2, \ldots, R_N$ on the individual bonds in the portfolio. These yields satisfy the equations

$$P_i + A_i = f_i(R_i), \qquad i = 1, 2, \ldots, N \tag{13.7}$$

We can think of the problem of computing the portfolio yield as the problem of computing a set of yield increments $\Delta R_1, \Delta R_2, \ldots, \Delta R_N$ such that

$$R_1 + \Delta R_1 = R_2 + \Delta R_2 = \cdots = R_N + \Delta R_N \tag{13.8a}$$

and such that

$$\sum_{i=1}^{N} Q_i \cdot (P_i + A_i) = \sum_{i=1}^{N} Q_i \cdot f_i(R_i + \Delta R_i) \tag{13.8b}$$

The portfolio yield R is any of the yields $R_i + \Delta R_i$ for $i = 1$ or $2 \ldots$ or N (these are all the same from equation 13.8a). It follows from equation (13.8b) that this yield satisfies equation (13.6).

To compute the values of the ΔR_i's consider a first-order approximation to the right-hand side of equation (13.8b):

$$\sum_{i=1}^{N} Q_i \cdot (P_i + A_i) = \sum_{i=1}^{N} Q_i \cdot f_i(R_i) + \sum_{i=1}^{N} Q_i \cdot f_i'(R_i) \cdot \Delta R_i \tag{13.9}$$

where $f_i'(R_i)$ is the derivative of the yield-dependent value function $f_i(\cdot)$ evaluated at the yield R_i. (This is proportional to the value of a basis point for \$100 principal amount of the bond.) From equation (13.7) we have

$$P_i + A_i = f_i(R_i), \qquad i = 1, 2, \ldots, N$$

Multiplying both sides of each equation by Q_i and summing from $i = 1$ to $i = N$ gives

$$\sum_{i=1}^{N} Q_i \cdot (P_i + A_i) = \sum_{i=1}^{N} Q_i \cdot f_i(R_i) \tag{13.10}$$

so that equation (13.9) becomes

$$0 = \sum_{i=1}^{N} Q_i \cdot f_i'(R_i) \cdot \Delta R_i \tag{13.11}$$

For notational simplicity let V_i denote the value of a basis point for the ith bond so that, up to a factor of proportionality, $V_i = f_i'(R_i)$. Equation (13.11) becomes

$$0 = \sum_{i=1}^{N} Q_i \cdot V_i \cdot \Delta R_i \tag{13.12}$$

Since $R = R_i + \Delta R_i$ for $i = 1, 2, \ldots, N$, this becomes

$$0 = \sum_{i=1}^{N} Q_i \cdot V_i \cdot (R - R_i) \tag{13.13}$$

or

$$R \cdot \sum_{i=1}^{N} Q_i \cdot V_i = \sum_{i=1}^{N} Q_i \cdot V_i \cdot R_i \tag{13.14}$$

Thus we can write the approximate yield on the portfolio as

$$R_a = \frac{\sum_{i=1}^{N} Q_i \cdot V_i \cdot R_i}{\sum_{i=1}^{N} Q_i \cdot V_i} \tag{13.15}$$

Comments

The approximation of portfolio yield in equation (13.15) is similar to that in equation (13.5) *except* that the yield on a bond is weighted by the aggregate value of a basis point of the position in that bond ($Q_i \cdot V_i$) rather than by the aggregate market value of the position ($Q_i \cdot (P_i + A_i)$). This shows that value sensitivity, rather than simple value, is a better way to weight bond yields when approximating portfolio yield.

13.4   Some Examples

The preceding section suggested that the yield on a portfolio of bonds can be better approximated as a value of a basis point-weighted average of the yields on the bonds in the portfolio rather than as a value-weighted average of those yields. This section illustrates the significance of our contention with some numerical examples.

Evaluating a Dumbbell Position

Suppose that an investor contemplates buying a position in $100 million principal amount of each of two Treasury bonds: the $8\frac{1}{8}\%$ 2-year note of

Table 13.1
Characteristics of two Treasury bonds and a portfolio of those bonds

---

Bond 1: $8\frac{1}{8}$% of May 31, 1990
Quoted at $99\frac{26}{32}$, plus .0222 points of accrued interest, for settlement on June 1, 1988
Invoice price = 99.8347
Yield = 8.23%
Duration = 1.88 years
Value of a basis point = $180.58 per $1 million principal amount

Bond 2: $8\frac{3}{8}$% of April 15, 1995
Quoted at $96\frac{18}{32}$, plus 1.0755 points of accrued interest, for settlement on June 1, 1988
Invoice price = 97.6380
Yield = 9.05%
Duration = 5.28 years
Value of a basis point = $492.87 per $1 million principal amount

Portfolio: $100 million principal amount each of bond 1 and bond 2
Portfolio yield = 8.83%
(computed from equation 13.3)
Portfolio duration = 3.56 years

May 31, 1990 (issued May 31, 1988), and the $8\frac{3}{8}$% 7-year note of April 15, 1995 (issued April 15, 1988). Assume the bonds are quoted at $99\frac{26}{32}$ and $96\frac{18}{32}$, respectively, for settlement on June 1, 1988.

Table 13.1 shows relevant data on the two bonds. The table indicates that the yield on the 2-year note is 8.23% per annum and that the yield on the 7-year note is 9.05%. The table further shows that the exact yield on the portfolio of both bonds, computed with equation (13.3), is 8.83%.

If we approximate the portfolio yield as a value-weighted average with equation (13.5), we get $R_a = 8.64\%$. If, on the other hand, we approximate the yield as a value of a basis point-weighted average with equation (13.15), we get $R_a = 8.83\%$. The calculations are displayed in example 1.

Comments

It may be helpful to examine this example in a bit more detail in order to appreciate why the value of a basis point-weighted average leads to a better approximation.

As shown in figure 13.1, we can think of the process of approximating the portfolio yield as a matter of choosing yield changes ΔR_1 and ΔR_2 such that $R_1 + \Delta R_1 = R_2 + \Delta R_2 = R$, where R is the portfolio yield and where R_1 and R_2 are the yields on the 2-year note and the 7-year note, respectively. We clearly need $\Delta R_1 > 0$ and $\Delta R_2 < 0$; that is, the portfolio yield R is greater than the yield $R_1 = 8.23\%$ on the 2-year note and less than the yield $R_2 = 9.05\%$ on the 7-year note. Moreover we want to choose ΔR_1 and ΔR_2 such that the change in value of the 2-year notes associated with the yield change ΔR_1 just offsets the change in value of the

Example 1
Two approximations to the yield on the portfolio in table 13.1

Value-weighted average

$$Ra = \frac{Q_1 \cdot (P_1 + A_1) \cdot R_1 + Q_2 \cdot (P_2 + A_2) \cdot R_2}{Q_1 \cdot (P_1 + A_1) + Q_2 \cdot (P_2 + A_2)}$$

$$= \frac{(100.) \cdot (99.8347) \cdot (8.23) + (100.) \cdot (97.6380) \cdot (9.05)}{(100.) \cdot (99.8347) + (100.) \cdot (97.6380)}$$

$$= 8.64\%$$

Value of a basis point-weighted average

$$Ra = \frac{Q_1 \cdot V_1 \cdot R_1 + Q_2 \cdot V_2 \cdot R_2}{Q_1 \cdot V_1 + Q_2 \cdot V_2}$$

$$= \frac{(100.) \cdot (180.58) \cdot (8.23) + (100.) \cdot (492.87) \cdot (9.05)}{(100.) \cdot (180.58) + (100.) \cdot (492.87)}$$

$$= 8.83\%$$

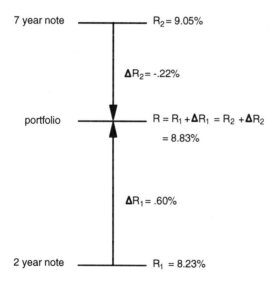

Figure 13.1
Approximating the yield on the portfolio in table 13.1

7-year notes associated with the yield change ΔR_2. (This ensures that the aggregate present value of the future payments on both bonds computed at the common discount rate R is the same as the sum of the present values computed at the discount rates R_1 and R_2 for the 2-year and 7-year notes, respectively.) In other words, we want $\Delta R_1 \cdot 100 \cdot 180.58 + \Delta R_2 \cdot 100 \cdot 492.87 = 0$, where \$180.58 is the value of a basis point for \$1 million principal amount of the 2-year note and \$492.87 is the value of a basis point for the 7-year note. It is not difficult to verify that $\Delta R_1 = .60\%$ and $\Delta R_2 = -.22\%$ satisfy this condition and lead to a portfolio yield of $R = R_1 + \Delta R_1 = 8.23 + .60 = 8.83\%$, or $R = R_2 + \Delta R_2 = 9.05 - .22 = 8.83\%$.

It is interesting to note that even though the portfolio is essentially equally divided between 2-year notes and 7-year notes the portfolio yield is much closer to the yield on the 7-year note. This stems from the greater price sensitivity of that longer note. In particular, ΔR_2 has a smaller absolute magnitude than ΔR_1 because the value of a basis point is greater for the second security.

This illustrates an important point: approximating the yield on a bond portfolio with a value-weighted average tends to underweight yields on bonds with longer durations (and hence larger values of a basis point). As a result, the conventional approximation tends to understate portfolio yield when, as in the example, the yield curve is positively sloped. (Conversely, it will overstate portfolio yield when the yield curve is inverted.)

Evaluating a Butterfly Trade

Our method of approximating the yield on a bond portfolio also has implications for evaluating a butterfly trade.

Suppose an investor owns the $8\frac{1}{4}\%$ Treasury note of August 15, 1992 (originally issued as a 5-year note on June 3, 1987) and contemplates selling that note in order to buy the portfolio in table 13.1. Assume he can sell the old 5-year note at a price of $98\frac{14}{32}$ and a yield of 8.70% for settlement on June 1, 1988. It is not hard to show that the duration of the old 5-year note and the duration of the portfolio are both about $3\frac{1}{2}$ years. Thus the proposed trade is a matter of selling one bond against buying a combination of shorter and longer bonds without changing duration; that is, it is a "butterfly" trade.

Using the actual portfolio yield of 8.83% the butterfly trade produces a yield pickup of 13 basis points. However, using the value-weighted average portfolio yield of 8.64% the trade appears to produce a yield give-up of 6 basis points. This shows that it can be quite important, when assessing butterfly trades, to compute correctly the yield on the portfolio of shorter and longer bonds.

A Comment on the Price of Convexity

The primary analytical difference between the old 5-year note (the $8\frac{1}{4}\%$ note of August 15, 1992) and the portfolio of 2-year and 7-year notes is that the portfolio has greater convexity. (For a discussion of convexity, see chapter 6.) If we compare the value-weighted average portfolio yield of 8.64% to the 8.70% yield on the old 5-year note we would erroneously conclude that more convex positions (of a given duration) have lower yields, i.e., that convexity is valued positively by the bond market. However, the actual portfolio yield was shown to be 8.83%. This suggests that, in fact, more convex positions are cheaper and that convexity is valued negatively by the market.

13.5 Conclusions

This paper examined the problem of approximating the yield on a portfolio of several different bonds from the yields on the bonds in the portfolio. Most market participants use a value-weighted average of the bond yields. We showed, however, that a value of a basis point-weighted average leads to a better approximation of the actual portfolio yield.

The results of this paper have relevance whenever an analyst computes a portfolio yield as some average of the yields on the bonds in the portfolio. Such a computation appears, e.g., in the course of optimizing an immunized portfolio (see chapter 15). It also appears in evaluating a butterfly swap where an investor sells a single bond and concurrently buys two other bonds with the same average duration. These swaps are frequently evaluated in terms of the spread between the yield on the bond that is sold and the yield on the portfolio that is purchased. We saw in section 13.4 that a value-weighted approximation to that portfolio yield will usually understate the actual yield if the yield curve is positively sloped.

13.6 Subsequent Remarks

A bond portfolio can be characterized by its duration as well as by its yield. It is therefore of some interest to inquire how we might compute the duration of a portfolio of several different bonds from the durations of the bonds in the portfolio.

Supposes that we have a portfolio of N different bonds. Let

$P_i + A_i =$ quoted market price plus accrued interest for $1 million principal amount of the ith bond,

$V_i(r)$ = dollar value of a basis point for the ith bond when the yield on the bond is r, expressed as the change in value of $1 million principal amount of the bond associated with a change in yield of 1 basis point, or a change in yield from r to $r + .0001$,

R_i = yield on the ith bond,

R = yield on the portfolio of bonds, computed as the value of R that satisfies equation (13.3) or approximated as in equation (13.15).

We can compute the duration $D_i(R)$ of the ith bond at yield R as

$$D_i(R) = \frac{V_i(R) \cdot (1 + \frac{1}{2}R)}{.0001 \cdot (P_i + A_i)} \tag{S13.1}$$

(This expression for duration uses equation S4.2 in chapter 4; ΔV in that equation becomes $V_i(R)$ in equation (S13.1), ΔR becomes .0001, and V becomes $P_i + A_i$.) We can similarly compute the duration $D(R)$ of the portfolio at yield R as

$$D(R) = \frac{[\sum_{i=1}^{N} Q_i \cdot V_i(R)] \cdot (1 + \frac{1}{2}R)}{.0001 \cdot \sum_{i=1}^{N} Q_i \cdot (P_i + A_i)} \tag{S13.2}$$

where Q_i is the quantity of the ith bond in the portfolio, expressed in units of millions of dollars of principal value.

From equation (S13.1) we have

$$V_i(R) = \frac{D_i(R) \cdot (P_i + A_i)}{(1 + \frac{1}{2}R) \cdot 1000.} \tag{S13.3}$$

Substituting this expression for $V_i(R)$ into equation (S13.2) gives

$$D(R) = \frac{\sum_{i=1}^{N} Q_i \cdot (P_i + A_i) \cdot D_i(R)}{\sum_{i=1}^{N} Q_i \cdot (P_i + A_i)} \tag{S13.4}$$

This shows quite directly that the duration of the portfolio can be computed as a value-weighted average of the durations of the bonds in the portfolio.

It should be noted that the duration of the ith bond in equation (S13.4) is computed at the portfolio yield R rather than at the bond yield R_i. Most analysts ignore this detail and approximate the duration of the portfolio as

$$D^a = \frac{\sum_{i=1}^{N} Q_i \cdot (P_i + A_i) \cdot D_i(R_i)}{\sum_{i=1}^{N} Q_i \cdot (P_i + A_i)} \tag{S13.5}$$

Equations (S13.4) and (S13.5) give similar results if yields on individual bonds are not too different from the yield on the portfolio or if the durations of the individual bonds are not too sensitive to the yields on the bonds.

14 Butterfly Trades: A Critical Assessment of Yield, Convexity, and Risk

During the past five years an increasing quantity of funds allocated to fixed income securities has been directed to "indexed" portfolios. Although details vary, these portfolios are generally structured to maintain a target duration continuously through time. The target may be either a fixed number, such as 4 years, or the duration of a well-known representative bond portfolio, such as the portfolio of all out standing Treasury securities.

Indexing is widely viewed as a device to limit discretionary money management based on interest rate forecasting. A manager running an indexed portfolio cannot extend out along the yield curve when he thinks rates are going to fall nor can he contract back into shorter maturities if he thinks rates will rise. As a result money managers have had to search for other ways to demonstrate superior investment skill.

So-called "butterfly" trades are return-enhancement devices that have become popular in the context of indexed portfolio management. A butterfly trade consists of the sale of one issue, such as a 5-year Treasury note, and simultaneous purchase of shorter and longer maturity issues, such as 2-year and 10-year notes. The trade is structured so that the proceeds from the sale match the aggregate cost of the purchases and so that the duration (or some related risk measure) of the portfolio remains the same. Butterfly trades fit nicely within the framework of indexed portfolio management precisely because they leave both value and duration unchanged.

Roughly speaking, a butterfly trade is deemed beneficial if the average yield on the securities purchased exceeds the yield on the security which is sold. Some portfolio managers will accept a yield give-up if they can acquire a bond position with significantly greater convexity.

This chapter presents a critical assessment of several analytical aspects of butterfly trades involving U.S. Treasury bonds. Section 14.1 describes how to weight a butterfly trade and compares weighting schemes based on duration and the value of a basis point. Section 14.2 reviews the premise of a butterfly trade: to increase yield and/or convexity while keeping both value and risk unchanged. The implies that a portfolio manager needs good measures of yield, convexity, and risk. These three topics are discussed in sections 14.3, 14.4, and 14.5. Section 14.6 concludes the paper with a restatement of the trade-offs implicit in a butterfly trade.

14.1 Weighting a Butterfly

As noted in the introduction, a butterfly trade consists of the sale of one security and simultaneous purchase of shorter and longer maturity issues.

Written in April 1989.

Table 14.1
Characteristics of bonds in a butterfly trade for settlement on January 5, 1988

	Bond 1 (2-year)	Bond 2 (5-year)	Bond 3 (10-year)
Coupon	$7\frac{7}{8}\%$	$8\frac{1}{4}\%$	$8\frac{7}{8}\%$
Maturity	12/31/1989	2/15/1993	11/15/1997
Quoted price	$100\frac{7}{32}$	$99\frac{18}{32}$	$100\frac{12}{32}$
Accrued interest	.1082	.7847	1.2435
Invoice price	100.3269	100.3472	101.6185
Conventional yield	7.753%	8.342%	8.814%
Value of a basis point	$181.53	$409.29	$652.07
Modified duration	1.809	4.079	6.417
Conventional duration	1.879	4.249	6.700

"Weighting" a butterfly is a matter of deciding how much of the shorter maturity issue and how much of the longer issue should be purchased.

Consider, for example, the three securities described in table 14.1. Suppose that an investor owns $1 million par amount of the 5-year note and decides to swap into weighted amounts of the 2-year and 10-year notes for settlement on January 5, 1988. He needs to compute the appropriate par amounts of his purchases.

This section describes how to weight a butterfly trade. We first present a scheme based on the value of a basis point and then show that using modified duration gives identical results. We also show that the scheme is nearly equivalent to one based on conventional or Macaulay duration.

Weighting with the Value of a Basis Point

There are two unknowns in weighting a butterfly trade: the amount of the shorter issue to be purchased and the amount of the longer issue. To solve for these two unknowns, we have to specify two conditions.

The first condition on a butterfly trade stipulates that the aggregate cost of the purchases must equal the proceeds from the sale. In other words, the trade should neither generate nor require any cash.

Suppose that an investor contemplates selling $1 million par amount of the 5-year note in table 14.1 and buying $.507567 million par amount of the 2-year note and $.486374 million of the 10-year note. From the invoice prices in table 14.1 we have that the proceeds from the sale of the 5-year note are

Proceeds = $(1.0) \cdot (\$1,003,472)$

$= \$1,003,472$

The aggregate cost of $.507567 million of the 2-year note and $.486374 million of the 10-year note is

$$\text{Cost} = (.507567) \cdot (\$1,003,269) \cdot (.486374) \cdot (\$1,016,185)$$

$$= \$509,226 + \$494,246$$

$$= \$1,003,472$$

This shows that the contemplated trade satisfies the proceeds constraint.

The second condition on a butterfly trade stipulates that the aggregate value of a basis point for the bonds purchased must equal the aggregate value of a basis point for the bonds sold. In other words, the value of the 2-year/10-year portfolio should change like the value of the 5-year note for small parallel shifts in bond yields.

Consider again the example of an investor selling $1 million par amount of the 5-year note and buying $.507567 million of the 2-year note and $.486374 million of the 10-year note. From the data in table 14.1, we have that the value of a basis point on the 5-year note is

$$\text{vbp} = (1.0) \cdot (409.29)$$

$$= \$409.29 \text{ per basis point}$$

The aggregate value of a basis point on the 2 year/10 year portfolio is

$$\text{vbp} = (.507567) \cdot (181.53) + (.486374) \cdot (652.07)$$

$$= 92.14 + 317.15$$

$$= \$409.29 \text{ per basis point}$$

This shows directly that a change in yield of one basis point will change the value of the 5-year note and the value of the 2-year/10-year portfolio by the same amounts. Thus the contemplated swap also satisfies the risk constraint on a butterfly trade.

An Analytical Derivation of the Weighting of a Butterfly Trade

It is not difficult to derive an algebraic expression for weighting a butterfly trade.

Assume that we have three bonds indexed as $i = 1, 2,$ and 3, and assume that we want to sell bond 2 and buy bonds 1 and 3. Let P_i denote the invoice price (quoted price plus accrued interest) on bond i, expressed as a percent of par value, and let Q_i denote the par value of bond i, expressed in millions of dollars. The proceeds constraint on a butterfly trade requires that

$$Q_2 \cdot P_2 = Q_1 \cdot P_1 + Q_3 \cdot P_3 \tag{14.1}$$

Now let V_i denote the value of a basis point for bond i, expressed as the change in value of $1 million par amount of the bond for a change in the yield on the bond of one basis point. The risk constraint on a butterfly trade requires that

$$Q_2 \cdot V_2 = Q_1 \cdot V_1 + Q_3 \cdot V_3 \tag{14.2}$$

Equations (14.1) and (14.2) specify two equations in two unknowns. The equations can be reduced to

$$Q_1 = \frac{P_2 \cdot V_3 - P_3 \cdot V_2}{P_1 \cdot V_3 - P_3 \cdot V_1} \cdot Q_2 \tag{14.3a}$$

$$Q_3 = \frac{P_1 \cdot V_2 - P_2 \cdot V_1}{P_1 \cdot V_3 - P_3 \cdot V_1} \cdot Q_2 \tag{14.3b}$$

If we use $Q_2 = \$1.0$ million par amount and the following values from table 14.1,

$$P_1 = 100.3269 \quad V_1 = \$181.53$$

$$P_2 = 100.3472 \quad V_2 = 409.29$$

$$P_3 = 101.6185 \quad V_3 = 652.07$$

in equation (14.3a) we get

$$Q_1 = \frac{(100.3472) \cdot (652.07) - (101.6185) \cdot (409.29)}{(100.3269) \cdot (652.07) - (101.6185) \cdot (181.53)} \cdot (1.0)$$

$$= .507567 \tag{14.4a}$$

If we use the same values in equation (14.3b), we get

$$Q_3 = \frac{(100.3269) \cdot (409.29) - (100.3472) \cdot (181.53)}{(100.3269) \cdot (652.07) - (101.6185) \cdot (181.53)} \cdot (1.0)$$

$$= .486374 \tag{14.4b}$$

Thus a properly weighted butterfly trade requires the purchase of $.507567 million par amount of the 2-year note and the purchase of $.486374 million par amount of the 10-year note for each $1.0 million par amount of the 5-year note sold.

Other Weighting Schemes

It should be noted that maintaining value and the aggregate value of a basis point are not the only two conditions that can be imposed on a butterfly trade. Other pairs of conditions lead to different weighting schemes.

For example, in section 14.5 we will examine an "arbitrage butterfly" which is weighted to maintain (1) the aggregate value of a basis point and (2) the sensitivity of value to change in the slope of the yield curve. The weighting of an arbitrage butterfly is quite different from the weighting of a conventional, or investor's, butterfly which is the primary focus of this chapter.

Weighting with Modified Duration

In some cases an investor may prefer to work with modified duration rather than with the value of a basis point in weighting a butterfly trade. It turns out that the two techniques produce identical results.

The modified duration of a bond measures the relative change in the bond's value per basis point of yield change. (This can be compared to the value of a basis point, which measures the dollar change in value per basis point of yield change.) Modified duration can be computed as the bond's value of a basis point divided by the invoice price of the bond. Thus, the modified duration of the 2-year note in table 14.1 is

$$D_1^{mod} = \frac{V_1}{P_1}$$

$$= \frac{181.53}{100.3269}$$

$$= 1.809 \tag{14.5}$$

The biggest difference in weighting a butterfly trade with modified duration is that the sizes of the bond positions are denominated in terms of market value. As noted above, bond positions are expressed in terms of par value when weighting with the value of a basis point.

Let q_i denote the total market value of the position in bond i for $i = 1$, 2, and 3. Assuming, as above, that the investor wants to sell bond 2 against buying bonds 1 and 3 the proceeds constraint is

$$q_2 = q_1 + q_3 \tag{14.6}$$

The risk constraint says that the modified duration of the bonds sold must equal the average modified duration of the bonds purchased:

$$D_2^{mod} = \frac{q_1 \cdot D_1^{mod} + q_3 \cdot D_3^{mod}}{q_1 + q_3} \tag{14.7}$$

In other words, the butterfly trade must leave unchanged the relative sensitivity of value to changes in yield.

It is not difficult to show that equations (14.6) and (14.7) are identical to equations (14.1) and (14.2). Observe first that, by definition, the total market value of a bond is its invoice price times the quantity of the bond. This implies that $q_i = Q_i \cdot P_i$ for $i = 1, 2, 3$. Equation (14.6) is therefore equivalent to

$$Q_2 \cdot P_2 = Q_1 \cdot P_1 + Q_3 \cdot P_3 \tag{14.8}$$

which is exactly equation (14.1). Next note that from equation (14.6), equation (14.7) can be written as

$$D_2^{\text{mod}} = \frac{q_1 \cdot D_1^{\text{mod}} + q_3 \cdot D_3^{\text{mod}}}{q_2}$$

or

$$q_2 \cdot D_2^{\text{mod}} = q_1 \cdot D_1^{\text{mod}} + q_3 \cdot D_3^{\text{mod}}$$

Using $q_i = Q_i \cdot P_i$ and $D_i^{\text{mod}} = V_i / P_i$, this becomes

$$(Q_2 \cdot P_2) \cdot \left(\frac{V_2}{P_2} \right) = (Q_1 \cdot P_1) \cdot \left(\frac{V_1}{P_1} \right) + (Q_3 \cdot P_3) \cdot \left(\frac{V_3}{P_3} \right)$$

or

$$Q_2 \cdot V_2 = Q_1 \cdot V_1 + Q_3 \cdot V_3 \tag{14.9}$$

which is exactly equation (14.2). Thus weighting a butterfly trade with modified duration is identical to weighting a butterfly trade with the value of a basis point.

Weighting with Conventional Duration

An investor might also choose to weight a butterfly trade with conventional, or Macaulay, duration.

The conventional duration of a bond can be computed as

$$D_i^{\text{con}} = \frac{V_i \cdot (1 + \frac{1}{2} R_i)}{P_i} \tag{14.10}$$

where V_i is the value of a basis point for the bond, P_i is the invoice price of the bond, and R_i is the yield on the bond assuming semi-annual compounding. Thus the conventional duration of the 2-year note in table 14.1 is

$$D_1^{\text{con}} = \frac{(181.53) \cdot (1 + \frac{1}{2}(.07753))}{100.3269}$$

$$= 1.879 \tag{14.11}$$

The size of a bond position is expressed in terms of market value when weighting a butterfly trade with conventional duration. Let q_i again denote the total market value of bond i for $i = 1, 2,$ and 3. The proceeds constraint is then

$$q_2 = q_1 + q_3 \tag{14.12}$$

and the risk constraint is

$$D_2^{con} = \frac{q_1 \cdot D_1^{con} + q_3 \cdot D_3^{con}}{q_1 + q_3} \tag{14.13}$$

The weightings from equations (14.12) and (14.13) are slightly different than the weightings derived from equations (14.1) and (14.2) or from equations (14.6) and (14.7). From the observation that $q_i = Q_i \cdot P_i$, equation (14.12) becomes

$$Q_2 \cdot P_2 = Q_1 \cdot P_1 + Q_3 \cdot P_3 \tag{14.14}$$

From the definition of conventional duration in equation (14.10) equation (14.13) becomes

$$Q_2 \cdot V_2 \cdot (1 + \tfrac{1}{2}R_2) = Q_1 \cdot V_1 \cdot (1 + \tfrac{1}{2}R_1) + Q_3 \cdot V_3 \cdot (1 + \tfrac{1}{2}R_3) \tag{14.15}$$

Equation (14.14) is identical to equation (14.1) but equation (14.15) differs from equation (14.2) unless the yield curve is flat and $R_1 = R_2 = R_3$.

As a practical matter the difference between equations (14.2) and (14.15) has trivial consequences. Using the data from table 14.1 and $Q_2 = \$1.0$ million par amount, equations (14.14) and (14.15) give the weightings

$$Q_1 = .508541$$

$$Q_3 = .485412$$

This is quite close to the values of $Q_1 = .507567$ and $Q_3 = .486374$ derived from weighting with the value of a basis point or modified duration. (See equations 14.4a and 14.4b.)

It follows that a correctly weighted butterfly trade leaves value, the aggregate value of a basis point, and modified duration unchanged, and (to a very close approximation) leaves conventional duration unchanged.

14.2   Why Do a Butterfly Trade?

Having considered in some detail the mechanics of weighting a butterfly trade, we are ready to appreciate a careful restatement of the premise for such a trade. The restatement will serve to motivate the assessments of yield, convexity, and risk in the following sections.

By construction, a butterfly trade leaves two characteristics of a bond position unchanged: value and the aggregate value of a basis point. The second constraint is sometimes expressed by saying that a butterfly maintains the *risk* of the position.

A butterfly trade can be interpreted as a swap of one security for a "synthetic" substitute or for a pair of different securities with the same aggregate market value and the same aggregate risk. The swap is usually motivated by a desire to increase yield or convexity.

These characteristics of a butterfly trade raise several questions:

1. Is keeping the aggregate value of a basis point unchanged equivalent to keeping risk unchanged? For example, is the 2-year/10-year portfolio calculated in section 14.1 really a synthetic substitute for the 5-year note?

2. How should the yield on a bond be measured if we intend to compare yields on different bonds? (This is a matter of recognizing things like weekend maturities and different day counts.)

3. How should the yield on a portfolio of several bonds be calculated?

4. How important is convexity for the relative price performance of, for example, a 2-year/10-year portfolio versus a 5-year note?

We address these issues in the following sections.

14.3   A Critical Assessment of Yield

This section examines several aspects of the problem of measuring yield on fixed income securities in the context of butterfly trades. We first present a general definition of yield and then show how that definition can be applied to individual bonds and bond portfolios.

We suggest that the conventional definition of the yield on a Treasury bond is not completely appropriate for assessing yield pickups and give-ups on butterfly trades. We also argue that the usual definition of the yield on a portfolio of bonds—as value-weighted average of the yields on the bonds in the portfolio—has serious shortcomings which dramatically affect the assessment of a butterfly trade.

A General Definition of Yield

Consider a collection of N future payments of money where the ith payment is for the amount F_i and will occur in x_i semi-annual periods (or in $\frac{1}{2}x_i$ years). Let P denote the present cost or invoice price of acquiring the payments.

We define the yield on the collection of cash flows as the discount rate at which the present value of the future payments equals the invoice price P. That is, the yield is the value of R that satisfies the equation

$$P = \sum_{i=1}^{N} F_i \cdot (1 + \tfrac{1}{2}R)^{-x_i} \tag{14.16}$$

R is compounded semi-annually in this expression.

The only ambiguity in equation (14.16) is how the x_is should be computed. Suppose, for example, that the first payment occurs 177 days after purchase. What is the resulting value of x_1 in semi-annual periods?

We propose that the time to a future payment, measured in semi-annual periods, be defined as the number of days to that payment divided by 182.625. This is equivalent to defining a standard semi-annual interval as 182.625 days or a standard year as 365.25 days. (The extra $\tfrac{1}{4}$ day accounts for a leap day every four years.) Thus $x_1 = .969199$ semi-annual periods if a payment is received 177 days after purchase ($.969199 = \frac{177}{182.625}$).

Example 1 illustrates the use of equation (14.16) with a numerical example.

The Conventional Yield on a Treasury Bond

The conventional yield on a Treasury bond is defined in a manner similar to equation (14.16). We first describe some essential features of the definition and then suggest why those features limit the usefulness of conventional yield in assessing yield pickups and give-ups on butterfly trades. Further details on conventional yields appear in chapter 1.

It is helpful to refer to a specific example in describing the conventional yield on a Treasury bond. Consider therefore the yield on the $6\tfrac{1}{4}\%$ bond

Example 1
Application of the definition of yield in equation (14.16)

Suppose that we can purchase at an invoice price of $P = 99.023352$ for settlement on January 5, 1988, the following two future payments:

Date of payment	Amount	Days to payment	x_i
Jun. 30, 1988	3.125	177	.969199
Jan. 3, 1989	103.125	364	1.993155

The yield on the future payments, computed using equation (14.16), is the value of R that satisfies the equation:

$$99.023352 = 3.125 \cdot (1 + \tfrac{1}{2}R)^{-.969199} + 103.125 \cdot (1 + \tfrac{1}{2}R)^{-1.993155}$$

or $R = .07309$, or 7.309% per annum, compounded semi-annually.

of December 31, 1988, quoted at $98\frac{30}{32}$ for settlement on January 5, 1988. This bond is scheduled to make two future payments: 3.125% of principal on June 30, 1988, and 103.125% of principal on December 31, 1988. The invoice price of the bond is 99.023352 (99.023352 = $98\frac{30}{32}$ quoted price, plus .085852 points of accrued interest from the last coupon payment on December 31, 1987, to settlement on January 5, 1988).

The conventional yield on the bond is the value of Y that satisfies the equation

$$99.023352 = 3.125 \cdot (1 + \tfrac{1}{2}Y)^{-w_1} + 103.125 \cdot (1 + \tfrac{1}{2}Y)^{-w_2} \qquad (14.17)$$

where w_i is the time to the ith payment in semi-annual periods.

Equation (14.17) looks identical to equation (14.16). The difference is in the calculation of w_1 and w_2. w_1 is calculated as the number of days from settlement on January 5, 1988, to the first coupon payment on June 30, 1988 (177 days) divided by the number of days in the current coupon period of December 31, 1987 to June 30, 1988 (182 days). Thus $w_1 = \frac{177}{182} = .972527$. The second payment (of 103.125) is assumed to occur exactly one semi-annual period after the first payment, so $w_2 = 1 + w_1 = 1.972527$. Substituting these values in equation (14.17) gives a yield of $Y = .07385$, or 7.385% per annum, compounded semi-annually.

Problems with Conventional Yield

There are three problems with the foregoing calculation of yield. First, the calculation fails to take account of the fact that the payment of 103.125 scheduled for December 31, 1988, will actually be made three days later. (December 31, 1988, is a Saturday. The following Monday is a bank holiday for New Year's Day, so the payment is made on Tuesday, January 3, 1989.) Second, the calculation defines the length of a semi-annual period as the number of days in the current coupon interval of a bond. Depending on the bond and the settlement date, this could be 181, 182, 183, or 184 days. Third, the calculation defines all payments after the first payment as exactly one semi-annual interval apart, even though the day counts between payments are not all identical.

As a consequence of these features the conventional yield of 7.385% on the $6\frac{1}{4}\%$ notes of December 31, 1988, is 7.6 basis points greater than the yield on the same set of cash flows calculated with equation (14.16) in example 1.

The difference between the conventional yield on a Treasury bond and the yield calculated with equation (14.16), which we will call the "true" yield, can be either positive or negative. Thus a conventional assessment of any particular butterfly trade can either understate or overstate the true yield pickup or give-up on the trade. The net effect depends, for example, on whether bonds with a Saturday maturity date are being bought or sold. However, the significance of the problems with conventional yield are *de minimis* for bonds maturing in more than three years (see chapter 5).

The Yield on a Portfolio of Bonds

Conceptually a portfolio of bonds is the same as a single bond: a collection of future payments that can be purchased at some invoice price. Thus the true yield on a portfolio can be calculated with equation (14.16).

As a practical matter, most market participants like to compute the yield on a bond portfolio as a weighted average combination of the yields on the individual bonds in the portfolio. We suggest that the best way to compute such an average yield is weighting bond yields by the aggregate value of a basis point rather than by market value. The analytical basis for this suggestion has been examined in chapter 13. We present here a numerical example illustrating the merits of the suggestion.

Consider again the butterfly trade described in section 14.1, where an investor sells \$1.0 million par amount of the 5-year note in table 14.1 and buys \$.507567 million of the 2-year note and \$.486374 million of the 10-year note. Table 14.2 summarizes the yields on the three bonds.

The true yield on the 2-year/10-year portfolio, calculated with equation (14.16), is 8.572% per annum, compounded semi-annually. The value-weighted average of the true yields on the 2-year note and 10-year note is

$$R_a = \frac{Q_1 \cdot P_1 \cdot R_1 + Q_3 \cdot P_3 \cdot R_3}{Q_1 \cdot P_1 + Q_3 \cdot P_3}$$

$$= \frac{(.507567) \cdot (100.3269) \cdot (7.737) + (.486374) \cdot (101.6185) \cdot (8.810)}{(.507567) \cdot (100.3269) + (.486374) \cdot (101.6185)}$$

$$= 8.265\% \tag{14.18}$$

Table 14.2
Yield characteristics of bonds in a butterfly trade for settlement on January 5, 1988

	Bond 1 (2-year)	Bond 2 (5-year)	Bond 3 (10-year)
Coupon	$7\frac{7}{8}\%$	$8\frac{1}{4}\%$	$8\frac{7}{8}\%$
Maturity	12/31/1989	2/15/1993	11/15/1997
Quoted price	$100\frac{7}{32}$	$99\frac{18}{32}$	$100\frac{12}{32}$
Accrued interest	.1082	.7847	1.2435
Invoice price	100.3269	100.3472	101.6185
Conventional yield	7.753%	8.342%	8.814%
True yield	7.737	8.338	8.810

The value of a basis point-weighted average of the true yields on the 2 year and 10 year notes is:

$$R_a = \frac{Q_1 \cdot V_1 \cdot R_1 + Q_3 \cdot V_3 \cdot R_3}{Q_1 \cdot V_1 + Q_3 \cdot V_3}$$

$$= \frac{(.507567) \cdot (181.53) \cdot (7.737) + (.486374) \cdot (652.07) \cdot (8.810)}{(.507567) \cdot (181.53) + (.486374) \cdot (652.07)}$$

$$= 8.568\% \tag{14.19}$$

This illustrates that weighting with the value of a basis point (as in equation 14.19) produces a value closer to the value from equation (14.16) than weighting with market value.

More specifically, the butterfly trade described in section 14.1 is seen to produce a yield pickup of 23.0 basis points ($.230 = 8.568 - 8.338$) rather than a yield give-up of 7.3 basis points ($-.073 = 8.265 - 8.338$).

Summary

This section criticized two aspects of conventional measures of the yield pickup on a butterfly trade. First, we pointed out that the conventional yield on a bond fails to recognize weekend maturities and makes arbitrary assumptions on the length of a semi-annual period and the number of semi-annual periods between coupon payments. This can affect bond yield by as much as several basis points. Second, we showed that computing the yield on a portfolio as a value-weighted average of the yields on the bonds in the portfolio can affect portfolio yield by several tens of basis points.

We suggested that bond yields be computed with equation (14.16), which dates payments to when they are made and which uses a standard definition of the length of a semi-annual period. We also suggested that the yield on a portfolio of bonds be computed either with equation (14.16) or as a value of a basis point-weighted average of the true yields on the bonds in the portfolio.

14.4   A Critical Assessment of Convexity

By construction, the aggregate value of a basis point of the bond portfolio purchased in a butterfly trade equals the aggregate value of a basis point of the bonds sold. As a result the value of the portfolio of shorter and longer maturity issues changes by the same amount as the value of the middle issue for small, parallel, yield shifts. However, if the general level of interest rates changes (up *or* down) by a *substantial* amount, the portfolio will outperform the middle security. The superior performance is a mani-festation of greater convexity.

This section illustrates the implications of convexity for relative price performance and points out that the phenomenon is grounded in the way in which the value of a basis point changes as yields vary. We also show that the convexity pickup on a butterfly trade is related to the difference between the maturities of the shorter and longer issues. A butterfly trade out of a 5-year note into a portfolio of 2-year and 10-year notes increases convexity by more than a butterfly trade out of the same 5-year note into a portfolio of 4-year and 7-year notes.

Relative Price Performance as a Manifestation of Convexity

Consider again the butterfly trade described in section 14.1 where an investor sells $1.0 million par amount of the 5-year note in table 14.1 and buys $.507567 million of the 2-year note and $.486374 million of the 10-year note. The value of the 5-year note (including accrued interest) is $1,003,472 for settlement on January 5, 1988. The butterfly trade is con-structed so that the value of the 2-year/10-year portfolio is also $1,003,472 on that settlement date.

Table 14.3 and figure 14.1 show how the value of the 5-year note varies as a function of change in the yield on the note. As expected, the note becomes more valuable as yields fall and conversely. Table 14.3 and figure 14.1 also show how the value of the 2-year/10-year portfolio changes as a function of change in the yields on the notes in the portfolio.

Table 14.3
Value as a function of changes in yields

Change from base yields	Value of 5-year note[a]	Value of 2-year/10-year portfolio[b]	Difference
+3.00%	$ 889,479	$ 892,807	$3,328
+2.00	925,595	927,160	1,566
+1.00	963,557	963,971	414
0	1,003,472	1,003,472	0
−1.00	1,045,454	1,045,919	465
−2.00	1,089,624	1,091,598	1,973
−3.00	1,136,111	1,140,822	4,711

a. $1.0 million par amount of $8\frac{1}{4}\%$ of 2/15/1993, base true yield of 8.338% for settlement January 5, 1988.
b. $.507567 million par amount of $7\frac{7}{8}\%$ of 12/31/1989, base true yield of 7.737%, and $.486374 million par amount of $8\frac{7}{8}\%$ of 11/15/1997, base true yield of 8.810%, for settlement January 5, 1988.

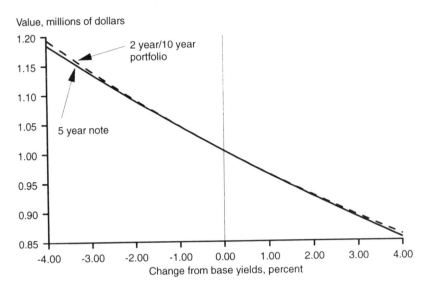

Figure 14.1
Value versus change from base yields (data taken from table 14.3)

What is remarkable about the data in table 14.3 and figure 14.1 is the observation that the value of the portfolio rises faster than the value of the 5-year note as yields fall and that it falls more slowly as yields rise. Thus the portfolio outperforms the 5-year note *regardless* of whether interest rates go up or down. This is a result of the greater convexity of the portfolio.

Table 14.3 suggests that an investor might do a butterfly trade, even without a pickup in yield, to increase the convexity of his portfolio. However, it is evident from figure 14.1 that greater convexity is a valuable attribute only in the context of large yield changes. If yields vary by only a few tens of basis points, the superior performance of a more convex position is negligible.

Why More Convex Portfolios Exhibit Superior Price Performance

It is instructive to consider why the 2-year/10-year portfolio outperforms the 5-year note regardless of whether interest rates go up or down.

Table 14.4 shows the value of a basis point for $1.0 million par amount of each of the securities in table 14.1 as a function of changes in yield. In all three cases the value of a basis point rises as yields fall, and conversely.

The 2-year/10-year portfolio consists of $.507567 million par amount of the 2-year note, and $.486374 million of the 10-year note. The aggregate value of a basis point of the portfolio is therefore

Table 14.4
Value of a basis point as a function of changes in yields

Change from base yield	Value of a basis point			
	2-year note[a]	5-year note[b]	10-year note[c]	2-year/ 10-year portfolio[d]
+3.00%	$169.26	$352.27	$505.89	$331.96
+2.00	173.24	370.22	550.04	355.45
+1.00	177.33	389.20	589.61	381.15
0.0	181.53	409.29	652.07	409.29
−1.00	185.87	430.55	710.96	440.13
−2.00	190.32	453.07	775.87	473.96
−3.00	194.91	476.91	847.47	511.11

a. $1.0 million par amount of $7\frac{7}{8}\%$ of 12/31/1989, base true yield of 7.737%.
b. $1.0 million par amount of $8\frac{1}{4}\%$ of 2/15/1993, base true yield of 8.338%.
c. $1.0 million par amount of $8\frac{7}{8}\%$ of 11/15/1997, base true yield of 8.810%.
d. $.507567 million par amount of 2-year note, and $.486374 million par amount of 10-year note.

$$.507567 \cdot V_1 + .486374 \cdot V_3 \tag{14.20}$$

where V_1 is the value of a basis point for $1.0 million par amount of the 2-year note and V_3 is the value of a basis point for $1.0 million of the 10-year note.

Table 14.4 shows that the value of a basis point for the 2-year/10-year portfolio rises faster than the value of a basis point of the 5-year note as yields fall. This is why the portfolio outperforms the 5-year note when interest rates decline. Conversely, the value of a basis point of the portfolio declines faster than the value of a basis point of the 5-year note as rates rise. This explains why the portfolio also outperforms the 5-year note in a bear market.

Different Butterfly Trades Exhibit Different Relative Price Behavior

It is important to keep in mind that different butterfly trades will exhibit different relative price behavior in rising and falling markets.

Consider, for example, a butterfly trade based on the securities in table 14.5 where an investor sells $1.0 million of the 5-year note and buys $.519971 million of the 4-year note and $.453231 million of the 7-year note. This is similar to the butterfly trade based on the securities in table 14.1 except that the shorter maturity issue is not as short (a 4-year note instead of a 2-year note) and the longer maturity issue is not as long (a 7-year note instead of a 10-year note).

As shown in table 14.6, the 4-year/7-year portfolio does not outperform the 5-year note by as much as the 2-year/10-year portfolio in either bull or

Table 14.5
Characteristics of bonds in a butterfly trade for settlement January 5, 1988

	Bond 1 (4-year)	Bond 2 (5-year)	Bond 3 (7-year)
Coupon	$8\frac{1}{4}\%$	$8\frac{1}{4}\%$	$9\frac{1}{2}\%$
Maturity	12/31/1991	2/15/1993	10/15/1994
Quoted price	$100\frac{3}{32}$	$99\frac{18}{32}$	$104\frac{10}{32}$
Accrued interest	.1133	.7847	2.1284
Invoice price	100.2071	100.3472	106.4409
Conventional yield	8.221%	8.342%	8.641%
True yield	8.220	8.338	8.634
Value of a basis point	$334.40	$409.29	$519.41

Table 14.6
Value of a 5-year note and a 4-year/7-year portfolio as a function of changes in yields

Change from base yields	Value of 5-year note[a]	Value of 4-year/7-year portfolio[b]	Difference
+3.00%	$ 889,479	$ 889,999	$521
+2.00	925,595	925,839	244
+1.00	963,557	963,621	65
0	1,003,472	1,003,472	0
−1.00	1,045,454	1,045,526	72
−2.00	1,089,624	1,089,925	301
−3.00	1,135,111	1,136,826	715

a. $1.0 million par amount of $8\frac{1}{4}\%$ of 2/15/1993, base true yield of 8.338% for settlement January 5, 1988.
b. $.519971 million par amount of $8\frac{1}{4}\%$ of 12/31/1991, base true yield of 8.220%, and $.453231 million par amount of $9\frac{1}{2}\%$ of 10/15/1994, base true yield of 8.634%, for settlement January 5, 1988.

bear markets. That is, the butterfly into the 4-year/7-year portfolio does not pick up as much convexity as the butterfly into the 2-year/10-year portfolio.

A Comment on Convexity Pickups and Yield Pickups

Many market participants believe that convexity is a valuable attribute and that, to increase convexity, they usually have to give up yield. The examples presented thus far suggest that this belief is not well founded.

We already demonstrated that the 2-year/10-year portfolio of table 14.1 has more convexity than the 4-year/7-year portfolio of table 14.5. It turns out that the former portfolio also has a higher yield and thus a greater yield pickup.

The value of a basis point-weighted average yield on the 4-year/7-year portfolio is 8.458%, giving a yield pickup of 12.0 basis points over the 8.338% yield on the 5-year note. We showed in section 14.3 that the value of a basis point-weighted average yield on the 2-year/10-year portfolio is 8.568%, giving a yield pickup of 23.0 basis points. Thus more convex positions do not necessarily have lower yields.

14.5   A Critical Assessment of Risk

We observed in section 14.2 that a butterfly trade is sometimes represented as a swap of one security for a "synthetic" substitute, where the swap is motivated by a yield and/or convexity pickup. The concept of a synthetic substitute is predicated on the two constraints of a butterfly trade: that value and the aggregate value of a basis point remain unchanged.

This section critically examines the proposition that the securities purchased in a butterfly trade constitute a *bona fide* substitute for the security sold. We point out that even for small yield shifts, changes in the value of the purchased portfolio are not always identical to changes in the value of the security sold. This implies that the portfolio bears a somewhat different kind of risk than the original security.

At least some of this different risk can be identified as the risk of change in the slope of the yield curve. In particular, the portfolio of securities purchased in a butterfly trade can be expected to outperform the security sold if the yield curve flattens and to underperform the security sold if the curve steepens.

More generally, a butterfly trade should not be viewed as a swap of one security for a genuine substitute. Instead, it must be viewed as a swap that maintains the sensitivity of value to small parallel yield shifts but that increases the sensitivity of value to change in the slope of the curve.

Comparative Fluctuations in the Values of the Legs of a Butterfly Trade

The cleanest way to express analytically the notion that one security is a substitute for another security (in a risk sense) is to require that the values of the two securities always change dollar for dollar. This concept can be applied to butterfly trades.

Consider, for example, three securities indexed as $i = 1$, 2, and 3. An investor contemplates selling Q_2 units of security 2 and buying Q_1 and Q_3 units of securities 1 and 3, respectively, in weighted amounts as described in section 14.1, where Q_i is denominated in millions of dollars of par value. If the yield on security i changes by the amount ΔR_i, the change in the value of the security sold will, to a first-order approximation, be

$$\Delta W_2 = -Q_2 \cdot V_2 \cdot \Delta R_2 \tag{14.21}$$

and the change in the value of the purchased portfolio will, to a first-order approximation, be

$$\Delta W_{1,3} = -Q_1 \cdot V_1 \cdot \Delta R_1 - Q_3 \cdot V_3 \cdot \Delta R_3 \tag{14.22}$$

where V_i is the value of a basis point for \$1.0 million par amount of security i. The portfolio of securities 1 and 3 can be considered a perfect substitute (in a first-order risk sense) for security 2 if $\Delta W_{1,3} = \Delta W_2$ for all possible values of ΔR_1, ΔR_2, and ΔR_3.

To begin to explore the implications of this definition, suppose that all bond yields always change by the same amount. Let ΔR denote the size of a particular yield change so that $\Delta R_1 = \Delta R_2 = \Delta R_3 = \Delta R$. Equation (14.21) then becomes

$$\Delta W_2 = -(Q_2 \cdot V_2) \cdot \Delta R \tag{14.23}$$

and equation (14.22) becomes

$$\Delta W_{1,3} = -(Q_1 \cdot V_1 + Q_3 \cdot V_3) \cdot \Delta R \tag{14.24}$$

Since the trade was structured as a butterfly trade it follows from equation (14.2) that $\Delta W_2 = \Delta W_{1,3}$ for all values of ΔR. More specifically, the purchased portfolio is a perfect substitute (in a first-order risk sense) for the security sold if yields always move in parallel.

In general, of course, yields do not always move in parallel so the portfolio purchased in a butterfly trade is not necessarily a genuine substitute for the security sold. It is possible to quantify the degree of substitutability by examining the statistical relationship between ΔW_2 and $\Delta W_{1,3}$.

Suppose that the yield changes ΔR_1, ΔR_2, and ΔR_3 are normally distributed over a one-week interval with zero means. Let σ_i denote the standard deviation of ΔR_i, and let ρ_{ij} denote the correlation of ΔR_i with ΔR_j.

It can be shown from equations (14.21) and (14.22) that ΔW_2 and $\Delta W_{1,3}$ will also be normally distributed with zero means. The standard deviation of ΔW_2, denoted S_2, is

$$S_2 = Q_2 \cdot V_2 \cdot \sigma_2 \tag{14.25}$$

The standard deviation of $\Delta W_{1,3}$ denoted $S_{1,3}$ is

$$S_{1,3} = (Q_1^2 \cdot V_1^2 \cdot \sigma_1^2 + Q_3^2 \cdot V_3^2 \cdot \sigma_3^2 + 2 \cdot Q_1 \cdot Q_3 \cdot V_1 \cdot V_3 \cdot \rho_{1,3} \cdot \sigma_1 \cdot \sigma_3)^{1/2} \tag{14.26}$$

The correlation of ΔW_2 with $\Delta W_{1,3}$, denoted ρ, is

$$\rho = (Q_1 \cdot Q_2 \cdot V_1 \cdot V_2 \cdot \rho_{1,2} \cdot \sigma_1 \cdot \sigma_2 + Q_3 \cdot Q_2 \cdot V_3 \cdot V_2 \cdot \rho_{3,2} \cdot \sigma_3 \cdot \sigma_2)/(S_2 \cdot S_{1,3}) \tag{14.27}$$

In general, ρ will be less than unity if $\rho_{1,2}$, $\rho_{1,3}$, or $\rho_{2,3}$ is less than unity. That is, change in the value of the purchased portfolio will not be perfectly correlated with change in the value of the security sold if *any* of the pairwise bond yield changes are imperfectly correlated. It follows that a butterfly trade is not a swap of genuine substitute securities unless the *only* way interest rates can fluctuate is by parallel shifts of all bond yields.

An Example

It may be helpful to illustrate the foregoing ideas with an example based on the butterfly trade of section 14.1, where an investor sells $1.0 million par amount of the 5-year note in table 14.1 and buys $.507567 million of the 2-year note and $.486374 million of the 10-year note.

Table 14.7 shows the standard deviations and correlations of yield changes over weekly intervals for the three securities. Observe that none of the correlations are perfect. This reflects the fact that the yield curve changed in shape as well as in level over the sample interval.

Using equations (14.25), (14.26), and (14.27) and the values of a basis point from table 14.1, the standard deviation of the change in value of the 5-year note over one week is

$$S_2 = \$8,142 \tag{14.28}$$

The standard deviation of the change in value of the 2-year/10-year portfolio is

$$S_{1,3} = \$8,066 \tag{14.29}$$

The correlation of the change in value of the 5-year note with the change

Table 14.7
Standard deviations and correlations of weekly yield changes for bonds in the sectors of the bonds in table 14.1, January 8, 1986, to November 16, 1988

	Bond 1	Bond 2	Bond 3
Standard deviation	18.3 bp	19.9	20.5
Correlation with			
Bond 1	1.000	.958	.903
Bond 2	.958	1.000	.984
Bond 3	.903	.984	1.000

in value of the portfolio is

$$\rho = .994 \qquad\qquad (14.30)$$

It follows that the value of the portfolio is slightly less volatile than the value of the 5-year note (compare $S_{1,3}$ with S_2) and that change in the value of the portfolio is not perfectly correlated with change in the value of the 5-year note.

As a quantitative matter, the difference in volatilities in the example above is small and the correlation is very nearly unity. Thus the 2-year/10-year portfolio is a "nearly" perfect substitute (in a first-order risk sense) for the 5-year note. However, it is not difficult to construct butterfly trades where the substitutability is much poorer. Example 2 shows a butterfly trade out of a 7-year note into a portfolio of 2-year notes and 30-year bonds where the correlation of change in value is only .957.

In general, the substitutability of the portfolio purchased in a butterfly trade for the security sold will be poorer (1) the greater the difference between the maturities of the shorter issue purchased and the security sold and (2) the greater the difference between the maturities of the longer issue purchased and the security sold. This follows because yield changes on Treasury bonds are less highly correlated the more dissimilar the maturities of the bonds (see chapter 16).

This observation implies that there is a connection between the convexity pickup on a butterfly trade and the substitutability of the portfolio purchased for the security sold. A greater spread between the maturities of the securities in the portfolio will (1) increase the convexity pickup (see section 14.4) but (2) reduce the substitutability of the portfolio for the security sold. As a result greater convexity is obtained at the "cost" of a greater change in risk characteristics.

The Nature of the Change in Risk on a Butterfly Trade

This section has suggested that a butterfly trade alters an investor's risk exposure because the portfolio purchased is not a perfect substitute (in a first-order risk sense) for the security sold. It is instructive to examine the nature of the change in risk.

The easiest way to appreciate how a butterfly trade changes risk is to consider a different type of trade: an arbitrage butterfly. An arbitrage butterfly is structured to maintain the sensitivity of the value of a position to change in the slope of the yield curve as well as to change in the level of the curve. (It does not, however, maintain the value of the position, and it usually requires cash.) An arbitrage butterfly will make money if the yield curve becomes more convex and will lose money if the curve straightens. That is, it is exposed to the risk of change in the curvature of the yield curve.

Example 2
A butterfly trade out of a 7-year note into a 2-year note and a 30-year bond

Consider a butterfly trade out of the 7-year note and into the 2-year note and 30-year bond for settlement on January 5, 1988:

	Bond 1 (2-year)	Bond 2 (7-year)	Bond 3 (30-year)
Coupon	$7\frac{7}{8}\%$	$9\frac{1}{2}\%$	$8\frac{7}{8}\%$
Maturity	12/31/1989	10/15/1994	8/15/2017
Quoted price	$100\frac{7}{32}$	$104\frac{10}{32}$	$99\frac{7}{32}$
Accrued interest	.1082	2.1284	3.4487
Invoice price	100.3269	106.4409	102.6675
Value of a basis point	$181.53	$519.41	$1027.39

From equations (14.3a) and (14.3b) we can calculate that an investor should buy $.663564 million par amount of bond 1 and $.388317 million of bond 3 for each $1.0 million of bond 2 sold.

The standard deviations and correlations of weekly yield changes for the three bonds are

	Bond 1	Bond 2	Bond 3
Standard deviation	18.3 bp	20.2	19.7
Correlation with			
Bond 1	1.000	.938	.829
Bond 2	.938	1.000	.926
Bond 3	.829	.926	1.000

Using this data in equations (14.25), (14.26), and (14.27) gives the standard deviation of the change in value of the 7-year note:

$$S_2 = \$10,487$$

the standard deviation of the change in value of the 2-year/30-year portfolio:

$$S_{1,3} = \$9,786$$

and the correlation of the change in value of the 7-year note with the change in value of the portfolio:

$$\varrho = .957$$

Note that this correlation is substantially lower than that shown at equation (14.30) for a butterfly trade out of a 5-year note into 2-year and 10-year notes.

Following the notation of section 14.1, the constraint on maintaining the sensitivity of the value of a position to change in the level of the yield curve can be written

$$Q_2 \cdot V_2 = Q_1 \cdot V_1 + Q_3 \cdot V_3 \tag{14.31}$$

This is a restatement of equation (14.2).

The constraint that an arbitrage butterfly maintains the sensitivity of the value of a position to change in the slope of the curve is more difficult to express. For simplicity, let us think of the yield curve pivoting around the conventional duration of security 2, denoted D_2^{con} such that the yield on a security with conventional duration D_i^{con} changes by an amount $\Delta R_i = (D_i^{con} - D_2^{con}) \cdot \Delta R$, where ΔR is an arbitrary factor. If ΔR is positive, then yields on securities with a duration greater than D_2^{con} will go up and yields on securities with a duration less than D_2^{con} will go down. In other words, the slope of the yield curve increases. The reverse will be true if ΔR is negative.

Note that the yield on security 2 is unchanged for all values of ΔR. This is what is meant by saying that the yield curve pivots around the conventional duration of security 2.

If the arbitrage butterfly is to maintain the sensitivity of the value of a position to the above type of change in the yield curve, then we must have

$$Q_2 \cdot V_2 \cdot \Delta R_2 = Q_1 \cdot V_1 \cdot \Delta R_1 + Q_3 \cdot V_3 \cdot \Delta R_3 \tag{14.32}$$

when

$$\Delta R_1 = (D_1^{con} - D_2^{con}) \cdot \Delta R \tag{14.33a}$$

$$\Delta R_2 = (D_2^{con} - D_2^{con}) \cdot \Delta R = 0 \tag{14.33b}$$

$$\Delta R_3 = (D_3^{con} - D_2^{con}) \cdot \Delta R \tag{14.33c}$$

This implies that the arbitrage butterfly must satisfy the constraint

$$Q_1 \cdot V_1 (D_1^{con} - D_2^{con}) + Q_3 \cdot V_3 (D_3^{con} - D_2^{con}) = 0 \tag{14.34}$$

Equations (14.31) and (14.34) are two equations in two unknowns that specify the constraints on an arbitrage butterfly. The equations can be solved for the par amounts of the securities to be purchased:

$$Q_1 = \frac{V_2 \cdot (D_3^{con} - D_2^{con})}{V_1 \cdot (D_3^{con} - D_1^{con})} \cdot Q_2 \tag{14.35}$$

$$Q_3 = \frac{V_2 \cdot (D_2^{con} - D_1^{con})}{V_3 \cdot (D_3^{con} - D_1^{con})} \cdot Q_2 \tag{14.36}$$

If we use the values of a basis point and conventional durations in table 14.1 and assume the investor is selling $Q_2 = \$1.0$ million par amount of the 5-year note, we get

$$Q_1 = 1.146253$$

$$Q_3 = .308567$$

Compared to the conventional butterfly weighting of $Q_1 = .507567$ and $Q_3 = .486374$, we see that an arbitrageur would buy more of the shorter maturity (2-year) issue and less of the longer (10-year) issue. Since the arbitrage butterfly has no risk with respect to a change in the slope of the yield curve, it follows that the portfolio purchased in a conventional butterfly (with more of the 10-year note and less of the 2-year note) will decline in value if the yield curve steepens and will appreciate in value if the curve flattens.

An Example

The claim that a conventional butterfly is exposed to the risk of loss of value from a steepening of the yield curve can be illustrated with a simple example.

Suppose that the yield curve changes slope by pivoting at the duration D_2^{con} so that the change in yield on security i is $\Delta R_i = (D_i^{con} - D_2^{con}) \cdot \Delta R$. Assume that $\Delta R = 5$ basis points per year.

From the data in table 14.1 we have

$$\Delta R_1 = (D_1^{con} - D_2^{con}) \cdot \Delta R$$

$$= (1.879 - 4.249) \cdot (5.0)$$

$$= -11.9 \text{ bp} \tag{14.37a}$$

and

$$\Delta R_3 = (D_3^{con} - D_2^{con}) \cdot \Delta R$$

$$= (6.700 - 4.249) \cdot (5.0)$$

$$= 12.3 \text{ bp} \tag{14.37b}$$

The general expression for the change in value of the 2-year/10-year portfolio is given by equation (14.22). For the case of the conventional butterfly, we have $Q_1 = \$.507567$ million and $Q_3 = \$.486374$ million. Using the values of a basis point from table 14.1, equation (14.22) becomes

$$\Delta W_{1,3} = -(.507567) \cdot (181.53) \cdot (-11.9)$$

$$- (.486374) \cdot (652.07) \cdot (12.3)$$

$$= -\$2,804 \tag{14.38}$$

Thus, as claimed, the conventional butterfly will lose value if the yield curve steepens.

By comparison the arbitrage butterfly is weighted so that $Q_1 = \$1.146253$ million and $Q_3 = \$.308567$ million. In this case equation (14.22) becomes

$$\Delta W_{1,3} = -(1.146253) \cdot (181.53) \cdot (-11.9)$$

$$-(.308567) \cdot (652.07) \cdot (12.3)$$

$$= 0 \qquad\qquad\qquad (14.39)$$

Thus, again as claimed, the arbitrage butterfly does not change in value as the slope of the curve changes.

14.6   Conclusions

This chapter has presented a critical examination of the analytical concepts used to assess a butterfly trade. We pointed out several flaws in the conventional wisdom concerning such trades.

First, the yield pickup, or give-up, on a butterfly trade is poorly measured in comparing a value-weighted average of the conventional yields on the bonds purchased to the conventional yield on the bond sold. This stems primarily from the observation that a value-weighted average is a poor way to approximate the yield on a bond portfolio. Using a value of a basis point-weighted average gives a much better approximation.

Second, greater convexity pickup on a butterfly trade does not necessarily require a reduced yield pickup or a yield give-up. Indeed the reverse seems true (at least when the yield curve has a positive slope): Greater convexity is associated with greater yield. This casts doubt on the claim that convexity is positively valued by the market.

Third, butterfly trades are not true risk maintenance trades. They do maintain (to a first-order approximation) the risk of a position with respect to parallel yield shifts. However, they increase the risk of loss due to a steepening of the yield curve.

Finally, the magnitude of the increase in slope risk on a butterfly trade appears to be positively associated with the convexity pickup on the trade. This means that an investor cannot look simply at the yield and convexity changes on alternative butterfly trades but that he must also consider the concurrent changes in exposure to slope risk.

15 Managing Yield Curve Risk: A Generalized Approach to Immunization

In the language of classical fixed income investment analysis, a bond portfolio is said to "immunize" a liability if the duration of the portfolio matches the time remaining before the liability comes due. For example, a portfolio with a 4-year duration is said to immunize a liability payable in 4 years.

Immunization is widely advertised as a device to eliminate risk because an immunizing portfolio is considered functionally equivalent to a zero coupon security that matures contemporaneously with the immunized liability. Thus an investor who has immunized a liability is purportedly indifferent about the future behavior of interest rates.

Unfortunately, this simple conception of immunization is incorrect. Merely matching the duration of a bond portfolio to an investor's liability horizon does not eliminate risk, and it does not leave the investor indifferent about future changes in interest rates. Such matching will eliminate the risk associated with parallel shifts in the yield curve, but it will not eliminate other risks associated with changes in the shape of the curve, such as a steepening or flattening (see chapter 5).

This chapter presents a reconstruction of immunization theory that extends and generalizes the rather special approach of simply matching portfolio duration to investment horizon. The extended theory shows how to solve the problem of immunizing a future liability against arbitrary changes in the shape of the yield curve. It also shows how to immunize a sequence of multiple liabilities. Thus the theory extends existing immunization techniques with respect to both the liabilities that can be immunized and the class of interest rate changes that can be immunized against.

Section 15.1 begins the analysis with a discussion of the problem of characterizing a sequence of cash flows with simple summary measures. (The cash flows can be either income received from a portfolio of bonds or a schedule of liabilities.) Duration is one of the proposed measures, but duration is shown to be only one member of a much larger family of characteristics. Understanding the proposed characteristics is crucial to the subsequent analysis because the characteristics provide a "vocabulary" for the generalized theory of immunization.

Section 15.2 examines the effect of an arbitrary change in the structure of interest rates on the present value of a sequence of cash flows. The effect is shown to be intimately connected to the characteristics defined in section 15.1. Indeed we can describe the effect entirely in terms of those characteristics, and we do not have to know any additional information about the underlying cash flows. This observation provides the insight needed to extend immunization theory.

Written in August 1985.

The general immunization strategy is presented in section 15.3. Immunization is viewed as the problem of allocating a bond portfolio such that *any* change in the structure of interest rates has an identical effect on the present value of the portfolio and the present value of the liability schedule to be immunized. If such complete immunization can be accomplished, an investor will be truly indifferent about the future behavior of interest rates. Section 15.3 demonstrates that a liability schedule can be immunized by constructing a bond portfolio whose characteristics match the corresponding characteristics of the liabilities. This demonstrates the central role of the proposed characteristics for bond immunization.

The analysis in section 15.3 has several interesting implications. First, simply matching the conventional duration of a portfolio to a given investment horizon produces only a first-order approximation to a complete immunization. In particular, it leaves an investor open to risk stemming from changes in the shape of the yield curve. Second, a portfolio that completely immunizes a liability schedule is actually a dedicated portfolio. Income received from the assets in the portfolio match precisely, in timing and amount, the payments required to satisfy the liabilities.

These two results suggest that a sequence of bond portfolios can be constructed to partially immunize a given liability schedule where successive portfolios provide progressively greater risk protection. At one extreme we can simply match the duration of the assets to the duration of the liabilities and achieve a basic, or first-order, immunization. At the other extreme we can construct a completely immunizing, or dedicated, portfolio. The analysis in section 15.3 shows how partially immunizing portfolios which fall between these extremes can be constructed.

Section 15.4 discusses some practical aspects of applying the general theory of immunization. In particular, it establishes a simple relation between the characteristics of the individual bonds in a portfolio and the characteristics of the portfolio as a whole. It also shows how a general immunization problem can be solved with linear programming techniques. This is important because there exist efficient computer programs for solving even quite large linear programs.

Section 15.5 applies the concepts of general immunization to a concrete example. It demonstrates how risk is reduced by progressively more complete immunization and how it can be eliminated by full immunization or by construction of a dedicated portfolio.

15.1   Characterizing a Schedule of Cash Flows

Consider a schedule of cash flows consisting of payments of prescribed amounts of money on a sequence of future dates. Such a schedule is ordinarily specified by the dates and amounts of each of the payments. In some cases, however, it is desirable to characterize the schedule with simple summary measures, such as the duration of the payments. We can then ask whether the schedule has the same risk as some other schedule, that is, whether two schedules have similar durations. More generally, measures like duration provide a convenient way to summarize possibly complex schedules of cash flows.

This section defines a series of characteristics of a cash flow schedule that constitute a "vocabulary" for the general analysis of immunization in the following sections. The characteristics are natural extensions of the conventional duration measure familiar to participants in the fixed income markets.

Specifying a Schedule

The first step in defining the characteristics is specifying an actual schedule of cash flows. The schedule can be, for example, the interest and principal payments from a particular bond or from a portfolio of many different bond, or it can be a schedule of disbursements such as retirement benefits from a pension fund.

Suppose that the schedule consists of n future payments, where the ith payment is for an amount F_i and occurs y_i years in the future. The schedule thus consists of the sequence

Date	Amount
y_1	F_1
y_2	F_2
y_3	F_3
$\vdots$	$\vdots$
y_{n-1}	F_{n-1}
y_n	F_n

Table 15.1 shows a simple example consisting of the payment of $100 million on November 15, 1985, and every six months thereafter until May 15, 1990.

Characterizing a Schedule

Assume now that each of the cash flows in the schedule are discounted at some yield R, where R is compounded semi-annually. (This is equivalent to assuming a flat spot yield curve, and hence a flat bond yield curve. Spot yields and their relation to bond yields are described in chapter 10.)

Table 15.1
Schedule of cash flows

Payment date[a]	Payment amount
11/15/85	$100. million
5/15/86	100.
11/17/86	100.
5/15/87	100.
11/16/87	100.
5/16/88	100.
11/15/88	100.
5/15/89	100.
11/15/89	100.
5/15/90	100.

a. Payments scheduled for 15th of the month are actually made the following Monday if the 15th is a Saturday or Sunday.

The most basic characteristic of the schedule is its present value V, computed as

$$V = F_1 \cdot (1 + \tfrac{1}{2}R)^{-2 \cdot y_1} + F_2 \cdot (1 + \tfrac{1}{2}R)^{-2 \cdot y_2} \cdots + F_n \cdot (1 + \tfrac{1}{2}R)^{-2 \cdot y_n}$$

(15.1)

or, in a more compact notation, as

$$V = \sum_{i=1}^{n} F_i \cdot (1 + \tfrac{1}{2}R)^{-2 \cdot y_i}$$

(15.2)

Equation (15.2) says that the present value of the schedule is the sum of the present values of the future payments. The first payment is for an amount F_1 and is paid in y_1 years or in $2 \cdot y_1$ semi-annual periods. Its discounted value is $F_1/(1 + \tfrac{1}{2}R)^{2 \cdot y_1}$. The discounted values of the subsequent payments are computed in a similar fashion.

Another familiar characteristic of the schedule is its duration D, defined as

$$D = (V)^{-1} \cdot \sum_{i=1}^{n} y_i \cdot F_i \cdot (1 + \tfrac{1}{2}R)^{-2 \cdot y_i}$$

(15.3)

Equation (15.3) says that the duration of the schedule is a weighed average of the times to the future payments, where the time to a given payment is weighted by the present value of that payment.

It is well-known that a bond or bond portfolio with a duration of D years is essentially equivalent to a zero coupon security maturing in D years if the yield curve can change only by small parallel movements of the entire curve. It is also known that this equivalence does not hold if the curve can change shape (see chapter 5).

Table 15.2
Present value, moments, and generalized durations of the schedule of cash flows in table 15.1

k	Moment W_k	Generalized duration $(W_k)^{1/k}$
1	2.53	2.53 yr
2	8.47	2.91
3	32.16	3.18
4	132.07	3.39
5	571.81	3.56
6	2,524.40	3.69
7	11,441.56	3.80
8	53,520.09	3.90
9	244,970.94	3.97

Note: All calculations assume a 10% yield, compounded semi-annually, as of a May 15, 1985, valuation date. Present value = \$771.1 million.

Characteristic Moments

The form of equation (15.3) suggests a sequence of additional characteristics of the cash flow schedule. These characteristics are called "moments." The kth moment of the schedule is defined as

$$W_k = (V)^{-1} \cdot \sum_{i=1}^{n} y_i^k \cdot F_i \cdot (1 + \tfrac{1}{2}R)^{-2 \cdot y_i} \tag{15.4}$$

Equation (15.4) says that the kth moment is a weighted average of the times (raised to the kth power) to the future payments, where the weights are the present values of the payments. Thus the second moment of the schedule is a weighted average of the squared times to the future payments:

$$W_2 = (V)^{-1} \cdot \sum_{i=1}^{n} y_i^2 \cdot F_i \cdot (1 + \tfrac{1}{2}R)^{-2 \cdot y_i} \tag{15.5}$$

The third moment is a weighted average of the cubed times to the future payments:

$$W_3 = (V)^{-1} \cdot \sum_{i=1}^{n} y_i^3 \cdot F_i \cdot (1 + \tfrac{1}{2}R)^{-2 \cdot y_i} \tag{15.6}$$

Note that the zero moment is identically equal to unity and that the first moment is the duration of the schedule. That is, $W_0 = 1$ and $W_1 = D$, where D is as defined in equation (15.3).

Table 15.2 tabulates some of the moments of the schedule of cash flows in Table 1 at a 10% yield.

An Interpretation of the Characteristic Moments

The moments characterizing a schedule of cash flows may seem abstract and unrelated to any concept familiar in fixed income investment analysis. They can, however, be interpreted as generalized measures of duration.

This interpretation is suggested by the observation that the kth moment of a zero coupon security is identically equal to its term to maturity raised to the kth power. More specifically, if a security makes only a single payment in y years, equation (15.4) becomes

$$W_k = y^k \tag{15.7}$$

It follows that the kth root of the kth moment of an arbitrary schedule of cash flows, or $(W_k)^{1/k}$, might be viewed as a kind of effective duration of the schedule.

Since $W_1 = D$, the first moment is clearly the conventional duration of the schedule, corresponding to the case of a parallel shift in the yield curve. Thus the schedule in table 15.1 is equivalent to a single payment due in 2.53 years if the yield curve can shift only by parallel movements. (This follows because $W_1 = 2.53$ years in table 15.2.)

The square root of the second moment, $(W_2)^{1/2}$, turns out to be the effective duration of the cash flow schedule for the case where the change in a yield used to discount a payment is *proportional* to the time remaining to that payment. This corresponds to a steepening or flattening shift in the yield curve, with longer-term yields varying more than shorter-term yields. The schedule in table 15.1 is therefore equivalent to a single payment due in 2.91 years if yields can change only in proportion to their times to payments, $(W_2)^{1/2} = 2.91$.

Similarly the cube root of the third moment, $(W_3)^{1/3}$, is the effective duration for the case where the change in a yield is proportional to the *square* of the time remaining to the associated payment. For this type of more sharply steepening or flattening shift in the yield curve the schedule in table 15.1 is equivalent to a single payment due in 3.18 years, $(W_3)^{1/3} = 3.18$.

In general, the kth root of W_k can be interpreted as an effective duration when the change in a yield is proportional to the time to the associated payment raised to the $(k-1)$st power. Thus each successive moment is a duration measure for a case where the yield curve "bends" more sharply. The proof of this assertion is given in appendix A.

The generalized durations tabulated in table 15.2 show that the effective duration of a schedule of cash flows is longer the greater the hypothesized bending of the yield curve. This follows because longer-term yields are progressively more volatile than shorter yields the greater the bending of the curve. The greater relative volatility exacerbates the market risk of a schedule with multiple payments relative to the reinvestment risk and hence pushes out the term at which the two risks balance, namely the schedule's effective duration. (This analysis, and the general notion that effective duration depends on how the yield curve can shift, is elaborated more completely in chapter 5.)

15.2 The Effect of a Change in the Structure of Yields on the Present Value of a Schedule of Cash Flows

We now want to assess the impact of a change in the structure of yields on the present value of a schedule of cash flows. More particularly, we want to analyze the effect on the present value of the schedule of an arbitrary change in the original (flat) spot yield curve, including changes in both the level and shape of the curve. This analysis is important because immunization requires construction of a bond portfolio whose present value changes in the same way as the present value of a specified liability schedule for an arbitrary change in the structure of yields.

We show in this section that the effect on present value of a change in the structure of yields can be expressed in terms of (1) the nature of the change in the yield curve and (2) the initial value and the moments of the cash flows. In particular, we do not require any information about the cash flow schedule *other than* its present value and its moments.

First Steps

Consider again a cash flow schedule of n payments where the ith payment is for an amount F_i and will be made in y_i years. Assuming a flat yield curve at yield R, the present value of the schedule is

$$V = \sum_{i=1}^{n} F_i \cdot (1 + \tfrac{1}{2}R)^{-2 \cdot y_i} \tag{15.8}$$

Now suppose the yield curve changes from a flat curve to a new curve such that the yield discounting a payment due in y years shifts from R to $R + t \cdot S(y)$, where t is a scalar and S is a function of the time to payment. In rough terms $S(y)$ represents the "direction" and relative magnitude of the shift at a term of y years, and t is a scale factor that represents the magnitude of the shift. If $S(y) = 1$ for all y, all yields change by the same amount and in the same direction. If $S(y) = y$, the change in the yield used to discount a payment is proportional to the time remaining to the payment. If $S(y) = y^2$, the change is proportional to the square of the remaining time. If $t = 0$, there is no shift anywhere along the curve. If $t > 0$, the curve shifts in the direction specified by the function $S(y)$ at a term of y years. If $t < 0$, the curve shifts in the opposite direction.

The present value of the schedule of cash flows using the new yield curve is

$$V' = \sum_{i=1}^{n} F_i \cdot (1 + \tfrac{1}{2}(R + t \cdot S(y_i)))^{-2 \cdot y_i} \tag{15.9}$$

Note that the ith payment is now discounted at the yield $R + t \cdot S(y_i)$. This reflects the shift in the curve from a flat curve at R to the new curve.

Let ΔV denote the change in present value resulting from the shift in the yield curve, so that $\Delta V = V' - V$. To a first-order approximation ΔV is a linear function of the magnitude t of the shift in the curve. It can be shown that this function is

$$\Delta V = -t \cdot \sum_{i=1}^{n} y_i \cdot S(y_i) \cdot F_i \cdot (1 + \tfrac{1}{2}R)^{-2 \cdot y_i - 1} \tag{15.10}$$

An Alternative Representation of the Effect of a Shift in the Structure of Yields

Equation (15.10) is not terribly useful as it stands because it gives the change in present value as a function of the original schedule of cash flows. That is, the dates and amounts of the cash flows (the y_i's and the F_i's) appear as explicit arguments in the expression for ΔV.

It would be preferable to express the change in present value as a function of summary characteristics of the cash flows, such as a function of the moments defined in section 15.1. This would facilitate an analysis of whether or not the present values of two quite different cash flow schedules might be affected in the same way by a particular change in the structure of yields.

Decomposing the Shift in the Yield Curve

If we assume the shift in the spot yield curve represented by $S(y)$ is a smooth function of the time to a payment y, we can recast equation (15.10) in a more interesting form.

We first rewrite the function S in a power, series:

$$S(y) = S(0) + S^1(0) \cdot y + \tfrac{1}{2}S^2(0) \cdot y^2 + \tfrac{1}{6}S^3(0) \cdot y^3 + \cdots \tag{15.11}$$

where $S(0)$ is the shift function at a maturity of zero years, $S^1(0)$ is the first derivative of the shift function at a maturity of zero years, and so on. In a more compact form, equation (15.11) can be written as

$$S(y) = \sum_{k=0}^{\infty} (k!)^{-1} \cdot S^k(0) \cdot y^k \tag{15.12}$$

where $k! = 1 \cdot 2 \cdot 3 \cdot \ldots \cdot k$ and $S^k(0)$ is the kth derivative of S evaluated at a maturity of zero years.

Equation (12) says that the general function $S(y)$ defining the shift in the yield curve can be expressed as a weighted sum of special shift functions. The first special function is a parallel shift of the curve and receives weight $S(0)$. The second special function is a change in yield proportional to the time remaining to a payment and receives weight $S^1(0)$. The third function is a change in yield proportional to the squared time to a payment and receives weight $\frac{1}{2}S^2(0)$. This continues progressively so that the $(k + 1)$st shift function is a change in yield proportional to the time to a payment raised to the power k and receives weight $(k!)^{-1} \cdot S^k(0)$. Each successive special function represents a greater bending of the original yield curve.

Re-expressing the Change in Value

Now substitute the expression for $S(y)$ on the right hand side of equation (15.12) into equation (15.10):

$$\Delta V = -t \cdot \sum_{i=1}^{n} y_i \cdot \left[\sum_{k=0}^{\infty} (k!)^{-1} \cdot S^k(0) \cdot y_i^k \right] \cdot F_i \cdot (1 + \tfrac{1}{2}R)^{-2 \cdot y_i - 1} \tag{15.13}$$

Reversing the order of the summations this becomes:

$$\Delta V = -t \cdot \sum_{k=0}^{\infty} (k!)^{-1} \cdot S^k(0) \cdot \left[\sum_{i=1}^{n} y_i^{k+1} \cdot F_i \cdot (1 + \tfrac{1}{2}R)^{2 \cdot y_i - 1} \right] \tag{15.14}$$

Noting the definition of the kth moment of the cash flow schedule given in equation (15.4), we observe that the term in brackets in equation (15.14) is $V \cdot W_{k+1} \cdot (1 + \tfrac{1}{2}R)^{-1}$. Thus the change in present value is

$$\Delta V = -t \cdot \sum_{k=0}^{\infty} (k!)^{-1} \cdot S^k(0) \cdot V \cdot W_{k+1} \cdot (1 + \tfrac{1}{2}R)^{-1}$$

or

$$\Delta V = -t \cdot V \cdot (1 + \tfrac{1}{2}R)^{-1} \sum_{k=0}^{\infty} (k!)^{-1} \cdot S^k(0) \cdot W_{k+1} \tag{15.15}$$

Equation (15.15) is exceedingly important to the general theory of immunization. It says that the change in the value of a schedule of cash flows that results from a shift in the yield curve depends on three things. First, of course it depends on the original value V of the schedule. Second, it depends on the nature of the shift in the curve. This is reflected in the values of t and the $S^k(0)$ terms. Third, it depends on the structure of the cash flows as represented by the W_k moments of the schedule.

Of equal significance, equation (15.15) says that the change in present value does not depend on any aspect of the schedule of cash flows *other than* its initial value and its moments. Thus, to compute the change in value, we can work either with the original schedule, as in equation (15.10), or we can work with the initial value and moments of the schedule, as in equation (15.15).

It follows from this analysis that the present values of two cash flow schedules will behave in a similar fashion with respect to an arbitrary change in the structure of yields *if* those schedules have similar present values and moments, *even if* the underlying schedules appear quite different. This conclusion brings us to the general theory of immunization.

15.3   The General Theory of Immunization

Having established an analytical foundation, we can now state the general theory of immunization quite simply. Suppose that we have a schedule of liabilities such as specified in table 15.1 and the present value and moments characterizing that schedule as in table 15.2. A bond portfolio of equal present value will more completely immunize the liability schedule the more precisely the moments of the portfolio receipts match the moments of the liabilities.

The simplest type of immunization is constructing a bond portfolio with a present value and duration matched to the present value and duration of the liabilities. This matching of initial value and first moments is in fact the way immunization is commonly understood. However, such simple immunization does not eliminate all of the risk associated with changes in interest rates. As suggested by equation (15.15), a change in the structure of interest rates may not affect the value of the bond portfolio the same as it affects the value of the liability schedule if the moments beyond the first moment do not match.

Depending on the set of bonds available for purchase, it may be possible to construct a bond portfolio to match the second as well as the first moment of the liability schedule, and hence to achieve a second-order immunization of the liabilities. More generally, it may be possible to match the first K moments of the liability schedule, and thus to achieve a "Kth order" immunizing bond portfolio. Each successive match of a portfolio moment to the corresponding moment of the liability schedule can be expected to enhance the immunization, that is, to reduce risk. In the limit, complete immunization will be obtained if *every* moment of the liability schedule can be matched.

An Interpretation of Generalized Immunization

The present proposal for generalizing the conventional concept of immunization can be given an illuminating interpretation.

Recall from section 15.1 that the successive moments of a schedule of cash flows are related to the generalized durations of the schedule, classified by progressively greater bindings of the yield curve. Matching moments is therefore equivalent to matching generalized durations.

If we construct a bond portfolio so that its first moment matches the first moment of a liability schedule, the conventional durations of the assets and liabilities will be the same. (This follows because the first moment is a conventional duration.) More particularly, the present values of the assets and liabilities will behave the same for parallel shifts of the yield curve.

If we construct a bond portfolio so that its first and second moments match the first and second moments, respectively, of the liability schedule, the present values will behave the same for *both* a parallel shift of the yield curve *and* a shift where the yield used to discount a payment changes in proportion to the time remaining to the payment. In other words, since the bond portfolio and the liability schedule have the same effective duration for *both* types of shifts in the structure of yields, their present values will change in tandem for *both* type of shifts.

This interpretation shows that generalized immunization, viewed as matching the generalized durations of a bond portfolio to the corresponding generalized durations of a liability schedule, is a form of enhanced risk management. The more extensive the matching, the more protection is available against more extreme changes in the shape of the yield curve.

Where Do We Go From Here?

At this point there are three important questions about generalized immunization that need to be addressed:

1. How, as a practical matter, can we construct an immunizing portfolio of a given order?

2. What are the costs of higher-order immunization?

3. What are the advantages of higher-order immunization?

The next two sections consider these issues.

15.4   Practical Aspects of Generalized Immunization

At first impression, constructing a bond portfolio whose moments match the moments of a given liability schedule might seem complicated. The moments of the payments from a bond portfolio depend on the dates and amounts of those payments (see equation 15.4), and hence depend on the precise composition of the portfolio. However, the portfolio moments may not be a simple function of any characteristics of the bonds in the portfolio. As a result it may be difficult to relate the portfolio moments directly to the composition of the portfolio.

This section shows that such concerns are unfounded. In fact it is quite easy to relate the composition of a bond portfolio to the portfolio's moments. This is attributable to a convenient "averaging" property of the moments of two cash flow schedules. We will first examine this averaging property and then describe an efficient way to construct an immunizing portfolio of arbitrary order.

Averaging Cash Flow Moments

Cash flow moments have an averaging property that is important for the practical construction of immunizing portfolios. Specifically the kth moment of a portfolio is a weighted average of the kth moments of the individual bonds in the portfolio, where the weight on the moment of a particular bond is the value of the bond (including accrued interest) divided by the value of the whole portfolio.

To appreciate this claim, consider two cash flow schedules:

Schedule 1:

Date	Amount
y_1'	F_1'
y_2'	F_2'
$\vdots$	$\vdots$
y_n'	F_n'

Schedule 2:

Date	Amount
y_1''	F_1''
y_2''	F_2''
$\vdots$	$\vdots$
y_m''	F_m''

Schedule 1 has n payments where the ith payment is for amount F_i' and occurs in y_i' years. Schedule 2 specifies m payments where the ith payment is for amount F_i'' and occurs in y_i'' years. The schedules may be thought of as payments from two bond positions, such as a 10-year bond and a 20-year bond.

The present value and kth moment of schedule 1 at yield R are

$$V' = \sum_{i=1}^{n} F_i' \cdot (1 + \tfrac{1}{2}R)^{-2 \cdot y_i'} \tag{15.16a}$$

$$W_k' = (V')^{-1} \cdot \sum_{i=1}^{n} (y_i')^k \cdot F_i' \cdot (1 + \tfrac{1}{2}R)^{-2 \cdot y_i'} \tag{15.16b}$$

Similarly the present value and kth moment of schedule 2 at the same yield are

$$V'' = \sum_{i=1}^{m} F_i'' \cdot (1 + \tfrac{1}{2}R)^{-2 \cdot y_i''} \tag{15.17a}$$

$$W_k'' = (V'')^{-1} \cdot \sum_{i=1}^{m} (y_i'')^k \cdot F_i'' \cdot (1 + \tfrac{1}{2}R)^{-2 \cdot y_i''} \tag{15.17b}$$

Finally, the present value and kth moment of the composite of the two schedules are

$$V = \sum_{i=1}^{n} F_i' \cdot (1 + \tfrac{1}{2}R)^{-2 \cdot y_i'} + \sum_{i=1}^{m} F_i'' \cdot (1 + \tfrac{1}{2}R)^{-2 \cdot y_i''} \tag{15.18a}$$

$$W_k = (V' + V'')^{-1}$$

$$\cdot \left[\sum_{i=1}^{n} (y_i')^k \cdot F_i' \cdot (1 + \tfrac{1}{2}R)^{-2 \cdot y_i'} + \sum_{i=1}^{m} (y_i'')^k \cdot F_i'' \cdot (1 + \tfrac{1}{2}R)^{-2 \cdot y_i''} \right] \tag{15.18b}$$

These expressions follow from the definitions in equations (15.2) and (15.4).

From the equations for W_k' and W_k'', we can rewrite the equation for the kth moment of the composite schedule as

$$W_k = (V' + V'')^{-1} \cdot [V' \cdot W_k' + V'' \cdot W_k'']$$

or as

$$W_k = \left(\frac{V'}{V' + V''} \right) \cdot W_k' + \left(\frac{V''}{V' + V''} \right) \cdot W_k'' \tag{15.19}$$

Equation (15.19) says that the kth moment of the composite schedule of cash flows can be computed as a weighted average of the kth moments of the component schedules. The weights are the fractional contributions of the individual schedules to the value of the composite schedule.

This result can be extended readily to a portfolio of bonds. Suppose there are M bonds in the portfolio, where $W_{k,i}$ is the kth moment of the ith bond and where the ith bond has a value weight of a_i in the portfolio. (Note that $a_1 + a_2 + \cdots + a_M = 1$.) The kth moment of the portfolio is:

$$W_k = \sum_{i=1}^{M} a_i \cdot W_{k,i} \tag{15.20}$$

Thus, a portfolio moment is a simple linear combination of the corresponding moments of the bonds in the portfolio.

Computing the Moments of a Bond with the Bond's Yield

The result stated in equation (15.20) on averaging the moments of the bonds in a portfolio applies, in a strict sense, only when all cash flows are discounted at the same yield. As a practical matter, however, it is usually adequate to compute the moments of a bond using the conventionally defined yield on the bond. (See similarly the Subsequent Remarks section of chapter 13.) This means that the moments of different bonds will be computed from different yields and that equation (15.20) will not be strictly true, but the significance of the error is usually quite small.

Constructing an Immunizing Portfolio of Order K

We can use the results above on the averaging of cash flow moments to state a simple way to construct an immunizing portfolio of arbitrary order.

Suppose that we want to immunize a liability schedule by matching the first three moments of that schedule. This problem can be solved by allocating a bond portfolio such that the portfolio has a maximum yield subject to the linear constraints that the first three portfolio moments match the first three moments of the liability schedule.

To a close approximation the yield on the portfolio is a weighted average of the yields on the bonds in the portfolio, where each bond yield is weighted by the product of the bond's duration relative to the duration of the portfolio and by its fractional contribution to the total value of the portfolio (see appendix B). Thus the problem of allocating a third-order immunizing portfolio is a matter of maximizing a linear objective function subject to three linear constraints. This is a problem in the well-studied area of linear programming (see appendix C).

More generally, an efficient immunizing portfolio of order K can be constructed by maximizing average portfolio yield subject to K linear constraints. The next section examines some solutions to this problem.

15.5   An Example of Generalized Immunization

Having described the concept of generalized immunization and having demonstrated how as a computational matter an immunizing portfolio of

Table 15.3
Treasury bonds includable in an immunizing portfolio

Coupon	Maturity	Price	Yield	Duration
$11\frac{3}{4}\%$	11/15/85	$101\frac{21}{32}$	8.237%	.50 yr
$13\frac{3}{4}$	5/15/86	$104\frac{25}{32}$	8.660	.97
$16\frac{1}{8}$	11/15/86	$109\frac{9}{32}$	9.298	1.40
14	5/15/87	$107\frac{30}{32}$	9.549	1.82
$12\frac{5}{8}$	11/15/87	$106\frac{6}{32}$	9.755	2.23
$9\frac{7}{8}$	5/15/88	$100\frac{4}{32}$	9.813	2.67
$11\frac{3}{4}$	11/15/88	$104\frac{26}{32}$	10.070	2.99
$11\frac{3}{4}$	5/15/89	$104\frac{30}{32}$	10.212	3.32
$12\frac{3}{4}$	11/15/89	$108\frac{4}{32}$	10.431	3.60
$11\frac{3}{8}$	5/15/90	$103\frac{26}{32}$	10.347	3.90

Note: All prices from May 14, 1985, all yields and durations computed for settlement on May 15, 1985.

arbitrary order can be constructed, we are now ready to examine an example in some detail. The examination is useful because it illustrates the costs and benefits of generalized immunization while clarifying the methodology.

As a concrete example we will immunize the liability schedule shown in table 15.1. For simplicity we will restrict the immunization to the Treasury bonds listed in table 15.3.

A Basic Immunization

The simplest type of immunization is to construct, from the bonds in table 15.3, a portfolio with as high a yield as possible, a value of $771 million, and a conventional duration of 2.53 years. Such a portfolio matches the present value and first moment of the liability schedule in table 15.1 and hence is a first-order immunizing portfolio.

The appropriate portfolio is shown in the first column of table 15.4. It consists of positions in only two bonds: $261.7 million principal value of the $11\frac{3}{4}\%$ bond of November 15, 1985, and $467.1 million principal value of the $12\frac{3}{4}\%$ bond of November 15, 1989.

The yield on the portfolio is 10.281% per annum, which represents a nontrivial spread over the 10.00% yield at which the liability schedule was evaluated. This suggests that, over time, simple immunization may generate significantly more cash than what is required to satisfy the immunized liabilities.

The drawback to a simple immunization strategy is suggested by the distribution of cash flows shown at the bottom lines of the first column of

Table 15.4
Portfolios that immunize the liability schedule of table 15.1

		Order of immunizing portfolio					
		1st	2nd	3rd	4th	5th	Dedicated
Portfolio allocation (principal value, millions $)							
$11\frac{3}{4}\%$	11/85:	261.7	62.4	84.2	86.8	59.1	52.3
$13\frac{3}{4}$	5/86:	0	0	0	0	0	57.6
$16\frac{1}{8}$	11/86:	0	0	0	0	180.8	61.5
14	5/87:	0	326.2	188.6	162.8	0	66.5
$12\frac{5}{8}$	11/87:	0	0	135.0	166.0	46.2	71.1
$9\frac{7}{8}$	5/88:	0	0	0	0	0	75.6
$11\frac{3}{4}$	11/88:	0	0	0	0	265.8	79.3
$11\frac{3}{4}$	5/89:	0	0	0	0	0	84.0
$12\frac{3}{4}$	11/89:	467.1	328.9	313.2	294.9	60.8	89.0
$11\frac{3}{8}$	5/90:	0	0	0	11.4	113.1	94.6
Portfolio yield (%)		10.281%	10.107%	10.105%	10.099%	10.024%	10.000%
Cash flows from portfolio (million $)							
	11/15/85:	306.9	109.9	130.8	133.5	108.7	100.0
	5/15/86:	29.8	43.8	41.7	41.3	43.4	100.0
	11/17/86:	29.8	43.8	41.7	41.3	224.2	100.0
	5/15/87:	29.8	369.9	230.3	204.1	28.8	100.0
	11/16/87:	29.8	21.0	163.4	195.9	75.0	100.0
	5/16/88:	29.8	21.0	20.0	19.4	25.9	100.0
	11/15/88:	29.8	21.0	20.0	19.4	291.7	100.0
	5/15/89:	29.8	21.0	20.0	19.4	10.3	100.0
	11/15/89:	496.9	349.9	333.2	314.4	71.1	100.0
	5/15/90:	0	0	0	12.0	119.5	100.0

table 15.1. Instead of anything like an even distribution of $100 million every six months, the first-order immunizing portfolio pays out on a highly irregular schedule. The irregularity of the payouts suggests that the investor has a significant amount of risk even though he holds a purportedly riskless portfolio.

From the analysis in sections 15.2 and 15.3, we might conjecture that this risk is attributable to the possibility of change in the shape of the yield curve. (Parallel shifts of the curve do not matter because a first-order portfolio immunizes against such shifts.) Comparing some of the generalized durations of the liability schedule (see table 15.2) with the corresponding generalized durations of the cash flows in the first column of table 15.4 shows this is indeed the case:

Table 15.5
Generalized durations of portfolios that immunize the liability schedule of table 15.1

Order of generalized duration	Liability schedule	Order of immunizing portfolio				
		1st	2nd	3rd	4th	5th
1st	2.53 yr	2.53[a] yr	2.53[a] yr	2.53[a] yr	2.53[a] yr	2.53[a] yr
2nd	2.91	3.13	2.91[a]	2.91[a]	2.91[a]	2.91[a]
3rd	3.18	3.47	3.19	3.18[a]	3.18[a]	3.18[a]
4th	3.39	3.68	3.41	3.39	3.39[a]	3.39[a]
5th	3.56	3.81	3.57	3.55	3.55	3.56[a]

a. Match between generalized duration of liability schedule and generalized duration of portfolio required by construction of the portfolio.

Order of generalized duration	Generalized durations	
	Liability schedule	Bond portfolio
1st	2.53 yr	2.53 yr
2nd	2.91	3.13
3rd	3.18	3.47
4th	3.39	3.68
5th	3.56	3.81

Observe that each generalized duration of the bond portfolio exceeds the corresponding generalized duration of the liability schedule by a significant margin (except for the first or conventional duration, which must match in a first-order immunization). This implies that the value of the bond portfolio will depreciate faster than the value of the liability schedule if the yield curve steepens as a result of long-term rates rising more than short-term yields. Conversely, the value of the portfolio will appreciate faster than the value of the liabilities if long-term yields fall more than short-term yields.

Higher-Order Immunizations

The problem of risk due to change in the shape of the yield curve can be addressed by generalized immunization. The second through fifth columns of table 15.4 show the consequences of matching the second through fifth moments of the liability schedule in table 15.1.

Note that the distribution of the cash flows from the bond portfolio becomes more regularly spaced as the order of immunization increases. This is a direct reflection of the reduction in yield curve risk provided by higher-order immunization. The same characteristic of lower curve risk is evident in table 15.5 in the progressively better match between the generalized durations of the liability schedule and the generalized durations of the immunizing bond portfolios.

Table 15.4 shows that high-order immunization is not costless. The yield on an immunizing portfolio goes down when the order of immunization is increased. For example, the move from first- to second-order immunization "costs" about 17.4 basis points in yield. Going to fourth-order immunization costs only .8 basis points more, but going on to fifth-order immunization lowers the portfolio yield by another 7.5 basis points.

It is reasonable that the yield on an immunizing portfolio goes down as the order of immunization is increased. A first-order immunizing portfolio only has to satisfy one constraint, but a fifth-order immunizing portfolio must satisfy five constraints. (This follows from the discussion at the end of section 15.4). Thus there is less freedom in constructing a higher-order portfolio. The loss of flexibility is reflected in a reduction of yield.

Another way to appreciate the cost of high-order immunization is to note that any portfolio that immunizes to order k must, by definition, immunize to order $k - 1$. Thus the set of immunizing portfolios of order $k - 1$ is at least as large as, and includes all the members of, the set of immunizing portfolios of order k. It follows that the highest yield among all immunizing portfolios of order k cannot exceed the highest yield among all immunizing portfolios of order $k - 1$.

The Extreme Case of a Dedicated Portfolio

If we continue in the direction of constructing immunizing portfolios of progressively higher order, we ultimately reach the extreme case of a dedicated portfolio. This is exhibited in the last column of table 15.4.

As shown in the lower lines of that column, the cash flows from the dedicated portfolio match exactly the disbursements specified in the liability schedule of table 15.1. This portfolio is clearly an absolutely riskless way to fund those liabilities. In particular, the liability schedule is immunized not only in a present value sense (i.e., identical change in the present values of future receipts and future disbursements for an arbitrary change in the structure of interest rates) but also in a cash flow sense (i.e., each and every future disbursement can be funded from a contemporaneous receipt of cash).

Note, however, that the yield on the dedicated portfolio is less than the yields on the immunizing portfolios of lower order. This is not unexpected because the requirement of exact cash flow matching is extremely stringent.

Some General Comments

This example serves to illustrate several aspects of generalized immunization:

1. Conventional immunization hedges against loss due to a parallel shift in the yield curve, but it often produces cash flows that do not match at all closely the purportedly immunized liability schedule. Thus, while first-order immunizing portfolios often look quite attractive on a yield basis, they may not protect against loss due to changes in the shape of the curve.

2. Higher-order immunization reduces yield curve risk by producing payments more nearly synchronous with disbursements, but it does so at the cost of lower portfolio yield.

3. The only way to eliminate all risk is to construct a dedicated portfolio.

15.6   Conclusions

This chapter has addressed the general problem of hedging interest rate risk by immunization. The essence of the chapter is the distinction between immunizing a liability schedule against a parallel shift of the yield curve by conventional immunization and immunizing a schedule against more general deformations in the shape of the yield curve.

We saw that conventional immunization can leave an investor exposed to substantial risk due to change in the shape of the yield curve. We also saw how this risk can be reduced by applying a generalized and extended concept of immunization.

Two caveats remain to be noted. First, generalized immunization, like conventional immunization, requires continuous monitoring over time. The need for periodic rebalancing of an immunizing portfolio arises because generalized durations change with the level of interest rates (see equation 15.4) and because they change when payments occur as a result of cash receipts from the bond portfolio or cash disbursements to satisfy the liabilities (see chapter 4).

Second, immunization does not provide any hedge against changes in the "basis" of difference bonds. For example, including very high and very low coupon Treasury bonds in an immunizing portfolio can lead to unanticipated gains and losses as a result of changes in the yield spreads between those bonds and par Treasury bonds. (The effect of high and low coupon rates on Treasury bond yields is examined in chapter 7.)

15.7   Appendix A: Interpreting the kth Root of the kth Moment of a Schedule of Cash Flows as a Duration

This appendix proves the claim stated in section 15.1 that the kth root of the kth moment of a schedule of cash flows is the duration of the schedule for the case where the yield used to discount a payment changes in proportion to the time to that payment raised to the $(k-1)$st power.

Let us assume the following:

1. The schedule specifies n payments where the ith payment is for an amount F_i and occurs in y_i years.

2. The yield curve is initially flat at yield R.

3. Following the shift in the curve the yield used to discount a payment due in y years is $R + t \cdot y^{k-1}$.

The initial value of the schedule is

$$V = \sum_{i=1}^{n} F_i \cdot (1 + \tfrac{1}{2}R)^{-2y_i} \tag{A15.1}$$

The kth moment of the schedule is

$$W_k = (V)^{-1} \cdot \sum_{i=1}^{n} y_i^k \cdot F_i \cdot (1 + \tfrac{1}{2}R)^{-2y_i} \tag{A15.2}$$

We want to show that the value of the schedule computed to a date $(W_k)^{1/k}$ years in the future using the new yield curve is invariant to first order with respect to the value of t.

Appendix B of chapter 5 shows that the value of the schedule computed to an arbitrary date h years in the future using the new yield curve is

$$FV = (1 + \tfrac{1}{2}R + \tfrac{1}{2}t \cdot h^{k-1})^{2h} \cdot \sum_{i=1}^{n} F_i \cdot (1 + \tfrac{1}{2}R + \tfrac{1}{2}t \cdot y_i^{k-1})^{-2y_i} \tag{A15.3}$$

The claim on the first-order invariance of FV will be proved if the derivative $d(FV)/dt$ evaluated at $t = 0$ is zero when $h = (W_k)^{1/k}$.

From the expression for FV in equation (A15.3) we have

$$\frac{d(FV)}{dt} = -(1 + \tfrac{1}{2}R + \tfrac{1}{2}t \cdot h^{k-1})^{2h} \cdot \sum_{i=1}^{n} F_i \cdot y_i^k \cdot (1 + \tfrac{1}{2}R + \tfrac{1}{2}t \cdot y_i^{k-1})^{-2y_i-1}$$

$$+ h^k \cdot (1 + \tfrac{1}{2}R + \tfrac{1}{2}t \cdot h^{k-1})^{2h-1} \cdot \sum_{i=1}^{n} F_i \cdot (1 + \tfrac{1}{2}R + \tfrac{1}{2}t \cdot y_i^{k-1})^{-2y_i} \tag{A15.4}$$

At $t = 0$ the derivative will vanish if

$$(1 + \tfrac{1}{2}R)^{2h} \cdot \sum_{i=1}^{n} F_i \cdot y_i^k \cdot (1 + \tfrac{1}{2}R)^{-2y_i-1}$$

$$= h^k \cdot (1 + \tfrac{1}{2}R)^{2h-1} \cdot \sum_{i=1}^{n} F_i \cdot (1 + \tfrac{1}{2}R)^{-2y_i} \tag{A15.5}$$

or if

$$h^k = \frac{\sum_{i=1}^{n} F_i \cdot y_i^k \cdot (1 + \frac{1}{2}R)^{-2y_i}}{\sum_{i=1}^{n} F_i \cdot (1 + \frac{1}{2}R)^{-2y_i}} \tag{A15.6}$$

or, by the definition of W_k in equation (A15.2), if

$$h^k = W_k \tag{A15.7}$$

This proves the claim.

15.8   Appendix B: An Alternative Expression for the Yield on a Portfolio of Bonds

This appendix demonstrates that the yield on a bond portfolio of a specified duration can be expressed as a linear combination of the product of (1) bond yield and (2) relative bond duration, where each product is weighted by the fractional contribution of the corresponding bond to the aggregate value of the portfolio.

Suppose that we have a portfolio of M different bonds. Let

R_i = yield on the ith bond,

Q_i = quantity of the ith bond in the portfolio, expressed in millions of dollars of principal value,

V_i = value of a basis point for the ith bond, expressed in dollars per \$1 million of principal value,

$P_i + A_i$ = quoted market price plus accrued interest for the ith bond, expressed in percent of principal,

D_i = duration of the ith bond.

We then have

$$D_i = \frac{V_i \cdot (1 + \frac{1}{2}R_i)}{P_i + A_i}, \qquad i = 1, 2, \ldots, N \tag{A15.8}$$

The yield on the portfolio can be approximated as a value of a basis point-weighted average of the yields on the bonds in the portfolio:

$$R = \frac{\sum_{i=1}^{M} Q_i \cdot V_i \cdot R_i}{\sum_{i=1}^{M} Q_i \cdot V_i} \tag{A15.9}$$

The duration of the portfolio can be approximated as a value-weighted average of the durations of the bonds in the portfolio:

$$D = \frac{\sum_{i=1}^{M} Q_i \cdot (P_i + A_i) \cdot D_i}{\sum_{i=1}^{M} Q_i \cdot (P_i + A_i)} \tag{A15.10}$$

(Equations A15.9 and A15.10 follow from the analyses in chapter 13.)
From equation (A15.8) we have

$$V_i = \frac{D_i \cdot (P_i + A_i)}{1 + \frac{1}{2}R_i}, \qquad i = 1, 2, \ldots, N \tag{A15.11}$$

Substituting this expression for V_i into equation (A15.9) gives

$$R = \frac{\sum_{i=1}^{M} Q_i \cdot (P_i + A_i) \cdot (1 + \frac{1}{2}R_i)^{-1} \cdot D_i \cdot R_i}{\sum_{i=1}^{M} Q_i \cdot (P_i + A_i) \cdot (1 + \frac{1}{2}R_i)^{-1} \cdot D_i} \tag{A15.12}$$

or, ignoring the $1 + \frac{1}{2}R_i$ terms,

$$R = \frac{\sum_{i=1}^{M} Q_i \cdot (P_i + A_i) \cdot D_i \cdot R_i}{\sum_{i=1}^{M} Q_i \cdot (P_i + A_i) \cdot D_i} \tag{A15.13}$$

From equation (A15.10) we have

$$\sum_{i=1}^{M} Q_i \cdot (P_i + A_i) \cdot D_i = D \cdot \sum_{i=1}^{M} Q_i \cdot (P_i + A_i) \tag{A15.14}$$

Substituting the right-hand side of equation (A15.14) into the denominator of equation (A15.13) gives

$$R = \frac{\sum_{i=1}^{M} Q_i \cdot (P_i + A_i) \cdot D_i \cdot R_i}{D \cdot \sum_{i=1}^{M} Q_i \cdot (P_i + A_i)} \tag{A15.15}$$

This shows that the yield on the portfolio can be written as a value-weighted average of the product of (1) bond yield and (2) relative bond duration:

$$R = \frac{\sum_{i=1}^{M} Q_i \cdot (P_i + A_i) \cdot (D_i/D) \cdot R_i}{\sum_{i=1}^{M} Q_i \cdot (P_i + A_i)} \tag{A15.16}$$

15.9 Appendix C: Constructing an Efficient Immunizing Portfolio of Order K

Suppose that we want to construct an efficient immunizing portfolio of order K from a set of M bonds where the yield on the ith bond is R_i and the kth characteristic moment of the ith bond is $W_{k,i}$.

Let a_i denote the fractional contribution of the ith bond to the aggregate value of the portfolio, so that $a_1 + a_2 + \cdots + a_M = 1$. From equation (15.20) we have that the kth characteristic moment of the portfolio is

$$W_k = \sum_{i=1}^{M} a_i \cdot W_{k,i} \qquad\qquad (A15.17)$$

From equation (A15.16) we have that the yield on the portfolio is

$$R = \sum_{i=1}^{M} a_i \cdot \left[\frac{W_{1,i}}{W_1} \right] \cdot R_i \qquad\qquad (A15.18)$$

The problem of constructing an efficient immunizing portfolio of order K for specified, or target, characteristic moments $W_1^*, W_2^*, \ldots, W_K^*$ is a matter of choosing $a_1, a_2, \ldots, a_M$ to maximize the portfolio yield:

$$R = \sum_{i=1}^{M} a_i \cdot \left[\frac{W_{1,i}}{W_1^*} R_i \right] \qquad\qquad (A15.19)$$

subject to the constraints

$$W_k^* = \sum_{i=1}^{M} a_i \cdot W_{k,i}, \qquad k = 1, 2, \ldots, K \qquad\qquad (A15.20)$$

$$a_i \geq 0, \qquad i = 1, 2, \ldots, M \qquad\qquad (A15.21)$$

This is a linear programming problem of choosing the $a_1, a_2, \ldots, a_M$ to maximize the value of a linear objective function (equation A15.19) subject to linear equality and inequality constraints (equations A15.20 and A15.21).

15.10   Subsequent Remarks

The analyses presented in this chapter have two flaws and one omission.

First, we assumed in the text preceding equation (15.1) that the initial spot yield curve was flat at some interest rate R. It would be preferable to assume instead an initial spot yield curve derived from the contemporaneous par bond yield curve as described in chapter 10.

Second, we assumed that the "best" portfolio within the class of immunizing portfolios of order K was the portfolio that had the highest yield (e.g., see the specification of the linear programming problem in appendix C). This assumption may seem quite natural to many market participants, but it has not been justified. In particular, we have criticized previously the proposition that yield is a good measure of average rate of return on capital when the yield curve is not flat (see chapter 5). It would be interesting to examine the matter of assessing the average rate of return on capital in the context of immunizing a complex liability schedule, where an investor wants to fund multiple future disbursements rather than a single disbursement and where he or she does not have a well-defined investment horizon.

Finally, the chapter observed that higher-order immunization has costs (in terms of reduced portfolio yield) and benefits (in terms of more complete risk reduction) but it failed to consider how those costs and benefits should be weighed. In particular, is second-order immunization "enough" or is it important to specify nothing less than fourth- or fifth-order immunization? This important issue is examined in chapter 16.

IV   MODES OF FLUCTUATION OF THE YIELD CURVE

The five chapters that constitute this part address the characteristics of fluctuations in the shape of the Treasury yield curve. Two related issues motivated the research reported in these chapters.

First, even a cursory appraisal of the behavior of Treasury yields shows that the shape as well as the level of the yield curve changes over time. It follows that interest rate risk is not simply a matter of parallel shifts of the curve and that deformations in the shape of the curve must also be recognized. This raises the threshold question of how to express analytically the nature of such deformations.

Chapter 16 opens the inquiry by separating changes in yields on securities of different maturities into independent modes of fluctuation. We show that shifts in the curve can be characterized broadly as changes in level, slope, and curvature and that these changes are statistically independent of each other. Chapter 17 extends the analysis by depicting the yield curve as a continuous function (rather than as a set of yields on a finite number of discrete securities) and by describing how the level and shape of the function varies through time.

The second issue that motivated the research reported in this part concerns the practice of relating yield to duration as measures of return and risk, respectively. Yield is a characteristic that has a nontrivial time dimension (e.g., the assessment of yield as a measure of average rate of return on capital over an interval of time equal to the duration of a bond in chapter 5). Duration also has a time dimension but the practical significance of any particular value is (outside of zero coupon securities) ambiguous when the level and shape of the yield curve can change in a variety of ways. Thus the analytical basis for relating bond yield to bond duration is ambiguous. (However, there is a clear practical reason for positing such a relationship, at least as a first approximation, as shown in chapters 7–10.) The basis for relating the yield on a portfolio of bonds to the duration of the portfolio is similarly suspect.

Chapter 18 examines an alternative proposition: that the shape of the yield curve reflects a relationship between (1) the *short-run* expected rate of return on a bond (or bond portfolio) and (2) the *short-run* risks of the bond (or bond portfolio) that stem from fluctuations in the level and shape of the curve. The chapter shows that it may be impossible to specify the shape of the yield curve independently of its modes of fluctuation. Chapter 19 uses the resulting analytical framework to price a yield-contingent claim, that is, a security whose future payments or payoffs depend on (or vary with) future yields, such as a call option on a bond.

Last, chapter 20 examines whether the modes of fluctuation of the yield curve are stationary through time.

Modes of Fluctuation in Bond Yields: An Analysis of Principal Components

This chapter addresses an issue at the heart of the market for fixed income securities: how yields on bonds of different maturities fluctuate. The importance of the topic can be appreciated by considering briefly how market participants describe changes in interest rates.

Most analysts understand that it may sometimes be crude to characterize the bond market as if it were a single entity, with yields on all bonds moving in parallel. An examination of figure 16.1, for example, suggests that it would be misleading to state simply that "Treasury bond yields fell" from July 1985 to March 1986. Although not untrue, the statement hardly reflects the most striking aspect of the change in the fixed income market over that interval.

When circumstances dictate more precision in characterizing the bond market than a crude, single-entity view, analysts sometimes choose to speak of individual market "sectors," such as the front end, the intermediate sector, and the long end. Thus one could describe the change in the market shown in figure 16.1 as an essentially unchanged front end, lower intermediate maturity yields, and dramatically lower long bond yields. More narrowly defined sectors, such as the 2-year sector or the 3-year sector, can be invoked if still greater precision is required.

As an alternative to, or in conjunction with, the sector approach, some analysts speak in terms of change in the level and slope of the curve. With this choice of characterization, we would say that the curve flattened dramatically between July 1985 and March 1986, with the flattening occuring as a result of unchanged short-term yields and sharply lower long-term yields. Similarly from figure 16.2 we would say that the level of the curve fell from late 1984 to early 1986 and that the decline in level was accompanied by a sharp reduction in curvature.

This paper addresses the utility of speaking of "the yield curve" in characterizing change in the bond market. The analysis begins in section 16.1 by examining the behavior of yields on actively traded, on-the-run Treasury securities. The results suggest that to a good approximation, we can summarize yield changes in an array of maturity sectors with comments on change in the level, slope, and curvature of the curve. More important, changes in level, slope, and curvature are found to be nearly independent phenomena. Thus the curve is equally likely to steepen or flatten, or to become more or less curved, in an environment of either rising or falling interest rates.

Defining the yield curve with yields on active Treasury issues, like the on-the-run 2-year note or 3-year note, is convenient, but it can be

Written in June 1986.

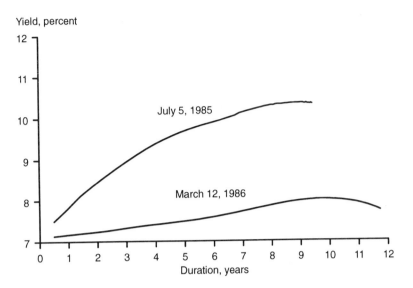

Figure 16.1
Treasury bond yield curves on July 5, 1985, and March 12, 1986

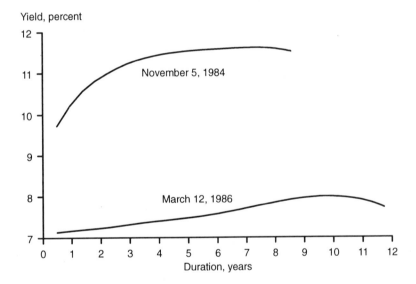

Figure 16.2
Treasury bond yield curves on November 5, 1984, and March 12, 1986

Table 16.1
Standard deviations and correlations of weekly yield changes for on-the-run Treasury securities from June 1983 to December 1985

	Sector								
	1 year	2 year	3 year	4 year	5 year	7 year	10 year	20 year	30 year
Standard deviation	20.0 bp	20.3	20.5	21.2	21.0	20.8	20.3	19.2	18.3
Correlation with									
1 yr	1.000	.964	.942	.927	.906	.873	.863	.832	.834
2	.964	1.000	.984	.973	.956	.927	.921	.891	.886
3	.942	.984	1.000	.983	.970	.945	.939	.909	.904
4	.927	.973	.983	1.000	.988	.972	.965	.940	.933
5	.906	.956	.970	.988	1.000	.985	.978	.953	.949
7	.873	.927	.945	.972	.985	1.000	.993	.973	.969
10	.863	.921	.939	.965	.978	.993	1.000	.982	.982
20	.832	.891	.909	.940	.953	.973	.982	1.000	.988
30	.834	.886	.904	.933	.949	.969	.982	.988	1.000

misleading. There is no stable measure of the intrinsic difference between, say, the active 2-year note and the active 20-year bond. Duration is the most natural measure, but it is not stable. In May 1984, for example, the 2-year note had a duration of 1.8 years and the 20-year bond had a duration of 7.0 years. By March 1986 the duration of the active 20-year bond had increased to 9.9 years (as a result of a lower coupon and lower yield), while the duration of the 2-year note had increased to only 1.9 years.

As noted in section 16.2, this difficulty can be resolved by using yields on single payment spot claims instead of conventional bond yields to define a yield curve. Section 16.3 repeats the analysis of section 16.1, using spot yields instead of yields on active issues. The qualitative results are the same: Change in the spot yield curve can be well represented as independently occurring changes in the level, slope, and curvature of the curve.

16.1 Modes of Fluctuation in Yields on Actively Traded Treasury Bonds

The problem of characterizing fluctuations in interest rates can be addressed by examining the relationship among changes in yields on bonds in different maturity sectors. Table 16.1 shows the standard deviations and correlations of yield changes over weekly intervals for actively traded, on-the-run, Treasury securities from June 1983 to December 1985. Two aspects of the data are worth noting.

First, yield volatility varied across different sectors of the Treasury market. The standard deviation of weekly yield change was 20.0 basis points for 1-year bills, increased to a high of 21.2 basis points for 4-year notes, and then declined to a low of 18.3 basis points for 30-year bonds.

Second, changes in yields on bonds in different maturity sectors were imperfectly correlated. The correlations were highest for "near-by" issues, such as the 7-year note and 10-year note (.993), and lowest for the most "distant" pairings, such as the 1-year bill and 30-year bond (.834). The correlations are generally smaller, the greater the difference in maturity between two securities. This is of course quite reasonable. We expect a 2-year note to behave nearly the same as a 3-year note but less like a 7-year note, and even less like a 30-year bond.

The correlations in table 16.1 suggest that yields on bonds of different maturities are subject to similar influences. That is, the correlations are generally high but not perfect. To understand the data more fully, we need a methodology for identifying the evident variety of influences on yields on bonds of different maturities.

The remainder of this section describes a technique for separating changes in bond yields into a set of independent factors (sometimes called "principal components"). We will see that to a good approximation, these factors can be identified as shifts in the level of the yield curve, the slope of the curve, and the curvature of the curve. The results imply that the vocabulary of yield curve analysis provides an adequate and efficient way to characterize change in the Treasury bond market.

Factoring Yield Changes into Independent Components

Let ΔRy be the change in yield (in basis points) over a one week interval on an active Treasury issue with a maturity of y years, for $y = 1, 2, 3, 4, 5, 7, 10, 20,$ or 30. Using the technique described in Appendix A we can write ΔRy as a weighted sum of nine random, statistically independent components:

$$\Delta Ry = a_{y,1} \cdot e_1 + a_{y,2} \cdot e_2 + \cdots + a_{y,9} \cdot e_9$$

$$\text{for } y = 1, 2, 3, 4, 5, 7, 10, 20, \text{ and } 30 \qquad (16.1)$$

where e_i is the value of the ith component and $a_{y,i}$ is a fixed coefficient denoting the "weighting" of component i for the yield change ΔRy. Each e_i is a random variable with a mean of zero and a standard deviation of unity.

Equation (16.1) provides a decomposition of the change in the yield on a bond into a weighted sum of statistically independent random components with equal standard deviations. Table 16.2 shows the values of the weighting coefficients for each Treasury issue. From the table we can, for example, write the change in the yield on a 2-year note over a one week

Table 16.2
Weighting coefficients of principal components of weekly yield changes for on-the-run treasury securities

Weighting on	Component								
	e_1	e_2	e_3	e_4	e_5	e_6	e_7	e_8	e_9
1 yr	18.6	−6.5	3.2	−1.2	.3	.3	−.2	.1	.1
2	19.7	−4.3	−.3	1.3	−1.2	−1.2	.4	.0	−.1
3	20.1	−3.0	−1.6	1.6	.1	1.5	−.3	.3	−.1
4	21.0	−1.1	−1.7	−.1	1.2	−.6	−.3	−1.1	.1
5	20.8	.5	−1.7	−1.2	.6	−.4	.9	1.1	.1
7	20.5	2.7	−.8	−1.6	−.9	.2	−.7	−.1	−.8
10	19.9	3.3	.1	−.5	−.9	.5	.1	−.4	1.0
20	18.5	4.4	1.5	1.2	.4	−.7	−1.0	.7	.1
30	17.6	4.3	2.1	.8	.4	.4	1.1	−.5	−.5

Table 16.3
Weighting coefficients (from table 16.2) of the first, second, and third principal components of weekly yield changes for on-the-run Treasury securities

Sector	Component		
	e_1	e_2	e_3
1 yr	18.6	−6.5	3.2
2	19.7	−4.3	−.3
3	20.1	−3.0	−1.6
4	21.0	−1.1	−1.7
5	20.8	.5	−1.7
7	20.5	2.7	−.8
10	19.9	3.3	.1
20	18.5	4.4	1.5
30	17.6	4.3	2.1

interval as

$$\Delta R_2 = 19.7 \cdot e_1 - 4.3 \cdot e_2 - .3 \cdot e_3 + 1.3 \cdot e_4$$
$$- 1.2 \cdot e_5 - 1.2 \cdot e_6 + 0.4 \cdot e_7 - 0.1 \cdot e_9 \tag{16.2}$$

This means that a realization of the first component of $e_1 = +1.0$ will lead to an increase in the yield on the 2-year note of 19.7 basis points. A realization of the second component of $e_2 = -.5$ will lead to an increase in the yield on the note of 2.15 basis points ($2.15 = (-4.3) \cdot (-.5)$).

The most interesting way to look at the data in table 16.2 is to examine how a particular component affects the yield on each Treasury issue. This is summarized in table 16.3 for the first three components.

Observe in table 16.3 that the first component affects all bond yields in a roughly comparable fashion. A positive realization of e_1 leads to an increase in all yields and a negative realization leads to a decrease in all yields. To a good approximation, the first component can thus be identified as a parallel movement of all yields. It should be noted, however, that this is only an approximation. The first component affects intermediate maturity issues somewhat more strongly than it affects short-term and long-term bonds. Consequently an increase in the general level of interest rates is associated with an increase in the slope of the yield curve out to about the 4-year sector and with a reduction in the slope of the curve from 4-year notes to 30-year bonds. Thus higher yields are associated with an increase in the curvature of the curve. Conversely, a negative realization of the first component tends to reduce the curvature of the yield curve as well as reduce interest rates generally.

The second component affects bond yields in a very different fashion. A positive realization of e_2 leads to a fall in short-term yields, an increase in long-term yields, and leaves yields in the intermediate sector of the market pretty much unchanged. This is equivalent to an increase in the slope of the yield curve. Conversely, a negative realization of e_2 leads to a flattening of the curve, with short-term yields going up and long-term interest rates falling. Thus, the second component can be identified as a factor which changes the slope of the curve.

In a similar fashion the third component can be identified as a factor which changes the curvature of the yield curve. A positive realization of e_3 will tend to "straighten out" a convex curve, with short and long-term interest rates rising and intermediate maturity yields falling.

Implications

The characterization of the first three components of bond yield changes as a level effect (e_1), a slope effect (e_2), and a curvature effect (e_3) is interesting for two reasons. First, it supports the use of those terms in the vocabulary that market participants use to describe change in the Treasury bond market.

Second, because of the way in which the components are constructed (see appendix A), change in the level, slope, and curvature of the yield curve are identified as largely independent phenomena. Knowing that, say, the level of the curve fell (a negative first component) implies little about the concurrent change in the slope (second component) and curvature (third component) of the curve. This means that a securities dealer can divide the trading of Treasury securities among traders who focus on level changes, a trader who focuses on change in the slope of the curve, and a trader who focuses on the curvature of the curve. To a large extent these are separable functions because they focus on uncorrelated, or statistically independent, phenomena.

The Unimportance of Higher Components

At this point the reader might wonder why we have focused attention on the first three components of the decomposition in equation (16.1) and ignored the six remaining components. The answer is that the remaining components are quantitatively unimportant.

Appendix B describes how we can allocate the total volatility of the yield on a bond to each component that makes up the change in the bond's yield. Averaging across all nine bond maturity sectors, change in the first component (which we have identified as a shift in the level of the yield curve) contributes 95.1% of the volatility of bond yields. Change in the second (slope) component contributes 3.2% of the average bond's yield volatility, and change in the third (curvature) component contributes .7% of yield volatility. Thus the first three components account for 99.0% of total bond yield volatility, leaving 1.0% to be allocated among the remaining six components.

16.2   Bond Yields and Spot Yields

To the extent that an analyst is willing to think of "the yield curve" being defined by yields on active Treasury bonds of sequential maturities, the analysis presented in section 16.1 is complete. However, in recent years many analysts have chosen to define the yield curve in terms of yields on securities of sequential *duration*. Bond yields are not wholly appropriate for examining change in the latter type of curve because the duration of a bond of a particular maturity will vary with the bond's coupon—lower coupon implies longer duration—and yield—lower yield implies longer duration.

The most natural way to define a yield curve in terms of duration is to use securities whose durations do not vary with the level of interest rates. The only securities satisfying this requirement are those that make a single future payment and for which duration is always and identically equal to term to maturity.

Zero coupon strips are one class of security that makes a single payment. However, using yields on zeros confounds change in the basic Treasury yield curve with change in the yield spread between zeros and Treasury bonds. What we need are instruments that, like zeros, make only a single payment but whose yields are more closely related to yields on whole Treasury bonds.

We will use yields on single payment spot Treasury claims to define a yield curve in terms of duration. The process of extracting a sequence of

Table 16.4
Standard deviations and correlations of weekly yield changes for selected spot Treasury claims from June 1983 to December 1985

	Sector									
	2 year	4 year	6 year	8 year	10 year	12 year	14 year	16 year	18 year	20 year
Standard deviation	20.8 bp	22.5	22.8	22.4	21.5	20.7	19.9	19.4	19.1	19.1
Correlation with										
2 yr	1.000	.972	.931	.892	.860	.844	.834	.816	.790	.769
4	.972	1.000	.987	.963	.939	.926	.914	.892	.861	.832
6	.931	.987	1.000	.993	.979	.969	.955	.930	.896	.863
8	.892	.963	.993	1.000	.996	.988	.974	.948	.912	.877
10	.860	.939	.979	.996	1.000	.996	.982	.955	.919	.883
12	.844	.926	.969	.988	.996	1.000	.994	.975	.945	.913
14	.834	.914	.955	.974	.982	.994	1.000	.993	.974	.951
16	.816	.892	.930	.948	.955	.975	.993	1.000	.993	.979
18	.790	.861	.896	.912	.919	.945	.974	.993	1.000	.995
20	.769	.832	.863	.877	.883	.913	.951	.979	.995	1.000

spot yields from the market prices and coupon rates of a sequence of Treasury bonds was described in chapter 10. We use coupon rates equal to par bond yields (computed as described in chapter 7) and hence assume bond prices equal to 100% of principal.

16.3   Modes of Fluctuation in Spot Yields

To examine the behavior of the spot yield curve, we computed the weekly changes in yields on spot Treasury claims with maturities of 1 to 20 years during the interval from June 1983 to December 1985. Table 16.4 reports the standard deviations and correlations of the yield changes for a selected subset of the obligations. As with active Treasury issues (see table 16.1), yields are less volatile at the short and long ends of the curve than in the middle of the curve, and yield changes on spot obligations of more similar maturities are more highly correlated.

Using the methodology described in appendix A, we can decompose the change in a spot yield into a weighted sum of statistically independent random factors, each with a mean of zero and variance of unity. Table 16.5 reports the weightings of the first three factors on spot obligations with maturities of 1 to 20 years. Figure 16.3 shows the same information graphically.

As in section 16.1, we can identify the first component e_1 as a factor that alters the level of the yield curve. It is not, however, a pure level effect because it affects spot yields in the 4-year to 9-year sectors more strongly

Table 16.5
Weighting coefficients of the first, second, and third principal components of weekly yield changes for spot Treasury claims

Term to maturity	Component		
	e_1	e_2	e_3
1 yr	15.8	−10.5	5.4
2	19.0	−8.1	2.6
3	20.6	−6.5	.9
4	21.8	−5.2	−.3
5	22.3	−3.7	−1.4
6	22.6	−2.4	−2.1
7	22.5	−1.2	−2.6
8	22.2	−.4	−3.0
9	21.7	.4	−3.2
10	21.2	1.1	−3.3
11	20.8	1.7	−2.8
12	20.4	2.3	−2.1
13	20.0	2.8	−1.2
14	19.6	3.2	−.2
15	19.2	3.8	.7
16	18.9	4.1	1.7
17	18.5	4.5	2.6
18	18.2	4.8	3.5
19	17.9	5.1	4.3
20	17.7	5.3	4.9

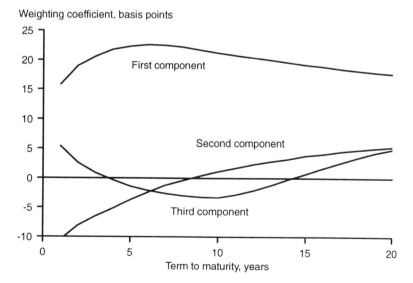

Figure 16.3
Weighting coefficients of the first, second, and third principal components of weekly yield changes for spot Treasury claims

than shorter or longer maturity spot yields. Thus, the first factor also affects the curvature of the yield curve. The second component e_2 is seen to affect the slope of the yield curve. A positive value of e_2 leads to a steepening of the curve, and vice versa. The third component affects the curvature of the curve.

These results on the principal modes of fluctuation in the spot yield curve closely parallel the results in section 16.1. In particular, we find that changes in spot yields are well represented by changes in the level, slope, and curvature of the spot yield curve and that these factors are largely statistically independent of each other.

16.4   Implications for Hedging

Consider a dealer firm which, from time to time, has to hedge the risk of a bond position which it has acquired from customers. Chapter 12 showed how to calculate the *size* of an optimal hedge for a *given* set of hedge bonds, but it did not address the problem of how to select the most appropriate set of hedge bonds.

If the dealer firm wants to use only a small number of Treasury issues to hedge an arbitrary position, it will want to select issues that, as a group, can be expected to reflect change in each of the major factors affecting bond yields. In particular, the hedge bonds should reflect changes in the level, slope, and curvature of the yield curve.

Any bond can be expected to reflect change in the level of the Treasury yield curve. As shown in table 16.3, the first component of bond yield change affects yields on all bonds in a comparable fashion. Change in the second component, or the slope of the yield curve, is best reflected in a short-maturity issue like a 1-year bill or a 2-year note coupled with a long-term issue like the 30-year bond. Finally, change in the curvature of the curve is well represented with a short-term issue, an intermediate maturity security like the active 5-year note, and the 30-year bond.

Taken together, a dealer can expect to insulate an arbitrary bond position against the quantitatively important classes of interest rate change by hedging with (1) 1-year bills or 2-year notes, and (2) 5-year notes, and (3) 30-year bonds. These three maturity sectors "span" the bond market with respect to change in the level, slope, and curvature of the yield curve. More particularly, it is not necessary to deal in 3-year notes, 7-year notes, 10-year notes, or 20-year bonds to hedge efficiently an arbitrary bond position.

16.5   Implications for Immunization

Basic immunization theory suggests than an investor can insulate his net worth against gains and losses due to changes in interest rates by holding a portfolio of bonds whose value and duration matches the value and duration of his liabilities. It is widely recognized that this basic view is not correct if the yield curve shifts in something other than a parallel fashion, but that a more general view of immunization can insulate an investor against nonparallel as well as parallel shifts of the curve (see chapters 5 and 15).

The more general view of immunization assumes the spot yield curve can shift in any of a variety of ways:

1. All spot yields change by the same amount, and/or

2. a spot yield changes in proportion to the time remaining to payment of the respective spot obligation, and/or

3. a spot yield changes in proportion to the *square* of the time remaining to payment of the respective spot obligation, and so on.

This generalized view of yield curve change does not, however, identify which members of the sequence are important and should be immunized and which members can be ignored. This is not a trivial problem because immunization against more classes of change in the yield curve can be obtained only at the cost of a lower average yield on the immunizing portfolio.

The question of what classes of change in the spot yield curve must, as a practical matter, be immunized can be answered with the analysis in section 16.3. We have already established the three principal modes of fluctuation in the spot yield curve (see table 16.5 and figure 16.3 above). Figure 16.4 shows that *each* of these modes can be approximated to within about 1 basis point by a quadratic function of the time to payment of a spot obligation. If we immunize against parallel shifts of the spot curve, shifts of the curve that are proportional to the time to a payment, and shifts that are proportional to the square of the time to a payment, we will have immunized against *all* linear combinations of those shifts. Thus we will have immunized against those particular linear combinations that make up the three principal modes of fluctuation in the spot yield curve.

16.6   Conclusions

This chapter has examined the principal modes of fluctuation in Treasury bond and spot yields. We found that the common vocabulary of the bond

Weighting coefficient, basis points

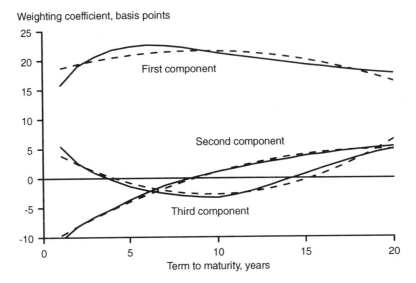

Figure 16.4
Actual (solid lines) and fitted (dashed lines) weighting coefficients of the first, second, and third principal components of weekly yield changes for spot Treasury claims (fitted coefficients are from a quadratic approximation of the actual coefficients)

market—which speaks of change in the level, slope, and curvature of the yield curve—is adequate and efficient for characterizing change in the structure of interest rates. Those three components account for the bulk of yield changes and, since they are largely statistically independent, are not redundant.

The results of the analysis also allowed us to answer two important questions in fixed income analysis. First, we find that an arbitrary bond position can be hedged efficiently with 1-year bills or 2-year notes, 5-year notes, and 30-year bonds. It is unnecessary to deal in bonds of other maturities and hence unnecessary to have hedges more elaborate than a three-bond hedge. Second, we find that a generalized bond immunization program need not be concerned with shifts in the spot yield curve beyond shifts that are proportional to the square of the time to payment of a spot obligation. More complex forms of immunization will not reduce risk significantly.

16.7   Appendix A: Identifying Modes of Interest Rate Fluctuation

This appendix describes how the changes in yields on a set of securities can be decomposed into a linear combination of statistically independent random variables, each with a mean of zero and unit variance.

Assume there are n securities and that the changes in yields on the securities have the $n \times n$ covariance matrix C, where $[C]_{i,j}$ is the covariance of the change in yield on security i with the change in yield on security j for $i = 1, 2, \ldots, n$ and $j = 1, 2, \ldots, n$. Since C is a symmetric matrix, there exists an orthogonal matrix V and a diagonal matrix D such that $C = V \cdot D \cdot V'$, where V' is the transpose of V. The ith column of V is an eigenvector of C with an eigenvalue equal to $[D]_{ii}$.

Let ΔR be an n-dimensional column vector of changes in yields on the n securities. By hypothesis, ΔR has an expected value of zero and a covariance matrix C. Let $D^{-1/2}$ denote the diagonal matrix whose ith diagonal element is $([D]_{ii})^{-1/2}$.

Consider now the n-dimensional vector $e = D^{-1/2} \cdot V' \cdot \Delta R$. e has an expected value of zero and a covariance matrix $D^{-1/2} \cdot V' \cdot C \cdot V \cdot D^{-1/2}$, or $D^{-1/2} \cdot D \cdot D^{-1/2}$, or just the identity matrix. Thus e is a vector of statistically independent random variables, each with a mean of zero and a variance of unity. Since $\Delta R = V \cdot D^{1/2} \cdot e$, we have that the vector ΔR can be written as a linear combination of statistically independent random variables, each with a mean of zero and unit variance. The element $[V \cdot D^{-1/2}]_{ij}$ is the weighting of the jth component on the change in yield of the ith security.

16.8   Appendix B: Allocating the Volatility of the Yield on a Bond among Its Components

This appendix shows how we can allocate the volatility of the yield on a bond among the components that make up the change in yield.

Following the results in appendix A, we can write the change in the yield on a bond, denoted ΔR, as a linear combination of n statistically independent random variables, each with a mean of zero and unit variance:

$$\Delta R = a_1 \cdot e_1 + a_2 \cdot e_2 + \cdots + a_n \cdot e_n \qquad (A16.1)$$

Since the e_i variables are independently distributed with unit variance, the variance σ^2 of ΔR can be written.

$$\sigma^2 = a_1^2 + a_2^2 + \cdots + a_n^2 \qquad (A16.2)$$

It follows that a_i^2/σ^2 is the fractional contribution of the ith factor to the total volatility of the yield on the bond.

Several of the preceding chapters depicted a yield curve as a sequence of yields on debt instruments with specified maturities, or as a finite set of discrete points in a graph of yield versus maturity. In some cases the points were connected to form a piecewise linear graph and occasionally the points were so close together that the graph looked smooth, but the real data was always a finite set of discrete points (e.g., see chapter 7). Statistically independent modes of fluctuation of a yield curve were similarly represented in terms of the variation in yields on bonds or spot claims of particular maturities (see chapter 16).

Despite the evident utility of representing a yield curve and modes of fluctuation in a yield curve with a set of descrete points, there are occasions when it is desirable to represent the curve and its modes of fluctuation with *continuous functions*. This chapter examines the problem of representing a yield curve and modes of fluctuation in a yield curve with *polynomial* functions of maturity. This is a matter of expressing the yield on a debt instrument as a power function of the maturity of the instrument and, more particularly, of obtaining numerical estimates of the coefficients of the power function. Section 17.1 describes the estimation methodology and Section 17.2 applies the technique to spot Treasury yield curves.

17.1 Methodology

We first state some general assumptions on the structure of the curve and its variation through time. We then specialize the structure to the case where the functions that make up the curve are polynomial functions. The heart of the section is the description of the method for estimating the coefficients of the polynomials.

Basic Assumptions on the Structure and Variation of the Yield Curve

Let $R(y, t)$ denote the yield at time t on a debt instrument with a term to maturity of y years. The instrument can be a single payment security like a Treasury bill, a zero coupon security, or a spot claim, or it can be a multiple payment security like a par Treasury bond.

The yield curve is a description of the variation of yield with term to maturity. One way to represent the curve at time t is with a set of yields of the form $R(y_i, t)$, where the index i runs from 1 to n. This represents the curve with a sequence of yields on discrete debt instruments with maturities of $y_1, y_2, \ldots, y_n$ years.

Written in July 1989.

Another way to represent the yield curve at time t is with a function of the form $R(y, t)$, where t is fixed and the maturity y runs *continuously* from zero to some upper limit such as 30 years. This chapter is concerned with the latter representation.

We assume the yield curve at time t can be expressed as

$$R(y, t) = R_0(y) + \sum_{j=1}^{J} w_j(t) \cdot f_j(y) \tag{17.1}$$

where $R_0(y)$ and $f_1(y), \ldots, f_J(y)$ are time-invariant, or stationary, functions of maturity. Equation (17.1) says that the curve at time t can be constructed as a "baseline" function $R_0(y)$ plus a linear combination of "shift" functions $f_1(y), \ldots, f_J(y)$. $w_j(t)$ is the weight on the jth shift function at time t.

The yield curve in equation (17.1) varies over time, in shape as well as level, as a result of temporal variation in the $w_j(t)$ weights. We assume that each weight evolves as a Gaussian (or normal) random walk with zero drift and a variance of unity per week and that change in one weight is uncorrelated with changes in other weights; that is, the random walks are statistically independent of each other.

It is useful to examine the implications of the behavior of the $w_j(t)$s in more detail. Let $t_0, t_1, t_2, \ldots$, be a sequence of times one week apart. Looking only at these points in time, equation (17.1) can be written

$$R(y, t_k) = R_0(y) + \sum_{j=1}^{J} w_j(t_k) \cdot f_j(y), \qquad k = 0, 1, 2, \ldots \tag{17.2}$$

The change in yield from time t_{k-1} to time t_k at a term of y years is

$$\Delta R(y, t_k) = R(y, t_k) - R(y, t_{k-1}) \tag{17.3}$$

(Note that this is not the change in yield on a particular debt instrument but rather the change in yield at a particular point along the curve.) Using equation (17.2), equation (17.3) can be rewritten

$$\Delta R(y, t_k) = R_0(y) + \sum_{j=1}^{J} w_j(t_k) \cdot f_j(y) - R_0(y) - \sum_{j=1}^{J} w_j(t_{k-1}) \cdot f_j(y)$$

$$= \sum_{j=1}^{J} f_j(y) \cdot [w_j(t_k) - w_j(t_{k-1})] \tag{17.4}$$

We can denote the change from time t_{k-1} to time t_k in the jth weight as

$$e_j(t_k) = w_j(t_k) - w_j(t_{k-1}) \tag{17.5}$$

so equation (17.4) becomes

$$\Delta R(y, t_k) = \sum_{j=1}^{J} f_j(y) \cdot e_j(t_k) \tag{17.6}$$

Thus the function describing the shift in the yield curve from time t_{k-1} to time t_k is a linear combination of the shift functions $f_1(y), \ldots, f_J(y)$. (This is why we called the $f_j(y)s$ "shift" functions.)

Based on the assumed behavior of the $w_j(t)$ weights, we have that the $e_j(t_k)$ terms are normally distributed random variables with the characteristics:

$$\exp[e_j(t_k)] = 0 \tag{17.7a}$$

$$\text{var}[e_j(t_k)] = 1 \tag{17.7b}$$

$$\text{cov}[e_j(t_k), e_i(t_h)] = 0 \quad \text{if } j \neq i \text{ or } k \neq h \tag{17.7c}$$

Thus the shift functions represent normalized (see equation 17.7b) and statistically independent (see equation 17.7c) modes of fluctuation in the yield curve.

The Problem

We can now state concisely the problem of interest in the chapter: What are the $R_0(y)$ and the $f_1(y), \ldots, f_J(y)$ *functions*, and what are the $w_1(t), \ldots, w_J(t)$ weights at any point in time?

Polynomial Functions

In general, estimating a function is quite difficult. To make our problem analytically tactable, we assume that the $R_0(y)$ baseline function and the $f_j(y)$ shift functions are polynomials in y.

More particularly, we assume that

$$R_0(y) = \sum_{i=1}^{I} \beta_{i0} y^{i-1} \tag{17.8a}$$

$$f_j(y) = \sum_{i=1}^{I} \beta_{ij} y^{i-1}, \quad j = 1, \ldots, J \tag{17.8b}$$

where the $\beta_{i0}s$ are the coefficients of the baseline polynomial and the $\beta_{ij}s$ are the coefficients of the shift polynomials. The polynomials in equations (17.8a) and (17.8b) are all polynomials of degree (or power) $I - 1$. If $I = 3$, the polynomials are second degree or quadratic polynomials.

We can assume $J \leq I$ without loss of generality. That is, there are no more shift functions than the number of coefficients in a polynomial. If $J > I$, then $J - I$ of the shift functions can be written as linear combinations of the other I shift functions. More specifically, we can specify a new set of just I functions which satisfy all of the assumptions of our model of the yield curve.

The Problem Restated

As a result of the introduction of the polynomials in equations (17.8a) and (17.8b), we can restate the problem as: What are the β_{i0} coefficients and the β_{ij} coefficients and what are the $w_j(t)$ weights at some arbitrary time t?

Estimating the β_{ij} Coefficients

As a first step in our analysis, we consider the problem of estimating the β_{ij} coefficients of the shift polynomials.

Equation (17.6) provides an expression for the change in yield over one week from time t_{k-1} to time t_k at a term of y years:

$$\Delta R(y, t_k) = \sum_{j=1}^{J} f_j(y) \cdot e_j(t_k) \tag{17.9}$$

Replacing the shift functions with their polynomial forms as given in equation (17.8b), equation (17.9) becomes

$$\Delta R(y, t_k) = \sum_{j=1}^{J} \left[\sum_{i=1}^{I} \beta_{ij} \cdot y^{i-1} \right] \cdot e_j(t_k)$$

or

$$\Delta R(y, t_k) = \sum_{i=1}^{I} y^{i-1} \cdot \left[\sum_{j=1}^{J} \beta_{ij} \cdot e_j(t_k) \right] \tag{17.10}$$

Now suppose that we focus on a set of n specific and distinct (but arbitrary) maturities denoted $y_1, y_2, \ldots, y_n$, where $n \geq I$. Define the vectors:

$$\Delta R(t_k) = \begin{bmatrix} \Delta R(y_1, t_k) \\ \vdots \\ \Delta R(y_n, t_k) \end{bmatrix} \tag{17.11}$$

$$e(t_k) = \begin{bmatrix} e_1(t_k) \\ \vdots \\ e_J(t_k) \end{bmatrix} \tag{17.12}$$

and the matrices:

$$Y = \begin{bmatrix} 1 & y_1 & y_1^2 & \cdots & y_1^{I-1} \\ \vdots & \vdots & \vdots & & \vdots \\ 1 & y_n & y_n^2 & \cdots & y_n^{I-1} \end{bmatrix} \tag{17.13}$$

$$B = \begin{bmatrix} \beta_{11} & \cdots & \beta_{1J} \\ \vdots & & \vdots \\ \beta_{I1} & \cdots & \beta_{IJ} \end{bmatrix} \tag{17.14}$$

From equation (17.10) we can write

$$\Delta R(t_k) = Y \cdot B \cdot e(t_k) \tag{17.15}$$

Equation (17.15) says that the vector of one week yield changes $\Delta R(t_k)$ is a linear function of the random vector $e(t_k)$. Note that from the discussion at equations (17.7a, b, c), the vector $e(t_k)$ is normally distributed with a mean vector of zero and a covariance matrix equal to the J-by-J identity matrix.

Let $\Omega_{\Delta R}$ denote the n-by-n covariance matrix of $\Delta R(t_k)$. We can write $\Omega_{\Delta R}$ in the form

$$\Omega_{\Delta R} = \tilde{V}_{\Delta R} \cdot \tilde{D}_{\Delta R} \cdot \tilde{V}'_{\Delta R} \tag{17.16}$$

where $\tilde{V}_{\Delta R}$ is an $n \times J$ matrix and $\tilde{D}_{\Delta R}$ is a $J \times J$ diagonal matrix. Equation (17.16) is crucial to the analysis. We show below that it is justified.

Consider now a J-dimensional normally distributed random vector e with a mean vector of zero and covariance matrix equal to the identity matrix; that is, the elements of e are independently distributed with unit variances. Further define the n-dimensional vector ΔR

$$\Delta R = \tilde{V}_{\Delta R} \cdot \tilde{D}_{\Delta R}^{1/2} \cdot e \tag{17.17}$$

where $\tilde{D}_{\Delta R}^{1/2}$ is a $J \times J$ diagonal matrix with entries of the form $[\tilde{D}_{\Delta R}^{1/2}]_{ii} = ([\tilde{D}_{\Delta R}]_{ii})^{1/2}$; that is, the entries on the diagonal of $\tilde{D}_{\Delta R}^{1/2}$ are the square roots of the corresponding entries on the diagonal of $\tilde{D}_{\Delta R}$.

The covariance matrix of ΔR is

$$\begin{aligned} \text{cov}[\Delta R] &= \exp[\Delta R \cdot \Delta R'] \\ &= \exp[\tilde{V}_{\Delta R} \cdot \tilde{D}_{\Delta R}^{1/2} \cdot e \cdot e' \cdot \tilde{D}_{\Delta R}^{1/2} \cdot \tilde{V}'_{\Delta R}] \\ &= \tilde{V}_{\Delta R} \cdot \tilde{D}_{\Delta R}^{1/2} \cdot \exp[e \cdot e'] \cdot \tilde{D}_{\Delta R}^{1/2} \cdot \tilde{V}'_{\Delta R} \\ &= \tilde{V}_{\Delta R} \cdot \tilde{D}_{\Delta R}^{1/2} \cdot I \cdot D_{\Delta R}^{1/2} \cdot \tilde{V}'_{\Delta R} \\ &= \tilde{V}_{\Delta R} \cdot \tilde{D}_{\Delta R} \cdot \tilde{V}'_{\Delta R} \end{aligned}$$

or, from equation (17.16),

$$\text{cov}[\Delta R] = \Omega_{\Delta R} \tag{17.18}$$

Now compare equations (17.15) and (17.17):

$$\Delta R(t_k) = Y \cdot B \cdot e(t_k) \tag{17.19a}$$

$$\Delta R = \tilde{V}_{\Delta R} \cdot \tilde{D}_{\Delta R}^{1/2} \cdot e \tag{17.19b}$$

The vectors on the left-hand side of both equations are normally distributed with a mean of zero and a covariance matrix of $\Omega_{\Delta R}$. The vectors on the right-hand side of both equations are normally distributed with a mean of zero and a covariance matrix equal to the $J \times J$ identity matrix. It follows that we can identify the matrices on the right-hand side of the two equations:

$$Y \cdot B = \tilde{V}_{\Delta R} \cdot \tilde{D}_{\Delta R}^{1/2} \tag{17.20}$$

We want to solve equation (17.20) for the matrix B. This is not too difficult. First pre-multiply both sides of the equation by Y':

$$Y' \cdot Y \cdot B = Y' \cdot \tilde{V}_{\Delta R} \cdot \tilde{D}_{\Delta R}^{1/2}$$

Then pre-multiply again by $(Y' \cdot Y)^{-1}$:

$$B = (Y' \cdot Y)^{-1} \cdot Y' \cdot \tilde{V}_{\Delta R} \cdot \tilde{D}_{\Delta R}^{1/2} \tag{17.21}$$

Equation (17.21) gives an expression for the matrix B in terms of the matrix Y (which is known; see equation 17.13) and the matrices $\tilde{V}_{\Delta R}$ and $\tilde{D}_{\Delta R}$ (which were assumed known at equation 17.16).

Thus we have reduced the problem of estimating the β_{ij} coefficients to the problem of computing the covariance matrix $\Omega_{\Delta R}$ and expressing that matrix in the form of equation (17.16). We consider next a solution to this new problem.

Computing $\Omega_{\Delta R}$ and Expressing It in the Form of Equation (17.16)

Consider again the representation of the yield curve given by equation (17.2):

$$R(y, t_k) = R_0(y) + \sum_{j=1}^{J} f_j(y) \cdot w_j(t_k) \tag{17.22}$$

Replacing the baseline function and the shift functions with their polynomial forms as given by equations (17.8a, b), this becomes

$$R(y, t_k) = \sum_{i=1}^{I} \beta_{i0} \cdot y^{i-1} + \sum_{j=1}^{J} \left[\sum_{i=1}^{I} \beta_{ij} \cdot y^{i-1} \right] \cdot w_j(t_k) \tag{17.23}$$

$$R(y, t_k) = \sum_{i=1}^{I} \left[\beta_{i0} + \sum_{j=1}^{J} \beta_{ij} \cdot w_j(t_k) \right] \cdot y^{i-1} \tag{17.24}$$

Now define a "composite" coefficient $a_i(t_k)$ as:

$$a_i(t_k) = \beta_{i0} + \sum_{j=1}^{J} \beta_{ij} \cdot w_j(t_k), \qquad i = 1, 2, \ldots, I \tag{17.25}$$

With this definition the representation of the yield curve in equation (17.24) can be written

$$R(y, t_k) = \sum_{i=1}^{I} a_i(t_k) \cdot y^{i-1} \tag{17.26}$$

Equation (17.26) says that the yield curve is a polynomial function of maturity, of degree $I - 1$, where the $a_i(t_k)$ coefficients of the polynomial vary through time.

We want to examine in more detail how the composite coefficients fluctuate. The change in the ith composite coefficient over one week, from time t_{k-1} to time t_k, is

$$\Delta a_i(t_k) = a_i(t_k) - a_i(t_{k-1}) \tag{17.27}$$

From the definition of $a_i(t_k)$ in equation (17.25), this becomes

$$\Delta a_i(t_k) = \beta_{i0} + \sum_{j=1}^{J} \beta_{ij} \cdot w_j(t_k)$$

$$- \beta_{i0} - \sum_{j=1}^{J} \beta_{ij} \cdot w_j(t_{k-1})$$

$$= \sum_{j=1}^{J} \beta_{ij} \cdot [w_j(t_k) - w_j(t_{k-1})]$$

or, from the definition of $e_j(t_k)$ in equation (17.5),

$$\Delta a_i(t_k) = \sum_{j=1}^{J} \beta_{ij} \cdot e_j(t_k), \qquad i = 1, 2, \ldots, I \tag{17.28}$$

Defining the I-dimensional vector:

$$\Delta a(t_k) = \begin{bmatrix} \Delta a_1(t_k) \\ \vdots \\ \Delta a_I(t_k) \end{bmatrix} \tag{17.29}$$

allows us to write equation (17.28) as

$$\Delta a(t_k) = B \cdot e(t_k) \tag{17.30}$$

where B is as defined in equation (17.14) and $e(t_k)$ is as defined in equation (17.12).

Equation (17.30) says that the vector $\Delta a(t_k)$ of composite coefficient changes is a linear function of the normally distributed random vector $e(t_k)$. Thus $\Delta a(t_k)$ is also a normally distributed random vector. The expected value of $\Delta a(t_k)$ is the zero vector. Let $\Omega_{\Delta a}$ denote the covariance matrix of $\Delta a(t_k)$. We assume here that $\Omega_{\Delta a}$ is known, and we show below how it can be estimated.

Now consider again equation (17.15) for the change from time t_{k-1} to time t_k in yields at n specified maturities:

$$\Delta R(t_k) = Y \cdot B \cdot e(t_k) \tag{17.31}$$

Comparing equations (17.30) and (17.31) shows that we can write $\Delta R(t_k)$ as

$$\Delta R(t_k) = Y \cdot \Delta a(t_k) \tag{17.32}$$

From equation (17.32) we can compute the covariance matrix of $\Delta R(t_k)$ as

$$\Omega_{\Delta R} = \mathrm{cov}[\Delta R(t_k)]$$

$$= \exp[\Delta R(t_k) \cdot \Delta R(t_k)']$$

$$= \exp[Y \cdot \Delta a(t_k) \cdot \Delta a(t_k)' \cdot Y']$$

$$= Y \cdot \exp[\Delta a(t_k) \cdot \Delta a(t_k)'] \cdot Y'$$

or

$$\Omega_{\Delta R} = Y \cdot \Omega_{\Delta a} \cdot Y' \tag{17.33}$$

Equation (17.33) provides a method for computing $\Omega_{\Delta R}$ from the known matrix Y and the presently assumed to be known matrix $\Omega_{\Delta a}$.

Having proposed a scheme for computing $\Omega_{\Delta R}$, we now have to show that $\Omega_{\Delta R}$ can be expressed in the form of equation (17.16). Since $\Omega_{\Delta R}$ is a symmetric matrix it can certainly be written as

$$\Omega_{\Delta R} = V_{\Delta R} \cdot D_{\Delta R} \cdot V_{\Delta R}' \tag{17.34}$$

where the columns of $V_{\Delta R}$ are the eigenvectors of $\Omega_{\Delta R}$ and where $D_{\Delta R}$ is a diagonal matrix whose entries are the eigenvalues of $\Omega_{\Delta R}$.

Since $\Delta R(t_k)$ has the form of equation (17.31), $\Omega_{\Delta R}$ will have only J positive eigenvalues. (Observe that $e(t_k)$ is a J-dimensional vector and $\Delta R(t_k)$ is an n-dimensional vector, where $n > I \geq J$.) Without loss of generality, we can assume a partitioning of $V_{\Delta R}$ and $D_{\Delta R}$ of the form

$$V_{\Delta R} = [\tilde{V}_{\Delta R} \mid \tilde{\tilde{V}}_{\Delta R}] \tag{17.35a}$$

$$D_{\Delta R} = \left[\begin{array}{c|c} \tilde{D}_{\Delta R} & 0 \\ \hline 0 & 0 \end{array}\right] \tag{17.35b}$$

where there are J column vectors in $\tilde{V}_{\Delta R}$ and where $\tilde{D}_{\Delta R}$ is a $J \times J$ diagonal matrix with positive values on its diagonal. It follows that

$$\Omega_{\Delta R} = \tilde{V}_{\Delta R} \cdot \tilde{D}_{\Delta R} \cdot \tilde{V}'_{\Delta R} \tag{17.36}$$

which is exactly equation (17.16).

We have now shown that we can compute $\Omega_{\Delta R}$ and express it in the form of equation (17.16) if we know $\Omega_{\Delta a}$. We consider next how to estimate $\Omega_{\Delta a}$.

Estimating $\Omega_{\Delta a}$

$\Omega_{\Delta a}$ is the covariance matrix of weekly changes in the composite coefficients $a_1(t_k), \ldots, a_I(t_k)$. We can estimate $\Omega_{\Delta a}$ from time series data on those coefficients.

Recall from equation (17.26) that the representation of the yield curve at time t_k can be written

$$R(y, t_k) = \sum_{i=1}^{I} a_i(t_k) \cdot y^{i-1} \tag{17.37}$$

The composite coefficients at time t_k can be estimated from data on a set of contemporaneous yields at known maturities. (The estimation procedure for a spot yield curve is elaborated in the appendix.) A time series of these estimates can then be used to estimate $\Omega_{\Delta a}$.

Summary

At this point it might be useful to summarize step by step, our proposed methodology for estimating the β_{ij} coefficients of the shift polynomials.

1. For each date t_k in a sequence of dates $t_0, t_1, \ldots, t_K$ at weekly intervals, estimate the values of the composite coefficients $a_1(t_k), \ldots, a_I(t_k)$ in equation (17.37).

2. Use the estimated values of the composite coefficients to estimate the covariance matrix of weekly changes in the composite coefficients. This gives an estimate $\hat{\Omega}_{\Delta a}$ of $\Omega_{\Delta a}$.

3. For a sequence of maturities $y_1, \ldots, y_n$, construct the matrix Y defined in equation (17.13), and compute an estimate $\hat{\Omega}_{\Delta R}$ of the covariance matrix $\Omega_{\Delta R}$ as $\hat{\Omega}_{\Delta R} = Y \cdot \hat{\Omega}_{\Delta a} \cdot Y'$ as in equation (17.33).

4. Compute the eigenvalues and eigenvectors of $\hat{\Omega}_{\Delta R}$ and identify $V_{\Delta R}$ and $D_{\Delta R}$ as in equation (17.34).

5. Extract $\tilde{V}_{\Delta R}$ and $\tilde{D}_{\Delta R}$ from $V_{\Delta R}$ and $D_{\Delta R}$ according to the partitionings in equations (17.35a, b).

6. Compute the desired β_{ij} coefficients as in equation (17.21).

A Problem

Let us step back a moment and compare what we wanted to obtain with what we have done.

We began by saying that there were J shift functions and that each function was a polynomial with I coefficients. Thus we wanted to estimate a total of $J \cdot I$ coefficients.

The values of J and I are presumably to be specified by an analyst. It is of interest to identify exactly where those values first appear in our methodology.

A review of the summary above shows that the value of I is introduced *exogenously* in step 1, where an analyst chooses the number of coefficients in the composite polynomial function of equation (17.37) representing the yield curve on any given date. The value of J appears *endogenously* in step 5, where J is the number of positive eigenvalues of the matrix $\tilde{\Omega}_{\Delta R} = Y \cdot \tilde{\Omega}_{\Delta a} \cdot Y'$ and hence is the dimension of the diagonal submatrix $\tilde{D}_{\Delta R}$. This shows that the value of J is *not* subject to exogenous specification and raises a question about how the value is determined in practice.

We argued in the analysis above that $\Omega_{\Delta R}$ will have exactly J positive eigenvalues. However, that argument was predicated on knowing the "true" value of $\Omega_{\Delta R}$. In fact we have to work with an estimate of that matrix, computed in step 3 as $\hat{\Omega}_{\Delta R} = Y \cdot \hat{\Omega}_{\Delta a} \cdot Y'$, where $\hat{\Omega}_{\Delta a}$ is the estimated covariance matrix constructed in step 2.

Suppose that the $I \times I$ estimated covariance matrix $\hat{\Omega}_{\Delta a}$ has rank M, where $M \le I$. Since $n \ge I$ (see the remark preceding equation 17.11), the estimated $n \times n$ covariance matrix $\hat{\Omega}_{\Delta R}$ will, outside of exceptional cases, have rank M as well. More particularly, the number of positive eigenvalues of $\hat{\Omega}_{\Delta R}$ (which is the value assigned endogenously to J by our methodology) equals the rank of $\hat{\Omega}_{\Delta a}$. We therefore have to investigate carefully the rank of $\hat{\Omega}_{\Delta a}$.

Equation (17.30) says that

$$\Delta a(t_k) = B \cdot e(t_k) \tag{17.38}$$

The "true" covariance matrix $\Omega_{\Delta a}$ can be calculated as

$$\Omega_{\Delta a} = \text{cov}[\Delta a(t_k)]$$

$$= \exp[\Delta a(t_k) \cdot \Delta a(t_k)']$$

$$= \exp[B \cdot e(t_k) \cdot e(t_k)' \cdot B']$$

$$= B \cdot \exp[e(t_k) \cdot e(t_k)'] \cdot B'$$

$$= B \cdot I \cdot B'$$

or

$$\Omega_{\Delta a} = B \cdot B' \tag{17.39}$$

Since B is an I-by-J matrix (see equation 17.14) and since $J \le I$, it follows that the rank of the "true" matrix $\Omega_{\Delta a}$ will be the "true" value of J.

However, the method used to construct $\Omega_{\Delta a}$ is not to form the product $B \cdot B'$ as in equation (17.39) (we are, after all, trying to estimate the matrix B) but to use our time series estimates of the $a_i(t_k)$ composite coefficients as in step 2 of the summary. It follows that $\hat{\Omega}_{\Delta a}$ will, in general, have full rank, or $M = I$.

This implies that the number of positive eigenvalues of $\hat{\Omega}_{\Delta R}$ computed in step 3 will equal the number of coefficients specified in step 1. If we choose to represent the shift functions as polynomials of degree 5 ($I = 6$), then M will equal 6 and the proposed methodology will endogenously assign the value $J = 6$ as well. More particularly, we will extract six statistically independent shift functions.

The inability of an analyst to specify a value for J independently of his specification of a value for I is something of a drawback to the proposed methodology. However, we will see shortly that there are some advantages to having $J = I$.

Estimating the β_{i0} Coefficients

The next step in our analysis of polynomial representations of the yield curve is examining the problem of estimating the β_{i0} coefficients of the baseline polynomial function $R_0(y)$ in equation (17.8a).

This step is quite short because those coefficients can not be estimated. More particularly, any polynomial representation of the yield curve (of the form of equation 17.26) is consistent with any polynomial representation of the baseline function (of the form of equation 17.8a). The reason for this will become clear when we consider the problem of estimating the $w_j(t)$ weights.

Estimating the $w_j(t)$ Weights

Recall the basic representation of the yield curve given by equation (17.1):

$$R(y,t) = R_0(y) + \sum_{j=1}^{J} f_j(y) \cdot w_j(t) \tag{17.40}$$

We now want to examine the problem of computing the $w_j(t)$ weights on the $f_j(y)$ shift functions.

We showed at equation (17.26) that with the assumption of polynomial forms for $R_0(y)$ and $f_j(y)$, the representation of the yield curve in equation

(17.40) can be written as a polynomial in term to maturity:

$$R(y, t) = \sum_{i=1}^{I} a_i(t) \cdot y^{i-1} \tag{17.41}$$

The appendix describes how the composite coefficients in equation (17.41) can be estimated from yields at time t on spot claims of known maturities. We show here how the estimates of the $a_i(t)$ coefficients can be used to compute the values of the $w_j(t)$ weights.

From equation (17.25) a composite coefficient can be written

$$a(t) = \beta_{i0} + \sum_{j=1}^{J} \beta_{ij} \cdot w_j(t), \qquad i = 1, 2, \ldots, I \tag{17.42}$$

Defining the vectors

$$a(t) = \begin{bmatrix} a_1(t) \\ \vdots \\ a_I(t) \end{bmatrix} \tag{17.43a}$$

$$\beta_0 = \begin{bmatrix} \beta_{10} \\ \vdots \\ \beta_{I0} \end{bmatrix} \tag{17.43b}$$

$$w(t) = \begin{bmatrix} w_1(t) \\ \vdots \\ w_J(t) \end{bmatrix} \tag{17.43c}$$

and using the matrix B as defined in equation (17.14), equation (17.42) can be written

$$a(t) = \beta_0 + B \cdot w(t) \tag{17.44}$$

Equation (17.44) shows how the $a(t)$ vector of composite coefficients is related to the $w(t)$ vector of weights.

We showed above that as a matter of practical application, the number of shift functions J will equal the number of coefficients in each shift function I. The matrix B will therefore be an $I \times I$ matrix. Outside of exceptional cases its estimate (computed as described earlier) will be nonsingular. Thus we can solve equation (17.44) for the unique weights at time t as

$$w(t) = B^{-1} \cdot (a(t) - \beta_0) \tag{17.45}$$

This calculation of the $w_j(t)$ weights has an interesting interpretation which illuminates the reason why we can not estimate the vector β_0 of coefficients of the baseline function. Equation (17.40) says that the yield curve at time t can be represented as a baseline function plus a linear combination of shift functions. If the yield curve is a polynomial of degree $I - 1$ (as in equation (17.41)) and if the baseline function is also a polynomial of degree $I - 1$ (as in equation 17.8a), then the difference between those functions, $R(y, t) - R_0(y)$, must be a polynomial of degree $I - 1$. This difference polynomial can be expressed exactly as a linear combination of an arbitrary set of I linearly independent polynomials of degree $I - 1$. If the matrix B is nonsingular, then the shift functions defined in equation (17.8b) are linearly independent polynomials. Thus the difference function $R(y, t) - R_0(y)$ can be expressed exactly as a linear combination of the shift functions. The coefficients of the linear combination are as shown in equation (17.45).

The validity of the foregoing argument does not depend on the details of the baseline function $R_0(y)$ as long as that function is a polynomial of degree $I - 1$. Thus we can calculate a vector $w(t)$ of weights for *any* baseline function or for any coefficient vector β_0 in equation (17.45).

The inability to identify a unique baseline function or to estimate the β_{i0} coefficients is not useless because it means we can specify exogenously the benchmark against which we want to measure fluctuations in the yield curve. For example, we can define a baseline function that is flat at 9% per annum so that $R_0(y) = 9.0$ or $\beta_{10} = 9.0$ and $\beta_{i0} = 0$ for $i > 1$. In this case the weights calculated in equation (17.45) would show the movement of the yield curve relative to a flat yield curve at 9%. Alternatively we could define the baseline function as the actual yield curve at an initial time so that $R_0(y) = R(y, t_0)$ or $\beta_{i0} = a_i(t_0)$ for $i = 1, 2, \ldots, I$. The weights would then reflect the movement of the yield curve relative to the curve which prevailed at time t_0.

17.2 Representing Spot Yield Curves

This section applies the methodology described in the preceding section to the problem of representing a spot Treasury yield curve. We begin by reviewing briefly the concept of a spot claim and then report our empirical results. It should be noted that the methodology can be applied as easily to represent yield curves for zero coupon securities or par Treasury bonds.

Spot Yields

A spot claim is an obligation for a specified amount of money payable at a single date in the future. A spot yield is a discount rate which relates the present value of a spot claim to its maturity payment.

Consider, for example, a spot claim for \$100 payable in $y = 4$ years. If the present value of the claim is $P = \$67.6839$, we can compute its semi-annually compounded yield as the value of R_{sa} that satisfies the equation:

$$P = 100. \cdot (1 + \tfrac{1}{2}R_{sa})^{-2 \cdot y}$$

$$67.6839 = 100. \cdot (1 + \tfrac{1}{2}R_{sa})^{-2 \cdot 4}$$

(17.46)

or

$R_{sa} = .10$, or 10% per annum

Similarly we can compute its continuously compounded yield as the value of R that satisfies the equation:

$$P = 100. \cdot e^{-R \cdot y}$$

$$67.6839 = 100. \cdot e^{-R \cdot 4}$$

(17.47)

or

$R = .09758$, or 9.758% per annum

Data

Our data consist of spot Treasury yields computed from yields on par Treasury bonds on one business day (usually Thursday) each week between January 5, 1984, and December 29, 1988. There are 261 weeks in our data set. Chapter 10 describes how the spot yields were constructed from data on actual Treasury bonds. For each day in the data set spot yields were calculated at 40 equally spaced maturities from 6 months to 20 years.

The spot yields were originally calculated as semi-annually compounded rates of return and then converted to continuously compounded rates by the equation

$$R = 2 \cdot \ln[1 + \tfrac{1}{2}R_{sa}]$$

(17.48)

This equation can be derived by equating the right hand sides of equations (17.46) and (17.47) and solving for R.

Weekly Estimates of the Composite Coefficients

The first step in the methodology is to choose a value for I (the number of coefficients in the polynomial form of the shift functions in equation (17.8b) and to estimate values of the composite coefficients $a_1(t_k), \ldots, a_I(t_k)$ in equation (17.37) for each date in our data set. We chose $I = 6$ (so that the polynomials are all fifth degree). The appendix reports the details of the procedure for estimating the composite coefficients.

As noted in the appendix, the estimated values of the coefficients on the higher order terms, such as $a_5(t)$ and $a_6(t)$, are quite small. It is convenient to write equation (17.37) in the form:

$$R(y, t_k) = \sum_{i=1}^{I} a_i(t_k) \cdot 20^{i-1} \cdot \left(\frac{y}{20}\right)^{i-1} \tag{17.49}$$

and to estimate the scaled composite coefficients $\tilde{a}_i(t_k)$ in the equation

$$R(y, t_k) = \sum_{i=1}^{I} \tilde{a}_i(t_k) \cdot \left(\frac{y}{20}\right)^{i-1} \tag{17.50}$$

The original composite coefficients can be recovered by the identities

$$a_i(t_k) = \frac{\tilde{a}_i(t_k)}{20^{i-1}}, \qquad i = 1, 2, \ldots, I \tag{17.51}$$

Note that the first scaled composite coefficient $\tilde{a}_1(t_k)$ is identical to the first composite coefficient $a_1(t_k)$.

Figure 17.1 shows weekly estimates of the first composite coefficient. From equation (17.49) this is an estimate of the continuously compounded spot yield at a term of $y = 0$ years. The behavior of the coefficient is quite similar to the behavior of short-term interest rates over the sample interval. The two panels of figure 17.2 show weekly estimates of four of the five remaining scaled composite coefficients.

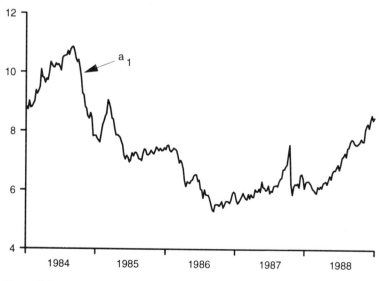

Figure 17.1
Estimates of composite coefficient a_1 at weekly intervals

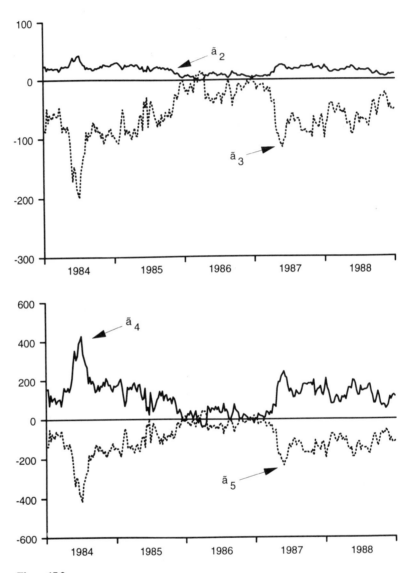

Figure 17.2
Estimates of scaled composite coefficients at weekly intervals

Table 17.1
Estimated standard deviations and correlations of weekly changes in composite coefficients, January 1984 to December 1988

	Composite coefficient					
	Δa_1	Δa_2	Δa_3	Δa_4	Δa_5	Δa_6
Standard deviation	.188	$2.503 \cdot 20^{-1}$	$13.092 \cdot 20^{-2}$	$29.410 \cdot 20^{-3}$	$29.228 \cdot 20^{-4}$	$10.582 \cdot 20^{-5}$
Correlation with						
Δa_1	1.00	.37	.33	−.32	.32	−.31
Δa_2	−.37	1.00	−.98	.96	−.94	.93
Δa_3	.33	−.98	1.00	−.99	.99	−.98
Δa_4	−.32	.96	−.99	1.00	−.99	.99
Δa_5	.32	−.94	.99	−.99	1.00	−.99
Δa_6	−.31	.93	−.98	.99	−.99	1.00

Table 17.2
Constructed (from $Y \cdot \hat{\Omega}_{\Delta a} \cdot Y'$) standard deviations and correlations of weekly spot yield changes, January 1984 to December 1988

	Sector								
	6 month	1 year	2 year	3 year	4 year	5 year	7 year	10 year	20 year
Standard deviation	.175%	.176	.189	.198	.200	.198	.194	.194	.203
Correlation with									
6 mo	1.00	.97	.87	.80	.77	.76	.74	.69	.56
1 yr	.97	1.00	.96	.92	.89	.88	.85	.80	.66
2	.87	.96	1.00	.99	.98	.96	.92	.88	.75
3	.80	.92	.99	1.00	.99	.99	.95	.91	.78
4	.77	.89	.98	.99	1.00	.99	.97	.94	.80
5	.76	.88	.96	.99	.99	1.00	.99	.96	.82
7	.74	.85	.92	.95	.97	.99	1.00	.99	.85
10	.69	.80	.88	.91	.94	.96	.99	1.00	.89
20	.56	.66	.75	.78	.80	.82	.85	.89	1.00

Estimate of $\Omega_{\Delta a}$

We now have 261 weeks of estimated values of the six composite coefficients in equation (17.37). We can use this data to calculate 260 weekly changes in each composite coefficient and hence to calculate an estimate $\hat{\Omega}_{\Delta a}$ of the covariance matrix of weekly change in the composite coefficients.

Table 17.1 shows the estimated standard deviations and correlations of the weekly changes in the composite coefficients. Note that changes in the first coefficient are only weakly correlated with changes in the higher-order coefficients. In contrast, the absolute value of the correlation of change in any two higher-order coefficients is quite high, over .90 in every case. This high correlation is also evident in the two panels of figure 17.2.

Table 17.3
Estimated (from original data) standard deviations and correlations of weekly spot yield changes, January 1984 to December 1988

| | Sector | | | | | | | | |
	6 month	1 year	2 year	3 ye:r	4 year	5 year	7 year	10 year	20 year
Standard deviation	.175%	.178	.189	.195	.196	.196	.196	.196	.192
Correlation with									
6 mo	1.00	.95	.87	.82	.79	.77	.73	.68	.59
1 yr	.95	1.00	.97	.94	.92	.90	.85	.81	.71
2	.87	.97	1.00	.99	.98	.96	.92	.88	.79
3	.82	.94	.99	1.00	.99	.98	.95	.91	.82
4	.79	.92	.98	.99	1.00	.99	.98	.94	.84
5	.77	.90	.96	.98	.99	1.00	.99	.96	.86
7	.73	.85	.92	.95	.98	.99	1.00	.99	.89
10	.68	.81	.88	.91	.94	.96	.99	1.00	.94
20	.59	.71	.79	.82	.84	.86	.89	.94	1.00

Estimate of $\Omega_{\Delta R}$

The third step in the methodology is to use our estimate of $\Omega_{\Delta a}$ to compute an estimated spot yield change covariance matrix $\hat{\Omega}_{\Delta R} = Y \cdot \hat{\Omega}_{\Delta a} \cdot Y'$, where the matrix Y is as defined in equation (17.13).

To construct the matrix Y, we have to choose a set of n matuities: y_1, $y_2, \ldots, y_n$ where $n > I$. We choose $n = 20$ and set $y_i = i/2$ for $1 \le i \le 10$, $y_i = i - 5$ for $10 < i \le 15$, and $y_i = 10 + 2 \cdot (i - 15)$ for $15 < i \le 20$. This gives a distribution of maturities at semi-annual increments out to 5 years, annual increments out to 10 years, and 2 year increments out to 20 years.

Table 17.2 shows a selected set of estimated standard deviations and correlations of spot yield changes. Table 17.3 shows the same statistics calculated directly from the original spot yield data. The constructed covariance matrix in table 17.2 seems to be quite similar to the directly estimated covariance matrix in table 17.3.

Estimates of the β_{ij} Coefficients

The next steps in the methodology are computing the eigenvalues and eigenvectors of $\hat{\Omega}_{\Delta R}$, extracting the $\tilde{V}_{\Delta R}$ and $\tilde{D}_{\Delta R}$ matrices according to the partitionings in equations (17.35a, b) and computing the coefficients of the β_{ij} shift polynomials as in equation (17.21).

Table 17.4 reports scaled values of the β_{ij} coefficients where the scalings follow the form of equation (17.50). That is, the shift polynomials are of the form

Table 17.4
Scaled coefficients $\tilde{\beta}_{ij}$ of the first three shift function polynomials

Coefficient index	Shift function f_j		
	$j = 1$	$j = 2$	$j = 3$
$i = 1$	.113	−.094	−.097
$i = 2$	1.101	.552	1.439
$i = 3$	−5.239	−1.518	−6.211
$i = 4$	11.044	3.125	12.190
$i = 5$	−10.602	−3.141	−11.315
$i = 6$	3.760	1.156	3.951

Note: β_{ij} coefficients are $\beta_{ij} = \tilde{\beta}_{ij} \cdot 20^{1-i}$

$$f_j(y) = \sum_{i=1}^{I} \beta_{ij} \cdot y^{i-1}$$

$$= \sum_{i=1}^{I} \beta_{ij} \cdot 20^{i-1} \left(\frac{y}{20}\right)^{i-1}$$

$$= \sum_{i=1}^{I} \tilde{\beta}_{ij} \cdot \left(\frac{y}{20}\right)^{i-1} \tag{17.52}$$

where the scaled coefficient $\tilde{\beta}_{ij}$ is

$$\tilde{\beta}_{ij} = \beta_{ij} \cdot 20^{i-1} \tag{17.53}$$

Figure 17.3 shows the shapes of the first three shift functions. Observe that the first shift function f_1 is essentially a parallel shift of the entire spot yield curve. The second function f_2 changes the slope of the yield curve, with short-term yields moving down (up) and longer-term yields moving up (down) as $w_2(t)$ increases (decreases). The third function f_3 affects the curvature of the curve, with short and long term yields moving down (up) and yields in the middle of the curve moving up (down) as $w_3(t)$ increases (decreases). The three remaining shift functions (f_4, f_5, and f_6) cause more complex "twistings" of the spot yield curve. The absolute magnitudes of these higher order shifts are quite small throughout the curve and are never greater than $2\frac{1}{2}$ basis points.

Estimates of the $w_j(t)$ Weights

The last step in our representation of the behavior of the spot Treasury yield curve is computing the time series of weights on each of the six shift functions.

We choose to report the shifts relative to the spot yield curve as it existed on January 5, 1984, the first day, denoted t_0, in our sample interval.

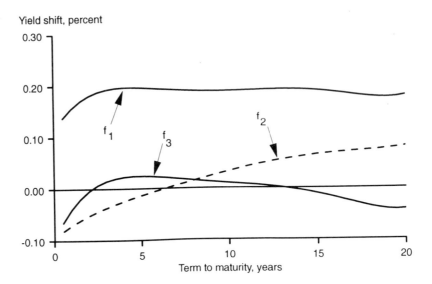

Figure 17.3
Shift functions

As described in section 17.1, this means we assign the baseline function $R_0(y)$ as the spot yield curve function $R(y, t_0)$ or that we assign the β_{i0} coefficients of the baseline polynomial as the respective composite coefficients $a_i(t_0)$.

Figure 17.4 shows the evolution of the first three weights over our sample interval. By the assumption of the preceding paragraph each weight has an initial value of exactly zero on January 5, 1984.

Recall that the first shift function was essentially a parallel shift of the entire spot yield curve. The top panel of figure 17.4 shows clearly the secular decline in the level of the yield curve, that is, the decline in the value of $w_1(t)$, from mid-1984 to the spring of 1986 and the subsequent increase during 1987 (punctuated by the sharp drop associated with the October 1987 break in the stock market).

The middle panel figure 17.4 shows the behavior of the slope of the yield curve over the sample interval. Positive values of w_2 indicate an increase in slope, relative to the slope on January 5, 1984, and negative values indicate a flattening or inversion of the yield curve. The flattening of the curve in mid-1984 and again in 1988 is quite evident.

The lower panel of figure 17.4 shows the change in the curvature of the yield curve. A positive value of w_3 indicates a more convex curve, and a negative value indicates a straighter, or possibly concave, curve.

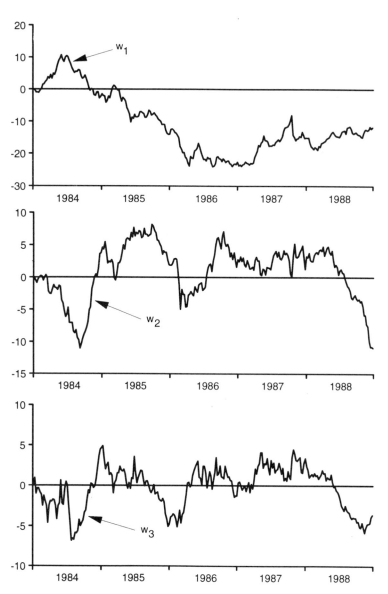

Figure 17.4
Weightings w_1, w_2, and w_3 at weekly intervals

17.3   Conclusion

This chapter has examined the problem of representing a yield curve and statistically independent modes of fluctuation in a yield curve with polynomial functions of maturity. We saw how the yield curve on a given date can be represented with a polynomial, and we saw how a time series of such polynomials can be used to extract polynomial shift functions representing the modes of fluctuation of the curve. Finally, we saw that the shift functions can be combined to reconstruct the individual yield curves, and we saw how to compute the weightings on the shift functions.

The methodology of this chapter is useful when an analyst needs to represent a yield curve and modes of fluctuation in the curve with functions rather than with tabulations of the behavior of yields at a finite number of discrete maturities.

17.4   Appendix: Estimating the Coefficients of a Polynomial Representation of the Spot Yield Curve

This appendix describes a procedure for estimating the coefficients of a polynomial representation of the spot yield curve. We assume that the polynomial is of the form

$$R(y) = \sum_{i=1}^{I} a_i \cdot y^{i-1} + e \tag{A17.1}$$

where $R(y)$ denotes the yield on a spot claim with a term to maturity of y years, the a_i are the coefficients to be estimated, and e is a random error term.

As described in section 17.2, our data consist of continuously compounded yields, measured in percent per anum, on 40 spot Treasury claims with maturities ranging from 6 months to 20 years. Let R_i denote the yield on the ith claim, and let y_i denote the term to maturity of the ith claim so that $y_1 = .5$, $y_2 = 1.0$, ..., $y_{40} = 20.0$. Define the vector R of observed yields as

$$R = \begin{bmatrix} R_1 \\ \vdots \\ R_{40} \end{bmatrix} \tag{A17.2}$$

the vector ε of error terms as

$$\varepsilon = \begin{bmatrix} e_1 \\ \vdots \\ e_{40} \end{bmatrix} \tag{A17.3}$$

and the matrix Z of regressors as

$$Z = \begin{bmatrix} 1 & \dfrac{y_1}{20} & \left(\dfrac{y_1}{20}\right)^2 & \cdots & \left(\dfrac{y_1}{20}\right)^{I-1} \\ \vdots & \vdots & \vdots & & \vdots \\ 1 & \dfrac{y_{40}}{20} & \left(\dfrac{y_{40}}{20}\right)^2 & \cdots & \left(\dfrac{y_{40}}{20}\right)^{I-1} \end{bmatrix} \tag{A17.4}$$

Using equation (A17.1), we write

$$R = Z \cdot \gamma + \varepsilon \tag{A17.5}$$

where γ is a vector of scaled coefficients related to the original coefficients as

$$\gamma = \begin{bmatrix} \gamma_1 \\ \gamma_2 \\ \vdots \\ \gamma_I \end{bmatrix} = \begin{bmatrix} a_1 \\ a_2 \cdot 20 \\ \vdots \\ a_I \cdot 20^{I-1} \end{bmatrix} \tag{A17.6}$$

Scaling the coefficients is convenient because the original coefficients become quite small for values of i greater than 3 or 4.

We assume that the vector of error terms in equation (A17.5) is normally distributed with a mean equal to the zero vector and a covariance matrix of $\sigma^2 \Phi_R$ where σ^2 is an unknown scalar and Φ_R is a known positive definite matrix. That is, we assume that

$$\varepsilon \sim N(0, \sigma^2 \Phi_R) \tag{A17.7}$$

Estimating the coefficient vector γ in equation (A17.5) for the error structure in (A17.7) is a problem in generalized least squares (see Arthur Goldberger, *Econometric Theory*, 1964, pp. 231–48). The best linear unbiased estimator of γ is

$$\hat{\gamma} = (Z' \cdot \Phi_R^{-1} \cdot Z)^{-1} \cdot Z' \cdot \Phi_R^{-1} \cdot R \tag{A17.8}$$

and the unbiased estimator of σ^2 is

$$s^2 = \frac{\hat{\varepsilon}' \cdot \Phi_R^{-1} \cdot \hat{\varepsilon}}{40 - I} \tag{A17.9}$$

where $\hat{\varepsilon}$ is the vector of regression errors: $\hat{\varepsilon} = R - Z \cdot \hat{\gamma}$.

The foregoing estimation methodology is straight forward once the matrix Φ_R is known. We first describe how we constructed Φ_R and then exhibit our results.

Constructing Φ_R

Our spot yield data is derived from estimates of yields on Treasury bonds priced at par, as described in chapter 10. Errors, or noise, in the estimates of the par bond yields will induce errors in the estimates of spot yields.

Let C_i denote the coupon rate on a par Treasury bond with i coupons remaining to be paid or with a remaining term to maturity of $i/2$ years. By definition of spot yields, we must have

$$100 = \sum_{k=1}^{i} \tfrac{1}{2} C_i \cdot e^{-.005 \cdot k \cdot R_k} + 100 \cdot e^{-.005 \cdot i \cdot R_i} \tag{A17.10}$$

Equation (A17.10) says that the invoice price of the par bond (100) equals the present discounted value of the bond's future cash flows, where each payment is discounted at its "own" spot yield. The coupon rate on the par bond can be computed by solving equation (A17.10) for C_i:

$$C_i = \frac{100 \cdot (1 - e^{-.005 \cdot i \cdot R_i})}{\tfrac{1}{2} \sum_{k=1}^{i} e^{-.005 \cdot k \cdot R_k}} \tag{A17.11}$$

Since equation (A17.11) is true for $i = 1, 2, \ldots, 40$, we can use it to define a function that computes a vector of 40 coupon rates (or equivalently, semi-annually compounded yields on par bonds) from a vector of 40 continuously compounded spot yields:

$$C = f(R) \tag{A17.12}$$

where C is the vector

$$C = \begin{bmatrix} C_1 \\ \vdots \\ C_{40} \end{bmatrix} \tag{A17.13}$$

and R is as defined in equation (A17.2).

Now let $\bar{R}$ and $\bar{C}$ denote vectors of "true" or errorless spot yields and bond yields which satisfy equation (A17.12), so that $\bar{C} = f(\bar{R})$. Let e_R denote a vector of estimation errors for the spot yields and e_C a vector of related estimation errors for the bond yields. $\bar{R} + e_R$ and $\bar{C} + e_C$ must also satisfy equation (A17.12):

$$\bar{C} + e_c = f(\bar{R} + e_R) \tag{A17.14}$$

Taking a first-order approximation to the right-hand side of equation (A17.14) at the vector $\bar{R}$ gives

$$\bar{C} + e_C = f(\bar{R}) + df \cdot e_R \qquad (A17.15)$$

or, since $\bar{C} = f(\bar{R})$,

$$e_C = df \cdot e_R \qquad (A17.16)$$

where df is the 40×40 matrix of partial derivatives of the function f:

$$[df]_{ij} = \frac{\partial C_i}{\partial R_j} \qquad (A17.17)$$

with C_i depending on R_j as in the equation (A17.11).

Equation (A17.16) tells us how estimation errors for spot yields are related to estimation errors for bond yields. If e_C and e_R have the distributions

$$e_C \sim N(o, \Phi_C) \qquad (A17.18a)$$

$$e_R \sim N(o, \Phi_R) \qquad (A17.18b)$$

then from equation (A17.16) we have

$$\Phi_C = df \cdot \Phi_R \cdot df' \qquad (A17.19)$$

or

$$\Phi_R = (df)^{-1} \cdot \Phi_C \cdot (df')^{-1} \qquad (A17.20)$$

Using equation (A17.20), we can construct a covariance matrix for spot yield estimation errors from any specified covariance matrix for par bond yield estimation errors. For purposes of this chapter, we assume the standard deviation of the estimation error on a par bond yield is 3 basis points and that the correlation between two errors is $.8^n$, where n is the absolute value of the difference in bond maturities measured in units of half years.

Table 17.5 shows selected parts of the resulting spot yield error covariance matrix, assuming a spot yield curve that is flat at 10% per annum. Note, in particular, that the standard deviation of the estimation error grows from 2.85 basis points at a maturity of 6 months to 8.05 basis points at a maturity of 20 years. This shows quite clearly that longer-term spot yields are not measurable with nearly the same accuracy as shorter-term spot rates.

Results

Having constructed a spot yield error covariance matrix, we can now implement the estimation procedure described in the beginning of this

Table 17.5
Constructed standard deviations and correlations of spot yield estimation errors

	Sector								
	6 month	1 year	2 year	3 year	4 year	5 year	7 year	10 year	20 year
Standard deviation	2.85 bp	2.87	2.93	3.01	3.13	3.26	3.60	4.26	8.05
Correlation with									
6 mo	1.00	.79	.48	.28	.15	.07	−.01	−.03	−.01
1 yr	.79	1.00	.61	.35	.19	.09	−.01	−.04	−.02
2	.48	.61	1.00	.58	.32	.16	.00	−.05	−.03
3	.28	.35	.58	1.00	.57	.30	.04	−.07	−.03
4	.15	.19	.32	.57	1.00	.55	.11	−.07	−.04
5	.07	.09	.16	.30	.55	1.00	.27	−.05	−.05
7	−.01	−.01	.00	.04	.11	.27	1.00	.08	−.08
10	−.03	−.04	−.05	−.07	−.07	−.05	.08	1.00	−.11
20	−.01	−.02	−.03	−.03	−.04	−.05	−.08	−.11	1.00

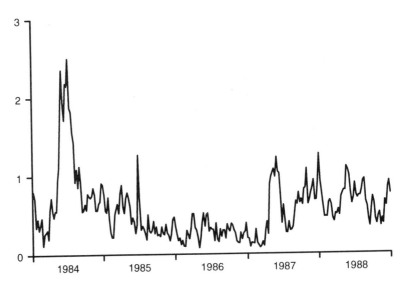

Figure 17.5
Estimates of σ at weekly intervals

appendix. The values of the estimated scaled coefficients computed by equation (A17.8) are shown in figures 17.1 and 17.2.

Figure 17.5 shows the estimated value of σ computed by equation (A17.9) for each day in our sample interval. Note that $\hat{\sigma}$ averages about .6. This implies that the distribution of spot yield regression errors is somewhat more compact than expected given our assumption on bond yield estimation errors. In general, lower values of I (the number of coefficients in the approximating polynomial) will shift up the graph of $\hat{\sigma}$ and higher values of I will lower the graph. This reflects the greater (lesser) relative representation errors associated with polynomials of lower (higher) order.

18 Consistency between the Shape of the Yield Curve and Its Modes of Fluctuation

This chapter addresses the connections between two individually innocuous observations. The first is that at most points in time the yield curve has shape, so yields to maturity and short-run expected rates of return on fixed income securities of different maturities are not all identical. The second observation is that the level and shape of the curve changes over time, so fixed income securities bear risk and the risks vary across different securities. We will assume that the short-run expected rate of return on a portfolio of fixed income securities is a function of the risks borne by that portfolio, and we will show that this implies a relationship between the shape of the yield curve and the ways in which the curve can fluctuate.

The chapter is divided into two parts. The first part, consisting of sections 18.1 through 18.5, analyzes some theoretical aspects of the relationship between the shape of the yield curve and its modes of fluctuation. The most important results are a demonstration that the risks and returns on *all* fixed income securities can be replicated with a small number of *arbitrary* securities and the statement of a "consistency condition" linking the shape of the curve to its modes of fluctuation.

The second part, consisting of sections 18.6 and 18.7, restates the consistency condition derived in the early sections on theory in the special case where the yield curve and its modes of fluctuation are polynomial functions of maturity. The very special case where the curve always shifts in parallel is examined in detail. Finally, we present an empirical application of the polynomial model to the U.S. Treasury securities market.

THEORY

The five sections in the first part of this chapter examine some theoretical aspects of the relationship between the shape of the yield curve and fluctuations in the curve. We use single payment spot claims rather than multiple payment bonds as the fundamental unit of analysis. As a result we will be concerned with the shape and modes of fluctuation of the spot yield curve.

Section 18.1 describes single payment spot claims and the spot yield curve. Section 18.2 observes that the price of a spot claim changes as a result of (1) the approach of its maturity date (i.e., the passage of time) and (2) change in the level and shape of the curve. These effects are identified analytically by constructing a linear approximation to the change in the price of a spot claim as a function of the passage of time and change in the shape of the curve. The approximation leads to measures of

Written in December 1989.

the short-run expected rate of return and the risks of a spot claim. Section 18.3 extends our measures of risk and expected return to portfolios of spot claims.

Section 18.4 sets forth a key assumption of the analysis: The expected rate of return on a portfolio of spot claims is a function of the risks of the portfolio but does not otherwise depend on the details of the composition of the portfolio. Section 18.5 explores two important implications of the assumption. The first is that the risk and return characteristics of any spot claim or portfolio of spot claims can be replicated with an (almost) arbitrary set of spot claims. The second is a consistency condition relating the shape of the spot yield curve to its modes of fluctuation.

18.1   The Spot Yield Curve

A spot claim is a promise to pay a specified amount of money on a specified date in the future. This section introduces some important assumptions on the structure of the spot yield curve and its variation through time.

Spot Yields

A spot yield is a discount rate used to compute the present value, or market price, of a spot claim.

Consider, for example, a spot claim for $100 payable in $y = 4$ years. If the yield on the claim is $R = 10\%$ per annum, compounded semi-annually, its present value is

$$P = 100 \cdot (1 + \tfrac{1}{2}R)^{-2 \cdot y}$$
$$= 100 \cdot (1 + \tfrac{1}{2}(.10))^{-2 \cdot 4}$$
$$= 67.6839 \tag{18.1}$$

Continuous Compounding

For our purposes we measure in this chapter the yield on a spot claim with continuous rather than semi-annual compounding. Continuous compounding is not widely used in the marketplace, though it has the advantage of simplifying the notation and derivations below.

The continuously compounded yield on a spot claim priced at $P = \$67.6839$ for $100 payable in $y = 4$ years is the value of R that satisfies the equation

$$P = 100 \cdot e^{-y \cdot R} \tag{18.2}$$

or

$$R = y^{-1} \cdot \ln\left[\frac{100}{P}\right]$$

$$= 4^{-1} \cdot \ln\left[\frac{100}{67.6839}\right]$$

$$= .097580, \text{ or } 9.7580\% \text{ per annum,}$$
compounded continuously   (18.3)

This yield is lower than the 10% semi-annually compounded yield on the same claim because of the more frequent compounding (continuous rather than semi-annual).

The Spot Yield Curve

A spot yield curve is a function that describes how the yield R on a spot claim varies with the time y remaining to payment of the claim, where R is measured in fractional terms (so that $R = .10$ means 10% per annum, compounded continuously) and y is measured in years.

Structure of the Spot Yield Curve

We assume that the spot yield curve at any point in time can be expressed in the form

$$R(y, w) = R_0(y) + \sum_{j=1}^{J} w_j \cdot f_j(y) \qquad (18.4)$$

where $R_0(y)$ and $f_1(y), \ldots, f_J(y)$ are known time-invariant functions of maturity and where $w_1, \ldots, w_J$ are scalar coefficients. The ensemble or vector of coefficients is denoted w.

Equation (18.4) says that the yield curve can be constructed as a "baseline" function $R_0(y)$ plus a linear combination of "shift" functions $f_1(y), \ldots, f_J(y)$. The weight, or coefficient, on the jth shift function is w_j. Yield curves with a structure similar to equation (18.4) were examined in chapter 17.

Temporal Variation in the Spot Yield Curve

We assume that the yield curve in equation (18.4) varies over time, in shape as well as level, as a result of temporal variation in the w_j weights. In particular, we assume that each weight evolves as a Gaussian random walk with zero drift and a variance of unity per year and that change in one weight is uncorrelated with changes in other weights; that is to say, the random walks are statistically independent of each other. We will sometimes write the jth weight as $w_j(t)$ and the ensemble of weights as $w(t)$ to emphasize this temporal variation.

It is useful to explore the implications of the temporal behavior of the $w_j(t)$ weights in further detail. Consider two points in time, denoted t_0 and t_1, where $t_0 < t_1$. The change in yield from time t_0 to time t_1 at a term of y years is $R(y, w(t_1)) - R(y, w(t_0))$. (Note that this is not the change in yield on a particular debt instrument but rather the change in yield at a particular point along the spot curve.) Using equation (18.4), we have

$$R(y, w(t_1)) - R(y, w(t_0))$$

$$= R_0(y) + \sum_{j=1}^{J} w_j(t_1) \cdot f_j(y) - R_0(y) - \sum_{j=1}^{J} w_j(t_0) \cdot f_j(y)$$

$$= \sum_{j=1}^{J} (w_j(t_1) - w_j(t_0)) \cdot f_j(y) \qquad (18.5)$$

Thus the shift in the yield curve from time t_0 to time t_1 is a linear combination of the shift functions where the coefficients in the linear combination are the changes in the $w_j(t)$ weights.

From our assumption on the behavior of the $w_j(t)$ weights, we have that the changes in the weights from time t_0 to time t_1 are normally distributed with the characteristics

$$\exp[w_j(t_1) - w_j(t_0)] = 0, \qquad j = 1, \ldots, J \qquad (18.6a)$$

$$\mathrm{var}[w_j(t_1) - w_j(t_0)] = t_1 - t_0, \qquad j = 1, \ldots, J \qquad (18.6b)$$

$$\mathrm{cov}[w_j(t_1) - w_j(t_0), w_k(t_1) - w_k(t_0)] = 0, \qquad j = 1, \ldots, J,$$

$$k = 1, \ldots, J,$$

$$k \neq j \qquad (18.6c)$$

Thus the shift functions represent trendless (see equation 18.6a), normalized (see equation 18.6b), and statistically independent (see equation 18.6c) *modes of fluctuation* in the spot yield curve.

Observe that as a result of equations (18.5) and (18.6a), we have

$$\exp[R(y, w(t_1)) - R(y, w(t_0))] = 0$$

This implies that market participants never expect yields to change. More specifically, a positively sloped yield curve is not associated with expectations of rising rates and a negatively sloped curve is not associated with expectations of falling rates.

The present chapter can be viewed broadly as an exercise in deriving the implications of equation (18.4). It should be noted that other models of yield fluctuation are possible, such as the statement that the natural logs of spot yields follow a Gaussian random walk or the statement that expectations of rising or falling rates affect the shape of the yield curve. These other models may have different implications, but the method of deriving those implications will parallel the present analysis.

18.2   Risk and Return for Spot Claims

This section defines quantitative measures of (1) the short-run expected rate of return on a spot claim and (2) the risks of the claim attributable to each of the modes of fluctuation in the yield curve. The definitions follow from a linear approximation to the change in the price of a spot claim as a function of the passage of time and change in the shape of the curve.

Pricing a Spot Claim

Given the pricing of a spot claim in equation (18.2) and our model of the spot yield curve in equation (18.4), it is not difficult to appreciate that the price of a spot claim depends on time and the level and shape of the curve.

Let $P(t, w_1, \ldots, w_J; t_m)$ represent the price at time t of a spot claim for \$100 maturing at time t_m $(t_m > t)$ when the weights in equation (18.4) are $w_1, \ldots, w_J$. (Observe that the w_j weights suffice to describe completely the level and shape of the yield curve because the functions $R_0(y)$ and $f_1(y)$, $\ldots, f_J(y)$ are assumed to be known and time invariant.) From our definition of the yield on a spot claim in equation (18.2), we have

$$P(t, w_1, \ldots, w_J; t_m) = 100 \cdot e^{-(t_m - t) \cdot \tilde{R}(t, w_1, \ldots, w_J; t_m)} \tag{18.7a}$$

where $\tilde{R}(t, w_1, \ldots, w_J; t_m)$ is the yield at time t on a spot claim maturing at time t_m when the weights are $w_1, \ldots, w_J$:

$$\tilde{R}(t, w_1, \ldots, w_J; t_m) = R_0(t_m - t) + \sum_{j=1}^{J} w_j \cdot f_j(t_m - t) \tag{18.7b}$$

Equations (18.7a, b) are the fundamental equations describing the price of a spot claim.

A Linear Approximation to the Change in the Price of a Spot Claim

Equations (18.7a, b) give an exact expression for the price P of a spot claim paying \$100 at time t_m as a function of time (denoted t) and the level and shape of the spot yield curve (as described by the w_j weights).

Appendix A shows that the linear approximation to the price change ΔP that occurs over an interval of time Δt when the jth weight changes by

Δw_j is

$$\Delta P = \left[\frac{\partial P}{\partial t} + \frac{1}{2} \sum_{j=1}^{J} \frac{\partial^2 P}{\partial w_j^2} \right] \cdot \Delta t + \sum_{j=1}^{J} \frac{\partial P}{\partial w_j} \cdot \Delta w_j \tag{18.8}$$

where $\partial P/\partial t$ is the partial derivative of price with respect to time, $\partial P/\partial w_j$ is the partial derivative of price with respect to the jth weight, and $\partial^2 P/\partial w_j^2$ is the second partial derivative of price with respect to the jth weight.

The partial derivatives in equation (18.8) can be constructed by differentiating the price function of equations (18.7a, b). It follows that

$$\frac{\partial P}{\partial t} = P \cdot \left[\tilde{R} - (t_m - t) \cdot \frac{\partial \tilde{R}}{\partial t} \right]$$

$$= P \cdot \left[R_0 + \sum_{j=1}^{J} w_j \cdot f_j - (t_m - t) \cdot \left[-R_0' - \sum_{j=1}^{J} w_j \cdot f_j' \right] \right] \tag{18.9a}$$

$$\frac{\partial P}{\partial w_j} = P \cdot \left[-(t_m - t) \cdot \frac{\partial \tilde{R}}{\partial w_j} \right]$$

$$= P \cdot [-(t_m - t) \cdot f_j], \qquad j = 1, \dots, J \tag{18.9b}$$

$$\frac{\partial^2 P}{\partial w_j^2} = P \cdot [(t_m - t)^2 \cdot f_j^2], \qquad j = 1, \dots, J \tag{18.9c}$$

where in equation (18.9a), R_0' is the derivative of the baseline function R_0 and f_j' is the derivative of the shift function f_j. It is understood that the functions R_0, R_0', f_j, and f_j' are all evaluated at $t_m - t$.

Substituting the derivatives of equations (18.9a, b, c) into equation (18.8) gives the linear approximation

$$\frac{\Delta P}{P} = \left[R_0 + \sum_{j=1}^{J} w_j \cdot f_j + (t_m - t) \cdot \left[R_0' + \sum_{j=1}^{J} w_j \cdot f_j' \right] \right]$$

$$+ \frac{1}{2}(t_m - t)^2 \cdot \sum_{j=1}^{J} f_j^2 \right] \cdot \Delta t - (t_m - t) \cdot \sum_{j=1}^{J} f_j \cdot \Delta w_j \tag{18.10}$$

Risk and Expected Return

The short-run expected rate of return on a spot claim can be defined as the rate of change in the price of the claim expected over some short interval of time. Any measure of the risk of the claim quantifies the relationship between change in the price of the claim and the change in the shape of the yield curve produced by a specified change in the w_j weights.

Let us denote the expected rate of return on a spot claim as μ and the risk of the claim with respect to change in the jth weight as σ_j. The form of equation (18.10) suggests the structure

$$\frac{\Delta P}{P} = \mu \cdot \Delta t - \sum_{j=1}^{J} \sigma_j \cdot \Delta w_j \tag{18.11}$$

Since the expected value of Δw_j is zero for $j = 1, \ldots, J$, equation (18.11) implies that the expectation of the rate of change in the price of the spot claim, $\exp[\Delta P/(P \cdot \Delta t)]$, is just μ.

Identifying the corresponding terms in equations (18.10) and (18.11) gives

$$\mu = \left[R_0 + \sum_{j=1}^{J} w_j \cdot f_j \right] + (t_m - t) \cdot \left[R_0' + \sum_{j=1}^{J} w_j \cdot f_j' \right]$$

$$+ \frac{1}{2}(t_m - t)^2 \cdot \sum_{j=1}^{J} f_j^2 \tag{18.12a}$$

$$\sigma_j = (t_m - t) \cdot f_j, \qquad j = 1, \ldots, J \tag{18.12b}$$

These are our measures of the risks and expected rate of return on a spot claim.

Risk and Expected Return as Functions of the Maturity of a Spot Claim and the Shape of the Yield Curve

Up to now the analysis in this section has addressed the behavior of the price of a spot claim as a function of the passage of time and fluctuations in the spot yield curve *given* the maturity of the claim and the initial shape of the curve. The primary result was equation (18.11), which expresses the relative change in the price of the claim in terms of the expected rate of return on the claim—μ as defined in equation (18.12a)—and the risks of the claim— the σ_j terms defined in equation (18.12b).

We now want to broaden the scope of the analysis and examine the variation of risk and expected return for spot claims with different maturities and yield curves with different shapes. As in section 18.1, let y denote the remaining term to maturity at time t of a spot claim maturing at time t_m, so that $y = t_m - t$.

The generalized risk *function* for a spot claim with respect to the jth mode of fluctuation in the spot yield curve follows easily from equation (18.12b):

$$\sigma_j(y) = y \cdot f_j(y), \qquad j = 1, \ldots, J \tag{18.13}$$

This equation indicates that our risk measures vary with the maturity of a spot claim but do not vary with the shape of the yield curve.

Before we define the generalized expected rate of return function, it will be helpful to make a brief digression. Recall from equation (18.4) that we can express the yield on a spot claim as a function of the maturity of the claim and the shape of the yield curve as

$$R(y, w) = R_0(y) + \sum_{j=1}^{J} w_j \cdot f_j(y) \tag{18.14}$$

Note that the expression on the right-hand side of equation (18.14) is identical to the term in the first set of brackets in equation (18.12a). It further follows from equation (18.14) that the derivative of the function $R(y, w)$ with respect to y, denoted $R'(y, w)$, is

$$R'(y, w) = R_0'(y) + \sum_{j=1}^{J} w_j \cdot f_j'(y) \tag{18.15}$$

Note that the expression on the right-hand side of equation (18.15) is identical to the term in the second set of brackets in equation (18.12a).

On the basis of the foregoing digression, we can define from equation (18.12a) the generalized expected rate of return function for spot claims of different maturities and yield curves with different shapes as

$$\mu(y, w) = R(y, w) + y \cdot R'(y, w) + \tfrac{1}{2} y^2 \cdot \sum_{j=1}^{J} f_j(y)^2 \tag{18.16}$$

where $R(y, w)$ is as specified in equation (18.14) and $R'(y, w)$ is as defined in equation (18.15).

The measures of risk and expected return in equations (18.13) and (18.16), respectively, are the crucial building blocks of our subsequent analysis.

18.3 Risk and Return for Portfolios of Spot Claims

The preceding section developed measures of the expected rates of return and risks of single payment spot claims. We now want to extend those measures to portfolios of spot claims. The first step in the extension is to specify how the market values a portfolio.

Valuing a Portfolio of Spot Claims

We assume that the market values a portfolio of spot claims as the sum of the values of the individual claims.

Consider a portfolio of K spot claims where the size of the payment on the kth claim is F_k. Let t_k denote the time of the kth payment, where $t_1 < t_2 < \cdots < t_K$. In view of our assumption on portfolio valuation, the market value of the portfolio at time t can be computed as

$$V = \sum_{k=1}^{K} F_k \cdot e^{-(t_k - t) \cdot \tilde{R}(t, w_1, \ldots, w_J; t_k)} \tag{18.17}$$

where $w_1, \ldots, w_J$ are the contemporaneous weights for the spot yield curve. The yield function $\tilde{R}$ is as defined in equation (18.7b). Observe in equation (18.17) that each of the K payments is discounted at its "own" spot yield.

A Linear Approximation to the Change in the Value of a Portfolio

The next step in the analysis is to construct a linear approximation to the change in the value of the portfolio as a function of the passage of time and change in the w_j weights.

The approximation has the same structure as equation (18.8):

$$\Delta V = \left[\frac{\partial V}{\partial t} + \frac{1}{2} \sum_{j=1}^{J} \frac{\partial^2 V}{\partial w_j^2} \right] \cdot \Delta t + \sum_{j=1}^{J} \frac{\partial V}{\partial w_j} \cdot \Delta w_j \tag{18.18}$$

The relevant partial derivatives can be constructed by differentiating the value function of equation (18.17) just as we differentiated the price function of equations (18.7a, b) in equations (18.9a, b, c).

Risk and Expected Return

The last step in the analysis is to define the expected rate of return on the portfolio and the risks of the portfolio with respect to different modes of fluctuation of the spot yield curve.

Following the analysis in section 18.2, we want the expected rate of return $\bar{\mu}$ and the risk measures $\bar{\sigma}_1, \ldots, \bar{\sigma}_J$ to conform to the expression

$$\frac{\Delta V}{V} = \bar{\mu} \cdot \Delta t - \sum_{j=1}^{J} \bar{\sigma}_j \cdot \Delta w_j \tag{18.19}$$

Comparing this to equation (18.18) shows that

$$\bar{\mu} = V^{-1} \cdot \left[\frac{\partial V}{\partial t} + \frac{1}{2} \sum_{j=1}^{J} \frac{\partial^2 V}{\partial w_j^2} \right] \tag{18.20}$$

and

$$\bar{\sigma}_j = -V^{-1} \cdot \frac{\partial V}{\partial w_j}, \qquad j = 1, \ldots, J \tag{18.21}$$

After working out the derivatives in equations (18.20) and (18.21), we can express the expected rate of return on the portfolio as a value-weighted average of the contemporaneous expected rates of return on the spot claims in the portfolio:

$$\bar{\mu} = \sum_{k=1}^{K} x_k \cdot \mu(y_k, w) \tag{18.22}$$

where y_k is the time to payment of the kth claim, the function $\mu(\cdot, \cdot)$ is as defined in equation (18.16), and where the kth value weight is

$$x_k = V^{-1} \cdot F_k \cdot e^{-(t_k-t) \cdot \tilde{R}(t, w_1, \dots, w_J; t_k)}$$

or

$$x_k = V^{-1} \cdot F_k \cdot e^{-y_k \cdot R(y_k, w)} \tag{18.23}$$

Observe that by definition of the value V of the portfolio in equation (18.17), the value weights sum to unity:

$$\sum_{k=1}^{K} x_k = V^{-1} \cdot \sum_{k=1}^{K} F_k \cdot e^{-y_k \cdot R(y_k, w)}$$

$$= V^{-1} \cdot V$$

$$= 1 \tag{18.24}$$

Similarly we can express the portfolio risk measure $\bar{\sigma}_j$ as a value-weighted average of the corresponding risk measures for the spot claims in the portfolio:

$$\bar{\sigma}_j = \sum_{k=1}^{K} x_k \cdot \sigma_j(y_k), \qquad j = 1, \dots, J \tag{18.25}$$

where the function $\sigma_j(\cdot)$ is as defined in equation (18.13).

Bonds and Bond Portfolios

The analysis in this section has examined the risks and expected rate of return on a portfolio of spot claims. It should be clear that the results extend immediately to bonds and portfolios of bonds. This follows because a bond is just a particular portfolio of spot claims and because a bond portfolio is just a larger portfolio of such claims. Our results apply as well to portfolios where some spot claims or some bonds are held short. The only consequence of a short position is that some of the future cash flows; that is, some of the F_k's, will be negative.

18.4   An Assumption on the Relationship between Risk and Expected Return

Having defined measures of the risks and expected rate of return on spot claims and portfolios of spot claims, we are now ready to set forth the crucial assumption of this chapter.

We assume that the expected rate of return on *any* portfolio of spot claims is a function (which may vary with the shape of the yield curve) only of the risks of the portfolio and that it does not otherwise depend on the details of the composition of the portfolio. That is, we assume that there exists a function G such that

$$\bar{\mu} = G(\bar{\sigma}_1, \ldots, \bar{\sigma}_J; w) \tag{18.26}$$

Equation (18.36) says that all portfolios with risk measures $\bar{\sigma}_1, \ldots, \bar{\sigma}_J$ have the same expected rate of return $\bar{\mu}$, where $\bar{\mu}$ is related to $\bar{\sigma}_1, \ldots, \bar{\sigma}_J$ through the function G. Note that the expected rate of return can also depend on the contemporaneous shape of the yield curve as reflected by the ensemble w of shift function weights.

Equation (18.26) is not a trivial statement. We can imagine a market with hundreds of different spot claims but with only $J = 3$ modes of fluctuation of the spot yield curve. There will be a great many different portfolios that have some specified triplet of risk measures. All of these portfolios will have the same expected rate of return.

Equation (18.26) is not as arbitrary as it may appear. Suppose, contrary to the assumption, that we had two portfolios of spot claims with equal values and identical risks but different expected rates of return. We could then form a composite (or "hedged") portfolio with zero net value and zero net risk such that the net value of the portfolio would, with certainty, increase over time. This would imply the existence of "arbitrage" profits, or riskless revenues without any commitment of capital.

In view of the linear structure of portfolio risk and return in equations (18.22) and (18.25), it can be shown (see appendix C) that the function G must be affine with respect to the risk measures or of the form

$$\bar{\mu} = g_0(w) + \sum_{j=1}^{J} g_j(w) \cdot \bar{\sigma}_j \tag{18.27}$$

The coefficient g_0 is the expected rate of return on any portfolio of spot claims with zero risk, that is, where $\bar{\sigma}_1 = 0, \ldots, \bar{\sigma}_J = 0$. The coefficient g_j can be interpreted as the "price" (in terms of expected rate of return) of the risk of the jth mode of fluctuation of the spot yield curve.

Note that g_0 and the g_j's are, in general, functions of the level and shape of the yield curve, that is, of the ensemble of shift function weights. At this point in the analysis, we cannot identify the forms of these functions. All we can say is that their existence is a necessary consequence of the absence of arbitrage profits.

Since equation (18.27) holds for all portfolios of spot claims, it must hold in particular for all spot claims. This implies that the expected rate of return *function* defined in equation (18.16) is related to the risk *functions* in equation (18.13) as

$$\mu(y, w) = g_0(w) + \sum_{j=1}^{J} g_j(w) \cdot \sigma_j(y) \tag{18.28}$$

The next section derives two important implications of equation (18.28).

18.5   Two Implications of the Assumption

We have now completed construction of a framework for analyzing risk and expected return on fixed income securities. The key elements of the construction were

1. the specification of the structure of the spot yield curve and its modes of fluctuation in equation (18.4) and

2. the assumption that the shape of the yield curve and the risks of a portfolio of spot claims completely determine the expected rate of return on the portfolio.

What remains is to explore the consequences of this analytical framework.

This section examines two implications. The first says that an (almost) arbitrary set of $J + 1$ spot claims (where J is the number of shift functions in equation 18.4) can replicate the behavior of *all* other spot claims and portfolios of spot claims. This is a strong result because it says that any fixed income security or portfolio of fixed income securities, however complex, can be replicated (and hence hedged) in a simple fashion.

The second implication is a consistency condition linking the shape of the spot yield curve with its modes of fluctuation. This result is important because it limits the set of admissable shift functions and baseline functions.

Replication

Consider, on the one hand, a spot claim with a remaining term to maturity of y_0 years (where y_0 is arbitrary) and, on the other hand, a set S of $J + 1$ spot claims with maturities of $y_1, \ldots, y_{J+1}$ years (where these maturities are also arbitrary but distinct). We say we can "replicate" the first claim with a portfolio of claims from the set S if we can choose a portfolio with the same risks and expected rate of return as the risks and expected rate of return on the first claim. It turns out that this is (almost always) possible.

The expected rate of return on the first claim is $\mu(y_0, w)$ and the risks of the first claim are $\sigma_1(y_0), \ldots, \sigma_J(y_0)$, where (from equation 18.28)

$$\mu(y_0, w) = g_0(w) + \sum_{j=1}^{J} g_j(w) \cdot \sigma_j(y_0) \tag{18.29}$$

Similarly the expected rates of return on the claims in the set S are $\mu(y_k, w)$, and the risks of the claims are $\sigma_1(y_k), \ldots, \sigma_J(y_k)$ for $k = 1, \ldots, J + 1$, where

$$\mu(y_k, w) = g_0(w) + \sum_{j=1}^{J} g_j(w) \cdot \sigma_j(y_k), \qquad k = 1, \ldots, J + 1 \qquad (18.30)$$

Suppose that we can find values of $x_1, \ldots, x_{J+1}$ to satisfy the system of simultaneous equations

$$\begin{bmatrix} \sigma_1(y_0) \\ \vdots \\ \sigma_J(y_0) \\ 1 \end{bmatrix} = \begin{bmatrix} \sigma_1(y_1) & \cdots & \sigma_1(y_{J+1}) \\ \vdots & & \vdots \\ \sigma_J(y_1) & \cdots & \sigma_J(y_{J+1}) \\ 1 & \cdots & 1 \end{bmatrix} \begin{bmatrix} x_1 \\ \vdots \\ x_J \\ x_{J+1} \end{bmatrix} \qquad (18.31)$$

That is, suppose we can find a portfolio allocation of the claims in the set S such that the value weights $x_1, \ldots, x_{J+1}$ of the allocation satisfy the adding-up constraint of equation (18.24):

$$1 = \sum_{k=1}^{J+1} x_k$$

and such that the risks of the portfolio replicate the risks of the first spot claim:

$$\sigma_j(y_0) = \sum_{k=1}^{J+1} x_k \cdot \sigma_j(y_k), \qquad j = 1, \ldots, J$$

This is seen to be a matter of the nonsingularity of the matrix on the right-hand side of equation (18.31). In particular, the existence of the desired allocation does not depend on the maturity of the first claim or on the risks of that claim.

Assuming that values of $x_1, \ldots, x_{J+1}$ can be found that satisfy equation (18.31), we can compute the expected rate of return on the portfolio by applying equations (18.22), (18.30), and (18.29):

$$\bar{\mu} = \sum_{k=1}^{J+1} x_k \cdot \mu(y_k, w)$$

$$= \sum_{k=1}^{J+1} x_k \cdot \left[g_0(w) + \sum_{j=1}^{J} g_j(w) \cdot \sigma_j(y_k) \right]$$

$$= g_0(w) \cdot \sum_{k=1}^{J+1} x_k + \sum_{j=1}^{J} g_j(w) \cdot \left[\sum_{k=1}^{J+1} x_k \cdot \sigma_j(y_k) \right]$$

$$= g_0(w) + \sum_{j=1}^{J} g_j(w) \cdot \sigma_j(y_0)$$

$$= \mu(y_0, w) \qquad (18.32)$$

Thus the expected rate of return on the portfolio will replicate the expected rate of return on the first claim.

It follows from this analysis that *any* set of $J + 1$ spot claims for which the matrix of risk factors in equation (18.31) is nonsingular can replicate the risks and expected return on *any* spot claim and hence on any bond (since a bond is just a portfolio of spot claims) and hence on any portfolio of bonds. More generally, *any* set of $J + 1$ spot claims (with a nonsingular risk matrix) can replicate the entire universe of fixed income securities.

Consistency

Recall from equation (18.4) our original description of the structure of the spot yield curve:

$$R(y, w) = R_0(y) + \sum_{j=1}^{J} w_j \cdot f_j(y) \tag{18.33}$$

Nothing in the analysis to this point suggests that there are any restrictions on either the baseline function $R_0(y)$ or the $f_j(y)$ shift functions. However, this is not quite the case.

Equation (18.28) showed that (in the absence of opportunities for riskless arbitrage profits) we can express the expected rate of return on a spot claim with y years to maturity when the yield curve has the structure described by the ensemble w of shift function weights as

$$\mu(y, w) = g_0(w) + \sum_{j=1}^{J} g_j(w) \cdot \sigma_j(y) \tag{18.34}$$

where $g_0(w)$ is the risk-free rate of return and $g_j(w)$ is the price of the risk of the jth mode of fluctuation of the spot yield curve. Replacing $\mu(y, w)$ and $\sigma_j(y)$ with their equivalent expressions from equations (18.16) and (18.13), equation (18.34) becomes

$$R(y, w) + y \cdot R'(y, w) + \tfrac{1}{2}y^2 \cdot \sum_{j=1}^{J} f_j(y)^2$$

$$= g_0(w) + \sum_{j=1}^{J} g_j(w) \cdot y \cdot f_j(y) \tag{18.35}$$

Now consider the following integral:

$$\int_0^y [R(z, w) + z \cdot R'(z, w)] \cdot dz = \int_0^y R(z, w) \cdot dz + \int_0^y z \cdot R'(z, w) \cdot dz$$

Using integration by parts on the second term, this becomes

$$\int_0^y [R(z,w) + z \cdot R'(z,w)] = \int_0^y R(z,w) \cdot dz + \Big|_0^y z \cdot R(z,w) - \int_0^y R(z,w) \cdot dz$$

$$= y \cdot R(y,w)$$

It follows that

$$R(y,w) = y^{-1} \cdot \int_0^y [R(z,w) + z \cdot R'(z,w)] \cdot dz$$

Replacing the term in brackets with the equivalent expression from equation (18.35) gives:

$$R(y,w) = y^{-1} \cdot \int_0^y \left[g_0(w) + \sum_{j=1}^J g_j(w) \cdot z \cdot f_j(z) - \tfrac{1}{2} z^2 \cdot \sum_{j=1}^J f_j(z)^2 \right] \cdot dz$$

or

$$R(y,w) = g_0(w) + \sum_{j=1}^J g_j(w) \cdot \left[y^{-1} \cdot \int_0^y z \cdot f_j(z) \cdot dz \right]$$

$$- \tfrac{1}{2} y^{-1} \cdot \sum_{j=1}^J \left[\int_0^y z^2 \cdot f_j(z)^2 \cdot dz \right] \tag{18.36}$$

Equation (18.36) provides an alternative construction of the spot yield curve in terms of the risk-free rate of return and the prices of the different categories of risk.

The issue of consistency between the shape of the spot yield curve and its modes of fluctuation is whether the yield curves in equations (18.33) and (18.36) are mutually consistent. That is, do there exist functions $g_0(w)$, $g_1(w), \ldots, g_J(w)$ such that, for any choice of the ensemble w of shift function weights, equations (18.33) and (18.36) are identical functions of maturity? The requirement of consistency places restrictions on the $R_0(y)$ and $f_j(y)$ functions. Arbitrary choices of the baseline and shift functions will, in general, result in an inconsistent specification of the structure of the yield curve in the sense that there will not be any functions $g_0(w)$, $g_1(w), \ldots,$ $g_J(w)$ such that equations (18.33) and (18.36) are identical functions of maturity.

An Example

To understand more fully the issue of consistency, it may be helpful to consider a simple example.

Let us assume that the spot yield curve is always flat and always shifts in parallel. (This assumption is quite common in fixed income analysis and underlies basic duration analysis; see chapters 3 and 5.) In this case we have only $J = 1$ mode of fluctuation, and we can write the baseline and shift functions as

$$R_0(y) = R_0 \quad \text{for all } y \tag{18.37a}$$

$$f_1(y) = f_1 \quad \text{for all } y \tag{18.37b}$$

In addition the ensemble w of shift function weights is just the first weight w_1. The spot yield curve is

$$R(y, w_1) = R_0(y) + w_1 \cdot f_1(y)$$

or, since $R_0(y)$ and $f_1(y)$ are constant-valued functions,

$$R(y, w_1) = R_0 + w_1 \cdot f_1 \quad \text{for all } y \tag{18.38}$$

From equation (18.36) the alternative construction of the spot yield curve is

$$R(y, w_1) = g_0(w_1) + g_1(w_1) \cdot \left[y^{-1} \cdot \int_0^y z \cdot f_1 \cdot dz \right]$$

$$- \tfrac{1}{2} y^{-1} \cdot \int_0^y z^2 \cdot f_1^2 \cdot dz$$

$$= g_0(w_1) + \tfrac{1}{2} g_1(w_1) \cdot f_1 \cdot y - \tfrac{1}{6} f_1^2 \cdot y^2 \tag{18.39}$$

Consistency requires that there exist functions $g_0(w_1)$ and $g_1(w_1)$ such that for any value of w_1 equations (18.38) and (18.39) are identical functions of maturity, or that

$$R_0 + w_1 \cdot f_1 = g_0(w_1) + \tfrac{1}{2} g_1(w_1) \cdot f_1 \cdot y - \tfrac{1}{6} f_1^2 \cdot y^2 \tag{18.40}$$

Equation (18.40) cannot be true (outside of the degenerate case where $f_1 = 0$ and the yield curve is stationary through time) because the right-hand side of the equation has terms involving y and y^2, while the left-hand side has no such terms. Thus we can conclude that equations (18.37a, b) constitute an inconsistent representation of the spot yield curve that provides opportunities for riskless arbitrage profits.

Summary

This section has derived two implications of our analytical framework. First, we saw that the risks and expected return on all fixed income securities and portfolios of fixed income securities can be replicated with a portfolio constructed from an arbitrary set of $J + 1$ spot claims (as long as the risk matrix for those claims is nonsingular). This implies that any fixed income security can be hedged perfectly with a position in $J + 1$ spot claims.

Second, we developed an alternative construction of the spot yield curve (equation 18.36) that must be consistent with the original construction (equation 18.33). The requirement of consistency limits the baseline and shift functions that can form the building blocks of the spot yield curve.

THE SPECIAL CASE OF POLYNOMIAL FUNCTIONS

The analyses in the first part of this chapter began with a general specification for the spot yield curve (see equation 18.4) and ended with the statement of a consistency condition relating the shape of the curve to its modes of fluctuation (see the discussion following equation 18.36). Given specific choices for the baseline function $R_0(y)$ and the shift functions $f_1(y)$, $\ldots, f_J(y)$, it is not too difficult to test directly whether there exist functions $g_0(w), g_1(w), \ldots, g_J(w)$ that satisfy equation (18.36) and hence to determine whether or not the baseline and shift functions are consistent and provide an arbitrage-free representation of the yield curve. However, it would be more useful if we could use equation (18.36) to *derive* specific functional forms for the baseline and shift functions that are necessarily consistent and whose parameters can be estimated from empirical data.

The first section in this part restates the consistency condition of equation (18.36) in the special case where the baseline and shift functions are polynomial functions of maturity with a finite number of coefficients. This case is interesting for two reasons. First, it is more tractable because a polynomial function is fully specified by its coefficients. (Technically the domain of analysis collapses from an infinite dimensional vector space of functions to a finite dimensional space of polynomial coefficients.) Second, the restated consistency condition leads to nontrivial restrictions on the class of admissable shift functions and to an expression for part of the baseline function in terms of the shift functions.

Section 18.7 reports on an empirical application of the polynomial model.

18.6   Consistency with Polynomial Functions

This section restates the consistency condition derived in section 18.5 for the special case where the baseline and shift functions are polynomials of finite degree and derives the restrictions that the polynomials must satisfy to produce a consistent representation of the spot yield curve and its modes of fluctuation. At the end of the section we examine the very special case where the yield curve always shifts in parallel.

Polynomial Functions

We assume that the baseline function is a polynomial with I' coefficients, and we assume that each of the shift functions is a polynomial with I coefficients. We do not assume any relationship between I' and I—although we will soon show they must be related as a result of the consistency condition.

More particularly, we can write

$$R_0(y) = \sum_{i=1}^{I'} b_{i0} \cdot y^{i-1} \tag{18.41a}$$

$$f_j(y) = \sum_{i=1}^{I} b_{ij} \cdot y^{i-1}, \qquad j = 1, \dots, J \tag{18.41b}$$

where the b_{i0}s are the coefficients of the baseline polynomial and the b_{ij}s are the coefficients of the shift functions.

Without loss of generality we can assume that $J \leq I$. That is, there are no more shift functions than the number of coefficients in a shift function polynomial. If $J > I$, then $J - I$ of the shift functions can be written as linear combinations of the other I functions, and we can specify an equivalent set of just I shift function that satisfy all the assumptions of our model of the yield curve set forth in section 18.1.

The Yield Curve with Polynomial Functions

Recall from equation (18.4) that the yield on a spot claim with y year remaining to maturity can be written as

$$R(y, w) = R_0(y) + \sum_{j=1}^{J} w_j \cdot f_j(y)$$

where the w_j are the weights on the respective shift functions.

In view of our assumption on the polynomial structure of the baseline and shift functions the yield curve $R(y, w)$ is also a polynomial function of maturity:

$$R(y, w) = \sum_{i=1}^{I'} b_{i0} \cdot y^{i-1} + \sum_{j=1}^{J} w_j \cdot \left[\sum_{i=1}^{I} b_{ij} \cdot y^{i-1} \right]$$

$$= \sum_{i=1}^{I'} b_{i0} \cdot y^{i-1} + \sum_{i=1}^{I} \left[\sum_{j=1}^{J} b_{ij} \cdot w_j \right] \cdot y^{i-1} \tag{18.42}$$

More specifically, the spot yield curve is a polynomial where the number of coefficients is the greater of I and I'.

The Alternative Construction of the Yield Curve

We next examine the alternative construction of the yield curve given by equation (18.36):

$$R(y, w) = g_0(w) + \sum_{j=1}^{J} g_j(w) \cdot \left[y^{-1} \cdot \int_0^y z \cdot f_j(z) \cdot dz \right]$$

$$- \tfrac{1}{2} y^{-1} \cdot \sum_{j=1}^{J} \left[\int_0^y z^2 \cdot f_j(z)^2 \cdot dz \right] \tag{18.43}$$

in the special case of polynomial shift functions.

Since each of the $f_j(y)$ shift functions is a polynomial the integrals in equation (18.43) can be evaluated. The term in the first set of brackets is

$$y^{-1} \cdot \int_0^y z \cdot f_j(z) \cdot dz = y^{-1} \cdot \int_0^y z \cdot \left[\sum_{i=1}^{I} b_{ij} \cdot z^{i-1} \right] \cdot dz$$

$$= y^{-1} \cdot \sum_{i=1}^{I} b_{ij} \cdot \int_0^y z^i \cdot dz$$

$$= y^{-1} \cdot \sum_{i=1}^{I} b_{ij} \cdot (i+1)^{-1} \cdot y^{i+1}$$

$$= \sum_{i=1}^{I} \left(\frac{b_{ij}}{i+1} \right) \cdot y^i$$

$$= \sum_{i=2}^{I+1} \left(\frac{b_{i-1,j}}{i} \right) \cdot y^{i-1} \tag{18.44}$$

Evaluating the last term in equation (18.43) is a little more difficult. We begin by writing $f_j(z)^2$ in a more convenient form:

$$f_j(z)^2 = \left[\sum_{i=1}^{I} b_{ij} \cdot z^{i-1} \right]^2$$

$$= \sum_{i=1}^{2I-1} a_{ij} \cdot z^{i-1} \tag{18.45}$$

where the a_{ij} coefficients are computed as:

$$a_{kj} = \sum_{i=L_k}^{U_k} b_{ij} \cdot b_{k+1-i,j}, \qquad k = 1, 2, \ldots, 2 \cdot I - 1 \tag{18.46}$$

with $L_k = \max[1, k+1-I]$ and $U_k = \min[k, I]$. Using equation (18.45), we can evaluate the last term in equation (18.43) as

$$-\tfrac{1}{2}y^{-1}\cdot\sum_{j=1}^{J}\left[\int_0^y z^2\cdot f_j(z)^2\cdot dz\right] = -\tfrac{1}{2}y^{-1}\cdot\sum_{j=1}^{J}\left[\int_0^y z^2\cdot\sum_{i=1}^{2I-1} a_{ij}\cdot z^{i-1}\cdot dz\right]$$

$$= -\tfrac{1}{2}\cdot\sum_{i=1}^{2I-1} y^{-1}\cdot\sum_{j=1}^{J} a_{ij}\cdot\int_0^y z^{i+1}\cdot dz$$

$$= -\tfrac{1}{2}\sum_{i=1}^{2I-1} y^{-1}\cdot\sum_{j=1}^{J} a_{ij}\cdot(i+2)^{-1}\cdot y^{i+2}$$

$$= \sum_{i=1}^{2I-1}\left[-\tfrac{1}{2}\sum_{j=1}^{J} a_{ij}\cdot(i+2)^{-1}\right]\cdot y^{i+1}$$

$$= \sum_{i=3}^{2I+1} c_i\cdot y^{i-1} \tag{18.47}$$

$$c_i = -\frac{\tfrac{1}{2}\sum_{j=1}^{J} a_{i-2,j}}{i}, \qquad i = 3, 4, \ldots, 2I + 1 \tag{18.48}$$

Substituting the expressions in equations (18.44) and (18.47) into equation (18.43) the alternative construction can be written

$$R(y, w) = g_0(w) + \sum_{j=1}^{J} g_j(w)\cdot\left[\sum_{i=2}^{I+1}\left(\frac{b_{i-1,j}}{i}\right)\cdot y^{i-1}\right] + \sum_{i=3}^{2I+1} c_i\cdot y^{i-1}$$

$$= g_0(w) + \sum_{i=2}^{I+1}\left[\sum_{j=1}^{J}\left(\frac{b_{i-1,j}}{i}\right)\cdot g_j(w)\right]\cdot y^{i-1} + \sum_{i=3}^{2I+1} c_i\cdot y^{i-1} \tag{18.49}$$

Thus the alternative construction of the spot yield curve is a polynomial function of maturity with $2I + 1$ coefficients.

Consistency

Consistency between the shape of the yield curve and its modes of fluctuation requires that the yield curves in equations (18.42) and (18.49) must be identical functions of maturity for any choice of the w_j weights. Since those functions are polynomials, they will be identical if and only if (1) the polynomials have the same *number* of coefficients and (2) corresponding coefficients have the same *value*. These requirements place nontrivial restrictions on the baseline and shift functions.

Equal Numbers of Coefficients

We have already indicated that the polynomial in equation (18.42) has $\max[I, I']$ coefficients and that the polynomial in equation (18.49) has $2I + 1$ coefficients. Thus we have

$$\max[I, I'] = 2I + 1$$

or

$$I' = 2I + 1 \tag{18.50}$$

For example, if the shift functions are second degree polynomials with $I = 3$ coefficients, then the baseline function must be a sixth degree polynomial with $I' = 7$ coefficients.

Equal Values of Corresponding Coefficients

To say that the corresponding coefficients of the polynomials in equations (18.42) and (18.49) have the same value is to say that the coefficient on y^{i-1} in equation (18.42) is the same as the coefficient on y^{i-1} in equation (18.49) for $i = 1, 2, \ldots, I'$. For example, for $i = 1$ we have

$$b_{10} + \sum_{j=1}^{J} b_{1j} \cdot w_j = g_0(w) \tag{18.51}$$

Similarly, for $i = 2$, we have

$$b_{20} + \sum_{j=1}^{J} b_{2j} \cdot w_j = \sum_{j=1}^{J} \left(\frac{b_{1j}}{2} \right) \cdot g_j(w) \tag{18.52}$$

This matching of coefficients continues through $i = I'$. The ultimate result is that we must have functions $g_0(w), g_1(w), \ldots, g_J(w)$ such that the system of equations in box 1 is satisfied for all values of $w_1, \ldots, w_J$.

The equations in box 1 are divided into two sets. The "low-order" equations come from the equality of the coefficients on y^{i-1} for $i = 1, \ldots, I + 1$. The "high-order" equations come from the equality of the coefficients on y^{i-1} for $i = I + 2, \ldots, I'$. We next examine each set of equations.

Equal Values of the High-Order Coefficients

As shown in the high-order equations in box 1, equality of the coefficients on y^{i-1} for $i = I + 2, \ldots, I'$ requires

$$b_{i0} = c_i, \qquad i = I + 2, \ldots, I' \tag{18.53}$$

or, by definition of c_i in equation (18.48),

$$b_{i0} = -\frac{\frac{1}{2} \sum_{j=1}^{J} a_{i-2,j}}{i}, \qquad i = I + 2, \ldots, I' \tag{18.54}$$

Since the a_{ij} terms are constructed from the b_{ij} coefficients of the shift function polynomials (see equation 18.46), equation (18.54) implies that the high-order coefficients of the baseline polynomial cannot be specified independently of the description of the modes of fluctuation of the spot yield curve.

Box 1
Consistency equations for polynomial baseline and shift functions

---

Low-order equations, coefficients on y^{i-1} for $i = 1, \ldots, I + 1$. These equations can be written in vector notation as $b_0 + B \cdot w = \Phi \cdot g(w) + c$.

$$
\begin{bmatrix} b_{10} \\ b_{20} \\ b_{30} \\ b_{40} \\ \vdots \\ b_{I0} \\ b_{I+1,0} \end{bmatrix}
+
\begin{bmatrix} b_{11} & b_{12} & \cdots & b_{1J} \\ b_{21} & b_{22} & \cdots & b_{2J} \\ b_{31} & b_{32} & \cdots & b_{3J} \\ b_{41} & b_{42} & \cdots & b_{4J} \\ \vdots & \vdots & & \vdots \\ b_{I1} & b_{I2} & \cdots & b_{IJ} \\ 0 & 0 & \cdots & 0 \end{bmatrix}
\begin{bmatrix} w_1 \\ w_2 \\ \vdots \\ w_J \end{bmatrix}
=
\begin{bmatrix}
1 & 0 & 0 & \cdots & 0 \\
0 & \dfrac{b_{11}}{2} & \dfrac{b_{12}}{2} & \cdots & \dfrac{b_{1J}}{2} \\
0 & \dfrac{b_{21}}{3} & \dfrac{b_{22}}{3} & \cdots & \dfrac{b_{2J}}{3} \\
0 & \dfrac{b_{31}}{4} & \dfrac{b_{32}}{4} & \cdots & \dfrac{b_{3J}}{4} \\
\vdots & \vdots & \vdots & & \vdots \\
0 & \dfrac{b_{I-1,1}}{I} & \dfrac{b_{I-1,2}}{I} & \cdots & \dfrac{b_{I-1,J}}{I} \\
0 & \dfrac{b_{I1}}{I+1} & \dfrac{b_{I2}}{I+1} & \cdots & \dfrac{b_{IJ}}{I+1}
\end{bmatrix}
\begin{bmatrix} g_0(w) \\ g_1(w) \\ g_2(w) \\ \vdots \\ g_J(w) \end{bmatrix}
+
\begin{bmatrix} 0 \\ 0 \\ c_3 \\ c_4 \\ \vdots \\ c_I \\ c_{I+1} \end{bmatrix}
$$

High-order equations, coefficients on y^{i-1} for $i = I + 2, \ldots, I'$

$$
\begin{bmatrix} b_{I+2,0} \\ \vdots \\ b_{I'0} \end{bmatrix}
=
\begin{bmatrix} c_{I+2} \\ \vdots \\ c_{I'} \end{bmatrix}
$$

Equal Values of the Low-Order Coefficients

As noted at the top of box 1, the low-order equations can be written in vector notation as

$$b_0 + B \cdot w = \Phi \cdot g(w) + c \tag{18.55}$$

where the matrix B is of dimension $(I + 1)$-by-J and the matrix Φ is of dimension $(I + 1)$-by-$(J + 1)$. Consistency requires that for any choice of the J-dimensional vector w, the value of the $J + 1$ dimensional vector-valued function $g(w)$ satisfies the $I + 1$ conditions in equation (18.55).

We have already observed that $I \geq J$. Suppose that I is strictly greater than J. Equation (18.55) will then have more equations than the number of elements of $g(w)$ and, outside of exceptional choices of $w_1, \ldots, w_J$, we will be unable to satisfy all the equations simultaneously. We conclude that

$$I = J \tag{18.56}$$

is necessary for consistency. This means that the number of shift functions (J) must equal the number of coefficients in each shift function polynomial (I).

If $I = J$, then the matrix Φ is square. Outside of exceptional cases it will also be nonsingular. If Φ is nonsingular, we will clearly be able to compute a solution value for $g(w)$ as

$$g(w) = \Phi^{-1} \cdot [b_0 + B \cdot w - c] \tag{18.57}$$

Thus $I = J$ is both necessary and, as a practical matter, sufficient to satisfy the low-order equations in box 1. (It is interesting to note that equation 18.57 implies that $g_0(w)$, $g_1(w)$, ..., $g_J(w)$ are *linear* functions of the shift function weights.)

Summary

We have now identified three restrictions on the baseline and shift function polynomials that must hold in a consistently specified polynomial model of the spot yield curve:

$$I' = 2I + 1 \tag{18.58a}$$

$$I = J \tag{18.58b}$$

$$b_{i0} = c_i, \qquad i = I + 2, \ldots, I' \tag{18.58c}$$

Moreover, if these restrictions are satisfied, then in almost all cases we will be able to find functions $g_0(w)$, $g_1(w)$, ..., $g_J(w)$ such that equations (18.42) and (18.49) are identical polynomial functions of maturity for all possible ensembles of shift function weights.

A Comment on $g_0(w)$

We remarked in section 4 that $g_0(w)$ is the rate of return on a portfolio of spot claims with zero risk. Equation (18.51) allows us to interpret $g_0(w)$ in a slightly different fashion.

Consider the yield on a spot claim with an arbitrarily short maturity or (in the limit) on a spot claim with a maturity of $y = 0$ years. From equation (18.42) we have

$$R(0, w) = b_{10} + \sum_{j=1}^{J} b_{1j} \cdot w_j \tag{18.59}$$

Comparing equations (18.51) and (18.59) shows that $g_0(w)$ is exactly $R(0, w)$. Thus $g_0(w)$ can also be interpreted as the yield on a spot claim with an arbitrarily short maturity. This yield is commonly called "the" short-term interest rate.

It should also be noted that since each w_j follows a Gaussian random walk, equation (18.51) implies that the short-term interest rate follows a Gaussian random walk. From equations (18.51) and (18.6a, b, c), we can deduce that over an interval from time t_0 to time t_1, during which the ensemble of shift function weights changes from $w(t_0)$ to $w(t_1)$ we have

$$\exp[g_0(w(t_1)) - g_0(w(t_0))] = 0 \tag{18.60a}$$

$$\text{var}[g_0(w(t_1)) - g_0(w(t_0))] = (t_1 - t_0) \cdot \sum_{j=1}^{J} b_{1j}^2 \tag{18.60b}$$

The Very Special Case of Parallel Shifts

To deepen our understanding of consistency in the special case of polynomial baseline and shift functions, it is useful to examine the very special case where the yield curve only shifts in parallel.

In this case we have only one mode of fluctuation ($J = 1$) and the shift function for that mode is a constant (so that $I = 1$ as well):

$$f_1(y) = b_{11} \tag{18.61}$$

The analysis earlier in this section established that $I' = 2I + 1$, so the baseline polynomial function must have three coefficients. (Note how this differs from the assumption of $I' = 1$ in the *inconsistent* representation of equation 18.37a.)

The system of equations in box 1 for the present case can be written

$$b_{10} + b_{11} \cdot w_1 = g_0(w_1) \tag{18.62a}$$

$$b_{20} = \tfrac{1}{2}b_{11} \cdot g_1(w_1) \tag{18.62b}$$

$$b_{30} = c_3 = -\tfrac{1}{6}a_{11}$$

or from equation (18.46),

$$b_{30} = -\tfrac{1}{6}b_{11}^2 \tag{18.62c}$$

Recall that $g_1(w_1)$ is the market price (in terms of expected rate of return) of the risk associated with the first mode of fluctuation of the spot yield curve. Equation (18.62b) implies that this price must be constant so that $g_1(w_1) = g_1$. More particularly, if the yield curve can only shift in parallel, then the aversion of market participants to the risk of such shifts must be constant.

The Level and Shape of the Yield Curve

For the present (very special) case of $I = J = 1$ and $I' = 3$, the spot yield curve can, from equation (18.42), be expressed as

$$R(y, w_1) = b_{10} + b_{20} \cdot y + b_{30} \cdot y^2 + w_1 \cdot b_{11}$$

or

$$R(y, w_1) = [b_{10} + w_1 \cdot b_{11}] + b_{20} \cdot y + b_{30} \cdot y^2$$

or, from equations (18.62a, b, c) and the preceding comment on $g_1(w_1)$,

$$R(y, w) = g_0(w_1) + \tfrac{1}{2} b_{11} \cdot g_1 \cdot y - \tfrac{1}{6} b_{11}^2 \cdot y^2 \qquad (18.63)$$

Equation (18.63) says that the yield curve must be a quadratic function of maturity. Assuming that $g_1 > 0$ (or that market participants have a positive aversion to interest rate fluctuations), the curve will be positively sloped at short maturities but will ultimately turn down. The *level* of the curve will vary in parallel with changes in the short-term interest rate $g_0(w_1)$, but the *shape* of the curve will be constant through time. The yield curve in equation (18.63) has also been derived, with a different methodology, in Jonathan Ingersoll, Jr., *Theory of Financial Decision Making*, (Rowman & Littlefield, 1987, 395–96).

The Shape of the Yield Curve When Market Participants Are Indifferent to Risk

It is instructive to examine in detail the shape of the yield curve when market participants are indifferent to risk or when $g_1 = 0$ in equation (18.63). In this case we have:

$$R(y, w_1) = g_0(w_1) - \tfrac{1}{6} b_{11}^2 \cdot y^2 \qquad (18.64)$$

A reasonable value for b_{11} is .0133405. (This follows because the standard deviation of the change in U.S. Treasury yields is about .00185 over one week (or 18.5 basis points), or .0133405 over one year (.0133405 = .00185 $\cdot$ (52.)$^{1/2}$).) Using this value in equation (64) gives:

$$R(y, w_1) = g_0(w_1) - \tfrac{1}{6}(.0133405)^2 \cdot y^2$$

$$= g_0(w_1) - .0000296617 \cdot y^2 \qquad (18.65)$$

At several representative maturities we have the following yields:

$$R(10, w_1) = g_0(w_1) - .0030 \qquad (18.66a)$$

$$R(20, w_1) = g_0(w_1) - .0119 \qquad (18.66b)$$

$$R(30, w_1) = g_0(w_1) - .0267 \qquad (18.66c)$$

Thus, the yield to maturity on a 10-year spot claim is about 30 basis points below the short term rate, the yield on a 20-year claim is about 119 basis points below that rate, and the yield on a 30-year claim is about 267 basis points lower.

These yields on longer-term securities raise an important question: If market participants do not expect yields to change and are indifferent to any changes that might occur, then why are they willing to hold, for example, 10-year spot claims at a yield lower than the short-term yield. More broadly, why isn't the yield curve flat at the short-term yield?

To answer this question, we have to examine the short-run expected rate of return on spot claims of different maturities. From equation (18.16) the expected rate of return on a security with y years remaining to maturity is

$$\mu(y, w) = R(y, w) + y \cdot R'(y, w) + \tfrac{1}{2} y^2 \cdot \sum_{j=1}^{J} f_j(y)^2 \qquad (18.67)$$

In the present case of $J = 1$ mode of fluctuation (with $f_1(y) = b_{11}$) and no risk aversion, we have from equation (18.64),

$$R(y, w_1) = g_0(w_1) - \tfrac{1}{6} b_{11}^2 \cdot y^2$$

so that

$$R'(y, w_1) = -\tfrac{1}{3} b_{11}^2 \cdot y$$

Substituting these expressions into equation (18.67) gives the expected rate of return function:

$$\mu(y, w_1) = (g_0(w_1) - \tfrac{1}{6} b_{11}^2 \cdot y^2) + y \cdot (-\tfrac{1}{3} b_{11}^2 \cdot y) + \tfrac{1}{2} y^2 \cdot b_{11}^2$$

or

$$\mu(y, w_1) = g_0(w_1) \qquad \text{for all } y \qquad (18.68)$$

Thus, if the yield curve has the form of equation (18.64), then *every* spot claim can be expected to appreciate (in the short run) at the short-term interest rate. This *is* a reasonable characterization of a market where interest rates are not expected to change and where market participants are indifferent to any changes that might occur.

It is also interesting to observe that the *curvature* of the yield curve in equation (18.64) is proportional to the squared volatility of interest rate fluctuations, to b_{11}^2. This shows that even in a simple consistent model of interest rates, the shape of the curve is inseparably linked to interest rate volatility.

The Shape of the Yield Curve When Market Participants Are Risk Averse

Having examined the shape of the yield curve when market participants are indifferent to risk ($g_1 = 0$), it is illuminating to reconsider the shape of the curve when they are risk averse ($g_1 > 0$).

As stated in equation (18.63) the yield curve when $I = J = 1$ and $I' = 3$ can be written

$$R(y, w_1) = g_0(w_1) + \tfrac{1}{2}b_{11} \cdot g_1 \cdot y - \tfrac{1}{6}b_{11}^2 \cdot y^2 \tag{18.69}$$

Using equation (18.67), it is easy to show from equation (18.69) that the expected rate of return on a spot claim with y years remaining to maturity is

$$\mu(y, w_1) = g_0(w_1) + g_1 \cdot b_{11} \cdot y \tag{18.70}$$

The implies that longer maturity claims can be expected to appreciate in value at a faster rate than shorter maturity claims and that the rate of appreciation in excess of the risk free rate is proportional to both the volatility of interest rates b_{11} and investor risk aversion g_1. More generally, the humped yield curve in equation (18.69) has the shape necessary to provide a greater expected rate of return to risk averse holders of longer term securities.

18.7   An Empirical Application

This section applies the polynomial structure described in section 18.6 to the problem of representing the U.S. Treasury spot yield curve and its modes of fluctuation in a consistent fashion. We begin by outlining some assumptions of the application and then examine estimates of the baseline and shift function polynomials. The section concludes with a test of whether the polynomial specification is correct and an appraisal of the consequences of using a misspecified structure.

Assumptions

For purposes of this application, we assume that there are $J = 3$ modes of fluctuation of the spot yield curve. We show below that these modes can be described heuristically as changes in the level, slope, and curvature of the curve. Our focus on just three modes of fluctuation is based on the analysis in chapter 16.

Since we have assumed that $J = 3$, consistency between the shape of the curve and its modes of fluctuation requires that $I = 3$ (meaning that each shift function is a polynomial with three coefficients) and $I' = 7$ (so the baseline function is a polynomial with seven coefficients).

Data

Our data consist of spot Treasury yields at semi-annual maturities from 6 months to 10 years (derived from yields on par Treasury bonds) on one business day (usually Thursday) each week between January 5, 1984, and December 29, 1988. Chapter 10 describes the methodology for constructing par bond yields and spot yields from data on actual bonds.

Estimates of the Shift Functions

We first examine the estimates of the shift function polynomials

$$f_j(y) = \sum_{i=1}^{I} b_{ij} \cdot y^{i-1}, \qquad j = 1, \ldots, J \tag{18.71}$$

The general problem of estimating the coefficients in these polynomials was addressed at length in chapter 17. The estimation technique used in this chapter differs slightly from that described in the earlier chapter and is outlined in appendix B.

Table 18.1 shows the estimated values of the coefficients of the shift function polynomials. Using those estimates, we can write the shift functions as

$$f_1(y) = \quad .10695 \cdot 10^{-1} + .11884 \cdot 10^{-2} \cdot y - .91417 \cdot 10^{-4} \cdot y^2 \tag{18.72a}$$

$$f_2(y) = -.79051 \cdot 10^{-2} + .27277 \cdot 10^{-2} \cdot y - .16164 \cdot 10^{-3} \cdot y^2 \tag{18.72b}$$

$$f_3(y) = -.14431 \cdot 10^{-2} + .10028 \cdot 10^{-2} \cdot y - .10890 \cdot 10^{-3} \cdot y^2 \tag{18.72c}$$

Note that the values of these functions are shifts in interest rates expressed in fractional terms so that a shift of 1.0 percent is written as .01. For example, the value of the first shift function at a term of $y = 0$ years is $f_1(0) = .010695$, or 1.0695%.

Figure 18.1 shows the values of the shift functions at maturities up to ten years. The basis for describing the first shift as a change in level, the second shift as a change in slope, and the third shift as a change in curvature is clear from the figure. Appendix B observes that these shift functions "fit" week-to-week fluctuations in the spot Treasury yield curve to within a standard error of 1 or 2 basis points.

Table 18.1
Estimated coefficients of the shift function polynomials (b_{ij}), based on weekly data from January 5, 1984, to December 29, 1988

Coefficient index	Shift function f_j		
	$j = 1$	$j = 2$	$j = 3$
$i = 1$	$.10695 \cdot 10^{-1}$	$-.79051 \cdot 10^{-2}$	$-.14431 \cdot 10^{-2}$
$i = 2$	$.11884 \cdot 10^{-2}$	$.27277 \cdot 10^{-2}$	$.10028 \cdot 10^{-2}$
$i = 3$	$-.91417 \cdot 10^{-4}$	$-.16164 \cdot 10^{-3}$	$-.10890 \cdot 10^{-3}$

Estimate of the Baseline Function

We next examine an estimate of the baseline polynomial:

$$R_0(y) = \sum_{i=1}^{I'} b_{i0} \cdot y^{i-1} \qquad\qquad (18.73)$$

It will be convenient to consider the low-order coefficients $(b_{10}, \ldots, b_{I+1,0})$ and the high-order coefficients $(b_{I+2,0}, \ldots, b_{I',0})$ separately.

High-Order Coefficients

The high-order coefficients of the baseline polynomial are computed directly from the coefficients of the shift function polynomials as shown at equations (18.46), (18.48), and (18.53). Using the values of the shift function coefficients in table 18.1, we obtain

$$b_{50} = -.10773 \cdot 10^{-5} \qquad\qquad (18.74a)$$

$$b_{60} = \quad .10979 \cdot 10^{-6} \qquad\qquad (18.74b)$$

$$b_{70} = -.33104 \cdot 10^{-8} \qquad\qquad (18.74c)$$

Low-Order Coefficients

The low-order coefficients of the baseline polynomial are estimated from observed spot yield data.

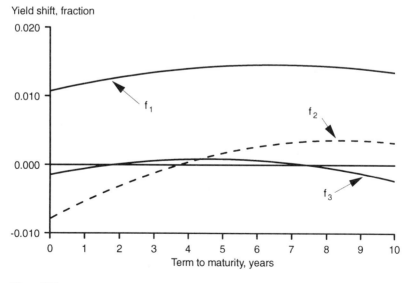

Figure 18.1
Spot yield curve shift functions

Say we decide to benchmark our model of the yield curve to the structure of interest rates at time $t^* = $ November 5, 1987 (this date was chosen arbitrarily). By definition, the weights on the shift functions at time t^* are zero (so that $w_1(t^*) = \cdots = w_J(t^*) = 0$) and the baseline function is equal to the yield curve function at t^*:

$$R_0(y) = R(y, w(t^*))$$

so that

$$R(y, w(t^*)) = \sum_{i=1}^{I'} b_{i0} \cdot y^{i-1} \tag{18.75}$$

We have data at time t^* on spot yields at semi-annual maturities out to 10 years, and we want to estimate the low-order coefficients in equation (18.75) while constraining the high-order coefficients to the values shown in equations (18.74a, b, c). Let $R(t^*)_h$ denote the observed yield at time t^* on a spot claim with a maturity of y_h years, where $y_1 = .5$ years, ..., $y_{20} = 10.0$ years. We assume these observed yields were generated by the model

$$R(t^*)_h = R(y_h, w(t^*)) + e_h, \qquad h = 1, \ldots, 20 \tag{18.76}$$

where e_h is random observation noise. It follows from equation (18.75) that

$$R(t^*)_h = \sum_{i=1}^{I'} b_{i0} \cdot y_h^{i-1} + e_h, \qquad h = 1, \ldots, 20 \tag{18.77}$$

The desired coefficient estimates can be obtained by defining a new set of variables:

$$v(t^*)_h = R(t^*)_h - \sum_{i=I+2}^{I'} b_{i0} \cdot y_h^{i-1}, \qquad h = 1, \ldots, 20 \tag{18.78}$$

We then have, from equation (18.77),

$$v(t^*)_h = \sum_{i=1}^{I+1} b_{i0} + y_h^{i-1} + e_h, \qquad h = 1, \ldots, 20 \tag{18.79}$$

The coefficients in equation (18.79) can be estimated with conventional regression techniques.

Using spot yield data from $t^* = $ November 5, 1987, we estimated the low-order coefficients of the baseline function as

$$b_{10} = \quad .62865 \cdot 10^{-1} \tag{18.80a}$$

$$b_{20} = \quad .68220 \cdot 10^{-2} \tag{18.80b}$$

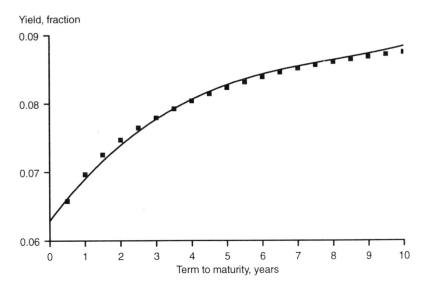

Figure 18.2
Spot yield curve baseline function (line) and observed spot Treasury yields (boxes) on November 5, 1987

$$b_{30} = -.71346 \cdot 10^{-3} \tag{18.80c}$$

$$b_{40} = .31785 \cdot 10^{-4} \tag{18.80d}$$

Combining these estimates with the high-order coefficient estimates in equations (18.74a, b, c) gives the baseline polynomial function on November 5, 1987:

$$
\begin{aligned}
R_0(y) = \quad & .62865 \cdot 10^{-1} \quad + .68220 \cdot 10^{-2} \cdot y \\
& -.71346 \cdot 10^{-3} \cdot y^2 + .31785 \cdot 10^{-4} \cdot y^3 \\
& -.10773 \cdot 10^{-5} \cdot y^4 + .10979 \cdot 10^{-6} \cdot y^5 \\
& -.33104 \cdot 10^{-8} \cdot y^6
\end{aligned}
\tag{18.81}
$$

Figure 18.2 shows the values of this baseline function at maturities up to ten years and also shows the actual spot yields on November 5, 1987. The standard error of the baseline function is .000341, or 3.41 basis points.

Testing the Specification of the Model

The preceding results suggest that a relatively simple ($J = 3$ modes of fluctuation) consistent polynomial representation of the spot yield curve can provide a reasonably accurate reflection of both the shape of the

Treasury curve on an arbitrarily chosen benchmark date ($t^* =$ November 5, 1987) and the modes of fluctuations in the curve over our sample interval (January 5, 1984, to December 29, 1988). However, the results do not shed any light on the important question of whether our assumption of three modes of fluctuation is unnecessarily large (an even simpler model of one or two modes might work just as well), or too small (four or five modes might be more appropriate), or just right. Moreover we do not know whether the estimate of the baseline polynomial is extremely sensitive or quite robust with respect to the choice of the benchmark date.

A Test Procedure

It is not too difficult to develop a procedure for testing the hypothesis that our choice of the number of modes of fluctuation was not too small and which also indicates the sensitivity of our results to the choice of the benchmark date.

Recall from equation (18.4) the basic model of the spot yield curve:

$$R(y, w(t)) = R_0(y) + \sum_{j=1}^{J} w_j(t) \cdot f_j(y) \tag{18.82}$$

In this equation we note explicitly that the ensemble of shift function weights varies through time.

When the baseline and shift functions are polynomials as in equations (18.73) and (18.71), equation (18.82) becomes

$$R(y, w(t)) = \sum_{i=1}^{I'} b_{i0} \cdot y^{i-1} + \sum_{j=1}^{J} \left[\sum_{i=1}^{I} b_{ij} \cdot y^{i-1} \right] \cdot w_j(t)$$

$$= \sum_{i=1}^{I} \left[b_{i0} + \sum_{j=1}^{J} b_{ij} \cdot w_j(t) \right] \cdot y^{i-1}$$

$$+ b_{I+1,0} \cdot y^I + \sum_{i=I+2}^{I'} b_{i0} \cdot y^{i-1}$$

$$= \sum_{i=1}^{I} a_i(t) \cdot y^{i-1} + b_{I+1,0} \cdot y^I + \sum_{i=I+2}^{I'} b_{i0} \cdot y^{i-1} \tag{18.83}$$

where

$$a_i(t) = b_{i0} + \sum_{j=1}^{J} b_{ij} \cdot w_j(t), \qquad i = 1, \ldots, I \tag{18.84}$$

Equation (18.83) shows that the yield curve is a polynomial with I' coefficients, where the first I coefficients can vary through time and the last $I' - I$ coefficients are stationary. As noted previously, the last $I' - I - 1$ coefficients (i.e., $b_{I+2,0}, \ldots, b_{I',0}$) are linked to the b_{ij} coefficients of the shift function polynomials by consistency (see equations 18.46, 18.48, and

18.53). The coefficient on y^I in equation (18.83) is not similarly determined, but it is constant.

This suggests that we can test the specification of the model by examining whether estimated values of the coefficient on y^I in equation (18.83) vary significantly through time when we constrain the coefficients on y^k for $k > I$ to their consistent values. A time series of the estimated coefficients will show directly whether there have been deformations in the shape of the yield curve involving powers of maturity greater than $I - 1$ and will also indicate the reliability of the estimate of $b_{I+1,0}$ derived from data on the benchmark date t^*.

Recall that on each day in our sample set we have data on spot yields at semi-annual maturities out to 10 years. Let $R(t)_h$ denote the observed yield at time t on a spot claim with a remaining maturity of y_h years. We assume that these observed yields were generated by the model

$$R(t)_h = R(y_h, w(t)) + e_h, \qquad h = 1, \ldots, 20 \tag{18.85}$$

where e_h again denotes observation noise. It follows from equation (18.83) that

$$R(t)_h = \sum_{i=1}^{I} a_i(t) \cdot y_h^{i-1} + b_{I+1,0} y_h^I$$

$$+ \sum_{i=I+2}^{I'} b_{i0} \cdot y_h^{i-1} + e_h, \qquad h = 1, \ldots, 20 \tag{18.86}$$

The desired coefficient estimates can be obtained by defining a new set of variables:

$$v(t)_h = R(t)_h - \sum_{i=I+2}^{I'} b_{i0} \cdot y_h^{i-1}, \qquad h = 1, \ldots, 20 \tag{18.87}$$

where the high-order coefficients $b_{I+2,0}, \ldots, b_{I',0}$ are computed from the coefficients of the shift function polynomials. We then have, from equation (18.86),

$$v(t)_h = \sum_{i=1}^{I} a_i(t) \cdot y_h^{i-1} + b_{I+1,0} \cdot y_h^I + e_h, \qquad h = 1, \ldots, 20 \tag{18.88}$$

The coefficients in equation (18.88) can be estimated with conventional regression techniques at each date in our data set. The estimates of the first I coefficients may vary through time, but the estimates of the coefficient on y^I will not vary significantly if our model is specified correctly.

Figure 18.3 shows the estimated values of the coefficient on y^I over our sample interval. The average standard error of estimate for the coefficient was .00000386. Even a casual appraisal of figure 18.3 supports the

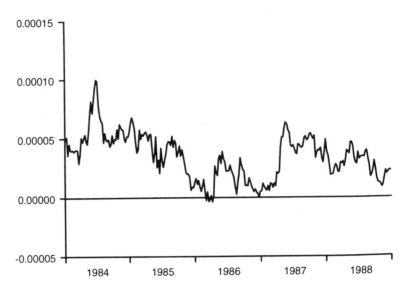

Figure 18.3
Estimated coefficients on y^I in equation (18.88)

conclusion that the coefficient on y^I was not stationary. We conclude that our simple polynomial model with $J = 3$ modes of fluctuation is misspecified and that we should have allowed for additional modes.

Using a Misspecified Model

We have concluded that our simple polynomial model with $J = 3$ modes of fluctuation is misspecified and that a well-specified model should have additional modes. However, it is conceivable that a user may have good reasons for not wanting to increase the number of modes, such as avoiding the computational burden of a more complex model. It is therefore of some interest to inquire how well our misspecified (but nonetheless consistent) model reflects the shape of the spot Treasury yield curve at times other than the benchmark date t^*.

Consider again the polynomial form of the yield curve at time t from equation (18.83):

$$R(y, w(t)) = \sum_{i=1}^{I} a_i(t) \cdot y^{i-1} + \sum_{i=I+1}^{I'} b_{i0} \cdot y^{i-1} \tag{18.89}$$

As noted above, the first I coefficients can vary through time and the last $I' - I$ coefficients are stationary. We are interested in how well the model of equation (18.89) can "fit" empirically observed yield curves when the values of the last $I' - I$ coefficients are held constant. (The

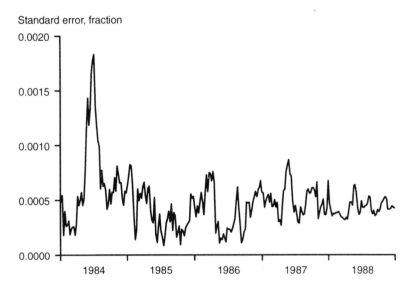

Figure 18.4
Standard errors of fit for equation (18.91)

value of $b_{I+1,0}$ is held constant at the estimate derived from data on the benchmark date, equation (18.80d), and the values of the high-order coefficients are fixed through the consistency condition, equations (18.74a, b, c).

The desired statistics can be obtained by defining a new set of variables on each date in our data set:

$$u(t)_h = R(t)_h - \sum_{i=I+1}^{I'} b_{i0} \cdot y_h^{i-1}, \qquad h = 1, \dots, 20 \tag{18.90}$$

We then have, from equation (18.89),

$$u(t)_h = \sum_{i=1}^{I} a_i(t) \cdot y_h^{i-1} + e_h, \qquad h = 1, \dots, 20 \tag{18.91}$$

The coefficients in equation (18.91) can be estimated with conventional regression techniques. The estimates can be used to produce yield curves on each date in our data set, which can in turn be used to assess standard errors of fit on each date.

Figure 18.4 shows the resulting standard errors and maximum errors of fit over the sample interval. Except for a brief episode in mid-1984, we were able to fit observed spot Treasury yields with our misspecified model to within a standard error of about 4 or 5 basis points. For many purposes this may be a sufficiently accurate reflection of the empirically observed shapes of the yield curve.

18.8   Conclusions

A "good" representation of the yield curve and its modes of fluctuation should satisfy at least three criteria. First, it should be flexible enough to fit empirically observed curves rather closely. A model that presumes that the yield curve is a quadratic function of maturity with a constant shape will clearly fail to provide an adequate approximation of many curves that have appeared in the recent past. Second, the representation should include a rich set of possible future curves. A model that presumes the yield curve can only shift in parallel will not satisfy this criterion. Third, any fitted curve should be consistent with the associated set of possible future curves, in the sense that the representation excludes the possibility of riskless arbitrage profits.

Many of the earlier chapters examined the separate problems of representing the shape of a yield curve and representing the modes of fluctuation of a curve. The present chapter has examined the composite problem of representing *consistently* both shape and modes of fluctuation and hence can be viewed as a synthesis and extension of those chapters.

The major theoretical result was a consistency condition linking the shape of the spot yield curve to its modes of fluctuation. This condition was derived initially in a general framework and then restated for the special case where the baseline and shift functions are polynomial functions of maturity. The last section of the chapter has presented an empirical application which showed that a fairly simple consistent polynomial structure can well describe both the shape and modes of fluctuation of the spot Treasury yield curve.

18.9   Appendix A: Linear Expansion of a Stochastic Equation

This appendix describes the linear expansion of a stochastic equation. The exposition is based on "Theoretical Valuation Models" by Stephen Figlewski in appendix A to chapter 3 in *Financial Options from Theory to Practice* (S. Figlewski, W. Silber, and M. Subrahmanyam, eds., Homewood, IL: Business One Irwin, 1990).

Consider the equation

$$x = f(t, w_1, \dots, w_n) \tag{A18.1}$$

where x is a scalar, t denotes time, and the w_j are random variables that follow independent Gaussian random walks in continuous time with zero means and variances of unity per unit time.

The second order expansion of equation (A18.1) is

$$\Delta x = \frac{\partial f}{\partial t} \cdot \Delta t + \sum_{i=1}^{n} \frac{\partial f}{\partial w_i} \cdot \Delta w_i + \frac{1}{2} \frac{\partial^2 f}{\partial t^2} \cdot \Delta t^2$$

$$+ \frac{1}{2} \sum_{i=1}^{n} \frac{\partial^2 f}{\partial t \cdot \partial w_i} \cdot \Delta w_i \cdot \Delta t + \frac{1}{2} \sum_{i=1}^{n} \sum_{j=1}^{n} \frac{\partial^2 f}{\partial w_i \cdot \partial w_j} \cdot \Delta w_i \cdot \Delta w_j \qquad (A18.2)$$

The term involving Δt^2 is clearly of second order and can be ignored in a linear expansion. The terms involving only Δt or only Δw_i are clearly of first order and must be retained. However, we need to examine the terms involving $\Delta t \cdot \Delta w_i$ and $\Delta w_i \cdot \Delta w_j$ more carefully.

From the stochastic process for w_i, we can write

$$\Delta w_i = (\Delta t)^{1/2} \cdot z_i, \qquad i = 1, \ldots, n \qquad (A18.3)$$

where the z_i are uncorrelated standard normal variates with zero means and unit variances.

It follows that

$$\Delta w_i \cdot \Delta t = (\Delta t)^{3/2} \cdot z_i \qquad (A18.4)$$

This product is of an order greater than first order in Δt. Terms involving $\Delta w_i \cdot \Delta t$ in equation (A18.2) can therefore be ignored.

It also follows that

$$\Delta w_i \cdot \Delta w_j = \Delta t \cdot z_i \cdot z_j \qquad (A18.5)$$

so that:

$$\exp[\Delta w_i^2] = \Delta t \qquad (A18.6a)$$

$$\mathrm{var}[\Delta w_i^2] = 2 \cdot \Delta t^2 \qquad (A18.6b)$$

$$\exp[\Delta w_i \cdot \Delta w_j] = 0, \qquad i \neq j \qquad (A18.6c)$$

Equations (A18.6a, b) show that terms involving Δw_i^2 have expected values equal to Δt and variances of order Δt^2. Thus, for small values of Δt, we can approximate Δw_i^2 with its expected value.

In view of the foregoing, the linear expansion of (A18.2) is

$$\Delta x = \frac{\partial f}{\partial t} \cdot \Delta t + \sum_{i=1}^{n} \frac{\partial f}{\partial w_i} \cdot \Delta w_i + \frac{1}{2} \sum_{i=1}^{n} \frac{\partial^2 f}{\partial w_i^2} \cdot \Delta t$$

or

$$\Delta x = \left[\frac{\partial f}{\partial t} + \frac{1}{2} \sum_{i=1}^{n} \frac{\partial^2 f}{\partial w_i^2} \right] \cdot \Delta t + \sum_{i=1}^{n} \frac{\partial f}{\partial w_i} \cdot \Delta w_i \qquad (A18.7)$$

18.10   Appendix B: Estimating the Coefficients of the Shift Function Polynomials

This appendix describes the methodology for estimating the b_{ij} coefficients of the shift function polynomials:

$$f_j(y) = \sum_{i=1}^{I} b_{ij} \cdot y^{i-1}, \qquad j = 1, \ldots, J \tag{A18.8}$$

Assume that we have data on H spot yields at semi-annual maturities (denoted $y_1, y_2, \ldots, y_H$) for each date in a sequence of $K + 1$ weekly dates (denoted $t_0, t_1, \ldots, t_K$). Assume also that, as required by consistency, $I = J$.

Polynomial Approximation of Weekly Yield Changes

From the general structure of the spot yield curve at equation (18.4), we can express the change in yield from time t_{k-1} to time t_k at a maturity of y_h years as

$$\Delta R(y_h, t_k) = R(y_h, t_k) - R(y_h, t_{k-1})$$

$$= R_0(y_h) + \sum_{j=1}^{J} w_j(t_k) \cdot f_j(y_h)$$

$$- R_0(y_h) - \sum_{j=1}^{J} w_j(t_{k-1}) \cdot f_j(y_h)$$

$$= \sum_{j=1}^{J} f_j(y_h) \cdot (w_j(t_k) - w_j(t_{k-1}))$$

$$= \sum_{j=1}^{J} f_j(y_h) \cdot \Delta w_j(t_k) \tag{A18.9}$$

The change in the jth weight from time t_{k-1} to time t_k, denoted $\Delta w_j(t_k)$, is normally distributed with mean zero and a variance of $1/52$. (The variance follows because the variance of the change in a weight is unity per year or $1/52$ per week.) Contemporaneous changes in different weights are uncorrelated.

In the special case of polynomial shift functions (as in equation A18.8), equation (A18.9) becomes

$$\Delta R(y_h, t_k) = \sum_{j=1}^{J} \left[\sum_{i=1}^{I} b_{ij} \cdot y_h^{i-1} \right] \cdot \Delta w_j(t_k) \tag{A18.10}$$

$$= \sum_{i=1}^{I} \left[\sum_{j=1}^{J} b_{ij} \cdot \Delta w_j(t_k) \right] \cdot y_h^{i-1}$$

$$= \sum_{i=1}^{I} \Delta a_i(t_k) \cdot y_h^{i-1} \tag{A18.11}$$

where

$$\Delta a_i(t_k) = \sum_{j=1}^{J} b_{ij} \cdot \Delta w_j(t_k), \qquad i = 1, \ldots, I \tag{A18.12}$$

For each date in our data set from t_1 to t_K, the polynomial coefficients $\Delta a_1(t_k), \ldots, \Delta a_I(t_k)$ in equation (A18.11) can be estimated with conventional regression techniques. For example, for the interval from $t_{k-1} =$ December 1, 1988 to $t_k =$ December 8, 1988, we estimated:

$$\Delta a_1(t_k) = \quad .24083 \cdot 10^{-2}$$

$$\Delta a_2(t_k) = -.38369 \cdot 10^{-3}$$

$$\Delta a_3(t_k) = \quad .13322 \cdot 10^{-4}$$

so the yield shift function can be written

$$\Delta R(y, t_k) = .24083 \cdot 10^{-2} - .38369 \cdot 10^{-3} \cdot y + .13322 \cdot 10^{-4} \cdot y^2$$

Figure 18.5 shows the values of this function over a range of maturities up to ten years and also shows the actual spot yield changes over the same week. The standard error of estimate of the yield shift function is .000065, or .65 basis points.

Figure 18.6 shows comparable standard errors for each weekly interval in our data set. We were generally able to fit observed spot Treasury yield changes to within a standard error of about 1 or 2 basis points. The implies that a simple quadratic structure provides a good representation of week to week changes in Treasury yields.

Shift Function Coefficients

At this point it will be helpful to switch to vector notation. Define

$$\Delta R(t_k) = \begin{bmatrix} \Delta R(y_1, t_k) \\ \vdots \\ \Delta R(y_H, t_k) \end{bmatrix}, \qquad k = 1, \ldots, K \tag{A18.13a}$$

$$Y = \begin{bmatrix} 1 & y_1 & y_1^2 & \cdots & y_1^{I-1} \\ \vdots & \vdots & \vdots & & \vdots \\ 1 & y_H & y_H^2 & \cdots & y_H^{I-1} \end{bmatrix} \tag{A18.13b}$$

$$B = \begin{bmatrix} b_{11} & \cdots & b_{1J} \\ \vdots & & \vdots \\ b_{I1} & \cdots & b_{IJ} \end{bmatrix} \tag{A18.13c}$$

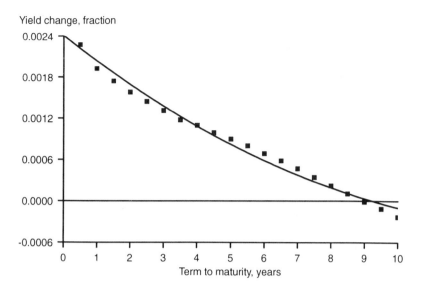

Figure 18.5
Estimated yield shift function (line) and observed changes in spot Treasury yields (boxes) for
the interval from December 1, 1988, to December 8, 1988

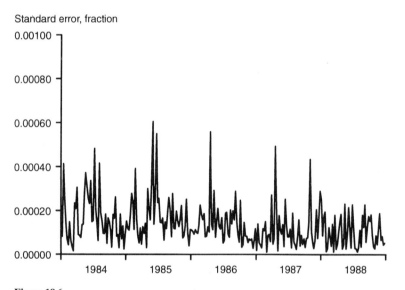

Figure 18.6
Standard errors of fit for equation (A18.11)

$$\Delta w(t_k) = \begin{bmatrix} \Delta w_1(t_k) \\ \vdots \\ \Delta w_J(t_k) \end{bmatrix}, \qquad k = 1, \ldots, K \tag{A18.13d}$$

$$\Delta a(t_k) = \begin{bmatrix} \Delta a_1(t_k) \\ \vdots \\ \Delta a_I(t_k) \end{bmatrix}, \qquad k = 1, \ldots, K \tag{A18.13e}$$

Equation (A18.10) can then be rewritten as

$$\Delta R(t_k) = Y \cdot B \cdot \Delta w(t_k) \tag{A18.14a}$$

and equation (A18.11) can be rewritten as

$$\Delta R(t_k) = Y \cdot \Delta a(t_k) \tag{A18.14b}$$

Given the statistical distribution of the $\Delta w(t_k)$ vector equation (A18.14a) can also be rewritten as

$$\Delta R(t_k) = Y \cdot B \cdot (52)^{-1/2} \cdot e \tag{A18.15}$$

where e is a J-dimensional random vector whose elements have zero means, unit variances, and zero covariances.

Now consider the $H \times H$ covariance matrix for $\Delta R(t_k)$, denoted $\Omega_{\Delta R}$. Let $\Omega_{\Delta a}$ denote the $I \times I$ covariance matrix for $\Delta a(t_k)$. From equation (A18.14b) we have

$$\Omega_{\Delta R} = Y \cdot \Omega_{\Delta a} \cdot Y' \tag{A18.16}$$

We can form an estimate $\hat{\Omega}_{\Delta a}$ of $\Omega_{\Delta a}$ from the time series of estimated values of $\Delta a(t_k)$. We can consequently compute an estimate of $\Omega_{\Delta R}$ as

$$\hat{\Omega}_{\Delta R} = Y \cdot \hat{\Omega}_{\Delta a} \cdot Y' \tag{A18.17}$$

For the reasons noted in chapter 17, we can write $\hat{\Omega}_{\Delta R}$ as

$$\hat{\Omega}_{\Delta R} = \tilde{V}_{\Delta R} \cdot \tilde{D}_{\Delta R} \cdot \tilde{V}'_{\Delta R} \tag{A18.18}$$

where $\tilde{D}_{\Delta R}$ is an $I \times I$ diagonal matrix of the I nonzero eigenvalues of $\hat{\Omega}_{\Delta R}$ and $\tilde{V}_{\Delta R}$ is an $H \times I$ matrix of the associated eigenvectors.

From equation (A18.18) it follows that we can write

$$\Delta R(t_k) = \tilde{V}_{\Delta R} \cdot \tilde{D}_{\Delta R}^{1/2} \cdot e \tag{A18.19}$$

where $\tilde{D}_{\Delta R}^{1/2}$ is an $I \times I$ diagonal matrix with entries of the form $[\tilde{D}_{\Delta R}^{1/2}]_{ii} = ([\tilde{D}_{\Delta R}]_{ii})^{1/2}$; in words, the entries on the diagonal of $\tilde{D}_{\Delta R}^{1/2}$ are the square roots of the corresponding entries on the diagonal of $\tilde{D}_{\Delta R}$, where e is an I-dimensional random vector whose elements have zero means, unit variances, and zero covariances.

Comparing equations (A18.15) and (A18.19) and noting that $I = J$ shows that we can make the identification

$$(52)^{-1/2} \cdot Y \cdot B = \tilde{V}_{\Delta R} \cdot \tilde{D}_{\Delta R}^{1/2} \tag{A18.20}$$

The estimated value of the B matrix is therefore

$$B = (52)^{1/2} \cdot (Y' \cdot Y)^{-1} \cdot Y' \cdot \tilde{V}_{\Delta R} \cdot \tilde{D}_{\Delta R}^{1/2} \tag{A18.21}$$

18.11 Appendix C: The Function $G(\bar{\sigma}_1, \ldots, \bar{\sigma}_J; w)$ is Affine with Respect to $\bar{\sigma}_1, \ldots, \bar{\sigma}_J$

This appendix shows that the function $G(\bar{\sigma}_1, \ldots, \bar{\sigma}_J; w)$ in equation (18.26) has the form of equation (18.27) when equations (18.22) and (18.25) hold.

Consider an arbitrary portfolio of K spot claims with $K > J + 1$, where the kth spot claim is payable in y_k years and where x_k is the fractional contribution of the kth claim to the aggregate value of the portfolio (see equation 18.23). Write the expected rate of return on the portfolio (equation 18.22) as

$$\bar{\mu} = \mu(w)' \cdot x \tag{A18.22}$$

where

$$\mu(w) = \begin{bmatrix} \mu(y_1, w) \\ \mu(y_2, w) \\ \vdots \\ \mu(y_K, w) \end{bmatrix}, \quad x = \begin{bmatrix} x_1 \\ x_2 \\ \vdots \\ x_K \end{bmatrix} \tag{A18.23}$$

and write the risks of the portfolio (equation 18.25) as

$$\bar{\sigma} = \Sigma \cdot x \tag{A18.24}$$

where

$$\bar{\sigma} = \begin{bmatrix} \bar{\sigma}_1 \\ \bar{\sigma}_2 \\ \vdots \\ \bar{\sigma}_J \end{bmatrix}, \quad \Sigma = \begin{bmatrix} \sigma_1(y_1) & \sigma_1(y_2) & \cdots & \sigma_1(y_K) \\ \sigma_2(y_1) & \sigma_2(y_2) & \cdots & \sigma_2(y_K) \\ \vdots & \vdots & & \vdots \\ \sigma_J(y_1) & \sigma_J(y_2) & \cdots & \sigma_J(y_K) \end{bmatrix} \tag{A18.25}$$

The vector x must satisfy equation (18.24) and hence may be written

$$x = \phi + \Phi \cdot \tilde{x} \tag{A18.26}$$

where $\tilde{x}$ is an unrestricted $(K-1)$-dimensional vector, ϕ is a K-dimensional vector with unity in the last element and zeros elsewhere and Φ is a $K \times (K-1)$ matrix of the form

$$\Phi = \left[\begin{array}{c} I_{K-1} \\ \hline -1 - 1 \ldots -1 \end{array} \right] \tag{A18.27}$$

where I_{K-1} is the $(K-1) \times (K-1)$ identity matrix. It follows that we can write equation (A18.22) as

$$\bar{\mu} = \mu(w)' \cdot [\phi + \Phi \cdot \tilde{x}]$$

or

$$\bar{\mu} = \mu(w)' \cdot \phi + \mu(w)' \cdot \Phi \cdot \tilde{x} \tag{A18.28}$$

It follows similarly that we can rewrite equation (A18.24) as

$$\bar{\sigma} = \Sigma \cdot [\phi + \Phi \cdot \tilde{x}]$$

or

$$\bar{\sigma} = \Sigma \cdot \phi + \Sigma \cdot \Phi \cdot \tilde{x} \tag{A18.29}$$

Now define the $(K-1)$-dimensional vector $[\bar{\sigma}]^{\text{ext}}$ as

$$[\bar{\sigma}]^{\text{ext}} = \begin{bmatrix} \bar{\sigma} \\ x_{J+1} \\ x_{J+2} \\ \vdots \\ x_{K-1} \end{bmatrix} \tag{A18.30}$$

the $(K-1)$-dimensional vector $[\Sigma \cdot \phi]^{\text{ext}}$ as

$$[\Sigma \cdot \phi]^{\text{ext}} = \begin{bmatrix} \Sigma \cdot \phi \\ 0 \\ 0 \\ \vdots \\ 0 \end{bmatrix} \tag{A18.31}$$

and the $(K-1)$-by-$(K-1)$ matrix $[\Sigma \cdot \Phi]^{\text{ext}}$ as

$$[\Sigma \cdot \Phi]^{\text{ext}} = \left[\begin{array}{c|c} \Sigma \cdot \Phi \\ \hline 0 & I_{K-1-J} \end{array} \right] \tag{A18.32}$$

where I_{K-1-J} is the $(K - 1 - J) \times (K - 1 - J)$ identity matrix. We can then write equation (A18.29) as

$$[\bar{\sigma}]^{\text{ext}} = [\Sigma \cdot \phi]^{\text{ext}} + [\Sigma \cdot \Phi]^{\text{ext}} \cdot \tilde{x} \tag{A18.33}$$

Without loss of generality, we can assume that $[\Sigma \cdot \Phi]^{\text{ext}}$ is nonsingular, so we can solve equation (A18.33) for $\tilde{x}$ as

$$\tilde{x} = \left[[\Sigma \cdot \Phi]^{\text{ext}} \right]^{-1} \cdot \left[[\bar{\sigma}]^{\text{ext}} - [\Sigma \cdot \phi]^{\text{ext}} \right] \tag{A18.34}$$

Using this expression for $\tilde{x}$ in equation (A18.28) gives $\bar{\mu}$ as an affine function of $[\bar{\sigma}]^{\text{ext}}$ or as an affine function of $(\bar{\sigma}_1, \bar{\sigma}_2, \ldots, \bar{\sigma}_J, x_{J+1} x_{J+2}, \ldots, x_{K-1})$. However, equation (18.26) says that $\bar{\mu}$ does not depend on any x_i once $\bar{\sigma}_1, \bar{\sigma}_2, \ldots, \bar{\sigma}_J$ are given. Thus equation (A18.28), with $\tilde{x}$ replaced by the right-hand side of equation (A18.34), must be of the form of equation (18.27).

18.12   Subsequent Remarks

An evident problem with the analysis in this chapter is that the original specification of the spot yield curve in equation (18.4) does not logically exclude the possibility that the yield on a spot claim can fall below zero.

The easiest way to avoid this difficulty is to specify that the right-hand side of equation (18.4) defines the *natural logarithm* of the yield on a spot claim with y years to maturity when the ensemble of shift function weights is w:

$$\ln[R(y, w)] = R_0(y) + \sum_{j=1}^{J} w_j \cdot f_j(y) \tag{S18.1}$$

However, equation (S18.1) implies that the standard deviation of the arithmetic change in the yield on a spot claim over a short interval of time is a linear function of that yield. There is ample evidence that interest rate volatility varies through time (see chapter 20) but no evidence to support the proposition that the variation is solely (or even largely) a matter of change in the level of yields. Moreover the problem of negative yields can be avoided with any monotonically increasing function $h[\cdot]$ that maps the set of positive real numbers onto the set of real numbers such that

$$h[R(y, w)] = R_0(y) + \sum_{j=1}^{J} w_j \cdot f_j(y) \tag{S18.2}$$

The natural log function is only one such function and there is no obvious reason to prefer it over the alternatives.

A second problem with the analysis in this chapter is our assumption that the shift functions $f_1(y), \ldots, f_J(y)$ are stationary through time. This issue is examined in detail in chapter 20.

Fixed income securities pay specified amounts of money on specified dates with no uncertainty. They include simple single payment Treasury bills as well as more complex coupon-bearing Treasury bonds. Excluding (admittedly not unimportant) considerations like differential taxation of capital gains and ordinary income, secondary market liquidity, and transient technical conditions (e.g., squeezes on short sellers), the market price of a fixed income security is strictly a matter of the time value of money— as reflected in the Treasury yield curve.

An important class of related securities consists of instruments whose prices depend on *prospective* interest rates as well as current yields. These securities include put and call options on bonds and putable and callable bonds. The instruments are readily distinguished from fixed income securities because they make *different payments* at specified dates and/or make specified payments at *different dates* depending on the future evolution of interest rates.

This chapter examines the pricing of claims whose payments (or, more generally, payoffs) depend on future interest rates. We will call these claims "yield-dependent contingent claims" or "contingent claims." The first part, sections 19.1 through 19.3, examines contingent claim pricing when yields vary continuously in continuous time. Our primary result is a partial differential equation characterizing the price behavior of all contingent claims. We observe that it is usually quite difficult to solve this equation. The second part, sections 19.4 through 19.8, addresses contingent claim pricing when interest rates and time vary in discrete increments rather than continuously. This alternative framework leads to practical numerical valuation procedures. We suggest that the resulting prices converge to the prices which arise out of a continuous framework as the time and yield increments grow small.

A Comment on Riskless Arbitrage

At several points in this chapter, we make reference to riskless arbitrage profits or revenue derived from a transaction that requires no commitment of capital and that does not expose the transactor to any risk of loss. We assume that the markets do not provide opportunities for such profits. More specifically, we use the assumption of "no riskless arbitrage" to logically exclude situations that give rise to such profits.

CONTINUOUS TIME/CONTINUOUS STATE ANALYSIS

The three sections in this part examine the valuation of fixed income securities and contingent claims when the level and shape of the yield

Written in February 1990.

curve varies continuously through time and when time itself is a continuous variable.

Section 19.1 begins by describing the yield curve and fluctuations in the curve. We use single payment spot claims rather than multiple payment bonds as the fundamental unit of analysis. As a result we will be concerned with the structure of the *spot* yield curve.

Section 19.2 observes that the price of a spot claim changes as a result of the passage of time and change in the level and shape of the yield curve. These effects are identified analytically by constructing a linear approximation to the change in the price of the claim as a function of the passage of time and change in the curve. The approximation leads to measures of the risks and expected rate of return on the claim. The section concludes with the statement of an equilibrium relationship between risk and return.

Section 19.3 considers the problem of pricing a contingent claim. Building on the relationship between risk and return expressed in section 19.2, we derive a partial differential equation that must be satisfied by all contingent claims. The section concludes with the observation that it is quite difficult to solve the equation and hence quite difficult to obtain a closed-form expression for the price of a contingent claim. This sets the stage for the discrete time/discrete state analysis presented in the second part of the chapter.

19.1   Spot Yields and the Spot Yield Curve

This section describes yields on spot claims and the spot yield curve. In particular, it introduces some important assumptions on the structure of the spot curve and its variation through time. The section concludes with explicit expressions for the price of a spot claim and for the prices of other fixed income securities as functions of time and the level and shape of the yield curve.

Spot Yields

A spot yield is a discount rate used to compute the present value or market price of a spot claim.

Consider, for example, a spot claim for $100 payable in $y = 4$ years. If the yield on the claim is $R = 10\%$ per annum, compounded semi-annually, its present value is

$$P = 100 \cdot (1 + \tfrac{1}{2}R)^{-2 \cdot y}$$

$$= 100 \cdot (1 + \tfrac{1}{2}(.10))^{-2 \cdot 4}$$

$$= 67.6839 \tag{19.1}$$

Continuous Compounding

For purposes of this discussion, we measure the yield on a spot claim with continuous compounding.

The continuously compounded yield on a spot claim priced at $P = \$67.6839$ for \$100 payable in $y = 4$ years is the value of R that satisfies the equation

$$P = 100 \cdot e^{-y \cdot R} \tag{19.2}$$

or

$$R = y^{-1} \cdot \ln \left[\frac{100}{P} \right]$$

$$= 4^{-1} \cdot \ln \left[\frac{100}{67.6839} \right]$$

$$= .097580, \text{ or } 9.7580\% \text{ per annum, compounded continuously} \tag{19.3}$$

This yield is lower than the 10% semi-annually compounded yield on the same claim because of the more frequent compounding (continuous rather than semi-annual).

The Spot Yield Curve

A spot yield curve is a function that describes how the yield R on a spot claim varies with the time y remaining to payment of the claim, where R is measured in fractional terms (so that $R = .10$ means 10% per annum, compounded continuously) and y is measured in years.

Structure of the Spot Yield Curve

We assume that the spot yield curve at any point in time can be expressed in the form

$$R(y, w) = R_0(y) + \sum_{j=1}^{J} w_j \cdot f_j(y) \tag{19.4}$$

where $R_0(y)$ and $f_1(y), \ldots, f_J(y)$ are known time-invariant functions of maturity and where $w_1, \ldots, w_J$ are scalar coefficients. The ensemble, or vector, of coefficients is denoted w.

Equation (19.4) says that the yield curve can be constructed as a "baseline" function $R_0(y)$ plus a linear combination of "shift" functions $f_1(y), \ldots, f_J(y)$. The weight, or coefficient, on the jth shift function is w_j. Yield curves with the structure of equation (19.4) were examined in chapter 18.

Temporal Variation in the Spot Yield Curve

We assume that the yield curve in equation (19.4) varies over time, in shape as well as level, as a result of temporal variation in the w_j weights. In particular, we assume that each weight evolves as a Gaussian random walk with zero drift and a variance of unity per year and that change in one weight is uncorrelated with changes in other weights; in other words, the random walks are statistically independent of each other. We will sometimes write the jth weight as $w_j(t)$ and the ensemble of weights as $w(t)$ to emphasize this temporal variation.

It is useful to explore the implications of the temporal behavior of the $w_j(t)$ weights in further detail. Consider two points in time, denoted t_0 and t_1, where $t_0 < t_1$. The change in yield from time t_0 to time t_1 at a term of y years is $R(y, w(t_1)) - R(y, w(t_0))$. Using equation (19.4), we have

$$R(y, w(t_1)) - R(y, w(t_0))$$

$$= R_0(y) + \sum_{j=1}^{J} w_j(t_1) \cdot f_j(y) - R_0(y) - \sum_{j=1}^{J} w_j(t_0) \cdot f_j(y)$$

$$= \sum_{j=1}^{J} (w_j(t_1) - w_j(t_0)) \cdot f_j(y) \tag{19.5}$$

Thus the shift in the yield curve from time t_0 to time t_1 is a linear combination of the shift functions, where the coefficients in the linear combination are the changes in the $w_j(t)$ weights.

From our assumption on the behavior of the $w_j(t)$ weights, we have that the changes in the weights from time t_0 to time t_1 are normally distributed with the characteristics

$$\exp[w_j(t_1) - w_j(t_0)] = 0, \qquad j = 1, \ldots, J \tag{19.6a}$$

$$\text{var}[w_j(t_1) - w_j(t_0)] = t_1 - t_0, \qquad j = 1, \ldots, J \tag{19.6b}$$

$$\text{cov}[w_j(t_1) - w_j(t_0), w_k(t_1) - w_k(t_0)] = 0, \qquad j = 1, \ldots, J$$

$$k = 1, \ldots, J$$

$$k \neq j \tag{19.6c}$$

Thus the shift functions represent trendless (see equation 19.6a), normalized (see equation 19.6b), and statistically independent (see equation 19.6c) *modes of fluctuation* in the spot yield curve.

Consistency

The baseline function $R_0(y)$ and the $f_j(y)$ shift functions in equation (19.4) cannot be specified arbitrarily by an analyst. It was demonstrated in chapter 18 that, by the exclusion of opportunities for riskless arbitrage, there exist $J + 1$ scalar-valued functions of the shift weights, denoted $g_0(w), g_1(w), \ldots, g_J(w)$, such that the following equation is true for all values of the shift weights and for all maturities $y \geq 0$:

$$R_0(y) + \sum_{j=1}^{J} w_j \cdot f_j(y) = g_0(w) + \sum_{j=1}^{J} g_j(w) \cdot \left[y^{-1} \cdot \int_0^y z \cdot f_j(z) \cdot dz \right]$$

$$- \frac{1}{2} y^{-1} \cdot \sum_{j=1}^{J} \left[\int_0^y z^2 \cdot f_j(z)^2 \cdot dz \right] \tag{19.7}$$

Equation (19.7) is a "consistency" condition relating the shape of the yield curve (the left-hand side of the equation) to its modes of fluctuation. We can exclude the possibility that particular choices of the baseline function and shift functions will ever be observed if we can show that, for those choices, there are *no* $g_j(w)$ functions satisfying equation (19.7). (Section 18.5 gave an example of baseline and shift functions with this characteristic.)

Pricing Spot Claims

Given the pricing of a spot claim in equation (19.2) and our model of the spot yield curve in equation (19.4), it is clear that the price of a spot claim depends on time and the level and shape of the yield curve. This dependence can be expressed with a simple equation.

Let $P(t, w; t_m)$ denote the price at time t of a spot claim paying \$100 at time t_m $(t_m > t)$ when the shift function weights in equation (19.4) have the value of the ensemble w. (Observe that the ensemble of weights describes the level and shape of the yield curve completely because the $R_0(y)$ and $f_j(y)$ functions are assumed to be known.) It follows that

$$P(t, w; t_m) = 100 \cdot e^{-(t_m - t) \cdot R(t_m - t, w)} \tag{19.8}$$

where the function R is as specified in equation (19.4), so that

$$R(t_m - t, w) = R_0(t_m - t) + \sum_{j=1}^{J} w_j \cdot f_j(t_m - t) \tag{19.9}$$

The analysis in the first three sections of this chapter is executed in a continuous time/continuous state framework because we allow time and each of the shift function weights to vary continuously. (The shift function weights are sometimes called "state" variables because they describe the state of the fixed income markets or the level and shape of the spot yield curve.) In section 19.4 we change to a discrete time/discrete state frame-work where time and each of the shift function weights changes only in discrete increments.

The pricing of a spot claim with equation (19.8) can be extended to pricing portfolios of spot claims. Consider a portfolio of K spot claims, where the size of the payment on the kth claim is F_k and where the kth claim will be paid at time t_k. The price of the portfolio at time t when the shift function weights in equation (19.4) have the value of the ensemble w is the sum of the prices of the individual spot claims:

$$\bar{P}(t, w) = \sum_{k=1}^{K} F_k \cdot e^{-(t_k - t) \cdot R(t_k - t, w)} \tag{19.10}$$

The bar over the letter P in equation (19.10) denotes the fact that we are speaking of the price of a portfolio of spot claims whose payment dates and amounts are not described explicitly through the function arguments.

Pricing Other Fixed Income Securities

We observed in the introduction to this chapter that a fixed income secu-rity is defined as an instrument that pays specified amounts of money on specified dates. It follows that the payment structure of any fixed income security is identical to the payment structure of some particular portfolio of spot claims. For example, if a bond pays the amount F_k at time t_k for $k = 1, \ldots, K$ payments, then the payments on the bond are identical to the payments on a portfolio of K spot claims where the kth claim pays the amount F_k at time t_k.

We assume the market values a fixed income security at the same price it places on the portfolio of spot claims with an identical payment struc-ture. Thus equation (19.10) is the general equation for pricing any fixed income security. By extension, equation (19.10) can also be used to price portfolios of fixed income securities.

It should be noted that this assumption is demonstrably false. Treasury bills have higher prices than comparable maturity Treasury bonds and some Treasury bonds have higher prices than portfolios of zero coupon Treasury securities with the same payment structure. These price differ-ences are usually attributed to tax effects and differences in secondary market liquidity. We ignore these factors in this chapter.

19.2   Risk and Return for Fixed Income Securities

The preceding section demonstrated how the price of a fixed income security depends on time and the level and shape of the spot yield curve.

It follows that *change* in the price of a fixed income security depends on the *passage* of time and *change* in the level and shape of the curve. The relationship between price change and the passage of time is usually identified as rate of return. The relationship between price change and change in the yield curve is usually identified as risk.

This section begins by defining quantitative measures of the risks and the short-run expected rate of return of a spot claim and other fixed income securities. We then argue that there exists a particular relationship between risk and return. The section concludes with a discussion of two implications of that relationship.

Measuring Risk and Return

Consider a security whose price depends on time, denoted t, and the level and shape of the spot yield curve, as reflected by the ensemble w of shift function weights and whose price does not depend on any other variable (e.g., the market price of a stock or tangible commodity). We can express the price P of the security as a function of the form

$$P = P(t, w) \qquad (19.11)$$

Spot claims and portfolios of spot claims are examples of such securities, as indicated by equations (19.8) and (19.10).

It can be shown (see appendix A in chapter 18) that the linear approximation to the price change ΔP that occurs over an interval of time Δt when the jth weight changes by Δw_j is

$$\Delta P = \left[\frac{\partial P}{\partial t} + \frac{1}{2} \sum_{j=1}^{J} \frac{\partial^2 P}{\partial w_j^2} \right] \cdot \Delta t + \sum_{j=1}^{J} \frac{\partial P}{\partial w_j} \cdot \Delta w_j \qquad (19.12)$$

where $\partial P/\partial t$ is the partial derivative of price with respect to time, $\partial P/\partial w_j$ is the partial derivative of price with respect to the jth weight, and $\partial^2 P/\partial w_j^2$ is the second partial derivative of price with respect to the jth weight.

Let $\mu(t, w)$ denote the expected short-run rate of return on the security at time t when the shift function weights are w, and let $\sigma_j(t, w)$ denote the risk of the security with respect to the jth mode of fluctuation of the spot yield curve. Given the form of equation (19.12), it is reasonable to write

$$\frac{\Delta P}{P} = \mu(t, w) \cdot \Delta t - \sum_{j=1}^{J} \sigma_j(t, w) \cdot \Delta w_j \qquad (19.13)$$

Since the expected value of the change in the jth weight is zero for $j = 1$, ..., J, equation (19.13) implies that the expected value of the rate of change in the price of the security, $\exp[\Delta P/(P \cdot \Delta t)]$, is just $\mu(t, w)$.

Comparing the corresponding terms in equations (19.12) and (19.13) allows us to identify the expected rate of return on the security as

$$\mu(t, w) = P^{-1} \cdot \left[\frac{\partial P}{\partial t} + \frac{1}{2} \sum_{j=1}^{J} \frac{\partial^2 P}{\partial v_j^2} \right] \tag{19.14}$$

and the risk of the security with respect to the jth mode of fluctuation of the spot curve as

$$\sigma_j(t, w) = -P^{-1} \cdot \frac{\partial P}{\partial w_j}, \qquad j = 1, \ldots, J \tag{19.15}$$

where it is understood that the price function and its derivatives are to be evaluated at the specified values of t and w.

Equations (19.14) and (19.15) are important because they show explicitly how we can measure the expected rate of return and the risks of a fixed income security. This is best understood in the context of some specific examples.

Risk and Return for a Spot Claim

Equation (19.8) gives the price of a spot claim as a function of t and the ensemble w. After working out the relevant partial derivatives (this is done in detail in chapter 18), we obtain the expected rate of return on a spot claim maturing at time t_m:

$$\mu(t, w; t_m) = R(t_m - t, w) + (t_m - t) \cdot R'(t_m - t, w)$$

$$+ \frac{1}{2}(t_m - t)^2 \cdot \sum_{j=1}^{J} f_j(t_m - t)^2 \tag{19.16}$$

The yield function $R(t_m - t, w)$ is as given in equation (19.9), and the function R' is the derivative of R with respect to its first (maturity) argument

$$R'(t_m - t, w) = R_0'(t_m - t) + \sum_{j=1}^{J} w_j \cdot f_j'(t_m - t) \tag{19.17}$$

where R_0' is the derivative of the baseline function and f_j' is the derivative of the jth shift function. Equation (19.16) shows that the expected rate of return on a spot claim depends on the level and slope of the yield curve at the term to maturity of the claim $(t_m - t)$ and that it also depends on the squared volatility of the yield curve at the term to maturity of the claim.

It also follows from equations (19.8) and (19.15) that the risk of a spot claim with respect to the jth mode of fluctuation of the yield curve is

$$\sigma_j(t; t_m) = (t_m - t) \cdot f_j(t_m - t), \qquad j = 1, \ldots, J \tag{19.18}$$

This shows that risk depends on the volatility of the spot yield curve at the term to maturity of the spot claim. It should be noted that the risk of a spot claim does not depend on the ensemble w of shift function weights or, more generally, on either the level or shape or the yield curve.

Risk and Return for a Portfolio of Spot Claims

Equation (19.10) gives the price of a portfolio of spot claims as a function of t and w. After working out the relevant partial derivatives, we find that we can express the expected rate of return on the portfolio, denoted $\bar{\mu}(t, w)$, as a linear combination of the expected rates of return on the spot claims in the portfolio:

$$\bar{\mu}(t, w) = \sum_{k=1}^{K} x_k(t, w) \cdot \mu(t, w; t_k) \tag{19.19}$$

where the function μ is as defined in equation (19.16) and where x_k is the fractional allocation of the kth spot claim in the portfolio:

$$x_k(t, w) = \frac{F_k \cdot e^{-(t_k - t) \cdot R(t_k - t, w)}}{\sum_{i=1}^{k} F_i \cdot e^{-(t_i - t) \cdot R(t_i - t, w)}}, \qquad k = 1, \ldots, K \tag{19.20}$$

Note that the fractional allocations always sum to unity:

$$\sum_{k=1}^{K} x_k(t, w) = 1 \tag{19.21}$$

In a similar fashion we can express the risk of the portfolio with respect to the jth mode of fluctuation of the spot yield curve, denoted $\bar{\sigma}_j(t, w)$, as a weighted combination of the risks of the constituent spot claims:

$$\bar{\sigma}_j(t, w) = \sum_{k=1}^{K} x_k(t, w) \cdot \sigma_j(t; t_k), \qquad j = 1, \ldots, J \tag{19.22}$$

Recall from section 19.1 that the price of a fixed income security or portfolio of fixed income securities is equal to the price of the portfolio of spot claims with an identical payment structure. It follows that equations (19.19) and (19.22) are the general equations for the expected rate of return and risks of any fixed income security or portfolio of fixed income securities.

The Relationship between Risk and Return

Having defined measures of risk and expected rate of return, we now want to examine the relationship between risk and return.

We assume that the expected rate of return on any portfolio of fixed income securities is a function (which may vary with the level and shape of the yield curve) only of the risks of the portfolio and that it does not otherwise depend on the details of the composition of the portfolio. That is, we assume there exists a function G such that the expected return on a portfolio with risk measures $\sigma_1, \ldots, \sigma_J$ when the ensemble of shift function weights is w is

$$\mu = G(\sigma_1, \ldots, \sigma_J, w) \tag{19.23}$$

Equation (19.23) is not as arbitrary as it may appear. Suppose, contrary to the assumption, that we had two portfolios of fixed income securities with equal values and identical risks but different expected rates of return. We could then form a composite (or "hedged") portfolio with zero net value and zero net risks such that the net value of the portfolio would, with certainty, increase over time. Thus, by the exclusion of riskless arbitrage profits, we can conclude that the function G exists.

In view of the linear dependence of portfolio risk and return on portfolio allocation in equations (19.19) and (19.22), it can be shown (see appendix C in chapter 18) that the function G must be affine with respect to the risk measures or of the form

$$\mu = g_0(w) + \sum_{j=1}^{J} g_j(w) \cdot \sigma_j \tag{19.24}$$

The coefficient g_0 is the expected rate of return on any portfolio with zero risk, where $\sigma_1 = 0, \ldots, \sigma_J = 0$. (It was shown in chapter 18 that g_0 can also be interpreted as the expected rate of return on a spot claim with a vanishingly short maturity or as "the" short-term interest rate.) The coefficient g_j can be interpreted as the "price" (in terms of expected rate of return) of the risk of the jth mode of fluctuation of the spot yield curve.

Equation (19.24) indicates that g_0 and the g_j are functions of the ensemble w of shift function weights. The specific forms of these functions have been derived for one important class of baseline and shift functions. See chapter 18, equation (18.57).

Since equation (19.24) holds for all portfolios of fixed income securities, it must hold in particular for all spot claims. This implies that

$$\mu(t, w; t_m) = g_0(w) + \sum_{j=1}^{J} g_j(w) \cdot \sigma_j(t; t_m) \tag{19.25}$$

where $\mu(t, w; t_m)$ is the expected rate of return at time t on a spot claim maturing at time t_m as set forth at equation (19.16) and where $\sigma_j(t; t_m)$ is the risk of the claim with respect to the jth mode of fluctuation of the spot yield curve as set forth at equation (19.18).

Implications of the Affine Relationship between Risk and Return

The affine relationship between the risks of a spot claim and the expected rate of return on the claim shown in equation (19.25) has two important implications. First, as shown in chapter 18, it implies the validity of the consistency condition in equation (19.7). Second, it implies that an (almost) arbitrary set of $J + 1$ spot claims (where J is the number of shift functions in equation 19.4) can replicate the behavior of all other fixed income securities. We will examine the second implication in some detail and then comment briefly on the significance of the first implication.

Replication

Consider, on the one hand, a fixed income security with an expected rate of return $\hat{\mu}$ and risk measures $\hat{\sigma}_1, \ldots, \hat{\sigma}_J$ and, on the other hand, a set S of $J + 1$ spot claims where the jth claim matures at time t_j for $j = 1, \ldots, J + 1$. We can "replicate" the first security with a portfolio of claims from the set S if we can choose a portfolio with an expected rate of return equal to $\hat{\mu}$ and with risk measures equal to the $\hat{\sigma}_j S$. It turns out that this is (almost) always possible.

From equation (19.24) the expected rate of return on the security is related to the risks of the security as

$$\hat{\mu} = g_0(w) + \sum_{j=1}^{J} g_j(w) \cdot \hat{\sigma}_j \tag{19.26}$$

Similarly the expected rates of return on the spot claims are related to the risks of the claims by equation (19.25):

$$\mu(t, w; t_k) = g_0(w) + \sum_{j=1}^{J} g_j(w) \cdot \sigma_j(t; t_k), \qquad k = 1, \ldots, J + 1 \tag{19.27}$$

Suppose that we find values of $x_1, \ldots, x_{J+1}$ to satisfy the system of simultaneous equations:

$$\begin{bmatrix} \hat{\sigma}_1 \\ \vdots \\ \hat{\sigma}_J \\ 1 \end{bmatrix} = \begin{bmatrix} \sigma_1(t; t_1) & \cdots & \sigma_1(t; t_{J+1}) \\ \vdots & & \vdots \\ \sigma_J(t; t_1) & \cdots & \sigma_J(t; t_{J+1}) \\ 1 & \cdots & 1 \end{bmatrix} \begin{bmatrix} x_1 \\ \vdots \\ x_J \\ x_{J+1} \end{bmatrix} \tag{19.28}$$

That is, we find a portfolio allocation of the claims in the set S such that the allocation weights satisfy the adding-up constraint

$$1 = \sum_{k=1}^{J+1} x_k \tag{19.29}$$

and such that the risks of the portfolio replicate the risks of the fixed income security

$$\hat{\sigma}_j = \sum_{k=1}^{J+1} x_k \cdot \sigma_j(t; t_k), \qquad j = 1, \ldots, J \tag{19.30}$$

This is seen to be a matter of the nonsingularity of the matrix on the right-hand side of equation (19.28).

Assuming that values of $x_1, \ldots, x_{J+1}$ can be found that satisfy equation (19.28), we can compute the expected rate of return on the portfolio by applying equations (19.27), (19.29), (19.30), and (19.26):

$$\sum_{k=1}^{J+1} x_k \cdot \mu(t, w; t_k) = \sum_{k=1}^{J+1} x_k \cdot \left[g_0(w) + \sum_{j=1}^{J} g_j(w) \cdot \sigma_j(t; t_k) \right]$$

$$= g_0(w) \cdot \sum_{k=1}^{J+1} x_k + \sum_{j=1}^{J} g_j(w) \cdot \left[\sum_{k=1}^{J+1} x_k \cdot \sigma_j(t; t_k) \right]$$

$$= g_0(w) + \sum_{j=1}^{J} g_j(w) \cdot \hat{\sigma}_j$$

$$= \hat{\mu} \tag{19.31}$$

Thus the expected rate of return on the portfolio of spot claims will replicate the expected rate of return on the fixed income security.

It follows from this analysis that *any* set of $J + 1$ spot claims for which the matrix of risk factors in equation (19.28) is nonsingular can replicate the risks and expected return on any fixed income security and hence on any portfolio of fixed income securities.

Consistency

We have already observed that equation (19.25) implies that the consistency condition of equation (19.7) is true. The significance of this implication lies in its logical converse.

If equation (19.7) does *not* hold then equation (19.25) must also be false, thereby invalidating equation (19.23) as well. This in turn means that the expected rate of return on a fixed income security depends on the details of the dates and amounts of the future payments of the security as well as on the risks of the security and the level and shape of the yield curve. We will see below that this has important consequences for pricing contingent claims.

19.3   Pricing a Contingent Claim

Up to this point we have set the stage for the analysis of contingent claim valuation by describing the behavior of fixed income securities prices. In particular, we presented a model of the spot yield curve (equation 19.4) and showed how spot claims and other fixed income securities are priced with that model (equations 19.8 and 19.10), we defined the risks and expected rates of return on spot claims and other fixed income securities (equations 19.16, 19.18, 19.19, and 19.22), and we derived a relationship between risk and return (equations 19.24 and 19.25). This section extends the structure of fixed income securities pricing to contingent claims. We begin by setting forth a key assumption concerning the behavior of the price of a contingent claim.

An Assumption

Let C denote the price of a contingent claim such as a call option on a bond. We assume that the only *variables* that can affect the price of the claim are time and the level and shape of the spot yield curve. More specifically, we assume that C is a function of t and the ensemble w of shift function weights:

$$C = C(t, w) \tag{19.32}$$

In writing the price of the contingent claim as a function of t and w, we are *not* saying that nothing else matters. For example, the price of a call option on a bond depends on the option's expiration date and exercise price as well as on whether it can be exercised before expiration (an American option) or only at expiration (a European option). However, these factors are *fixed* for a particular option and are not variable.

On the other hand, the form of equation (19.32) does exclude securities whose prices depend on *variables* other than t and w. Thus we are not here concerned with options on stock or bonds convertible into stock because the market prices of those instruments clearly depend on the prices of the underlying stocks.

Risk and Return for Contingent Claims

Since we have assumed that the price of a contingent claim can be written as a function of t and w, we can construct a linear approximation to the change in the price of the claim over an interval of time Δt when the jth shift weight changes by Δw_j. The approximation has the same form as equation (19.12):

$$\Delta C = \left[\frac{\partial C}{\partial t} + \frac{1}{2} \sum_{j=1}^{J} \frac{\partial^2 C}{\partial w_j^2} \right] \cdot \Delta t + \sum_{j=1}^{J} \frac{\partial C}{\partial w_j} \cdot \Delta w_j \tag{19.33}$$

Reasoning by analogy with the analysis of fixed income securities in section 19.2, we can define the expected short-run rate of return on the contingent claim as

$$\mu^c(t, w) = C^{-1} \cdot \left[\frac{\partial C}{\partial t} + \frac{1}{2} \sum_{j=1}^{J} \frac{\partial^2 C}{\partial w_j^2} \right] \tag{19.34}$$

and we can define the risk of the contingent claim with respect to the jth mode of fluctuation of the spot yield curve as

$$\sigma_j^c(t, w) = -C^{-1} \cdot \frac{\partial C}{\partial w_j}, \qquad j = 1, \dots, J \tag{19.35}$$

These definitions parallel the definitions of the risks and expected rate of return for a fixed income security (see equations 19.14 and 19.15).

The Relationship between Risk and Return for Contingent Claims

The next step in the analysis of contingent claim pricing is to argue that the expected rate of return and the risks of a contingent claim must have the *same affine relationship* as the expected rate of return and the risks of a fixed income security.

As in section 19.2, let $g_0(w)$ denote the expected rate of return on a risk-free fixed income security, and let $g_j(w)$ denote the price of the risk of the jth mode of fluctuation of the spot yield curve. By the exclusion of opportunities for riskless arbitrage, we must have

$$\mu^c(t, w) = g_0(w) + \sum_{j=1}^{J} g_j(w) \cdot \sigma_j^c(t, w) \tag{19.36}$$

The basis for equation (19.36) is not difficult to establish. Suppose that the expected rate of return μ^c is not an affine function of the σ_j^c risk measures as provided in equation (19.36). We could then form a portfolio of $J + 1$ spot claims that has the same value and the same risks as the contingent claim but a different expected rate of return. Going further, we could combine the contingent claim and the portfolio of spot claims into a composite (or "hedged") portfolio with zero net value and zero net risk such that the net value of the composite portfolio would, with certainty, increase over time. Since this would produce riskless arbitrage profits, we can logically exclude the possibility that risk and return for a contingent claim are not related by equation (19.36).

A Characteristic Partial Differential Equation for Contingent Claims

The last step in the analysis of contingent claim pricing is to substitute the definitions of risk and expected rate of return for a contingent claim from equations (19.34) and (19.35) into equation (19.36). Rewriting the result slightly gives the characteristic partial differential equation that must be satisfied by any contingent claim:

$$\frac{\partial C}{\partial t} + \frac{1}{2} \sum_{j=1}^{J} \frac{\partial^2 C}{\partial w_j^2} = g_0(w) \cdot C - \sum_{j=1}^{J} g_j(w) \cdot \frac{\partial C}{\partial w_j} \tag{19.37}$$

This equation states how the variation of the price of a contingent claim with respect to time must be related to the variation of the price of the claim with respect to the level and shape of the spot yield curve. If a particular functional form for $C(t, w)$ does not satisfy equation (19.37), then we can exclude the possibility of ever observing a contingent claim with that price behavior (because the functional form, in violating equation 19.37), admits the possibility of riskless arbitrage profits).

Distinguishing Different Contingent Claims with Boundary Conditions

It might seem odd that a single differential equation characterizes *all* contingent claims. What then distinguishes claims with different terms? Phrased more narrowly, how does the exercise price and expiration date of a call option on a bond affect the price of the option?

Different contingent claims are distinguished by the so-called boundary conditions that particular functional forms for $C(t, w)$ must satisfy in addition to satisfying the partial differential equation of equation (19.37). The role of these boundary conditions can be clarified most easily with an example.

Consider a call option (on a bond) with expiration date t_x that can be exercised at price $E(t)$ at time t on or before the expiration date. (Accrued interest is included in the exercise price.) This specification of the exercise price allows for different exercise prices at different points in time. If the option is a European option, then $E(t)$ will be infinite at all dates prior to the expiration date.

Let K denote the number of future payments on the underlying bond at original issue, where the kth payment is for amount F_k and will be paid at time t_k. Let $\phi(t)$ denote the index number at time t of the *next* payment, so payments $1, 2, \ldots, \phi(t) - 1$ have already been made at time t. The invoice price of the bond at time t when the shift function weights in equation (19.4) have the value of the ensemble w is (from equation 19.10)

$$B(t, w) = \sum_{k=\phi(t)}^{K} F_k \cdot e^{-(t_k - t) \cdot R(t_k - t, w)} \tag{19.38}$$

where the spot yield function R is given by equation (19.9).

The price of the call option as a function of t and w must satisfy the boundary conditions

$$C(t_x, w) = \max[0, B(t_x, w) - E(t_x)] \tag{19.39a}$$

$$C(t, w) \geq \max[0, B(t, w) - E(t)], \qquad t < t_x \tag{19.39b}$$

Equation (19.39a) says that on its expiration date the option must be worth the greater of zero and the excess of the price of the underlying bond over the option's exercise price. Equation (19.39b) says that at dates prior to expiration the option must not be worth less than the greater of zero and the excess of the contemporaneous price of the bond over the option's contemporaneous exercise price. (Note that if the option is European so that $E(t)$ is infinite for all t less than t_x, then equation 19.39b becomes $C(t, w) \geq 0$ for $t < t_x$.)

In general, different contingent claims are distinguished by the different boundary conditions that their price functions must satisfy in addition to satisfying the partial differential equation of equation (19.37).

A Difficulty

As a practical matter it appears to be quite difficult to solve the characteristic partial differential equation of equation (19.37) subject to some specified set of boundary conditions and hence quite difficult to derive a closed form expression for the price of a contingent claim as a function of t and w and the contractual provisions of the claim. This has prompted a search for numerical algorithms for pricing contingent claims. The next three sections describe one such algorithm.

DISCRETE TIME/DISCRETE STATE ANALYSIS

Sections 19.4 through 19.6 examine contingent claim pricing when the level and shape of the spot yield curve vary in discrete shifts through time and when time itself is a discrete variable.

The analysis in section 19.4 considers yield fluctuations in a discrete time/discrete state framework. Section 19.5 shows that the risks and return on a contingent claim over finite intervals of time can be replicated, to a linear approximation, with a portfolio of (almost) any set of $J + 1$ spot claims, where J is the number of modes of fluctuation of the spot yield curve in equation (19.4). The process of replication is turned inside out in section 19.6, where we exhibit a numerical algorithm for pricing a contingent claim.

Section 19.7 illustrates the concepts developed in this chapter by computing the price of a 2-year American call option on a 10-year bond when the spot yield curve has $J = 2$ modes of fluctuation. The example is important because it shows that the price of the option is *not* a well-defined function of only the price of the underlying bond. That is, many different option prices are consistent with a single bond price. This has important implications for hedging options with bonds.

19.4   A Discrete Time/Discrete State Framework

This section presents a framework for describing discrete fluctuations in interest rates over finite intervals of time. As in section 19.1 we assume that the yield at time t on a spot claim maturing at time t_m can be expressed as

$$R(y, w(t)) = R_0(y) + \sum_{j=1}^{J} w_j(t) \cdot f_j(y) \tag{19.40}$$

where $y = t_m - t$ is the time to maturity of the spot claim and $w(t)$ is the ensemble of shift function weights at time t. However, we will now look at the yield curve only at discrete points in time rather than continuously through time. Similarly we will assume the yield curve moves in discrete jumps rather than smoothly and continuously.

Time as a Discrete Variable

Within the discrete time framework we assume that the value of t is of the form $k \cdot \Delta t$, where k is an integer and Δt is any positive real number. More particularly, time moves sequentially through the set $\{\ldots, -2 \cdot \Delta t, -\Delta t, 0, \Delta t, 2 \cdot \Delta t, \ldots\}$.

The quantity Δt is the length of an "epoch" or the length of the interval between two consecutive points in time. In most applications the length of an epoch is a day ($\Delta t = 1/365.25$ years), a week ($\Delta t = 1/52$ years), or a month ($\Delta t = 1/12$ years). It can, however, assume any positive value.

Shift Function Weights as Discrete Variables

Paralleling our discretization of time we assume that the w_j shift function weight for the jth mode of fluctuation is a discrete variable of the form $w_j^0 + k \cdot h$, where w_j^0 is an arbitrary constant, k is an integer, and h is a step-size common to all modes and equal to

$$h = (\Delta t)^{1/2} \tag{19.41}$$

The reason for this choice of h will become evident shortly.

The Lattice of Time and Shift Function Weights

As a result of the discrete structure of time and the shift function weights, we can represent temporal fluctuations in the spot yield curve as the motion of a point in a lattice of dimension $J + 1$. Each point in the lattice is identified by a set of $J + 1$ numbers, $(w_1, w_2, \ldots, w_J, t)$, where t is an integral multiple of Δt and each w_j weight is some arbitrary constant plus an integral multiple of h. Each point represents a spot yield curve with a particular level and shape at a particular point in time.

Movement through the Lattice

Movement through the lattice is subject to two rules. First, as noted above, the value of the time coordinate moves sequentially through the set $\{\ldots, -2 \cdot \Delta t, -\Delta t, 0, \Delta t, 2 \cdot \Delta t, \ldots\}$.

Second, the value of each shift function weight depends (in a random fashion) on its value one epoch earlier:

$$w_j(t + \Delta t) = w_j(t) + \begin{cases} +h \text{ with probability } \frac{1}{2} \\ -h \text{ with probability } \frac{1}{2}, \end{cases} \quad j = 1, \ldots, J \qquad (19.42)$$

This implies that each weight either increases or decreases by one unit of h over each epoch of time.

We also assume that the random changes in the weights are serially and cross-sectionally independent processes. Thus the individual weights follow independent binomial random walks in discrete time. (This can be compared with the statement in section 19.1 that the individual weights follow independent Gaussian random walks in continuous time.)

Statistical Characteristics of Changes in Shift Function Weights

From the stochastic process stated at equation (19.42), it is easy to show that the expected value of the change in a weight over one epoch is

$$\exp[w_j(t + \Delta t) - w_j(t)] = 0, \quad j = 1, \ldots, J$$

and that the variance of the change in a weight over one epoch is

$$\mathrm{var}[w_j(t + \Delta t) - w_j(t)] = h^2, \quad j = 1, \ldots, J$$

The length of an epoch is Δt years, so there are $1/\Delta t$ epochs in each year. It follows from the serial independence of weight changes that the variance of the change in a weight is $h^2/\Delta t$ per year. Since $h = (\Delta t)^{1/2}$, the variance of the change in a weight is unity per year. (This is why we defined $h = (\Delta t)^{1/2}$.)

As the length of an epoch becomes ever smaller, the lattice model of fluctuations in the spot yield curve converges to our continuous time/continuous state model. More particularly, as Δt goes to zero, each binomial random walk with zero drift and unit variance per year converges to a Gaussian random walk with zero drift and unit variance per year.

19.5 Replicating a Contingent Claim with a Portfolio of Spot Claims

To a linear approximation a portfolio of (almost) any set of $J + 1$ spot claims can replicate the risks and return on a contingent claim over an interval of time equal to one epoch. Phrased more loosely, a contingent claim is (to a linear approximation) economically indistinguishable from a portfolio of spot claims. This is an important result because it provides the basis for the pricing algorithm described in the next section.

The Meaning of Replication in a Discrete Time/Discrete State Framework

It may be helpful to begin our analysis with a clear statement of what we mean when we speak of "replicating the risks and return on a contingent claim with a portfolio of spot claims."

Suppose that at some time t we have a contingent claim and a set S of $J + 1$ spot claims (where J is the number of modes of fluctuation of the spot yield curve in equation (19.4). The spot claims have arbitrary (but distinct) maturity dates, denoted $\tau_1, \tau_2, \ldots, \tau_{J+1}$.

We can replicate the contingent claim if we can construct a portfolio of spot claims from the set S such that

1. the value of the portfolio at time t is the same as the price of the contingent claim at time t,

2. the value of the portfolio one epoch later (at time $t + \Delta t$) is the same as the price of the contingent claim one epoch later *regardless* of how the spot yield curve shifts during the epoch.

It should be clear that if we can replicate the contingent claim, then we cannot distinguish (in an economic sense) between the claim and its replicating portfolio.

Some Preliminaries

Before we examine the problem of constructing a replicating portfolio of spot claims, it is necessary to establish some preliminary characteristics of the behavior of the prices of the contingent claim and the spot claims.

Price of the Contingent Claim at Times t and $t + \Delta t$

As in Section 19.3, let $C(t, w)$ denote the price of the contingent claim at time t when the ensemble of shift function weights has the value w.

Define C_0 as the price of the contingent claim at time t so that

$$C_0 = C(t, w(t)) \tag{19.43}$$

and let C_1 denote the price of the contingent claim one epoch later:

$$C_1 = C(t + \Delta t, w(t + \Delta t)) \tag{19.44}$$

Finally, let Δw_j denote the change in the jth shift function weight over the epoch so that $\Delta w_j = w_j(t + \Delta t) - w_j(t)$. Observe that by our assumption on the discrete dynamics of the shift function weights (see equation 19.42), we have

$$\Delta w_j = +h \quad \text{or} \quad -h, \qquad j = 1, \ldots, J \tag{19.45}$$

From the analysis in section 19.3 (see equation 19.33), the relative change in the price of the contingent claim over the epoch can be written, to a linear approximation, as

$$\frac{C_1 - C_0}{C_0} = \mu^c(t, w(t)) \cdot \Delta t - \sum_{j=1}^{J} \sigma_j^c(t, w(t)) \cdot \Delta w_j \tag{19.46}$$

where μ^c is the expected rate of return on the claim (defined at equation 19.34) and σ_j^c is the risk of the claim with respect to the jth mode of fluctuation of the spot yield curve (defined at equation 19.35).

Equation (19.46) implies that to a linear approximation the value of the contingent claim at the end of the epoch is

$$C_1 = C_0 \cdot \left[1 + \mu^c(t, w(t)) \cdot \Delta t - \sum_{j=1}^{J} \sigma_j^c(t, w(t)) \cdot \Delta w_j \right] \tag{19.47}$$

Note that C_1 depends on the length of the epoch and on the realized changes in the shift function weights.

Price of a Spot Claim at Times t and $t + \Delta t$

As in section 19.1, let $P(t, w; \tau_m)$ denote the price of a spot claim at time t when the ensemble of shift function weights has the value w, where the spot claim pays \$100 at time τ_m.

Define P_{0k} as the initial price of the kth spot claim in the set S so that

$$P_{0k} = P(t, w(t); \tau_k), \qquad k = 1, \ldots, J + 1 \tag{19.48}$$

and let P_{1k} denote the price of the same claim one epoch later:

$$P_{1k} = P(t + \Delta t, w(t + \Delta t); \tau_k), \qquad k = 1, \ldots, J + 1 \tag{19.49}$$

From the analysis in section 19.2 (see equation 19.12) the relative change in the price of the kth spot claim over the epoch can be written, to a linear approximation, as

$$\frac{P_{1k} - P_{0k}}{P_{0k}} = \mu(t, w(t); \tau_k) \cdot \Delta t - \sum_{j=1}^{J} \sigma_j(t; \tau_k) \cdot \Delta w_j, \qquad k = 1, \ldots, J + 1 \tag{19.50}$$

where μ is the expected rate of return on the claim (defined at equation 19.14) and σ_j is the risk of the claim with respect to the jth mode of fluctuation of the spot yield curve (defined at equation 19.15).

Equation (19.50) implies that to a linear approximation the value of the kth spot claim at the end of the epoch is

$$P_{1k} = P_{0k} \cdot \left[1 + \mu(t, w(t); \tau_k) \cdot \Delta t - \sum_{j=1}^{J} \sigma_j(t; \tau_k) \cdot \Delta w_j \right], \qquad k = 1, \ldots, J+1$$

$$(19.51)$$

Here again the price of the claim at time $t + \Delta t$ depends on the length of the epoch and the realized changes in the shift function weights.

A Replicating Portfolio of Spot Claims

We are now ready to examine the problem of constructing a portfolio of spot claims to replicate the risks and return on the contingent claim over the epoch from time t to time $t + \Delta t$.

Let Q_k denote the number of units of the kth spot claim in the replicating portfolio. A unit quantity of a spot claim is a promise to pay \$100 at maturity. If $Q_k = 1.2$, then the portfolio includes a spot claim for \$120 payable at time τ_k.

Choose values of $Q_1, \ldots, Q_{J+1}$ to satisfy the equations

$$C_0 = \sum_{k=1}^{J+1} Q_k \cdot P_{0k} \tag{19.52a}$$

$$C_0 \cdot \sigma_j^c(t, w(t)) = \sum_{k=1}^{J+1} Q_k \cdot P_{0k} \cdot \sigma_j(t; \tau_k), \qquad j = 1, \ldots, J \tag{19.52b}$$

Note that this is a system of $J + 1$ linear equations in $J + 1$ unknowns. We will demonstrate that this portfolio replicates, to a linear approximation, the risks and return on the contingent claim.

The easy part of the demonstration is to observe from equation (19.52a) that the value of the portfolio at time t equals the price of the contingent claim at time t.

The hard part of the demonstration is verifying that the value of the portfolio at time $t + \Delta t$ is, to a linear approximation, equal to the price of the contingent claim at time $t + \Delta t$, regardless of how the yield curve shifts during the epoch. To verify this claim, we first need to show that

$$C_0 \cdot \mu^c(t, w(t)) = \sum_{k=1}^{J+1} Q_k \cdot P_{0k} \cdot \mu(t, w(t); \tau_k) \tag{19.53}$$

is a consequence of equations (19.52a,b).

Deriving Equation (19.53)

For the portfolio of spot claims $Q_1, \ldots, Q_{J+1}$ define the fractional value allocation to the kth claim as

$$x_k = \frac{Q_k \cdot P_{0k}}{C_0} = \frac{Q_k \cdot P_{0k}}{\sum_{i=1}^{J+1} Q_i \cdot P_{0i}}, \qquad k = 1, \ldots, J+1 \tag{19.54}$$

Dividing both sides of equations (19.52a,b) by C_0 gives

$$1 = \sum_{k=1}^{J+1} x_k \tag{19.55a}$$

$$\sigma_j^c(t, w(t)) = \sum_{k=1}^{J+1} x_k \cdot \sigma_j(t; \tau_k), \qquad j = 1, \ldots, J \tag{19.55b}$$

From the analysis in section 19.3, the expected rate of return on the contingent claim is an affine function of the risks of the claim (see equation 19.36):

$$\mu^c(t, w(t)) = g_0(w(t)) + \sum_{j=1}^{J} g_j(w(t)) \cdot \sigma_j^c(t, w(t)) \tag{19.56}$$

Substituting the values of σ_j^c from equation (19.55b) into equation (19.56) gives

$$\mu^c(t, w(t)) = g_0(w(t)) + \sum_{j=1}^{J} g_j(w(t)) \cdot \left[\sum_{k=1}^{J+1} x_k \cdot \sigma_j(t; \tau_k) \right]$$

$$= g_0(w(t)) + \sum_{k=1}^{J+1} x_k \cdot \left[\sum_{j=1}^{J} g_j(w(t)) \cdot \sigma_j(t; \tau_k) \right]$$

Using equation (19.55a), this becomes

$$\mu^c(t, w(t)) = \sum_{k=1}^{J+1} x_k \cdot \left[g_0(w(t)) + \sum_{j=1}^{J} g_j(w(t)) \cdot \sigma_j(t; \tau_k) \right]$$

or, from the affine relationship between the expected rate of return on a spot claim and the risks of the claim (see equation 19.27),

$$\mu^c(t, w(t)) = \sum_{k=1}^{J+1} x_k \cdot \mu(t, w(t); \tau_k) \tag{19.57}$$

Multiplying both sides of equation (19.57) by C_0 and observing from equation (19.54) that $x_k \cdot C_0 = Q_k \cdot P_{0k}$ gives equation (19.53).

The Main Result

We can now verify that the value at time $t + \Delta t$ of a portfolio of spot claims which satisfies equations (19.52a,b) is, to a linear approximation, equal to the price of the contingent claim at time $t + \Delta t$ regardless of how the yield curve shifts.

The value of the portfolio at time $t + \Delta t$, denoted V_1, is

$$V_1 = \sum_{k=1}^{J+1} Q_k \cdot P_{1k} \tag{19.58}$$

or, from the approximations of equation (19.51),

$$V_1 = \sum_{k=1}^{J+1} Q_k \cdot P_{0k} \cdot \left[1 + \mu(t, w(t); \tau_k) \cdot \Delta t - \sum_{j=1}^{J} \sigma_j(t; \tau_k) \cdot \Delta w_j \right]$$

$$= \sum_{k=1}^{J+1} Q_k \cdot P_{0k} + \sum_{k=1}^{J+1} Q_k \cdot P_{0k} \cdot \mu(t, w(t); \tau_k) \cdot \Delta t$$

$$- \sum_{j=1}^{J} \left[\sum_{k=1}^{J+1} Q_k \cdot P_{0k} \cdot \sigma_j(t; \tau_k) \cdot \Delta w_j \right]$$

From equations (19.52a,b) and (19.53), this becomes

$$V_1 = C_0 + C_0 \cdot \mu^c(t, w(t)) \cdot \Delta t - \sum_{j=1}^{J} C_0 \cdot \sigma_j^c(t, w(t)) \cdot \Delta w_j$$

or

$$V_1 = C_0 \cdot \left[1 + \mu^c(t, w(t)) \cdot \Delta t - \sum_{j=1}^{J} \sigma_j^c(t, w(t)) \cdot \Delta w_j \right] \tag{19.59}$$

Comparing equations (19.47) and (19.59) shows that to a linear approximation the value V_1 of the portfolio of spot claims at time $t + \Delta t$ equals the price C_1 of the contingent claim at time $t + \Delta t$ regardless of the realized values of $\Delta w_1, \ldots, \Delta w_J$, that is, regardless of how the yield curve shifts.

A Comment

Constructing the replicating portfolio of spot claims requires solving equations (19.52a,b) for $Q_1, \ldots, Q_{J+1}$ or, equivalently, solving equations (19.55a,b) for $x_1, \ldots, x_{J+1}$ or, again equivalently, solving the system of simultaneous linear equations:

$$\begin{bmatrix} \sigma_1^c(t, w(t)) \\ \vdots \\ \sigma_J^c(t, w(t)) \\ 1 \end{bmatrix} = \begin{bmatrix} \sigma_1(t; \tau_1) & \cdots & \sigma_1(t; \tau_{J+1}) \\ \vdots & & \vdots \\ \sigma_J(t; \tau_1) & \cdots & \sigma_J(t; \tau_{J+1}) \\ 1 & \cdots & 1 \end{bmatrix} \begin{bmatrix} x_1 \\ \vdots \\ x_J \\ x_{J+1} \end{bmatrix} \tag{19.60}$$

This is seen to be a matter of the nonsingularity of the matrix on the right-hand side of equation (19.60). Thus *any* set of $J + 1$ spot claims that gives rise to a nonsingular risk matrix at time t can be used to replicate, to a linear approximation, the risks and return on *any* contingent claim over the epoch from time t to time $t + \Delta t$.

Another Comment

The accuracy with which the replicating spot claim portfolio duplicates the prices of the contingent claim at time $t + \Delta t$ depends on the length of an epoch. Specifically, the ratio of (1) the difference between V_1 in equation (19.58) and C_1 in equation (19.44) and (2) the length of an epoch Δt will go to zero as Δt grows small. In mathematical notation,

$$\lim_{\Delta t \to 0} \left[\frac{V_1 - C_1}{\Delta t} \right] = 0 \tag{19.61}$$

Equation (19.61) says that the pricing error associated with the replicating portfolio goes to zero *faster* than the length of an epoch. This follows because the replicating portfolio duplicates the contingent claim to a linear approximation.

19.6   Pricing a Contingent Claim

This section presents an algorithm for pricing a contingent claim in a discrete time/discrete state framework.

Recall from section 19.3 that in a continuous time/continuous state framework the pricing problem is a matter of deriving a *function $C(t, w)$* that satisfies the characteristic partial differential equation for any contingent claim (equation 19.37) and that also satisfies the boundary conditions for the particular claim being priced. In a discrete time/discrete state framework the pricing problem can be viewed as a matter of computing the *value* of that function at times (or values of t) that are integral multiples of Δt and at shift function weights (or values of w_j) that, up to additive constants, are integral multiples of h. We do not have to derive the function itself. We only have to be able to compute its values at different times and ensembles of shift function weights.

We begin our analysis with a more precise statement of the contingent claim pricing problem in a discrete time/discrete state framework and then present an overview of the solution. The balance of the section describes the details of the solution.

A Restatement of the Problem

Assume we are interested in the price of a contingent claim between some initial time t_0 and an expiration date t_x after which the claim ceases to exist. We assume that t_0 and t_x are both integral multiples of the length of an epoch. (The initial date is conventionally assigned the value $t_0 = 0$ and the length of an epoch is chosen such that the ratio $t_x/\Delta t$ is an integer.)

The contingent claim pricing problem is solved if we can compute the price of the claim at all discrete times in the set $\{t_0, t_0 + \Delta t, \ldots, t_x - \Delta t, t_x\}$ and at all shift function weights in the set $\{\ldots, w_j^0 - 2 \cdot h, w_j^0 - h, w_j^0, w_j^0 + h, w_j^0 + 2 \cdot h, \ldots\}$ for $j = 1, \ldots, J$.

Overview of the Solution

The contingent claim pricing problem can be solved by a recursion algorithm proceeding backward in time from the expiration date.

We first show how the contingent claim can be priced at time t_x for all ensembles of shift function weights. We then show that *if* the claim can be priced at time $t + \Delta t$ for all ensembles of shift function weights, *then* it can be priced at time t for all ensembles of shift function weights. It follows by induction that the claim can be priced at all times in the set $\{t_0, t_0 + \Delta t, \ldots, t_x - \Delta t, t_x\}$ for all ensembles of shift function weights.

Pricing the Contingent Claim at the Expiration Date

The price of a contingent claim on its expiration date is established from the boundary conditions that characterize the claim.

For example, in section 19.3 we observed at equation (19.39a) that the price of a call option on a bond on its expiration date is

$$C(t_x, w) = \max[0, B(t_x, w) - E(t_x)] \tag{19.62}$$

The exercise price of the option on the expiration date, denoted $E(t_x)$, is specified by the terms of the option. The contemporaneous price of the underlying bond, denoted $B(t_x, w)$, can be computed from our general equation for the price of a fixed income security (as in equation 19.38).

Pricing the Contingent Claim at Dates prior to Expiration

Assume now that we can compute the price of a contingent claim at time $t + \Delta t$ for any ensemble of shift function weights. We have to show that we can also compute the price of the claim at time t for any ensemble.

Say we want to compute the price of the claim at time t when the ensemble of shift function weights has the value $w(t)^*$. Let C_0 denote this (presently unknown) price.

From the specification of the discrete time/discrete state stochastic dynamics of the shift function weights, we know that the jth weight at time $t + \Delta t$ must be either $w_j(t)^* + h$ or $w_j(t)^* - h$. This implies that there are 2^J values for the ensemble $w(t + \Delta t)$ that can follow the given value of $w(t)^*$. Index these possible ensembles as $i = 1, \ldots, 2^J$, and let C_{1i} denote the (known—by the induction assumption) price of the contingent claim at time $t + \Delta t$ for the ith possible ensemble.

Now choose a set S of $J + 1$ spot claims where the kth spot claim matures at time $\tau_k > t + \Delta t$. The maturity dates are distinct but otherwise arbitrary. Let P_{0k} denote the (known) price of the kth claim at time t when the ensemble of shift function weights has the value $w(t)^*$. Let P_{1ki} denote the (known) price of the kth claim at time $t + \Delta t$ for the ith possible ensemble.

We showed in section 19.5 that there (almost always) exists a replicating portfolio of spot claims from the set S that at time t has a value equal to the price of the contingent claim at time t and that at time $t + \Delta t$ has a value equal, to a linear approximation, to the price of the contingent claim at time $t + \Delta t$ regardless of how the spot yield curve shifts during the epoch. That is, there (almost always) exists a portfolio $Q_1, \ldots, Q_{J+1}$ of spot claims from the set S that satisfies the equation

$$C_0 = \sum_{k=1}^{J+1} Q_k \cdot P_{0k} \tag{19.63}$$

and that, to a linear approximation, also satisfies the equations

$$C_{1i} = \sum_{k=1}^{J+1} Q_k \cdot P_{1ki}, \qquad i = 1, \ldots, 2^J \tag{19.64}$$

If we can identify the values of $Q_1, \ldots, Q_{J+1}$, then we can compute the unknown price C_0 from the known prices $P_{01}, \ldots, P_{0,J+1}$ with equation (19.63).

The composition of the replicating portfolio can be established by computing an approximate solution to equation (19.64). (Note that, by assumption, all of the C_{1i} prices and all of the P_{1ki} prices in equation 19.64 are known.) Define the vectors

$$C_1 = \begin{bmatrix} C_{1,1} \\ \vdots \\ C_{1,2}^J \end{bmatrix}, \quad Q = \begin{bmatrix} Q_1 \\ \vdots \\ Q_{J+1} \end{bmatrix} \tag{19.65a}$$

and the matrix

$$P_1 = \begin{bmatrix} P_{1,1,1} & \cdots & P_{1,J+1,1} \\ \vdots & & \vdots \\ P_{1,1,2}^J & \cdots & P_{1,J+1,2}^J \end{bmatrix} \tag{19.65b}$$

so that equation (19.64) can be written

$$C_1 = P_1 \cdot Q \tag{19.66}$$

The portfolio that "solves" equation (19.66) with minimum mean square error is

$$\hat{Q} = (P_1' \cdot P_1)^{-1} \cdot P_1' \cdot C_1 \tag{19.67}$$

We approximate C_0 with the value $\hat{C}_0$ of the portfolio in equation (19.67) at time t:

$$\hat{C}_0 = \sum_{k=1}^{J+1} \hat{Q}_k \cdot P_{0k} \tag{19.68}$$

Observe that as the length of an epoch goes to zero, the portfolio in equation (19.67) will converge to the portfolio that satisfies equations (19.52a,b) so that $\hat{C}_0$ will converge to $C_0 = C(t, w(t)^*)$ as desired.

Boundary Conditions Prior to Expiration

The foregoing algorithm must be modified in one respect if the contingent claim is characterized by boundary conditions at times prior to expiration.

Suppose, for example, that the contingent claim is an American call option on a bond with exercise price $E(t)$ at time t. We observed at equation (19.39b) in section 19.3 that the price of the option must satisfy the inequality

$$C(t, w) \geq \max[0, B(t, w) - E(t)], \qquad t < t_x \tag{19.69}$$

where $B(t, w)$ is the price of the underlying bond at time t when the ensemble of shift function weights has the value w. It follows that we should then approximate the value of C_0 as

$$\hat{\hat{C}}_0 = \max[0, B(t, w(t)^*) - E(t), \hat{C}_0] \tag{19.70}$$

where $\hat{C}_0$ is as given in equation (19.68).

A Comment on the Consistency Condition

As a computational matter the pricing algorithm described in this section can be implemented for *any* baseline function R_0 and for *any* set of shift functions $f_1, \ldots, f_J$ in the model of the yield curve given in equation (19.4). However, if those functions do not satisfy the consistency condition of equation (19.7), then we know that the choice of baseline and shift functions allows riskless arbitrage profits. More particularly, the expected rate of return on a portfolio of spot claims will depend on the details of the composition of the portfolio as well as on the risks of the portfolio. This implies that the calculated prices of a contingent claim will depend on the particular choices of spot claims in the set S at each point in time and at each ensemble of shift function weights. More generally, the price of the contingent claim will not be a well-defined function of only time and the level and shape of the spot yield curve. This of course invalidates the key assumption of section 19.3 that we can write the price of the contingent claim as $C(t, w)$.

19.7   An Illustrative Example

This section illustrates the ideas presented above by pricing a 2 year call option on a 10 year bond when the spot yield curve has two modes of fluctuation. The most interesting result is that the price of the option is not a well-defined function of the price of the underlying bond. This implies that the risks of a position in the option can not be hedged completely with a position in the bond alone.

The Bond and the Option

We assume the bond has 10.0 years remaining to maturity at time $t_0 = 0$ and that it has a coupon of 10% per annum, payable semi-annually. Thus the bond pays interest equal to 5% of its principal value at .5 years, 1.0 years, and so on, to 10.0 years.

The call option expires at time $t_x = 2.0$ years. It can be exercised at any time prior to expiration at a price equal to 100% of the principal value of the bond plus accrued interest to the exercise date. Interest accrues linearly between coupon payments.

The Spot Yield Curve

We assume that the spot yield curve has $J = 2$ modes of fluctuation. This value was chosen for simplicity of exposition rather than realism. In fact, it was suggested in chapter 18 that the spot Treasury yield curve may have at least four quantitatively significant modes of fluctuation.

We further assume that the baseline function $R_0(y)$ is a polynomial with I' coefficients and that the shift functions $f_1(y)$ and $f_2(y)$ are both polynomials with I coefficients. It was shown in chapter 18 that the consistency condition requires $I = J$ and $I' = 2 \cdot I + 1$, so we have $I = 2$ and $I' = 5$ in our example.

More specifically, we assume that the baseline function is

$$R_0(y) = .78989 \cdot 10^{-1} + .43087 \cdot 10^{-2} \cdot y$$
$$- .22537 \cdot 10^{-3} \cdot y^2 + .72530 \cdot 10^{-6} \cdot y^3$$
$$- .11572 \cdot 10^{-6} \cdot y^4 \tag{19.71}$$

This function is shown in figure 19.1 for values of y out to 10 years. The baseline function is positively sloped and convex, as has been characteristic of the U.S. Treasury yield curve at most recent points in time. Note that yields are measured as a fraction per annum, so $R_0(y) = .09$ is equivalent to a yield of 9% per annum, compounded continuously.

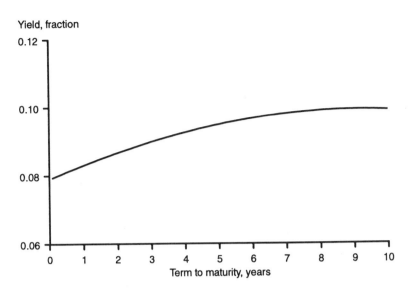

Figure 19.1
Baseline function from equation (19.71)

The shift functions, shown in figure 19.2, are

$$f_1(y) = .12318 \cdot 10^{-1} + .18519 \cdot 10^{-3} \cdot y \qquad (19.72a)$$

$$f_2(y) = -.48905 \cdot 10^{-2} + .10597 \cdot 10^{-2} \cdot y \qquad (19.72b)$$

The first shift function is, essentially, a parallel shift of the level of the yield curve. Higher values of w_1 imply a higher curve, and lower values of w_1 imply a lower curve. The second shift function is a shift in the slope of the yield curve. Higher values of w_2 imply a steeper curve with lower short-term yields and higher long-term yields. Lower values of w_2 imply a flatter, or even negatively sloped, curve.

It should be noted the baseline function and the two shift functions cannot be specified independently. As noted above, the consistency condition requires that $I = J$ and $I' = 2 \cdot I + 1$. The consistency condition also links the high-order coefficients of the baseline function to the coefficients of the shift functions. This linkage was derived in chapter 18. Equations (19.71) and (19.72a,b) satisfy all of the conditions imposed by the consistency condition.

We have presented only qualitative justifications for our illustrative baseline and shift functions: The baseline function is positively sloped and convex, and the shift functions reflect changes in the level and slope of the yield curve, respectively. No further justification is needed for our present purposes. Chapter 18 discusses several aspects of the problem of

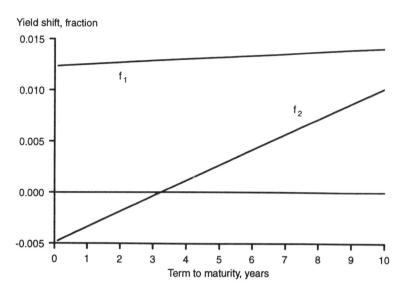

Figure 19.2
Shift functions from equations (19.72a,b)

estimating from empirical data baseline and shift functions that satisfy the consistency condition.

Spot Yield Curves at Time t_0

We are interested in pricing the bond and the call option on the bond at a variety of different spot yield curves at time t_0. It will therefore be helpful to have some way of representing systematically the spectrum of possible initial curves.

In general, the yield on a spot claim with y years to maturity at time t_0 when the shift function weights have the values $w_1(t_0)$ and $w_2(t_0)$ is

$$R(y, w(t_0)) = R_0(y) + w_1(t_0) \cdot f_1(y) + w_2(t_0) \cdot f_2(y) \qquad (19.73)$$

where $R_0(y)$ is the polynomial in equation (19.71) and $f_1(y)$ and $f_2(y)$ are the polynomials in equations (19.72a,b).

Figure 19.3 shows several different spot yield curves at time t_0. Curve A corresponds to the case where $w_1(t_0) = 0$ and $w_2(t_0) = 0$ in equation (19.73), or where the initial spot yield curve is just the baseline function $R_0(y)$. Curve B corresponds to the case where $w_1(t_0) = 1$ and $w_2(t_0) = 0$. This is essentially an upward parallel shift of curve A. Curve C is the case where $w_1(t_0) = -1$ and $w_2(t_0) = 0$ and is a downward parallel shift of curve A.

Figure 19.4 shows a different set of initial spot yield curves. Curve A is the baseline function as in figure 19.3. Curve D corresponds to the case

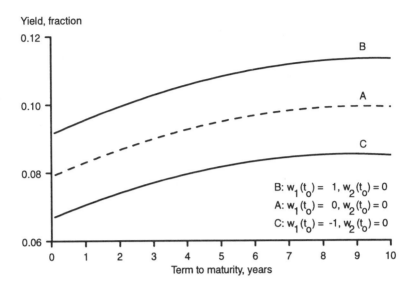

Figure 19.3
Several spot yield curves at time t_0

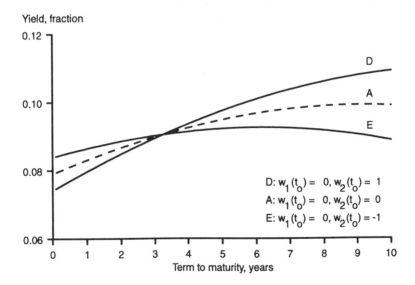

Figure 19.4
Several spot yield curves at time t_0

where $w_1(t_0) = 0$ and $w_2(t_0) = 1$ and is a steeper curve. Curve E is a flatter curve where $w_1(t_0) = 0$ and $w_2(t_0) = -1$.

It should be clear that each choice of the shift function weights $w_1(t_0)$ and $w_2(t_0)$ in equation (19.73) leads to a unique spot yield curve at time t_0. Larger values of $w_1(t_0)$ imply higher curves, and larger values of $w_2(t_0)$ imply curves with steeper slopes.

It will be convenient to represent a particular choice of initial shift function weights on a coordinate grid like figure 19.5. The value of $w_1(t_0)$ is plotted along the horizontal axis, and the value of $w_2(t_0)$ is plotted along the vertical axis of that figure. The points labeled A, B, C, D, and E identify the shift function weights that produced the similarly labeled spot yield curves in figures 19.3 and 19.4. Movement from left to right in figure 19.5, such as from points C to A to B, reflects a higher initial curve. Movement from bottom to top, such as from point E to A to D, reflects a steeper curve.

Bond Prices at Time t_0

Pricing the 10-year 10% bond at time t_0 is a simple problem in computing the price of a fixed income security.

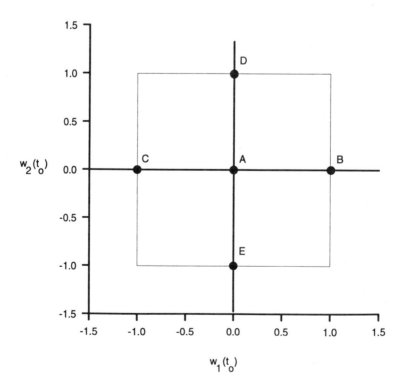

Figure 19.5
Grid of shift function weights at time t_0

Let $B(t_0, w(t_0))$ denote the price of the bond as a percent of principal value at time t_0 when the ensemble of shift function weights has the value $w(t_0)$. We then have

$$B(t_0, w(t_0)) = \sum_{k=1}^{20} 5 \cdot e^{-(\tau_k - t_0) \cdot R(\tau_k - t_0, w(t_0))}$$

$$+ 100 \cdot e^{-(\tau_{20} - t_0) \cdot R(\tau_{20} - t_0, w(t_0))} \tag{19.74}$$

where $t_0 = 0$, $\tau_1 = .5$, $\tau_2 = 1.0, \ldots, \tau_{20} = 10.0$, and where the function R is as given in equation (19.73). This follows because the bond pays 20 semi-annual coupons of 5% of principal and repays principal at maturity.

With equation (19.74) we can calculate the price of the bond at time t_0 for any initial spot yield curve or for any choice of $w_1(t_0)$ and $w_2(t_0)$. Figure 19.6 shows that the variation in price as $w_1(t_0)$ and $w_2(t_0)$ vary within the unit box of figure 19.5, where $|w_1(t_0)| \leq 1.0$ and $|w_2(t_0)| \leq 1.0$. The points labeled A, B, C, D, and E in figure 19.6 correspond to the similarly labeled points in figure 19.5 and to the similarly labeled yield

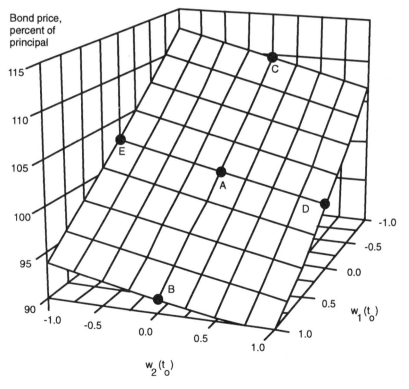

Figure 19.6
Price of the 10-year 10% bond at time t_0 as a function of the initial shift function weights

curves in figure 19.3 and 19.4. The constant term in the baseline function of equation (19.71) was chosen so that the bond has a price of par, or 100.0, when $w_1(t_0) = 0$ and $w_2(t_0) = 0$ (point A).

Figure 19.6 shows that the price of the bond rises as the level of the yield curve falls (or as $w_1(t_0)$ moves from $+1.0$ to -1.0; compare points B, A, and C). The figure also shows that the price of the bond rises (albeit not as rapidly) as the curve flattens (or as $w_2(t_0)$ moves from $+1.0$ to -1.0; compare points D, A, and E). Note finally that the pricing surface in figure 19.6 has no visible curvature, so the price of the bond is very nearly an affine function of the shift function weights within the unit box of figure 19.5.

Call Option Prices at Time t_0

Pricing the 2-year American call option on the 10-year bond at time t_0 is not simple but can be accomplished with the algorithm described in section 19.6.

Figure 19.7 shows the price of the option (expressed as a percent of the principal value of the bond) as $w_1(t_0)$ and $w_2(t_0)$ vary within the dotted box of figure 19.5. The figure shows that the price of the option rises as the level of the spot yield curve falls (or as $w_1(t_0)$ moves from $+1.0$ to -1.0; compare points B, A, and C). The price also rises as the curve flattens (or as $w_2(t_0)$ moves from $+1.0$ to -1.0; compare points D, A, and E). These variations in option price with respect to change in the level and slope of the curve are qualitatively similar to the variations in the price of the bond observed in figure 19.6.

The option pricing surface in figure 19.7 exhibits significant curvature with respect to change in the level of the yield curve but virtually no curvature with respect to change in the slope of the curve.

Joint Variation in Bond and Call Option Prices at Time t_0

Thus far we have examined how the price of the 10-year bond and the price of the call option on that bond vary with the level and slope of the spot yield curve at time t_0. Most important, both prices rise as the curve falls or flattens.

We now want to examine the *joint* variation in the price of the bond and the price of the call option as a function of the level and slope of the yield curve. In particular, we want to examine whether a *unique* option price is associated with each different bond price.

The easiest way to address this issue is to construct "iso-bond price curves" on the grid in figure 19.5. Each curve represents the set of initial shift function weights that leads to a given price for the bond. Five such

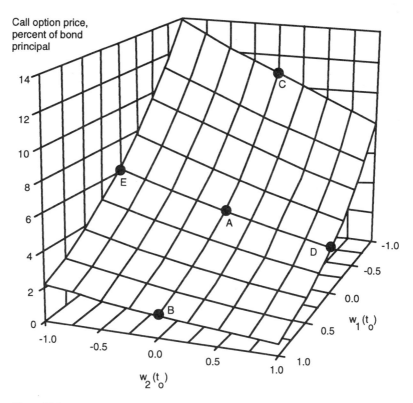

Figure 19.7
Price of the 2-year American call option at time t_0 as a function of the initial shift function weights

curves are shown in figure 19.8. All of the $w_1(t_0)$ and $w_2(t_0)$ combinations along curve **a** produce a bond price at time t_0 equal to 109.56 percent of principal value. Similarly all of the combinations along curve **d** produce a bond price of 95.63% of principal value. Figure 19.8 shows that the price of the bond remains unchanged if the yield curve flattens (as a result of a declining value of $w_2(t_0)$) as it rises (as a result of a rising value of $w_1(t_0)$). That is, the iso-bond price curves run from northwest to southeast.

Now suppose that we look at the behavior of the price of the call option at different initial shift function weights on a *common* iso-bond price curve. Figure 19.9 shows that the option has a price of 10.4% of the principal value of the bond at point a_1 and a price of 11.2% of the principal value of the bond at point a_2. Thus the option becomes more valuable (even while the price of the bond remains unchanged) as the yield curve rises and flattens or as the initial shift function weights move from point a_1 to point a_2 along curve **a**. The same pattern is repeated along each of the iso-bond price curves in figure 19.9.

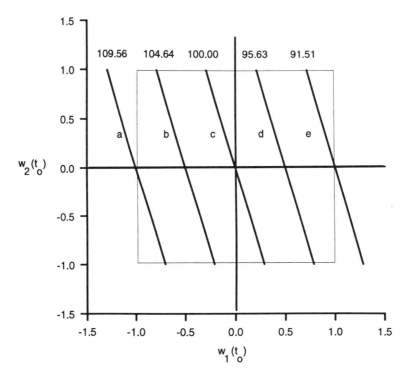

Figure 19.8
Five iso-bond price curves at time t_0

The foregoing analysis shows that the price of the call option is *not* a well-defined (or single-valued) function of only the price of the underlying bond. This implies that the yield curve can shift in ways that change the price of the option while leaving the price of the bond unchanged, and in ways that change the price of the bond while leaving the price of the option unchanged. It also implies that there are shifts in the yield curve that will increase the price of the option while decreasing the price of the bond, and vice versa.

These results further show that, for example, a long position in a bond cannot hedge away all of the risks associated with a short position in a call option on that bond. More particularly, "delta-neutral" hedging of a yield-dependent contingent claim with the underlying bond is a hedging strategy built on false premises.

19.8   Conclusions

This chapter has addressed several analytical and computational aspects of pricing claims whose payments (or payoffs) depend on fluctuations in

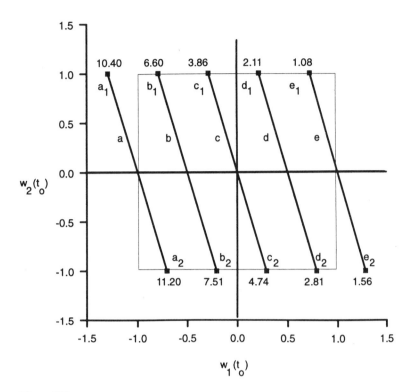

Figure 19.9
Prices of the 2-year American call option at time t_0 at selected points on five iso-bond price curves

interest rates. First, we introduced a model of the spot yield curve, defined measures of risk and expected return for spot claims, and characterized the relationship between risk and return. These results provided the foundation for analyzing the behavior of contingent claim prices and for deriving the characteristic partial differential equation of a contingent claim.

Since the differential equation is difficult to solve, we examined a numerical pricing algorithm. The basis of the algorithm is the observation that a portfolio of (almost) any set of $J + 1$ spot claims can replicate exactly the risks and expected return on a contingent claim in continuous time and hence can replicate to a linear approximation the risks and expected return on a contingent claim in discrete time.

The chapter concluded with a quantitative example of contingent claim pricing. We showed that the premise of delta-neutral hedging (that the price of an option is a well-defined function of the price of the underlying asset) is open to question in even a simple model of the spot yield curve with just two modes of fluctuation.

It should be noted that the analysis in this chapter is a natural extension of the results reported in chapter 18. Realistic analysis of yield-dependent contingent claims has to be based on models of the yield curve that are flexible and allow a close representation of empirically observed curves, have a rich set of possible future curves, and are specified to be free of opportunities for riskless arbitrage profits. Chapter 18 addressed these three issues and thereby laid the foundation for the present analysis.

19.9   Subsequent Remarks

The algorithm for computing the price of a contingent claim developed in this chapter relies on the model of the spot yield curve presented in chapter 18 and is consequently burdened with the problems of that model. In particular, as the length of an epoch Δt goes to zero in the discrete time/ discrete state framework, it becomes virtually certain that some yield curves examined by the algorithm at times prior to expiration of a contingent claim will exhibit negative interest rates. Negative interest rates do not present a computational problem, but they are inconsistent with the exclusion of riskless profits in the absence of a commitment of capital. (If interest rates were negative a market participant could borrow, e.g., \$110 against promising to repay \$100 in one year, maintain the borrowing in currency, and make a riskless profit of \$10 at the end of the year.) Thus the valuation procedure does not completely exclude riskless arbitrage profits. The only response to this criticism is the observation that the probability of evolving to a yield curve with negative interest rates is small if initial yields are not near zero and if the contingent claim does not have a long time remaining to expiration, implying the pricing error caused by the misspecification of the model is also small.

In addition the valuation procedure presented in this chapter assumes that the shift functions $f_1(y), \ldots, f_J(y)$ are stationary through time. (More particularly, it assumes that they are stationary until at least the expiration of the contingent claim.) Evidence presented in the next chapter suggests that this assumption is not justified.

20

Time Variation in the Modes of Fluctuation of the Spot Treasury Yield Curve

So far we have examined the decomposition of shifts in the yield curve into a small number of statistically independent modes of fluctuation. Chapters 17 through 19 assumed that the modes were stationary through time.

This chapter addresses the issue of time variation in the modes of fluctuation of the yield curve. We find that over the interval from January 1984 to mid-1990 the ways in which the yield curve fluctuated varied rapidly and significantly. This raises serious questions about the usefulness (for pricing contingent claim contracts) of models of interest rate variation that exhibit stationary modes of fluctuation. (See chapter 19 for an example of such a model.)

Section 20.1 begins our appraisal of time variation in the modes of fluctuation of the yield curve by presenting a model of the spot yield curve. Section 20.2 estimates the modes of fluctuation of the model under the assumption that the modes were stationary over the sample interval. Section 20.3 reestimates the modes without imposing the assumption of stationarity.

20.1 A Model of the Spot Yield Curve with Stationary Modes of Fluctuation

A spot claim is a promise to pay a specified amount of money on a single specified date in the future. This section describes yields on spot claims and presents a model of the spot yield curve.

Spot Yields

A spot yield is a discount rate used to compute the present value, or market price, of a spot claim. Consider, for example, a spot claim for $100 payable in $y = 4$ years. If the yield on the claim is $R = 10\%$ per annum, compounded semi-annually, its present value is

$$
\begin{aligned}
P &= 100 \cdot \left(1 + \frac{R}{2}\right)^{-2 \cdot y} \\
&= 100 \cdot \left(1 + \frac{.10}{2}\right)^{-2 \cdot 4} \\
&= 67.6839
\end{aligned}
\tag{20.1}
$$

Written in October 1989 and November 1990. This chapter combines two separate papers authored by Kenneth Baron and Kenneth Garbade. The appendix was written by Kenneth Baron and has benefited from contributions by Tom Daula.

Continuous Compounding

For purposes of this chapter we measure the yield on a spot claim with continuous rather than semi-annual compounding. The continuously compounded yield on a spo' claim priced at $P = \$67.6839$ for $100 payable in $y = 4$ years is the value of R which satisfies the equation:

$$P = 100 \cdot e^{-y \cdot R} \tag{20.2}$$

or

$$R = y^{-1} \cdot \ln\left[\frac{100}{P}\right]$$

$$= 4^{-1} \cdot \ln\left[\frac{100}{67.6839}\right]$$

$$= .097580, \text{ or } 9.7580\% \text{ per annum, compounded continuously} \tag{20.3}$$

The Spot Yield Curve

A spot yield curve is a function which describes how the yield R on a spot claim varies with the time y remaining to payment of the claim, where R is measured in percent per annum, compounded continuously, and y is measured in years.

A Model of the Spot Yield Curve

Our basic model of the spot yield curve assumes that at any point in time the curve can be expressed in the form

$$R(y, w) = R_0(y) + \sum_{j=1}^{J} w_j \cdot f_j(y) \tag{20.4}$$

where $R_0(y)$ and $f_1(y), \ldots, f_J(y)$ are known *time-invariant* functions of maturity and where $w_1, \ldots, w_J$ are scalar coefficients. The ensemble, or vector, of coefficients is denoted w.

    Equation (20.4) says that the yield curve can be constructed as a baseline function $R_0(y)$ plus a linear combination of shift functions $f_1(y), \ldots, f_J(y)$. The weight, or coefficient, on the jth shift function is w_j.

Temporal Variation in the Spot Yield Curve

The yield curve in equation (20.4) varies over time in shape as well as level as a result of temporal variation in the w_j weights. We assume that each weight evolves as a Gaussian random walk with zero drift and a variance of unity per year and that change in one weight is uncorrelated with changes in other weights; that is, the random walks are statistically independent of each other. We will write the jth weight as $w_j(t)$ and the ensemble of weights as $w(t)$ to emphasize this temporal variation.

It is useful to explore the implications of the temporal behavior of the w_j weights in further detail. Consider two points in time, denoted t_0 and t_1, where $t_0 < t_1$. The change in yield from time t_0 to time t_1 at a term of y years is $R(y, w(t_1)) - R(y, w(t_0))$. Using equation (20.4), we have

$$R(y, w(t_1)) - R(y, w(t_0))$$

$$= R_0(y) + \sum_{j=1}^{J} w_j(t_1) \cdot f_j(y) - R_0(y) - \sum_{j=1}^{J} w_j(t_0) \cdot f_j(y)$$

$$= \sum_{j=1}^{J} (w_j(t_1) - w_j(t_0)) \cdot f_j(y) \qquad (20.5)$$

Thus the shift in the yield curve from time t_0 to time t_1 is a linear combination of the f_j shift functions, where the coefficients in the linear combination are the *changes* in the w_j weights from time t_0 to time t_1.

From our assumption on the behavior of the w_j weights, we have that the changes in the weights from time t_0 to time t_1 are normally distributed with the characteristics

$$\exp[w_j(t_1) - w_j(t_0)] = 0, \qquad j > 1, \ldots, J \qquad (20.6\text{a})$$

$$\mathrm{var}[w_j(t_1) - w_j(t_0)] = t_1 - t_0, \qquad j = 1, \ldots, J \qquad (20.6\text{b})$$

$$\mathrm{cov}[w_j(t_1) - w_j(t_0), w_k(t_1) - w_k(t_0)] = 0, \qquad j = 1, \ldots, J$$
$$k = 1, \ldots, J$$
$$k \neq j \qquad (20.6\text{c})$$

Thus the f_j shift functions represent trendless (see equation 20.6a), normalized (see equation 20.6b), and statistically independent (see equation 20.6c) *modes of fluctuation* of the spot yield curve. Since the f_j functions are time invariant, equation (20.4) is a model of the spot yield curve with stationary modes of fluctuation.

The key question addressed in this chapter is whether the spot Treasury yield curve exhibited stationary modes of fluctuation over the interval from January 1984 to June 1990.

20.2   Estimating Stationary Modes of Fluctuation

Our analysis of time variation in the modes of fluctuation of the spot Treasury yield curve begins with a special case: What are the modes of fluctuation under the maintained hypothesis that the modes are stationary? This special case is important for two reasons. First, it provides a benchmark for addressing the more general problem of time variation in the modes of fluctuation. Second, it gives us the opportunity to develop an estimation methodology in a simple setting.

We begin the analysis of the special case by making the simplifying assumption that the modes of fluctuation are polynomial functions of maturity. We then show how the coefficients of the polynomials can be estimated from observed changes in interest rates. The estimation methodology is illustrated with data on spot Treasury yields at semi-annual maturities from 6 months to 10 years (derived from yields on par Treasury bonds) on one business day (usually Thursday) each week between January 5, 1984, and June 28, 1990. Chapter 10 described the methodology for constructing spot yields from data on actual bonds.

Polynomial Shift Functions

We assume that each of the f_j shift functions is a polynomial function of maturity with I coefficients. More particularly, we assume that

$$f_j(y) = \sum_{i=1}^{I} b_{ij} \cdot y^{i-1}, \qquad j = 1, \dots, J \tag{20.7}$$

Assuming that the f_j shift functions are stationary is equivalent to assuming that the b_{ij} coefficients of the polynomials in equation (20.7) are constant through time.

Shifts in the Yield Curve as Polynomial Functions

Given our assumption in equation (20.7) on the polynomial structure of the shift functions, it is easy to show that the shift in the yield curve from time t_0 to time t_1 is also a polynomial function of maturity.

From equation (20.5) the shift in the yield curve from time t_0 to time t_1 is

$$R(y, w(t_1)) - R(y, w(t_0)) = \sum_{j=1}^{J} (w_j(t_1) - w_j(t_0)) \cdot f_j(y) \tag{20.8}$$

Replacing the f_j shift functions in equation (20.8) with the polynomials in equation (20.7) gives

$$R(y, w(t_1)) - R(y, w(t_0)) = \sum_{j=1}^{J} \left[(w_j(t_1) - w_j(t_0)) \cdot \sum_{i=1}^{I} b_{ij} \cdot y^{i-1} \right]$$

$$= \sum_{i=1}^{I} \left[\sum_{j=1}^{J} b_{ij} \cdot (w_j(t_1) - w_j(t_0)) \right] \cdot y^{i-1} \tag{20.9}$$

Equation (20.9) says that the shift in the yield curve from time t_0 to time t_1 is a polynomial with I coefficients.

Estimating the Coefficients of the Shift Function Polynomials

We are now ready to examine the problem of estimating the b_{ij} coefficients of the shift function polynomials in equation (20.7). Suppose that we have data on H spot yields at semi-annual maturities (denoted $y_1, y_2, \ldots, y_H$) for each date in a sequence of $K + 1$ weekly dates (denoted $t_0, t_1, \ldots, t_K$). $R(y_h, t_k)$ denotes the continuously compounded yield observed at time t_k on a spot claim with y_h years remaining to maturity.

From equation (20.9) we write

$$\Delta R(y_h, t_k) = \sum_{i=1}^{I} \left[\sum_{j=1}^{J} b_{ij} \cdot \Delta w_j(t_k) \right] \cdot y_h^{i-1}, \qquad h = 1, \ldots, H; k = 1, \ldots, K \tag{20.10}$$

where $\Delta R(y_h, t_k)$ is the observed change in yield from time t_{k-1} to time t_k at a term of y_h years and where $\Delta w_j(t_k)$ is the unobserved change in the jth weighting coefficient from time t_{k-1} to time t_k. Defining the symbol $\Delta a_i(t_k)$,

$$\Delta a_i(t_k) = \sum_{j=1}^{J} b_{ij} \cdot \Delta w_j(t_k), \qquad i = 1, \ldots, I; k = 1, \ldots, K \tag{20.11}$$

we rewrite equation (20.10) as

$$\Delta R(y_h, t_k) = \sum_{i=1}^{I} \Delta a_i(t_k) \cdot y_h^{i-1}, \qquad h = 1, \ldots, H; k = 1, \ldots, K \tag{20.12}$$

Equation (20.12) expresses the change in yield from time t_{k-1} to time t_k at a term of y_h years as a polynomial function of y_h. The $\Delta a_i(t_k)$ terms are the coefficients of the polynomial. These coefficients are quite important to the estimation of the b_{ij}. We will call them "reduced shift coefficients."

Estimating the Time Series of Reduced Shift Coefficients

For each date in our data set from t_1 to t_K the reduced shift coefficients $\Delta a_1(t_k), \ldots, \Delta a_I(t_k)$ in equation (20.12) can be estimated with conventional regression techniques.

For example, for the interval from t_{k-1} = December 1, 1988, to t_k = December 8, 1988 we estimated (with $I = 3$)

$$\widehat{\Delta a_1}(t_k) = .2408 \tag{20.13a}$$

$$\widehat{\Delta a_2}(t_k) = -.03837 \tag{20.13b}$$

$$\widehat{\Delta a_3}(t_k) = .001332 \tag{20.13c}$$

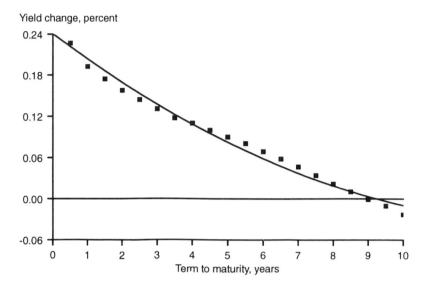

Figure 20.1
Estimated yield shift function (line) and observed changes in spot Treasury yields (boxes) for the interval from December 1, 1988, to December 8, 1988

so the yield shift function over that interval can be written

$$\Delta R(y, t_k) = .2408 - .03837 \cdot y + .001332 \cdot y^2 \tag{20.14}$$

Figure 20.1 shows the values of this function over a range of maturities up to ten years and also the actual spot yield changes over the same week. The standard error of estimate of the yield shift function in figure 20.1 is .0065% or .65 basis points.

Figure 20.2 shows comparable standard errors for each weekly interval from January 1984 to June 1990. We were generally able to fit observed spot Treasury yield changes to within a standard error of about 1 or 2 basis points. This implies that a simple quadratic structure ($I = 3$) provides a good representation of weekly changes in Treasury yields.

The Covariance Matrix of the Reduced Shift Coefficients

The next step in estimating the coefficients of the shift function polynomials is using the time series of reduced shift coefficients to estimate the covariance matrix of those coefficients.

At this point it will be convenient to switch to vector notation. Let

$$\Delta a(t_k) = \begin{bmatrix} \Delta a_1(t_k) \\ \vdots \\ \Delta a_I(t_k) \end{bmatrix}, \qquad k = 1, \ldots, K \tag{20.15a}$$

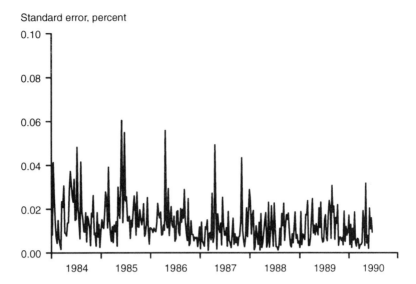

Figure 20.2
Standard errors of fit for equation (20.12), $I = 3$

$$B = \begin{bmatrix} b_{11} & \cdots & b_{1J} \\ \vdots & & \vdots \\ b_{I1} & \cdots & b_{IJ} \end{bmatrix} \tag{20.15b}$$

$$\Delta w(t_k) = \begin{bmatrix} \Delta w_1(t_k) \\ \vdots \\ \Delta w_J(t_k) \end{bmatrix}, \qquad k = 1, \ldots, K \tag{20.15c}$$

Equation (20.11) can then be rewritten as

$$\Delta a(t_k) = B \cdot \Delta w(t_k), \qquad k = 1, \ldots, K \tag{20.16}$$

We assumed in section 20.1 that each of the w_j shift function weights follows a Gaussian random walk with zero drift and a variance of unity per year and that the random walks are statistically independent of each other. Recalling that we are here concerned with weekly intervals, it follows that the $\Delta w(t_k)$ vector defined in equation (20.15c) has an expected value of zero and a covariance matrix of $52^{-1} \cdot \Phi_J$, where Φ_J is the $J \times J$ identity matrix.

The covariance matrix of the $\Delta a(t_k)$ vector, denoted $\Omega_{\Delta a}$, follows from equation (20.16):

$$\Omega_{\Delta a} = 52^{-1} \cdot B \cdot B' \tag{20.17}$$

The important feature of equation (20.17) is that the covariance matrix $\Omega_{\Delta a}$

Table 20.1
Standard deviations and correlations of reduced shift coefficients, over weekly intervals, January 5, 1984, to June 28, 1990, excluding the week of October 15 to October 22, 1987

	Coefficient		
	Δa_1	Δa_2	Δa_3
Standard deviation	.1567	.0328	.00221
Correlation with			
Δa_1	1.00	−.13	−.02
Δa_2	−.13	1.00	−.96
Δa_3	−.02	−.96	1.00

is stationary if the B matrix of coefficients of the shift function polynomials is stationary.

We can estimate the covariance matrix $\Omega_{\Delta a}$ with the time series estimates $\widehat{\Delta a}(t_1), \ldots, \widehat{\Delta a}(t_K)$ of the reduced shift coefficients. In the case where $\Omega_{\Delta a}$ is stationary, the estimate of the covariance matrix can be computed as

$$\hat{\Omega}_{\Delta a} = K^{-1} \cdot \sum_{k=1}^{K} \widehat{\Delta a}(t_k) \cdot \widehat{\Delta a}(t_k)' \tag{20.18}$$

Table 20.1 shows the standard deviations and correlations of $\hat{\Omega}_{\Delta a}$ based on data from January 1984 to June 1990, excluding the week of the stock market break in 1987 (October 15 to October 22). The week of the break was excluded because yield changes during that week were grossly uncharacteristic of yield changes during other weeks in the sample interval.

It should be noted that there are alternative estimators of the covariance matrix which are appropriate when the modes of fluctuation vary through time. We return to this observation in section 20.3.

Shift Function Coefficients

It remains only to show how we can use the estimate $\hat{\Omega}_{\Delta a}$ of the covariance matrix of the reduced shift coefficients to estimate the B matrix of the coefficients of the shift function polynomials.

First define

$$\Delta R(t_k) = \begin{bmatrix} \Delta R(y_1, t_k) \\ \vdots \\ \Delta R(y_H, t_k) \end{bmatrix}, \qquad k = 1, \ldots, K \tag{20.19a}$$

$$Y = \begin{bmatrix} 1 & y_1 & y_1^2 & \cdots & y_1^{I-1} \\ \vdots & \vdots & \vdots & & \vdots \\ 1 & y_H & y_H^2 & \cdots & y_H^{I-1} \end{bmatrix} \tag{20.19b}$$

Table 20.2
Estimated coefficients of the shift function polynomials (b_{ij}), based on weekly data from January 5, 1984, to June 28, 1990, excluding the week of October 15 to October 22, 1987

Coefficient index	Shift function f_j		
	$j = 1$	$j = 2$	$j = 3$
$i = 1$	.9454	−.6055	−.1310
$i = 2$	.1015	.1961	.0855
$i = 3$	−.008141	−.010281	−.009017

Equation (20.12) can then be rewritten as

$$\Delta R(t_k) = Y \cdot \Delta a(t_k), \qquad k = 1, \ldots, K \tag{20.20}$$

The covariance matrix of yield changes from time t_{k-1} to time t_k, denoted $\Omega_{\Delta R}$, follows from equation (20.20) as

$$\Omega_{\Delta R} = Y \cdot \Omega_{\Delta a} \cdot Y' \tag{20.21}$$

An estimate of $\Omega_{\Delta R}$ is

$$\hat{\Omega}_{\Delta R} = Y \cdot \hat{\Omega}_{\Delta a} \cdot Y' \tag{20.22}$$

For the reasons noted in chapter 17, we can decompose the matrix $\hat{\Omega}_{\Delta R}$ as

$$\hat{\Omega}_{\Delta R} = \tilde{V}_{\Delta R} \cdot \tilde{D}_{\Delta R} \cdot \tilde{V}_{\Delta R'} \tag{20.23}$$

where $\tilde{D}_{\Delta R}$ is an $I \times I$ diagonal matrix of the I nonzero eigenvalues of $\hat{\Omega}_{\Delta R}$ and $\tilde{V}_{\Delta R}$ is an $H \times I$ matrix of the associated eigenvectors. The estimator of the B matrix for $J = I$ modes of fluctuation is

$$\hat{B} = (52)^{1/2} \cdot (Y' \cdot Y)^{-1} \cdot Y' \cdot \tilde{V}_{\Delta R} \cdot \tilde{D}_{\Delta R}^{1/2} \tag{20.24}$$

where $\tilde{D}_{\Delta R}^{1/2}$ is an $I \times I$ diagonal matrix with entries of the form $[\tilde{D}_{\Delta R}^{1/2}]_{ii} = ([\tilde{D}_{\Delta R}]_{ii})^{1/2}$, i.e., the entries on the diagonal of $\tilde{D}_{\Delta R}^{1/2}$ are the square roots of the corresponding entries on the diagonal of $\tilde{D}_{\Delta R}$. Details of the derivation of equation (20.24) appear in chapter 17 and appendix B of chapter 18.

Table 20.2 shows estimated values of the b_{ij} coefficients based on data from January 1984 to June 1990, excluding the week of the stock market break in 1987. From the table we can write our estimates of the stationary modes of fluctuation of the spot Treasury yield curve as

$$f_1(y) = .9454 + .1015 \cdot y - .008141 \cdot y^2 \tag{20.25a}$$

$$f_2(y) = -.6055 + .1961 \cdot y - .010281 \cdot y^2 \tag{20.25b}$$

$$f_3(y) = -.1310 + .0855 \cdot y - .009017 \cdot y^2 \tag{20.25c}$$

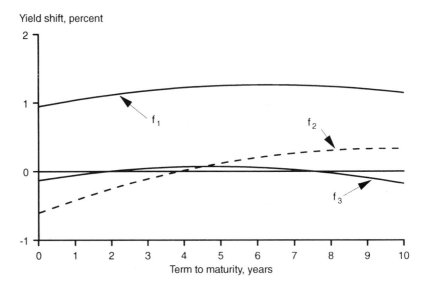

Figure 20.3
Spot yield curve shift functions

Figure 20.3 shows the values of these shift functions at maturities up to ten years. The basis for describing the first mode of fluctuation as a change in level, the second mode as a change in slope, and the third mode as a change in curvature is clear from the figure.

20.3   Estimating Time-Varying Modes of Fluctuation

This section addresses the question of whether the stationary modes of fluctuation shown in Figure 20.3 are an appropriate characterization of the behavior of changes in the spot Treasury yield curve since 1984 or whether it is more appropriate to allow for time variation in the modes of fluctuation. As in section 20.2 we assume that the modes of fluctuation of the yield curve are polynomial functions of maturity. Our problem is to identify and estimate time variation in the coefficients of the polynomials.

Estimating Time-Varying Coefficients of the Shift Function Polynomials

The methodology described in section 20.2 for estimating stationary coefficients of the shift function polynomials had three basic steps:

1. Estimating a time series of reduced shift coefficients.

2. Estimating the covariance matrix $\hat{\Omega}_{\Delta a}$ of the reduced shift coefficients with equation (20.18).

3. Estimating the coefficients of the shift function polynomials with equation (20.24).

The assumption of stationarity enters in the second step and, in particular, in the form of equation (20.18).

Equation (20.17) shows that time variation in the B matrix of polynomial coefficients will induce time variation in the covariance matrix $\Omega_{\Delta a}$. Thus, as a matter of estimation methodology, we can relax the assumption of stationary shift functions by allowing for time variation in $\Omega_{\Delta a}$.

More particularly, we replace the estimator of $\Omega_{\Delta a}$ in equation (20.18) with an estimator of a time-varying covariance matrix:

$$\hat{\Omega}_{\Delta a}(t_i) = \frac{\sum_{k=1}^{K} \widehat{\Delta a}(t_k) \cdot \widehat{\Delta a}(t_k)' \cdot \omega^{|i-k|}}{\sum_{k=1}^{K} \omega^{|i-k|}}, \qquad i = 1, \ldots, K \tag{20.26}$$

$\hat{\Omega}_{\Delta a}(t_i)$ is an estimate of the covariance matrix at time t_i of the reduced shift coefficients. The estimator in equation (20.26) has the form of a two-sided geometrically weighted average, where the weighting parameter ω is between zero and unity. Higher values of ω imply a less volatile and more stable covariance matrix. The basis for the form of the estimator and a technique for estimating ω are described in appendix A.

Once we have obtained a time series of covariance matrices for the reduced shift coefficients, we can form a time series of covariance matrices for changes in spot yields (compare with equation 20.22):

$$\hat{\Omega}_{\Delta R}(t_i) = Y \cdot \hat{\Omega}_{\Delta a}(t_i) \cdot Y', \qquad i = 1, \ldots, K \tag{20.27}$$

Each of these matrices can be decomposed in a manner similar to equation (20.23):

$$\hat{\Omega}_{\Delta R}(t_i) = \tilde{V}_{\Delta R}(t_i) \cdot \tilde{D}_{\Delta R}(t_i) \cdot \tilde{V}_{\Delta R}(t_i)', \qquad i = 1, \ldots, K \tag{20.28}$$

producing a time series of estimates of the coefficients of the shift function polynomials (compare with equation 20.24)

$$\hat{B}(t_i) = (52)^{1/2} \cdot (Y' \cdot Y)^{-1} \cdot Y' \cdot \tilde{V}_{\Delta R}(t_i) \cdot \tilde{D}_{\Delta R}(t_i)^{1/2}, \qquad i = 1, \ldots, K \tag{20.29}$$

Results

From our weekly data on spot Treasury yields from January 1984 to June 1990, we estimated a value of ω of .92. This implies immediately that the modes of fluctuation of the spot Treasury yield curve were not stationary over the sample interval.

Figure 20.4 shows the nature of the variation through time of the first mode of fluctuation of the spot yield curve. The figure clearly indicates that the first mode varied dramatically in shape as well as level over the

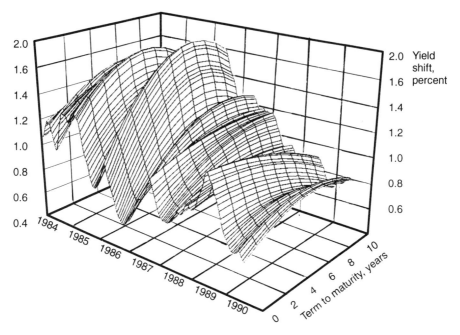

Figure 20.4
Time-varying first mode of fluctuation

sample period. It was high and had a steep positive slope in mid-1985, and it had a moderate negative slope in mid-1989. At all times, however, the first mode can be roughly characterized as a change in the level of the yield curve. That is, the first shift function always had positive values at maturities up to ten years.

This result implies that the first mode of fluctuation in figure 20.3 is only some kind of time series average of the actual first mode of fluctuation of the spot Treasury yield curve between 1984 and 1990. Most important, it appears that the actual mode exhibited substantial nonstationarities over the sample interval.

The second and third modes of fluctuation remained largely unchanged through time.

20.4   Conclusions

There are four areas in fixed income analysis where accurate characterizations of the volatilities and correlations of bond yield changes are necessary:

- Hedging (see chapter 12).
- Immunization (see chapter 15).
- Risk assessment.
- Pricing contingent claims (see chapter 19).

The results reported in this chapter have important implications for each of these areas.

Hedging and risk assessment require accurate estimates of contemporaneous volatilities and correlations of bond yield changes. These estimates should be derived with a methodology that recognizes that patterns of yield changes in the more distant past are not as relevant for estimating current behavior as more recent patterns.

Immunization and contingent claim pricing require accurate estimates of contemporaneous *and future* volatilities and correlations of bond yield changes. (This should be clear because, among other things, the value of an option on a bond depends on the prospective volatility of interest rates.) This chapter has shown that the first mode of fluctuation of the spot Treasury yield curve has varied substantially and in complex ways since 1984. This implies that models of the yield curve that exhibit stationary modes of fluctuation may result in mispriced options.

20.5   Appendix A: Estimating a Time-Varying Covariance Matrix

This appendix shows how we estimated, as in equation (20.26), the evolution of a time-varying covariance matrix. We first show how to estimate a single scalar element of the matrix and then extend the methodology to the entire matrix.

Estimating a Time-Varying Scalar

This section introduces the structure needed to represent a time-varying scalar variable, shows how to estimate the variable using current and past information, and finally develops an estimation algorithm that uses all available information.

The Structure of the Problem

We assume that time is a discrete variable, indexed as $t = 1, 2, \ldots, T$. We wish to estimate an *unobserved* scalar quantity β_t that evolves through time according to the process

$$\beta_t = \beta_{t-1} + p_t, \qquad t = 2, 3, \ldots, T \tag{A20.1}$$

We assume that the random variable p_t has mean zero, variance Π, and is uncorrelated with p_s for all $s \neq t$. We make no additional assumptions on the distribution of p_t. In particular, we do not assume that p_t is normally distributed. We write $p_t \sim (0, \Pi)$ to denote that "p_t is sampled from a distribution with mean zero and variance Π."

We receive information on β_t through an *observed* quantity d_t. The relationship between β_t and d_t is assumed to be

$$d_t = \beta_t + u_t, \qquad t = 1, 2, \ldots, T \tag{A20.2}$$

where $u_t \sim (0, \Psi)$. We further assume that u_t is uncorrelated with u_s for all $s \neq t$ and that u_t is uncorrelated with p_s for all t and all s.

This structure can be mapped into the estimation problem in the body of the chapter. Time is measured in weeks. The unobserved scalar β_t is the covariance at time t between two reduced shift coefficients. The observed scalar d_t is the product of the realized values of the reduced shift coefficients at time t.

Best Linear Unbiased Estimators and a Related Theorem

Suppose that we have a data set $D = \{d_1, \ldots, d_T\}$ of sample size T. Consider selecting an estimator $\hat{B}$ of a variable B from the class of estimators that are linear combinations of the observations in D. We can thus write $\hat{B}$ as

$$\hat{B} = \sum_{t=1}^{T} \theta_t \cdot d_t \tag{A20.3}$$

for weighting coefficients $\theta_1, \theta_2, \ldots, \theta_T$. If $\hat{B}$ is the unique estimator with the properties that (1) $E(\hat{B} - B) = 0$ so that $\hat{B}$ is an unbiased (as well as linear) estimator of B, and (2) $\hat{B}$ minimizes $\text{var}(\hat{B} - B)$ over the class of all such unbiased linear estimators, then we call $\hat{B}$ the best linear unbiased estimator (BLUE) of B using the data set D. We now present a theorem on how to construct BLUE estimators.

Theorem Let $\hat{B}_1$ be BLUE for estimating B using the data set D_1, and let $\hat{B}_2$ be BLUE for estimating B using another data set D_2. Assume that

$$\begin{bmatrix} \hat{B}_1 - B \\ \hat{B}_2 - B \end{bmatrix} \sim \left(\begin{bmatrix} 0 \\ 0 \end{bmatrix}, \begin{bmatrix} \sigma_1^2 & 0 \\ 0 & \sigma_2^2 \end{bmatrix} \right) \tag{A20.4}$$

Then the estimator

$$\hat{B} = \omega \cdot \hat{B}_1 + (1 - \omega) \cdot \hat{B}_2 \tag{A20.5}$$

is BLUE for B using the combined data set $D_1 \cup D_2$, where

$$\omega = \frac{\sigma_2^2}{\sigma_1^2 + \sigma_2^2} \tag{A20.6}$$

Further

$$\text{var}(\hat{B} - B) = (\sigma_1^{-2} + \sigma_2^{-2})^{-1} \tag{A20.7}$$

The theorem is proved in appendix B.

Forward Filtering

We now construct an estimator $\tilde{\beta}_t$ that is BLUE for β_t using observations up to and including time t. (This is sometimes called "forward filtering" or just "filtering.") Let D_t denote the set $\{d_1, d_2, \ldots, d_t\}$. Thus we wish to construct an estimator $\tilde{\beta}_t$ which is BLUE for β_t using D_t.

To initialize our procedure, set $\tilde{\beta}_1 = d_1$ and $S_1 = \Psi$. Trivially then $\tilde{\beta}_1$ is BLUE for β_1 using D_1, and from equation (A20.2), $\text{var}(\tilde{\beta}_1 - \beta_1) = S_1$. To estimate β_t for $t > 1$, assume that $\tilde{\beta}_{t-1}$ is BLUE for β_{t-1} using D_{t-1} and that $\text{var}(\tilde{\beta}_{t-1} - \beta_{t-1}) = S_{t-1}$. Then we can write

$$\tilde{\beta}_{t-1} = \beta_{t-1} + s_{t-1} \tag{A20.8}$$

where s_{t-1} is the estimation error $\tilde{\beta}_{t-1} - \beta_{t-1}$. Since $\tilde{\beta}_{t-1}$ is an unbiased estimate of β_{t-1}, we have $s_{t-1} \sim (0, S_{t-1})$.

We can combine equations (A20.1) and (A20.8) to get

$$\tilde{\beta}_{t-1} = \beta_t - p_t + s_{t-1} \tag{A20.9}$$

We can show that s_{t-1} is a linear function of $p_1, p_2, \ldots, p_{t-1}$ and $u_1, u_2, \ldots, u_{t-1}$. This implies that s_{t-1} is uncorrelated with p_t and u_t. Using this fact and equation (A20.2) we have

$$\begin{bmatrix} \tilde{\beta}_{t-1} - \beta_t \\ d_t - \beta_t \end{bmatrix} \sim \left(\begin{bmatrix} 0 \\ 0 \end{bmatrix}, \begin{bmatrix} S_{t-1} + \Pi & 0 \\ 0 & \Psi \end{bmatrix} \right) \tag{A20.10}$$

Now $\tilde{\beta}_{t-1}$ is BLUE for estimating β_t using D_{t-1}, and d_t is BLUE for estimating β_t using d_t. Further observe that

$$D_{t-1} \cup d_t = D_t \tag{A20.11}$$

Then the theorem implies that

$$\tilde{\beta}_t = \omega_t \cdot \tilde{\beta}_{t-1} + (1 - \omega_t) \cdot d_t \tag{A20.12}$$

is BLUE for estimating β_t using D_t, where

$$\omega_t = \frac{\Psi}{S_{t-1} + \Pi + \Psi} \tag{A20.13}$$

Equation (A20.12) provides a recursive updating procedure for $\tilde{\beta}_t$. We can also write $\tilde{\beta}_t$ as

$$\tilde{\beta}_t = \tilde{\beta}_{t-1} + (1 - \omega_t) \cdot (d_t - \tilde{\beta}_{t-1}) \tag{A20.14}$$

We refer to $d_t - \tilde{\beta}_{t-1}$ as the "innovation" or the new information revealed at time t.

We can compute the variance of $\tilde{\beta}_t - \beta_t$ using equation (A20.7):

$$
\begin{aligned}
S_t &= \mathrm{var}(\tilde{\beta}_t - \beta_t) \\
&= ((S_{t-1} + \Pi)^{-1} + \Psi^{-1})^{-1} \tag{A20.15}
\end{aligned}
$$

Thus

$$S_t^{-1} = (S_{t-1} + \Pi)^{-1} + \Psi^{-1} \tag{A20.16}$$

The Asymptotic Forward Filter

It can be shown from equation (A20.16) that S_t converges to S_* for $t \gg 1$, where S_* is the unique positive solution to the equation

$$S_*^{-1} = (S_* + \Pi)^{-1} + \Psi^{-1} \tag{A20.17}$$

We define

$$\omega_* = \frac{\Psi}{S_* + \Pi + \Psi} \tag{A20.18}$$

Then the estimator $\tilde{\beta}_t$ for $t \gg 1$ follows the equation

$$\tilde{\beta}_t = \omega_* \cdot \tilde{\beta}_{t-1} + (1 - \omega_*) \cdot d_t \tag{A20.19}$$

Substituting for $\tilde{\beta}_{t-1}$ gives

$$\tilde{\beta}_t = (1 - \omega_*) \cdot d_t + \omega_* \cdot (1 - \omega_*) \cdot d_{t-1} + \omega_*^2 \cdot \tilde{\beta}_{t-2} \tag{A20.20}$$

Repeating this process $k - 2$ times yields

$$\tilde{\beta}_t = (1 - \omega_*) \cdot \left(\sum_{s=0}^{k-1} \omega_*^s \cdot d_{t-s} \right) + \omega_*^k \cdot \tilde{\beta}_{t-k}$$

Letting k grow without bound, we have that

$$\tilde{\beta}_t = (1 - \omega_*) \cdot \left(\sum_{s=0}^{\infty} \omega_*^s \cdot d_{t-s} \right) \tag{A20.21}$$

or

$$\tilde{\beta}_t = \frac{\sum_{s=0}^{\infty} \omega_*^s \cdot d_{t-s}}{\sum_{s=0}^{\infty} \omega_*^s} \tag{A20.22}$$

Equation (A20.22) implies that the asymptotic forward filter is a one-sided geometrically declining weighted average of past and current observations.

The Reverse Filter

We now apply the forward filter methodology to estimate β_t using current and *future* observations. Let D^t denote the data set of current and future observations at time t so that $D^t = \{d_t, d_{t+1}, \ldots, d_T\}$.

To initialize this procedure, set $\tilde{\tilde{\beta}}_T = d_T$ and $R_T = \Psi$. Next let us consider an estimator $\tilde{\tilde{\beta}}_{t+1}$ that is BLUE for β_{t+1} using D^{t+1} where $\text{var}(\tilde{\tilde{\beta}}_{t+1} - \beta_{t+1}) = R_{t+1}$. We write

$$\tilde{\tilde{\beta}}_{t+1} = \beta_{t+1} + r_{t+1} \tag{A20.23}$$

where r_{t+1} is the estimation error of $\tilde{\tilde{\beta}}_{t+1}$ and $r_{t+1} \sim (0, R_{t+1})$. To update $\tilde{\tilde{\beta}}_t$, we observe that $\beta_{t+1} = \beta_t + p_{t+1}$, so equation (A20.23) can be rewritten as

$$\tilde{\tilde{\beta}}_{t+1} = \beta_t + p_{t+1} + r_{t+1} \tag{A20.24}$$

We can show that r_{t+1} is a linear function of $p_{t+2}, p_{t+3}, \ldots, p_T$ and u_{t+1}, $u_{t+2}, \ldots, u_T$, which implies that r_{t+1} is uncorrelated with u_t and p_{t+1}. This leads to

$$\begin{bmatrix} \tilde{\tilde{\beta}}_{t+1} - \beta_t \\ d_t - \beta_t \end{bmatrix} \sim \left(\begin{bmatrix} 0 \\ 0 \end{bmatrix}, \begin{bmatrix} R_{t+1} + \Pi & 0 \\ 0 & \Psi \end{bmatrix} \right) \tag{A20.25}$$

Observe that $\tilde{\tilde{\beta}}_{t+1}$ is BLUE for estimating β_t using D^{t+1} and that d_t is BLUE for estimating β_t using d_t. Note also that

$$D^{t+1} \cup d_t = D^t \tag{A20.26}$$

Then the theorem implies that

$$\tilde{\tilde{\beta}}_t = v_t \cdot \tilde{\tilde{\beta}}_{t+1} + (1 - v_t) \cdot d_t \tag{A20.27}$$

is BLUE for estimating β_t using D^t, where

$$v_t = \frac{\Psi}{R_{t+1} + \Pi + \Psi} \tag{A20.28}$$

Further equation (A20.7) implies that

$$R_t^{-1} = \text{var}(\tilde{\tilde{\beta}}_t - \beta_t)^{-1}$$

$$= (R_{t+1} + \Pi)^{-1} + \Psi^{-1} \tag{A20.29}$$

This equation for R_t is similar to equation (A20.16) for the forward filter's variance S_t.

The Asymptotic Reverse Filter

It can be shown that R_t converges to S_* for $t \ll T$ where S_* is as defined in equation (A20.17). It follows from equations (A20.27) and (A20.28) that the asymptotic reverse filtered estimator of β_t is

$$\tilde{\tilde{\beta}}_t = \omega_* \cdot \tilde{\tilde{\beta}}_{t+1} + (1 - \omega_*) \cdot d_t \tag{A20.30}$$

or, equivalently,

$$\tilde{\tilde{\beta}}_t = \frac{\sum_{s=0}^{\infty} \omega_*^s \cdot d_{t+s}}{\sum_{s=0}^{\infty} \omega_*^s} \tag{A20.31}$$

where ω_* is defined in equation (A20.18). The asymptotic reverse filter is a one-sided geometrically declining weighted average of current and future observations.

The Smoother

We now combine the forward and reverse filters to form a composite estimator of β_t using *all* observations—past, present, and future.

The filter and the reverse filter give

$$\tilde{\beta}_t = \beta_t + s_t \tag{A20.32}$$

$$\tilde{\tilde{\beta}}_{t+1} = \beta_t + p_{t+1} + r_{t+1} \tag{A20.33}$$

so that

$$\begin{bmatrix} \tilde{\beta}_t - \beta_t \\ \tilde{\tilde{\beta}}_{t+1} - \beta_t \end{bmatrix} \sim \left(\begin{bmatrix} 0 \\ 0 \end{bmatrix}, \begin{bmatrix} S_t & 0 \\ 0 & \Pi + R_{t+1} \end{bmatrix} \right) \tag{A20.34}$$

Recall that $\tilde{\beta}_t$ is BLUE for estimating β_t using D_t and that $\tilde{\tilde{\beta}}_{t+1}$ is BLUE for estimating β_t using D^{t+1}. Observe also that $D_t \cup D^{t+1} = D$. Then the theorem implies that

$$\hat{\beta}_t = \theta_t \cdot \tilde{\beta}_t + (1 - \theta_t) \cdot \tilde{\tilde{\beta}}_{t+1} \tag{A20.35}$$

is BLUE for estimating β_t using all observations where

$$\theta_t = \frac{\Pi + R_{t+1}}{S_t + \Pi + R_{t+1}} \tag{A20.36}$$

Further equation (A20.7) implies that

$$V_t^{-1} = \text{var}(\hat{\beta}_t - \beta_t)^{-1}$$
$$= S_t^{-1} + (\Pi + R_{t+1})^{-1} \tag{A20.37}$$

This shows that $V_t^{-1} > S_t^{-1}$, which implies that $V_t < S_t$, so the smoother is a more efficient estimator of β_t than the forward filter.

The Asymptotic Smoother

We noted above that S_t converges to S_* for $t \gg 1$ and that R_t converges to S_* for $t \ll T$, where S_* is defined in equation (A20.17). It follows from equation (A20.36) that for values of t such that $1 \ll t \ll T$, we have

$$\theta_t = \frac{\Pi + S_*}{2 \cdot S_* + \Pi} \tag{A20.38}$$

We show in appendix C that

$$\frac{\Pi + S_*}{2 \cdot S_* + \Pi} = \frac{1}{1 + \omega_*} \tag{A20.39}$$

where ω_* is defined in equation (A20.18), so equation (A20.38) becomes

$$\theta_t = \frac{1}{1 + \omega_*}$$

It follows from equation (A20.35) that for values of t such that $1 \ll t \ll T$, we can write

$$\hat{\beta}_t = \left[\frac{1}{1 + \omega_*} \right] \cdot \tilde{\beta}_t + \left[\frac{\omega_*}{1 + \omega_*} \right] \cdot \tilde{\tilde{\beta}}_{t+1} \tag{A20.40}$$

and from equations (A20.21) and (A20.31),

$$\begin{aligned}
\hat{\beta}_t &= \left[\frac{1}{1 + \omega_*} \right] \cdot (1 - \omega_*) \cdot \left(\sum_{s=0}^{\infty} \omega_*^s \cdot d_{t-s} \right) \\
&\quad + \left[\frac{\omega_*}{1 + \omega_*} \right] \cdot (1 - \omega_*) \cdot \left(\sum_{s=0}^{\infty} \omega_*^s \cdot d_{t+1+s} \right) \\
&= \left[\frac{1 - \omega_*}{1 + \omega_*} \right] \cdot \left[d_t + \sum_{s=1}^{\infty} \omega_*^s \cdot d_{t-s} + \sum_{s=0}^{\infty} \omega_*^{s+1} \cdot d_{t+1+s} \right]
\end{aligned}$$

or

$$\hat{\beta}_t = \left[\frac{1 - \omega_*}{1 + \omega_*} \right] \cdot \left[d_t + \sum_{s=1}^{\infty} \omega_*^s \cdot (d_{t-s} + d_{t+s}) \right] \tag{A20.41}$$

Now observe that

$$1 + 2 \cdot \sum_{s=1}^{\infty} \omega_*^s = -1 + 2 \cdot \sum_{s=0}^{\infty} \omega_*^s$$

$$= -1 + \frac{2}{1 - \omega_*}$$

$$= \frac{1 + \omega_*}{1 - \omega_*} \tag{A20.42}$$

It follows from equations (A20.41) and (A20.42) that

$$\hat{\beta}_t = \frac{d_t + \sum_{s=1}^{\infty} \omega_*^s \cdot (d_{t-s} + d_{t+s})}{1 + 2 \cdot \sum_{s=1}^{\infty} \omega_*^s} \tag{A20.43}$$

The asymptotic smoother is therefore a two-sided geometrically declining weighted average of all observations.

The asymptotic smoother in equation (A20.43) can also be written

$$\hat{\beta}_t = \frac{\sum_{s=-\infty}^{\infty} \omega_*^{|t-s|} \cdot d_s}{\sum_{s=-\infty}^{\infty} \omega_*^{|t-s|}} \tag{A20.44}$$

For finite samples we approximate the asymptotic smoother as

$$\hat{\beta}_t = \frac{\sum_{s=1}^{T} \omega_*^{|t-s|} \cdot d_s}{\sum_{s=1}^{T} \omega_*^{|t-s|}} \tag{A20.45}$$

This is the basis for the form of equation (20.26).

Estimating ω_*

$\hat{\beta}_t$ depends on ω_*, which depends only on Π and Ψ. (See equations A20.17 and A20.18.) Since we usually do not know Π and Ψ, we next suggest a way to estimate ω_* directly.

Serial Correlation of the Innovations

Let e_t be defined as

$$e_t = d_t - \tilde{\beta}_{t-1} \tag{A20.46}$$

and recall from the forward filter that e_t is called an "innovation." Suppose that filtered estimates are formed using the weight sequence η_t for $t = 2, 3, \ldots$. Then from equation (A20.12),

$$\tilde{\beta}_t = \eta_t \cdot \tilde{\beta}_{t-1} + (1 - \eta_t) \cdot d_t \tag{A20.47}$$

Using equations (A20.2) and (A20.47), we have

$$e_{t+1} = d_{t+1} - \tilde{\beta}_t$$

$$= (\beta_{t+1} + u_{t+1}) - (\eta_t \cdot \tilde{\beta}_{t-1} + (1 - \eta_t) \cdot d_t)$$

$$\begin{aligned}
&= (\beta_t + p_{t+1} + u_{t+1}) - \eta_t \cdot \tilde{\beta}_{t-1} - (1 - \eta_t) \cdot d_t \\
&= (\beta_t - d_t) + p_{t+1} + u_{t+1} + \eta_t \cdot (d_t - \tilde{\beta}_{t-1}) \\
&= -u_t + p_{t+1} + u_{t+1} + \eta_t \cdot e_t
\end{aligned}$$
(A20.48)

Then

$$\begin{aligned}
\text{cov}[e_{t+1}, e_t] &= \text{cov}[-u_t + p_{t+1} + u_{t+1} + \eta_t \cdot e_t, e_t] \\
&= \eta_t \cdot \text{var}[e_t] - \text{cov}[u_t, e_t]
\end{aligned}$$
(A20.49)

Now

$$\begin{aligned}
e_t &= d_t - \tilde{\beta}_{t-1} \\
&= \beta_t + u_t - \tilde{\beta}_{t-1} \\
&= \beta_{t-1} + p_t + u_t - \tilde{\beta}_{t-1} \\
&= p_t + u_t - (\tilde{\beta}_{t-1} - \beta_{t-1}) \\
&= p_t + u_t - s_{t-1}
\end{aligned}$$
(A20.50)

So

$$\text{var}[e_t] = \Pi + \Psi + S_{t-1}$$
(A20.51)

We also have

$$\begin{aligned}
\text{cov}[u_t, e_t] &= \text{cov}[u_t, p_t + u_t - s_{t-1}] \\
&= \text{var}[u_t] \\
&= \Psi
\end{aligned}$$
(A20.52)

From equation (A20.49),

$$\text{cov}[e_{t+1}, e_t] = \eta_t \cdot [\Pi + \Psi + S_{t-1}] - \Psi$$
(A20.53)

Recalling from equation (A20.13) that

$$\omega_t = \frac{\Psi}{\Psi + S_{t-1} + \Pi}$$
(A20.54)

it follows that

$$\text{cov}[e_{t+1}, e_t] > 0 \qquad \text{if } \eta_t > \omega_t$$
(A20.55a)

$$\text{cov}[e_{t+1}, e_t] < 0 \qquad \text{if } \eta_t < \omega_t$$
(A20.55b)

$$\text{cov}[e_{t+1}, e_t] = 0 \qquad \text{if } \eta_t = \omega_t$$
(A20.55c)

If $\eta_t > \omega_t$, then the weights decline too slowly and the innovations are positively serially correlated. If $\eta_t < \omega_t$, then the weights decline too quickly and the innovations are negatively serially correlated. If $\eta_t = \omega_t$, then the innovations are serially uncorrelated. We now extend this analysis to the asymptotic case.

Asymptotic Serial Correlation of the Innovations

From the asymptotic forward filter the innovations are

$$e_{t+1} = d_{t+1} - \tilde{\beta}_t \tag{A20.56}$$

where

$$\tilde{\beta}_t = \frac{\sum_{s=0}^{\infty} \omega_*^s \cdot d_{t-s}}{\sum_{s=0}^{\infty} \omega_*^s} \tag{A20.57}$$

$$\omega_* = \frac{\Psi}{\Psi + S_* + \Pi} \tag{A20.58}$$

If we choose η_* to be the weighting coefficient then,

$$\text{cov}[e_{t+1}, e_t] > 0 \qquad \text{if } \eta_* > \omega_* \tag{A20.59a}$$

$$\text{cov}[e_{t+1}, e_t] < 0 \qquad \text{if } \eta_* < \omega_* \tag{A20.59b}$$

$$\text{cov}[e_{t+1}, e_t] = 0 \qquad \text{if } \eta_* = \omega_* \tag{A20.59c}$$

This suggests a way to estimate ω_*. Choose ω as an estimate of ω_* such that ω is between zero and unity and such that the squared sample serial correlation of the innovations has minimum value. This requires no knowledge of Π or Ψ and can be computed with a simple grid search on the unit interval. Once ω is estimated, the asymptotic smoothed estimates of the $\beta_t s$ can be computed as in equation (A20.45).

Estimating the Time-Varying Covariance Matrix

We have seen how to run the smoother for the scalar case. We now generalize the smoother to the matrix case. This generalization relies on a crucial assumption about the time-varying covariance matrix. To motivate this assumption, we derive how ω_* depends on Π and Ψ.

How ω_* Relates to Π and Ψ

Recall from equation (A20.17) that S_* is the unique positive solution to

$$S_*^{-1} = \Psi^{-1} + (S_* + \Psi)^{-1} \tag{A20.60}$$

Using the quadratic formula, we can show that

$$S_* = \frac{-\Pi}{2} + \left[\frac{\Pi^2}{4} + \Pi \cdot \Psi\right]^{1/2}$$

(A20.61)

Writing S_* in terms of $x = \Pi/\Psi$ yields

$$S_* = \Psi \cdot \left[\frac{-x}{2} + \left[\frac{x^2}{4} + x\right]^{1/2}\right]$$

(A20.62)

Recall from equation (A20.18) that

$$\omega_* = \frac{\Psi}{\Psi + S_* + \Pi}$$

$$= \left[1 + \frac{S_*}{\Psi} + \frac{\Pi}{\Psi}\right]^{-1}$$

$$= \left[1 + \frac{x}{2} + \left[\frac{x^2}{4} + x\right]^{1/2}\right]^{-1}$$

(A20.63)

So ω_* is a function of x, the ratio of Π to Ψ, but does not otherwise depend on either variance.

An Assumption about the Covariance Matrix

We have shown that ω_* depends on Π and Ψ only through their ratio x. If the elements of the time-varying covariance matrix all follow (A20.1) and (A20.2) and have the same value of x than they have the same value of ω_*. In this case we can estimate ω_* using information from all the elements.

Let $P_{ij}(\eta)$ denote the sample serial correlation of the innovations for the time-varying scalar variable in the ith row and jth column of the time-varying covariance matrix when the weighting coefficient is η. If ω_* is the true weighting coefficient for some i and for some j, then $P_{ij}(\omega_*)$ should be near zero for that i and j. If ω_* is the true weighting coefficient for all i and j then $P_{ij}(\omega_*)$ should be near zero for all i and j.

We estimated ω_* by choosing ω on the unit interval to minimize the criterion function

$$\sum_{i=1}^{I} \sum_{j=1}^{i} P_{ij}(\omega)^2$$

(A20.64)

Thus we choose ω to minimize the total squared sample serial correlation of the innovations of all of the elements in the covariance matrix. As noted in the text following equation (20.29), this leads to $\omega = .92$.

20.6   Appendix B: Proof of the Theorem Stated in Appendix A

This appendix proves the theorem stated in appendix A.

Theorem   Let $\hat{B}_1$ be BLUE for estimating B using the data set D_1, and let $\hat{B}_2$ be BLUE for estimating B using another data set D_2. Further assume that

$$\begin{bmatrix} \hat{B}_1 - B \\ \hat{B}_2 - B \end{bmatrix} \sim \left(\begin{bmatrix} 0 \\ 0 \end{bmatrix}, \begin{bmatrix} \sigma_1^2 & 0 \\ 0 & \sigma_2^2 \end{bmatrix} \right) \tag{A20.65}$$

Then the estimator

$$\hat{B} = \omega \cdot \hat{B}_1 + (1 - \omega) \cdot \hat{B}_2 \tag{A20.66}$$

is BLUE for B using the combined data set $D_1 \cup D_2$, where

$$\omega = \frac{\sigma_2^2}{\sigma_1^2 + \sigma_2^2} \tag{A20.67}$$

Further

$$\text{var}(\hat{B} - B) = (\sigma_1^{-2} + \sigma_2^{-2})^{-1} \tag{A20.68}$$

Proof of Theorem   It can be shown that the BLUE estimator for B using the combined data set $D_1 \cup D_2$ takes the form

$$\hat{B} = \omega \cdot \hat{B}_1 + \tilde{\omega} \cdot \hat{B}_2 \tag{A20.69}$$

for some ω and $\tilde{\omega}$. Now

$$E(\hat{B} - B) = E(\omega \cdot \hat{B}_1 + \tilde{\omega} \cdot \hat{B}_2 - B) \tag{A20.70}$$

$$= E(\omega \cdot (\hat{B}_1 - B) + \tilde{\omega} \cdot (\hat{B}_2 - B) - (1 - \omega - \tilde{\omega}) \cdot B) \tag{A20.71}$$

Since $\hat{B}_1$ and $\hat{B}_2$ are unbiased estimators of B, we have

$$E(\hat{B} - B) = -E((1 - \omega - \tilde{\omega}) \cdot B) \tag{A20.72}$$

$\hat{B}$ is unbiased only if

$$E(\hat{B} - B) = 0 \tag{A20.73}$$

or only if

$$E((1 - \omega - \tilde{\omega}) \cdot B) = 0 \tag{A20.74}$$

For equation (A20.74) to hold for all values of B requires that

$$\tilde{\omega} = 1 - \omega \tag{A20.75}$$

Thus, without loss of generally, we can write the estimator $\hat{B}$ in equation (A20.69) as

$$\hat{B} = \omega \cdot \hat{B}_1 + (1 - \omega) \cdot \hat{B}_2 \tag{A20.76}$$

We wish to find ω to minimize the variance of $(\hat{B} - B)$. Now

$$\begin{aligned}
\operatorname{var}(\hat{B} - B) &= \operatorname{var}(\omega \cdot \hat{B}_1 + (1 - \omega) \cdot \hat{B}_2 - B) \\
&= \operatorname{var}(\omega \cdot (\hat{B}_1 - B) + (1 - \omega) \cdot (\hat{B}_2 - B))
\end{aligned} \tag{A20.77}$$

Since $\hat{B}_1 - B$ and $\hat{B}_2 - B$ are uncorrelated, we have

$$\begin{aligned}
\operatorname{var}(\hat{B} - B) &= \omega^2 \cdot \operatorname{var}(\hat{B}_1 - B) + (1 - \omega)^2 \cdot \operatorname{var}(\hat{B}_2 - B) \\
&= \omega^2 \cdot \sigma_1^2 + (1 - \omega)^2 \cdot \sigma_2^2
\end{aligned} \tag{A20.78}$$

Taking the derivative with respect to ω gives

$$\begin{aligned}
\frac{\partial \operatorname{var}(\hat{B} - B)}{\partial \omega} &= 2\omega \cdot \sigma_1^2 - 2(1 - \omega) \cdot \sigma_2^2 \\
&= 2\omega \cdot (\sigma_1^2 + \sigma_2^2) - 2\sigma_2^2
\end{aligned} \tag{A20.79}$$

Setting this derivative to zero and solving for ω, we get

$$\omega = \frac{\sigma_2^2}{\sigma_1^2 + \sigma_2^2} \tag{A20.80}$$

This confirms equation (A20.67).

We next compute the variance of $(\hat{B} - B)$. Recalling equation (A20.78) and substituting for ω from equation (A20.80) gives

$$\begin{aligned}
\operatorname{var}(\hat{B} - B) &= \omega^2 \cdot \sigma_1^2 + (1 - \omega)^2 \cdot \sigma_2^2 \\
&= \left(\frac{\sigma_2^2}{\sigma_1^2 + \sigma_2^2}\right)^2 \cdot \sigma_1^2 + \left(\frac{\sigma_1^2}{\sigma_1^2 + \sigma_2^2}\right)^2 \cdot \sigma_2^2 \\
&= \left(\frac{1}{\sigma_1^2 + \sigma_2^2}\right)^2 (\sigma_1^2 \cdot \sigma_2^4 + \sigma_1^4 \cdot \sigma_2^2) \\
&= \left(\frac{1}{\sigma_1^2 + \sigma_2^2}\right)^2 \cdot \sigma_1^2 \cdot \sigma_2^2 \cdot (\sigma_1^2 + \sigma_2^2) \\
&= \frac{\sigma_1^2 \cdot \sigma_1^2}{\sigma_1^2 + \sigma_2^2} \\
&= \left(\frac{1}{\sigma_1^2} + \frac{1}{\sigma_2^2}\right)^{-1}
\end{aligned} \tag{A20.81}$$

Thus equation (A20.68) holds.

20.7   Appendix C: Demonstration of Equation (A20.39)

We show in this appendix that

$$\frac{\Pi + S_*}{\Pi + 2 \cdot S_*} = \frac{1}{1 + \omega_*} \tag{A20.82}$$

where

$$\omega_* = \frac{\Psi}{S_* + \Pi + \Psi} \tag{A20.83}$$

and where S_* satisfies the equation

$$S_*^{-1} = (S_* + \Pi)^{-1} + \Psi^{-1} \tag{A20.84}$$

Multiplying both sides of equation (A20.84) by $(S_* + \Pi) \cdot \Psi$ gives

$$S_*^{-1} \cdot (S_* + \Pi) \cdot \Psi = \Psi + S^* + \Pi \tag{A20.85}$$

Substituting the left-hand side of equation (A20.85) into the denominator of the right-hand side of equation (A20.83) gives

$$\omega_* = \frac{\Psi}{S_*^{-1} \cdot (S_* + \Pi) \cdot \Psi}$$

$$= \frac{S_*}{\Pi + S_*}$$

or

$$\Pi + S_* = \frac{S_*}{\omega_*} \tag{A20.86}$$

It follows that

$$\frac{\Pi + S_*}{\Pi + 2 \cdot S_*} = \frac{(S_*/\omega_*)}{(S_*/\omega_*) + S_*}$$

$$= \frac{(S_*/\omega_*)}{(S_*/\omega_*) + \omega_* \cdot (S_*/\omega_*)}$$

or

$$\frac{\Pi + S_*}{\Pi + 2 \cdot S_*} = \frac{1}{1 + \omega_*} \tag{A20.87}$$

thus demonstrating equations (A20.82) and (A20.39).

Further Reading

Bierwag, G., G. Kaufman, and A. Toevs. 1983. Recent Developments in bond portfolio immunization strategies. In *Innovations in Bond Portfolio Management*, G. Kaufman, G. Bierwag, and A. Toevs, eds. Greenwich, CT: Jai Press.

Black, F., E. Derman, and W. Toy. 1990. A one-factor model of interest rates and its application to treasury bond options. *Financial Analysts Journal* 46:33.

Brennan, M., and E. Schwartz. 1977. Saving bonds, retractable bonds and callable bonds. *Journal of Financial Economics* 5:67.

Brennan, M., and E. Schwartz. 1979. A continuous time approach to the pricing of bonds. *Journal of Banking and Finance* 3:134.

Brennan, M., and E. Schwartz. 1980. Conditional predictions of bond prices and returns. *Journal of Finance* 35:405.

Brennan, M., and E. Schwartz. 1982. An equilibrium model of bond pricing and a test of market efficiency. *Journal of Financial and Quantitative Analysis* 17:301.

Brennan, M., and E. Schwartz. 1983. Duration, bond pricing, and portfolio management. In *Innovations in Bond Portfolio Management*, G. Kaufman, G. Bierwag and A. Toevs, eds. Greenwich, CT: Jai Press.

Burghardt, G., T. Belton, M. Lane, and J. Pappa. 1994. *The Treasury Bond Basis*, rev. ed. New York: Irwin.

Cox, J., J. Ingersoll, and S. Ross. 1985. A theory of the term structure of interest rates. *Econometrica* 53:385.

Fabozzi, F. 1993. *Fixed Income Mathematics*, rev. ed. Chicago: Probus Publishing.

Fisher, L., and M. Leibowitz. 1983. Effects of alternative anticipations of yield curve behavior on the composition of immunized portfolios and on their target returns. In *Innovations in Bond Portfolio Management*, G. Kaufman, G. Bierwag and A. Toevs, eds. Greenwich, CT: Jai Press.

Fong, H. G., and O. Vasicek. 1983. Return maximization for immunized portfolios. In *Innovations in Bond Portfolio Management*, G. Kaufman, G. Bierwag and A. Toevs, eds. Greenwich, CT: Jai Press.

Granito, M. 1984. *Bond Portfolio Immunization*. Lexington, MA: Lexington Books.

Heath, D., R. Jarrow, and A. Morton. 1992. Bond pricing and the term structure of interest rates: A new methodology for contingent claims valuation. *Econometrica* 60:77.

Ho, T. 1995. Evolution of interest rate models: A comparison. 2 *Journal of Derivatives* 2:9.

Ho, T., and S. Lee. 1986. Term structure movements and pricing interest rate contingent claims. *Journal of Finance* 41:1011.

Hull, J. 1993. *Options, Futures and Other Derivative Securities*, 2d ed. Englewood Cliffs, NJ: Prentice Hall.

Hull, J., and A. White. 1990. Pricing interest rate derivative securities. *Review of Financial Studies* 3:573.

Liebowitz, M. 1992. *Investing, The Collected Works of Martin L. Liebowitz*, F. Fabozzi, ed. Chicago: Probus Publishing.

Longstaff, F., and E. Schwartz. 1992. Interest rate volatility and the term structure: A two-factor general equilibrium model. *Journal of Finance* 47:1259.

McCulloch, J. H. 1975. An estimate of the liquidity premium. *Journal of Political Economy* 83:95.

McCulloch, J. H. 1975. The tax-adjusted yield curve. *Journal of Finance* 30:811.

Stigum, M. 1989. *The Repo and Reverse Markets*. New York: Irwin.

Vasicek, O. 1977. A equilibrium characterization of the term structure. *Journal of Financial Economics* 5:177.

Index